Lecture Notes in Computer Sc

Edited by G. Goos, J. Hartmanis, and J. v

T0230221

Springer

Berlin
Heidelberg
New York
Barcelona
Hong Kong
London
Milan
Paris
Tokyo

Thomas Eiter   Klaus-Dieter Schewe (Eds.)

Foundations
of Information and
Knowledge Systems

Second International Symposium, FoIKS 2002
Salzau Castle, Germany, February 20-23, 2002
Proceedings

 Springer

Series Editors

Gerhard Goos, Karlsruhe University, Germany
Juris Hartmanis, Cornell University, NY, USA
Jan van Leeuwen, Utrecht University, The Netherlands

Volume Editors

Thomas Eiter
Technical University of Vienna, Institute of Information Systems (E814)
Karlsplatz 13, 1040 Wien, Austria
E-mail: eiter@kr.tuwien.ac.at

Klaus-Dieter Schewe
Massey University , Department of Information Systems
Private Bag 11 222, Palmerston North, New Zealand
E-mail: K.D.Schewe@massey.ac.nz

Cataloging-in-Publication Data applied for

Die Deutsche Bibliothek - CIP-Einheitsaufnahme

Foundations of information and knowledge systems : second international
symposium ; proceedings / FoIKS 2002, Salzau Castle, Germany, February
20 - 23, 2002. Thomas Eiter ; Klaus-Dieter Schewe (ed.). - Berlin ; Heidelberg ;
New York ; Barcelona ; Hong Kong ; London ; Milan ; Paris ; Tokyo :
Springer, 2002
    (Lecture notes in computer science ; Vol. 2284)
    ISBN 3-540-43220-5

CR Subject Classification (1998): H.2, H.3, H.5, I.2.4, F.3.2, G.2

ISSN 0302-9743
ISBN 3-540-43220-5 Springer-Verlag Berlin Heidelberg New York

Springer-Verlag Berlin Heidelberg New York
a member of BertelsmannSpringer Science+Business Media GmbH

http://www.springer.de

© Springer-Verlag Berlin Heidelberg 2002
Printed in Germany

Typesetting: Camera-ready by author, data conversion by Olgun Computergrafik
Printed on acid-free paper   SPIN 10846301   06/3142   5 4 3 2 1 0

Preface

This volume contains the papers presented at the "Second International Symposium on Foundations of Information and Knowledge Systems" (FoIKS 2002), which was held in Schloß Salzau, Germany from February 20th to 23rd, 2002.

FoIKS is a biennial event focusing on theoretical foundations of information and knowledge systems. It aims to bring together researchers working on the theoretical foundations of information and knowledge systems and to attract researchers working in mathematical fields such as discrete mathematics, combinatorics, logics, and finite model theory who are interested in applying their theories to research on database and knowledge base theory. FoIKS took up the tradition of the conference series "Mathematical Fundamentals of Database Systems" (MFDBS) which enabled East-West collaboration in the field of database theory. The first FoIKS symposium was held in Burg, Spreewald (Germany) in 2000. Former MFDBS conferences were held in Dresden (Germany) in 1987, Visegrád (Hungary) in 1989, and in Rostock (Germany) in 1991. Proceedings of these previous events were published by Springer-Verlag as volumes 305, 364, 495, and 1762 of the LNCS series.

In addition the FoIKS symposium is intended to be a forum for intensive discussions. For this reason the time slot of long and short contributions is 60 and 30 minutes respectively, followed by 30 and 15 minutes for discussions, respectively. Furthermore, participants are asked in advance to prepare as correspondents to a contribution of another author. There are also special sessions for the presentation and discussion of open research problems.

The FoIKS 2002 call for papers solicited contributions dealing with any foundational aspect of information and knowledge systems, e.g.

- Mathematical Foundations: discrete methods, boolean functions, finite model theory, non-classical logics
- Database Design: formal models, dependency theory, schema translations, desirable properties, design primitives, design strategies
- Query Languages: expressiveness, computational and descriptive complexity, query languages for advanced datamodels, classification of computable queries
- Semi-structured Databases and WWW: models of web databases, querying semi-structured databases, web transactions and negotiations
- Security in Data and Knowledge Bases: cryptography, steganography, information hiding
- Integrity and Constraint Management: constraint checking, verification and validation of consistency, consistency enforcement, triggers
- Information Integration: heterogenous data, views, schema dominance and equivalence

- Data- and Knowledge Base Dynamics: models of transactions, models of interaction, updates in data and knowledge bases, consistency preservation, dynamic consistency, concurrency control, complexity of update propagation
- Intelligent Agents: multi-agent systems, autonomous agents, foundations of software agents, cooperative agents
- Logics in Databases and AI: non-classical logics, temporal logics, non-monotonic logics, spatial logics, probabilistic logics, deontic logic
- Logic Programming: declarative logic programming, constraint programming, inductive logic programming
- Knowledge Representation: planning, description logics, knowledge and belief, belief revision and update, non-monotonic formalisms, uncertainty
- Reasoning Techniques: automated reasoning, satisfiability testing, abduction, induction, theorem proving, constraint satisfaction, common-sense reasoning, probabilistic reasoning, reasoning about actions

The program committee received 55 submissions. Each paper was carefully reviewed by at least three experienced referees. Fifteen papers were chosen for long presentation, two papers for short presentation. This volume contains polished versions of these papers with respect to comments made in the reviews. A few papers will be selected for further extension and publishing in a special issue of the journal "Annals of Mathematics and Artificial Intelligence".

We would like to thank all authors who submitted papers and all workshop participants for the fruitful discussions. We are grateful to the members of the program committee and the external referees for their timely expertise in carefully reviewing the papers, and we would like to express our thanks to our hosts for the beautiful week in the pleasant surroundings of Schloß Salzau in Holstein.

February 2002   Thomas Eiter
                                                     Klaus-Dieter Schewe

Organization

Program Committee Co-chairs

Thomas Eiter   Technical University of Vienna (Austria)
Klaus-Dieter Schewe   Massey University (New Zealand)

Program Committee

Franz Baader	RWTH Aachen (Germany)
Leopoldo Bertossi	Carleton University (Canada)
Joachim Biskup	University of Dortmund (Germany)
Marco Cadoli	University of Rome La Sapienza (Italy)
Alexandre Dikovsky	Université de Nantes (France)
Jürgen Dix	University of Manchester (UK)
Fausto Giunchiglia	IRST Trento (Italy)
Sven Hartmann	University of Rostock (Germany)
Gyula Katona	Hungarian Academy of Sciences (Hungary)
Nicola Leone	University of Calabria (Italy)
Neil Lesley	Victoria University Wellington (New Zealand)
Bernhard Nebel	Albert Ludwigs University at Freiburg (Germany)
Vladimir Sazonov	University of Liverpool (UK)
Thomas Schwentick	Phillipps University at Marburg (Germany)
Dietmar Seipel	University of Würzburg (Germany)
V.S. Subrahmanian	University of Maryland (USA)
Bernhard Thalheim	Brandenburgian Technical University at Cottbus (Germany)
José Maria Turull Torres	Univerdidad de Luján (Argentina)
Jan Van den Bussche	University of Limburg (Belgium)
Alexei Voronkov	University of Manchester (UK)

External Referees

Marcelo Arenas	Joachim Baumeister
Piero Bonatti	Gerhard Brewka
David Coufal	Ingo Dahn
Alexander Dekhtyar	Michael Dekhtyar
Carlos Damasio	Johannes Fürnkranz
Jörg Gebhardt	Ulrich Geske
Giorgio Ghelli	Giovambattista Ianni
Christoph Koch	Michael Kohlhase
Rudolf Kruse	Joao Leite
Sebastian Link	Alexei Lisitsa
Vincenzo Loia	Elio Masciari
Frank Neven	Nikolaj S. Nikitchenko
Martin Otto	Flavio Rizzolo
Francesco Scarcello	M. P. Schellekens
Manfred Schmidt-Schauß	Emmanuel Stefanakis
Giorgio Terracina	Bernd Thomas
Hans Tompits	Alexei Tretiakov
D. Ursino	Mars Valiev
Emil Weydert	Jingtao Yao

Organization

Hans-Joachim Klein	Christian Albrechts University at Kiel (Germany)
Bernhard Thalheim	Brandenburgian Technical University at Cottbus (Germany)

Table of Contents

Modeling Paraconsistent Reasoning
by Classical Logic

Ofer Arieli[1] and Marc Denecker[2]

[1] Department of Computer Science, The Academic College of Tel-Aviv
Antokolski 4, Tel-Aviv 61161, Israel
oarieli@mta.ac.il
[2] Department of Computer Science, University of Leuven
Celestijnenlaan 200A, B-3001 Heverlee, Belgium
marcd@cs.kuleuven.ac.be

Abstract. We introduce a general method for paraconsistent reasoning in knowledge systems by classical second-order formulae. A standard technique for paraconsistent reasoning on inconsistent classical theories is by shifting to multiple-valued logics. We show how these multiple-valued theories can be "shifted back" to two-valued classical theories (through a polynomial transformation), and how preferential reasoning based on multiple-valued logic can be represented by classical circumscription-like axioms. By applying this process we manage to overcome the shortcoming of classical logic in properly handling inconsistent data, and provide new ways of implementing multiple-valued paraconsistent reasoning in knowledge systems. Standard multiple-valued reasoning can thus be performed through theorem provers for classical logic, and multiple-valued preferential reasoning can be implemented using algorithms for processing circumscriptive theories (such as DLS and SCAN).

1 Introduction

Any knowledge-based system for common-sense reasoning must be able to process incomplete and inconsistent information in a "proper" way. This implies, in particular, that (first-order) classical logic is inappropriate for such systems. Indeed, on one hand classical logic is too cautious in drawing conclusions from incomplete theories. This is so since classical logic is monotonic, thus it does not allow to retract previously drawn conclusions in light of new, more accurate information. On the other hand, classical logic is too liberal in drawing conclusions from inconsistent theories. This is explained by the fact that classical logic is not paraconsistent [7], therefore everything classically follows from a contradictory set of premises. If follows, therefore, that knowledge-based systems should use other (or more general) formalisms for handling uncertainty.

Preferential reasoning [23] is an elegant way to overcome classical logic's shortcoming for reasoning on uncertainty. It is based on the idea that in order to draw conclusions from a given theory one should not consider all the models of that theory, but only a subset of *preferred models*. This subset is usually

T. Eiter and K.-D. Schewe (Eds.): FoIKS 2002, LNCS 2284, pp. 1–14, 2002.
© Springer-Verlag Berlin Heidelberg 2002

determined according to some preference criterion, which is often defined in terms of partial orders on the space of valuations. This method of preferring some models and disregarding the others yields robust formalisms that allow to draw intuitive conclusions from partial knowledge.

In the context of classical logic, preferential semantics cannot help to overcome the problem of trivial reasoning with contradictory theories. Indeed, if a certain theory has no (two-valued) models, then it has no preferred models as well. A useful way of reasoning on contradictory classical theories is therefore by embedding them in multiple-valued logics in general, and Belnap's four-valued logic [5,6] in particular (which is the underlying multiple-valued semantics used here). There are several reasons for using this setting. The most important ones for our purposes are the following:

- In the context of four-valued semantics it is possible to define consequence relations that are not degenerated w.r.t. *any* theory (see, e.g., [1,2,6,20,21]); the fact that every theory has a nonempty set of four-valued models implies that four-valued reasoning may be useful for properly handling inconsistent theories. As shown e.g. in [1,2], this indeed is the case.
- Analysis of four-valued models can be instructive to pinpoint the causes of the inconsistency and/or the incompleteness of the theory under consideration. (See [1,2,5,6] for a detailed discussion on this property, as well as some relevant results).

However, Belnap's four-valued logic has its own shortcomings:

- As in classical logic, many theories have too many models, and as a consequence the entailment relation is often too weak. In fact, since Belnap's logic is weaker than classical logic w.r.t. consistent theories, we are even in a worse situation than in classical logic!
  A (partial) solution to this problem is by using preferential reasoning in the context of multiple-valued logic (see, e.g., [1,2,3,11,12,20,21]).
- At the computational level, implementing paraconsistent reasoning based on four-valued semantics poses important challenges. An effective implementation of theorem provers for one of the existing proof systems for Belnap's logic requires a major effort. The problem is even worse in the context of four-valued *preferential* reasoning, for which currently no (implementations of) proof systems are known.

Our goal in this paper is to show a way in which these problems can be avoided (or at least alleviated) altogether. In particular, we present a polynomial transformation back from four-valued theories to two-valued theories such that reasoning in preferential four-valued semantics can be implemented by standard theorem proving in two-valued logic. Moreover, preference criteria on four-valued theories are translated into 'circumscriptive-like" formulae [17,18], and thus paraconsistent reasoning may be automatically computed by some specialized methods for compiling circumscriptive theories (such as those described in

[10,22]), and incorporated into algorithms such as SCAN [19] and DLS [8,9], for reducing second-order formulae to their first-order equivalents[1].

2   Preliminaries

2.1   Preferential Reasoning

First we briefly review the basic notions of preferential reasoning [23].

Definition 2.1. A *preferential model* (w.r.t. a language Σ) is a triple $\mathcal{M} = (M, \models, \leq)$, where M is a set (of semantical objects, sometimes called *states*), $\models$ is a relation on $M \times \Sigma$ (called the *satisfaction relation*), and $\leq$ (the *preference relation*) is a binary relation on the elements of M.

Most often, the preference relation is a partial order or at least a pre-order (i.e., reflexive and transitive). In this paper this will always be the case.

Definition 2.2. Let $\mathcal{M} = (M, \models, \leq)$ be a preferential model, Γ a set of formulae in a language Σ, and $m \in M$. Then m *satisfies* Γ (notation: $m \models \Gamma$) if $m \models \gamma$ for every $\gamma \in \Gamma$. m *preferentially satisfies* Γ (alternatively, m is a $\leq$-*most preferred model* of Γ) if m satisfies Γ, and for each other $n \in M$ s.t. $n \leq m$ and n satisfies Γ, it holds that $m \leq n$. The set of the elements in M that preferentially satisfy Γ is denoted by $!(\Gamma, \leq)$.

Now we can define the preferential entailment relations:

Definition 2.3. Let $\mathcal{M} = (M, \models, \leq)$ be a preferential model, Γ a set of formulae in Σ, and ψ a formula in Σ. We say that ψ (preferentially) *follows* from Γ if every element of $!(\Gamma, \leq)$ satisfies ψ. We denote this by $\Gamma \models_{\leq} \psi$.

The idea that a non-monotonic deduction should be based on some preference criterion that reflects some normality relation among the relevant semantical objects is a very natural one, and may be traced back to [17]. Furthermore, this approach is the semantical basis of some well-known general patterns for non-monotonic reasoning, introduced in [13,14,15,16], and it is a key concept behind many formalisms for nonmonotonic and paraconsistent reasoning (see, e.g., [1,2,3,11,12,20,21]). Our purpose in this paper is to propose techniques of expressing preferential reasoning by formulae in the underlying language. Next we define the framework for doing so.

2.2   The Underlying Semantical Structure

The formalism that we consider here is based on Belnap's four-valued algebraic structure [5,6], denoted by $\mathcal{FOUR}$ (Figure 1). This structure is composed of four elements $FOUR = \{t, f, \bot, \top\}$, arranged in the following two lattice structures:

---

[1] For a longer version of this paper see [4].

- $(FOUR, \leq_t)$, in which t is the maximal element, f is the minimal one, and $\top, \bot$ are two intermediate and incomparable elements.
- $(FOUR, \leq_k)$, in which $\top$ is the maximal element, $\bot$ is the minimal one, and t, f are two intermediate and incomparable elements.

Here, t and f correspond to the classical truth values. The two other truth values may intuitively be understood as representing different cases of uncertainty: $\top$ corresponds to a contradictory knowledge, and $\bot$ corresponds to an incomplete knowledge. This interpretation of the meaning of the truth values will be useful in what follows for modeling paraconsistent reasoning[2]. According to this interpretation, the partial order $\leq_t$ reflects differences in the amount of *truth* that each element represents, and the partial order $\leq_k$ reflects differences in the amount of *knowledge* that each element exhibits.

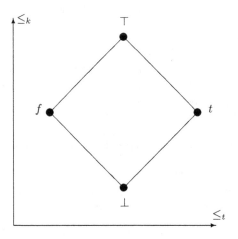

Fig. 1. $\mathcal{FOUR}$

In what follows we shall denote by $\wedge$ and $\vee$ the meet and join operations on $(FOUR, \leq_t)$. A negation, $\neg$, is a unary operation on $FOUR$, defined by $\neg t = f$, $\neg f = t$, $\neg \top = \top$, and $\neg \bot = \bot$. As usual in such cases, we take t and $\top$ as the *designated elements* in $FOUR$ (i.e., the elements that represent true assertions).

In the rest of this paper we denote by Σ a language with a finite alphabet, in which the connectives are $\vee, \wedge, \neg$. These connectives correspond to the operations on $FOUR$ with the same notations. ν and μ denote arbitrary four-valued *valuations*, i.e., functions that assign a value in $FOUR$ to every atom in Σ. The extension to complex formulae in Σ is defined in the standard way:

$$\nu(\psi \wedge \phi) = glb_{\leq_t}(\nu(\psi), \nu(\phi)), \quad \nu(\psi \vee \phi) = lub_{\leq_t}(\nu(\psi), \nu(\phi)), \quad \nu(\neg\psi) = \neg\nu(\psi).$$

---

[2] This was also the original motivation of Belnap when he introduced $\mathcal{FOUR}$.

The space of the four-valued valuations is denoted by $\mathcal{V}^4$. A valuation $\nu \in \mathcal{V}^4$ is a *model* of a formula ψ (alternatively, ν *satisfies* ψ) if $\nu(\psi) \in \{t, \top\}$. ν is a model of a set Γ of formulae if ν is a model of every $\psi \in \Gamma$. The set of the models of Γ is denoted by $mod(\Gamma)$.

2.3   Four-Valued Preferential Reasoning

A natural definition of a consequence relation on $\mathcal{FOUR}$ is the following:

Definition 2.4. Let Γ be a set of formulae and ψ a formula in Σ. Denote $\Gamma \models^4 \psi$ if every four-valued model of Γ is a four-valued model of ψ.

In [2] it is shown that $\models^4$ is a consequence relation in the sense of Tarski [24], i.e., it is reflexive, monotonic, and transitive. It is also shown there that $\models^4$ is paraconsistent, compact, and has cut-free, sound and complete Hilbert-type and Gentzen-type proof systems. However, the fact that $\models^4$ is a Tarskian consequence relation means, in particular, that it is monotonic, and as such it is "over-cautious" in drawing conclusions from incomplete theories. In what follows we therefore refine the reasoning process by using the techniques discussed above for preferential reasoning. Below are some useful preference criteria.

Definition 2.5. [2] Let $\nu, \mu \in \mathcal{V}^4$. Denote:

- $\nu \leq_k \mu$ if $\nu(p) \leq_k \mu(p)$ for every atom p.
- $\nu \leq_{\{\top\}} \mu$ if for every atom p, $\mu(p) = \top$ whenever $\nu(p) = \top$.
- $\nu \leq_{\{\top, \bot\}} \mu$ if for every atom p, $\mu(p) \in \{\top, \bot\}$ whenever $\nu(p) \in \{\top, \bot\}$.

It is easy to check that $\leq_k$ is a partial order and $\leq_{\{\top\}}$, $\leq_{\{\top, \bot\}}$ are pre-orders on $\mathcal{V}^4$. In what follows we shall write $\nu <_k \mu$ to denote that $\nu \leq_k \mu$ and $\mu \not\leq_k \nu$; similarly for $<_{\{\top\}}$ and $<_{\{\top, \bot\}}$.

Each one of the preference orders given in Definition 2.5 has its own rationality: according to $\leq_k$, for instance, one prefers valuations that reflect as minimal information as reasonably possible. This criterion may as well be viewed as an argumentation for consistency preserving, since as long as one keeps the amount of information (or belief) as minimal as possible, the tendency of getting into conflicts decreases.

The pre-order $\leq_{\{\top\}}$ states a somewhat more explicit preference of inconsistency minimization: it prefers those valuations that minimize the amount of inconsistent assignments. Similarly, $\leq_{\{\top, \bot\}}$, prefers those valuations that are as classical as possible. I.e., those ones that assign classical truth values whenever possible.

Given a set Γ of formulae in Σ, the minimal elements in $mod(\Gamma)$ w.r.t. $\leq_k$ (respectively, w.r.t $\leq_{\{\top\}}$, w.r.t. $\leq_{\{\top, \bot\}}$) are called the *k-minimal models* of Γ (respectively, the *most consistent models* of Γ, the *most classical models* of Γ).

Example 2.1. Let $\Gamma = \{p, \neg p \vee q, \neg q, r \vee q\}$. The four-valued models of Γ are given in Table 1.

The *k*-minimal models of Γ are $\{M_1, M_3\}$, the most consistent ones are $\{M_1, M_3, M_4, M_5\}$, and the most classical ones are $\{M_1, M_4, M_5\}$.

Table 1. The elements in $mod(\Gamma)$

Model	p	q	r	Model	p	q	r
M_1	$\top$	f	t	M_6	t	$\top$	$\top$
M_2	$\top$	f	$\top$	M_7	$\top$	$\top$	$\bot$
M_3	t	$\top$	$\bot$	M_8	$\top$	$\top$	f
M_4	t	$\top$	f	M_9	$\top$	$\top$	t
M_5	t	$\top$	t	M_{10}	$\top$	$\top$	$\top$

Each one of the preference criteria considered in Definition 2.5 induces a corresponding preferential consequence relation:

Definition 2.6. [2] Let Γ be a set of formulae and ψ a formula in Σ. Denote:

- $\Gamma \models_k^4 \psi$ if every k-minimal model of Γ is a model of ψ.
- $\Gamma \models_{\{\top\}}^4 \psi$ if every most consistent model of Γ is a model of ψ.
- $\Gamma \models_{\{\top,\bot\}}^4 \psi$ if every most classical model of Γ is a model of ψ.

Example 2.2. Consider again the set Γ of Example 2.1, and let $\psi = r \vee \neg r$. Then $\Gamma \models_{\{\top,\bot\}}^4 \psi$, while $\Gamma \not\models_k^4 \psi$ and $\Gamma \not\models_{\{\top\}}^4 \psi$.

Clearly, the consequence relations of Definition 2.6 are particular cases of the preferential entailment relations $\models_\leq$, given in Definition 2.3. It is also easy to see that all of these consequence relations are paraconsistent and have the following properties (see [2,3] for further details):

1. $\Gamma \models_k^4 \psi$ iff $\Gamma \models^4 \psi$.

   Thus $\models_k^4$ is a compact representation of $\models^4$; it is sufficient to consider only the k-minimal models of a given theory in order to simulate reasoning with $\models^4$.

2. *Denote by $\models^2$ the two-valued classical consequence relation. If Γ is classically consistent and ψ is a formula in CNF, none of its disjunctions is a tautology, then $\Gamma \models_{\{\top\}}^4 \psi$ iff $\Gamma \models^2 \psi$.*

3. *If Γ is classically consistent then $\Gamma \models_{\{\top,\bot\}}^4 \psi$ iff $\Gamma \models^2 \psi$.*

   Thus $\models_{\{\top,\bot\}}^4$ is equivalent to classical logic on consistent theories and is nontrivial w.r.t. inconsistent theories in the sense that not all formulas are entailed.

3   Paraconsistent Classical Reasoning

This section shows how to simulate paraconsistent reasoning by classical reasoning. We propose a transformation such that four-valued entailment for theories can be defined in terms of classical two-valued entailment for the transformed theories. Moreover, we show that four-valued preferential entailment can be defined in terms of classical entailment for the transformed theories augmented with circumscriptive axioms.

3.1   An Alternative Representation of Semantical Concepts

The elements of $\mathcal{FOUR}$ can be represented by pairs of components from the two-valued lattice $(\{0,1\}, 0 < 1)$ as follows: $t = (1,0)$, $f = (0,1)$, $\top = (1,1)$, $\bot = (0,0)$. In this representation the negation operator is defined in $\mathcal{FOUR}$ by $\neg(x,y) = (y,x)$, and the corresponding partial orders in $\mathcal{FOUR}$ are represented by the following rules: for every $x_1, x_2, y_1, y_2 \in \{0,1\}$,

$$(x_1, y_1) \leq_t (x_2, y_2) \text{ iff } x_1 \leq x_2 \text{ and } y_1 \geq y_2,$$

$$(x_1, y_1) \leq_k (x_2, y_2) \text{ iff } x_1 \leq x_2 \text{ and } y_1 \leq y_2.$$

It follows, in particular, that in the representation by pairs of two-valued components, the $\leq_t$-meet (i.e., the greatest lower bound w.r.t. $\leq_t$) and the $\leq_t$-join (i.e., the least upper bound w.r.t. $\leq_t$) in $\mathcal{FOUR}$ are defined as follows:

$$(x_1, y_1) \wedge (x_2, y_2) = (x_1 \wedge x_2,\ y_1 \vee y_2).$$

$$(x_1, y_1) \vee (x_2, y_2) = (x_1 \vee x_2,\ y_1 \wedge y_2),$$

It is obvious that there is a one-to-one correspondence between four-valued valuations and pairs of two-valued valuations. We shall denote these pairs of two-valued components by $\nu = (\nu_1, \nu_2)$. So if, for instance, $\nu(\psi) = t$, then $\nu_1(\psi) = 1$ and $\nu_2(\psi) = 0$.

The preference criteria considered in the previous section may now be reformulated as follows:

Lemma 3.1. *Let* $\nu, \mu \in \mathcal{V}^4$. *Then:*

- $\nu \leq_k \mu$ *iff for every atom* p, $\nu_1(p) \leq \mu_1(p)$ *and* $\nu_2(p) \leq \mu_2(p)$.
- $\nu \leq_{\{\top\}} \mu$ *iff for every atom* p, *if* $\nu_1(p) \wedge \nu_2(p) = 1$, *then* $\mu_1(p) \wedge \mu_2(p) = 1$ *as well.*
- $\nu \leq_{\{\top, \bot\}} \mu$ *iff for every atom* p, *if* $(\nu_1(p) \wedge \nu_2(p)) \vee (\neg \nu_1(p) \wedge \neg \nu_2(p)) = 1$, *then* $(\mu_1(p) \wedge \mu_2(p)) \vee (\neg \mu_1(p) \wedge \neg \mu_2(p)) = 1$ *as well.*

Proof: Immediately follows from the corresponding definitions.   □

Given the language Σ, define the language $\Sigma^\pm$ based on the alphabet consisting of symbols p^+, p^- for each atom p of Σ. Let ψ be a formula in Σ. Denote by $\widehat{\psi}$ the formula in $\Sigma^\pm$, obtained from ψ by first translating ψ to its negation normal form, ψ' (where the negation operator precedes atomic formulae only)[3], then substituting every occurrence in ψ' of an atomic formula p that is not preceded by a negation, by the new predicate symbol p^+, and replacing every other occurrence of p in ψ', together with the negation that precedes it, by the new predicate symbol p^-. For instance, if $\psi = \neg(p \vee \neg q)$, then $\psi' = \neg p \wedge q$, and so $\widehat{\psi} = p^- \wedge q^+$. Given a theory Γ, we shall write $\widehat{\Gamma}$ for the set $\{\widehat{\psi} \mid \psi \in \Gamma\}$. Note

---

[3] It is easy to verify that as in the two-valued case, also in $\mathcal{FOUR}$ ψ and ψ' are logically equivalent.

that $\widehat{\Gamma}$ can be obtained from Γ in a linear time. Moreover, for every Γ, $\widehat{\Gamma}$ is a positive theory, and hence it is consistent.

Given a four-valued valuation $\nu = (\nu_1, \nu_2)$, $\widehat{\nu}$ denotes the two-valued valuation on $\Sigma^\pm$, defined by $\widehat{\nu}(p^+) = \nu_1(p)$ and $\widehat{\nu}(p^-) = \nu_2(p)$. Extensions to complex formulae in $\Sigma^\pm$ are defined in the usual way[4].

Definition 3.1. Given a valuation $\nu = (\nu_1, \nu_2)$, denote $\overline{\nu} = (\neg\nu_2, \neg\nu_1)$.

Proposition 3.1. $\nu(\psi) = (\widehat{\nu}(\widehat{\psi}), \ \neg\widehat{\overline{\nu}}(\widehat{\psi}))$.

Proof: Let ψ' be the negation normal form of ψ. Since ψ and ψ' are logically equivalent in $\mathcal{FOUR}$, $\nu(\psi)$ is the same as $\nu(\psi')$. The rest of the proof is by an induction on the structure of ψ':

$\psi' = p$: $(\widehat{\nu}(\widehat{p}), -\widehat{\overline{\nu}}(\widehat{p})) = ((\widehat{\nu_1, \nu_2})(p^+), \neg(\widehat{\neg\nu_2, \neg\nu_1})(p^+)) = (\nu_1(p), \neg\neg\nu_2(p)) =$
         $(\nu_1(p), \nu_2(p)) = \nu(p)$.

$\psi' = \neg p$: $(\widehat{\nu}(\widehat{\neg p}), \neg\widehat{\overline{\nu}}(\widehat{\neg p})) = ((\widehat{\nu_1, \nu_2})(p^-), \neg(\widehat{\neg\nu_2, \neg\nu_1})(p^-)) =$
         $(\nu_2(p), \neg\neg\nu_1(p)) = (\nu_2(p), \nu_1(p)) = \neg(\nu_1(p), \nu_2(p)) = \neg\nu(p) = \nu(\neg p)$.

$\psi' = \phi_1 \vee \phi_2$: $\nu(\phi_1 \vee \phi_2) = \nu(\phi_1) \vee \nu(\phi_2) = (\widehat{\nu}(\widehat{\phi_1}), \neg\widehat{\overline{\nu}}(\widehat{\phi_1})) \vee (\widehat{\nu}(\widehat{\phi_2}), \neg\widehat{\overline{\nu}}(\widehat{\phi_2})) =$
         $(\widehat{\nu}(\widehat{\phi_1}) \vee \widehat{\nu}(\widehat{\phi_2}), \neg\widehat{\overline{\nu}}(\widehat{\phi_1}) \wedge \neg\widehat{\overline{\nu}}(\widehat{\phi_2})) = (\widehat{\nu}(\widehat{\phi_1} \vee \widehat{\phi_2}), \neg(\widehat{\overline{\nu}}(\widehat{\phi_1}) \vee \widehat{\overline{\nu}}(\widehat{\phi_2}))) =$
         $(\widehat{\nu}(\widehat{\phi_1 \vee \phi_2}), \neg\widehat{\overline{\nu}}(\widehat{\phi_1 \vee \phi_2})) = (\widehat{\nu}(\widehat{\phi_1 \vee \phi_2}), \neg\widehat{\overline{\nu}}(\widehat{\phi_1 \vee \phi_2}))$.

The case $\psi' = \phi_1 \wedge \phi_2$ is similar to that of $\phi_1 \vee \phi_2$. $\square$

3.2   Simulating (Preferential) Four-Valued Reasoning by Classical Logic

In what follows we use the pairwise representations, considered in the previous section, for the following goals:

1. Showing that four-valued reasoning can be simulated by classical reasoning,
2. Constructing circumscriptive formulae for defining four-valued preferential reasoning.

For item (1) above we first need the following lemma:

Lemma 3.2. *For every four-valued valuation ν and a formula ψ in Σ, $\nu(\psi)$ is designated iff $\widehat{\nu}(\widehat{\psi}) = 1$.*

Proof: $\nu(\psi)$ is designated iff $\nu_1(\psi) = 1$, iff (Proposition 3.1) $\widehat{\nu}(\widehat{\psi}) = 1$. $\square$

The following result is an immediate corollary of Lemma 3.2:

---

[4] Clearly, the converse construction is also possible: every two-valued valuation ν on $\Sigma^\pm$ corresponds to a unique four-valued valuation ν' on Σ defined, for every atom p, by $\nu'(p) = (\nu(p^+), \nu(p^-))$.

Theorem 3.1. $\Gamma \models^4 \psi$ iff $\widehat{\Gamma} \models^2 \widehat{\psi}$.

It follows, therefore, that four-valued reasoning may be implemented by two-valued theorem provers. Moreover, since $\widehat{\Gamma}$ is obtained from Γ in a polynomial time, the theorem above shows that four-valued entailment in the context of Belnap's logic is polynomially reducible to the classical entailment.

Another immediate consequence of this theorem is the next well-known result:

Corollary 3.1. *In the language without negations,* $\Gamma \models^4 \psi$ *iff* $\Gamma \models^2 \psi$.

We turn now to the preferential case. To extend the above technique to deal with preferential four-valued reasoning, we must express that the encoded four-valued interpretation is minimal with respect to a preference relation $\leq$. This can be accomplished by introducing a circumscription axiom. The proviso is that we are able to express the preference relation $\leq$ objectively, by a formula $\Psi_{\leq}$. The first point to check out is therefore how to express a semantical preference relation $\leq$ in an axiom.

Let $\boldsymbol{p} = \{p_1, .., p_n\}$ be the set symbols of our language Σ, and let $\boldsymbol{p}^{\pm}$ be the set of symbols $\{p_1^+, p_1^-, \ldots, p_n^+, p_n^-\}$. To be able to express for two valuations $\nu = (\nu_1, \nu_2)$ and $\mu = (\mu_1, \mu_2)$ that $\nu \leq \mu$ by one formula, we introduce new symbols $\boldsymbol{q}$ as renaming of the symbols of $\boldsymbol{p}$. With $(\boldsymbol{p}^{\pm} : \nu; \boldsymbol{q}^{\pm} : \mu)$, we denote the two-valued interpretation that interprets symbols p_i^+ as $\nu_1(p)$, p_i^- as $\nu_2(p)$, q_i^+ as $\mu_1(p)$ and q_i^- as $\mu_2(p)$ for every $1 \leq i \leq n$.

Definition 3.2. A preferential order $\leq$ is *represented* by a formula $\Psi_{\leq}(\boldsymbol{p}^{\pm}, \boldsymbol{q}^{\pm})$ if for every four-valued valuations ν and μ we have that $\nu \leq \mu$ iff $(\boldsymbol{p}^{\pm} : \nu, \boldsymbol{q}^{\pm} : \mu)$ satisfies $\Psi_{\leq}(\boldsymbol{p}^{\pm}, \boldsymbol{q}^{\pm})$.

Given a formula ψ of Σ, denote by $\widehat{\psi}(\boldsymbol{P}^{\pm})$ the formula that is obtained by substituting symbols $\boldsymbol{P}^{\pm}$ for symbols $\boldsymbol{p}^{\pm}$ in $\widehat{\psi}$.

Proposition 3.2. *Let* $\Psi_{\leq}(\boldsymbol{p}^{\pm}, \boldsymbol{P}^{\pm})$ *be a formula that represents a preferential order* $\leq$*. Then* ν *is a* $\leq$*-most preferred model of* ψ *(that is,* $\nu \in !(\{\psi\}, \leq)$*) iff* $\widehat{\nu}$ *satisfies* $\widehat{\psi}$ *and the following formula:*

$$\mathsf{Circ}_{\leq}(\boldsymbol{p}^{\pm}) \;=\; \forall(\boldsymbol{P}^{\pm})\,\{\,\widehat{\psi}(\boldsymbol{P}^{\pm}) \;\rightarrow\; (\,\Psi_{\leq}(\boldsymbol{P}^{\pm}, \boldsymbol{p}^{\pm}) \rightarrow \Psi_{\leq}(\boldsymbol{p}^{\pm}, \boldsymbol{P}^{\pm}))\,\}.$$

Proof: By Corollary 3.2, ν is a model of ψ iff $\widehat{\nu}$ satisfies $\widehat{\psi}$. It remains to show that the fact that $\widehat{\nu}$ satisfies $\mathsf{Circ}_{\leq}$ is a necessary and sufficient condition for assuring that ν is a $\leq$-minimal element in the set $mod(\psi)$ of the models of ψ. Indeed, $\widehat{\nu}$ satisfies $\mathsf{Circ}_{\leq}$ iff for every valuation μ that satisfies ψ and for which $\mu \leq \nu$, it is also true that $\nu \leq \mu$. Thus, for every $\mu \in mod(\psi)$, we have that $(\mu \leq \nu) \rightarrow (\nu \leq \mu)$ (alternatively, there is no $\mu \in mod(\psi)$ s.t. $\mu < \nu$). I.e., $\nu \in !(\psi, \leq)$. □

Note 3.1. Denote the formula $\bigwedge_{i=1}^{n} ((p_i^+ = P_i^+) \wedge (p_i^- = P_i^-))$ by $\boldsymbol{p}^{\pm} = \boldsymbol{P}^{\pm}$ [5], and let $\Psi_{<}(\boldsymbol{P}^{\pm}, \boldsymbol{p}^{\pm})$ be the following formula: $\Psi_{\leq}(\boldsymbol{P}^{\pm}, \boldsymbol{p}^{\pm}) \wedge \neg \Psi_{\leq}(\boldsymbol{p}^{\pm}, \boldsymbol{P}^{\pm})$. Then:

---

[5] In the context of two-valued logic, $p = q$ denotes $\forall \overline{x}.p(\overline{x}) \leftrightarrow q(\overline{x})$.

a) The formula $\mathsf{Circ}_{\leq}(\boldsymbol{p}^{\pm})$ of Proposition 3.2 may be rewritten as follows:

$$\forall(\boldsymbol{P}^{\pm})\ \{\ \widehat{\psi}(\boldsymbol{P}^{\pm})\ \rightarrow\ \neg\varPsi_{<}(\boldsymbol{P}^{\pm},\boldsymbol{p}^{\pm})\ \}$$

b) In case that $\leq$ is a partial order, $\mathsf{Circ}_{\leq}(\boldsymbol{p}^{\pm})$ can be rewritten as follows:

$$\forall(\boldsymbol{P}^{\pm})\ \{\ [\,\widehat{\psi}(\boldsymbol{P}^{\pm})\wedge\varPsi_{\leq}(\boldsymbol{P}^{\pm},\boldsymbol{p}^{\pm})\,]\rightarrow\boldsymbol{p}^{\pm}=\boldsymbol{P}^{\pm}\ \}$$

The following theorem is an immediate corollary of Proposition 3.2:

Theorem 3.2. *Let $\varGamma$ be a set of formulae and ψ a formula in $\varSigma$. Let $\mathsf{Circ}_{\leq}$ be the formula given in Proposition 3.2 for a preferential relation $\leq$. Then $\varGamma\models_{\leq}\psi$ iff $\widehat{\varGamma}\cup\mathsf{Circ}_{\leq}\models^2\widehat{\psi}$.*

Proposition 3.2 gives a general characterization in terms of "formula circumscription" [18] of the preferred models of a given theory: given a preferential relation $\leq$, in order to express $\leq$-preferential satisfaction of a theory, one should first formulate a corresponding formula $\varPsi_{\leq}$ that represents $\leq$, and then integrate $\varPsi_{\leq}$ with $\mathsf{Circ}_{\leq}$ as in Proposition 3.2. Again, this can be done in a polynomial time.

Next we define formulae that represent the preferential relations considered above.

Definition 3.3. In what follows we shall write $x \preceq y$ for $x \rightarrow y$, and $x \prec y$ for $(x\rightarrow y)\wedge\neg(y\rightarrow x)$.

Lemma 3.3. *Let n be the number of diffrent atomic formulae in $\varSigma$. Then:*

a) *The preferential relation $\leq_k$ is represented by the following formula:*

$$\varPsi_{\leq_k}(\boldsymbol{p}^{\pm},\boldsymbol{P}^{\pm})\ =\ \bigwedge_{i=1}^{n}\ ((p_i^+\preceq P_i^+)\wedge(p_i^-\preceq P_i^-))$$

b) *The preferential relation $\leq_{\{\top\}}$ is represented by the following formula:*

$$\varPsi_{\leq_{\{\top\}}}(\boldsymbol{p}^{\pm},\boldsymbol{P}^{\pm})\ =\ \bigwedge_{i=1}^{n}\ ((p_i^+\wedge p_i^-)\preceq(P_i^+\wedge P_i^-))$$

c) *The preferential relation $\leq_{\{\top,\bot\}}$ is represented by the following formula:*

$$\varPsi_{\leq_{\{\top,\bot\}}}(\boldsymbol{p}^{\pm},\boldsymbol{P}^{\pm})\ =\ \bigwedge_{i=1}^{n}\ (\ ((p_i^+\wedge p_i^-)\vee(\neg p_i^+\wedge\neg p_i^-))$$
$$\preceq((P_i^+\wedge P_i^-)\vee(\neg P_i^+\wedge\neg P_i^-))\ )$$

Proof: We show only part (a); the proof of the other parts is similar.

$$\nu \leq_k \mu \Longleftrightarrow \forall 1 \leq i \leq n \ \ \nu(p_i) \leq_k \mu(p_i)$$
$$\Longleftrightarrow \forall 1 \leq i \leq n \ \ \nu_1(p_i) \leq \mu_1(p_i) \text{ and } \nu_2(p_i) \leq \mu_2(p_i)$$
$$\Longleftrightarrow (\boldsymbol{p}^\pm{:}\nu, \ \boldsymbol{P}^\pm{:}\mu) \text{ satisfies } \bigwedge_{i=1}^n ((p_i^+ \preceq P_i^+) \wedge (p_i^- \preceq P_i^-))$$
$$\Longleftrightarrow (\boldsymbol{p}^\pm{:}\nu, \ \boldsymbol{P}^\pm{:}\mu) \text{ satisfies } \Psi_{\leq_k}(\boldsymbol{p}^\pm, \boldsymbol{P}^\pm).$$

$\square$

By Proposition 3.2, Lemma 3.3(a), and Note 3.1(b), we have the following corollary:

Corollary 3.2. *A valuation* $\nu = (\nu_1, \nu_2)$ *is a k-minimal model of ψ iff $\hat{\nu}$ satisfies $\hat{\psi}$ and* $\mathsf{Circ}_{\leq_k}(\boldsymbol{p}^\pm)$, *where* $\mathsf{Circ}_{\leq_k}(\boldsymbol{p}^\pm)$ *is the following formula*[6]:

$$\forall(\boldsymbol{P}^\pm) \ \left\{ \left[\hat{\psi}(\boldsymbol{P}^\pm) \wedge \bigwedge_{i=1}^n ((P_i^+ \preceq p_i^+) \wedge (P_i^- \preceq p_i^-)) \right] \right.$$
$$\left. \rightarrow \left[\bigwedge_{i=1}^n ((P_i^+ = p_i^+) \wedge (P_i^- = p_i^-)) \right] \right\}$$

As in Corollary 3.2, the most consistent models and the most classical models of a given theory can be represented by formulae of the form $\mathsf{Circ}_{\leq_{\{\mathbf{\square}\}}}(\boldsymbol{p}^\pm)$ and $\mathsf{Circ}_{\leq_{\{\mathbf{\square},\mathbf{\square}\}}}(\boldsymbol{p}^\pm)$, obtained by respectively integrating the formulae given in parts (b) and (c) of Lemma 3.3 with $\mathsf{Circ}_\leq$, given in Proposition 3.2.

In the remaining of this section we consider a uniform way of representing $\mathsf{Circ}_{\leq_{\{\mathbf{\square}\}}}(\boldsymbol{p}^\pm)$, $\mathsf{Circ}_{\leq_{\{\mathbf{\square},\mathbf{\square}\}}}(\boldsymbol{p}^\pm)$, and some other formulae that correspond to preferential criteria like $\leq_{\{\top\}}$ and $\leq_{\{\top,\bot\}}$. For this, let $\Delta \subseteq FOUR$. Define an order relation $<_\Delta$ on $FOUR$ by $x <_\Delta y$ iff $x \notin \Delta$ while $y \in \Delta$. A corresponding pre-order on $\mathcal{V}^4$ may now be defined as follows: for every $\nu, \mu \in \mathcal{V}^4$, $\nu \leq_\Delta \mu$ iff for every atom p, the fact that $\nu(p) \in \Delta$ entails that $\mu(p) \in \Delta$ as well. The $\leq_\Delta$-most preferred models of Γ are the $\leq_\Delta$-minimal elements in $mod(\Gamma)$, and $\Gamma \models_\Delta^4 \psi$ if every $\leq_\Delta$-most preferred model of Γ is a model of ψ.

Clearly, $\leq_{\{\top\}}$ and $\leq_{\{\top,\bot\}}$ are particular cases of $\leq_\Delta$, where $\Delta = \{\top\}$ and $\Delta = \{\top, \bot\}$, respectively. Now, the $\leq_\Delta$-most preferred models of a given theory can be represented by a circumscriptive formula in the following way:

Definition 3.4. For $\Delta \subseteq FOUR$, let $\Lambda_\Delta(p^+, p^-) = \bigvee_{x \in \Delta} \Lambda_x(p^+, p^-)$, where

$$\Lambda_t(p^+, p^-) = p^+ \wedge \neg p^-, \qquad \Lambda_f(p^+, p^-) = \neg p^+ \wedge p^-,$$
$$\Lambda_\bot(p^+, p^-) = \neg p^+ \wedge \neg p^-, \qquad \Lambda_\top(p^+, p^-) = p^+ \wedge p^-. \quad [7]$$

Similar arguments as those in Lemma 3.3 show that the formula

$$\Psi_{\leq_\Delta}(\boldsymbol{p}^\pm, \boldsymbol{P}^\pm) = \bigwedge_{i=1}^n (\Lambda_\Delta(p_i^+, p_i^-) \preceq \Lambda_\Delta(P_i^+, P_i^-))$$

represents the preferential relation $\leq_\Delta$. Therefore, by Proposition 3.2,

---

[6] Note that $\mathsf{Circ}_{\leq_k}(\boldsymbol{p}^\pm)$ is a standard circumscriptive axiom in the sense of [17].

[7] Intuitively, $\Lambda_x(p^+, p^-)$ expresses that $\nu(p) = x$ and $\Lambda_\Delta(p^+, p^-)$ means that $\nu(p) \in \Delta$.

Proposition 3.3. *A valuation ν is a $\leq_\Delta$-preferred model of ψ iff $\widehat{\nu}$ satisfies $\widehat{\psi}$ and the following formula:*

$$\mathsf{Circ}_{\leq_\Delta}(\boldsymbol{p}^\pm) \;=\; \forall(\boldsymbol{P}^\pm)\,\{\,\widehat{\psi}(\boldsymbol{P}^\pm) \;\rightarrow\; (\Psi_{\leq_\Delta}(\boldsymbol{P}^\pm,\boldsymbol{p}^\pm)\rightarrow\Psi_{\leq_\Delta}(\boldsymbol{p}^\pm,\boldsymbol{P}^\pm))\,\}.$$

4   Experimental Study

As we have already noted, all the formulae that are obtained by our method have a circumscriptive form. It is therefore possible to apply, for instance, the formula $\mathsf{Circ}_{\leq_k}$, given in Corollary 3.2, in algorithms for reducing circumscriptive axioms. Below are some simple results obtained by experimenting with such algorithm (We have used Doherty, Lukaszewicz and Szalas DLS algorithm [8,9], available at http://www.ida.liu.se/labs/kplab/projects/dls/circ.html)[8].

- Consider the theory $\Gamma = \{Q(a), Q(b), \neg Q(a)\}$, where Q denotes some predicate, and a, b are two constants. In our context, this theory is translated to $\widehat{\Gamma} = \{Q^+(a), Q^+(b), Q^-(a)\}$. Circumscribing $\widehat{\Gamma}$ where Q^+ and Q^- are simultaneously minimized, yields the following result:

$$\forall x\,\{\,(Q^-(x) \rightarrow x = a) \wedge (Q^+(x) \rightarrow (x = a \vee x = b))\,\}.$$

  It follows, then, that a is the only object for which both $Q^+(x)$ and $Q^-(x)$ hold (i.e., a is the only object that is inconsistent w.r.t. Q), and b is the only object for which only $Q^+(x)$ holds. For all the other objects neither $Q^+(x)$ nor $Q^-(x)$ holds. I.e., if $c \notin \{a, b\}$ then $Q(c)$ corresponds to $\bot$. This indeed is exactly the k-minimal semantics of Γ.
  Note that the fact that for every object x different from a and b neither $Q^+(x)$ nor $Q^-(x)$ holds means that the truth values of all the domain elements other than a or b do not matter in order to satisfy this formula. This information may be important from analysis point of view.

- Suppose that in the previous example one wants to impose the law of excluded middle. It is possible to do so by adding to Γ the restriction $\psi = \forall x(Q(x) \vee \neg Q(x))$, which is translated to $\widehat{\psi} = \forall x(Q^+(x) \vee Q^-(x))$. Circumscribing $\widehat{\Gamma} \cup \{\widehat{\psi}\}$ yields

$$\forall x\,\{\,[(Q^+(x) \wedge x \neq a \wedge x \neq b) \rightarrow \neg Q^-(x)] \wedge [(Q^-(x) \wedge x \neq a) \rightarrow \neg Q^+(x)]\,\},$$

  which has almost the same meaning as before, except that this time, the combination of this and $\widehat{\psi}$ means that if $c \notin \{a, b\}$ then either $Q^+(c)$ or $Q^-(c)$ holds, but not both. It follows, then, that for such c, $Q(c)$ must have some classical value. Again, this corresponds to what one expects when k-minimizing $\Gamma \cup \{\psi\}$.

---

[8] In what follows we deliberately consider very simple cases. Our experience is that for more complex theories the output quickly becomes more complicated, and so not comprehensible by humans (it *is* manageable in automated computations, though).

5 Conclusion

In this paper we have introduced a method for paraconsistent reasoning in knowledge systems by classical second-order formulae. Our method touches upon several important aspects. First, it shows that two-valued reasoning may be useful for simulating inference procedures in the context of many-valued semantics. Second, this approach demonstrates the usefulness of circumscription not only as a general method for non-monotonic reasoning, but also as an appealing technique for implementing paraconsistent reasoning. Finally, this is another evidence to the fact that in many cases concepts that are defined in a "meta-language" (such as preference criteria, etc.) can be expressed in the language itself (using, e.g., higher-order formulae). This enables a potentially wide area for practical implementations. For instance, we have shown that preferential multiple-valued reasoning can be incorporated with practical applications for automated reasoning and theorem proving.

References

1. O.Arieli, A.Avron. *The logical role of the four-valued bilattice.* Proc. LICS'98, pp.218–226, IEEE Press, 1998.
2. O.Arieli, A.Avron. *The value of the four values.* Artificial Intelligence 102(1), pp.97–141, 1998.
3. O.Arieli, A.Avron. *Bilattices and paraconsistency.* Frontiers of Paraconsistent Logic (D. Batens, C. Mortensen, G. Priest, J. Van Bendegem, editors), pp.11–27, Studies in Logic and Computation 8, Research Studies Press, 2000.
4. O.Arieli, M.Denecker. *Circumscriptive approaches to paraconsistent reasoning.* Technical Report CW-304, Department of Computer Science, University of Leuven, 2001.
5. N.D.Belnap. *A useful four-valued logic.* Modern Uses of Multiple-Valued Logic (G.Epstein, J.M.Dunn, editors), pp.7–37, Reidel Publishing Company, 1977.
6. N.D.Belnap. *How computer should think.* Contemporary Aspects of Philosophy (G.Ryle, editor), pp.30–56, Oriel Press, 1977.
7. N.C.A.da-Costa. *On the theory of inconsistent formal systems.* Notre Dame Journal of Formal Logic 15, pp.497–510, 1974.
8. P.Doherty, W.Lukaszewicz, A.Szalas. *Computing circumscription revisited: Preliminary report.* Proc. IJCAI'95, pp.1502–1508, 1995.
9. P.Doherty, W.Lukaszewicz, A.Szalas. *Computing circumscription revisited: A reduction algorithm.* Journal of Automated Reasoning 18, pp.297–334, 1997.
10. M.L.Ginsberg. *A circumscriptive theorem prover.* Artificial Intelligence 29, pp.209–230, 1989.
11. M.Kifer, E.L.Lozinskii. *RI: A logic for reasoning with inconsistency.* Proc. LICS'89, pp.253–262, IEEE Press, 1989.
12. M.Kifer, E.L.Lozinskii. *A logic for reasoning with inconsistency.* Journal of Automated Reasoning 9(2), pp.179–215, 1992.
13. S.Kraus, D.Lehmann, M.Magidor. *Nonmonotonic reasoning, preferential models and cumulative logics.* Artificial Intelligence 44(1–2) pp.167–207, 1990.
14. D.Lehmann, M.Magidor. *What does a conditional knowledge base entail?* Artificial Intelligence 55, pp.1–60, 1992.

15. D.Makinson. *General theory of cumulative inference.* Non-Monotonic Reasoning (M.Reinfrank, editor), LNAI 346, pp.1–18, Springer, 1989.
16. D.Makinson. *General patterns in nonmonotonic reasoning.* Handbook of Logic in Artificial Intelligence and Logic Programming 3 (D.Gabbay, C.Hogger, J.Robinson, editors) pp.35–110, Oxford Science Pub., 1994.
17. J.McCarthy. *Circumscription – A form of non monotonic reasoning.* Artificial Intelligence 13(1–2), pp.27–39, 1980.
18. J. McCarthy. *Applications of circumscription to formalizing common-Sense knowledge.* Artifical Intelligence 28, pp.89–116, 1986.
19. H.J.Ohlbach, *SCAN – Elimination of predicate quantifiers.* Proc. CADE'96, (M.A.McRobbie, J.Slaney, editors), LNAI 1104, pp.161–165, Springer, 1996.
20. G.Priest. *Reasoning about truth.* Artificial Intelligence 39, pp.231–244, 1989.
21. G.Priest. *Minimally Inconsistent LP.* Studia Logica 50, pp.321–331, 1991.
22. T.Przymusinski. *An algorithm to compute circumscription.* Artificial Intelligence 38, pp.49–73, 1991.
23. Y.Shoham. *Reasoning about change.* MIT Press, 1988.
24. A.Tarski. *Introduction to logic.* Oxford University Press, N.Y., 1941.

Implementing Term Algebra Syntactic Unification in Free Modules over Certain Rings

R.N. Banerjee and A. Bujosa

Dept. de Matemática Aplicada, E.T.S.I. Telecomunicación
Universidad Politécnica de Madrid, Ciudad Universitaria s/n 28040 Madrid, Spain
{rbf,abb}@mat.upm.es

Abstract. We have shown elsewhere how to introduce a concept of syntactic unification when terms are taken as the elements in a free module. This is done so as to obtain an m.g.u and its uniqueness modulo isomorphism. Here we introduce the concept of an *implementation*: An injective function from a term algebra into another object in a different category, both free over the same denumerable set of variables, but which carries over a generalised form of the so called Unification Axiom. We show that any implementation induces a faithful representation of the semi-group of substitutions of a term algebra in an appropriately chosen semi-group of homomorphisms in the target structure. We moreover show that this representation assigns unifiers to unifiers and, under certain conditions, an m.g.u. to an m.g.u. Moreover, when the target structure for an implementation is another term algebra, we show that a unification problem is solvable in the target if and only if it is so in the original term algebra. We qualify these implementations as *faithful*. However, when the target structure is a free module of the type mentioned, we show by means of a counter-example that there exist non-faithful implementations. We then give a necessary and sufficient condition for an implementation on one of these modules to be faithful. Strikingly, this condition is nothing but a translation into the language of the module of the well-known occurs–check property of usual syntactic unification. Finally we construct an example of a faithful implementation of a term algebra in one of our free modules.

1 Introduction

Unification of symbolic expressions has been widely studied (see [3] for an extensive review) both in its syntactic and equational forms. Well known properties of syntactic unification are the existence and uniqueness, up to composition with a variable renaming, of the so called *most general unifier* (m.g.u.) [13]. Deep results pertaining to equational unification, which address decidability, unification type (i.e. unitary, finite, infinite or zero) as well as unification procedures have been obtained for widely different equational theories (see [3, Section 3.4] for a survey), including results for commutative and Boolean rings. However, to the best of our knowledge, the case of unification in a module has not been addressed in the literature. This is the main topic of this paper.

T. Eiter and K.-D. Schewe (Eds.): FoIKS 2002, LNCS 2284, pp. 15–31, 2002.
© Springer-Verlag Berlin Heidelberg 2002

We have shown in a previous work [4], that it is possible to soundly introduce a concept of unification, where terms are understood to be the elements (called $\mathcal{M}$–terms) in a given free R–module $\mathcal{M}$ over certain kind of rings R, in such a manner as to obtain an m.g.u and its uniqueness modulo isomorphism. Thus, this unification concept satisfies the same properties as syntactic unification in term algebras. However, a connection between both concepts had not been established. This would provide a first step towards a geometric formulation of syntactic unification, which in turn would place this subject in a new context, thus making available the use of its many rich techniques.

Here we show that syntactic unification of terms may be embedded in a free module, provided certain conditions are met by the underlying ring. We do so by introducing the concept of an *implementation*. This is inspired on the well-known idea of a faithful non-trivial linear representation of a group, which is able to injectively and homomorphically transfer the abstract group properties to a set of linear transformations (see, for instance [16]). We thus define an implementation to be an injective function from a given term algebra into another free object in a different category, but which carries over a generalised form of the so called *Unification Axiom* (see [3] for a definition). In this work we consider two types of target structures for an implementation: Another (different) term algebra, and a free module over several different kind of rings, which are not assumed to be commutative. We show that any of these implementations induces a faithful representation of the semi-group of substitutions of a term algebra in an appropriately chosen semi-group of homomorphisms in the target structure and that this representation transforms syntactic unifiers into unifiers in the target structure. Moreover, when the target structure for an implementation is another term algebra, the syntactic m.g.u. for a given unification problem is carried over by any implementation into the syntactic m.g.u. for the implemented version of the unification problem. Further, in this case, a unification problem is solvable in the target algebra if and only if it is so in the original term algebra. We qualify these implementations as *faithful*. As a means of an example, we develop in detail the implementation of any term algebra in a term algebra representing Link-Lists, which is a well-known strategy from Computer Science.

However, when the target is a free module, we cannot guarantee, for a given unification problem, that the induced representation shall carry a syntactic m.g.u. to an m.g.u. in the module, unless the underlying ring is assumed to verify an additional hypothesis. Under it, we show that, though more than one m.g.u. may exist for the implemented terms, the implementation chooses one of them. If we strengthen the hypothesis, then we are able to provide uniqueness modulo isomorphism of the corresponding m.g.u. in the module. Despite, none of these hypotheses are enough to ensure the faithfulness of an implementation. We show that a necessary and sufficient condition for an implementation to be faithful is just a straight forward translation, into the language of the module, of the well-known occurs–check property for syntactic unification, i.e., a variable unifies with a term, which is not a variable, as long as the term does not contain that variable. Next we construct an example of an implementation of any term algebra in an appropriate free module over a so called *semi-group ring* [1], and show that it is faithful. Finally we give an example of an implementation of link-lists in the same module which is not faithful. We end up discussing our results and giving some suggestions for further work

2 Notations, Definitions and Previous Results

We devote this section to establish our notations and some previous results which are needed in the sequel. We refer the reader to the extensive review by Baader and Snyder [3] for the required definitions pertaining to unification. We just restate some of them here to ease the reading, while the slight modifications introduced to suit our needs are explicitly mentioned "in situ".

In this regard we place the reader in the realm of Universal Algebra and as usual, we let a **type** [5] be a pair (S, ar) where S is a set and $ar : S \to \mathbb{N}$ is a function[1]. Assuming we have fixed a type (S, ar) and a denumerable set of variables X such that $X \cap S = \emptyset$, we shall consider a fixed (S, ar)-algebra $T(X)$, free over X. Then a **term** is any element in $T(X)$. For any $t \in T(X)$ we let $var(t)$ denote the set of variables on which it depends, while $size(t)$ denote its size, defined as usual [14]. We let a **substitution** θ be any endomorphism $\theta : T(X) \to T(X)$ such that for almost all $x \in X$ verifies: $\theta(x) = x$. We further denote the set of all substitutions in $T(X)$ by $\mathcal{S}_{T(X)}$. Observe that though our definition of a substitution differs from the usual one [3], they are equivalent since for free objects, the homomorphisms are fixed by the images of the generators.

The term pairs $\{(t_n, t'_n)\}_{i=1,\ldots,n}$ **unify** (i.e. the syntactic unification problem $\Gamma \equiv \{t_1 =^? t'_1, \cdots, t_n =^? t'_n\}$ is solvable) if there exists $\theta \in \mathcal{S}_{T(X)}$ such that $\theta(t_i) = \theta(t'_i)$, $i = 1, \ldots, n$ and then θ is called a (syntactic) **unifier** of $\{(t_n, t'_n)\}_{i=1,\ldots,n}$. Finally, if $\{(t_n, t'_n)\}_{i=1,\ldots,n}$ unify, a unifier θ is an **m.g.u.** if for every other unifier θ', there exists an $\eta \in \mathcal{S}_{T(X)}$ such that $\theta' = \eta \circ \theta$, where $\circ$ denotes composition. Observe that our convention, contrary to [3], is that substitutions act on terms from the left. Moreover, this definition is only valid for syntactic unification (see section 4.4 of [3]).

2.1 Previous Results

We have shown in a previous work [4], that it is possible to introduce a concept of unification, where terms are understood to be the elements (called $\mathcal{M}$–terms) in a given free R–module $\mathcal{M}$ over certain kind of rings R, in such a manner as to obtain an m.g.u an its uniqueness modulo isomorphism. We state here the definitions and main results, and refer the reader to the above for the proofs.

In [4], we had let I be an infinite set and considered the left R–module, R an arbitrary ring (not necessarily commutative) with unit, free over I which we denoted by $\mathcal{M}$. This is (see, for instance [12]):

$$\mathcal{M} = \{\boldsymbol{t} : I \to R| \text{ for almost all } i \in I, \boldsymbol{t}(i) = 0\} \tag{1}$$

---

[1] We assume that 0 is natural, i.e. $0 \in \mathbb{N}$

i.e. the direct external sum (see [1]) $\oplus_I R_i$, where $i \in I$ and for all i, $R_i = R$. We let e_i denote the characteristic functions for the singletons, i.e., the elements of the form $\chi_{\{i\}}$ where $i \in I$ and denote by t^i the image $t(i)$, for any $t \in \mathcal{M}$. Clearly, then, with this notation: $t = \sum_{i \in I} t^i e_i$, the sum being finite by construction. Finally, we select a denumerable subset $X \subset I$.

With these definitions we defined precisely the objects to be dealt with:

Definition 2.1 ($\mathcal{M}$–terms and substitutions).

1. We let an $\mathcal{M}$–**term** be any element in $\mathcal{M}$.
2. We refer to the elements in $\{e_i | i \in X\}$ as "**variables**", while those in $\{e_i | i \in I - X\}$ as "**symbols**".
3. a **substitution** θ is any endomorphism $\theta : \mathcal{M} \to \mathcal{M}$ such that
   (a) for almost all $i \in X$: $\theta(e_i) = e_i$,
   (b) for all $i \in I - X$: $\theta(e_i) = e_i$.
   We further denote the set of all substitutions by $\mathcal{S}_\mathcal{M}$ and let θ_i denote the image $\theta(e_i)$, for any $\theta \in \mathcal{S}_\mathcal{M}$.

Note that, though X is assumed infinite, and substitutions are homomorphisms, thus defined for all variables, they affect only a finite number of them. Moreover, substitutions leave invariant all symbols.

The analogous of the standard concepts pertaining to unification were defined as follows:

Definition 2.2 (Unification and unifiers).

1. The collection of $\mathcal{M}$–term pairs $\{(t_i, t'_i)\}_{i=1...n}$ **unify** if there exists $\theta \in \mathcal{S}_\mathcal{M}$ such that: $\theta(t_i - t'_i) = 0, i = 1 \ldots n$, and then θ is called a **unifier** for the collection $\{(t_i, t'_i)\}_{i=1...n}$.
2. If the terms $\{(t_i, t'_i)\}_{i=1...n}$ unify, the substitution θ is a **most general unifier (m.g.u.)** if:
   (a) θ is a unifier $\{(t_i, t'_i)\}_{i=1...n}$ and
   (b) for any other unifier θ' of $\{(t_i, t'_i)\}_{i=1...n}$, there exists $\eta \in \mathcal{S}_\mathcal{M}$ such that $\theta' = \eta \circ \theta$

Observe that these definitions exactly match the corresponding ones for syntactic unification in term algebras.

We further showed in [4] that the key point for the existence and uniqueness of an m.g.u. for a given family of $\mathcal{M}$–terms is to have at our disposal a fundamental system of solutions to a certain linear system of equations. In this regard, we had let R be such that for any system of linear homogeneous equations there exists a fundamental solution set, i.e., it verified the following hypothesis:

Hypothesis 2.1 ($\mathcal{F}$–rings) For any matrix $A \in R^{m \times n}$, there exists a system $Z^1, \cdots, Z^r \in R^{n \times 1}$ such that $0 \leq r \leq n$ and

1. for all $X \in R^{n \times 1}$: $AX = 0 \Leftrightarrow \exists \lambda_1, \cdots, \lambda_r \in R$, such that $X = \sum_{i=1}^r Z^i \lambda_i$
2. For any $\lambda_1, \cdots, \lambda_r \in R$: $\sum_{i=1}^r Z^i \lambda_i = 0 \Rightarrow \lambda_1 = \cdots = \lambda_r = 0$

Condition 1 requires the set of column matrices $Z^1, \cdots, Z^r \in R^{n \times 1}$ to parametrically generate the solutions, while condition 2 requires this set of column matrices to be free on the right. This condition over the ring R is trivially satisfied by any field $\mathbb{K}$ since in this case we would have a finite dimensional vector space and thus an even stronger conditionwould hold, i.e. the well–known results regarding dimensionality of the solution subspace. This condition is also verified by some rings such as $\mathbb{Z}$, however, for general rings it is non–trivial (e.g. the ring $M_n(\mathbb{K})$ of square matrices of order $n > 1$ over the field $\mathbb{K}$). In absence, to the best of our knowledge, of a standard notation for this type of rings, we had termed them as $\mathcal{F}$–rings, for "rings with a fundamental set of solutions".

Under this hypothesis we were able to prove the following property which is the analogous of the a well-known property for syntactic unifiers:

Theorem 2.1 (Existence of m.g.u.). *Let $\{(t_i, t_i')\}_{i=1\ldots n}$ unify. Then, under hypothesis 2.1, there exists an m.g.u of $\{(t_i, t_i')\}_{i=1\ldots n}$.*

Uniqueness modulo isomorphism of the family of m.g.u.'s was rather more involved to show than the above result. It depends on a number of lemmas that essentially show how several well-known rank results in vector spaces, and thus the corresponding results for matrices, carry over to free modules over the kind of rings we are considering. We omit the required lemmas for brevity. Moreover, we found the need to tighten hypothesis 2.1 in order to prove uniqueness. In this regard we posed the following

Hypothesis 2.2 ($\mathcal{DF}$–rings) *We assume hypothesis 2.1 plus the following condition: If $A \neq 0$, then the fundamental system of solutions $Z^1, \cdots, Z^r \in R^{n \times 1}$ is such that $r < n$.*

As before, the set of column matrices $Z^1, \cdots, Z^r \in R^{n \times 1}$ generates the solutions and is free on the right, but now we require that there should be strictly less parameters than unknowns. This is well–known for vector spaces. We termed these rings as $\mathcal{DF}$–rings, for "rings with a dimension-like property". Under this hypothesis and aided by the lemmas we proved the following

Theorem 2.2 ("Uniqueness" of the m.g.u.). *Let $\theta, \theta' \in \mathcal{S}_\mathcal{M}$ be m.g.u.'s for $\{(t_i, t_i')\}_{i=1\ldots n}$. Then, under hypothesis 2.2, there exists a substitution $\eta \in \mathcal{S}_\mathcal{M}$ such that $\theta' = \eta \circ \theta$ and with η an isomorphism.*

This provides the analogous for the well-known result of uniqueness modulo isomorphism of the m.g.u in term algebras.

3   Implementations

So far, we know that it is possible to soundly speak about unification in a free module over an $\mathcal{F}$-ring for which there exists an m.g.u. for any finite collection of $\mathcal{M}$-terms that unify. Moreover, we may guarantee uniqueness modulo isomorphism of the m.g.u. for free modules over $\mathcal{DF}$-rings. However, the connection to usual syntactic unification in term algebras is lacking. In this regard we must be able to relate in a proper manner symbolic terms (or, for short, just terms) and the $\mathcal{M}$–terms. More precisely, we want to represent terms via $\mathcal{M}$–terms in such a way as to guarantee that unification is preserved, i.e. that, given a finite collection of terms, they unify if and only if the corresponding $\mathcal{M}$–terms do. Obviously, then, we need an injective function from terms to $\mathcal{M}$–terms that maintains unification properties. This function we call an *implementation*. We now formalise these ideas and start by considering the simpler case of implementations whose target structure is another term algebra, since it shall clarify many of the ideas to be developed when addressing implementations in free modules.

3.1   Implementations in Term Algebras

In this section we formalise the implementation of a given term algebra $T(X)$ in another, possibly different algebra $L(X)$, both free over the same set X. We denote the corresponding set of substitutions in the term algebras $T(X)$, $L(X)$ by $\mathcal{S}_{T(X)}$, $\mathcal{S}_{L(X)}$, respectively. We again omit the proofs for the sake of brevity.

Since we want to be able to represent all terms in $T(X)$ by terms in $L(X)$ via an implementation, such an implementation must be some injective function $i : T(X) \longrightarrow L(X)$, so as not to "loose" any terms. We further want an implementation to maintain unification properties, i.e. if $t_j, t'_j \in T(X)$ unify, we want at least $i(t_j), i(t'_j) \in L(X)$ to unify, and desirably we also would like the converse to be true. Now, terms unify in either algebras if and only if there exists a substitution that makes them equal, and since both algebras are free over X, substitutions are uniquely determined by the image of X. Thus, the obvious choice is to require that an implementation i should take every variable in X to itself.

In the spirit of the above discussion and of the so called *Unification Axiom* (see [3], Definition 2.11) we arrive at the following definition:

Definition 3.1 (Implementation in a term algebra). *Let $T(X)$ and $L(X)$ be term algebras over the same set X, but possibly of a diffrent signature. We then say that the function $i : T(X) \to L(X)$ is an **implementation** of $T(X)$ in $L(X)$ if:*

1. *$\forall x \in X,\ \ i(x) = x$*
2. *For any function symbols f and g of arities n and m, respectively, any $t_j, t'_j \in T(X)$ and $\theta, \theta' \in \mathcal{S}_{L(X)}$, we have:*

$$\left. \begin{array}{c} f = g \\ \theta(i(t_1)) = \theta'(i(t'_1)) \\ \vdots \\ \theta(i(t_n)) = \theta'(i(t'_n)) \end{array} \right\} \Leftrightarrow \theta(i(f(t_1, \cdots, t_n))) = \theta'(i(g(t'_1, \cdots, t'_m)))$$

The above function i may be easily shown to be injective, as required. The following proposition shows that any $T(X)$–endomorphism is uniquely mapped via i to an $L(X)$–endomorphism:

Proposition 3.1. *Let $i : T(X) \to L(X)$ be a given implementation. Then for any endomorphism $\theta : T(X) \to T(X)$, there exists a unique endomorphism $\overline{\theta} : L(X) \to L(X)$ such that: $\overline{\theta} \circ i = i \circ \theta$*

As an immediate corollary of the above we have that an implementation verifies the following important consistency properties:

Corollary 3.1. *Let $i : T(X) \to L(X)$ be an implementation. Then:*

1. $id_{L(X)} = \overline{id_{T(X)}}$
2. *For any $T(X)$–endomorphisms θ, η: $\overline{\theta \circ \eta} = \overline{\theta} \circ \overline{\eta}$*
3. *If θ is a unifier for $\{(t_j, t'_j)\}_{j=1..n}$ then $\overline{\theta}$ is a unifier for $\{(i(t_j), i(t'_j))\}_{j=1..n}$*

Thus, the identity and composition are preserved by our definition of implementation and, hence, an implementation i induces a representation [16] of the semi-group $(End(T(X)), \circ)$ in the semi-group $(End(L(X)), \circ)$. Moreover, it is a faithful representation since $\overline{\theta} = \overline{\theta'}$ iff $i \circ \theta = i \circ \theta'$, and since i is injective we must have $\theta = \theta'$ and thus the representation is injective. Moreover, property 3 in the above corollary shows that the unique endomorphism $\overline{\theta}$ that extends the unifier θ is also a unifier of the implemented terms. This is, of course, needed so as not to loose the meaning of unification of terms, when they are considered in their implemented version. But, what if we had started with an m.g.u. θ ? The following theorem shows that then $\overline{\theta}$ is also an m.g.u. for the implemented terms.

Theorem 3.1. *Let $i : T(X) \to L(X)$ be an implementation. Then, if θ is an m.g.u. for $\{(t_j, t'_j)\}_{j=1..n}$, $\overline{\theta}$ is an m.g.u. for $\{(i(t_j), i(t'_j))\}_{j=1..n}$*

A last question remains: Corollary 3.1 shows that whenever terms unify then their corresponding implemented terms do also. However, is the converse true? We formalise this idea via the following definition of a *faithful implementation*:

Definition 3.2 (Faithful implementation). *An implementation $i : T(X) \to L(X)$ is **faithful** if whenever the implemented terms $\{(i(t_j), i(t'_j))\}_{j=1..n}$ unify in $L(X)$ implies that $\{(t_j, t'_j)\}_{j=1..n}$ unify in $T(X)$.*

In this regard the following theorem shows that any implementation of a term algebra in another one is always faithful and thus, at least in this sense, trivial:

Theorem 3.2. *Let $T(X)$ and $L(X)$ be term algebras over the same denumerable set X but possibly of a diffrent signature, and let $i : T(X) \to L(X)$ be an implementation. Then $\{(i(t_j), i(t'_j))\}_{j=1..n}$ unify if an only if $\{(t_j, t'_j)\}_{j=1..n}$ unify and, therefore, i is a faithful implementation.*

The following example illustrates all the results above in a fairly well-known setting: Link-lists.

An Example: Implementation in Lists. It is well known that any term algebra may be implemented in a computer using a link-list data-structure. In the following we show how the framework above is adapted to this case. Though this is a rather trivial example it is worthwhile, since the techniques used shall appear again for other implementations shown in the forthcoming.

To implement a term algebra on lists, we first must view lists as a term algebra and then establish an implementation. Of course, once this is done we know by theorem 3.2 above that the implementation, no matter what, shall be faithful. In this regard, let $Atom$ and X be denumerable sets with $Atom \cap X = \emptyset$, and let $\emptyset \neq S \subset Atom$. Further, let $T(X)$ be the (S, ar)–algebra free over X. We then denote by $\mathbb{L}(X)$ the $(Atom \cup \{cons, nil\}, ar_{\mathbb{L}(X)})$–algebra free over X, where $cons, nil$ are symbols such that $Atom \cap \{cons, nil\} = \emptyset$, and $ar_{\mathbb{L}(X)}$ is the arity function:

$$ar_{\mathbb{L}(X)} : Atom \cup \{cons, nil\} \longrightarrow \mathbb{N}$$
$$\sigma \quad \rightarrow \quad \begin{cases} 2 \text{ if } \sigma = cons \\ 0 \text{ if } \sigma = nil \\ 0 \text{ if } \sigma \in Atom \end{cases} \tag{2}$$

The elements of $\mathbb{L}(X)$ are thus **lists** in the usual sense.

Now, for each symbol $s \in S$ of arity n in the signature of $T(X)$, we define a corresponding function $s_{\mathbb{L}(X)}$ of arity n, in the following way:

$$s_{\mathbb{L}(X)} : \quad \mathbb{L}(X)^n \quad \longrightarrow \mathbb{L}(X)$$
$$(x_1, \cdots, x_n) \rightarrow cons(s, cons(x_1, \cdots cons(x_n, nil) \cdots))$$

Observe that this is nothing but the element in $\mathbb{L}(X)$ corresponding to the usual link-list structure used to represent the function symbol s. Now, $\mathbb{L}(X)$ together with these new operations becomes an (S, ar)–algebra (in fact a realization in the sense of Plotkin [15]), and since $T(X)$ is a free object in the same category there exists a unique (S, ar)–algebra homomorphism $i : T(X) \to \mathbb{L}(X)$ such that, for all $x \in X$, $i(x) = x$. Our target, now, is to show that this homomorphism i is an implementation.

Indeed, observe that the first property in Definition 3.1 is fulfilled by construction. Thus we only need to show the second. Since both implications are shown similarly, we only give the "if" case:

$$\theta(i(f(t_1, \cdots, t_n))) = \theta(f_{\mathbb{L}(x)}(i(t_1), \cdots, i(t_n)))$$
$$= \theta(cons(f, cons(i(t_1), \cdots, cons(i(t_n), nil) \cdots)))$$
$$= cons(f, cons(\theta(i(t_1)), \cdots, cons(\theta(i(t_n)), nil)))$$
$$= cons(g, cons(\theta'(i(t'_1)), \cdots, cons(\theta'(i(t'_m)), nil)))$$
$$= \theta'(cons(g, cons(i(t'_1), \cdots, cons(i(t'_m), nil))))$$
$$= \theta'(g_{\mathbb{L}(x)}(i(t'_1), \cdots, i(t'_m)))$$
$$= \theta'(i(g(t'_1, \cdots, t'_m))).$$

Hence i is an implementation, and it is faithful, since $\mathbb{L}(X)$ is a term algebra.

Thus, whenever we use a term algebra, such as lists, as the target structure for an implementation of another term algebra, faithfulness is automatically guaranteed and things work properly. However we are interested in implementing in a free module over a certain ring. Hence, faithfulness for an implementation in a free module is a non-trivial issue. In the following section we address the core subject of our work, that is, implementations in free modules.

4   Implementation of Term Algebras in Free Modules

We know from our previous results that it is possible to soundly speak about unification in free modules over $\mathcal{F}$–rings. This unification concept satisfies the same properties as syntactic unification in term algebras. However, a connection between both concepts needs to be established. In this regard we shall use the ideas about implementations developed in the previous section to properly relate unification of symbolic terms (or, for short, just terms) to that of $\mathcal{M}$–terms. Thus, in the terminology introduced above, we want to build a fair implementation of a term algebra in a free module. However, the previous results on implementations in term algebras cannot be directly applied to this case, since a free module is not a term algebra. Indeed, observe that in a module there are no syntactic variables, and therefore, the definition of an implementation used before must be reformulated. Hence, all those results pertaining to the consistency of the implementation (see Corollary 3.1) must be re-obtained. Again, for brevity, we omit the proofs and therefore all technicalities. Only in some cases we give a brief hint. Though the proofs differ from the corresponding ones in the previous section, they share many common ideas.

Recall that in Definition 2.1 we had selected a denumerable subset $X \subset I$. Since in a free module there are no syntactic variables as such, we shall choose the set of generators e_i corresponding to the indices in X to represent "variables" while those corresponding to the indices in $I - X$ as "symbols". Indeed recall that we have required a substitution in $\mathcal{M}$ to leave invariant the "symbols" while affect only a finite number of "variables" (c.f.. definition 2.1). We thus force those sets of generators to behave as variables and symbols, respectively. In this spirit we introduce the following definition of an implementation in a free module, which is a straight forward adaptation of definition 3.1:

Definition 4.1 (Implementation in a free module). *Let I be an infinite set and R an arbitrary ring (not necessarily commutative), and let $\mathcal{M} = R^{(I)}$, i.e. the left R–module, free over I (recall (1)). Moreover, let $X \subset I$ be denumerable and $T(X)$ be a term algebra over the same set X. We then say that the function $i : T(X) \longrightarrow \mathcal{M}$ is an* **implementation** *of $T(X)$ in $\mathcal{M}$ if:*

1. *$\forall x \in X, \quad i(x) = e_x$*
2. *For any function symbols f and g of arities n and m, respectively, $t_j, t'_j \in T(X)$ and $\theta, \theta' \in \mathcal{S}_{\mathcal{M}}$, we have:*

$$\left.\begin{array}{c} f = g \\ \theta(i(t_1)) = \theta'(i(t'_1)) \\ \vdots \\ \theta(i(t_n)) = \theta'(i(t'_n)) \end{array}\right\} \Leftrightarrow \theta(i(f(t_1, \cdots, t_n))) = \theta'(i(g(t'_1, \cdots, t'_m)))$$

Again, the function i, as defined above, may be easily shown to be injective, as required.

4.1   Main Properties

We give here the main properties satisfied by implementations on free modules. They are given in order of increasing strength in the hypotheses pertaining the underlying ring. First, implementations in free modules over a ring with unit verify the following extension property:

Proposition 4.1. *Let $T(X)$ and $\mathcal{M}$ be as in definition 4.1, and let $i : T(X) \to \mathcal{M}$ be a given implementation. Then for any substitution $\theta \in \mathcal{S}_{T(X)}$, there exists a unique substitution $\bar{\theta} \in \mathcal{S}_{\mathcal{M}}$ such that: $\bar{\theta} \circ i = i \circ \theta$*

Again, as an immediate corollary of the above we may conclude that an implementation in the sense of definition 4.1 verifies the following important consistency properties:

Corollary 4.1. *Let $T(X)$ and $\mathcal{M}$ be as in definition 4.1, and let $i : T(X) \to \mathcal{M}$ be a given implementation. Then:*

1. *$id_{\mathcal{M}} = \overline{id_{T(X)}}$*
2. *For any θ, $\eta \in \mathcal{S}_{T(X)} : \overline{\theta \circ \eta} = \bar{\theta} \circ \bar{\eta}$*
3. *If $\theta \in \mathcal{S}_{T(X)}$ is a unifier for $\{(t_j, t'_j)\}_{j=1..n}$ then $\bar{\theta} \in \mathcal{S}_{\mathcal{M}}$ is a unifier for $\{(i(t_j), i(t'_j))\}_{j=1..n}$*

This result totally mimics corollary 3.1 and hence the meanings of identity and composition are again preserved when implementing in free modules. We remark further, that a close look at the proofs (not given here for brevity) shows that the above proposition and corollary may be shown without invoking hypothesis 2.1, and are therefore valid for an implementation in a free module over any ring with unit. Observe moreover that any implementation i again induces a faithful representation of the semi-group $(\mathcal{S}_{T(X)}, \circ)$ in the semi-group $(\mathcal{S}_{\mathcal{M}}, \circ)$.

Despite, when addressing properties pertaining to m.g.u.'s the ring hypotheses are needed. This is the case for the following main unification theorem, which shows that the extension of an m.g.u. into the module, via an implementation, is also an m.g.u. Its proof makes use of the following two results which show that, with respect to substitutions, variables are properly handled by an implementation:

Lemma 4.1. *For $t \in \mathcal{M}$, let $var(t) \equiv \{i \in X \mid t^i \neq 0\}$. Then, for any $t \in \mathcal{M}$ and $A \subset X$, the following conditions are equivalent:*

1. *$var(t) \subset A$*
2. *$\forall \theta, \theta' \in \mathcal{S}_{\mathcal{M}}, \theta_{|A} = \theta'_{|A} \Rightarrow \theta(t) = \theta'(t)$*

Proof. 1 $\Rightarrow$ 2 is trivial. 2 $\Rightarrow$ 1 is shown by "reductio ad absurdum"

Proposition 4.2. *Let $T(X)$ and $\mathcal{M}$ be as in definition 4.1 and $i : T(X) \to \mathcal{M}$ an implementation. Then, for any $t \in T(X) : var(t) = var(i(t))$*

Proof. The proof is by induction on $size(t)$ and makes use of the previous lemma.

Theorem 4.1 (Transfer of a syntactic m.g.u.). *Let $T(X)$ and $\mathcal{M}$ be as in definition 4.1 but where now R is assumed to be an $\mathcal{F}$–ring. Moreover, let $i : T(X) \to \mathcal{M}$ be a given implementation. Then, if θ is an m.g.u. for $\{(t_j, t'_j)\}_{j=1..n}$, $\overline{\theta}$ is an m.g.u. for the $\mathcal{M}$–terms $\{(i(t_j), i(t'_j))\}_{j=1..n}$.*

Proof. The proof is in two steps. First we show that for any $\{(t_j, t'_j)\}_{j=1..n}$ that unify there exists a certain m.g.u. $\theta_0 \in \mathcal{S}_{T(X)}$ in the corresponding family of m.g.u.'s such that its extension $\overline{\theta} \in \mathcal{S}_{\mathcal{M}}$ is also an m.g.u. for the corresponding $\mathcal{M}$–terms $\{(i(t_j), i(t'_j))\}_{j=1..n}$. This is done by induction on $(Var, Size)$, where $Var = \# \bigcup_{j=1}^{n}(var(t_j) \cup var(t'_j))$ and $Size = \sum_{j=1}^{n}(size(t_j) + size(t'_j))$, the pairs lexicographically ordered (which is a well order). The existence of an m.g.u. in $\mathcal{M}$ is assumed in the induction hypothesis, thus the need for hypothesis 2.1. The desired result now follows from Corollary 4.1: Indeed, if $\theta \in \mathcal{S}_{T(X)}$ is any other m.g.u. for the term pairs $\{(t_j, t'_j)\}_{j=1..n}$, there exists an isomorphism $\eta \in \mathcal{S}_{T(X)}$ such that: $\theta = \eta \circ \theta_0$. But then: $\overline{\theta} = \overline{\eta} \circ \overline{\theta_0}$. Hence, if $h \in \mathcal{S}_{\mathcal{M}}$ is a unifier for $\{(i(t_j), i(t'_j))\}_{j=1..n}$, there exists $f \in \mathcal{S}_{\mathcal{M}}$ such that $h = f \circ \overline{\theta_0} = (f \circ (\overline{\eta})^{-1}) \circ \overline{\theta}$ and thus $\overline{\theta}$ is an m.g.u. for $\{(i(t_j), i(t'_j))\}_{j=1..n}$.

In this way, an implementation of a term algebra in a free module over an $\mathcal{F}$–ring transfers a syntactic m.g.u. to an m.g.u. in the module. However, more than one m.g.u. may exist for the corresponding $\mathcal{M}$–terms in which case the implementation just picks up one of them. Of course, if instead of an $\mathcal{F}$–ring we use a $\mathcal{DF}$–ring we would have uniqueness modulo isomorphism for the m.g.u. in the module and the implementation would assign this m.g.u to the original syntactic m.g.u.

Thus far, the faithfulness of an implementation in a free module has not yet been addressed. The following theorem gives a necessary and sufficient condition for the faithfulness of an implementation in a free module over an $\mathcal{F}$–ring:

Theorem 4.2 (Faithfull implementations). *Let $T(X)$ and $\mathcal{M}$ be as in definition 4.1, with R an $\mathcal{F}$–ring. Then, the implementation $i : T(X) \to \mathcal{M}$ is faithful if and only if $\forall x \in X, \forall t \in (T(X) - X)$: If $(e_x, i(t))$ unify, then $x \notin var(i(t))$*

Proof. Necessity is trivial. Sufficiency is shown again by induction on the set of pairs $(Var, Size)$ of Theorem 4.1.

Observe that this condition is just the translation into the language of the module of the well-known "occurs-check" property of syntactic unification, i.e. if $x \in X$, $t \in (T(X) - X)$ and (x, t) unify, then $x \notin var(t)$.

We have as yet not provided an example to show that all of the concepts introduced thus far are non-void. We do so in the following section by constructing a faithful implementation for any term algebra on a free module over a so called *semi-group ring*.

4.2   A Faithful Implementation on a Free Module

In what follows we let $\mathbb{S}$ be a finite set (of symbols) $\mathbb{S} = \{u_1, \cdots, u_s\}$ and let $\mathbb{S}^*$ be the free monoid over $\mathbb{S}^*$, i.e. the set of words (including the empty word ϵ) formed with the symbols in $\mathbb{S}$. As usual, if $s, r \in \mathbb{S}^*$ are two words we shall denote by sr the word formed by concatenating the two symbols s and r, and by $len(w)$ the lenght of the word $w \in \mathbb{S}^*$.

Now, given a field $\mathbb{K}$, we shall denote by $\mathbb{K}\mathbb{S}^*$ the *semi-group ring [1, pag 25] of* $\mathbb{S}^*$ *over* $\mathbb{K}$ defined as follows[2]:

$$\mathbb{K}\mathbb{S}^* = \{\alpha : \mathbb{S}^* \to \mathbb{K}| \text{ for almost all } s \in \mathbb{S}^*, \ \alpha(s) = 0\}.$$

In $\mathbb{K}\mathbb{S}^*$ we define the following sum and product:

$$(\alpha + \beta)(s) = \alpha(s) + \beta(s) \quad , \quad (\alpha\beta)(s) = \sum_{rt=s} \alpha(r)\beta(t).$$

Note that we may regard the elements in $\mathbb{K}\mathbb{S}^*$ as a kind of non-commuting polynomials with coefficients in the field $\mathbb{K}$. In this sense, we denote by $\hat{y}_j = \chi(u_j), u_j \in \mathbb{S}$ an "indeterminate" and denote the set of all indeterminates as $\hat{Y}$. Moreover, for any $\alpha \in \mathbb{K}\mathbb{S}^*$ we define its **order** $o(\alpha)$ as:

$$o(\alpha) = \max\left(\{len(s) \mid \alpha(s) \neq 0\} \cup \{-\infty\}\right).$$

Obviously, $o(\alpha) = -\infty$ iff $\alpha = 0$. This clearly resembles a degree function[3] since it is positive (but for its minimum value $-\infty$), and verifies $o(\alpha\beta) = o(\alpha) + o(\beta)$. Therefore, $\mathbb{K}\mathbb{S}^*$ has no zero-divisors and it is hence an (non-commutative) integral domain (see [1, p. 11]).

This ring may be shown to be an $\mathcal{DF}$–ring. This is done in two steps: First we show that hypothesis 2.2 is verified for a single linear equation and then show that any system of linear equations has the desired property. Thus a first lemma:

Lemma 4.2. *Let the coefficients* $\alpha_1, \ldots, \alpha_n$, *be given elements in the ring* $\mathbb{K}\mathbb{S}^*$, *such that at least one of the* α_i *verifies* $\alpha_i(\epsilon) \neq 0$. *Then the equation*

$$\alpha_1\gamma_1 + \cdots + \alpha_n\gamma_n = 0 \tag{3}$$

has a fundamental system of solutions in $\mathbb{K}\mathbb{S}^*$ *with less than n elements.*

Proof. The proof follows the lines of that for the so called "Hilbert's Fundamental Theorem" which shows that any polynomial ring is noetherian (see, for instance [11, p. 16]). It is rather involved and a short description is not possible. It is thus fully omitted for brevity.

---

[2] Observe that this is $\mathbb{K}^{\left(\mathbb{S}^*\right)} = \oplus_{\mathbb{S}^*}\mathbb{K}$

[3] As in Euclidean rings, but not quite, since it is not associated to an Euclidean division algorithm. See [6, A III.197] for a precise definition of non-commuting polynomials with an Euclidean division and a proper degree function.

Now we may obtain the desired result as a corollary of the previous lemma:

Corollary 4.2. *For any non-zero matrix $A \in (\mathbb{KS}^*)^{m \times n}$ there exists a system $Z_1, \cdots, Z_r \in (\mathbb{KS}^*)^{n \times 1}$, free on the right, where $0 \leq r < n$, and being such that $\forall X \in (\mathbb{KS}^*)^{n \times 1}$, $AX = 0$ if and only if $\exists \alpha_1, \ldots, \alpha_r \in \mathbb{KS}^*$ such that $X = Z_1 \alpha_1 + \cdots + Z_r \alpha_r$*

Proof. The proof is by induction on $(n, o(A))$ where the order of a matrix $A \in (\mathbb{KS}^*)^{m \times n}$ is defined as $o(A) = \max\{o(\alpha_{ij}), \alpha_{ij} \in A\}$. It uses the previous lemma as well as an order reduction trick which is also used in its proof.

Thus, $\mathbb{KS}^*$ is indeed a $\mathcal{DF}$–ring and thus appropriate to build an implementation of a term algebra on a free module over it.

In this regard, let $T(X)$ be a term algebra, i.e. a (Σ, ar)-algebra free over a denumerable set of variables X. Further, let $\mathbb{M} = \mathbb{KS}^{*(J)}$ be the left $\mathbb{KS}^*$–module free over the set $J \equiv \Sigma \cup \{nil\} \cup X$ [4] and finally choose two "indeterminates" $\hat{y}_1, \hat{y}_2 \in \hat{Y} \subset \mathbb{KS}^*$. In the spirit of the construction we made for lists, we shall now build within $\mathbb{M}$ a (Σ, ar)-algebra (i.e. a realisation). We begin by defining in $\mathbb{M}$ the analogous of the *cons* operator for lists. To avoid confusion we denote by $CONS$ this new function:

$$
\begin{aligned}
CONS : \mathbb{M} \times \mathbb{M} &\longrightarrow \mathbb{M} \\
(\boldsymbol{a}, \boldsymbol{b}) &\rightarrow \hat{y}_1 \boldsymbol{a} + \hat{y}_2 \boldsymbol{b}
\end{aligned} \tag{4}
$$

$CONS$ has the two following important properties:

1. Since $\hat{y}_1, \hat{y}_2 \in \mathbb{KS}^*$ are a system of scalars free on the right, the function $CONS$ is injective.
2. Since no component of $CONS(\boldsymbol{a}, \boldsymbol{b})$ has order 0, its image doesn't contain neither "variables" nor "symbols" (recall definition 2.1), i.e.

$$
\{e_j | j \in J\} \cap CONS(\mathbb{M} \times \mathbb{M}) = \emptyset .
$$

As we did for lists, for each symbol $\sigma \in \Sigma$ of arity n we now define a function $\sigma_{\mathbb{M}}$ of the same arity, in the following way:

$$
\begin{aligned}
\sigma_{\mathbb{M}} : \quad \mathbb{M}^n &\longrightarrow \mathbb{M} \\
(\boldsymbol{x}_1, \cdots, \boldsymbol{x}_n) &\rightarrow CONS(e_\sigma, CONS(\boldsymbol{x}_1, \cdots CONS(\boldsymbol{x}_n, e_{nil}) \cdots))
\end{aligned}
$$

Now, since $\mathbb{M}$ together with these operations is a (Σ, ar)–algebra there exists a unique (Σ, ar)–homomorphism $i : T(X) \to \mathbb{M}$ such that for all $x \in X$, $i(x) = e_{\boldsymbol{x}}$. We now show that this i is an implementation. Since the first property is fulfilled by construction, we turn over to the second. We first observe that for any substitution $\theta \in \mathcal{S}_{\mathbb{M}}$ the following properties hold:

1. $\forall j \in J - X, \ \theta(e_j) = e_j$

---

[4] i.e. the external direct sum $\oplus_J (\mathbb{KS}^*)_j, j \in J$

2. For any $a, b \in \mathbb{M}$:

$$\theta(CONS(a, b)) = \theta(\hat{y}_1 a + \hat{y}_2 b) = \hat{y}_1 \theta(a) + \hat{y}_2 \theta(b)$$
$$= CONS(\theta(a), \theta(b))$$

3. For any $\sigma \in \Sigma$ of arity n, any terms $t_1, \cdots, t_n \in T(X)$, and any substitution $\theta \in \mathcal{S}_{\mathbb{M}}$:

$$\theta(i(\sigma(t_1, \cdots, t_n))) = \theta(\sigma_{\mathbb{M}}(i(t_1), \cdots, i(t_n)))$$
$$= \theta(CONS(e_\sigma, CONS(i(t_1), \cdots, CONS(i(t_n), e_{nil}) \cdots)))$$
$$= CONS(e_\sigma, CONS(\theta(i(t_1)), \cdots, CONS(\theta(i(t_n)), e_{nil}))))$$

That i is an implementation, now follows thus:

$$\theta(i(\sigma(t_1, \cdots, t_n))) = \theta'(i(\rho(t_1', \cdots, t_m')))$$

$$\Leftrightarrow \begin{cases} CONS(e_\sigma, CONS(\theta(i(t_1)), \cdots, CONS(\theta(i(t_n)), e_{nil}) \cdots)) = \\[2mm] CONS(e_\rho, CONS(\theta'(i(t_1')), \cdots, CONS(\theta'(i(t_m')), e_{nil}) \cdots)) \end{cases}$$

$$\Leftrightarrow \begin{cases} \sigma = \rho \\ \theta(i(t_1)) = \theta'(i(t_1')) \\ \vdots \\ \theta(i(t_n)) = \theta'(i(t_n')) \end{cases}$$

We therefore have an implementation of any term algebra in our special module $\mathbb{M}$. But, is this implementation faithful?. Since we have in hand theorem 4.2, which gives a necessary and sufficient condition, we shall show that the above implementation verifies the condition. To do so we first need a technical lemma, which is proven by induction on $size(t)$:

Lemma 4.3. *Let $t \in T(X)$ and $x \in var(t) \subset X \subset J$. Then, for any $\theta \in \mathcal{S}_\mathcal{M}$: $o(\theta(i(t))) \geq o(\theta(e_x))$ Moreover, if $size(t) > 1$ strict inequality holds.*

Now we may obtain the desired property as a corollary:

Corollary 4.3. *Let $t \in (T(X) - X)$ and $x \in var(t) \subset X \subset J$. Then, $(e_x, i(t))$ do not unify.*

Hence, by theorem 4.2 the above implementation $i : T(X) \to \mathbb{M}$ **is faithful**.

So far, all implementations we have found are faithful. Thus the question arises as to whether there exists non faithful implementations. That this is the case is shown below.

Indeed, let us consider the following natural implementation of the term algebra $\mathbb{L}(X)$ (recall the example in section 2) in the free module $\mathbb{M}$ above: Recall that $\mathbb{L}(X)$ is the $(Atom \cup \{cons, nil\}, ar_{\mathbb{L}(X)})$–algebra free over X, where $cons, nil$ are symbols, $ar_{\mathbb{L}(X)}$ is the arity function in Eq. (2), and we assume further that $Atom \cap \{cons, nil\} = \emptyset$. Now take as Σ the set $Atom \cup \{cons, nil\}$ and $J = \Sigma \cup X$, as above, and consider again the free module $\mathbb{M} = \mathbb{KS}^{*(J)}$.

However, now for each symbol $\sigma \in Atom \cup \{nil\}$ (i.e. of arity zero) we rather let $\sigma_{\mathbb{M}} = e_\sigma$, while, for the symbol $cons$ we now let:

$$cons_{\mathbb{M}} : (\mathbb{M})^2 \longrightarrow \mathbb{M}$$
$$(\boldsymbol{a}, \boldsymbol{b}) \rightarrow CONS(\boldsymbol{a}, \boldsymbol{b}) = \hat{y_1}\boldsymbol{a} + \hat{y_2}\boldsymbol{b}$$

Hence, we are considering the most straight forward possibility for an implementation of lists, i.e., take the constants to constants and the $cons$ function to the $CONS$ function. Now, $\mathbb{M}$ together with these operations is an $(\Sigma, ar_{\mathbb{L}(X)})$–algebra and thus there exists a unique $(\Sigma, ar_{\mathbb{L}(X)})$–homomorphism $i : \mathbb{L}(X) \to \mathbb{M}$ such that for all $x \in X$, $i(x) = e_{\boldsymbol{x}}$. It may be easily shown as above that this i is an implementation. However, observe that while the terms in $\mathbb{L}(X)$ (i.e the lists) x and $cons(x, x)$ do not unify in $\mathbb{L}(X)$, the corresponding $\mathcal{M}$-terms $(e_{\boldsymbol{x}}, \hat{y_1}e_{\boldsymbol{x}} + \hat{y_2}e_{\boldsymbol{x}})$ are unified by the substitution that applies $e_x \to \boldsymbol{0}$. Thus this implementation is **not faithful**.

5 Discussion and Suggestions for further Work

Our work shows that it is possible to soundly speak about implementations of term algebras in free modules over $\mathcal{F}$–rings by means of which any syntactic m.g.u. is transfered to an m.g.u. for the corresponding $\mathcal{M}$–terms in the module. In general, under hypothesis 2.1, several different m.g.u.'s for the corresponding $\mathcal{M}$–term unification problem may exist, however, the implementation just picks one of them. Moreover, if hypothesis 2.2 is assumed instead, and thus we work with a $\mathcal{DF}$–ring, then the uniqueness modulo isomorphism of the m.g.u. for the corresponding $\mathcal{M}$–terms is ensured. Moreover, if the implementation is faithful, both unification concepts, syntactic in term algebras and ours in free modules **may be regarded as equivalent**.

The logical dependencies of the hypotheses regarding the rings have not been studied. Indeed, we don't know if hypothesis 2.1 implies hypothesis 2.2. However, it is clear that for a ring to be $\mathcal{DF}$ it must be an integral domain[5]. Thus one should look for an $\mathcal{F}$–ring with zero divisors, though clearly not every ring with zero divisors is an $\mathcal{F}$–ring (recall $M_n(\mathbb{K}), n > 1$). Moreover, sufficient conditions for a ring to be either $\mathcal{F}$ or $\mathcal{DF}$ are unknown to us, but they would be, we think, of great interest. We should note that our hypotheses resemble, those used by Nutt and Baader for unification with constants in commutative theories (see [3] Theorem. 5.4 and forth). They find that a necessary and sufficient condition for such a theory to be unitary w.r.t. elementary unification is that the solution set to a certain system of linear equations in an appropriate semi-ring has a finite generating set. However, they don't seem to need the condition $r < n$. We have not addressed this matter further, but the similarities being striking, probably deserve future effort.

The example of the non-faithful implementation of $\mathbb{L}$ on $\mathbb{M}$ points out the critical importance of choosing the right realization for the function symbols in

---

[5] We thank Prof. R. Criado for remarking this fact

the term algebra to be implemented. Indeed, it is obviously easy to "repair" the implementation by choosing $cons_{\mathrm{M}}(\boldsymbol{a}, \boldsymbol{b}) = CONS(\boldsymbol{e_{cons}}, CONS(\boldsymbol{a}, CONS(\boldsymbol{b}, \boldsymbol{e_{nil}}))))$ instead. Moreover, the given is not the only example known to us of a non-faithful implementation, though it is a simple one. We have used in previous works a free module over the so called Ring of 2-tangles (see, [7]–[9]). This ring is built over the free monoid over a two symbol alphabet, and its elements are the subsets of the monoid. The set of subsets is endowed with two operations, and turned into a non-commutative characteristic two ring with unit a no zero divisors. Moreover it may be made into an ultra-metric space in which all elements of the form $1 + \alpha$, where α does not contain 1, and only these are invertible, the inverses being given in a power series form. This ring is easily shown to be local (see [1, Prop. 15.15] for a characterisation of such rings) and isomorphic to the ring of non-commuting formal power series in two variables over the field $\mathbb{Z}_2$. Moreover, it may be shown to verify hypothesis 2.2 and it is thus, according to our proposed naming, a $\mathcal{DF}$–ring. Thus the question about the relationship between our $\mathcal{DF}$–rings and local rings arises naturally. Moreover, for a free module over the Ring of 2-tangles we have shown that, for some toy examples, unification (as in Prolog) may be phrased in terms of the solution of a system of inhomogeneous linear equations in the module [10], and therefore a possible geometric context for unification had been hinted. Our present work opens the way to a geometric interpretation of unification through the obvious generalisation of this idea. Moreover, from the perspective of our present work, we may now realise that, for these examples, the corresponding implementations were not faithful. Despite, we know that the Ring of 2-tangles provides a natural algebraic description for infinite binary tress [2] and thus rational terms should properly fit within this framework. We hence foresee the possibility of extending the present work so as to embed unification of rational terms in one of our free modules, with the advantage that we would not be concerned by the occurs-check and thus the implementation would be expected to be fair.

References

1. Frank W. Anderson, Kent R.Fuller *Rings and Categories of Modules* Springer-Verlag, 1992
2. F. Arriaga, A. Bujosa, R. Criado *A constructive definition of the space of infinite p-trees*, Math. Japonica Vol 40, No 1 (1994), pp. 167-172
3. F. Baader and W. Snyder *Unification Theory* in "Handbook of Automated Reasoning" A. Robinson and A. Voronkov, Editors, Elsevier Sci. Publishers B.V., 2001
4. R. N. Banerjee and A. Bujosa *Syntactic Unification Concepts in Free Modules over Certain kind of Rings*, submitted to "Logic Programming for Artificial Intelligence and Information Systems", EPIA 2001
5. Donald W. Barnes, John M. Mack *An Algebraic Introduction to Mathematical Logic* Springer-Verlag, 1975
6. N. Bourbaki *Éléments de Mathématique: Algèbre I, Chapitres 1 à 3* Hermann, Paris (1970)
7. A. Bujosa, R. Criado *p-Tangles: A ring with identity which contains the space of infinite p-trees*, Math. Japonica Vol 42, No 1 (1995), pp. 153-163

8. A. Bujosa, R. Criado *Syntactic elements of declarative programming: Symbolic linear equations,* Fund. Informaticae Vol 25, No.1 (1996), pp. 39-48

9. A. Bujosa, R. Criado *A linear dependence condition which characterizes the p-trees* Math. Japonica Vol 43, No.2 (1996), pp.369-376

10. A. Bujosa, R. Criado and M. A. Hernández *Unification: Nothing but the Solution of a System Of Linear Equations* Fund. Informaticae Vol 32, (1997), pp. 267-280

11. W. Fulton *Curvas Algebraicas, Introducción a la geometría algebraica,* Ed. Reverté (1971).

12. Hungerford *Algebra,* Graduate Texts in Mathematics. Springer Verlag, 1974

13. J. -L. Lassez, M. Maher and K. Marriot *Unification Revisited* in "Foundations of Deductive Databases and Logic Programming", J. Minker Editor, Morgan Kaufman, Los Altos, California, 1987

14. M. J. Maher *Complete Axiomatisations of the Algebras of finite, Rational, and Infinite Trees* L.I.C.S. 1988, pp. 348-357

15. B. I. Plotkin *Universal Algebra, Algebraic Logic and Databases* Kluwer Academic Publishers (1994)

16. L. S. Pontriaguin *Grupos Continuos* Ed. Mir, Moscú (1978)

Analytic Tableaux and Database Repairs: Foundations

Leopoldo Bertossi[1] and Camilla Schwind[2]

[1] Carleton University,
School of Computer Science,
Ottawa, Canada K1S 5B6
bertossi@scs.carleton.ca
[2] LIM, Faculté des Sciences de Luminy,
163, Avenue de Luminy, Case 901,
13288 Marseille, Cedex 9, France
schwind@lim.univ-mrs.fr

Abstract. In this article, we characterize in terms of analytic tableaux the repairs of inconsistent relational databases, that is databases that do not satisfy a given set of integrity constraints. For this purpose we provide closing and opening criteria for branches in tableaux that are built for database instances and their integrity constraints. We use the tableaux based characterization as a basis for consistent query answering, that is for retrieving from the database answers to queries that are consistent wrt the integrity constraints.

1 Introduction

The notion of consistent answer to a query posed to an inconsistent database was defined in [1]: A tuple is a consistent answer if it is an answer, in the usual sense, in every possible repair of the inconsistent database. A repair is a new database instance that satisfies the integrity constraints and differs from the original instance by a minimal set of changes wrt set inclusion.

A computational methodology to obtain such consistent answers was also presented in [1]. Nevertheless, it has some limitations in terms of the syntactical form of integrity constraints and queries it can handle. In particular, it does not cover the case of existential queries and constraints.

In classical logic, analytic tableaux [4] are used as a formal deductive system for propositional and predicate logic. Similar in spirit to resolution, but with some important methodological and practical differences [8], they are mainly used for producing formal refutations from a contradictory set of formulas. Starting from a set of formulas, the system produces a tree with formulas in its nodes. The set of formulas is inconsistent whenever all the branches in the tableau can be closed. A branch closes when it contains a formula and its negation.

In this paper we extend the tableaux methodology to deal with a relational database instance plus a set of integrity constraints that the first fails to satisfy. Consequently, both inputs together can be considered as building an inconsistent

T. Eiter and K.-D. Schewe (Eds.): FoIKS 2002, LNCS 2284, pp. 32–48, 2002.

set of sentences. In this situation, we give criteria for closing branches in a tableau for a relational database instance.

The technique of "opening tableaux" was introduced in [11] for a solution to the frame problem, and in [14,15] for applying tableaux methods to default logic. In this paper we show how to open tableaux for database instances plus their constraints, and this notion of opening is applied to characterize and represent by means of a tree structure all the repairs of the original database. Finally, we sketch how this representation could be used to retrieve consistent query answers. At least at the theoretical level, the methodology introduced in this paper could be applied to any kind of first order queries and constraints.

2 Inconsistent Databases and Repairs

In this paper a database instance is given by a finite set of finite relations on a database schema. A database schema can be represented in logic by a typed first-order language, $\mathcal{L}$, containing a finite set of sorted predicates and a fixed infinite set of constants D. The language contains a predicate for each database relation and the constants in D correspond to the elements in the database domain, that we will also denote by D. That is every database instance has an infinite domain D. We also have a set of integrity constraints IC expressed in language $\mathcal{L}$. These are first-order formulas which the database instances are expected to satisfy. In spite of this, there are realistic situations where a database may not satisfy its integrity constraints [1]. If a database instance satisfies IC, we say that it is consistent (wrt IC), otherwise we say it is inconsistent. In any case, we will assume from now on that IC is a consistent set of first order sentences.

A database instance r can be represented by a finite set of ground atoms in the database language, or alternatively, as a Herbrand structure on this language. In consequence, we can say that a database instance is consistent, wrt IC, when its corresponding Herbrand structure is a model of IC.

The active domain of a database instance r is the set of those elements of D that explicitly appear in r. The active domain is always finite and we denote it by $Act(r)$. We may also have a set of built-in (or evaluable) predicates, like equality, arithmetical relations, etc. In this case, we have the language $\mathcal{L}$ possibly extended with these predicates. In all database instances each of these predicates has a fixed and possibly infinite extension. Of course, since we defined database instances as finite sets of ground atoms, we are not considering these built-in atoms as members of database instances.

An inconsistent database[1] has "most" of its data contents still consistent wrt IC and can still provide "consistent answers" to queries posed to it. The notion of consistent answer was defined and analyzed in [1]. This was done on the basis of considering all possible changes to r, in such a way that it becomes a consistent database instance. A consistent answer is an answer that can be retrieved from all those repairs that differ from the original instance in a minimal way.

---

[1] Sometimes we will simply say "database" instead of "database instance".

The notion of minimal change, defined in [1], is based on the notion of minimal distance between models using symmetric set difference Δ of sets of database tuples. This definition turns out to coincide with Winslett's definition of belief update [17].

Definition 2.1. *Given databases instances[2] r, r' and r'', we say that r' is closer than r'' to r, iff $r\Delta r' \subseteq r\Delta r''$. This is denoted by $r' \leq_r r''$.*

Only database predicates are taken into account for the notion of distance. In particular, built-in predicates are not subject to change; they have the same extension in all database instances. Now we can define the "repairs" of an inconsistent database instance.

Definition 2.2. *[1] (a) Given database instances r and r', r' is a* repair *of r, if $r' \models IC$ and r' is a minimal element in the set of instances wrt the order $\leq_r$. (b) Given a database instance r, a set IC and a first order query $Q(\bar{x})$, we say that a ground tuple $\bar{t}$ is a consistent answer to Q in r wrt IC iff $r' \models Q[\bar{t}]$ for every repair r' of r (wrt IC).*

Example 2.1. Consider the integrity constraint

$$IC : \forall x, y, z(Supply(x, y, z) \wedge Class(z, T_4) \rightarrow x = C),$$

stating that C is the only provider of items of class T_4; and the inconsistent database $r = \{Supply(C, D_1, I_1), Supply(D, D_2, I_2), Class(I_1, T_4), Class(I_2, T_4)\}$. We have only two possible (minimal) repairs of the original database instance, namely $r_1 = \{Supply(C, D_1, I_1), Class(I_1, T_4), Class(I_2, T_4)\}$ and $r_2 = \{Supply(C, D_1, I_1), Supply(D, D_2, I_2), Class(I_1, T_4)\}$.

Given the query $Q(x, y, z) : Supply(x, y, z)?$, the tuple (C, D_1, I_1) is a consistent answer because it can be obtained from every repair, but (D, D_2, I_2) is not, because it cannot be retrieved from r_1.   □

We have given a semantic definition of consistent answer to a query in an inconsistent database. We would like to compute consistent answers, but via computing all possible repairs and checking answers in common in **all** of them. Actually there may be an exponential number of repairs in the size of the database [2].

In [1,6] a mechanism for computing and checking consistent query answers was considered. It does not produce/use the repairs, but it queries the only explicitly available inconsistent database instance. The methodology can be applied to first-order queries and constraints. Given a query Q, to obtain the consistent answers, Q is qualified with appropriate information derived from the interaction between Q and the ICs. More precisely, if we want the consistent answers to $Q(\bar{x})$ in r, we rewrite the query, generating $\mathcal{T}(Q(\bar{x}))$; and then we retrieve from r the (ordinary) answers to $\mathcal{T}(Q(\bar{x}))$.

---

[2] We are assuming here and everywhere in the paper that all database instances have the same predicates and domain.

Example 2.2. (example 2.1 continued) Consider the query $Q : Supply(x, y, z)$? about the supplied items with the associated information. If we want the consistent answers, we generate the new query $\mathcal{T}(Q) : Supply(x, y, z) \wedge (Class(z, T_4) \rightarrow x = C)$ and pose it to the original database. The extra conjunct is the "residue" obtained from the interaction between the query and the constraint. Residues can be obtained automatically [1]. □

In general, $\mathcal{T}$ is an iterative operator. There are sufficient conditions on queries and ICs for soundness, completeness and termination of operator $\mathcal{T}$; and natural and useful syntactical classes satisfy those conditions. There are some limitations though: $\mathcal{T}$ does not work for some queries, actually is not defined for existential queries like $Q(X) : \exists Y\ Supplies(X, Y, I_1)$?. Nevertheless, this query does have consistent answers at the semantic level.

Notice that $\mathcal{T}$ is based on the interaction between the queries and the ICs. It does not consider the interaction between the ICs and the database instance. In this paper we concentrate mostly on this interaction. In particular, we wonder if we can obtain an implicit and compact representation of the database repairs.

Furthermore, the database seen as a set of logical formulas plus IC is an inconsistent first order theory; and we know that such an inconsistency can be detected and represented by means of an analytic tableau.

An analytic tableau is a syntactically generated tree-like structure that, starting from a set of formulas placed at the root, has all its branches "closed" when the initial set of formulas is inconsistent. This tableaux can show us how to repair inconsistencies, because closed branches can be opened by removing literals.

In this work, we show how to generate, close and open tableaux for database instances with their constraints; and we apply the notion of opening to characterize and represent by means of a tree structure all the repairs of the original database. Finally, we sketch how this representation could be used to retrieve consistent query answers. At least at the theoretical level, the methodology introduced here could be applied to any kind of first order queries and constraints.

3   Database Repairs and Analytic Tableaux

In order to use analytic tableaux to represent database repairs and characterize consistent query answers, we need a special form of tableaux, suitable for representing database instances and their integrity constraints.

Given a database instance r and a finite set of integrity constraints IC, we first compute the tableau, $TP(IC \cup r)$, for IC and r. This tableau has as root node the set of formulas $IC \cup r$. This tableau should be closed, that is the tableau has only closed branches, if and only if r is inconsistent. By removing database literals in every closed branch we can transform r into a consistent database instance and thus obtain a repair of the database. For all this to work, we must take into account, when computing the tableau, that r represents a database instance and not just a set of formulas, in particular, that the absence of positive information means negative information, etc. (see section 3.2). Next, we give a brief review of classical first order analytic tableaux [4,16,9].

3.1   Analytic Tableaux

The tableau of a set of formulas is obtained by recursively *breaking down* the formulas into subformulas, obtaining sets of sets of formulas. These are the usual Smullyan's classes of formulas:

α	α_1	α_2	β	β_1	β_2
$f \wedge g$	f	g	$f \vee g$	f	g
$\neg(f \vee g)$	$\neg f$	$\neg g$	$\neg(f \wedge g)$	$\neg f$	$\neg g$
$\neg(f \rightarrow g)$	f	$\neg g$	$f \rightarrow g$	$\neg f$	g

γ	$\gamma(p), p$ any constant	δ	$\delta(p), p$ a fresh constant
$(\forall x)f$	$f[x/p]$	$(\exists x)f$	$f[x/p]$
$\neg(\exists x)f$	$\neg f[x/p]$	$\neg(\forall x)f$	$\neg f[x/p]$

A tableaux prover produces a formula tree. An α-rule adds new formulas to branches, a β-rule splits the tableau and adds a new branch. Given a formula φ, we denote by $TP(\varphi)$ the tree produced by the tableaux system. We can think of this tree as the set of its branches.

Notice that the original set of constants in the language, in our case, D, is extended with a set of new constants, P, the so-called Skolem functions or parameters. These parameters, that we will denote by $p, p_1, \ldots$, have to be new at the point of their introduction in the tree in the sense that they have not appeared so far in the (same branch of the) tableau. When applying the γ-rule, the parameter can be any of the old or new constants.

A tableau branch is *closed* if it contains a formula and its negation, otherwise it is *open*. Every open branch corresponds to a model of the formula: If a branch $B \in TP(\varphi)$ is open, then the set of ground atoms on B is a model of φ. The completeness theorem for tableaux theorem proving [16] states that: F is a theorem iff $TP(\{\neg F\})$ is closed.

We consider TP not only as a theorem prover (or consistency checker) for formulae but also as an application from (sets of) formulas to trees which has some useful properties. Thus, operations on tableaux can be defined on the basis of the logical connectives occurring inside the formulas involved.

Lemma 1 *Let φ and ψ be any formulae. Then TP has the following properties.*

1. $TP(\{\varphi \vee \psi\}) = TP(\{\varphi\}) \cup TP(\{\psi\})$
2. $TP(\{\varphi \wedge \psi\}) = \{X \cup Y : X \in TP(\{\varphi\}) \text{ and } Y \in TP(\{\psi\})\}$
3. *If $B \in TP(\varphi \wedge \psi)$ then $B = B' \cup B''$ and $B' \in TP(\varphi)$ and $B'' \in TP(\psi)$.* □

Property 3. follows directly from properties 1. and 2. The properties in the lemma give rise to the following notation: $T \otimes T' = \{X \cup Y : X \in T \text{ and } Y \in T'\}$.

The properties above can be used to check whether a formula φ derives from a theory A. $A \models \varphi$ iff $A \rightarrow \varphi$ is a theorem, what will be proved if we derive a contradiction from assuming $\neg(A \rightarrow \varphi)$. Therefore we will have to compute $TP(\{\neg(A \rightarrow \varphi)\})$ and check for closure. Using the second property, we will check $TP(\{A\}) \otimes TP(\{\neg \varphi\})$ for closure, allowing us to compute $TP(A)$ only once for any number of requests.

3.2   Representing Database Instances by Tableaux

In database theory, we usually make the following assumptions[3]: (a) Unique Names Assumption (UNA): If a and b are different constants in D, then $a \neq b$ holds in r. (b) Closed World Assumption (CWA): If r is a database instance, then for any ground database atom $P(c)$, if $P(c) \notin r$, then $\neg P(c)$ holds for r, more precisely, implicitly $\neg P(c)$ belongs to r.

When computing a tableau for a database instance r, we do not add explicitly the formulas corresponding to the UNA and CWA, rather we keep them implicit, but taking them into account when computing the tableau. This means, for example, that the presence on a tableau branch of a formula $a = b$, for different constants a, b in D, closes the branch.

In consequence, if we see the relational database as the set of its explicit atoms plus its implicit negative atoms, we can always repair the database by removing ground database literals.

Given a database r and integrity constraints IC, we will generate the tableau $TP(IC \cup r)$. Notice that every branch B of this tableau will be of the form $I \cup r$, where $I \in TP(IC)$ (see lemma 1). I is the "IC-part" of the branch.

$TP(IC \cup r)$ is defined as in section 3.1, but we still have to define the closure conditions for tableaux associated to database instances. Before, we present some motivating examples.

Example 3.1. (example 2.1 continued) In this case, $TP(IC \cup r)$ is the tree in figure 1.

The last branch is closed because $D = C$ is false in the database (alternatively, because $D \neq C$ is implicitly in the database). We can see that $TP(IC \cup r)$ is closed. r is inconsistent wrt IC. The nodes $(Supply(C, D_1, I_1) \wedge Class(I_1, T_4) \rightarrow C = C)$ and $(Supply(D, D_2, I_2) \wedge Class(I_2, T_4) \rightarrow D = C)$ are obtained by applying the γ-rule to $\forall x, y, z(Supply(x, y, z) \wedge Class(z, T_4) \rightarrow x = C)$. Application of the β-rule to $(Supply(D, D_2, I_2) \wedge Class(I_2, T_4) \rightarrow D = C)$ produces the same subtree for all three leaves: $\neg Supply(C, D_1, I_1)$, $\neg Class(I_1, T_4)$ and $C = C$. In the figure, we indicate this subtree by "$\ldots$". We will see later (see section 3.3) that, in some cases, we can omit the development of subtrees that should develop under branches that are already closed. Here we can omit the explicit further development of the subtree from the first two leftmost branches, because these branches are already closed.   □

In tableaux with equality, we need extra rules. We will assume that we can always introduce equalities of the form $t = t$, for a term t, and that we can replace a term t in a predicate P by t' whenever $t = t'$ belongs to the same tableau branch [9]. It will be simpler to define the closure rules for database tableaux, if we skolemize existential formulas before developing the tableau [8]. We assume from now on that all integrity constraints are skolemized by means of a set of Skolem constants (the parameters in P) and new function symbols.

---

[3] Actually, it is possible to make all these assumptions explicit and transform the database instance into a first-order theory [12].

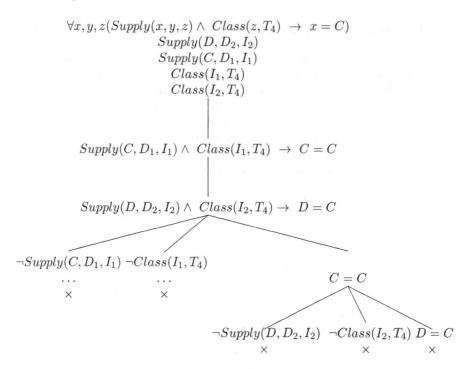

Fig. 1. Tableau for Example 3.1

Example 3.2. Consider the referential IC : $\forall x\ (P(x) \rightarrow \exists y\ Q(x,y))$, and the inconsistent database instance $r = \{P(a), Q(b,d)\}$, for $a, b, c \in D$. With an initial skolemization, we can develop the following tableau $TP(IC \cup r)$. In this tableau, the second branch closes because $Q(a, f(a))$ does not belong to the database instance. There is no x in the active database domain, such that r contains $Q(a, x)$. Implicitly, by the CWA, r contains $\neg Q(a, x)$ for any x. Hence the branch containing $Q(a, f(a))$ closes and r is inconsistent for IC.

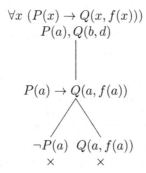

Example 3.3. Consider the inconsistent database $r_1 = \{Q(a), Q(b)\}$ wrt the IC: $\exists x\ P(x)$. After having skolemized $\exists x P(x)$ into $P(p)$, a tableau proof for the inconsistency is the following

$$P(p)$$
$$Q(a), Q(b)$$
$$\times$$

This branch closes because there is no x in D such that $P(x) \in r$ and therefore $\neg P(x)$ belongs to r for any x in D. $P(p)$ cannot belong to this database.

Example 3.4. Let us now change the database instance in example 3.3 to $r_2 = \{P(a), P(b)\}$, keeping the integrity constraint. Now, the database is consistent. and we have the following tableau $TP(IC \cup r_2)$:

$$P(p)$$
$$P(a), P(b)$$

This time we do not want the tableau to close, and thus sanctioning the inconsistency of the database. The reason is that we could make p take any of the values in the active domain $\{a, b\} \subseteq D$ of the database.   □

A similar situation can be found in a modified version of example 3.2.

Example 3.5. Change the database instance in example 3.2 to $\{P(a), Q(a, d)\}$. Now it is consistent wrt the same IC. We obtain

$$\forall x \ (P(x) \rightarrow Q(x, f(x)))$$
$$P(a), Q(a, d)$$

$$P(a) \rightarrow Q(a, f(a))$$

$$\neg P(a) \qquad Q(a, f(a))$$
$$\times$$

Now we do not close the rightmost branch because we may define f as a function from the active domain into itself that makes $Q(a, f(a))$ become a member of the database, actually by defining $f(a) = d$.

Example 3.6. Consider $IC : \ \exists x \ \neg P(x)$ and the consistent database instance $r = \{P(a)\}$. The tableau $TP(IC \cup r)$ after skolemization of IC is:

$$\neg P(p)$$
$$P(a)$$

This tableau cannot be closed, because p must be a new parameter, not occurring in the same branch of the tableau and it is not the case that $P(p) \in r$ (alternatively, we may think of p as a constant that can be defined as any element in $D \setminus \{a\}$, that is in the complement of the active domain of the database).   □

Usually, a tableau branch is closed whenever it contains a formula and its negation. For our purposes, we have taken into account that not all literals are explicit on branches due to the UNA and CWA. The following definition of closed branch modifies the standard definition, taking those assumptions into account.

Definition 3.1. *Let B be a tableau branch for a database instance r with integrity constraints IC, say $B = I \cup r$. B is closed iff one of the following conditions holds:*

1. *$a = b \in B$ for different constants a, b in D.*
2. *(a) $P(\bar{c}) \in I$ and $P(\bar{c}) \notin r$, for a ground tuple $\bar{c}$ containing elements of D only.*
   (b) $P(\bar{c}) \in I$ and there is no substitution σ for the parameters in $\bar{c}$ such that $P(\bar{c})\sigma \in r$ [4].
3. *$\neg P(\bar{c}) \in I$ and $P(\bar{c}) \in r$ for a ground tuple $\bar{c}$ containing elements of D only.*
4. *$\varphi \in B$ and $\neg \varphi \in B$, for an arbitrary formula φ.*
5. *$\neg t = t \in B$ for any term t.*

Condition 1. takes UNA into account. Notice that it is restricted to database constants, so that it does not consider new parameters[5]. Condition 2(a) takes CWA into account. Alternative condition 2(b) (actually it subsumes 2(a)) gives an account of examples 3.2, 3.3, 3.4, and 3.5.

In condition 3. one might miss a second alternative as in condition 2., something like "$\neg P(\bar{c}) \in I$ for a ground tuple containing Skolem symbols, when there is no way to define them considering elements of $D \setminus Act(r)$ in such a way that $P(\bar{c}) \notin r$". This condition can be never satisfied because we have an infinite database domain D, but a finite active domain $Act(r)$. So, it will never apply. This gives an account of example 3.6. Conditions 4. and 5. are the usual closure conditions. Conditions 2(a) and 3. are special cases of 4.

Now we can state the main properties of tableaux for database instances and their integrity constraints.

Proposition 3.1. *For a database instance r and integrity constraints IC, it holds:*

1. *r is inconsistent wrt to IC iff every branch of the tableau TP $(IC \cup r)$ is closed.*
2. *$TP(IC \cup r)$ is closed iff r is not a model of IC.*

3.3   Opening Tableaux

The inconsistency of a database r wrt IC is characterized by a tableau $TP(IC \cup r)$ which has only closed branches. In order to obtain a repair of r, we may remove the literals in the branches which are "responsible" for the inconsistencies, even implicit literals corresponding to the CWA. Every branch which can be "opened" in this way will possibly yield a repair. We can only repair inconsistencies due to literals in r. We cannot remove literals in I because, according to our approach, integrity constraints are rigid, we are not willing to give them up; we only allow

---

[4] A substitution is given as a pair $\sigma = (p, t)$, where p is a variable (parameter) and t is a term. The result of applying σ to formula F, noted $F\sigma$, is the formula obtained by replacing every occurrence of p in F by t.

[5] That is, elements of P are treated as null values in Reiter's logical reconstruction of relational databases [12].

changes in the database instances. We cannot suppress equalities $a = b$ neither built-in predicates.

According to definition 3.1, we can repair inconsistencies due only to cases 2. and 3. If B is closed because of the CWA (case 2.), it can be opened by inserting $P(\bar{c})$ into r, equivalently removing implicit literal $\neg P(\bar{c})$ from r. If B is closed because of contradictory literals $\neg P(\bar{c}) \in I$ and $P(\bar{c}) \in r$, then it can be opened by removing $P(\bar{c})$ from r.

Example 3.7. (example 3.1 continued) The tableau has 9 closed branches: (we display the literals within the branches only)

B_1	B_2	B_3
$Supply(C, D_1, I_1)$	$Supply(C, D_1, I_1)$	$Supply(C, D_1, I_1)$
$Supply(D, D_2, I_2)$	$Supply(D, D_2, I_2)$	$Supply(D, D_2, I_2)$
$Class(I_1, T_4)$	$Class(I_1, T_4)$	$Class(I_1, T_4)$
$Class(I_2, T_4)$	$Class(I_2, T_4)$	$Class(I_2, T_4)$
$\neg Supply(C, D_1, I_1)$	$\neg Supply(C, D_1, I_1)$	$\neg Supply(C, D_1, I_1)$
$\neg Supply(D, D_2, I_2)$	$\neg Class(I_2, T_4)$	$D = C$

B_4	B_5	B_6
$Supply(C, D_1, I_1)$	$Supply(C, D_1, I_1)$	$Supply(C, D_1, I_1)$
$Supply(D, D_2, I_2)$	$Supply(D, D_2, I_2)$	$Supply(D, D_2, I_2)$
$Class(I_1, T_4)$	$Class(I_1, T_4)$	$Class(I_1, T_4)$
$Class(I_2, T_4)$	$Class(I_2, T_4)$	$Class(I_2, T_4)$
$\neg Class(I_1, T_4)$	$\neg Class(I_1, T_4)$	$\neg Class(I_1, T_4)$
$\neg Supply(D, D_2, I_2)$	$\neg Class(I_2, T_4)$	$D = C$

B_7	B_8	B_9
$Supply(C, D_1, I_1)$	$Supply(C, D_1, I_1)$	$Supply(C, D_1, I_1)$
$Supply(D, D_2, I_2)$	$Supply(D, D_2, I_2)$	$Supply(D, D_2, I_2)$
$Class(I_1, T_4)$	$Class(I_1, T_4)$	$Class(I_1, T_4)$
$Class(I_2, T_4)$	$Class(I_2, T_4)$	$Class(I_2, T_4)$
$C = C$	$C = C$	$C = C$
$\neg Supply(D, D_2, I_2)$	$\neg Class(I_2, T_4)$	$D = C$

The first four tuples in every branch correspond to the initial instance r. Each branch B_i consists of an I-part and the r-part $B_i = r \cup I_i$. And we have

I_1	I_2	I_3
$\neg Supply(C, D_1, I_1)$	$\neg Supply(C, D_1, I_1)$	$\neg Supply(C, D_1, I_1)$
$\neg Supply(D, D_2, I_2)$	$\neg Class(I_2, T_4)$	$D = C$

I_4	I_5	I_6
$\neg Class(I_1, T_4)$	$\neg Class(I_1, T_4)$	$\neg Class(I_1, T_4)$
$\neg Supply(D, D_2, I_2)$	$\neg Class(I_2, T_4)$	$D = C$

I_7	I_8	I_9
$C = C$	$C = C$	$C = C$
$\neg Supply(D, D_2, I_2)$	$\neg Class(I_2, T_4)$	$D = C$

In order to open this closed tableau, we can remove literals in the closed branches. Since a tableau is open whenever it has an open branch, each opened branch of the closed tableau might produce one possible transformed open tableau. Since we want to modify the database r, which should become consistent, we should try to remove a minimal set of literals in the r-part of the branches in order to open the tableau. This automatically excludes branches B_3, B_6 and B_9, because they close due to the literals $D = C$, which do not correspond to database literals, but come from the constraints.

In this example we observe that the sets of database literals of some of the I_j are included in others. Let us denote by I'_j the set of literals in I_j corresponding to database atoms. We have then $I'_1 \supset I'_7$, $I'_2 \supset I'_8$, $I'_3 \supset I'_9$, $I'_4 \supset I'_7$, $I'_5 \supset I'_8$, $I'_6 \supset I'_9$. This shows that in order to open B_1, for example, we have to remove a bigger set of atoms from r than for opening B_7. Hence, we can decide that the branches whose database part contains the database part of another branch can be ignored: they will not produce any (minimal) repairs. This allows us not to consider B_1 through B_6 in our example. Then, B_7 and B_8 are the only branches that can lead us to repairs.   □

Definition 3.2. *Let $B = I \cup r$ be a closed branch of the tableau $TP(IC \cup r)$ such that I is not closed. r' is called* opening *of r iff $r' = (r \setminus L) \cup K$ where $L = \{l : l \in r \text{ and } \neg l \in I\}$ and $K = \{l : l \in I \text{ and there is no substitution } \sigma \text{ such that } l\sigma \in r\}$.*

Proposition 3.2. *Let r' be an opening of r. Then r' is consistent with IC.*

In consequence, for an opening $I \cup r'$ of a branch $I \cup r$ it holds:(a) If $P(\bar{c}) \in I$ and $P(\bar{c}) \notin r$, then $P(\bar{c}) \in r'$. (b) If $\neg P(\bar{c}) \in I$ and $P(\bar{c}) \in r$, then $P(\bar{c}) \notin r'$. Notice that we only open branches which are closed because of conflicting database literals. Every opening is related to a possibly non minimal repair of the original database instance. For repairs, we are only interested in "minimally" opened branches, i.e. in open branches which are as close as possible to r. Openings of r are obtained by deletion of literals from r, or, equivalently, by deletion/insertion of atoms from/into r. In order to obtain minimal repairs, we have to make a minimal set of changes, therefore we do not keep openings associated to an r'', such that $r'\Delta r \subsetneqq r''\Delta r$, where r' is associated to another opening. We will show subsequently that these are the openings where L and K are minimal in the sense of set inclusion wrt all other openings in the same tree.

The following theorem establishes a relationship between the order of repairs defined in definition 2.1 and the set inclusion of the database atoms that have been inserted or deleted when opening a database instance.

Lemma 2 *For any opening $r' = (r \setminus L) \cup K$, we have $r\Delta r' = L \cup K$.*

Theorem 3.1. *Let $r_1 = (r \setminus L_1) \cup K_1$ and $r_2 = (r \setminus L_2) \cup K_2$. Then r_1 is closer to r than r_2, i.e. $r_1 \leq_r r_2$ iff $L_1 \subseteq L_2$ and $K_1 \subseteq K_2$.*

Theorem 3.2. *Let r be an inconsistent database wrt IC. Then r' is a repair of r iffhere is an open branch I of $TP(IC)$, such that $I \cup r$ is closed and $I \cup r'$ is a minimal opening of $I \cup r$ in $TP(IC \cup r)$.*

Example 3.8. (example 3.7 continued) $TP(IC \cup r)$ has two minimal openings:

$$
\begin{array}{cc}
r'_7 & r'_8 \\
Supply(C, D_1, I_1) & Supply(C, D_1, I_1) \\
Class(I_1, T_4) & Class(I_1, T_4) \\
Class(I_2, T_4) & Supply(D, D_2, I_2)
\end{array}
$$

The rightmost closed branch cannot be opened because it is closed by the atom $D = C$ which is not a database predicate.

3.4   Complexity Considerations

The number of branches of a fully developed tableaux is very high: in the worst case, it contains $o(2^n)$ branches where n is the length of the formula. Moreover, we have to find minimal elements within this exponential set which increases the complexity to $\sum_2^P$ (see [10]). Theorem 3.1 tells us that we do not need to compare the entire branches but only parts of them, namely the literals which have been removed in order to open the tableau. This reduces the size of the sets we have to compare, but not their number. Let us reconsider in example 3.1 the point just before applying the tableaux rule which develops formula $Supply(D, D_2, I_2) \wedge Class(I_2, T_4) \rightarrow D = C$. As we pointed out in the discussion of example 3.1, under some conditions, it is possible to avoid the development of closed branches because we know that they will not be minimal without developing them.

Example 3.9. (example 3.1 continued) In this case, $TP(IC \cup r)$ is the tree in figure 2. This tree has two closed branches, b_1 and b_2, and one open branch b_3. Each of these branches will receive an identical subtree due to the application of the tableaux rules to the formulas not yet developed on the tree, namely $(Supply(D, D_2, I_2) \wedge Class(I_2, T_4) \rightarrow D = C)$. We know at this stage of the development that b_1 is closed due to $\neg Supply(C, D_1, I_1)$ and b_2 is closed due to $\neg Class(I_1, T_4)$; b_3 is not closed.   □

In this example, we can see that if we further develop the tree, every b_i will have the same sets of subbranches, say $L_1, L_2, \ldots$, where L_i is a set of literals. The final fully developed tableau will then consist of the branches $b_1 \cup L_1, b_1 \cup L_2,$ $\ldots, b_2 \cup L_1, b_2 \cup L_2, \ldots b_3 \cup L_1, b_3 \cup L_2, \ldots, \ldots$. If the final tableau is closed, since b_3 is not closed, every $b_3 \cup L_j$ will be closed due to literals within L_j, say K_j.

We have then two cases: either the literals in K_j close due to literals in r (which is the original inconsistent database instance) or they close due to literals in the part of b_3 not in r. In the first case, these literals from K_j will close every branch of the tree (also b_1 and b_2). Since b_1 and b_2 were already closed, they will be closed due to a set of literals that is strictly bigger than before, and therefore they will not produce minimally closed branches (and no repairs). In this situation, those branches can immediately be ignored and not further developed. This can considerably reduce the size of the tableau. In this example, at the end of the development, only b_3 will produce repairs (see example 3.1).

In the second case, the literals in K_j close due to literals in the part of b_3 that are not in r. If these literals are not database literals (we have called them built-in predicates), the branch cannot be opened, we cannot repair inconsistencies that are not due to database instances. Then, we only have to consider the case of database literals that are not in r.

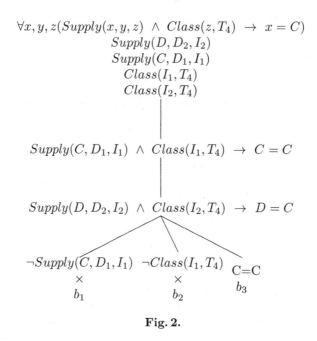

$$\forall x, y, z(Supply(x, y, z) \ \wedge \ Class(z, T_4) \ \rightarrow \ x = C)$$
$$Supply(D, D_2, I_2)$$
$$Supply(C, D_1, I_1)$$
$$Class(I_1, T_4)$$
$$Class(I_2, T_4)$$

$$Supply(C, D_1, I_1) \ \wedge \ Class(I_1, T_4) \ \rightarrow \ C = C$$

$$Supply(D, D_2, I_2) \ \wedge \ Class(I_2, T_4) \ \rightarrow \ D = C$$

$\neg Supply(C, D_1, I_1)$ $\neg Class(I_1, T_4)$ C=C
$\times$ $\times$ b_3
b_1 b_2

Fig. 2.

Since b_3 is open, those literals are negative literals (in the other case, b_3 would not have been open, due to condition 2. in definition 3.1). This is the only situation where the subbranches which are closed at a previous point of development may still become minimal. In consequence, a reasonable heuristics will be to suspend the explicit development of already closed branches unless we are sure that this case will not occur.

4   Consistent Query Answering

In order to determine consistent answers to queries, we can also use, at least at the theoretical level, a tableaux theorem prover that is able to produce $TP(IC \cup r)$ and its openings. Let us denote by $op(TP(IC \cup r))$ the tableau $TP(IC \cup r)$, with its minimal openings: All branches which cannot be opened or which cannot be minimally opened are pruned and all branches which can be minimally opened are kept (and opened).

We claim that, according to definition 2.2, $\bar{t}$ is a consistent answer to the open query $Q(\bar{x})$ when $op(TP(IC \cup r)) \otimes TP(\neg Q(\bar{t}))$ is, again, a closed tableau, where $T \otimes T' = \{X \cup Y : X \in T$ and $Y \in T'\}$ is the combined tableau. In consequence, we might use the tableau $op(TP(IC \cup r)) \otimes TP(\neg Q(\bar{x}))$ in order to retrieve those values for $\bar{x}$ that restore the closure of all the opened branches in the tableau.

Example 4.1. Consider the functional dependency

$$IC : \quad \forall(x, y, z, u, v)(Student(x, y, z) \wedge Student(x, u, v) \rightarrow y = u \wedge z = v);$$

and the inconsistent students database instance

$$r$$
$$Student(S_1, N_1, D_1)$$
$$Student(S_1, N_2, D_1)$$
$$Course(S_1, C_1, G_1)$$
$$Course(S_1, C_2, G_2)$$

which has the two repairs

r_1	r_2
$Student(S_1, N_1, D_1)$	$Student(S_1, N_2, D_1)$
$Course(S_1, C_1, G_1)$	$Course(S_1, C_1, G_1)$
$Course(S_1, C_2, G_2)$	$Course(S_1, C_2, G_2)$

We can distinguish two types of queries, the first type (see definition 2.2) yields a database tuple as answer. This type of query is a first order formula containing free variables (not quantified).

Consider now the query $Course(x, y, z)?$. We want the consistent answers. Here we have that $op(TP(IC \cup r)) \otimes TP(\neg Course(x, y, z))$ is closed for the tuples (S_1, C_1, G_1) and (S_1, C_2, G_2).

The other type of queries correspond to queries without free variables. They should get the answer "yes" or "no". For example, consider the query $Course(S_1, C_2, G_2)?$. Here $op(TP(IC \cup r)) \otimes TP(\neg Course(S_1, C_2, G_2))$ is closed. The answer is "yes", meaning that the sentence is true in all repairs.

Now, consider the query $Student(S_1, N_2, D_1)?$. The tableau $op(TP(IC \cup r)) \otimes TP(\neg Student(S_1, N_2, D_1))$ is not closed, and $Student(S_1, N_2, D_1)$ is not a member of both repairs. The answer is "no", meaning that the query is not true in all repairs. □

The following example shows that, as opposed to [1], we are able to treat existential queries in a proper way.

Example 4.2. Consider the query $\exists x Course(x, C_2, G_2)$ for the database in example 4.1. Here we have that $op(TP(IC \cup r)) \otimes TP(\neg \exists x Course(x, C_2, G_2))$ is closed. The second tableau introduces the formulas $\neg Course(p, C_2, G_2)$, for every $c \in D \cup P$ in every branch. The answer is "yes". This answer has been obtained by replacing p by the same constant S_1 in both branches. This does not need to be always the case. For example, with the query $\exists x\ Student(S_1, x, D_1)?$, that introduces the formulas $\neg Student(S_1, p, D_1)$ in every branch of $op(TP(IC \cup r)) \otimes TP(\neg \exists x\ Student(S_1, x, D_1))$, the tableau closes, the answer is "yes", but one repair has been closed for $p = N_1$ and the other repair has been closed for $p = N_2$.

We can also handle open existential queries. Let $Q(y) : \exists z Course(S_1, y, z)?$ be a query. The tableaux for $op(TP(IC \cup r)) \otimes TP(\neg \exists z Course(S_1, y, z))$, which introduces the formulas $\neg Course(S_1, y, p)$ in every branch, is closed, actually by $y = C_1$, and also by $y = C_2$, but for two different values for p, namely G_1 and G_2, resp. □

Theorem 4.1. *Let r be an inconsistent database wrt to the set of integrity constraints IC.*

1. *Let $Q(\bar{x})$ be an open query with the free variables $\bar{x}$. A ground tuple $\bar{t}$ is a consistent answer to $Q(\bar{x})$ iffp $(TP(IC \cup r)) \otimes TP(\neg Q(\bar{x}))$ is closed for the substitution $\bar{x} \mapsto \bar{t}$.*
2. *Let Q be query without free variables. The answer is "yes", meaning that the query is true in all repairs, iffp $(TP(IC \cup r)) \otimes TP(\neg Q)$ is closed.*

5   Conclusions

This paper presents ongoing work and some – as we believe – promising ideas and methodologies that deserve and require further investigation.

We have presented the theoretical basis for a treatment of consistent query answering in relational databases by means of analytic tableaux. We have mainly concentrated on the interaction of the database instance and the integrity constraints; and in the problem of representing database repairs by means of opened tableaux.

The methodology for answering queries deserves further investigation. In particular, it would be interesting to compare it with the methodology for consistent query answering presented in the more restricted syntactical scenario of [6], which relies on denials and disjunctive forms for constraints. As example 4.2 shows, one advantage of the methodology proposed here is that we can answer existential queries, what is not possible with the approach in [6].

There are many open issues. One of them has to do with the possibility to obtain from the tableau the right "residues" in order to rewrite the original query as in [1]. Another one has to do with the fact that Skolem parameters are treated as null values. It would be interesting to study the applicability of a methodology for query evaluation of queries in databases with null values [13].

Most interesting open problems have to do with implementation and efficiency issues, more specifically, the main challenge consists in developing heuristics and mechanisms for using a tableaux theorem prover to generate/store/represent $TP(IC \cup r)$ in a compact form with the purpose of: (a) applying the database assumptions, (b) interacting with a DBMS on request, in particular, without replicating the whole database instance at the tableau level, (c) detecting and producing the minimal openings (only), (d) using a theorem prover (in combination with a DBMS) in order to consistently answer queries.

Once we have $op(TP(IC \cup r))$, we need to be able to: (a) use it for different queries Q, (b) process the combined tableau $op(TP(IC \cup r)) \otimes TP(\neg Q)$ in an "reasonable and practical" way.

With respect to related work, [7] presents a general logic framework for reasoning about contradictory information which is based on an axiomatization in modal propositional logic. Instead, our approach is based on classical first order logic. A purely proof-theoretic notion of consistent query answer is presented in [5]. This notion, described only in the propositional case, corresponds to our notion of core answer. In [1] connections of the notion of consistent query answers with belief revision/update can be found.

Acknowledgments

Work supported by FONDECYT Grant # 1000593; ECOS /CONICYT Grant C97E05, and Grant # 9364-01 from Carleton University. A preliminary version of this paper appeared in [3]; we are grateful to anonymous referees for their remarks.

References

1. M. Arenas, L. Bertossi and J. Chomicki. Consistent Query Answers in Inconsistent Databases. Proc. ACM Symposium on Principles of Database Systems (ACM PODS'99), 1999, pp. 68–79.
2. M. Arenas, L. Bertossi and J. Chomicki. Scalar Aggregation in FD-Inconsistent Databases. In Database Theory - ICDT 2001 (Proc. International Conference on Database Theory, ICDT'2001). Springer LNCS 1973, 2001, pp. 39 – 53.
3. L. Bertossi and C. Schwind. An Analytic Tableaux based Characterization of Database Repairs for Consistent Query Answering (preliminary report). In Working Notes of the IJCAI'01 Workshop on Inconsistency in Data and Knowledge, AAAI Press, 2001, pp. 95 – 106.
4. E. W. Beth. The Foundations of Mathematics. North Holland, 1959.
5. F. Bry. Query Answering in Information Systems with Integrity Constraints. In Proc. IFIP WG 11.5 Working Conference on Integrity and Control in Information Systems, Chapman & Hall, 1997.
6. A. Celle and L. Bertossi. Querying Inconsistent Databases: Algorithms and Implementation. In 'Computational Logic - CL 2000', J. Lloyd et al. (eds.). Stream: 6th International Conference on Rules and Objects in Databases (DOOD'2000). Lecture Notes in Artificial Intelligence 1861, Springer 2000, pp. 942 – 956.
7. L. Cholvy. A General Framework for Reasoning about Contradictory Information and some of its Applications. In Proceedings of ECAI Workshop "Conflicts among Agents", Brighton, England, August 1998.
8. M. Fitting. First Order Modal Tableaux. Journal of Automated Reasoning, 4(2), 191–213, 1988.

9. M. Fitting. *First Order Logic and Automated Theorem Proving*. Texts and Monographs in Computer Science. Springer Verlag, 1990.
10. G. Gottlob. Complexity results for nonmonotonic logics. *Journal of Logic and Computation*, 2(3), 1992.
11. E. Lafon and C. B. Schwind. A Theorem Prover for Action Performance. In Y. Kodratoff, editor, *Proceedings of the 8th European Conference on Artificial Intelligence*, pages 541–546. Pitman Publishing, 1988.
12. R. Reiter. Towards a Logical Reconstruction of Relational Database Theory. In 'On Conceptual Modeling', Brodie, M. L. and Mylopoulos, J. and Schmidt, J. W. (eds.), Springer-Verlag, 1984, pp. 191–233.
13. R. Reiter. A Sound and Sometimes Complete Query Evaluation Algorithm for Relational Databases with Null Values. Journal of the ACM, 33(2): 349–370, 1986.
14. C. B. Schwind. A Tableau-based Theorem Prover for a Decidable Subset of Default Logic. In M. E. Stickel, editor, *Proceedings of the 10th International Conference on Automated Deduction*, number 449 in Lecture Notes in Artificial Intelligence, pages 541–546. Springer Verlag, July 1990.
15. C. B. Schwind and V. Risch. Tableau-based Characterisation and Theorem Proving for Default Logic. *Journal of Automated Reasoning*, 13(4):223–242, 1994.
16. R. M. Smullyan. *First Order Logic*. Springer, 1968.
17. M. Winslett. Reasoning about Action with a Possible Models Approach. In *Proceedings of the 8th National Conference on Artificial Intelligence*, pages 89–93, 1988.

Controlled Query Evaluation for Known Policies by Combining Lying and Refusal

Joachim Biskup[1] and Piero Bonatti[2]

[1] Fachbereich Informatik, Universität Dortmund, D-44221 Dortmund, Germany
biskup@ls6.informatik.uni-dortmund.de
[2] Dipartimento di Tecnologie dell'Informazione, Università di Milano,
I-26013 Crema, Italy
bonatti@dti.unimi.it

Abstract. Controlled query evaluation enforces security policies for confidentiality in information systems. It deals with users who may apply background knowledge to infer additional information from the answers to their queries. For each query the correct answer is first judged by some censor and then – if necessary – appropriately modified to preserve security. In previous approaches, modification has been done uniformly, either by lying or by refusal. A drawback of lying is that all disjunctions of secrets must always be protected. On the other hand, refusal may hide an answer even when the correct answer does not immediately reveal a secret.

In this paper we introduce a hybrid answer modification method that appropriately combines lying and refusal. We prove that the new method is secure under the models of known potential secrets and of known secrecies, respectively. Furthermore, we demonstrate that the combined approach can be more cooperative than uniform lies and uniform refusal, and enjoys the advantages of both.

Keywords: Inference control; Controlled query evaluation; Secrecy; Potential secret; User log; Refusal; Lying; Reliability

1   Introduction

An important goal of security in information systems is to protect the *confidentiality* of specific information according to some policy. Using a logic-oriented model of information systems, including the relational model and Datalog, this goal has to be enforced even if users are able to *infer* more information than what is explicitly returned as an answer to their queries.

Most practical enforcement mechanisms use a static approach, where an adminstrator sets up (hopefully) appropriate access rights in advance, based on a complete analysis of the protection requirements. Examples of the static approach can be found in [10, 9, 6, 4]. On the contrary, the *dynamic approach* aims at loading the burden of analyzing the requirements to the system, that has to decide how to deal with each query based on the current query history. The dynamic approach has been pioneered in [8] and [3]. There, *refusal* and *lying*

T. Eiter and K.-D. Schewe (Eds.): FoIKS 2002, LNCS 2284, pp. 49–66, 2002.

have been introduced as basic means to protect confidential information. These means have been further investigated and compared in [1, 2].

These studies show that protection can be seeked under two different models for security policies. Under the model of *secrecies*, a policy requires that users should not be able to infer the truth values of a given set of assertions with respect to the current instance of the information system. Under the model of *potential secrets*, a policy requires only that, for a given set of assertions, if any of these assertions is true in the current instance of the information system then the user should not be able to infer that fact. But he is allowed to believe the opposite truth value. Thus under the former model, query answers should not suggest any truth value at all for the given set of assertions, while under the latter model, a predetermined alternative of the truth values should be suggested.

Finally, under each of the models, security can be seeked either under the assumption that the user *knows the policy*, i.e. the specific assertions that are to be protected, or under the assumption that the user is not aware of this policy.

In this paper we further contribute to the formal study of the *dynamic approach* for *known policies* under both the model of *secrecies* and the model of *potential secrets*.

We start with a review of the disadvantages of using refusals or lies uniformly, respectively. Uniform refusal has to sometimes refuse answers even if the correct answer would not violate the policy, while uniform lies must always protect also the disjunction of the assertions under consideration. As a consequence, each approach is sometimes more restrictive than the other one, and thus less cooperative to the user.

Based on these observations we suggest a new method that appropriately *combines* refusals and lies. Roughly speaking, the combined method avoids to be unnecessarily restrictive by returning lies, if required by the assertions to be protected but *without* considering their disjunction *and* as long as a lie in turn would not reveal a protected assertion; otherwise, if both the correct answer and the false answer, i.e. a lie, would result in a security violation, then the answer is refused. This new combined method is precisely defined and investigated in depth. In particular we formally prove that it is secure under both models.

Moreover, for the model of potential secrets we extensively compare the new combined method with the uniform methods.

First, we demonstrate that the combined method is "more cooperative" as any of the uniform methods in the following sense. After starting the system, the former method returns correct answers always at least as long as the latter ones. We refer to this property as the "longest honeymoon". Afterwards, after a first modified answer, the behaviors might become incomparable in general. However, we can guarantee, that all correct answers under a uniform method can also be got by the combined method using an appropriate reordering of the query sequence.

Second, we characterize the cases where the combined method actually coincides with one of the uniform methods. For uniform lying, coincidence occurs if the set of potential secrets is closed under disjunction. For uniform refusal, coincidence occurs if, roughly speaking, the set of potential secrets has some strong closure property related to negation such that, in particular, each potential secret has a counterpart in the potential secrets such that both sentences together form a tautology.

Third, since the combined method allows lies, the problem of reliability of answers is studied. Intuitively, an answer is reliable if the user can be sure that the database has not modified the actual query result. We prove that the combined method yields the longest prefix of reliable answers.

A similar comparison for the case of secrecies has been postponed for further elaboration. In this paper, we only present a corresponding "longest honeymoon" result.

The proofs in Section 5 have been omitted due to space limitations.

2   Controlled Query Evaluation Reconsidered

First we summarize the underlying models for *ordinary query evaluation* and for *controlled query evaluation*, respectively. Then we shortly review *policies based on known secrecies* and *policies based on known potential secrets*, thereby introducing formal definitions of their security requirements.

2.1   Ordinary Query Evaluation

An *information system* maintains two kinds of data: A *schema DS* captures the universe of discourse for the intended application and is formally defined as the set of all allowed instances. An *instance db* is a *structure* which *interprets* the symbols of some logic, i.e. of the universe of discourse (see e.g. [7, 5]). We only consider the most elementary kind of query, namely a sentence in the language of the logic. Given a structure *db* (stored as an instance) and a sentence Φ (issued as a query), Φ is either *true* (*valid*) or *false* in *db*, or in other words, the structure is either a *model* of the sentence or not. When a user issues a query Φ against the schema *DS*, the (ordinary) *query evaluation* $eval(\Phi)$ determines the pertinent case for the current instance *db*. Thus we formally define

$$eval(\Phi) : DS \rightarrow \{true, false\} \text{ with } eval(\Phi)(db) := db \text{ model\_of } \Phi, \quad (1)$$

where the boolean operator model_of is assumed to be appropriately specified for the logic under consideration[1]. We also use an equivalent formalization where either the queried sentence or its negation is returned:

$$eval^*(\Phi) : DS \rightarrow \{\Phi, \neg\Phi\} \text{ with}$$

$$eval^*(\Phi)(db) := \text{if } db \text{ model\_of } \Phi \text{ then } \Phi \text{ else } \neg\Phi. \quad (2)$$

The symbols of the logic comprise both the negation symbol (as implicitly assumed above) and disjunction. We assume that both connectives have their classical semantics, namely,

---

[1] The reader who prefers classical reasoning may always replace model_of with its equivalent $\models$ in first-order logic.

db model_of $\neg\Phi$ iff it does not hold that db model_of Φ;

db model_of $\Phi_1 \vee \Phi_2$ iff db model_of Φ_1 or db model_of Φ_2.

More generally, for all (potentially infinite) sets of sentences S,

db model_of $\bigvee_{\Phi \in S} \Phi$ iff there exists $\Phi \in S$ such that db model_of Φ.

In this paper we always follow the convention that a sequence of two negation symbols is automatically discarded. Our definition trivially implies that for all instances db and for all queries Φ we have db model_of $eval^*(\Phi)(db)$.

We also define the semantic relationship $\models$ for logical implication in a standard way: $\Phi \models \Psi$ iff for every structure db such that db model_of Φ we also have db model_of Ψ. The complementary relationship is denoted with $\not\models$.

As usual, we say that a set of sentences S is *consistent* if there exists an instance db such that for all $\Phi \in S$, db model_of Φ. S is *inconsistent* if it is not consistent. As a final assumption, we assume the logic to be *compact*, that is, an infinite set of sentences is inconsistent iff it contains a finite inconsistent subset[2].

2.2   Controlled Query Evaluation for Known Policies

Controlled query evaluation consists of two steps. First, the correct answer is judged by some *censor* and then, depending on the output of the censor, some *modificator* is applied. In order to assist the censor, the system maintains a *user log*, denoted by *log*, which represents the explicit part ot the *user's assumed knowledge*. Formally, *log* is declared to be a set of sentences. Practically, the user log comprises any collection of sentences that the user is assumed to hold true in the instance, in particular publicly known *semantic constraints*. Additionally, the log records the sentences returned as *answers to previous queries*.

Formally we will describe an approach to *controlled query evaluation* by a family of functions of form *control_eval*(Q, log_0), each of which has a (possibly infinite) query sequence $Q = \langle \Phi_1, \Phi_2, \ldots, \Phi_i, \ldots \rangle$ and an initial user log log_0 as parameters. The inputs to any such function are appropriate pairs (db, *policy*) where db is an instance of the information system, and *policy* is a suitably formalized security policy. The function returns an answer sequence to the user, and updates the user log as a side effect. In symbols,

$$control\_eval(Q, log_0)(db, policy) =$$
$$\langle (ans_1, log_1), (ans_2, log_2), \ldots, (ans_i, log_i), \ldots \rangle .$$

Throughout the paper we deal with the case that the user knows the security policy *policy*. But, of course, the user does not know the instance db, rather he only sees the answer sequence to his queries.

---

[2] This assumption is not restrictive for practical purposes, as it is strictly connected to the computability of entailment.

2.3   Policies Based on Known Secrecies

A *secrecy* consists of a pair of complementary sentences $\{\Psi, \neg\Psi\}$. A security policy based on a known set *secr* of secrecies states the following requirements:

- For every secrecy in *secr* the user should not be able to determine – whether by explicit answers or by inferences – which alternative of the secrecy is true (with respect to the current instance).
- Moreover, for any sequence of queries the answers should be consistent with any belief on the truth values for a secrecy in *secr*.

Such policies have been introduced in [8] for refusal and further studied in [1].

Definition 2.1. *Let* $control\_eval(Q, log_0)$ *describe a specific controlled query evaluation for the query sequence* $Q = \langle \Phi_1, \Phi_2, \ldots, \Phi_i, \ldots \rangle$ *and an initial user log* log_0, *and let secr be a set of secrecies.*

1. $control\_eval(Q, log_0)$ *is defined to be* secure *with respect to secr iff for all finite prefixes* Q' *of* Q, *the following conditions hold: for all* Ψ *with* $\{\Psi, \neg\Psi\} \in secr$ *and for all "appropriate" arguments* $(db_1, secr)$ *such that* db_1 model_of Ψ *but* $log_0 \not\models \Psi$, *there exists an "appropriate" argument* $(db_2, secr)$ *such that:*
    (a) [same answers]

    $$control\_eval(Q', log_0)(db_1, secr) = control\_eval(Q', log_0)(db_2, secr);$$

    (b) [different secrets]

    $$eval^*(\Psi)(db_1) \neq eval^*(\Psi)(db_2).$$

2. *More generally,* $control\_eval(Q, log_0)$ *is defined to be* secure *iff it is secure with respect to all "appropriate" sets of secrecies.*

This formal definition of the security requirement can be paraphrased by saying that the controlled query evaluation functions should be "nowhere injective with respects to secrecies", i.e. for every secrecy in *secr* and any finite subsequence of query answers there are two different instances producing these answers and having opposite truth values for the secrecy. The first property says that the instances are "indistinguishable" for the user, and the second property says that the instances are "essentially different".

For *refusal*, the so-called secrecy censor can meet the requirements though in a highly restrictive way. The *secrecy censor* demands for refusing the answer to a query whenever the correct result or the false result, together with additional knowledge based on initial assumptions and previous answers, would imply an alternative of a (known) secrecy. For further details on the rationale behind this censor, the reader is referred to [8, 1].

For *lying*, under the assumption of known secrecies, we obviously cannot meet the requirements, since the system would be forced to *always* return the false alternative of a secrecy (cf. [1]).

2.4   Policies Based on Known Potential Secrets

A *potential secret* is just a sentence Ψ. Such a sentence determines a corresponding secrecy, $\{\Psi, \neg\Psi\}$. In the context of potential secrets, however, one of the alternatives of a secrecy is distinguished as a potential secret, and the other alternative is considered to be harmless. Accordingly, on the one hand a specified potential secret should never appear as a logical consequence of the system's answers to queries, whereas on the other hand the system is allowed to suggest that the harmless alternative is true. Thus a security policy based on a known set *pot_sec* of potential secrets states the following requirements:

- For every potential secret $\Psi \in pot\_sec$, the user should not be able to determine – whether by explicit answers or by inferences – that Ψ is true in the current instance.
- Moreover, for any sequence of queries the answers should be consistent with the belief that an arbitrary potential secret is false.

Basically, the first requirement applies when the potential secret Ψ is an actual secret, i.e., if for the current instance *db* we have *db* model_of Ψ. Surely it can happen that a sentence of *pot_sec* is not true in the current instance. In this case, the user is allowed to see or to conclude that the *negation* of such a sentence is true in the current instance, as expressed by the second requirement.

Such policies have been implicitly introduced in [3] for lying and further studied in [2] for both refusal and lying.

Definition 2.2. Let *control_eval*(Q, log_0) *describe a specific controlled query evaluation for the query sequence* $Q = \langle \Phi_1, \Phi_2, \ldots, \Phi_i, \ldots \rangle$ *and an initial user log* log_0, *and let pot_sec be a set of potential secrets.*

1. *control_eval*(Q, log_0) *is defined to be* secure *with respect to pot_sec iff for all finite prefixes* Q' *of* Q, *the following conditions hold: for all potential secrets* $\Psi \in pot\_sec$ *and for all "appropriate" arguments* (db_1, pot_sec) *such that* $log_0 \not\models \Psi$, *there exists an "appropriate" argument* (db_2, pot_sec) *such that:*
   (a) [same answers]

   $$control\_eval(Q', log_0)(db_1, pot\_sec) = control\_eval(Q', log_0)(db_2, pot\_sec)\,;$$

   (b) [the potential secret is false]

   $$eval^*(\Psi)(db_2) = \neg\Psi\,.$$

2. *More generally, control_eval*(Q, log_0) *is defined to be* secure *iff it is secure with respect to all "appropriate" sets of potential secrets.*

This formal definition can be paraphrased by saying that the controlled query evaluation functions should have a "surjective restriction on false potential secrets", i.e. for every potential secret in *pot_sec* and any finite subsequence of query answers there is an instance producing these answers and assigning the truth value *false* to the potential secret. Thus for any instance producing the query answers there exists another instance, possibly identical with the first one, such that according to the first property both instances are "indistinguishable" for the user, and according to the second property the second instance makes the potential secret false.

For *refusal*, the so-called refusal censor can meet the requirements. The *refusal censor* demands for refusing the answer to a query whenever the correct result or the false result, together with additional knowledge based on initial assumptions and previous answers, would imply a potential secret:

$$censor^R(db, pot\_sec, log, \Phi) := (\text{exists}\,\Psi)[\Psi \in pot\_sec \text{ and}$$
$$[\,log \cup \{eval^*(\Phi)(db)\} \models \Psi \text{ or } log \cup \{\neg eval^*(\Phi)(db)\} \models \Psi\,]\,].$$

Observe that the censor's condition is independent from the actual instance *db*, since the censor can be equivalently rewritten as

$$censor^R(db, pot\_sec, log, \Phi) := (\text{exists}\,\Psi)[\Psi \in pot\_sec \text{ and}$$
$$[\,log \cup \{\Phi\} \models \Psi \text{ or } log \cup \{\neg\Phi\} \models \Psi\,]\,].$$

Intuitively, the refusal censor could not block an answer only when it entails a potential secret, because then the answer could be reconstructed (it would always be the one that entails the secret). So this censor blocks also those answers whose negation entails a potential secret.

For *lying*, the so-called lying censor can meet the requirements. The *lying censor* demands for modifying the answer to a query whenever the correct result, together with additional knowledge based on initial assumptions and previous answers, would imply the *disjunction of all potential secrets*:

$$censor^L(db, pot\_sec, log, \Phi) := log \cup \{eval^*(\Phi)(db)\} \models pot\_sec\_disj\,,$$

where

$$pot\_sec\_disj := \bigvee_{\Psi \in pot\_sec} \Psi\,.$$

Clearly, this censor should at least ask for a lie when the answer entails a potential secret. This condition is strengthened to the entailment of *pot_sec_disj* in order to avoid situations that – informally speaking – would put the query answering mechanism in a corner, forcing it to reveal some secret (cf. [3]).

2.5 "Appropriate" Arguments

Refusal and lying need different notions of an "appropriate" argument, as required in Definition 2.1 and Definition 2.2.

In the context of *refusal*, we have to ensure that also the initial user log log_0 contains only correct data, i.e., an argument $(db_i, policy)$ is "appropriate" if db_i model_of log_0. Moreover, if already the initial user log implied an alternative of a secrecy, then the system would *always* refuse the answer. Thus the system can "appropriately" be applied only if the following precondition holds:

$$\text{for all } \{\Psi, \neg\Psi\} \in secr, log_0 \not\models \Psi \text{ and } log_0 \not\models \neg\Psi . \tag{3}$$

In the context of *lying*, we have to ensure that the initial user log log_0 does not already imply the disjunction of all potential secrets, i.e., an argument (db_i, pot_sec) is "appropriate" if $log_0 \not\models pot\_sec\_disj$, and thus, in particular the following precondition must hold:

$$\text{for all } \Psi \in pot\_sec, log_0 \not\models \Psi . \tag{4}$$

3 Combining Lying and Refusal for Known Potential Secrets

As sketched above in Section 2.4, refusal and lying both have disadvantages. In particular, refusal needs to hide the correct answer also if the *false* answer would violate the policy, and lying needs to *protect disjunctions*. In order to avoid these disadvantages, we are now going to combine refusal and lying. This combined method is outlined as follows:

Given a query Φ, there are three possible reactions:

1. refusal,
2. lying, and
3. correct answer.

Case 1, *refusal* applies iff the current log and the correct answer would imply a potential secret, and, additionally, the current log and the false answer would also imply a potential secret. Clearly, once we have reached this situation, refusal is the only option to protect the potential secrets.

Case 2, *lying* applies iff the current log and the correct answer would imply a potential secret, but the current log and the false answer do *not* imply a potential secret. Thus we lie, if there is a need to do so, and, additionally, we can assure that the lie will not be "harmful".

Case 3, *correct answer* applies for the remaining cases, i.e., iff the current log and the correct answer do *not* imply any potential secret[3].

In the rest of this section we will show that, following this outline, we can achieve both security in the sense of Definition 2.2 and the advantages of uniform refusal and of uniform lying.

---

[3] This condition holds vacuously when there are no potential secrets. In that case, only true answers are returned, as expected, since there is nothing to protect. Note that in this case the log may become inconsistent, but only if the current instance is not a model of log_0, i.e., the initial (estimated) beliefs of the user contain some wrong belief. Intuitively, log inconsistency is not perceived as a problem because in the absence of potential secrets there is no need to craft believable lies.

3.1   Procedure

Given a security policy as a set of potential secrets pot_sec and a query sequence $Q = \langle \Phi_1, \Phi_2, \ldots, \Phi_i, \ldots \rangle$ and an initial user log log_0, we aim at maintaining the following *invariant* for the user log log_i:

$$\text{for all } \Psi \in pot\_sec,\ log_i \not\models \Psi. \tag{5}$$

Surely, on initialization, i.e. for $i = 0$, we need this property as a *precondition*.

The new combined method, i.e. the *controlled query evaluation by combining refusal and lying*, $control\_eval^C(Q, log_0)$, is defined as

$$control\_eval^C(Q, log_0)(db, pot\_sec) =$$
$$\langle (ans_1, log_1), (ans_2, log_2), \ldots, (ans_i, log_i), \ldots \rangle,$$

where the i-th answer ans_i and the i-th user log log_i are given by

$ans_i := $ if $(\text{exists } \Psi_1)[\Psi_1 \in pot\_sec \text{ and } log_{i-1} \cup \{eval^*(\Phi_i)(db)\} \models \Psi_1]$
            then
                 if $(\text{exists } \Psi_2)[\Psi_2 \in pot\_sec \text{ and } log_{i-1} \cup \{\neg eval^*(\Phi_i)(db)\} \models \Psi_2]$
                 then mum
                 else $\neg eval^*(\Phi_i)(db)$
            else $eval^*(\Phi_i)(db)$

and

$$log_i := \text{if } ans_i = \text{mum then } log_{i-1} \text{ else } log_{i-1} \cup \{ans_i\}.$$

3.2   Examples

We reconsider the examples given in section 5.2 of [2]. Throughout the examples let $pot\_sec = \{s_1, s_2, s_3\}$, $log_0 = \{p \to s_1 \vee s_2,\ p \wedge q \to s_3\}$.

Example 3.1. Let the query sequence be $Q = \langle p, q \rangle$, and the instance be $db = \{p, q, s_1, s_2, s_3\}$. The correct answer to p, together with log_0, entails no potential secret (so the answer is not distorted by the refusal mechanism), but it does entail a disjunction of secrets ($s_1 \vee s_2$), and hence the lying mechanisms returns $\neg p$. At the next step, the two methods have different logs, $log_1^R = log_0 \cup \{p\}$ and $log_1^L = log_0 \cup \{\neg p\}$. Now, log_1^R and q together imply a potential secret (s_3), so refusal must block this answer, while log_1^L and q together don't even imply pot_sec_disj. Therefore, the answers based upon refusal are $\langle p, \text{mum} \rangle$, while using lies we get $\langle \neg p, q \rangle$. The combined method yields $\langle p, \neg q \rangle$ and thus avoids the early lying on query p, which is due in order to protect the disjunction.

Example 3.2. If the query sequence were given in reverse order, i.e. $Q = \langle q, p \rangle$, then the answers based upon refusal would be $\langle q, \text{mum} \rangle$, while both those based upon lies and those under the combined method would be $\langle q, \neg p \rangle$. In this case all approaches return the same correct answers.

Example 3.3. Now let $Q = \langle p, r \rangle$. Both refusals and the combined method yield answers $\langle p, \neg r \rangle$; lies yield $\langle \neg p, \neg r \rangle$. In this case, refusals produce more correct answers than lies, and so does the combined method.

Example 3.4. Finally, let $Q = \langle q, \neg p \rangle$, and $db = \{q\}$. Here refusals yield $\langle q, \text{mum} \rangle$, and both lies and the combined method yield $\langle q, \neg p \rangle$. In this case, lies produce more correct answers than refusals, and so does the combined method.

Summarizing these examples we observe that whenever refusals or lies outperforms the other approach, then the combined method shares the advantages of the better performing approach and avoids the disadvantages of the worse one.

3.3 Security

Based on the introductory explanations we can easily derive the required security property for the combined method.

Theorem 3.1 (combined method of lying and refusal is secure). *Under the model of known potential secrets, the controlled query evaluation by combining lying and refusal $control\_eval^C(Q, log_0)$ is secure in the sense of Definition 2.2, where we consider an argument as "appropriate" iff the precondition (4) holds.*

Proof. Consider a potential secret $\Psi \in pot\_sec$ and an "appropriate" argument (db_1, pot_sec) such that $log_0 \not\models \Psi$, and let $\{log_i^1\}_{i \geq 0}$ be the set of logs produced by $control\_eval^C(Q, log_0)(db_1, pot\_sec)$. By the declaration of the combined method, the invariant (5) is maintained, and hence

$$\text{for all } i \geq 0, \; log_i^1 \not\models \Psi . \tag{6}$$

Let Q' be an arbitrary prefix of Q, and let k be the length of Q'. By (6), some instance db_2 is a model of $log_k^1 \cup \{\neg\Psi\}$, and this instance is "appropriate" too.

Since for $i \leq k$ the *non-refused* answers ans_i^1 produced by $control\_eval^C(Q, log_0)(db_1, pot\_sec)$ are contained in log_k^1, we have that for all such i, $db_2 \; \text{model\_of} \; ans_i^1$, and hence

$$eval^*(\Phi_i)(db_2) = ans_i^1 . \tag{7}$$

Now we prove by induction on i that for all $i \leq k$ the pairs (ans_i^2, log_i^2) in the sequence $control\_eval^C(Q, log_0)(db_2, pot\_sec)$ coincide with their counterparts in $control\_eval^C(Q, log_0)(db_1, pot\_sec)$.

For $i = 0$ we have $log_0^1 = log_0^2 = log_0$ (ans_0^1 and ans_0^2 are not defined).

For $i > 0$, we consider the ith query Φ_i. According to the declaration of the combined method, there are three cases w.r.t. the instance db_1:

Case 1, *refusal*: Then we have $log_{i-1}^1 \cup \{eval^*(\Phi_i)(db_1)\} \models \Psi_1$ and $log_{i-1}^1 \cup \{\neg eval^*(\Phi_i)(db_1)\} \models \Psi_2$ for some $\Psi_1, \Psi_2 \in pot\_sec$. The same property holds if we replace db_1 by db_2, since for each of the instances both sentences, Φ_i and $\neg\Phi_i$, occur as ordinary query result and as negated ordinary query result. Thus, refusal also applies for the instance db_2.

Case 2, *lying*: Then we have $log_{i-1}^1 \cup \{eval^*(\Phi_i)(db_1)\} \models \Psi_1$ for some $\Psi_1 \in pot\_sec$, but $log_{i-1}^1 \cup \{\neg eval^*(\Phi_i)(db_1)\} \not\models \Psi_2$ for all $\Psi_2 \in pot\_sec$. Hence

$$\neg eval^*(\Phi_i)(db_1) = ans_i^1 = eval^*(\Phi_i)(db_2),$$

and the correct answer applies for the instance db_2, i.e., $ans_i^1 = ans_i^2$.

Case 3, *correct answer*: Then we have $log_{i-1}^1 \cup \{eval^*(\Phi_i)(db_1)\} \not\models \Psi_1$ for all $\Psi_1 \in pot\_sec$. Hence

$$eval^*(\Phi_i)(db_1) = ans_i^1 = eval^*(\Phi_i)(db_2),$$

and the correct answer also applies for the instance db_2, i.e., $ans_i^1 = ans_i^2$.

Since for all cases, each of the instances returns the same answer, they also produce the same user log.

This completes the proof that

$$control\_eval^L(Q', log_0)(db_1, pot\_sec) = control\_eval^L(Q', log_0)(db_2, pot\_sec).$$

Finally, by construction, we have db_2 `model_of` $\neg\Psi$, as required by Definition 2.2, property (b). $\square$

3.4   Comparison with Uniform Refusal and Uniform Lying

We now investigate our observations about the examples given in Section 3.2 in more general terms. First, we can easily verify the following lemma.

Lemma 3.1 (combined method enjoys "longest honeymoon"). *Under the model of known potential secrets, the controlled query evaluation by combining lying and refusal $control\_eval^C(Q, log_0)$ returns the first modified answer not earlier than uniform refusal or uniform lying.*

Proof. We assume that the argument under consideration is "appropriate" for the method to be compared. Consider the smallest i such that the combined method returns a modified answer. Then the claim directly follows from the observations, that up to $i-1$ the answers are identical and thus the logs are identical, and that the request of the combined method to modify, namely $(exists\ \Psi_1)[\Psi_1 \in pot\_sec$ and $log_i \cup \{eval^*(\Phi_i)(db)\} \models \Psi_1]$, entails the request to modify for the uniform method. $\square$

Next, we study the general situation. It turns out that after a first modified answer the methods might in general become incomparable. The examples presented in section 5 below for the study of reliability also justify this observation. However, we can show, that all correct answers under a uniform method can also be got by the combined method using an appropriate reordering of the query sequence. In order to prove this result, we first consider such reorderings.

Lemma 3.2 (reordering of correctly answered queries). *Under the model of known potential secrets, for uniform refusal as well as for uniform lying, any query sequence $Q = \langle \Phi_1, \Phi_2, \ldots, \Phi_i, \ldots \rangle$ can be rearranged into a query sequence $Q' = \langle \Phi'_1, \Phi'_2, \ldots, \Phi'_i, \ldots \rangle$ such that all correctly answered queries in Q occur in the prefix of Q'.*

Proof. We consider uniform refusal first. Define Φ'_i as the i-th query in Q that is correctly answered. If there are infinitely many such queries then Q' is completely defined, otherwise we append the queries in Q not added to Q' so far. Then answers for Q and for Q' are the same for the prefix of the queries correctly answered in Q. This claim can be justified by an easy induction. We just have to observe that for uniform refusal the user log remains unchanged for a modified answer, i.e., both query sequences produce the same log values for corresponding queries.

For uniform lying essentially the same reasoning applies. The only difference is that now a log value for the rearranged query sequence is a (possibly strict) subset of the original value for the corresponding query. But if the larger log does not imply the disjunction of all secrets, so does not the contained log. □

Theorem 3.2 (combined method is "more cooperative" than others). *Let M denote either $R(efusal)$ or $L(ying)$, and let log_0 and (db, pot_sec) be any appropriate parameters. Then, for all query sequences Q^M for the uniform method M there exists a query sequence Q^C for the combined method such that the following properties hold:*

1. *$control\_eval^C(Q, log_0)(db, pot\_sec)$ delivers all answers that are correct under $control\_eval^M(Q, log_0)(db, pot\_sec)$, and possibly more correct answers.*
2. *Q^C is defined by a reordering that shifts correctly answered queries towards the beginning of the query sequence.*

Proof. We first apply Lemma 3.2, yielding a reordering for which we then apply the "Honeymoon Lemma" 3.1. □

By definition, the combined method exploits both lies and refusal. In some cases, however, only one of the modifications is actually used. In the rest of this section we fully characterize these cases.

Theorem 3.3 (coincidence with uniform lying). *The combined method coincides with uniform lying if and only if the set of of potential secrets pot_sec is closed under disjunction.*

Proof. Suppose that $pot\_sec\_disj \in pot\_sec$. Then we show that the combined method never refuses. Otherwise, for some current log log, some query Φ and some instance db there exist potential secrets $\Psi_1, \Psi_2 \in pot\_sec$ such that $log \cup \{eval^*(\Phi)(db)\} \models \Psi_1$ and $log \cup \{eval^*(\neg\Phi)(db)\} \models \Psi_2$. Then we have also $log \cup \{eval^*(\Phi)(db)\} \models pot\_sec\_disj$ and $log \cup \{eval^*(\neg\Phi)(db)\} \models pot\_sec\_disj$. But this means that already $log \models pot\_sec\_disj$, which together with the supposition contradicts the security property of the combined method.

Now suppose that $pot\_sec\_disj \notin pot\_sec$. Let $\{\Psi_1, ..., \Psi_k\}$ be a minimal set of potential secrets such that $\Psi_1 \vee ... \vee \Psi_k \notin pot\_sec$. Then we consider an empty initial log, an instance which makes $\Psi_1 \vee ... \vee \Psi_k$ true, and as queries first $\Psi_1 \vee ... \vee \Psi_k$ and then Ψ_1. The combined method returns the correct answer for the first query but has to supply a modified answer for the second query. This must be a refusal. For assume otherwise. Then a lie is returned, and the resulting log would be $\{\Psi_1 \vee ... \vee \Psi_k, \neg\Psi_1\}$. This log, however, implies $\Psi_2 \vee ... \vee \Psi_k$, which is an element of pot_sec by supposition. So we have derived a contradiction to the security of the combined method.   □

Theorem 3.4 (coincidence with uniform refusal). *The combined method coincides with uniform refusal if and only if the set of of potential secrets pot_sec is closed under the following property:*

for all instances db, for all sets of sentences $log \supseteq log_0$ such that (i) db model_of *log and (ii) for all $\Psi \in pot\_sec$, $log \not\models \Psi$; for all queries Φ, if there exists $\Psi_1 \in pot\_sec$ such that $log \cup \{eval^*(\Phi)(db)\} \models \Psi_1$, then there exists $\Psi_2 \in pot\_sec$ such that $log \cup \{\neg eval^*(\Phi)(db)\} \models \Psi_2$.*

Proof. (Sketch) Clearly, by the definition of the combined method, if the condition of the theorem holds, then no lies can occur. (It can be proved by induction, with the extra inductive hypothesis that each log_i satisfies (i) and (ii)).

Conversely, suppose the condition does not hold. Then there exist db and $log \supseteq log_0$ satisfying (i) and (ii), and there exists a query Φ and $\Psi_1 \in pot\_sec$ such that $log \cup \{eval^*(\Phi)(db)\} \models \Psi_1$, and for all $\Psi_2 \in pot\_sec$, $log \cup \{\neg eval^*(\Phi)(db)\} \not\models \Psi_2$. Then the query sequence $\langle \bigwedge log, \Phi \rangle$ leads to a lie.   □

The following observations are easy consequences of theorem. Suppose that the combined method coincides with uniform refusal, and consider an instance db such that for all $\Psi \in pot\_sec$, db model_of Ψ. Then we have:

1. log_0 entails a disjunction of secrets. In particular, if $log_0 = \emptyset$ then pot_sec contains two sentences Ψ_1, Ψ_2 such that $\Psi_1 \vee \Psi_2$ is a tautology.
2. For all $\Psi_1 \in pot\_sec$ there exists a $\Psi_2 \in pot\_sec$ such that $log_0 \cup \{\neg\Psi_1\} \models \Psi_2$ and thus also $log_0 \cup \{\neg\Psi_2\} \models \Psi_1$.
3. If pot_sec contains only atoms, then we have $\Psi \in pot\_sec$ if and only if $\neg\Psi \in pot\_sec$.

4   Combining Lying and Refusal for Known Secrecies

As sketched in Section 2.3, under the model of known secrecies uniform refusal can be succesfully applied but requires a highly restrictive censor, and lying cannot be used at all. Somehow surprisingly, as shown in this section, even under this model we can combine refusal and lying, thereby weakening the censor at the price of some lies. In fact, after a straightforward modification we can basically reuse the combined method for the model of potential secrets.

4.1   Procedure

The modification comes from a different *invariant* and *precondition*. Now we need, given a security policy as a set of secrecies *secr* and a query sequence $Q = \langle \Phi_1, \Phi_2, \ldots, \Phi_i, \ldots \rangle$ and an initial user log log_0:

$$\text{for all } \{\Psi, \neg\Psi\} \in secr, \; log_i \not\models \Psi \text{ and } log_i \not\models \neg\Psi . \tag{8}$$

For conciseness, we introduce the operator `secrecy` which maps any sentence Ψ on the corresponding secrecy $\{\Psi, \neg\Psi\}$. Then we can restate (8) as

$$\text{for all } \Psi \text{ with } \texttt{secrecy}(\Psi) \in secr, \; log_i \not\models \Psi . \tag{9}$$

Finally, for this model of known secrecies the *controlled query evaluation by combining* refusal and lying, $control\_eval^C(Q, log_0)$, is redefined as

$$control\_eval^C(Q, log_0)(db, secr) =$$
$$\langle (ans_1, log_1), (ans_2, log_2), \ldots, (ans_i, log_i), \ldots \rangle ,$$

where the i-th answer ans_i and the i-th user log log_i are given by

```
ans_i := if  (exists Ψ_1)[ secrecy(Ψ_1) ∈ secr and log_{i-1} ∪ {eval*(Φ_i)(db)} ⊨ Ψ_1]
         then
             if  (exists Ψ_2)[ secrecy(Ψ_2) ∈ secr and
                               log_{i-1} ∪ {¬eval*(Φ_i)(db)} ⊨ Ψ_2]
             then mum
             else ¬eval*(Φ_i)(db)
         else eval*(Φ_i)(db)
```

and

$$log_i := \texttt{if } ans_i = \texttt{mum then } log_{i-1} \texttt{ else } log_{i-1} \cup \{ans_i\} .$$

4.2   Examples

We resume an example given in Section 3.2, now suitably modified for the model of known secrecies, where the method of uniform lying is not applicable. Let $secr = \{\{s_1, \neg s_1\}, \{s_2, \neg s_2\}, \{s_3, \neg s_3\}\}$, and $log_0 = \{p \rightarrow s_1 \vee s_2, \; p \wedge q \rightarrow s_3\}$, and consider the query sequence $Q = \langle p, q \rangle$.

Example 4.1. First, let the instance be $db = \{p, q, s_3\}$. The answers based upon refusal are $\langle p, \texttt{mum} \rangle$, since for the second query the correct answer q, together with $log_1 = log_0 \cup \{p\}$, would imply the correct alternative of a secrecy (s_3). Accordingly, the combined method would return $\langle p, \neg q \rangle$, i.e., the refusal would be replaced by a lie.

Example 4.2. Now let the instance be $db = \{p, \neg q, s_3\}$. Again, the answers based upon refusal are $\langle p, \texttt{mum} \rangle$, since for the second query now the false answer would imply the correct alternative of a secrecy. The combined method, however, would return only correct answers, namely $\langle p, \neg q \rangle$.

Example 4.3. Finally, let the instance be $db = \{p, \neg q, \neg s_3\}$. Then refusals would again return $\langle p, \mathtt{mum} \rangle$, whereas the combined method again yields the corrrect answers $\langle p, \neg q \rangle$.

Summarizing these examples we observe that the combined method is as cooperative as refusals and gives strictly more correct answers, on the price of replacing some refusals by lies and thus raising the issue of reliability.

4.3   Security

Basically, all results under the model of potential secrets can be tranferred to the model under secrecies.

Theorem 4.1 (combined method of lying and refusal is secure). *Under the model of known secrecies, the controlled query evaluation by combining lying and refusal $control\_eval^C(Q, log_0)$ is secure in the sense of Definition 2.1, where we consider an argument as "appropriate" iff the p recondition (3) holds.*

Proof. Consider a sentence Ψ with $\mathtt{secrecy}(\Psi) \in secr$ and an "appropriate" argument $(db_1, secr)$ such that db_1 $\mathtt{model\_of}$ Ψ and both $log_0 \not\models \Psi$ and $log_0 \not\models \neg\Psi$. Again, we study the set $\{log_i^1\}_{i \geq 0}$ of logs produced by $control\_eval^C(Q, log_0)$ $(db_1, secr)$. By the declaration of the combined method, the invariant (8) is maintained, and hence

$$\text{for all } i \geq 0, \ log_i^1 \not\models \Psi \text{ and } log_i \not\models \neg\Psi. \tag{10}$$

Let Q' be an arbitrary prefix of Q, and let k be the length of Q'. By (10), some instance db_2 is a model of $log_k^1 \cup \{\neg\Psi\}$, and this instance is "appropriate" too.

Since for $i \leq k$ the *non-refused* answers ans_i^1 produced by $control\_eval^C(Q, log_0)(db_1, secr)$ are contained in log_k^1, we have that for all such i, db_2 $\mathtt{model\_of}$ ans_i^1, and hence

$$eval^*(\Phi_i)(db_2) = ans_i^1. \tag{11}$$

Using the same arguments as under the model of known potential secrets, we can now prove by induction on i that for all $i \leq k$ the pairs (ans_i^2, log_i^2) in the sequence $control\_eval^C(Q, log_0)(db_2, secr)$ coincide with their counterparts in $control\_eval^C(Q, log_0)(db_1, secr)$.

Finally, by construction, while db_1 $\mathtt{model\_of}$ Ψ we have db_2 $\mathtt{model\_of}$ $\neg\Psi$, and thus $eval^*(\Psi)(db_1) \neq eval^*(\Psi)(db_2)$ as required by Definition 2.1, property (b). $\qquad\qquad\square$

4.4   Comparison with Uniform Refusal

Again we can easily verify the following lemma.

Lemma 4.1 (combined method enjoys "longest honeymoon"). *Under the model of known secrecies, the controlled query evaluation by combining lying and refusal $control\_eval^C(Q, log_0)$ returns the first modified answer not earlier than uniform refusal.*

5 Reliability

In this section we study the issue of answer reliability. Roughly speaking, an answer is reliable if the user can be sure that the query answer has not been modified by the database. From this point of view, a mum is an unreliable answer, because it does not report the correct value of the query in the database. In the presence of lies, subtler cases arise. For example an answer may be *correct but unreliable* if the answer is true in the current instance but false in another instance with the same observable behavior. Then even a well-informed user could not be sure that the answer is correct, given the external behavior of the database and knowledge about the initial log and the set of potential secrets.

5.1 The Case of Potential Secrets

In the framework based on potential secrets, reliability is formalized as follows.

Definition 5.1 (Reliability). *Let Q be a (possibly infinite) sequence of queries and $control\_eval(Q, log_0)(db, pot\_sec) = \langle (a_1, log_1), \ldots, (a_j, log_j), \ldots \rangle$. In this context, we say that a_j is* reliable *iff $a_j \neq$ mum and for all instances db' that return the same answers to Q as db (i.e., such that $control\_eval(Q, log_0)(db', pot\_sec) = \langle (a_1, log_1'), \ldots, (a_j, log_j'), \ldots \rangle$), it holds that db' model_of a_j.*

Note that only db' may vary, while log_0 and pot_sec are fixed. This models the worst-case assumption that the user knows both the initial log and the set of potential secrets. Note also that uniform refusal never lies, so all answers different from mum are reliable by definition. Finally, note that since the answers $a_1, \ldots, a_j, \ldots$ are the same for db and db', then also $log_i = log_i'$ for all indexes i in the sequence.

Example 5.1. Let $pot\_sec = \{s\}$ and $log_0 = \{p \to s\}$. Suppose db is a model of $q, \neg p$ and s, and consider the query sequence $Q = \langle q, p, s \rangle$. The answers are $\langle q, \neg p, \neg s \rangle$. Here the first answer is correct and reliable (given pot_sec and log_0 no database instance would need to lie on q), while the second answer is correct but unreliable (as any instance db' satisfying both q and p would return the same answers, i.e., $\langle q, \neg p, \neg s \rangle$; the second one would be a lie). The third answer is both incorrect and unreliable.

In [2] it was proved that uniform lies and refusals return the same reliable answers when the set of potential secrets is closed under disjunction. From this result and Theorem 3.3 we obtain a similar result for the combined approach.

Corollary 5.1. *If pot_sec is closed under disjunction, then uniform refusal, uniform lies and the combined approach return the same reliable answers.*

The above correspondence does not always hold. In general, the three approaches are incomparable (w.r.t. reliability) when the set of potential secrets is not closed under disjunction. In a previous paper we have proved that uniform lies and uniform refusal methods may yield incomparable sequences of reliable answers [2]. Here we show that each of the two methods is incomparable with the combined method.

Example 5.2. Let $pot\_sec = \{s_1, s_2, s_3\}$ and $log_0 = \{p \rightarrow s_1, q \rightarrow p \vee s_2, r \wedge q \rightarrow s_3\}$. Suppose that db satisfies p, q, r and s_1, s_2, s_3. Consider the query sequence $Q = \langle p, q \rangle$. Uniform refusal yields the answers $\langle \texttt{mum}, q \rangle$, while the combined approach yields $\langle \neg p, \neg q \rangle$. In this case uniform refusal yields one reliable answer (q) while the combined method returns none. Next consider the query sequence $Q = \langle p, q, r \rangle$. Uniform refusal yields the answers $\langle \texttt{mum}, q, \texttt{mum} \rangle$, while the combined approach yields $\langle \neg p, \neg q, r \rangle$. In this case the combined approach yields one correct answer, too (r), that turns out to be reliable (after answering $\neg q$ no database db' would need to lie on r). The sets of reliable answers returned by the two approaches are not comparable.

Example 5.3. Let $pot\_sec = \{s_1, s_2, s_3\}$ and $log_0 = \{p \rightarrow s_1 \vee s_2, p \wedge q \rightarrow s_3\}$. Suppose that db satisfies p, q and consider the query sequence $Q = \langle p, q \rangle$. Uniform lies return answers $\langle \neg p, q \rangle$, where $\neg p$ is clearly unreliable, while q is reliable in the context of uniform lies. On the contrary, the combined approach returns $\langle p, \neg q \rangle$ where p is reliable in the combined context and $\neg q$ is clearly unreliable. In this example, the set of reliable answers of the two approaches are incomparable.

Still, a form of "longest honeymoon lemma" holds w.r.t. reliability. We deal first with uniform refusals.

Lemma 5.1. *Let* $Q = \langle \Phi_1, \ldots, \Phi_i, \ldots \rangle$ *and*

$$control\_eval^R(Q, log_0)(db, pot\_sec) = \langle (a_1, log_1), \ldots, (a_i, log_i), \ldots \rangle$$
$$control\_eval^C(Q, log_0)(db, pot\_sec) = \langle (a'_1, log'_1), \ldots, (a'_i, log'_i), \ldots \rangle.$$

Let m be the least index such that a_m is unreliable (in the context of the sequence $control\_eval^R(Q, log_0)(db, pot\_sec)$) and let n be the least index such that a'_n is unreliable (in the context of $control\_eval^C(Q, log_0)(db, pot\_sec)$). Then $m \leq n$.

The relationships between the combined approach and uniform lies are more complex. Some queries may have *backward reliability* effects, as illustrated by the following example.

Example 5.4. Let $pot\_sec = \{\neg p\}$, and $log_0 = \emptyset$. Consider the following databases:

$$db_1 = \emptyset, \ db_2 = \{p\}, \ db_3 = \{q\}, \ db_4 = \{p, q\}.$$

Given the query sequence $Q = \langle p \rangle$ all the databases respond with the answer sequence $\langle p \rangle$, under both the combined method and uniform lies. Clearly, answer p is unreliable in this context, as db_1 and db_3 do not satisfy p. However, the response to an extended sequence $Q' = \langle p, p \wedge q \rangle$ equals $\langle p, p \wedge q \rangle$ only for db_4. Then, if the second answer is $p \wedge q$, a user who knows pot_sec and log_0 may conclude that the first answer was reliable. This shows how in general the reliability of a query may emerge after some time, under both kinds of controlled evaluation.

Because of such backward reliability effects, it is hard to extend the previous lemma to uniform lies. Currently we can prove a honeymoon lemma restricted to finite query sequences.

Lemma 5.2. *Let* $Q = \langle \Phi_1, \ldots, \Phi_n \rangle$ *and*

$$control\_eval^L(Q, log_0)(db, pot\_sec) = \langle (a_1, log_1), \ldots, (a_n, log_n) \rangle$$
$$control\_eval^C(Q, log_0)(db, pot\_sec) = \langle (a'_1, log'_1), \ldots, (a'_n, log'_n) \rangle \, .$$

If the answers $a'_1, \ldots, a'_{n-1}$ *are all reliable and* a'_n *is unreliable in the context of* $control\_eval^C(Q, log_0)(db, pot\_sec)$, *then for some* $1 \leq k \leq n$, a_k *is unreliable in the context of* $control\_eval^L(Q, log_0)(db, pot\_sec)$.

6   Conclusions

The combined approach introduced here enjoys the advantages of both uniform refusal and uniform lies. The honeymoon lemmata prove that the combined method yields the longest prefixes of correct and reliable answers of all the three methods. Moreover, if the query sequence does not make different methods converge to incomparable solutions, then the combined method returns at least as many correct answers as the other methods (Theorem 3.2). This property can be exploited to enforce *information availability constraints*. This will be the subject of future work.

Our results include a honeymoon lemma for the case of known secrecies, and comprise a formal characterization of the notion of *reliability*. For the case of known potential secrets we have completely characterized the relationships between the combined methods and the uniform ones.

References

1. Biskup, J.: For unknown secrecies refusal is better than lying, Data and Knowledge Engineering, 33 (2000), pp. 1-23.
2. Biskup, J., Bonatti, P.A. : Lying versus refusal for known potential secrets, Data and Knowledge Engineering, 38 (2001), pp. 199-222.
3. Bonatti, P.A., Kraus, S., Subrahmanian, V.S.: Foundations of secure deductive databases, IEEE Transactions on Knowledge and Data Engineering 7,3 (1995), pp. 406-422.
4. Dawson, S., De Capitani di Vimercati, S., Lincoln, P., Samarati, P.: Minimal data upgrading to prevent inference and association attacks, Proc. of the 18th ACM SIGMOD-SIGACT-SIGART Symposium on Principles of Database Systems (PODS), 1999, pp. 114-125.
5. Lloyd, J.W.: Foundations of Logic Programming, Springer, 1987.
6. Quian, X.: View-based access control with high assurance. Proc. of the 1996 IEEE Symp. on Security and privacy, 1996, pp. 85-93.
7. Shoenfield, J.R.: Mathematical Logic, Addison-Wesley, Reading etc., 1967.
8. Sicherman, G.L., de Jonge, W., van de Riet, R.P.: Answering queries without revealing secrets, ACM Transactions on Database Systems 8,1 (1983), pp. 41-59.
9. Stickel, M.E.: Elimination of inference channels by optimal upgrading. In Proc. of the 1994 IEEE Symposium on Security and Privacy, 1994, pp. 168–174.
10. Su, T.A., Ozsoyoglu, G.: Controlling FD and MVD inferences in multilevel relational database systems. IEEE Trans. on Knowledge and Data Engineering, 3(4):474-485, (1991).

A Logical Framework for Integrating Inconsistent Information in Multiple Databases[*]

Sandra de Amo[1], Walter A. Carnielli[2], and João Marcos[3]

[1] Faculty of Computer Science
Federal University of Uberlândia
Uberlândia, Brazil
deamo@ufu.br
[2] Group of Theoretical and Applied Logic
CLE/IFCH – State University of Campinas
Campinas, Brazil
carniell@cle.unicamp.br
[3] Centre for Logic and Philosophy of Science
Ghent University, Belgium
vegetal@cle.unicamp.br

Abstract. When integrating data coming from multiple different sources we are faced with the possibility of inconsistency in databases. In this paper, we use one of the paraconsistent logics introduced in [9,7] (**LFI1**) as a logical framework to model possibly inconsistent database instances obtained by integrating different sources. We propose a method based on the sound and complete tableau proof system of **LFI1** to treat both the integration process and the evolution of the integrated database submitted to users updates. In order to treat the integrated database evolution, we introduce a kind of generalized database context, the *evolutionary databases*, which are databases having the capability of storing and manipulating inconsistent information and, at the same time, allowing integrity constraints to change in time. We argue that our approach is sufficiently general and can be applied in most circumstances where inconsistency may arise in databases.

1   Introduction

The treatment of inconsistencies arising from the integration of multiple sources has been a topic increasingly studied in the past years and has become an important field of research in databases. Since some pioneer work on database updates and belief revision in the eighties [17,20], a great deal of work on multidatabases and inconsistency management has been done during the last decade. Two basic

[*] Author (1) was supported by an individual research grant from CNPq (Brazil). Author (2) was partially supported by a grant from the Alexander von Humboldt Foundation (Germany), by CAPES (Brazil) and by an individual research grant from CNPq (Brazil). Author (3) was supported by the Research Fund of Ghent University, project BOF2001/GOA/008.

T. Eiter and K.-D. Schewe (Eds.): FoIKS 2002, LNCS 2284, pp. 67–84, 2002.

approaches have been followed in solving the inconsistency problem in knowledge bases: belief revision ([21,22]) and paraconsistent logic ([10,12,6]). The goal of the first approach is to make an inconsistent theory consistent, either by revising it or by representing it by a consistent semantics. So, the main concern there is to avoid contradictions. On the other hand, the paraconsistent approach allows reasoning in the presence of inconsistency, and contradictory information can be derived or introduced without trivialization. In this paper, we propose to treat inconsistencies arising from the integration of multiple databases by introducing a method based on the paraconsistent approach. We argue that in most situations inconsistent information can be useful, unavoidable and even desirable, like for instance in airline booking systems.

In recent work ([9,7]), a family of paraconsistent logics called *Logics of Formal Inconsistency* (**LFI**s) has been introduced, and sound and complete axiomatic proof systems for this class of logics have been provided. The most important feature of these logics consists in the internalization of the concepts of consistency and inconsistency inside the object language. In this paper, we focus our attention in one of these logics, which we call **LFI1**, and use it as a logical framework to model integrated databases. We present the method REPAIR based on the inference mechanism of the sound and complete tableau system of **LFI1**, introduced in [8]. The method consists basically in constructing a repaired version of the integrated database where inconsistent information may appear. **LFI1** (with its 3-valued semantics) is used as the logical framework for the underlying model of this repaired version, which we call *paraconsistent databases*. We focus our attention on a particular class of integrity constraints and show that, as far as this particular class of constraints is concerned, the method is sound and complete: all paraconsistent databases returned by the method are repairs of the integrated database, i.e. they satisfy the integrity constraints and are as close as possible to the original (possibly) inconsistent integrated instance, and all possible repairs can be obtained through this procedure.

Example 1.1 (Running Example). Let us consider the local databases $\mathbf{R}_1 = \{R(a), Q(a), Q(b)\}$ and $\mathbf{R}_2 = \{R(c), Q(b)\}$. The first database verifies the condition $C_1 = \forall x(\neg R(x) \vee Q(x))$ and the second one verifies $C_2 = \forall x(\neg R(x) \vee \neg Q(x))$. However, the integrated database $\{R(a), R(c), Q(a), Q(b)\}$ violates both conditions C_1 and C_2. So, local databases may be consistent but when they are integrated, inconsistencies may appear. Even worse, the conditions may be mutually inconsistent or be only satisfied by an empty database as in the following situation: Let us consider a third local database $\mathbf{R}_3 = \{R(b), Q(b)\}$ and the condition $C_3 = \forall x(\neg Q(x) \vee R(x))$. This database satisfies C_3 but the integrated database $\mathbf{I} = \{R(a), R(b), R(c), Q(a), Q(b)\}$ violates conditions C_1 and C_2. The three conditions C_1, C_2 and C_3 are rather incompatible in the sense that they are simultaneously satisfied only by empty databases.

The method REPAIR can be applied to $\mathbf{I}$ and produces the following database:

$$\mathbf{J} = \{\ R(a), R(b), \bullet R(c), \bullet Q(a), \bullet Q(b)\ \}$$

The symbol $\bullet$ preceding a ground atomic formula means that the information represented by the formula is controversial. Intuitively, the condition stated by C_1 enforces that each element in R must appear in Q. This condition is violated in the integrated database **I** because c belongs to R but not to Q. However, if the information "$c \in$ R" was taken as controversial, then C_1 would be verified (at least as far as the instantiation $x = c$ is concerned). In the same way, the condition stated by C_2 enforces that elements in R should not appear in Q. So, this condition is violated in **I** because a and b belong to R and Q simultaneously. If the two facts "$a \in$ Q" and "$b \in$ Q" were taken as controversial, then C_2 would be verified. The database **J** containing inconsistent information is called *paraconsistent database* and we can show that it satisfies (within **LFI1**) the integrity constraints IC. Besides, it constitutes a *repair* of the original instance, i.e., it is a paraconsistent database containing *minimal changes* w.r.t. the original integrated database **I** and which is consistent w.r.t. IC. As we will see in section 3, repairs are not unique, i.e., there are other paraconsistent databases satisfying the constraints and containing minimal changes w.r.t. the original (possibly inconsistent) database. For instance, $\mathbf{J}_1 = \{R(a), \bullet R(b), R(c), \bullet Q(a), Q(b), \bullet Q(c)\}$ is another repair of **I**. By using a *backtracking* mechanism, the method REPAIR can produce the set of repairs corresponding to a given database **I**.

Our notion of *repair* is more *refined* than the one introduced in [3], in the sense that it is closer to the original database. This follows from the fact that, contrarily to [3], in our approach inconsistent information are always kept inside the repaired database.

The method REPAIR is suitable to treat both static and dynamic aspects of inconsistency management in databases. The static aspect deals only with the integration of different database instances, by constructing the repaired version. The dynamic aspect of our approach deals with the evolution of the integrated databases submitted to user updates. In order to treat the dynamics of paraconsistent database evolution, we introduce a kind of generalized database context, the *evolutionary databases*, which are databases having the capability of storing and handling inconsistent information and, at the same time, allowing integrity constraints to change in time. The method REPAIR interacts with user updates (which may be a data or an integrity constraint update) in order to build a repaired version of the paraconsistent database produced after the user update.

We argue that our approach is sufficiently general and can be applied in most circumstances where inconsistency may arise in databases. It could be suitable for managing inconsistency in active and reactive databases and datawarehouses.

This paper is organized as follows: In section 2 we describe the syntax and the three-valued semantics of our Logic of Formal Inconsistency **LFI1** and present a sound and complete proof system for this logic. In section 3, we introduce the notion of *paraconsistent databases* and repairs. In section 4 we give the method for constructing repairs for paraconsistent databases obtained by the integration of different local consistent databases. In section 5 we generalize this method in order to treat the dynamic aspects of paraconsistent databases as well as more general situations where inconsistency may appear in a database context, these situations being captured by the notion of *evolutionary databases*. Finally, in section 6 we discuss our perspectives for further work and compare our method with some other methods treating the problem of inconsistency in multiple databases. For lack of space, the proofs are just outlined.

2   LFI1: A Three-Valued Logic for Formal Inconsistency

In this section we describe the syntax and semantics of our Logic of Formal Inconsistency (**LFI1**). A detailed presentation can be found in our former paper [9].

Let **R** be a finite signature without functional symbols and **Var** a set of variables symbols. We assume the formulas of our logic to be defined in the usual way, as in the classical first-order logic, with the addition of a new symbol • (read "it is inconsistent"). So, a formula of **LFI1** is defined inductively by the following statements (and only by them):

- If R is a predicate symbol of arity k and $x_1, ..., x_k$ are constants or variables, then $R(x_1, ..., x_k)$ and $x_1 = x_2$ are atomic formulas or atoms. The former is called a *relational* atom and the later an *equality* atom.

- If F, G are formulas and x is a variable then $F \vee G$, $\neg F$, $\forall x F$, $\exists x F$ and $\bullet F$ are formulas.

The notions of free and bound variables are defined as usual. If $x_1, \ldots, x_n$ are free variables of a formula F and $c_1, \ldots, c_n$ are constants or variables, we denote by $F[c_1, \ldots, c_n / x_1, \ldots, x_n]$ the formula obtained by replacing each occurrence of the variable x_i by c_i, for $i = 1, \ldots, n$. A *sentence* is a formula without free variables. In particular, an *atomic ground formula* or *ground atom* is an atomic formula which is a sentence. We denote by $\mathcal{G}$ and $\mathcal{S}$, the set of all ground atoms and the set of all sentences respectively.

We next define *interpretations* for formulas of **LFI1**, using *three-valued valuations* which are homomorphisms between sentences and the truth-values 0 (for "false"), 1 (for "true"), $\frac{1}{2}$ (for "partially true"). These homomorphisms are induced by the *connective matrices* and *distribution quantifiers* introduced below. It is important to notice that in a database context, one only considers *Herbrand interpretations*, those for which **Dom** (the set of constants of the language) is the domain of valuation of the variables and where each constant symbol is interpreted by itself.

Definition 2.1. *Let* **R** *be a finite signature. An* interpretation *over* **R** *is an application* $\delta : \mathcal{G} \to \{0 \ (false), 1 \ (true), \frac{1}{2} \ (inconsistent)\}$.

An interpretation of ground atoms can be extended to the propositional sentences of $\mathcal{S}$ *in a natural way by using the connective matrices in figure 1(a). The connective* $\wedge$ *is derived from of* $\vee, \neg :$ A$\wedge$ B $\equiv \neg(\neg A \vee \neg B)$. *The derived matrix for* $\wedge$ *is given in figure 1 (b). The connective* $\to$ *is defined in* **LFI1** *as* $A \to B \equiv B \vee \neg(A \vee \bullet A)$.[1] *It is easy to show ([9]) that* • *cannot be derived from the other propositional connectives* $\vee$ *and* $\neg$. *So,* $\vee, \neg, \bullet, \forall$ *can be taken as the primitive logical symbols of our language.*

The extension of δ *to the quantified sentences in* $\mathcal{S}$ *is obtained by means of the concept of* distribution quantifiers, *introduced in [13]. Basically, this concept translates our basic intuition that an universal quantifier should work as*

---

[1] In this paper, we omit the matrix for $\to$, since the class of **LFI1**-formulas we will be interested in (the *integrity constraints*) does not use this connective.

∨	1	½	0
1	1	1	1
½	1	½	½
0	1	½	0

	¬	•
1	0	0
½	½	1
0	1	0

∧	1	½	0
1	1	½	0
½	½	½	0
0	0	0	0

(a)   (b)

Fig. 2.1.

a kind of unbounded conjunction and an existential quantifier as an unbounded disjunction. A valuation is an application $v : \mathbf{Var} \to \mathbf{Dom}$. We extend δ to the quantified sentences as follows:

- $\delta(\forall x A(x)) = 1$ iff for all valuations v we have $\delta(A[v(x)/x]) = 1$,
- $\delta(\forall x A(x)) = 0$ iff there exists a valuation v such that $\delta(A[v(x)/x]) = 0$,
- $\delta(\forall x A(x)) = \frac{1}{2}$ iff for all valuations v we have $\delta(A[v(x)/x]) = 1$ or $\frac{1}{2}$, and there exists a valuation v' such that $\delta(A[v'(x)/x]) = \frac{1}{2}$,
- $\delta(\exists x A(x)) = 1$ iff there exists a valuation v such that $\delta(A[v(x)/x]) = 1$,
- $\delta(\exists x A(x)) = 0$ iff for all valuations v we have $\delta(A[v(x)/x]) = 0$,
- $\delta(\exists x A(x)) = \frac{1}{2}$ iff for all valuations v we have $\delta(A[v(x)/x]) = 0$ or $\frac{1}{2}$, and there exists a valuation v' such that $\delta(A[v'(x)/x]) = \frac{1}{2}$.

It is easy to see that $\delta(\forall x A(x)) = \delta(\neg \exists x \neg A(x))$ as usual in classical first-order logic.

Definition 2.2. Let $F(x_1, ..., x_n)$ be a formula of **LFI1** with free variables $x_1, \ldots, x_n, v$ a valuation and δ an interpretation. We say that (δ, v) satisfies $F(x_1, ..., x_n)$ (denoted by $(\delta, v) \models F(x_1, ..., x_n)$) iff $\delta(F[v(x_1), ..., v(x_n)/x_1, ..., x_n])$ is 1 or $\frac{1}{2}$.

Example 2.1. Let R be a binary predicate symbol. Let δ be the interpretation $\delta(R(a, b)) = 1, \delta(R(c, b)) = \frac{1}{2}$ and $\delta(R(p, q)) = 0$ for all (p, q) such that $p \neq c$ and $p \neq a$, or $q \neq b$. Then, $(\delta, v) \models (\exists x \bullet R(x, y) \wedge \neg \forall x R(x, y))$, where v is a valuation such that $v(y) = b$.

If $(\delta, v) \models F$ for each valuation v, we say that δ is a *model* of F (denoted $\delta \models F$). In this case, F is **LFI1**-*satisfiable*. A formula is **LFI1**-*valid* if for each interpretation δ, $\delta \models F$. An **LFI1** sentence F is a *logical consequence* of a set of **LFI1** sentences Γ if all models of F are also models of all formulas in Γ (we denote this by $\Gamma \models F$).

The logic **LFI1** is a *paraconsistent logic* since it does not verify the *principle of explosion*, i.e., $A, \neg A \not\models B$ for all B. In fact, if we take the interpretation δ of example 2.1, we see that $\delta \models R(c, b)$ and $\delta \models \neg R(c, b)$ but $\delta \not\models R(b, a)$.

A Tableau Proof System for **LFI1**. Before introducing our proof system, we need some definitions concerning the tableaux terminology:

Definition 2.3. A signed *formula of* **LFI1** *is an expression of the form* $T(A)$ *or* $F(A)$, *where* A *is a formula of* **LFI1**, *or the special symbol* $\perp$. *If* A *is atomic (resp. ground), the signed formula is said to be atomic (resp. ground).*

Table 1. A tableau proof system for **LFI1**

and-rule			or-rule		
α	α_1	α_2	α	α_1	α_2
(1) T(A∧B)	T(A)	T(B)	(5) F(A∧B)	F(A)	F(B)
(2) F(A∨B)	F(A)	F(B)	(6) T(A∨B)	T(A)	T(B)
(3) F(¬A)	T(A)	F(•A)	(7) T(¬A)	F(A)	T(•A)
(4) T(¬¬A)	T(A)	T(A)	(8) F(¬¬A)	F(A)	F(A)
(9) T(•A)	T(A)	T(¬A)			
(10) T(•• A)	⊥	⊥	(11) F(•A)	F(A)	F(¬A)
(12) F(•(A∧B))	F(•A∧B)	F(•B∧A)	(14) T(•(A∧B))	T(•A∧B)	T(•B∧A)
(13) F(•(A∨B))	F(•A∧¬B)	F(•B∧¬A)	(15) T(•(A∨B))	T(•A∧¬ B)	T(•B∧¬A)
(16) T(∀xA(x))	T(A(t))	T(A(t))	(20) F(∀xA(x))	F(A(s))	F(A(s))
(17) T(∃xA(x))	T(A(s′))	T(A(s′))	(21) F(∃xA(x))	F(A(t))	F(A(t))
(18) T(¬∀xA))	T(∃x¬A)	T(∃x¬A)	(22) F(¬∀xA)	F(∃x¬A)	F(∃x¬A)
(19) T(¬∃xA)	T(∀x¬A)	T(∀x¬A)	(23) F(¬∃xA)	F(∀x¬A)	F(∀x¬A)
(24) T(•(∀xA))	T(∃x•A)	T(∀xA)	(26) F(•(∀xA))	F(∃x•A)	F(∀xA)
(25) T(•(∃xA))	T(∃x•A)	T(∀x¬A)	(27) F(•(∃xA))	F(∃x•A)	F(∀x¬A)
(28) T (A[x])	T(A[x/y])	T(A[x/y]) (*)	(29) F(A[x])	F(A[x/y])	F(A[x/y]) (*)

t, t' are arbitrary terms; s is a new term w.r.t. $\forall x$ A(x), i.e., it does not appear in any branch containing $\forall x$ A(x); and s' is a new term w.r.t. $\exists x$ A(x), i.e., it does not appear in any branch containing $\exists x$ A(x).
(*) if T$(x = y)$ is in S.

In what follows S is a finite set of atomic signed formulas, α and α_i (i ∈ {1, 2}) are signed formulas. An inference rule *is an expression of one the following forms:*

$S : \alpha$ **and-rules :** *from* $S \cup \{\alpha\}$ *we can*
$S : \alpha_1, S : \alpha_2$ *infer* $S \cup \{\alpha_1, \alpha_2\}$

$S : \alpha$ **or-rules:** *from* $S \cup \{\alpha\}$ *we can*
$S : \alpha_1 \quad S : \alpha_2 \quad S \cup \{\alpha_2\}$ *infer* $S \cup \{\alpha_1\}$ *or*

If r is an **and-rule** *(resp. an* **or-rule***) then we define* $r(S \cup \{\alpha\}) = S \cup \{\alpha_1, \alpha_2\}$ *(resp.* $r(S \cup \alpha) = S \cup \{\alpha_1\}$ *or* $r(S) = S \cup \{\alpha_2\})$.

The inferences rules[2] of our proof system are listed in table 1.

We now describe the *tableaux method* underlying the proof system:

Definition 2.4. *A tableau for a set S of signed formulas is a (finite) tree* $\mathcal{T}$ *whose nodes are sets of signed formulas and which is constructed as follows:*

1. *the root of* $\mathcal{T}$ *is the set S.*
2. *a node is said to be* closed *(open otherwise) if it contains signed formulas of the form T(A) and F(A) for some A, or if it contains F(x = x) or if it contains the special symbol* ⊥*.*

---

[2] In fact, in order to simplify the presentation and for the purposes of the restricted class of sentences we treat in this paper, we have omitted the rules for → which are present in the original logic **LFI1** [9].

3. *a node S_2 is an* and-*successor (resp. an* or-*successor) of an* **open** *node S_1 if it is obtained by applying one* and-*rule (resp. one* or-*rule) r to an arbitrary element α of S_1. ($S_2 = (S_1 - \{\alpha\}) \cup r(S_1 : \alpha)$). Closed nodes have no successors.*

A tableau is closed *if all its leaves are closed. It is* open *if at least one leaf is open. A* proof *of a formula A is a closed tableau for the singleton $\{F(A)\}$. We say that A is* provable *(denoted by $\vdash A$) if there is a proof of A. A* derivation *of a formula A from a finite set Γ is a closed tableau for the set $\Gamma_T \cup F(A)$, where $\Gamma_T = \{T(X) \mid X \in \Gamma\}$. We say that A is* derived *from Γ (denoted $\Gamma \vdash A$) if there is a derivation of A from Γ.*

Example 2.2. $\vdash A \vee \neg A$ and $\bullet A \vdash \neg A$. Indeed:

$$
\begin{array}{l}
F(A \vee \neg A) \\
\hline \quad \text{(by (2))} \\
F(A), F(\neg A) \\
\hline \quad \text{(by (3))} \\
F(A), T(A), F(\bullet A)
\end{array}
\qquad
\begin{array}{l}
F(\neg A), T(\bullet A) \\
\hline \quad \text{(by (9))} \\
F(\neg A), T(A), T(\neg A)
\end{array}
$$

$$
\qquad\qquad\text{closed}\qquad\qquad\qquad\qquad\text{closed}
$$

The following result guarantees the soundness and completeness of the proof system with respect to the logic **LFI1**:

Theorem 2.1 ([8,13]). *Let Γ be a set of* **LFI1** *formulas and A be a* **LFI1** *formula. Then, $\Gamma \vdash A$ if and only if $\Gamma \models A$.*

Remark. We notice that in our paraconsistent logic **LFI1**, the third truth-value $\frac{1}{2}$ should not be read as "undefined" as in Kleene's logic, but rather as "over-defined". Our logic is paraconsistent, while Kleene's system is not. The two approaches are conceptually incomparable.

3   Paraconsistent Databases

In this section we use the logical formalism of **LFI1** to generalize the notion of database instance so as to allow the storage of inconsistent information in our databases. We assume the reader to be familiar with traditional database terminology [1].

Definition 3.1 (p-instance). *Let* **R** *be a database schema[3]. A paraconsistent instance (p-instance) over* **R** *is an interpretation* **I** *such that for each $R \in \mathbf{R}$ the set $\mathbf{I}_R = \{u : \mathbf{I}(R(u)) = 1 \text{ or } \mathbf{I}(R(u)) = \frac{1}{2}\}$ is finite. So, an instance over* **R** *can be viewed as a finite set of relations where each relation is a finite set of tuples (those having truth-values 1 or $\frac{1}{2}$). A tuple u over R such that $\mathbf{I}(R(u)) = \frac{1}{2}$ is intended to be* controversial, *i.e. there may be evidence in favor of $R(u)$ and also*

---

[3] A set of relational names of a given arity.

evidence against $R(u)$.[4] *On the other hand, if $\mathbf{I}(R(u)) = 1$, $R(u)$ is intended to be a safe information. A p-instance where all tuples have truth-value 1 is called simply an* instance. *We denote by* adom($\mathbf{I}$) *the active domain of* $\mathbf{I}$, *i.e. the set of constants appearing in the relations of* $\mathbf{I}$. *For the sake of simplification, we use the informal notation of example 1.1 for denoting p-instances, with the obvious translation.*

Definition 3.2 (Integrity Constraints). *An* integrity constraint *over a database schema* $\mathbf{R}$ *is an* **LFI1** *sentence of the form*

$$\forall x_1 \forall x_2 \ldots \forall x_n (\bigvee_{i=0}^{p} R_i(u_i) \vee \bigvee_{j=1}^{q} \neg Q_j(v_j) \vee \bigvee_{l=0}^{s} \varphi_l)$$

where R_i and Q_j are relational atoms, u_i, v_j are tuples of variables appearing in $\{x_1, \ldots, x_n\}$ and φ_l are equality atoms or negations of equality atoms.

Several important constraints that appear in databases fit into this form. Indeed, this class of sentences coincides with the class of *full dependencies* described in [1] (including functional dependencies, set inclusion dependencies, transitivity dependencies). However, inclusion dependencies of the form $\forall x(\neg P(x) \vee \exists y Q(x,y))$ do not belong to this class.

Example 3.1 (Running Example - Continued). Let IC = $\{C_1, C_2, C_3\}$ and $\mathbf{I}$ be, respectively, the set of formulas and the integrated database instance mentioned in example 1.1. It is clear that each C_i is an integrity constraint (accordingly to definition 3.2). The two instances $\mathbf{J}$ and $\mathbf{J}_1$ introduced in this example are p-instances (where the notation $\bullet R(u)$ means $\mathbf{J}(R(u)) = \frac{1}{2}$). A simple calculation using the matrices in figure 1 will convince us that the p-instances $\mathbf{J}$ and $\mathbf{J}_1$ satisfy IC.

In section 4 we will present a method for repairing instances which are possibly inconsistent w.r.t. a given set of integrity constraints. This method is based on the tableau proof system for **LFI1** which has been introduced in the previous section. The soundness and completeness of this proof system w.r.t. *finite* structures (one reminds that a database instance is a finite structure) is essential for proving the soundness of the method. Theorem 2.1 guarantees the completeness of the tableau system but it is important to emphasize that this result is achieved when "$\Gamma \models A$" means *all unrestricted interpretations (not necessarily finite) satisfying Γ also satisfy A.* Unfortunately, due to Trakhtenbrot's Theorem [23], this completeness result cannot be proven for finite structures in general. However, for the special class of integrity constraints one can prove the following theorem which is essential in the remainder of the paper:

Theorem 3.1. *Let IC be a set of integrity constraints and C be an integrity constraint over $\mathbf{R}$. Then, $IC \vdash C$ if and only if $IC \models_{fin} C$ (all finite models of IC are also models of C).*

---

[4] These tuples must be understood as "overdefined" instead of "undefined" as in Kleene's logic.

This follows from a well-known theorem for first-order logic (which can be extended to **LFI1** using the techniques of [19]), stating that the satisfiability problem (SAT) for the Bernays-Schönfinkel class $\exists^*\forall^*$ is decidable and so unrestricted and finite satisfiability are equivalent [15].

The following definition will be helpful in the remainder of the paper:

Definition 3.3. *Let IC be a set of integrity constraints. A tableau is called reduced for F(IC) if (a) each of its leaves is either closed or is a set of signed formulas of the form T(X), F(X) or F(•X), where X is an atomic formula, (b) rule (11) has not been used in the derivation of the tableau nodes and (c) rules (28) and (29) cannot be applied to any leaf.*

The proof of the following result is straightforward and is omitted.

Proposition 3.1. *Let IC be a a set of integrity constraints. Then:*

1. *There is a unique reduced tableau for F(IC), which we call the reduced tableau for F(IC).*
2. *If $\mathcal{X}$ is an open leaf of the reduced tableau for F(IC) and $T(X) \in \mathcal{X}$ then $F(\bullet X) \in \mathcal{X}$.*

We denote by reduction *(IC) the set $\{L - \{F(\bullet X) \mid F(\bullet X) \in L\} \mid L$ is an open leaf of the reduced tableau for F(IC)$\}$ (i.e., the set of the open leaves of the reduced tableau for F(IC) without the signed formulas of the form $F(\bullet X)$).*

Example 3.2 (Running Example - Continued). Let C_1 be the integrity constraint $\forall x(\neg R(x) \vee Q(x))$ of example 1.1. A simple calculation shows that the reduced tableau for $F(C_1)$ contains only the leaf $\{T(R(s)), F(Q(s)), F(\bullet R(s))\}$ Hence, reduction(C_1)= $\{\{T(R(s)), F(Q(s))\}\}$.

Repair Databases. Let us suppose the situation we have described in example 1.1: we are given (1) a database specification which is the integration of several local databases, and (2) an instance which violates the integrity constraints. We want to build a repaired version "as close as possible" to the given instance which will verify the integrity constraints (w.r.t. the semantics of **LFI**). Our presentation generalizes the ideas presented in [3] which we have suitably adapted to our paraconsistent environment. The following definition aims at specifying what we mean by *as close as possible*:

Definition 3.4. *Let **I** and **J** be p-instances over a database schema **R**.*

*The distance between **I** and **J** (a generalization of the well-known Hamming-distance) is given by:*

$$d(\mathbf{I}, \mathbf{J}) = \sum_{u \in \mathbf{I}_R \cup \mathbf{J}_R, R \in \mathbf{R}} \mid \mathbf{I}(R(u)) - \mathbf{J}(R(u)) \mid$$

*For p-instances **J** and **K**, we define $\mathbf{J} \leq_\mathbf{I} \mathbf{K}$ if $d(\mathbf{I},\mathbf{J}) \leq d(\mathbf{I},\mathbf{K})$.*

Obviously, our definition of *distance* satisfies the desirable properties of a *distance* in measure theory: (1) $d(\mathbf{I},\mathbf{J}) = 0$ iff $\mathbf{I} = \mathbf{J}$, (2) $d(\mathbf{I},\mathbf{J}) = d(\mathbf{J},\mathbf{I})$ and (3) $d(\mathbf{I},\mathbf{K}) \leq d(\mathbf{I},\mathbf{J}) + d(\mathbf{J},\mathbf{K})$.

Definition 3.5. *Let* **R** *be a database schema, IC a finite set of integrity constraints over* **R** *and* **I** *an instance over* **R** *(***I** *does not necessarily satisfy the integrity constraints in IC). A* repair *of* **I** *is a p-instance* **J** *satisfying IC which is* $\leq_{\mathbf{I}}$*-minimal among those satisfying IC.*

*Example 3.3 (*Running Example - Continued*).* Let us consider the situation described in example 1.1. A simple calculation yields: $d(\mathbf{J},\mathbf{I}) = 1.5$, $d(\mathbf{J}_1,\mathbf{I}) = 1.5$. Let now consider the p-instance $\mathbf{J}_2 = \{\bullet R(a), \bullet R(b), R(c), \bullet Q(a), Q(b), \bullet Q(c)\}$. We can easily verify that $\mathbf{J}_2$ satisfies the integrity constraints IC and $d(\mathbf{J}_2,\mathbf{I}) = 2$. So, $\mathbf{J}_2$ is not a repair, even though it satisfies the constraints. It can be shown that **J** and $\mathbf{J}_1$ are repairs.

The definition of repair database we have just introduced satisfies some desirable properties. Firstly, we notice that if **I** satisfies the constraints IC then it does not need to be repaired ($d(\mathbf{I},\mathbf{I}) = 0$). Moreover,

Proposition 3.2. *The repair of an instance always exists and, in general, is not unique.*

Proof. As IC is **LFI1**-satisfiable (see Theorem 5.1) there exists a p-instance **J** which satisfies IC. If **J** is a repair of **I**, we are done. If not, there exists a p-instance **J'** satisfying $\mathcal{C}$ such that $d(\mathbf{I},\mathbf{J'}) < d(\mathbf{I},\mathbf{J})$. We repeat the argument for **J'**. Eventually, we will find a repair of **I** (which can be **I** itself if **I** satisfies IC). The repair, in general, is not unique, as it is illustrated in example 3.3. Obviously, if $\mathbf{J}_1$ and $\mathbf{J}_2$ are repairs of **I** then $d(\mathbf{I},\mathbf{J}_1) = d(\mathbf{I},\mathbf{J}_2)$.

We notice that in our definition of repair we have assumed that the instance being repaired is a (classical) instance (the integrity constraints are first-order sentences). We did so because our first concern was the development of a logical framework to treat inconsistencies arising from the integration of local databases. However, this assumption can be dropped and the notion of repair can be easily extended to p-instances.

4   A Method for Building Repair Databases

In this section we introduce a method to construct repair databases. This method can be viewed as a *static repairing process* because it concerns only the process of data integration: it takes as input a possibly inconsistent database instance resulting from the integration of several local consistent databases and produces a repaired version of this integrated instance. However, future updates over this (paraconsistent) repair version have to be monitored to insure a repairing process after each transaction. These *dynamic repairing process* will be treated in section 5, where we will generalize the "static" method we propose in the present section. The most important feature of our method relies on the fact that no information is lost in the repaired instance, but some information which was safe before may become controversial.

The method we propose here is based on the tableau proof system for **LFI1** presented in section 2. In general, the advantage of proof methods based on analytic tableaux is that, when a proof is not possible, in some cases counterexamples can be read from the derivation tree. We will explore this issue in order to construct a repair instance for a given database instance. For the sake of simplifying the presentation, we will consider only integrity constraints without constant symbols. Nevertheless, the method we present in this section can be extended to treat integrity constraints with constants.

Some Notations. Let **R** be a database schema and **I** be a p-instance over a relation schema $R \in \mathbf{R}$. We denote by S(**I**) the set of the signed formulas obtained as follows: To each tuple v over R such that $\mathbf{I}(v) = 1$ (resp. 0, $\frac{1}{2}$), we associate the signed formula T(R(v)) (resp. F(R(v)), T($\bullet$R(v))). If **I** is a p-instance over **R**, we define S(**I**) $= \bigcup_{R \in \mathbf{R}}$ S(**I**(R)) $\cup$ {T($a = a$) | $a \in$ adom(**I**)} $\cup$ {F($a = b$) | $a, b \in$ adom(**I**) and $a \neq b$}. For instance, in example 1.1, S(**I**) $=$ {T($R(a)$),T($R(b)$),T($R(c)$),T($Q(a)$),T($Q(b)$),F($Q(c)$)} $\cup$ {T($a = a$),T($b = b$),T($c = c$),F($a = b$),F($a = c$),...}.[5]

Conversely, let D $\subseteq$ **Dom** be a finite set of constants. To each set $\mathcal{S}$ of signed ground formulas over **R** and D satisfying the condition:

- if A is an atomic ground formula over **R** and D then $\mathcal{S}$ contains one and only one of the signed formulas T(A), F(A) or T($\bullet$A),

a p-instance is associated in the obvious way. We denote this p-instance by $\mathrm{S}^{-1}(\mathcal{S})$.

Let IC be a set of integrity constraints and **I** be an instance. Then reduction(IC) $= \{L_1, \ldots, L_m\}$[6], where each L_i is a set of signed atomic formulas without constants. For each valuation of variables v_j (within adom(**I**)), let $\mathcal{X}_j^i = v_j(L_i)$ be the set of signed ground formulas instantiated accordingly to v_j. So, for each i all the $\mathcal{X}_j^i$ have the same number k_i of signed atoms. Let $\mathcal{X}_1^i, \ldots, \mathcal{X}_{j_i}^i$ be the set of instantiations of L_i. In what follows, we will fix an enumeration for the set $\{L_1, \ldots, L_m\}$ and an enumeration for each set of ground atoms $\mathcal{X}_j^i$.[7] So, we can assume that reduction(IC) is a list $[L_1, \ldots, L_m]$ and each $\mathcal{X}_j^i$ is also a list of signed atomic formulas.

Let L_i be a leaf in reduction(IC). A function $f : \{1, \ldots, j_i\} \rightarrow \{1, \ldots, k_i\}$ determines a choice of one signed ground atom in each instantiation $\mathcal{X}_j^i$ ($j = \{1, \ldots, j_i\}$) of L_i.

Example 4.1 (Running Example – Continued). Let us consider the set of integrity constraints IC $= \{C_1, C_2, C_3\}$ and the integrated instance **I** introduced in example 1.1. A simple calculation yields:
reduction(IC) $= [[\mathrm{T}(R(x_1)), \mathrm{F}(Q(x_1))], [\mathrm{T}(R(x_2)), \mathrm{T}(Q(x_2))],$
$\qquad\qquad [\mathrm{T}(Q(x_3)), \mathrm{F}(R(x_3))]].$

---

[5] In the remainder of the paper, we will omit the signed tuples T($a = a$), F($a = b$) (for a and $b \in$ adom(**I**), $a \neq b$) in the description of S(**I**), presuming they are implicitly contained in this set.

[6] One reminds that reduction(IC) is the set of the open leaves of the reduced tableau for F(IC) without the signed formulas F($\bullet$X).

[7] It can be shown that these choices do not affect the result of the method REPAIR.

Let us consider the first leaf, $[T(R(x_1)), F(Q(x_1))]$. As adom($\mathbf{I}$) $= \{a, b, c\}$, we have three instantiations for this leaf: $\mathcal{X}_1^1 = [T(R(a)), F(Q(a))]$, $\mathcal{X}_2^1 = [T(R(b)), F(Q(b))]$, $\mathcal{X}_3^1 = [T(R(c)), F(Q(c))]$. The function f such that $f(1) = 1$, $f(2) = 2$ and $f(3) = 2$ determines the choice of the first element in $\mathcal{X}_1^1$ ($T(R(a))$), the second element in $\mathcal{X}_2^1$ ($F(Q(b))$) and the second element in $\mathcal{X}_3^1$ ($F(Q(c))$).

We are ready now for the description of the method:

Input: a database schema $\mathbf{R}$, a finite set IC $= \{C_1, \ldots, C_n\}$ of integrity constraints over $\mathbf{R}$, an instance $\mathbf{I}$ over $\mathbf{R}$.
Output: a set $\mathcal{K}$ of repairs of $\mathbf{I}$ and $n = $ d($\mathbf{I},\mathbf{J}$), for all $\mathbf{J} \in \mathcal{K}$.

Method REPAIR:
(1) Leaves := reduction(IC);
     % A list of lists containing signed atomic formulas T(X) or F(X)
(2) **If** Leaves $= \emptyset$ **then** return $\mathcal{K} = \{\mathbf{I}\}$ and $n = 0$ *% $\mathbf{I}$ is a valid formula*
(3) **else** $\mathcal{K} := \emptyset$; $n := 0$;
(4) **For each** $f_1, f_2, \ldots, f_m$ **do**
     % for each choice of one element in each instantiated leaf
(5) $\mathcal{S} := $ S($\mathbf{I}$); $d := 0$;
(6)   **For each** $l = 1, \ldots, m$ **do** *% for each leaf*
(7)   **For each** $k = 1, \ldots, j_l$ **do** *% for each of its instantiations*
(8)   **If** $\mathcal{X}_k^l \subseteq \mathcal{S}$ **then**
(9)   choose the $f_l(k)$-th element A $\in \mathcal{X}_k^l$
                 (A $=$ T(X) or A $=$ F(X), X a relational atom);
(10) $\mathcal{S} := (\mathcal{S} - \{A\}) \cup \{ T(\bullet X) \}$;
(11) $d := d + \frac{1}{2}$;
(12)   **If** $n = 0$ or $d = n$ **then** $\mathcal{K} := \mathcal{K} \cup \{S^{-1}(\mathcal{S})\}$; n:= d;
(13)   **elseif** $d < n$ **then** $\mathcal{K} := \{S^{-1}(\mathcal{S})\}$; n:= d

Example 4.2 (Running Example - Continued). Let us consider the situation of example 4.1. We have:
Leaves $= [[T(R(x_1)), F(Q(x_1))], [T(R(x_2)), T(Q(x_2))], [T(Q(x_3)), F(R(x_3))]]$

$$\mathcal{X}_1^1 = [T(R(a)), F(Q(a))] \ \mathcal{X}_2^1 = [T(R(b)), F(Q(b))] \ \mathcal{X}_3^1 = [T(R(c)), F(Q(c))]$$
$$\mathcal{X}_1^2 = [T(R(a)), T(Q(a))] \ \mathcal{X}_2^2 = [T(R(b)), T(Q(b))] \ \mathcal{X}_3^2 = [T(R(c)), T(Q(c))]$$
$$\mathcal{X}_1^3 = [T(Q(a)), F(R(a))] \ \mathcal{X}_2^3 = [T(Q(b)), F(R(b))] \ \mathcal{X}_3^3 = [T(Q(c)), F(R(c))]$$

The number m of leaves is 3, $k_1 = k_2 = k_3 = 2 = $ number of atoms in each leaf and $j_1 = j_2 = j_3 = 3 = $ number of instantiations for each leaf. Let us consider the following choice in step (4): $f_1(1) = f_1(2) = f_1(3) = f_2(1) = f_2(2) = f_2(3) = f_3(1) = f_3(2) = f_3(3) = 1$. In step (5) we have: $\mathcal{S} = $ S($\mathbf{I}$) $= \{T(R(a))$, $T(R(b)), T(R(c)), T(Q(a)), T(Q(b)), F(Q(c))\}$. Only the instantiations $\mathcal{X}_3^1, \mathcal{X}_1^2$ and $\mathcal{X}_2^2$ may verify the condition in step (8). The choice (f_1, f_2, f_3) (step (4)) implies that the first elements in each instantiation will be chosen. By repeating steps (10) and (11) for each of these instantiations, we obtain at the end of the iteration (7) $\mathcal{S} = $ S($\mathbf{I}$) $= \{\bullet T(R(a)), \bullet T(R(b)), \bullet T(R(c)), T(Q(a)), T(Q(b)),$ $F(Q(c))\}$ and $d = 1.5$. As $n = 0$, the associated instance is inserted into $\mathcal{K}$ and n is instantiated with 1.5. All these calculations are repeated for each choice of

(f_1, f_2, f_3). If, for the next choice one obtains a value for d greater than 1.5, then the set S will not be included in $\mathcal{K}$. On the other hand, if d is smaller than 1.5, then $\mathcal{K}$ is instantiated with the unary set $\{S\}$.

We notice that if IC is a **LFI1**-valid formula or if **I** satisfies IC then the repair returned by the method coincides with **I**. In fact, in the first case, the algorithm stops in step (2) and in the second case, the algorithm stops in step (8) for each iteration: as **I** satisfies IC, then in each element of Leaves and for all instantiations of its variables, we have a signed ground atomic formula T(A) (resp. F(A)) which matches with F(A) (resp. T(A)) in S(**I**). So T(A) (resp. F(A)) cannot appear in S(**I**). We notice also that the active domain of the repairs obtained by the method is the same as the one of the input instance **I** (no new constants are created).

Now, we will state and give sketchs of proofs of the main results of this section. The first one tells us that our method is sound, i.e. its result is a set of repairs of **I** and the second one guarantees that all repairs of **I** are contained in the output of REPAIR. The essential part of the proof of these two results is contained in Lemma 4.1 below. This lemma is a consequence of the fact that the tableau system for the class $\forall^*$ is sound and complete w.r.t. finite structures (Theorem 3.1). In what follows, **R** is a database schema, IC is a finite set of integrity constraints and **I** a safe instance over **R**.

Theorem 4.1. *All elements of the set $\mathcal{K}$ returned by executing the method RE-PAIR is a repair of* **I**.

The proof of this theorem follows immediately from Lemmas 4.1, 4.2 and 4.3 below.

Lemma 4.1. *Let* **J** *be a p-instance over* **R**. *Then, there exists a closed tableau for $S(\mathbf{J}) \cup F(IC)$ if and only if* $\mathbf{J} \models IC$.

Proof. It can be shown that there exists a **LFI1**-sentence $\sigma_{\mathbf{J}}$ which characterizes **J** (a finite structure), i.e., for every arbitrary interpretation $\mathcal{I}$, $\mathcal{I} \models \sigma_{\mathbf{J}}$ if and only if $\mathcal{I}$ is isomorphic to **J** (this is due to an extension to **LFI1** of a well-known theorem for first-order logic ([18]). It can be shown that there is a closed tableau for $T(\sigma_{\mathbf{J}}) \cup F(IC)$ if and only if there exists a closed tableau for $S(\mathbf{J}) \cup F(IC)$. The existence of a closed tableau for $T(\sigma_{\mathbf{J}}) \cup F(IC)$ is equivalent to affirming that $\sigma_{\mathbf{J}} \models_{fin} IC$, by Theorem 3.1. Let us suppose that $\mathbf{J} \models IC$ and let **J'** be a p-instance such that $\mathbf{J'} \models \sigma_{\mathbf{J}}$. Then, **J'** and **J** are isomorphic and so, $\mathbf{J'} \models IC$. This proves that $\sigma_{\mathbf{J}} \models_{fin} IC$. Conversely, suppose that $\sigma_{\mathbf{J}} \models_{fin} IC$. Using the fact that $\mathbf{J} \models \sigma_{\mathbf{J}}$, we can conclude that $\mathbf{J} \models IC$.

Lemma 4.2. *Let $\mathcal{K}$ be the output of the method REPAIR and $\mathbf{J} \in \mathcal{K}$. Then, there exists a closed tableau for $S(\mathbf{J}) \cup F(IC)$.*

Proof. Let us suppose without loss of generality that IC = $\{C\}$. So m = number of leaves = 1. If **J** = **I** : either Leaves = $\emptyset$ (the reduced tableau for F(IC) is closed) or for each instantiation there exists A $\in \mathcal{X}$ such that A $\notin$ S(**I**). Let A = T(X) (resp. F(X)). Then F(X) (resp. T(X)) is in S(**I**). So, in order to obtain a closed tableau for $S(\mathbf{I}) \cup F(IC)$, we simply apply the rules of the reduced tableau for $F(IC)$. If $\mathbf{J} \neq \mathbf{I}$: For each instantiation $\mathcal{X}$ (step (7)) where there is a modification in $\mathcal{S}$, we have necessarily that $\mathcal{X} \subseteq \mathcal{S}$ (step (8)). A signed atomic formula A is chosen in $\mathcal{X}$ (step (9)). Let A = T(X). A is replaced by $\underline{T(\bullet X)}$ in $\mathcal{S}$ (step (9)). From proposition 3.1(b), we know that $F(\bullet X)$ appears in the leaf corresponding to $\mathcal{X}$. So, the resulting tableau for $S(\mathbf{J}) \cup F(IC)$ closes. Now, let A = $\underline{F(X)}$ (remind that $A \in \mathcal{S}$ and $A \in \mathcal{X}$). A is replaced by $T(\bullet X)$ in $\mathcal{S}$. We consider the same rules applied in order to obtain the reduced tableau for $F(IC)$, and then we apply the rule (9) to $T(\bullet X)$, obtaining $\underline{T(X)}$ and $T(\neg X)$. Hence, the resulting tableau for $S(\mathbf{J}) \cup F(IC)$ closes.

Lemma 4.3. *Let $\mathcal{K}$ be the output of the method* REPAIR *and $\mathbf{J} \in \mathcal{K}$. For each p-instance $\mathbf{J}$' over $\mathbf{R}$ such that $\mathbf{J}$' $\models IC$ we have that $d(\mathbf{J},\mathbf{I}) \leq d(\mathbf{J}',\mathbf{I})$.*

Proof. If $\mathbf{J}$' $\models IC$ then there exists a closed tableau for $S(\mathbf{J}') \cup F(IC)$ (Lemma 4.1). All p-instances $\mathbf{K}$ which are closest to $\mathbf{I}$ and for which there exists a closed tableau for $S(\mathbf{K}) \cup F(IC)$ are obtained by the method. So, $d(\mathbf{J},\mathbf{I}) \leq d(\mathbf{J}',\mathbf{I})$.

We conclude this section with the following theorem which states the completeness of the method:

Theorem 4.2. *Let $\mathbf{I}$ be an instance (safe) over $\mathbf{R}$. If $\mathbf{J}$ is a repair of $\mathbf{I}$ then $\mathbf{J}$ is included in the output of the method* REPAIR.

Proof. If $\mathbf{J}$ is a repair of $\mathbf{I}$ then $\mathbf{J} \models IC$. By Lemma 4.1, there exists a closed tableau for $S(\mathbf{J}) \cup F(IC)$. But all p-instances $\mathbf{J}$' which are closest to $\mathbf{I}$ and for which there exists a closed tableau for $S(\mathbf{J}') \cup F(IC)$ are obtained by the method. So $\mathbf{J}$ is obtained by the method.

5   Updating Paraconsistent Databases

In this section we will study a dynamic repairing process for paraconsistent databases. This repairing process, which in fact is a simple adaptation of the method REPAIR for paraconsistent databases, will be executed after each update in order to control data inconsistencies. The method is sufficiently general and can treat two kinds of updates which possibly produce data inconsistencies: (1) data updates and (2) integrity constraints updates. It is important to notice that our update operations will not allow users to insert controversial information in the database. So, in our approach inconsistencies are viewed as an internal phenomenon and can only arise as a consequence of information conflict.

Example 5.1 (Running Example - Continued). Let $\mathbf{R}$, $\mathbf{J}$ and IC be respectively the database schema, the integrated p-instance and the integrity constraints of example 1.1. Let us suppose that the user executes the operation $ins_R(d)$. After the update, the resulting p-instance violates the integrity constraint C_1. Let us now suppose that, instead of a data update, the user executes an integrity constraint update by inserting the new integrity constraint $C_4 = \forall x \forall y (\neg R(x) \vee \neg R(y) \vee x = y)$. The p-instance $\mathbf{J}$, which satisfied the original integrity constraints IC before the update, now violates C_4.

The idea is to use the method REPAIR in order to build a repair for the updated inconsistent p-instance. So, the whole update process is composed of two steps: (1) the user update and (2) the repair process executed over the updated database.

Evolutionary Databases and Udpates. We introduce now the *evolutionary databases* which is a general database context where data and integrity constraints updates are allowed.

Definition 5.1. *Let* **R** *be a database schema. An* evolutionary instance (e-instance) *is a pair* **(I**,*IC) where* **I** *is a p-instance and IC is a finite set of integrity constraints such that* **I** $\models$ *IC.*

Definition 5.2. *Let* **R** *be a database schema. An* update *over* **R** *is an expression of the form* $ins_R(u)$, $del_R(u)$, $ins(\varphi)$ *or* $del(\varphi)$, *where* $R \in$ **R**, φ *is an integrity constraint over* **R**, *and u is a tuple over* **R**. *The first two updates are called* data updates *and the other two are called* constraint updates.

The semantics of an update t is given by its effect over an e-instance $(\mathbf{I},IC)$. We define $(\mathbf{J},IC') = t(\mathbf{I},IC)$, where **J** and IC' are defined by the following table:

t	J	IC'
$ins_R(u)$	$\mathbf{J}(R(u)) = 1$ if $\mathbf{I}(R(u)) = 0$ $\mathbf{J}(R(u)) = \mathbf{I}(R(u))$ otherwise $\mathbf{J}(S(v)) = \mathbf{I}(S(v))$ for all tuples v over S if S $\neq$ R	IC
$del_R(u)$	$\mathbf{J}(R(u)) = 0$	IC
$ins(\varphi)$	**I**	IC $\cup \{\varphi\}$
$del(\varphi)$	**I**	IC $- \{\varphi\}$

This quite natural semantics implicitly presumes the following assumptions: (1) no inconsistent information can be inserted in the database by an user insertion, (2) an inconsistent information cannot become a safe information unless it is deleted by a user deletion and inserted as a safe information later on. We notice that the result $(\mathbf{J},IC')$ of a user update does not necessarily produce an e-instance, i.e., the integrity constraints IC' may be violated by the p-instance **J**. Another important point is the following:

Theorem 5.1. *All sets of integrity constraints are* **LFI1**-*satisfiable.*

So, the resulting set of integrity constraints IC' is always **LFI1**-satisfiable. This means that in our framework, inconsistencies can appear only at data level.

Proof of Theorem 5.1. First we find the reduced tableau for F(IC). As there is at least a negative relational atom $\neg R(x_1, \ldots, x_n)$ in each sentence of IC, then all leaves in reduction(IC) contain a signed atomic formula of type $T(R(x_1, ..., x_n))$. For each leaf L_i, one considers one of these signed atoms A_i. Let $L = \{A_1, ..., A_k\}$. Let **Var** $= \{y_1, ..., y_m\}$ be the set of variables in L. Let $v : \{y_1, ..., y_m\} \to \{1, ..., m\}$. We consider the instance built in the following way: for each $A_i = T(R_i(z_1, ..., z_k))$, we define $\mathbf{I}(R_i)(v(z_1), ..., v(z_k)) = \frac{1}{2}$. It is easy to see that $S(\mathbf{I}) \cup F(IC)$ has a closed tableau, using the same techniques of the proof of Lemma 4.2.

The Method REPAIR *as a Repairing Technique for p-Instances.* Theorem 5.2 below guarantees that the method REPAIR executed over p-instances is correct and complete, and so, this method can be used as a repairing process after each update in order to control possible inconsistencies.

Theorem 5.2. *Let* **I** *be a p-instance and IC be a finite set of integrity constraints over a database schema* **R**. *Let* **J** $\in \mathcal{K}$, *where* $\mathcal{K}$ *is the output of the method* REPAIR. *Then* **J** *is a repair of* **I**. *Conversely, if* **J'** *is a repair of* **I** *then* **J'** *is contained in* $\mathcal{K}$.

Proof. The completeness proof uses the same arguments of the proof of Theorem 4.2 and the soundness proof uses Lemmas 4.1, 4.2 and 4.3. Lemma 4.1 was proved for p-instances and the proofs of Lemmas 4.2 and 4.3 can be easily extended to p-instances. In fact, the only part of its proof which should be adapted is the case when **J** = **I**. In this case, either Leaves = $\emptyset$ (the reduced tableau for F(IC) is closed) either for each instantiation there exists A $\in \mathcal{X}$ such that A $\notin$ S(**I**). Let A = T(X) (resp. F(X)). Then F(X) or T($\bullet$X) (resp. T(X) or T($\bullet$X)) is in S(**I**). If it is the case that T($\bullet$X) is in S(**I**) and A = F(X), in order to obtain a closed tableau for S(**I**) $\cup$ F(IC), we simply apply the rules of the reduced tableau for F(IC) and the rule (9) to T($\bullet$X). If it is the case that T($\bullet$X) is in S(**I**) and A = T(X): from proposition 3.1(b), we can affirm that F($\bullet$X) must also appear in the leaf corresponding to $\mathcal{X}$. The closure of S(**I**) $\cup$ F(IC) is then achieved. The other cases are treated as in the proof of Lemma 4.2.

6   Conclusion and Further Work

In this paper we have introduced the method REPAIR for the integration of multiple databases where inconsistencies are not eliminated from the integrated database. The method produces a set of repair versions of the integrated database where inconsistencies are kept under control, i.e., one knows exactly what part of the whole information is inconsistent w.r.t. the integrity constraints specified in the local sources. The method is complete, i.e., all possible repairs of the integrated database can be obtained. Besides being an effective procedure for the integration of multiple databases it can also be employed to deal with the dynamics of the integrated database. It is sufficiently general to treat also other situations where inconsistencies may arise in databases, such as when integrity constraints changes during the lifetime of the database. The method can be generalized to treat other classes $\mathcal{C}$ of integrity constraints for which IC $\models_{fin}$ C is equivalent to IC $\models$ C, where IC $\subseteq \mathcal{C}$ and C $\in \mathcal{C}$. For classes where this property is not satisfied, the method will not be complete and the p-instances produced would not necessarily verify the minimal distance.

We are currently pursuing the following lines of research: First, the complexity of the repair problem should be investigated and the adaptation of the method to a logic programming environment needs to be considered, by translating our tableau proof system into a resolution method. The logic **LFI1** may be used to specify a query language in a DATALOG style to query paraconsistent databases. It would be interesting to compare our three-valued semantics with the well-founded semantics of DATALOG¬ and obtain a fixpoint semantics for our paraconsistent query language. Finally, we plan to generalize our method for the creation and management of consistent materialized views (datawarehouses).

Some Related Work. In [10] we have proposed a paraconsistent logical framework having a two-valued semantics and a method for controlling inconsistencies in databases. Nevertheless, this method is not complete and does not guarantee that the instance produced contains minimal changes w.r.t. the original. In [3], a method for consistent answers to queries in relational databases (possibly violating a given set of integrity constraints) has been introduced. For this purpose, this paper introduces a notion of *repair* databases based on the minimal distance from the original database, similar to the one introduced in our approach. Consistent answers are then obtained from the minimally repaired versions of the original database. The class of integrity constraints treated there is the same considered in our approach. Even though the main purpose of our paper is not the problem of consistent query answer, we could point some differences between our approach and the one in [3] concerning repairs: (1) their method does not compute the repair databases; (2) our repairs are more *refined* in the sense that they are closer to the original database than the one in [3]; and (3) our repairs do not eliminate inconsistent information. In [4], the same authors present another method to compute consistent answers in possibly inconsistent databases where repairs are specified in a logic programming formalism. This method can treat a larger class of integrity contraints but does not compute the repairs. In [16,5,2], the semantics of integrating possibly inconsistent data is captured by the maximal consistent subsets of the union of the theories specifying the local sources. In [2] and [16], extensions of relational algebra and relational calculus, respectively, are introduced for manipulating and querying inconsistent data and inconsistent information is eliminated from the database. Our approach offers a much proper treatment of the whole question mainly because we do not waste information in the presence of contradiction.

References

1. Abiteboul, S., Hull, R. and Vianu, V.: Foundations of Databases, Addison-Wesley (1995).
2. Agarwal, S., Keller, A. M., Wiederhold, G., Saraswat, K.: Flexible Relation: An Approach for Integrating Data from Multiple, Possibly Inconsistent Databases. *Proceedings ICDE*, 1995.
3. Arenas, M., Bertossi, L., Chomicki, J.: Consistent Query Answers in Inconsistent Databases. In *Proc. of the 18th ACM Symposium on Principles of Database Systems*, June 1999, Philadelphia, USA, pp 68-79.
4. Arenas, M., Bertossi, L., Chomicki, J.: Specifying and Querying Database Repairs using Logic Programs with Exceptions. *In Proc. 4th International Conference on Flexible Query Aswering Systems*, October 2000, Warsaw, Poland, Springer-Verlag.
5. Baral,C., Kraus, S., Minker, J., Subrahmanian, V. S.: Combining knowledge bases consisting of first-order theories. *Computational Intelligence*, 8:45-71, 1992.

6. Blair, H., Subrahmanian, V.S.: Paraconsistent Logic Programming. *Theoretical Computer Science*, 68: 135-154, 1989. Also in *Proc. Conf. on Foundations of Software Technology and Theoretical Computer Science*, (LNCS 287), 340-360, 1987. Integrity

7. Carnielli, W.A. and Marcos, J.: A taxonomy of C-systems To appear in: W. A. Carnielli, M. E. Coniglio, and I. M. L. D'Ottaviano, editors, Paraconsistency: The logical way to the inconsistent. *Proceedings of the II World Congress on Paraconsistency* (WCP2000). Marcel Dekker, 2001.
http://www.cle.unicamp.br/e-prints/abstract_5.htm

8. Carnielli, W.A. and Marcos, J.: Tableau systems for logics of formal inconsistency. In: H.R.Arabnia, editor, *Proceedings of the 2001 International Conference on Artificial Intelligence*, (IC-AI 2001), v. II, p. 848-852. CSREA Press, USA, 2001.
http://logica.rug.ac.be/~joao/tableauxLFIs.ps.zip

9. Carnielli, W.A., Marcos, J., de Amo, S.: Formal Inconsistency and evolutionary databases. To appear in *Logic and Logical Philosophy*, 7/8, 2000.
http://www.cle.unicamp.br/e-prints/abstract_6.htm

10. Carnielli, W.A., de Amo, S.: A logic-based system for controlling inconsistencies in evolutionary databases. *Proc. of the VI Workshop on Logic, Language, Information and Computation*, (WoLLIC 99), Itatiaia, Brazil, 1998, pp.89-101.

11. Carnielli, Walter A.: Many-valued logics and plausible reasoning. *Proceedings of International Symp. on Multiple-valued Logic*, Charlotte, U.S.A.,pp. 328-335 IEEE Computer Society Press(1990)

12. Carnielli, W. A., Lima–Marques, M.: Reasoning under Inconsistent Knowledge. *Journal of Applied Non-classical Logics*, Vol. 2 (1), 1992, pp. 49-79.

13. Carnielli, Walter A.: Systematization of the finite many-valued through the method of tableaux.

14. da Costa, Newton C.A.: On the theory of inconsistent formal system, *Notre Dame Journal of Formal Logic* , v. 11, pp. 497-510 (1974).

15. Dreben, B., Goldburg, W.D.: The Decision Problem: Solvable Classes of Quantificational Formulas. Addison-Wesley, 1979.

16. Dung, P.M.: Integrating Data from Possibly Inconsistency Databases. *International Conference on Cooperative Information Systems*, Brussels, Belgium, 1996.

17. Fagin, R., Ullman, J. D., Vardi, M.: On the semantics of updates in databases. In *2nd ACM SIGACT-SIGMOD Symposium on Principles of Database Systems*, pages352-365, 1983.

18. Fagin, R.: Finite Model Theory: a Personal Perspective. *Theoretical Computer Science*, 116 (182):3-31, 1994.

19. Gallo, G., Rago, G.: The Satisfiability problem for the Schöenfinkel-Bernays fragment: Partial Instantiation and Hypergraph Algorithms TR 4/94, Dipartimento di Informatica, Università di Pisa, 1994.

20. Gärdenfors, P.: Knowledge in Flux - Modeling the Dynamics of Epistemic States. MIT Press, 1988.

21. Kifer, M., Lozinskii, E.L: A Logic for Reasoning with Inconsistency. *Journal of Automated Reasoning* 9: 179-215, 1992.

22. Subrahmanian, V.S.: Amalgamating knowledge bases. *ACM Transactions on Database Systems*, 19(2)-1994.

23. Trakhtenbrot, B.A.: The impossibility of an algorithm for the decision problem for finite domains. (Russian), *Doklady Akademii Nauk*, SSSR (N.S.) 70, pp 569-572, 1950.

Functional Dependencies in Presence of Errors

János Demetrovics[1], Gyula O.H. Katona[2,*], and Dezső Miklós[2]

[1] Comp. and Autom. Institute, Hungarian Academy of Sciences
Kende u. 13-17, H-1111, Hungary
dj@ilab.sztaki.hu
[2] Alfréd Rényi Institute of Mathematics
Hungarian Academy of Sciences
Budapest P.O.B. 127 H-1364 Hungary
{ohkatona,dezso}@renyi.hu

Abstract. A relational database D is given with Ω as the set of attributes. The rows (tuples, data of one individual) are transmitted through a noisy channel. It is supposed that at most one data in a row can be changed by the transmission. We say that $A \to b$ $(A \subset \Omega, b \in \Omega)$ is an error-correcting functional dependency if the data in A uniquely determine the data in b in spite of the error. We investigate the problem how much larger a minimal error-correcting functional dependency can be than the original one.

1 Introduction

Let us give some examples. Suppose that the pair of attributes (first name, last name) is a key in the database M. The values in M are the real data. However, some of the data can be erroneous: the information is misunderstood in a phone conversation, the typist makes a mistake or the informant simply lies. Say, if one of the first names "Mario" is replaced by "Maria" (M contains "Mario", M^* contains "Maria") then we might have two individual with names Maria Sklodowska in M^*, hence the individual (row) cannot be determined from these two attributes. The question raised here is what other additional attributes we need to make us able to determine the real person (row).

A database can be considered as an $m \times n$ matrix M, where the rows are the data of one individual, the data of the same sort (*attributes*) are in the same column. Denote the set of attributes (equivalently, the set of columns of the matrix) by Ω, its size is $|\Omega| = n$. It will be supposed that the data of two distinct individuals are different, that is, the rows of the matrix are different. Let $A, B \subset \Omega$. We say that B *funtionally depends* on A and write $A \to B$ if any two rows coinciding in the columns of A are also equal in the columns of B. Specially, if $K \to \Omega$ then K is called a *key*. In other words, there are no two distinct rows of the matrix which are equal in K. A key is a *minimal key* if no proper subset of it is a key. Denote the family of all minimal keys by $\mathcal{K}$.

* The work of the second and third author was supported by the Hungarian National Foundation for Scientific Research grant numbers T016389, T029255

T. Eiter and K.-D. Schewe (Eds.): FoIKS 2002, LNCS 2284, pp. 85–92, 2002.

Let M denote the matrix of the real data. These data are transmitted through a noisy channel. M^* ($m \times n$, again) denotes the matrix of the data obtained after the transmission. We know that M and M^* differ in at most e entries in each row. Although it is also supposed here that the real data of two distinct individuals are different, that is the rows of M are different, this cannot be stated about M^*.

We assume that the structure of M is known, on the other hand we only know the received rows of M^* and our aim is to make conclusions based on this information. Suppose for instance that $A \to a$ ($A \subset \Omega, a \in \Omega$) holds in M. Then the data in a row in the columns of A determine the data of the same row in the column a. We know however only the corresponding rows in M^*. The data in the columns of A do not necessarily determine the data in a, since these data are distorted. Can we enlarge A into an A' whose data (in M^*) already determine a? If yes, to what extent should it be enlarged?

For instance, if the number of errors in one row is at most one ($e = 1$) and sex is one of the attributes then either the first name or the sex is correct. Yet, (Maria, Sklodowska, M) can be found in two different rows of M^* (one was (Mario, Sklodowska, M) the other one was (Maria, Sklodowska, F)). Further attributes migh be needed to identify the individual. That is, (first name, last name, sex) is not a 1-error-correcting key.

Let us emphasize that the problem of data mining in case of errors is different. Then only M^* is known, nothing is known about M. In our case the keys, functional dependencies are known for us in M. We want to modify them only for the purposes in M^*. In case of data mining we have no prior information on M, the keys or error-correcting keys should be determined only on the base of M^*.

Formalize our notions. We write $C \to \{e\}B$ if the values of the matrix M^* in the columns of C determine the values in the columns B uniquely, assuming that at most e errors occur in every row. (Actually, it is determined in M, the data in M^* can be erronous.) In other words, for any row r of M^* there are no two rows s and t of M both having Hamming distance less then or equal to e from r in the columns of C but being different in the columns of B. This is called an e-error-correcting functional dependency. The aim of the present paper is to find inequalities between the sizes of the sets occuring in the real functional dependencies and the e-error-correcting ones. Our previous paper [4] dealt with the case of the keys. The results of the present paper are analogous.

It is worth mentioning that $\{a\} \to \{1\}a$ does not hold, since the knowledge of the data in the column a does not give any information, it can be erronous. It does not determine the value in column a.

The number of different entries in two rows is called the *Hamming distance* of these two rows. The $m \times |C|$ submatrix of M determined by the set C of its columns is denoted by $M(C)$. Suppose that the Hamming distance of any two rows of $M(C)$, which are different in $a \in \Omega$, is at least $2e+1$. Then the Hamming distance of any two rows of $M^*(C)$ is at least 1, that is, knowing the entries of the unreliable matrix in C determines the value in the column a, $C \to \{e\}a$ is an e-error-correcting functional dependency. Here we used the assumption that the functional dependencies of M are known. The converse is true, too: if the Hamming distance of two rows of $M(C)$, which are different in a, is at most $2e$ then it may happen that the rows are equal in $M^*(C)$, that is, $C \to \{e\}a$ is not true. We obtained the following proposition.

Proposition 1.1 $C \to \{e\}a$ $(C \subset \Omega, a \in \Omega)$ *is an e-error-correcting functional dependency iffthe pairwise Hamming distance of the rows of* $M(C)$, *which are diffrent in* a, *is at least* $2e + 1$. □

2   Error-Correcting Functional Dependencies

It is easy to see that if the pairwise Hamming distance of the rows of $M(C)$ being different in a is at least $2e$ then the knowledge of $M^*(C)$ detects the error (i.e. the presence of the error in M^*), but does not determine the data in a uniqely, i.e. there can be more then one rows of M having the same values in $M^*(C)$. This case is less interesting, but it makes worth introducing the more general definition: $C \to (d)a$ is called a d-*distance functional dependency* iff the pairwise Hamming distance of the rows of $M(C)$, which are different in a, is at least d.

The main aim of the present investigations is to find connections between the functional dependencies and the d-distance functional dependencies. The next proposition is the first step along this line. Let $\mathcal{F}_a$ be the family of minimal subsets F of Ω satisfying $F \to a$ (in $M!$).

Proposition 2.1 $C \to (d)a$ $(C \subset \Omega, a \in \Omega)$ *is a d-distance functional dependency ifffor any choice* $a_1, \ldots, a_{d-1} \in C$ *one can find an $F \in \mathcal{F}_a$ such that* $F \subseteq C - \{a_1, \ldots, a_{d-1}\}$.

Proof. The necessity will be proved in an indirect way. Suppose that there exist $a_1, \ldots, a_{d-1} \in C$ such that $C - \{a_1, \ldots, a_{d-1}\}$ contains no member of $\mathcal{F}_a$, that is, $C - \{a_1, \ldots, a_{d-1}\} \to a$ does not hold. Therefore there are two rows of M which are equal in $M(C - \{a_1, \ldots, a_{d-1}\})$ and are different in a. The Hamming distance of these two rows in $M(C)$ is less than d. The obvious contradiction completes this part of the proof.

To prove the sufficiency suppose, again in an indirect way, that $M(C)$ contains two rows with Hamming distance $< d$ and the rows are different in a. Delete those columns where these rows are different. We found a set $C - \{a_1, \ldots, a_{d-1}\}$ satisfying the condition that $M(C - \{a_1, \ldots, a_{d-1}\})$ contains two rows which are equal everywhere, but the rows are different in a. Therefore $C - \{a_1, \ldots, a_{d-1}\} \to a$ is not true in M, $C - \{a_1, \ldots, a_{d-1}\}$ cannot contain a member of $\mathcal{F}_a$. □

The systems of functional dependencies were characterized in [1]. We prefer an equivalent description (see e.g. [3]) by the closure

$$\mathcal{L}(A) = \{a : a \in \Omega, A \to a\} \ (A \subseteq \Omega).$$

It is easy to see that this closure satisfies the following 3 conditions.

$$A \subseteq \mathcal{L}(A), \tag{i}$$

$$A \subseteq B \text{ implies } \mathcal{L}(A) \subseteq \mathcal{L}(B), \tag{ii}$$

$$\mathcal{L}(\mathcal{L}(A)) = \mathcal{L}(A). \tag{iii}$$

It is well-known ([1], [2]) that there is a database for any closure, in which the system of functional dependencies is exactly the one defined by this closure. This is why it is sufficient to give a closure rather than constructing the complete database or matrix.

It is possible to give a characterization with the families $\mathcal{F}_a$ as well. It is easy to see that $\mathcal{F}_a$ consists of $\{a\}$ and a (possibly empty) *inclusion-free* family of subsets of $\Omega - \{a\}$. (Inclusion-free means that $F_1, F_2 \in \mathcal{F}_a, F_1 \neq F_2$ implies $F_1 \not\subseteq F_2$.) We need one more condition for the interrelation between these families. Howvere, since we did not find the shortest form and no such characterization is needed in this paper we prove only the following lemma, which will be needed later.

Lemma 2.2 *Given an inclusion-free family $\mathcal{F}$ of subsets of a $\Omega \setminus \{a\}$, there is a system of functional dependencies (and therefore, with the preceeding remark, a relation M) such that it defines $\mathcal{F}_a = \mathcal{F} \cup \{\{a\}\}$ for some $a \in \Omega$.*

Proof. Fix an $a \in \Omega$ and define $\mathcal{F}_a$ as the family consisting of $\{a\}$ and $\mathcal{F}$ placed in some way in the remaing part of Ω. Let $\mathcal{L}(A) = A \cup \{a\}$ if $F \subseteq A$ for some $F \in \mathcal{F}_a$ and $\mathcal{L}(A) = A$ otherwise. It is easy to see that this function satisfies conditions (i)-(iii), that is, it is a closure. □

In other words, Lemma 2.2 says that for any inclusion-free family $\mathcal{F}$ on an $n-1$-element set there is a database where the family of minimal sets F satisfying $F \to a$ is exactly exactly equal to $\mathcal{F}_a = \mathcal{F} \cup \{\{a\}\}$.

Proposition 2.1 makes us able to give an abstract combinatorial definition, independent of databases. Let X be an n-element set and $\mathcal{F}$ be an inclusion-free family of its subsets. The *d-blownup* of $\mathcal{F}$ (in notation $\mathcal{F}(d)$) is defined by

$$\mathcal{F}(d) = \{G \subseteq X : \text{ for any choice of } x_1, \ldots, x_{d-1} \in G \ \exists F \in \mathcal{F} \text{ such that}$$

$$F \subseteq G - \{x_1, \ldots, x_{d-1}\} \text{ and } G \text{ is minimal for this property}\}.$$

Note that $\mathcal{F}(1) = \mathcal{F}$ and that, as we will see later, for an inclusion-free family of sets $\mathcal{F}$ forming the left hand sides of the functional dependencies of a relation $\mathcal{F}(d)$ will be the left hand sides of minimal d-distance dependencies. set

Our first observation is that it may happen that the d-blownup of $\mathcal{F}$ is an empty family while the original $\mathcal{F}$ is not. Fix an element $a \in X$ and an integer $2 \leq k$. Define $\mathcal{F}$ as the family of all k-element sets ($\subset X$) containing a. Then for any $C \subseteq X \ C - \{a\}$ cannot contain any member of $\mathcal{F}$ therefore $\mathcal{F}(d)$ is empty for $2 \leq d$.

On the other hand, if $\mathcal{F}$ consists of all k-element subsets of X then all sets $G \subseteq X$ with $k + d - 1$ elements form $\mathcal{F}(d)$. Our last example suggests that the sizes of the members of $\mathcal{F}(d)$ do not exceed the sizes of the members of $\mathcal{F}$ by too much. We will show that this is not really true.

We say that the family $\mathcal{F}$ can be *pinned* by p elements if there are $x_1, \ldots, x_p$ such that no member of $\mathcal{F}$ avoids all of them, that is $F \cap \{x_1., \ldots, x_p\} \neq \emptyset \; \forall F \in \mathcal{F}$. We saw that if $\mathcal{F}$ can be pinned by $d-1$ elements then $\mathcal{F}(d)$ is empty. Otherwise $\mathcal{F}(d)$ is never empty since X always satisfies the first part of the definition of the blownup and if it is not minimal, one can reduce it until arriving to a minimal set.

Theorem 2.3 *Let $n_0(k, d) \leq n$ and let $\mathcal{F}$ be an inclusion-free family of subsets of size at most k of a given set of size n, such that $\mathcal{F}$ cannot be pinned by $d-1$ elements. Then the sizes of the members of $\mathcal{F}(d)$ are at most $c_1 k^d$. On the other hand there is such an $\mathcal{F}$ for which all members of $\mathcal{F}(d)$ have size at least $c_2 k^d$. Here c_1 and c_2 depend only on d.*

As mentioned earlier, define now $\mathcal{F}_a(d)$ as the family of the left hand sides of the minimal d-distance dependencies described by Proposition 2.1. The family $\mathcal{F}(d)$ will then be defined as the union of the families $\mathcal{F}_a(d)$ for all $a \in \Omega$. If $F \to a$ holds for some $(a \in \Omega, F \subseteq \Omega)$ and no proper subset F' of F satisfies $F' \to a$ then F is called a *minimal functional dependency set*. The following theorem will be obtained as an immediate consequence of the previous one.

Theorem 2.4 *Let $n_0(k, e) \leq n$. Suppose that all minimal functional dependency sets have sizes at most k. Then the members of $\mathcal{F}(2e+1)$ cannot be larger than $c_1 k^{2e+1}$. On the other hand there is a database with minimal functional dependency sets of size at most k in which all members of $\mathcal{F}(2e+1)$ have sizes at least $c_2 k^{2e+1}$. Here c_1 and c_2 depend on e, only.*

It is worth formulating the special case $e = 1$ with more specific constants.

Corollary 2.5 *Suppose that all minimal functional dependency sets have sizes at most k. Then the members of $\mathcal{F}(3)$ cannot be larger than $3k^3$. On the other hand there is a database with minimal functional dependency sets of size at most k in which all members of $\mathcal{F}(3)$ have sizes at least $c_2 k^3$ where c_2 is approximately $\frac{2}{27}$.*

Our conclusion is that the errors can considerably increase the sizes of the minimal fuctional dependencies, but the growth is only polynomial.

3 Proofs

Proof of Theorem 2.3. This proof is analogous to the proof of the main theorem of [4]. Let $\mathcal{F}$ be an inclusion-free family of subsets of X. The definition of $\mathcal{F}(d)$ implies that the family $\{F : F \in \mathcal{F}, F \subseteq G\}$ cannot be pinned by $d-1$ elements for members $G \in \mathcal{F}(d)$. On the other hand, by the minimality of a member $G \in \mathcal{F}(d)$, this is not true for $G - \{a\}$ where $a \in G$ is chosen arbitrarily. This gives the following proposition.

Proposition 3.1 $G \in \mathcal{F}(d)$ iff $\{F : F \in \mathcal{F}, F \subseteq G\}$ *cannot be pinned by* $d - 1$ *elements, but* $\{F : F \in \mathcal{F}, F \subseteq G - \{a\}\}$ *can be pinned by some* $d - 1$ *elements for every* $a \in G$. □

Lower Estimate. We give an inclusion-free family $\mathcal{F}$ consisting of $2 \leq k$-element sets which generates an $\mathcal{F}(d)$ consisting of one member having size at least $c_2 k^d$.

Fix an integer $1 \leq i < k$ and take a subset $A \subset X$ of size $i + d - 1$. Let $B_1, B_2, \ldots$ be all the $\binom{i+d-1}{i}$ i-element subsets of A and

$$\mathcal{G}^i = \{B_1 \cup C_1, B_2 \cup C_2, \ldots\},$$

where $C_1, C_2, \ldots$ are disjoint subsets of $X - A$ with $|C_1| = |C_2| = \cdots = k - i$. This can be carried out if

$$i + d - 1 + \binom{i + d - 1}{i}(k - i) \leq n. \tag{3.1}$$

Using Proposition 3.1 we next show that the only member of $\mathcal{G}^i(d)$ is $D = A \cup \bigcup_i C_i$. It is easy to see that $\mathcal{G}^i$ cannot be pinned by $d - 1$ elements.

On the other hand, if $a \in C_j$ for some j then the d-element $\{a\} \cup (A - B_j)$ pins all members of $\mathcal{G}^i$ in $D - \{a\}$. If, however, $a \in A$ then any d-element $E \subset A$ containing a pins the members of $\mathcal{G}^i$ in $D - \{a\}$. Therefore D is really a member of $\mathcal{G}^i(d)$. It is easy to see that there is no other member.

Choose $i = \lfloor k(1 - \frac{1}{d}) \rfloor$. Then the size of D, given by the left hand side of (3.1) asymptotically becomes

$$\frac{(d - 1)^{d-1}}{d^d(d - 1)!} k^d.$$

(3.1) gives a condition how large n has to be. □

Upper Estimate. Let $G \in \mathcal{F}(d)$ where $\mathcal{F} \subset \binom{X}{\leq k}$ (the latter one denotes the family of all subsets of X of size at most k). We will prove that $|G| \leq dk^d$. Since we have to consider only the subsets of G, so it can be supposed that all members of $\mathcal{F}$ are subsets of G.

Proposition 3.1 defines d-element subsets D of G each of them is pinning $\mathcal{F}$. Moreover, still by Proposition 3.1, their union is G. Denote this family by $\mathcal{D}$. We know

$$\cup_{D \in \mathcal{D}} D = G, \tag{3.2}$$

$$D \cap F \neq \emptyset \text{ for all } D \in \mathcal{D}, F \in \mathcal{F} \tag{3.3}$$

and $\mathcal{F}$ cannot be pinned by a set with less than d elements.

Let $I \subseteq G$. Define the I-degree of $\mathcal{D}$ as the number of members of $\mathcal{D}$ containing I, that is,

$$\deg_I(\mathcal{D}) = |\{D \in \mathcal{D} : I \subset D\}|.$$

Lemma 3.2 *If $|I| < d$ then*

$$\deg_I(\mathcal{D}) \leq k^{d-|I|}.$$

Proof. We use induction on $j = d - |I|$. Suppose that $j = d - |I| = 1$, that is, $|I| = d - 1$. If all members of $\mathcal{F}$ meet I then $\mathcal{F}$ can be pinned by $d - 1$ elements, a contradiction. Therefore there is an $F \in \mathcal{F}$ which is disjoint to I. By (3.3) all the sets D satisfying $I \subset D$ must intersect this F, therefore their number is $\leq |F| \leq k$. This case is settled.

Now suppose that the statement is true for $j = d - |I| \geq 1$ and prove it for $j + 1 = d - |I|$. Let $|I^*| = d - j - 1$. There must exist an $F \in \mathcal{F}, F \cap I^* = \emptyset$ otherwise $\mathcal{F}$ is pinned by less than d elements, a contradiction. Let $F = \{x_1, \ldots, x_l\}$ where $l \leq k$. By (3.3) we have

$$\{D \in \mathcal{D}: \; I^* \subset D\} = \cup_{i=1}^{l}\{D \in \mathcal{D}: \; (I^* \cup \{x_i\}) \subset D\}. \tag{3.4}$$

The sizes of the sets on the right hand side are $\deg_{I^* \cup \{x_i\}}(\mathcal{D})$ which are at most $k^{d-|I^*|-1} = k^j$ by the induction hypothesis. Using (3.4)

$$\deg_{I^*}(\mathcal{D}) \leq l k^{d-|I^*|-1} \leq k^{d-|I^*|}$$

is obtained, proving the lemma. □

Finally, consider any $F = \{y_1, \ldots, y_r\} \in \mathcal{F}$ where $r \leq k$. By (3.3), the families $\{D \in \mathcal{D}: y_i \in D\}$ cover $\mathcal{D}$. Apply the lemma for $I = \{y_i\}$:

$$|\{D \in \mathcal{D}: y_i \in D\}| \leq k^{d-1}.$$

This implies $|\mathcal{D}| \leq k^d$ and

$$|\cup_{D \in \mathcal{D}} D| \leq |\mathcal{D}| d \leq dk^d.$$

Application of (3.2) completes the proof: $|G| \leq dk^d$. □

Proof of Theorem 2.4 Let $d = 2e + 1$. Apply the results of Theorem 2.3 first for a family $\mathcal{F}_a$. Since its members are not larger than k, the theorem implies that all members of $\mathcal{F}_a(2e + 1)$ are of size at most $c_1 k^{2e+1}$. Since this is true for every a, the union of the families has the same property.

On the other hand, take the inclusion-free family $\mathcal{F}$ giving the optimum in the lower estimation in Theorem 2.3. Lemma 2.2 defines a system of functional dependencies (database) in which $\mathcal{F}_a = \mathcal{F} \cup \{a\}$ holds for some $a \in \Omega$. Therefore $\mathcal{F}(2e + 1)$ contains sets of size at least $c_2 k^{2e+1}$. □

4   Further Problems

1. Although Theorem 2.3 determines the order of magnitude of the smallest size in the "worst" family, it does give the exact value. We believe that the lower estimate is sharp, our construction is the best possible.

Conjecture 4.1 *If $\mathcal{F} \subseteq \binom{X}{\leq k}$ then $\mathcal{F}(d)$ has a member with size at most*

$$\max_i \{i + d - 1 + \binom{i + d - 1}{i}(k - i)\}.$$

for $n_0(k, d) \leq n$.

2. Can the systems of e-error-correcting dependencies be characterized?

3. The following problem sounds similar to the problem treated here, but it is actually very different. Suppose that the data go through a noisy channel, where each data can be distorted with a small probability. So, in this case only M^* is known, no information is available on the structure of M. What is the relationship between the "functional dependencies" found in M^* and the real functional dependencies in M? This is the real problem arising in data mining in a distorted database.

References

1. Armstrong, W.W., Dependency structures of data base relationship, in: *Information Processing 74*, North-Holland, Amsterdam, pp. 580-583.
2. Demetrovics, J., On the equivalence of candidate keys with Sperner systems, *Acta Cybernet.* **4**(1979) 247-252.
3. Demetrovics J., Füredi, Z, and Katona, G.O.H.: Minimum matrix representation of closure operations, *Discrete Appl. Math.* **11**(1985) 115-128.
4. Demetrovics J., G.O.H. Katona, Miklós, D.: Error-correcting keys in relational databases, in *Foundations of Informationn and Knowledge Systems, FoIKS 2000* (K.-D. Schewe and B. Thalheim eds.) Lecture Notes in Computer Science, **1762**, Springer, 2000, pp. 88-93.

A Context Model
for Constructing Membership Functions
of Fuzzy Concepts Based on Modal Logic

V.N. Huynh[1,3], Y. Nakamori[1], T.B. Ho[1], and G. Resconi[2]

[1] Japan Advanced Institute of Science and Technology
Tatsunokuchi, Ishikawa, 923-1292, Japan
{huynh,nakamori,bao}@jaist.ac.jp
[2] Department of Mathematics and Physics
Catholic University, Via Trieste 17, Brescia, Italy
resconi@numerica.it
[3] Department of Computer Science, Quinhon University
170 An Duong Vuong, Quinhon, Vietnam

Abstract. In this paper we show that the context model proposed by Gebhardt and Kruse (1993) can be semantically extended and considered as a data model for constructing membership functions of fuzzy concepts within the framework of meta-theory developed by Resconi et al. in 1990s. Within this framework, we integrate context models by using a model of modal logic, and develop a method for calculating the expressions for the membership functions of composed fuzzy concepts based on values $\{0, 1\}$, which correspond to the truth values $\{F, T\}$ assigned to a given sentence as the response of a context considered as a possible world. It is of interest that fuzzy intersection and fuzzy union operators by this model are truth-functional, and, moreover, they form a well-known dual pair of *Product t-norm T_P* and *Probabilistic Sum t-conorm S_P*.

Keywords: Context model, fuzzy concept, membership function, modal logic

1 Introduction

The mathematical model of vague concepts was firstly introduced by Zadeh in 1965 by using the notion of membership functions resulted in the so-called theory of fuzzy sets. Since then mathematical foundations as well as successful applications of fuzzy set theory have already been developed (Klir & Yuan, 1995). As pointed out by Klir et al. (1997), these applications became feasible only when the methods of constructing membership functions of relevant fuzzy sets were efficiently developed in given application contexts.

In this paper we consider a context model, which was originally introduced by Gebhardt and Kruse (1993) in fuzzy data analysis, for constructing membership functions of vague concepts within framework of the modal logic based meta-theory developed by Resconi et al. (1992, 1993, 1996). By this approach, we can

T. Eiter and K.-D. Schewe (Eds.): FoIKS 2002, LNCS 2284, pp. 93–104, 2002.

integrate context models by using a model of modal logic, and then develop a method for calculating the expressions for the membership functions of composed fuzzy concepts based on values $\{0,1\}$ corresponding to the truth values $\{F,T\}$ assigned to a given sentence as the response of a context considered as a possible world. It is of interest to note that fuzzy intersection and fuzzy union operators by this model are truth-functional, and, moreover, they are a well-known dual pair of *Product t-norm* T_P and *Probabilistic Sum t-conorm* S_P.

The paper is organized as follows. In the next section, we briefly present some preliminary concepts: context model, modal logic, and meta-theory (with a short introduction to the modal logic interpretation of various uncertainty theories). In Section 3, we introduce a context model for fuzzy concept analysis and propose a model of modal logic for formulating fuzzy sets within a context model. Finally, some concluding remarks will be given in Section 4.

2   Preliminaries: Context Model, Modal Logic, and Meta-theory

2.1   Context Model

In the framework of fuzzy data analysis, Gebhardt and Kruse (1993) have introduced the context model as an approach to the representation, interpretation, and analysis of imperfect data. Shortly, the motivation of this approach stems from the observation that the origin of imperfect data is due to situations, where we are not able to specify an object by an original tuple of elementary characteristics because of the presence of incomplete statistical observations.

Formally, a context model is defined as a triple $\langle D, C, A_C(D) \rangle$, where D is a nonempty *universe of discourse*, C is a nonempty *finite set of contexts*, and the set $A_C(D) = \{a | a : C \to 2^D\}$ which is called the set of all vague characteristics of D with respect to C. For $a_1, a_2 \in A_C(D)$, then a_1 is said to be *more specific* than a_2 iff $(\forall c \in C)(a_1(c) \subseteq a_2(c))$.

If there is a finite measure P_C on the measurable space $(C, 2^C)$, then $a \in A_C(D)$ is called a *valuated vague characteristic* of D w.r.t. P_C. Then we call a quadruple $\langle D, C, A_C(D), P_C \rangle$ a valuated context model.

In this approach, each characteristic of an observed object is described by a fuzzy quantity formed by context model (Kruse et al. 1993). More refinements of the context model as well as its applications could be referred to Gebhardt and Kruse (1998), Gebhardt (2000). In the connection with formal concept analysis, it is interesting to note that in the case where C is a single-element set, say $C = \{c\}$, a context model formally becomes a formal context in the sense of Wille (see Ganter and Wille 1999) as follows. Let $\langle D, C, A_C(D) \rangle$ be a context model such that $|C| = 1$. Then the triple (O, A, R), where $O = D, A = A_C(D)$ and $R \subseteq O \times A$ such that $(o, a) \in R$ iff $o \in a(c)$, is a formal context. Thus, a context model can be considered as a collection of formal contexts. Huynh and Nakamori (2001) have considered and introduced the notion of fuzzy concepts within a context model and the membership functions associated with these fuzzy concepts. It is shown that fuzzy concepts can be interpreted exactly as the collections of α-cuts of their membership functions.

2.2 Modal Logic

Propositional modal logic is an extension of classical propositional logic that adds to the propositional logic two unary modal operators, an operator of necessity, $\Box$, and an operator of possibility, $\Diamond$. Given a proposition p, $\Box p$ stands for the proposition "it is necessary that p", and similarly, $\Diamond p$ represents the proposition "it is possible that p". Modal logic is well developed syntactically (Chellas 1980).

In Resconi et al. (1992, 1993, 1996), the modal logic interpretation of various uncertainty theories is based on the fundamental semantics of modal logic using Kripke models.

A model, M, of modal logic is a triple $M = \langle W, R, V \rangle$, where W, R, V denote, respectively, a set of possible worlds, a binary relation on W, and a value assignment function, by which truth (T) or falsity (F) is assigned to each atom in each possible world, i.e.

$$V : W \times \mathcal{Q} \longrightarrow \{T, F\},$$

where $\mathcal{Q}$ is the set of all atoms. The value assignment function is inductively extended to all formulas in the usual way, the only interesting cases being

$$\begin{aligned} V(w, \Box p) = T &\Longleftrightarrow \forall w' \in W, (wRw') \Rightarrow V(w', p) = T \\ &\Longleftrightarrow \mathcal{R}_s(w) \subseteq \| p \|^M \end{aligned} \tag{1}$$

and

$$\begin{aligned} V(w, \Diamond p) = T &\Longleftrightarrow \exists w' \in W, (wRw') \text{ and } V(w', p) = T \\ &\Longleftrightarrow \mathcal{R}_s(w) \cap \| p \|^M \neq \emptyset \end{aligned} \tag{2}$$

where $\mathcal{R}_s(w) = \{w' \in W \mid wRw'\}$, and $\| p \|^M = \{w \mid V(w, p) = T\}$. The relation R is usually called an *accessibility relation*, and different systems of modal logic are characterised by different additional requirements on accessibility relation R. Some systems of modal logic are depicted as shown in Table 1.

Table 1. Acessibility relation and axiom schemas

No condition	**Df$\Diamond$.** $\Diamond p \leftrightarrow \neg \Box \neg p$
No condition	**K.** $\Box(p \to q) \to (\Box p \to \Box q)$
Serial: $\forall w \exists w'(wRw')$	**D.** $\Box p \to \Diamond p$
Reflexive: $\forall w(wRw)$	**T.** $\Box p \to p$
Symmetric: $\forall w \forall w'(wRw' \Rightarrow w'Rw)$	**B.** $p \to \Box \Diamond p$
Transitive: $\forall w \forall w' \forall w''(wRw' \text{ and } w'Rw'' \Rightarrow wRw'')$	**4.** $\Box p \to \Box \Box p$
Connected: $\forall w \forall w'(wRw' \text{ or } w'Rw)$	**4.3.** $\Box(\Diamond p \lor \Diamond q) \to (\Box \Diamond p \lor \Box \Diamond q)$
Euclidean: $\forall w \forall w' \forall w''(w'Rw \text{ and } w'Rw'' \Rightarrow wRw'')$	**5.** $\Diamond p \to \Box \Diamond p$

2.3   Meta-theory Based Upon Modal Logic

In a series of papers initiated by Resconi et al. (1992), the authors have developed a hierarchical uncertainty meta-theory based upon modal logic. Particularly, modal logic interpretations for several theories, including the mathematical theory of evidence[1], fuzzy set theory, possibility theory have been already proposed (Resconi et al. 1992, 1993, 1996; Harmanec et al. 1994, 1996; Klir and Harmanec 1994). These interpretations are based on Kripke models of modal logic. Moreover, Resconi et al. (1996) have suggested to add a weighting function $\Omega : W \to [0,1]$ such that $\sum_{i=1}^{n} \Omega(w_i) = 1$ as a component of model M. By such a way we obtain a new model $M_1 = \langle W, R, V, \Omega \rangle$.

With the model M_1, given a universe of discourse X we can consider propositions that are relevant to fuzzy sets having the following form

$$a_x : \text{``} x \text{ belongs to a given set } A \text{''}$$

where $x \in X$ and A denotes a subset of X that is based on a vague concept. Set A is then viewed as an ordinary fuzzy set whose membership function μ_A is defined, for all $x \in X$, by the following formula

$$\mu_A(x) = \sum_{i=1}^{n} \Omega(w_i)\, {}^i a_x$$

where

$$
{}^i a_x = \begin{cases} 1 & \text{if } V(w_i, a_x) = T, \\ 0 & \text{otherwise.} \end{cases}
$$

The set-theoretic operations such as complement, intersection and union defined on fuzzy sets are then formulated within the model M_1 based on logical connectives NOT, AND, OR respectively (see Resconi et al. 1992, 1996).

To develop the interpretation of Dempster-Shafer theory of evidence (Shafer 1987) in terms of modal logic, Resconi et al. (1992) and Harmanec et al. (1994, 1996) employed propositions of the form

$$e_A : \text{``A given incompletely characterized element } \epsilon \text{ is classified in set } A \text{''}$$

where X denotes a frame of discernment, $A \in 2^X$ and $\epsilon \in X$. Due to the inner structure of these propositions, it is sufficient to consider as atomic propositions only propositions $e_{\{x\}}$, where $x \in X$. Furthermore, for each world $w_i \in W$, it is assumed that $V(w_i, e_{\{x\}}) = T$ for one and only one $x \in X$ and that the accessibility relation R is serial. Then the model M_1 yields the following equations for the basic functions in the Dempster-Shafer theory:

$$
\begin{aligned}
Bel(A) &= \sum_{i=1}^{n} \Omega(w_i)\, {}^i(\Box e_A) \\
Pl(A) &= \sum_{i=1}^{n} \Omega(w_i)\, {}^i(\Diamond e_A) \\
m(A) &= \sum_{i=1}^{n} \Omega(w_i)\, {}^i[\Box e_A \wedge (\bigwedge_{x \in A} \Diamond e_{\{x\}})] \\
Com(A) &= \sum_{i=1}^{n} \Omega(w_i)\, {}^i(\bigwedge_{x \in A} \Diamond e_{\{x\}})
\end{aligned}
$$

---

[1] also called Dempster-Shafer theory

where Bel, Pl, m and Com denote the belief function, plausibility function, basic probability assignment, and commonality function in the Dempster-Shafer theory, respectively.

In the case where the basic probability assignment m in the Dempster-Shafer theory induces a nested family of focal elements, we obtain a special belief function called a *necessity measure*, along with a corresponding plausibility function called a *possibility measure* (Dubois and Prade 1987). It is shown by Klir and Harmanec (1994) that the accessibility relation R of models associated with possibility theory are transitive and connected, i.e. these models formally correspond to the modal system $S4.3$ (see Table 1). The authors also showed the completeness of modal logic interpretation for possibility theory.

3   Fuzzy Concepts by Context Model Based on Modal Logic

3.1   Single Domain Case

As noted by Resconi and Turksen (2001), the specific meaning of a vague concept in a proposition may and usually does evaluate in different ways for different assessments of an entity by different agents, contexts, etc. For example, consider a sentence such as: "John is tall", where "tall" is a linguistic term of a linguistic variable, the height of people (Zadeh 1975). Assume that the domain $D = [0, 3m]$ which is associated with the base variable of the linguistic variable *height*. Note that in the terms of fuzzy sets, we may know John's height but must determine to what degree he is considered "tall". Next consider a set of worlds W in the sense of the Kripke model in which each world evaluates the sentence as either *true* or *false*. That is each world in W responds either as true or false when presented with the sentence "John is tall". These worlds may be contexts, agents, persons, etc. This implicitly shows that each world w_i in W determines a subset of D given as being compatible with the linguistic term *tall*. That is this subset represents w_i's view of the vague concept "tall". At this point we see that the context model introduced by Gebhardt and Kruse (1993) can be semantically extended and considered as a data model for constructing membership functions of vague concepts based on modal logic.

Let us consider a context model $\mathcal{C} = \langle D, C, A_C(D) \rangle$, where D is a domain of an attribute at which is applied to objects of concern, C is a non-empty finite set of contexts, and $A_C(D)$ is a set of linguistic terms associated with the domain D considered now as vague characteristics in the context model. For example, consider $D = [0, 3m]$ which is interpreted as the domain of the attribute *height* for people, C is a set of contexts such as Japanese, American, Swede, etc., and $A_C(D) = \{$ *very short, short, medium, tall, more or less tall*, ...$\}$. Each context determines a subset of D given as being compatible with a given linguistic term. Formally, each linguistic term can be considered as a mapping from C to 2^D. For linguistic terms such as *tall* and *very tall*, there are two interpretations possible: it may either be meant that *very tall* implies *tall*, i.e. that every very tall person is also tall. Or *tall* is an abbreviation for "tall, but not very tall". These two interpretations have been used in the literature depending on the shape of membership functions of relevant fuzzy sets. The linguistic term *very tall* is more specific than *tall* in the first interpretation, but not in the second one.

Furthermore, we can also associate with the context model a weighting function or a probability distribution Ω defined on C. As such we obtain a valuated context model $\mathcal{C} = \langle D, C, A_C(D), \Omega \rangle$.

By this context model, each linguistic term $a \in A_C(D)$ may be semantically represented by the fuzzy set A as follows

$$\mu_A(x) = \sum_{c \in C} \Omega(c)\mu_{a(c)}(x),$$

where $\mu_{a(c)}$ is the characteristic function of $a(c)$. Intuitively, while each subset $a(c)$, for $c \in C$, represents the c's view of the vague concept a, the fuzzy set A is the result of a weighted combined view of the vague concept. For the sake of a further development in the next subsection, in the sequent we will formulate the problem in the terms of modal logic. To this end, we consider propositions that are relevant to a linguistic term have the following form

$$a_x : \text{``}x \text{ belongs to a given set } A\text{''},$$

where $x \in D$ and A denotes a subset of D that is based on a linguistic term a in $A_C(D)$. Assume that $C = \{c_1, \ldots, c_n\}$, we now define a model of modal logic

$$M = \langle W, R, V_D, \Omega \rangle,$$

where $W = C$, that is each context c_i is associated with a possible world w_i; R is a binary relation on W, in this case R is the identity, i.e. each world w_i only itself is accessible; and V_D is the value assignment function such that for each world in W, by which truth (T) or falsity (F) is assigned to each atomic proposition a_x by

$$V_D(w_i, a_x) = \begin{cases} 1 & \text{if } x \in a(c_i), \\ 0 & \text{otherwise.} \end{cases}$$

We now define the compatible degree of any value x in the domain D to the linguistic term a (and the set A is then viewed as an ordinary fuzzy set) as the membership expression of truthood of the atomic sentence a_x in M as follows

$$\mu_A(x) = \sum_{i=1}^{n} \Omega(w_i)V_D(w_i, a_x) \tag{3}$$

Similar as in Resconi et al. (1996), it is straightforward to define the set-theoretic operations such as complement, intersection, union on fuzzy sets induced from linguistic terms in $A_C(D)$ by the model M using logical connectives NOT, AND, and OR respectively. Apply (3) to the complement A^c of fuzzy set A we have

$$\mu_{A^c}(x) = \sum_{i=1}^{n} \Omega(w_i)V_D(w_i, \neg a_x) = \sum_{i=1}^{n} \Omega(w_i)(1 - V_D(w_i, a_x)) = 1 - \mu_A(x).$$

In addition to propositions a_x, let us also consider propositions

$$b_x : \text{``}x \text{ belongs to a given set } B\text{''},$$

where $x \in D$ and B denotes a subset of D that is based on another linguistic term b in $A_C(D)$. To define composed fuzzy sets $A \cap B$ and $A \cup B$, we now apply logical connectives AND, OR to propositions a_x and b_x as follows

$$\mu_{A \cap B}(x) = \sum_{i=1}^{n} \Omega(w_i)V_D(w_i, a_x \wedge b_x) \tag{4}$$

$$\mu_{A \cup B}(x) = \sum_{i=1}^{n} \Omega(w_i)V_D(w_i, a_x \vee b_x) \tag{5}$$

It is easily seen that if a is more specific than b, we have

$$\mu_{A \cap B}(x) = \mu_A(x), \text{ and } \mu_{A \cup B}(x) = \mu_B(x),$$

this interpretation of linguistic hedges such as *very*, *less*, etc., is in accordance with that considered by Zadeh (1975).

Following properties of the operations $\vee, \wedge$ in classical logic, we easily obtain

$$\mu_{A \cup B}(x) = \mu_A(x) + \mu_B(x) - \mu_{A \cap B}(x) \tag{6}$$

Furthermore, it follows directly by (4), (5) and (6) the following.

Proposition 3.1. *For any $x \in D$, we have*

$$\max(0, \mu_A(x) + \mu_B(x) - 1) \leq \mu_{A \cap B}(x) \leq \min(\mu_A(x), \mu_B(x))$$
$$\max(\mu_A(x), \mu_B(x)) \leq \mu_{A \cup B}(x) \leq \min(1, \mu_A(x) + \mu_B(x))$$

It should be noticed that under the constructive formulation of fuzzy sets by this context model, fuzzy intersection and fuzzy union operations are no longer truth-functional. Also, if there is a non-trivial relationship between contexts, we should take the relation R into account in defining of the fuzzy set A. A solution for this is by using modal operators $\Box$ and $\Diamond$, and results in an interval-valued fuzzy set defined as follows

$$\mu_A(x) = \left[\sum_{i=1}^{n} \Omega(w_i)V_D(w_i, \Box a_x), \sum_{i=1}^{n} \Omega(w_i)V_D(w_i, \Diamond a_x) \right].$$

In the next subsection we deal with the general case where composed fuzzy sets which represent linguistic combinations of linguistic terms of several context models are considered.

3.2   General Case

It should be emphasized that Kruse et al. (1993) considered the same set of contexts for many domains of concern. While this assumption is acceptable in the framework of fuzzy data analysis where the characteristics (attributes) of observed objects are considered simultaneously in the same contexts, it may not be longer suitable for fuzzy concept analysis. For example, let us consider two attributes *Height* and *Income* of a set of people. Then, a set of contexts used for formulating of vague concepts of the attribute *Height* may be given as in the preceding subsection; while another set of contexts for formulating of vague concepts of the attribute *Income* (like *high*, *low*, etc.), may be given as a set of kinds of employees or a set of residential areas of employees.

Given two context models $\mathcal{C}_i = \langle D_i, C_i, A_{C_i}(D_i) \rangle$ defined on D_i, for $i = 1, 2$, respectively. A pair $(x, y) \in D_1 \times D_2$ is then interpreted as the pair of values of two attributes at_1 and at_2 for objects of concern. Recall that each element in $A_{C_i}(D_i)$ is a linguistic term understood as a mapping from $C_i \to 2^{D_i}$. Assume that $\mid C_i \mid = n_i$, for $i = 1, 2$.

We now define a unified Kripke model as follows: $M = \langle W, R, V, \Omega \rangle$, where $W = C_1 \times C_2$, R is the identity relation on W, and

$$\Omega : C_1 \times C_2 \to [0, 1]$$
$$(c_i^1, c_j^2) \mapsto \omega_{ij} = \omega_i \omega_j.$$

where the simplified notations $\Omega(c_i^1, c_j^2) = \omega_{ij}, \Omega_1(c_i^1) = \omega_i, \Omega_2(c_j^2) = \omega_j$ are used.

For $a_i \in A_{C_i}(D_i)$, for $i = 1, 2$, we now formulate composed fuzzy sets, which represent combined linguistic terms like "a_1 *and* a_2" and "a_1 *or* a_2" within model M.

For simplicity of notation, let us denote O a set of objects of concern which we may apply for two attributes at_1, at_2 those values range on domains D_1 and D_2, respectively. Then instead of considering fuzzy sets defined on different domains, we can consider fuzzy sets defined only on a universal set, the set of objects O. As such, we now consider atomic propositions of the form

$$a_o : \text{``An object } o \text{ is in relation to a linguistic term } a\text{''}$$

where $a \in A_{C_1}(D_1) \cup A_{C_2}(D_2)$ or a is a linguistic combination of linguistic terms in $A_{C_1}(D_1) \cup A_{C_2}(D_2)$.

Notice that this constructive formulation of composed fuzzy sets is comparable with the notion of the translation of a proposition a_o into a *relational assignment equation* introduced by Zadeh (1978).

Single Term Case. Firstly we consider the case where $a \in A_{C_1}(D_1)$. For this case, we define the valuation function V in M for atomic propositions a_o by

$$V((c_i^1, c_j^2), a_o) = \begin{cases} 1 & \text{if } at_1(o) \in a(c_i^1), \\ 0 & \text{otherwise,} \end{cases}$$

where $at_1(o) \in D_1$ denotes the value of attribute at_1 for object o.

Then the fuzzy set A which represents the meaning of the linguistic term a is defined in the model M as follows

$$\mu_A^M(o) = \sum_{i=1}^{n_1} \sum_{j=1}^{n_2} w_{ij} V((c_i^1, c_j^2), a_o) \tag{7}$$

Set $W' = \{(c_i^1, c_j^2) \in C_1 \times C_2 \mid V((c_i^1, c_j^2), a_o) = 1\}$. It follows by definition of V that $W' = C_1' \times C_2$, where $C_1' = \{c_i^1 \in C_1 \mid at_1(o) \in a(c_i^1)\}$. Thus, we have

Proposition 3.2. *For any $o \in O$, we have $\mu_A^M(o) = \mu_A^{M_1}(o)$, where $\mu_A^{M_1}(o)$ is represented by $\mu_A^{M_1}(at_1(o))$ as in the preceding subsection.*

A similar result also holds for the case where $a \in A_{C_2}(D_2)$.

Composed Term Case. We now consider for the case where a is a composed linguistic term which is of the form like "a_1 *and* a_2" and "a_1 *or* a_2", where $a_i \in A_{C_i}(D_i)$, for $i = 1, 2$. To formulate the composed fuzzy set A corresponding to the term a in the model M, we need to define the valuation function V for propositions a_o. It is natural to express a_o by

$$a_o = \begin{cases} a_{1,o} \vee a_{2,o} & \text{if } a \text{ is "} a_1 \text{ or } a_2 \text{"} \\ a_{1,o} \wedge a_{2,o} & \text{if } a \text{ is "} a_1 \text{ and } a_2 \text{"}. \end{cases}$$

where $a_{i,o}$, for $i = 1, 2$, are propositions of the form

$$a_{i,o} : \text{"An object } o \text{ is in relation to a linguistic term } a_i.\text{"}$$

Consider the case where a is "a_1 *or* a_2". Then, the valuation function V for propositions a_o is defined as follows

$$V((c_i^1, c_j^2), a_{1,o} \vee a_{2,o}) = \begin{cases} 1 & \text{if } at_1(o) \in a_1(c_i^1) \vee at_2(o) \in a_2(c_j^2) \\ 0 & \text{otherwise.} \end{cases}$$

With this notation, we define the compatible degree of any object $o \in O$ to the composed linguistic term "a_1 *or* a_2" in the model M by

$$\mu_A(o) = \mu_{A_1 \cup A_2}(o) = \sum_{i=1}^{n_1} \sum_{j=1}^{n_2} w_{ij} V((c_i^1, c_j^2), a_{1,o} \vee a_{2,o}) \tag{8}$$

where A_1, A_2 denote fuzzy sets which represent component linguistic terms a_1, a_2, respectively.

Similar for the case where a is "a_1 *and* a_2". The valuation function V for propositions a_o is then defined as follows

$$V((c_i^1, c_j^2), a_{1,o} \wedge a_{2,o}) = \begin{cases} 1 & \text{if } at_1(o) \in a_1(c_i^1) \wedge at_2(o) \in a_2(c_j^2) \\ 0 & \text{otherwise,} \end{cases}$$

and the compatible degree of any object $o \in O$ to the composed linguistic term "a_1 and a_2" in the model M is defined by

$$\mu_A(o) = \mu_{A_1 \cap A_2}(o) = \sum_{i=1}^{n_1} \sum_{j=1}^{n_2} w_{ij} V((c_i^1, c_j^2), a_{1,o} \wedge a_{2,o}) \qquad (9)$$

Notice that in the case without the weighting function Ω in the model M, the membership expressions of composed fuzzy sets defined in (8) and (9) are comparable with those given by Resconi and Turksen (2001).

Now we examine the behaviours of operators $\cup, \cap$ in this formulation. Let us denote by

$$C_1' = \{c_i^1 \in C_1 \mid at_1(o) \in a_1(c_i^1)\},$$
$$C_2' = \{c_j^2 \in C_2 \mid at_2(o) \in a_2(c_j^2)\}.$$

It is easy to see that

$$V((c_i^1, c_j^2), (a_{1,o} \vee a_{2,o})) = \begin{cases} 1 & \text{if } (c_i^1, c_j^2) \in (C_1' \times C_2 \cup C_1 \times C_2'), \\ 0 & \text{otherwise,} \end{cases} \qquad (10)$$

$$V((c_i^1, c_j^2), (a_{1,o} \wedge a_{2,o})) = \begin{cases} 1 & \text{if } (c_i^1, c_j^2) \in (C_1' \times C_2'), \\ 0 & \text{otherwise.} \end{cases} \qquad (11)$$

Furthermore, we have the following representation

$$(C_1' \times C_2 \cup C_1 \times C_2') = (C_1' \times C_2 \uplus C_1 \times C_2') \setminus (C_1' \times C_2') \qquad (12)$$

where $\uplus$ denotes an joint union which permits an iterative appearance of elements.

It is immediately to follow from (8)–(12) and Proposition 3.2 that

Proposition 3.3. *For any $o \in O$, we have*

$$\mu_{A_1 \cap A_2}(o) = \mu_{A_1}(o)\mu_{A_2}(o) \qquad (13)$$
$$\mu_{A_1 \cup A_2}(o) = \mu_{A_1}(o) + \mu_{A_2}(o) - \mu_{A_1}(o)\mu_{A_2}(o) \qquad (14)$$

Expressions (13) and (14) show that fuzzy intersection and fuzzy union operators by this model are truth-functional, and, moreover, they form a well-known dual pair of *Product t-norm T_P* and *Probabilistic Sum t-conorm S_P* (Klement 1997).

4   Conclusions

A context model for constructing membership functions of fuzzy concepts based on modal logic has been proposed in this paper. It has been shown that fuzzy intersection and fuzzy union operators by this model are truth-functional, and, more precisely, they form a well-known dual pair of Product t-norm T_P and

Probabilistic Sum t-conorm S_P, respectively. It is worthwhile to note that for the purpose of finding new operators for using in the fuzzy expert system shell FLOPS, Buckley and Siler (1998) have used elementary statistical calculations on binary data for the truth of two fuzzy propositions to present new t-norm and t-conorm for computing the truth of AND, and OR propositions. Furthermore, their t-norm and t-conorm are also reduced to Product t-norm T_P and Probabilistic Sum t-conorm S_P in the case that the sample correlation coefficient equals to 0.

It should be worthwhile to note that the proposal in this paper can be developed as a method for evaluating queries, which contain vague predicates, in databases as well as for constructing membership functions for fuzzy concepts in mining fuzzy association rules from databases (Hong et al. 1999; Kuok et al. 1998). These problems are being the subject of our further work.

Acknowledgments

The authors would like to thank the anonymous referees for their very constructive comments. The first author is supported by Inoue Foundation for Science under a postdoctoral fellowship.

References

1998. J.J. Buckley & W. Siler, A new t-norm, *Fuzzy Sets and Systems* **100** (1998) 283–290.

1980. B.F. Chellas, *Modal Logic: An Introduction*, Cambridge University Press, 1980.

1987. D. Dubois & H. Prade, *Possibility Theory – An Approach to Computerized Processing of Uncertainty*, Plenum Press, New York, 1987.

1999. B. Ganter & R. Wille, *Formal Concept Analysis: Mathematical Foundations*, Springer-Verlag, Berlin Heidelberg, 1999.

1993. J. Gebhardt & R. Kruse, The context model: An integrating view of vagueness and uncertainty, *International Journal of Approximate Reasoning* **9** (1993) 283–314.

1998. J. Gebhardt & R. Kruse, Parallel combination of information sources, in D.M. Gabbay & P. Smets (Eds.), *Handbook of Defeasible Reasoning and Uncertainty Management Systems*, Vol. 3 (Kluwer, Doordrecht, The Netherlands, 1998) 393–439.

2000. J. Gebhardt, Learning from data – Possibilistic graphical models, in D.M. Gabbay & P. Smets (Eds.), *Handbook of Defeasible Reasoning and Uncertainty Management Systems*, Vol. 4 (Kluwer, Doordrecht, The Netherlands, 2000) 314–389.

1994. D. Harmanec, G. Klir & G. Resconi, On modal logic interpretation of Dempster-Shafer theory of evidence, *International Journal of Intelligent Systems* **9** (1994) 941–951.

1996. D. Harmanec, G. Klir & Z. Wang, Modal logic interpretation of Demspter-Shafer theory: an infinite case, *International Journal of Approximate Reasoning* **14** (1996) 81–93.

1999. T-P Hong, C-S Kuo & S-C Chi, Mining association rules from quantitative data, *Intelligent Data Analysis* **3** (1999) 363–376.

2001. V.N. Huynh & Y. Nakamori, Fuzzy concept formation based on context model, in: N. Baba et al. (Eds.), *Knowledge-Based Intelligent Information Engineering Systems & Allied Technologies* (IOS Press, 2001), pp. 687–691.

1997. E.P. Klement, Some mathematical aspects of fuzzy sets: Triangular norms, fuzzy logics, and generalized measures, *Fuzzy Sets and Systems* **90** (1997) 133–140.

1994. G. Klir, Multi-valued logic versus modal logic: alternate framework for uncertainty modelling, in: P.P. Wang (Ed.), *Advances in Fuzzy Theory and Technology*, vol. II, Duke University Press, Durham, NC, 1994, pp. 3–47.

1995. G. Klir & B. Yuan, *Fuzzy Sets and Fuzzy Logic: Theory and Applications*, Prentice-Hall PTR, Upper Saddle River, NJ, 1995.

1994. G. Klir & D. Harmanec, On modal logic interpretation of possibility theory, *International Journal of Uncertainty, Fuzziness and Knowledge-Based Systems* **2** (1994) 237–245.

1997. G. Klir, Z. Wang & D. Harmanec, Constructing fuzzy measures in expert systems, *Fuzzy Sets and Systems* **92** (1997) 251–264.

1993. R. Kruse, J. Gebhardt & F. Klawonn, Numerical and logical approaches to fuzzy set theory by the context model, in: R. Lowen and M. Roubens (Eds.), *Fuzzy Logic: State of the Art*, Kluwer Academic Publishers, Dordrecht, 1993, pp. 365–376.

1998. C. M. Kuok, Ada Fu, M. H. Wong, Mining Fuzzy Association Rules in Databases, *ACM SIGMOD Records* **27** (1998) 41–46.

1992. G. Resconi, G. Klir & U. St. Clair, Hierarchically uncertainty metatheory based upon modal logic, *International Journal of General Systems* **21** (1992) 23–50.

1993. G. Resconi, G. Klir, U. St. Clair & D. Harmanec, On the integration of uncertainty theories, *International Journal of Uncertainty, Fuzziness and Knowledge-Based Systems* **1** (1) (1993) 1–18.

1996. G. Resconi, G. Klir, D. Harmanec & U. St. Clair, Interpretations of various uncertainty theories using models of modal logic: a summary, *Fuzzy Sets and Systems* **80** (1996) 7–14.

2001. G. Resconi & I. B. Turksen, Canonical forms of fuzzy truthoods by meta-theory based upon modal logic, *Information Sciences* **131** (2001) 157–194.

1987. G. Shafer, *A Mathematical Theory of Evidence* (Princeton University Press, Princeton, 1976).

1965. L.A. Zadeh, Fuzzy sets, *Information and Control* **8** (1965) 338–353.

1975. L. A. Zadeh, The concept of linguistic variable and its application to approximate reasoning, *Information Sciences,* I: **8** (1975) 199–249; II: **8** (1975) 310–357.

1978. L. A. Zadeh, Fuzzy sets as a basis for a theory of possibility, *Fuzzy Sets and Systems* **1** (1978) 3–38.

The Principle of Conditional Preservation in Belief Revision

Gabriele Kern-Isberner

FernUniversität Hagen, Department of Computer Science,
P.O. Box 940, D-58084 Hagen, Germany
gabriele.kern-isberner@fernuni-hagen.de

Abstract. Although the crucial role of if-then-conditionals for the dynamics of knowledge has been known for several decades, they do not seem to fit well in the framework of classical belief revision theory. In particular, the propositional paradigm of minimal change guiding the AGM-postulates of belief revision proved to be inadequate for preserving conditional beliefs under revision. In this paper, we present a thorough axiomatization of a principle of conditional preservation in a very general framework, considering the revision of epistemic states by sets of conditionals. This axiomatization is based on a non-standard approach to conditionals, which focuses on their dynamic aspects, and uses the newly introduced notion of conditional valuation functions as representations of epistemic states. In this way, probabilistic revision as well as possibilistic revision and the revision of ranking functions can all be dealt with within one framework. Moreover, we show that our approach can also be applied in a merely qualitative environment, extending AGM-style revision to properly handling conditional beliefs.

1   Introduction

Knowledge is subject to change, either due to changes in the real world, or by obtaining new findings about the domain under consideration. New information may simply extend the prior knowledge base, or be in conflict with it, in which case its incorporation makes complex revision processes necessary. In any case, the modification of knowledge bases brought about by learning new information may drastically alter the response behavior of knowledge systems to queries; e.g. answers that were meaningful in the context of the prior knowledge base, might become irrelevant or even false in the light of new information.

Belief revision, the theory of dynamics of knowledge, has been mainly concerned with propositional beliefs for a long time. The most basic approach here is the *AGM-theory* presented in the seminal paper [1] as a set of postulates outlining appropriate revision mechanisms in a propositional logical environment. If-then-conditionals, on the other hand, seem to play an ambivalent role in belief revision: Although their dynamic power as *revision policies* has been appreciated (see e.g. [36,5]), Gärdenfors' *triviality result* [16] describes an obvious incompatibility between conditionals and *classical* AGM-approaches. This incompatibility, however, can be resolved by leaving the narrow framework of

T. Eiter and K.-D. Schewe (Eds.): FoIKS 2002, LNCS 2284, pp. 105–129, 2002.

classical logic – first, conditional beliefs must be understood as fundamentally different from propositional beliefs (cf. [31]) and hence be treated differently, and second, instead of focusing on belief sets (i.e. deductively closed propositional theories) containing all certain beliefs, one should consider belief states or epistemic states, respectively, as representations of cognitive states of intelligent agents. Although the close connections between belief revision and conditionals, on the one side, and between belief revision and epistemic orderings, on the other side, has been apparent for many years (cf. [36,19]), it was only quite recently that first approaches extending the AGM-theory to that broader framework have been brought forth: Darwiche and Pearl [8] reformulated the AGM-postulates for revising epistemic states by propositional beliefs and, moreover, they formulated four new postulates dealing explicitly with conditional beliefs. Instead of following the *minimal change paradigm* which guides propositional AGM-revision, Darwiche and Pearl's postulates vaguely outline how to preserve conditional beliefs under propositional revision. In [22], we then presented a complete set of axioms for revising epistemic states by conditional beliefs, extending propositional AGM-revision and covering the postulates of Darwiche and Pearl.

Instead of only regarding the results of belief change, as in AGM-theory, studying belief revision in the framework of epistemic states and conditionals means to observe the very process of belief dynamics. Perhaps the most important consequence of this is that, in overcoming classical borders and peculiarities, it opens up the view to a most general framework which unifies belief revision, nonmonotonic reasoning and inductive representation of complex, conditional knowledge. To be more precise, belief revision and nonmonotonic reasoning can be linked via conditionals in epistemic states in the following way: A nonmonotonically implies B, based on the knowledge given by the epistemic state Ψ, $(A \mathrel{|\!\sim}_\Psi B)$, iff the conditional $(B|A)$ is accepted in Ψ ($\Psi \models (B|A)$) iff revising Ψ by A yields belief in B ($\Psi * A \models B$). Note that here background knowledge represented by Ψ can be taken explicitly into account, in contrast to the purely propositional view in [33]. Furthermore, inductive knowledge representation can be understood as revising a uniform belief state, expressing complete ignorance, by the (conditional) knowledge to be represented.

For these reasons, revising epistemic states by conditional beliefs should not be considered as an artifact, but rather be understood as one of the most fundamental and powerful processes in formal knowledge management. A thorough axiomatization of an appropriate *principle of conditional preservation* in the sense of [8] and [22] will be able to serve as an important guideline for handling those revisions. To this end, we even go one step further: We leave the purely qualitative framework and enter into semi-quantitative (i.e. ordinal) and quantitative (i.e. probabilistic) environments, finding once again that more complex surroundings provide clearer, unifying views. In this paper, *conditional valuation functions* are introduced as quite general representation of epistemic states. Ordinal conditional functions, possibility distributions and probability functions are special instances of conditional valuation functions. We then formalize a most general principle of conditional preservation, dealing with the revision of conditional valuation functions by sets of (quantified) conditional beliefs. This principle is inspired by properties of optimal information-theoretical methods, and hence can be regarded as a most appropriate paradigm to deal with conditional information. As ordinal epistemic states (such as ordinal conditional functions and possibility distributions) also allow a purely qualitative view, we investigate the consequences of this quantitative principle of conditional preservation in a qualitative setting. We show that our quantitative principle of conditional preservation implies the validity of the axioms for conditional belief revision of [22] and hence also provides a high-level formalization of Darwiche and Pearl's ideas [8].

The principle of conditional preservation to be axiomatized in this paper is based on a non-standard theory of conditionals which captures the dynamic effects of establishing conditional relationships within epistemic states. *Conditional structures* make interactions of conditionals transparent and computable – a crucial problem when revising by sets of conditionals. This framework we consider conditionals in not only concerns belief revision, nonmonotonic reasoning and inductive knowledge representation, but also helps unifying qualitative and quantitative approaches. We clearly differentiate between numerical and structural aspects of conditionals, by first building up a formal, algebraic frame for conditionals and then linking this frame to numerical values. It is just this idea of separating structures from numbers that provides a solid basic theory of conditionals with applications in (apparently) very different domains.

This paper is organized as follows: Section 2 contains some formal preliminaries, and here we briefly explain the different types of epistemic states we are going to consider. In Section 3, conditional valuation functions are introduced as basic representations of (semi-)quantitative epistemic states. In Section 4, we present a new, dynamic view on conditionals; in particular, we define the notions of *subconditional* and of *perpendicular conditionals*, which are crucial for formalizing a qualitative principle of conditional preservation in Section 5. Section 6 prepares the axiomatization of the quantitative principle of conditional preservation in Section 7 by explaining *conditional structures* and *conditional indiffrence* . Finally, Section 8 shows that both principles are compatible. Section 9 concludes with highlighting the main results of this paper.

All proofs are omitted for the sake of brevity, but can be found in [27].

2 Conditionals, Epistemic States and Belief Revision

We start with a finitely generated propositional language $\mathcal{L}$, with atoms $a, b, c, \ldots$, and with formulas $A, B, C, \ldots$. For conciseness of notation, we will omit the logical *and*-connector, writing AB instead of $A \wedge B$, and barring formulas will indicate negation, i.e. $\overline{A}$ means $\neg A$. Let Ω denote the set of possible worlds over $\mathcal{L}$; Ω will be taken here simply as the set of all propositional interpretations over $\mathcal{L}$. $\omega \models A$ means that the propositional formula $A \in \mathcal{L}$ holds in the possible world $\omega \in \Omega$.

By introducing a new binary operator $|$, we obtain the set $(\mathcal{L} \mid \mathcal{L}) = \{(B|A) \mid A, B \in \mathcal{L}\}$ of conditionals over $\mathcal{L}$. $(B|A)$ formalizes "*if A then B*" and establishes a plausible, probable, possible etc connection between the *antecedent* A and the *consequent* B. Here, conditionals are supposed not to be nested, that is, antecedent and consequent of a conditional will be propositional formulas.

Conditionals are usually considered within richer structures such as *epistemic states*. Besides certain (logical) knowledge, epistemic states also allow the representation of preferences, beliefs, assumptions etc of an intelligent agent. In a purely qualitative setting, preferences are assumed to be given by an epistemic pre-ordering on $\mathcal{L}$ (reflexive and transitive, but not symmetrical, and mostly induced by pre-orderings on worlds). In a (semi-)quantitative setting, also degrees of plausibility, probability, possibility, necessity etc can be expressed. Here, most widely used representations of epistemic states are

- *probability functions* (or *probability distributions*) $P : \Omega \to [0,1]$ with $\sum_{\omega \in \Omega} P(\omega) = 1$. The probability of a formula $A \in \mathcal{L}$ is given by $P(A) = \sum_{\omega \models A} P(\omega)$. Note that, since $\mathcal{L}$ is finitely generated, Ω is finite, too, and we only need additivity instead of σ-additivity. Conditionals are interpreted via conditional probability, so we have $P(B|A) = \frac{P(AB)}{P(A)}$ for $P(A) > 0$, and $P \models (B|A)[x]$ iff $P(B|A) = x$ ($x \in [0,1]$).
- *ordinal conditional functions, OCFs,* (also called *ranking functions*) $\kappa : \Omega \to \mathbb{N} \cup \{\infty\}$ with $\kappa^{-1}(0) \neq \emptyset$, expressing degrees of plausibility of propositional formulas A by specifying degrees of disbeliefs of their negations $\overline{A}$ (cf. [38]). More formally, we have $\kappa(A) := \min\{\kappa(\omega) \mid \omega \models A\}$, so that $\kappa(A \vee B) = \min\{\kappa(A), \kappa(B)\}$. Hence, at least one of $\kappa(A), \kappa(\overline{A})$ must be 0. A proposition A is believed if $\kappa(\overline{A}) > 0$ (which implies particularly $\kappa(A) = 0$). Degrees of plausibility can also be assigned to conditionals by setting $\kappa(B|A) = \kappa(AB) - \kappa(A)$. A conditional $(B|A)$ is accepted in the epistemic state represented by κ, or κ *satisfies* $(B|A)$, written as $\kappa \models (B|A)$, iff $\kappa(AB) < \kappa(A\overline{B})$, i.e. iff AB is more plausible than $A\overline{B}$. We can also specify a numerical degree of plausibility of a conditional by defining $\kappa \models (B|A)[n]$ iff $\kappa(AB) + n < \kappa(A\overline{B})$ ($n \in \mathbb{N}$). OCF's are the qualitative counterpart of probability distributions. Their plausibility degrees may be taken as order-of-magnitude abstractions of probabilities (cf. [17,18]).
- *possibility distributions* $\pi : \Omega \to [0,1]$ with $\max_{\omega \in \Omega} \pi(\omega) = 1$. Each possibility distribution induces a *possibility measure* on $\mathcal{L}$ via $\pi(A) := \max_{\omega \models A} \pi(\omega)$. Since the correspondence between possibility distributions and possibility measures is straightforward and one-to-one, we will not distinguish between them. A *necessity measure* N_π can also be based on π by setting $N_\pi(A) := 1 - \pi(\overline{A})$. Possibility measures and necessity measures are dual, so it is sufficient to know only one of them. Furthermore, a possibility degree can also be assigned to a conditional $(B|A)$ by setting $\pi(B|A) = \frac{\pi(AB)}{\pi(A)}$, in full analogy to Bayesian conditioning in probability theory. Note that we also make use of the product operation in $[0,1]$. That means, that our approach is not only based upon comparing numbers, but also takes relations between numbers into account. These numerical relationships encode important information about the (relative) strength of conditionals which proves to be particularly crucial for representation and revision tasks. This amounts to

carrying over Spohn's argumentation in [38] to a possibilistic framework (see also [23] and [3]).

A conditional $(B|A)$ *is accepted in* π, $\pi \models (B|A)$, iff $\pi(AB) > \pi(A\overline{B})$ (which is equivalent to $\pi(\overline{B}|A) < 1$ and $N_\pi(B|A) = 1 - \pi(\overline{B}|A) > 0$) (cf. [12]). So, in accordance with intuition, a conditional $(B|A)$ is accepted in the epistemic state modeled by a possibility distribution, if its confirmation (AB) is considered to be more possible (or plausible) than its refutation $(A\overline{B})$. This definition can be generalized by saying that π *accepts* $(B|A)$ *with degree* $x \in (0,1]$, $\pi \models (B|A) [x]$, iff $N_\pi(B|A) \geqslant x$ iff $\pi(A\overline{B}) \leqslant (1-x)\pi(AB)$. Possibility distributions are similar to ordinal conditional functions (cf. [2]), but realize degrees of possibility (or plausibility) in a non-discrete, compact domain. They can be taken as fuzzy representations of epistemic states (cf. [30,11]), and are closely related to belief functions (cf. [4]).

With each epistemic state Ψ (either qualitative or (semi-)quantitative) one can associate the set $Bel(\Psi) = \{A \in \mathcal{L} \mid \Psi \models A\}$ of those beliefs the agent accepts as most plausible. $Bel(\Psi)$ is supposed to consist of formulas (or to be a formula, respectively) of $\mathcal{L}$ and hence is subject to classical belief revision theory which investigates the changing of propositional beliefs when new information becomes evident. Here, most important work has been done by Alchourron, Gärdenfors and Makinson in presenting in [1] a catalogue of postulates (the so-called *AGM-postulates*) which a well-behaved revision operator $*$ should obey. The revision of epistemic states, however, cannot be reduced to propositional revision, for two reasons: First, two *diffrent* epistemic states Ψ_1, Ψ_2 may have *equivalent* belief sets $Bel(\Psi_1) \equiv Bel(\Psi_2)$. Thus an epistemic state is not described uniquely by its belief set, and revising Ψ_1 and Ψ_2 by new (propositional) information A may result in different revised belief sets $Bel(\Psi_1 * A) \not\equiv Bel(\Psi_2 * A)$. Second, epistemic states may represent different kinds of beliefs, and beliefs on different levels of acceptance. So "information" in the context of epistemic state must be understood as a much more complex concept than provided by the propositional framework. Incorporating new information in an epistemic state means, for instance, to change degrees of plausibility, or to establish a new conditional relationship. Nevertheless, the revision of Ψ by $A \in \mathcal{L}$ also yields a revised belief set $Bel(\Psi * A) \subseteq \mathcal{L}$, and of course, this revision should obey the standards of the AGM theory. So, Darwiche and Pearl have reformulated the AGM-postulates for belief revision so as to comply with the framework of epistemic states (cf. [8]):

Suppose Ψ, Ψ_1, Ψ_2 to be epistemic states and $A, A_1, A_2, B \in \mathcal{L}$;

(R*1) A is believed in $\Psi * A$: $Bel(\Psi * A) \models A$.
(R*2) If $Bel(\Psi) \wedge A$ is satisfiable, then $Bel(\Psi * A) \equiv Bel(\Psi) \wedge A$.
(R*3) If A is satisfiable, then $Bel(\Psi * A)$ is also satisfiable.
(R*4) If $\Psi_1 = \Psi_2$ and $A_1 \equiv A_2$, then $Bel(\Psi_1 * A_1) \equiv Bel(\Psi_2 * A_2)$.
(R*5) $Bel(\Psi * A) \wedge B$ implies $Bel(\Psi * (A \wedge B))$.
(R*6) If $Bel(\Psi * A) \wedge B$ is satisfiable then $Bel(\Psi * (A \wedge B))$ implies $Bel(\Psi * A) \wedge B$.

Epistemic states, conditionals and revision are related by the so-called *Ramsey test*, according to which a conditional $(B|A)$ is accepted in an epistemic state Ψ, iff revising Ψ by A yields belief in B:

$$\Psi \models (B|A) \quad \text{iff } \Psi * A \models B. \tag{1}$$

The Ramsey test can be generalized for quantified beliefs and conditionals in a straightforward way:

$$\Psi \models (B|A)\,[x] \quad \text{iff } \Psi * A \models B\,[x].$$

In this paper, we will consider quantified as well as unquantified (structural) conditionals, where the quantifications are taken from the proper domain ($[0, 1]$ or $\mathbb{N} \cup \{\infty\}$, respectively). If $\mathcal{R}^* = \{(B_1|A_1)\,[x_1], \ldots, (B_n|A_n)\,[x_n]\}$ is a set of quantified conditionals, then $\mathcal{R} = \{(B_1|A_1), \ldots, (B_n|A_n)\}$ will be its structural counterpart and vice versa.

3   Conditional Valuation Functions

What is common to probability functions, ordinal conditional functions, and possibility measures is, that they make use of *two diffrent operations* to handle both purely propositional information and conditionals adequately. Therefore, we will introduce the abstract notion of a conditional valuation function to reveal more clearly and uniformly the way in which (conditional) knowledge may be represented and treated within epistemic states. As an adequate structure, we assume an algebra $\mathcal{A} = (\mathcal{A}, \oplus, \odot, 0^{\mathcal{A}}, 1^{\mathcal{A}})$ of real numbers to be equipped with two operations, $\oplus$ and $\odot$, such that

- $(\mathcal{A}, \oplus)$ is an associative and commutative structure with neutral element $0^{\mathcal{A}}$;
- $(\mathcal{A} - \{0^{\mathcal{A}}\}, \odot)$ is a commutative group with neutral element $1^{\mathcal{A}}$;
- the rule of distributivity holds, i.e. $x \odot (y \oplus z) = (x \odot y) \oplus (x \odot z)$ for $x, y, z \in \mathcal{A}$;
- $\mathcal{A}$ is totally ordered by $\leqslant_{\mathcal{A}}$ which is compatible with $\oplus$ and $\odot$ in that $x \leqslant_{\mathcal{A}} y$ implies both $x \oplus z \leqslant_{\mathcal{A}} y \oplus z$ and $x \odot z \leqslant_{\mathcal{A}} y \odot z$ for all $x, y, z \in \mathcal{A}$.

So $\mathcal{A}$ is close to be an ordered field, except that the elements of $\mathcal{A}$ need not be invertible with respect to $\oplus$.

Definition 3.1 (conditional valuation function). *A conditional valuation function is a function $V : \mathcal{L} \to \mathcal{A}$ from the set $\mathcal{L}$ of formulas into the algebra $\mathcal{A}$ satisfying the following conditions:*

1. *$V(\bot) = 0^{\mathcal{A}}, V(\top) = 1^{\mathcal{A}}$, and for exclusive formulas A, B (i.e. $AB \equiv \bot$), we have $V(A \vee B) = V(A) \oplus V(B)$;*
2. *for each conditional $(B|A) \in (\mathcal{L} \mid \mathcal{L})$ with $V(A) \neq 0^{\mathcal{A}}$, $V(B|A) = V(AB) \odot V(A)^{-1}$, where $V(A)^{-1}$ is the $\odot$-inverse element of $V(A)$ in $\mathcal{A}$.*

Conditional valuation functions assign degrees of certainty, plausibility, possibility etc to propositional formulas and to conditionals. Making use of two operations, they provide a framework for considering and treating conditional knowledge as fundamentally different from propositional knowledge, a point that is stressed by various authors and that seems to be indispensable for representing epistemic states adequately (cf. [8]). There is, however, a close relationship between propositions (facts) and conditionals – facts may be considered as conditionals of a degenerate form by identifying A with $(A|\top)$: Indeed, we have $V(A|\top) = V(A) \odot (1^V)^{-1} = V(A)$. Therefore, conditionals should be regarded as extending propositional knowledge by a new dimension.

For each conditional valuation function V, we have $V(A) = \sum_{\omega \models A}^{\oplus} V(\omega)$, so V is determined uniquely by its values on interpretations or on possible worlds, respectively, and we will also write $V : \Omega \to \mathcal{A}$. For all $A \in \mathcal{A}$, we have $0^{\mathcal{A}} \leqslant_{\mathcal{A}} V(A) \leqslant_{\mathcal{A}} 1^{\mathcal{A}}$. It is easy to see that any conditional valuation function $V : \mathcal{L} \to \mathcal{A}$ is a *plausibility measure*, in the sense of Friedman and Halpern, ([15,14]), that is, it fulfills $V(\bot) \leqslant_{\mathcal{A}} V(A)$ for all $A \in \mathcal{L}$, and $A \models B$ implies $V(A) \leqslant_{\mathcal{A}} V(B)$.

A notion which is well-known from probability theory may be generalized for conditional valuation functions: A conditional valuation function V is said to be *uniform* if $V(\omega) = V(\omega')$ for all worlds ω, ω', i.e. if it assigns the same degree of plausibility to each world.

The following examples show that the newly introduced notion of a conditional valuation function indeed covers probability functions, ordinal conditional functions and possibility distributions:

Example 3.1. Each *probability function* P may be taken as a conditional valuation function $P : \Omega \to (\mathbb{R}^+, +, \cdot, 0, 1)$, where $\mathbb{R}^+$ denotes the set of all nonnegative real numbers. Conversely, each conditional valuation function $V : \Omega \to (\mathbb{R}^+, +, \cdot, 0, 1)$ is a probability function.

Similarly, each *ordinal conditional function* κ is a conditional valuation function $\kappa : \Omega \to (\mathbb{Z} \cup \{\infty\}, \min, +, \infty, 0)$, where $\mathbb{Z}$ denotes the set of all integers, and any *possibility measure* π can be regarded as a conditional valuation function $\pi : \Omega \to (\mathbb{R}^+, \max, \cdot, 0, 1)$.

Conditional valuation functions not only provide an abstract means to quantify epistemological attitudes. Their extended ranges allow us to calculate and compare arbitrary proportions of values attached to single worlds. This will prove quite useful to handle complex conditional interrelationships.

By means of a conditional valuation function $V : \mathcal{L} \to \mathcal{A}$, we are able to validate propositional as well as conditional beliefs. We may say, for instance, that proposition A is *believed in* V, $V \models A$, iff $V(A) = 1^{\mathcal{A}}$, or that the conditional $(B|A)$ is *valid* or *accepted in* V, $V \models (B|A)$, iff $V(A) \neq 0^{\mathcal{A}}$ and $V(A\overline{B}) <_{\mathcal{A}} V(AB)$, i.e. iff AB is more plausible (probable, possible etc.) than $A\overline{B}$. In this way, conditional valuation functions are apt to represent epistemic states.

Note that there is a difference between taking a proposition A for granted or to be true, which would be properly expressed by $V(A) = 1^{\mathcal{A}}$, and considering A to be plausible, which amounts to stating $V(A) >_{\mathcal{A}} V(\overline{A})$. It is only from the second point of view, that propositions, A, can be consistently identified with degenerate conditionals, $(A|\top)$. Since belief revision is mostly concerned with revising plausible beliefs by new plausible beliefs, conditionals offer a most adequate framework to study revision methods in, and conditional valuation functions allow us to distinguish between true facts and plausible propositions.

4   A Dynamic View on Conditionals

As it is well-known, a conditional $(B|A)$ is an object of a three-valued nature, partitioning the set of worlds Ω in three parts: those worlds satisfying AB and thus *verifying* the conditional, those worlds satisfying $A\overline{B}$, thus *falsifying* the conditional, and those worlds not fulfilling the premise A and so which the conditional may not be applied to at all. The following representation of $(B|A)$ as a *generalized indicator function* goes back to de Finetti [9]:

$$(B|A)(\omega) = \begin{cases} 1 & : & \omega \models AB \\ 0 & : & \omega \models A\overline{B} \\ u & : & \omega \models \overline{A} \end{cases} \tag{2}$$

where u stands for *unknown* or *indeterminate*. Two conditionals are considered *equivalent* iff the corresponding indicator functions are identical, i.e. $(B|A) \equiv (D|C)$ iff $A \equiv C$ and $AB \equiv CD$ (see e.g. [6]). Usually, equation (2) is applied in a static way, namely, to check if possible worlds verify, or falsify a conditional, or are simply neutral with respect to it. In the context of inductive knowledge representation or belief revision, however, when conditionals are to be learned, it also provides a dynamic view on how to incorporate conditional dependencies adequately in a belief state (which might be the uniform one): The conditional $(B|A)$ distinguishes clearly between verifying, falsifying and neutral worlds, but it does not distinguish between worlds within one and the same of these partitioning sets. So, in order to establish $(B|A)$, if demanded with a suitable degree of certainty, the plausibilities or probabilities of worlds have to be shifted uniformly, depending on to which of the partitioning sets the worlds belong. In this sense, conditionals have effects on possible worlds, taking an active role (like *agents*) in the revision (or representation) process.

   To make things more precise, we define the *verifying set* $(B|A)^+ := Mod(AB)$, and the *falsifying set* $(B|A)^- := Mod(A\overline{B})$ of a conditional $(B|A)$. $Mod(\overline{A})$ is called the *neutral set* of $(B|A)$. Each of these sets may be empty. If $(B|A)^+ = \emptyset$, $(B|A)$ is called *contradictory*, if $(B|A)^- = \emptyset$, $(B|A)$ is called *tautological*, and if $Mod(\overline{A}) = \emptyset$, i.e. A is tautological, $(B|A)$ is called a *fact*. Verifying and falsifying set clearly identify a conditional up to equivalence. Note that, although $(B|A)$ and $(\overline{B}|A)$ induce the same partitioning on Ω, their verifying and falsifying sets are different, in that $(B|A)^+ = (\overline{B}|A)^-$ and $(B|A)^- = (\overline{B}|A)^+$.

Example 4.1. $(\overline{A}|A)$ is a contradictory conditional, $(A|A)$ is tautological and $(A|\top)$ is a fact.

   As usual, propositional formulas $A \in \mathcal{L}$ may be identified with factual conditionals $(A|\top)$. Hence, the results to be presented can be related to the theory of propositional revision, as will be done in Section 5. It should be emphasized, however, that in our framework, $(A|\top)$ should be understood as "A is plausible" or "A is believed", whereas A actually means "A is true". Hence a clear distinction between propositions as *logical* statements and propositions as *epistemic* statements is possible, and is indeed respected in our framework (see [26]).

Next, we introduce the notion of a subconditional:

Definition 4.1 (subconditional, $\sqsubseteq$). *A conditional* $(D|C)$ *is called a* subconditional *of* $(B|A)$, $(D|C) \sqsubseteq (B|A)$, *iff* $(D|C)^+ \subseteq (B|A)^+$ *and* $(D|C)^- \subseteq (B|A)^-$.

The $\sqsubseteq$-relation may be expressed using the standard ordering $\leqslant$ between propositional formulas: $A \leqslant B$ iff $A \models B$, i.e. iff $Mod(A) \subseteq Mod(B)$:

Lemma 4.1. *Let* $(B|A), (D|C) \in (\mathcal{L} \mid \mathcal{L})$. *Then* $(D|C)$ *is a subconditional of* $(B|A)$, $(D|C) \sqsubseteq (B|A)$, *iff* $CD \leqslant AB$ *and* $C\overline{D} \leqslant A\overline{B}$; *in particular, if* $(D|C) \sqsubseteq (B|A)$ *then* $C \leqslant A$.

Thus $(D|C) \sqsubseteq (B|A)$ if the effect of the former conditional on worlds is in line with the latter one, but $(D|C)$ possibly applies to fewer worlds. Furthermore, the well-known equivalence relation for conditionals can also be taken as to be induced by $\sqsubseteq$:

Lemma 4.2. *Two conditionals* $(B|A)$ *and* $(D|C)$ *are equivalent,* $(B|A) \equiv (D|C)$ *iff* $(B|A) \sqsubseteq (D|C)$ *and* $(D|C) \sqsubseteq (B|A)$.

We will now introduce another relation between conditionals that is quite opposite to the subconditional relation and so describes another extreme of possible conditional interaction:

Definition 4.2 (perpendicular conditionals, $\perp\!\!\!\perp$). *Suppose* $(B|A), (D|C) \in (\mathcal{L} \mid \mathcal{L})$ *are two conditionals.* $(D|C)$ *is called* perpendicular *to* $(B|A)$, $(D|C) \perp\!\!\!\perp (B|A)$, *iff either* $Mod\,(C) \subseteq (B|A)^+$, *or* $Mod(C) \subseteq (B|A)^-$, *or* $Mod(C) \subseteq Mod(\overline{A})$, *i.e. iff either* $C \leqslant AB$, *or* $C \leqslant A\overline{B}$, *or* $C \leqslant \overline{A}$.

The perpendicularity relation symbolizes a kind of *irrelevance* of one conditional for another one. We have $(D|C) \perp\!\!\!\perp (B|A)$ if $Mod(C)$, i.e. the range of application of the conditional $(D|C)$, is completely contained in exactly one of the sets $(B|A)^+, (B|A)^-$ or $Mod(\overline{A})$. So for all worlds which $(D|C)$ may be applied to, $(B|A)$ has the same effect and yields no further partitioning. Note, that $\perp\!\!\!\perp$ is not a symmetric relation; $(D|C) \perp\!\!\!\perp (B|A)$ rather expresses that $(D|C)$ is *not affected* by $(B|A)$, or, that $(B|A)$ is *irrelevant* for $(D|C)$.

Example 4.2. Suppose a, b, c are atoms of the language $\mathcal{L}$. Subconditionals of $(b|a)$ are typically obtained by strengthening the antecedent: $(b|ac)$ and $(b|a\overline{c})$ are both subconditionals of $(b|a)$, $(b|ac), (b|a\overline{c}) \sqsubseteq (b|a)$. As an example for perpendicularity, consider the conditionals $(c|ab), (c|a\overline{b})$ and $(c|\overline{a})$ which are all perpendicular to $(b|a)$: $(c|ab), (c|a\overline{b}), (c|\overline{a}) \perp\!\!\!\perp (b|a)$.

It should be remarked that neither $\sqsubseteq$ nor $\perp\!\!\!\perp$ provide new insights for (flat) propositions, when identifying propositions with factual conditionals. It is easily seen that $(B|\top) \sqsubseteq (A|\top)$ if and only if A and B are logically equivalent, and $(B|\top) \perp\!\!\!\perp (A|\top)$ can only hold if A is tautological or contradictory. Both relations need the richer epistemic framework of conditionals to show their usefulness. For a more thorough discussion of the relations $\sqsubseteq$ and $\perp\!\!\!\perp$, see [27].

5   A Principle of Conditional Preservation in a Qualitative Framework

In [8], Darwiche and Pearl discussed the problem of preserving conditional beliefs under (propositional) belief revision in an AGM-environment. They emphasized that conditional beliefs are different in nature from propositional beliefs, and that the *minimal change paradigm* which is crucial for the AGM-theory [1] should not be blindly applied when considering conditionals. They reformulated the AGM-postulates in the richer framework of epistemic states (cf. Section 2) and extended this approach by phrasing four new postulates explicitly dealing with the acceptance of conditionals in epistemic states, in the following denoted as *DP-postulates*:

DP-postulates for conditional preservation:

(C1) If $C \models B$ then $\Psi \models (D \mid C)$ iff $\Psi * B \models (D \mid C)$.
(C2) If $C \models \overline{B}$ then $\Psi \models (D \mid C)$ iff $\Psi * B \models (D \mid C)$.
(C3) If $\Psi \models (B \mid A)$ then $\Psi * B \models (B \mid A)$.
(C4) If $\Psi * B \models (\overline{B} \mid A)$ then $\Psi \models (\overline{B} \mid A)$.

The DP-postulates were supported by plausible arguments and many examples (for a further discussion, see the original paper [8]). They are crucial for handling iterated revisions via the Ramsey test (1). For instance, by applying (1), (C2) can be reformulated to guide iterated revisions, as follows: If $C \models \overline{B}$ then $\Psi * C \models D$ iff $\Psi * B * C \models D$. The DP-postulates are not indisputable. An objection often made is the following: Let $C = \overline{p}$ and $B = pq$ (p, q atoms), such that $C \models \overline{B}$. Then (C2) yields $\Psi * \overline{p} \models D$ iff $\Psi * pq * \overline{p} \models D$, which implies $Bel(\Psi * \overline{p}) = Bel(\Psi * pq * \overline{p})$ – the information conveyed by learning (p and) q has apparently been extinguished when $\overline{p}$ becomes evident. As atoms are assumed to be independent, this seems to be counterintuitive. Actually, this example does not really cast doubt on the DP-postulates, rather it proves the inappropriateness of a strictly propositional framework for belief revision. In such a framework, it is impossible to distinguish between revising by p *and* q, on the one hand, and $p \wedge q \equiv pq$, on the other hand, since sets of formulas are identified with the conjunction of the corresponding formulas. pq, however, suggests an intensional connection between p and q, whereas $\{p, q\}$ does not. Furthermore, (C2) does not demand the equivalence of the involved epistemic states $\Psi * \overline{p}$ and $\Psi * pq * \overline{p}$, but only the identity of the corresponding belief sets (cf. Section 2). Again, this distinction gets lost when focusing on propositional beliefs.

In [22], we considered conditionals under revision in an even broader framework, setting up *postulates for revising epistemic states by conditional beliefs*:

Postulates for conditional revision:

Suppose Ψ is an epistemic state and $(B|A), (D|C)$ are conditionals. Let $\Psi * (B|A)$ denote the result of revising Ψ by a non-contradictory conditional $(B|A)$.

(CR0) $\Psi * (B|A)$ is an epistemic state.
(CR1) $\Psi * (B|A) \models (B|A)$ *(success)*.
(CR2) $\Psi * (B|A) = \Psi$ iff $\Psi \models (B|A)$ *(stability)*.
(CR3) $\Psi * B := \Psi * (B|\top)$ induces a propositional AGM-revision operator.
(CR4) $\Psi * (B|A) = \Psi * (D|C)$ whenever $(B|A) \equiv (D|C)$.
(CR5) If $(D|C) \perp\!\!\!\perp (B|A)$ then $\Psi \models (D|C)$ iff $\Psi * (B|A) \models (D|C)$.
(CR6) If $(D|C) \sqsubseteq (B|A)$ and $\Psi \models (D|C)$ then $\Psi * (B|A) \models (D|C)$.
(CR7) If $(D|C) \sqsubseteq (\overline{B}|A)$ and $\Psi * (B|A) \models (D|C)$ then $\Psi \models (D|C)$.

The postulates (CR0)-(CR2) and (CR4) realize basic ideas of AGM-revision in this more general framework, and (CR3) links conditional belief revision to propositional AGM-revision. (CR5)-(CR7) are the proper axioms to formalize a qualitative principle of conditional preservation. They realize the idea of preserving conditional beliefs by use of the two relations $\sqsubseteq$ and $\perp\!\!\!\perp$, which reflect possible interactions between conditionals. In detail, (CR5) claims that revising by a conditional should preserve all conditionals to which that conditional is irrelevant, in the sense described by the relation $\perp\!\!\!\perp$. The rationale behind this postulate is the following: The validity of a conditional $(B|A)$ in an epistemic state Ψ depends on the relation between (some) worlds in $Mod(AB)$ and (some) worlds in $Mod(A\overline{B})$. So incorporating $(B|A)$ into Ψ may require a shift between $Mod(AB)$ on one side and $Mod(A\overline{B})$ on the other side, but should leave intact any relations between worlds within $Mod(AB)$, $Mod(A\overline{B})$, or $Mod(\overline{A})$. These relations may be captured by conditionals $(D|C)$ not affected by $(B|A)$, that is, by conditionals $(D|C) \perp\!\!\!\perp (B|A)$.

(CR6) states that conditional revision should bring about no change for conditionals that are already in line with the revising conditional, and (CR7) guarantees that no conditional change contrary to the revising conditional is caused by conditional revision.

In particular, by considering a propositional formula as a degenerated conditional with tautological antecedent, each conditional revision operator induces a propositional revision operator, as described by (CR3). For this propositional revision operator, the postulates (CR0)-(CR6) above are trivially fulfilled within an AGM-framework. Postulate (CR7) then reads

(CR7)$^{\textbf{prop}}$ If $\Psi * A \models \overline{A}$, then $\Psi \models \overline{A}$

An AGM-revision operator, obeying the postulate of success and yielding a consistent belief state, as long as the revising proposition A is not inconsistent, would never fulfill the precondition $\Psi * A \models \overline{A}$. Hence (CR7) is vacuous in an AGM-framework. If we only presuppose that $*$ satisfies the AGM-postulate of success, then $\Psi * A \models \overline{A}$ implies the inconsistency of $\Psi * A$, although A is assumed to be non-contradictory. A reasonable explanation for this would be that Ψ itself is inconsistent, in which case it would entail anything, particularly $\Psi \models \overline{A}$ would be fulfilled. The handling of an inconsistent prior belief state is one of the crucial differences between *revision* and *update*, as characterized in [20] by the so-called *KM-postulates*. An AGM-revision demands $\Psi * A$ to be consistent, regardless if the prior state Ψ is inconsistent or not, whereas update does not remedy the inconsistence of a prior state, even if the new information is consistent. So (CR7) would be trivially fulfilled for KM-updates. If we also give up the postulate of success, then (CR7) describes a reasonable behavior of a revision process in an extreme case: A revision should not establish the negation of the revising proposition if this negated proposition is not already implied by the prior belief state.

The following theorem shows that the postulates (CR0)-(CR7) cover the DP-postulates (C1)-(C4):

Theorem 5.1. *Suppose $*$ is a conditional revision operator obeying the postulates (CR0)-(CR7). Then for the induced propositional revision operator, postulates (C1)-(C4) are satisfied, too.*

Therefore, the idea of conditional preservation inherent to the postulates (C1)-(C4) of Darwiche and Pearl ([8]) is indeed captured by our postulates. While (CR0) - (CR4) only serve as basic, unspecific postulates, the last three postulates (CR5)-(CR7) can be taken as properly axiomatizing a *principle of conditional preservation in a qualitative framework*. Moreover, our framework provides further, formal justifications for the DP-postulates by making interactions of conditionals more precise.

6   Conditional Structures and Conditional Indifference

The notion of *conditional structures* has been presented and exemplified in several papers (see, e.g., [25,24,28]). Since they are basic to the results to be obtained in this paper, we will summarize the main ideas and definitions here. The concept of *conditional indiffrence*   has also been a major topic in [25]; in the present paper, however, it is developed in the general framework of conditional valuation functions.

In Section 4, we presented a dynamic approach to conditionals, focusing on the effects of only one conditional in the revision process. When considering sets $\mathcal{R} = \{(B_1|A_1), \ldots, (B_n|A_n)\} \subseteq (\mathcal{L} \mid \mathcal{L})$ of conditionals, the effects each of these conditionals exerts on worlds must be clearly identified. To this end, we replace the numbers 0 and 1 in (2) by formal symbols, one pair of symbols $\mathbf{a}_i^+, \mathbf{a}_i^-$ for each conditional $(B_i|A_i)$ in $\mathcal{R}$, giving rise to the functions $\sigma_i = \sigma_{(B_i|A_i)}, 1 \leqslant i \leqslant n$:

$$\sigma_i(\omega) = \begin{cases} \mathbf{a}_i^+ & \text{if} \quad (B_i|A_i)(\omega) = 1 \\ \mathbf{a}_i^- & \text{if} \quad (B_i|A_i)(\omega) = 0 \\ 1 & \text{if} \quad (B_i|A_i)(\omega) = u \end{cases} \tag{3}$$

$\sigma_i(\omega)$ represents the effects each conditional $(B_i|A_i)$ has on possible worlds ω. To make these conditional effects computable, we make use of a group structure, introducing the *free abelian group* $\mathcal{F}_{\mathcal{R}} = \langle \mathbf{a}_1^+, \mathbf{a}_1^-, \ldots, \mathbf{a}_n^+, \mathbf{a}_n^- \rangle$ with generators $\mathbf{a}_1^+, \mathbf{a}_1^-, \ldots, \mathbf{a}_n^+, \mathbf{a}_n^-$, i.e. $\mathcal{F}_{\mathcal{R}}$ consists of all elements of the form $(\mathbf{a}_1^+)^{r_1}(\mathbf{a}_1^-)^{s_1} \ldots (\mathbf{a}_n^+)^{r_n}(\mathbf{a}_n^-)^{s_n}$ with integers $r_i, s_i \in \mathbb{Z}$ (the ring of integers). Each element of $\mathcal{F}_{\mathcal{R}}$ can be identified by its exponents, so that $\mathcal{F}_{\mathcal{R}}$ is isomorphic to $\mathbb{Z}^{2n}$ (cf. [32,13]). The commutativity of $\mathcal{F}_{\mathcal{R}}$ corresponds to a simultaneous application of the conditionals in $\mathcal{R}$, without assuming any order of application. Note that the neutral element 1 of $\mathcal{F}_{\mathcal{R}}$ is assigned to possible worlds in the neutral sets of the conditionals. The function $\sigma_{\mathcal{R}} = \prod_{1 \leqslant i \leqslant n} \sigma_i : \Omega \to \mathcal{F}_{\mathcal{R}}$, given by

$$\sigma_{\mathcal{R}}(\omega) = \prod_{1 \leqslant i \leqslant n} \sigma_i(\omega) = \prod_{\substack{1 \leqslant i \leqslant n \\ \omega \models A_i B_i}} \mathbf{a}_i^+ \prod_{\substack{1 \leqslant i \leqslant n \\ \omega \models A_i \overline{B}_i}} \mathbf{a}_i^- \tag{4}$$

describes the all-over effect of $\mathcal{R}$ on ω. $\sigma_{\mathcal{R}}(\omega)$ is called *(a representation of) the conditional structure of ω with respect to $\mathcal{R}$*. For each world ω, $\sigma_{\mathcal{R}}(\omega)$ contains at most one of each $\mathbf{a}_i^+$ or $\mathbf{a}_i^-$, but never both of them because each conditional applies to ω in a well-defined way. The following simple example illustrates the notion of conditional structures and shows how to calculate in this framework:

Example 6.1. Let $\mathcal{R} = \{(c|a), (c|b)\}$, where a, b, c are atoms, and let $\mathcal{F}_{\mathcal{R}} = \langle \mathbf{a}_1^+, \mathbf{a}_1^-, \mathbf{a}_2^+, \mathbf{a}_2^- \rangle$. We associate $\mathbf{a}_1^{\pm}$ with the first conditional, $(c|a)$, and $\mathbf{a}_2^{\pm}$ with the second one, $(c|b)$. The following table shows the values of the function $\sigma_{\mathcal{R}}$ on worlds $\omega \in \Omega$:

ω	$\sigma_{\mathcal{R}}(\omega)$	ω	$\sigma_{\mathcal{R}}(\omega)$	ω	$\sigma_{\mathcal{R}}(\omega)$	ω	$\sigma_{\mathcal{R}}(\omega)$
abc	$\mathbf{a}_1^+ \mathbf{a}_2^+$	$\overline{a}bc$	$\mathbf{a}_2^+$	$ab\overline{c}$	$\mathbf{a}_1^- \mathbf{a}_2^-$	$\overline{a}b\overline{c}$	$\mathbf{a}_2^-$
$a\overline{b}c$	$\mathbf{a}_1^+$	$\overline{a}\overline{b}c$	1	$a\overline{b}\overline{c}$	$\mathbf{a}_1^-$	$\overline{a}\overline{b}\overline{c}$	1

We find that $\dfrac{\sigma_{\mathcal{R}}(abc)\sigma_{\mathcal{R}}(\overline{a}\overline{b}c)}{\sigma_{\mathcal{R}}(a\overline{b}c)\sigma_{\mathcal{R}}(\overline{a}bc)} = \dfrac{\mathbf{a}_1^+ \mathbf{a}_2^+ \cdot 1}{\mathbf{a}_1^+ \cdot \mathbf{a}_2^+} = 1$, which may be interpreted by stating that the sets of worlds $\{abc, \overline{a}\overline{b}c\}$ and $\{a\overline{b}c, \overline{a}bc\}$ are balanced with respect to the effects of the conditionals in $\mathcal{R}$.

To comply with the group theoretical structure of $\mathcal{F}_{\mathcal{R}}$, we also impose a multiplication on Ω, introducing the free abelian group $\widehat{\Omega} := \langle \omega \mid \omega \in \Omega \rangle$ generated by all $\omega \in \Omega$, and consisting of all products $\widehat{\omega} = \omega_1^{r_1} \ldots \omega_m^{r_m}$ with $\omega_1, \ldots, \omega_m \in \Omega$, and integers $r_1, \ldots r_m$. Now $\sigma_{\mathcal{R}}$ may be extended to $\widehat{\Omega}$ in a straightforward manner by setting

$$\sigma_{\mathcal{R}}(\omega_1^{r_1} \ldots \omega_m^{r_m}) = \sigma_{\mathcal{R}}(\omega_1)^{r_1} \ldots \sigma_{\mathcal{R}}(\omega_m)^{r_m},$$

yielding a *homomorphism of groups* $\sigma_{\mathcal{R}} : \widehat{\Omega} \to \mathcal{F}_{\mathcal{R}}$. We will often use fractional representations for the elements of $\widehat{\Omega}$, that is, for instance, we will write $\dfrac{\omega_1}{\omega_2}$ instead of $\omega_1 \omega_2^{-1}$. Having the same conditional structure defines an equivalence relation $\equiv_{\mathcal{R}}$ on $\widehat{\Omega}$: $\widehat{\omega}_1 \equiv_{\mathcal{R}} \widehat{\omega}_2$ iff $\sigma_{\mathcal{R}}(\widehat{\omega}_1) = \sigma_{\mathcal{R}}(\widehat{\omega}_2)$ The equivalence classes are in one-to-one correspondence to the elements of the quotient group $\widehat{\Omega}/_{ker\,\sigma_{\mathcal{R}}} = \{\widehat{\omega} \cdot$

$(ker\ \sigma_{\mathcal{R}}) \mid \widehat{\omega} \in \widehat{\Omega}\}$, where $ker\ \sigma_{\mathcal{R}} := \{\widehat{\omega} \in \widehat{\Omega} \mid \sigma_{\mathcal{R}}(\widehat{\omega}) = 1\}$ denotes the kernel of the homomorphism $\sigma_{\mathcal{R}}$, since $\widehat{\omega}_1 \equiv_{\mathcal{R}} \widehat{\omega}_2$ iff $\widehat{\omega}_1 \widehat{\omega}_2^{-1} \in ker\ \sigma_{\mathcal{R}}$. Therefore, the kernel plays an important role in identifying conditional structures. It contains exactly all group elements $\widehat{\omega} \in \widehat{\Omega}$ with a balanced conditional structure, that means, where all effects of conditionals in $\mathcal{R}$ on worlds occurring in $\widehat{\omega}$ are completely cancelled. For instance, in Example 6.1 above, the element $\dfrac{abc \cdot \overline{a}\overline{b}c}{\overline{a}\overline{b}c \cdot \overline{a}bc}$ is an element of the kernel of $\sigma_{\mathcal{R}}$.

Besides the conditional information in $\mathcal{R}$ (or $\mathcal{R}^*$, if one is concerned with quantified conditionals), one usually has to take normalization constraints such as $P(\top) = 1$ for probability distributions P, or $\kappa(\top) = 0$ for ordinal conditional functions κ, or $\pi(\top) = 1$ for possibility distributions π, into regard. This is done by focusing on the subgroup

$$\widehat{\Omega}_0 = ker\ \sigma_{(\top|\top)} = \{\widehat{\omega} = \omega_1{}^{r_1} \cdot \ldots \cdot \omega_m{}^{r_m} \in \widehat{\Omega} \mid \sum_{j=1}^{m} r_j = 0\}$$

of $\widehat{\Omega}$. Two elements $\widehat{\omega}_1 = \omega_1^{r_1} \ldots \omega_m^{r_m}$, $\widehat{\omega}_2 = \nu_1^{s_1} \ldots \nu_p^{s_p} \in \widehat{\Omega}$ are *equivalent modulo* $\widehat{\Omega}_0$, $\widehat{\omega}_1 \equiv_{\top} \widehat{\omega}_2$, iff $\widehat{\omega}_1 \widehat{\Omega}_0 = \widehat{\omega}_2 \widehat{\Omega}_0$, iff $\sum_{1 \leqslant j \leqslant m} r_j = \sum_{1 \leqslant k \leqslant p} s_k$. This means that $\widehat{\omega}_1 \equiv_{\top} \widehat{\omega}_2$ iff they both are a (cancelled) product of the same number of generators ω, each generator being counted with its corresponding exponent. Let $ker_0\ \sigma_{\mathcal{R}} := ker\ \sigma_{\mathcal{R}} \cap \widehat{\Omega}_0$ be the part of $ker\ \sigma_{\mathcal{R}}$ which is included in $\widehat{\Omega}_0$.

Finally, we will show how to describe the relations $\sqsubseteq$ and $\perp\!\!\!\perp$ between conditionals, introduced in Definitions 4.1 and 4.2, respectively, by considering the kernels of the corresponding σ-homomorphisms. As a convenient notation, for each proposition $A \in \mathcal{L}$, we define $\widehat{A} := \{\widehat{\omega} = \omega_1^{r_1} \ldots \omega_m^{r_m} \in \widehat{\Omega} \mid \omega_i \models A \text{ for all } i, 1 \leqslant i \leqslant m\}$.

Proposition 6.1. *Let* $(B|A), (D|C) \in (\mathcal{L} \mid \mathcal{L})$ *be conditionals.*

1. *$(D|C)$ is either a subconditional of $(B|A)$ or of $(\overline{B}|A)$ iff $C \leqslant A$ and $ker\ \sigma_{(D|C)} \cap \widehat{C} \subseteq ker\ \sigma_{(B|A)} \cap \widehat{C}$.*
2. *$(D|C) \perp\!\!\!\perp (B|A)$ iff $\widehat{C} \cap \widehat{\Omega}_0 \subseteq ker\ \sigma_{(B|A)}$.*

To study conditional interactions, we now focus on the behavior of conditional valuation functions $V : \mathcal{L} \to \mathcal{A}$ with respect to the "multiplication" $\odot$ in $\mathcal{A}$ (see Definition 3.1). Each such function may be extended to a homomorphism $V : \widehat{\Omega}_+ \to (\mathcal{A}, \odot)$ by setting $V(\omega_1^{r_1} \cdot \ldots \cdot \omega_m^{r_m}) = V(\omega_1)^{r_1} \odot \ldots \odot V(\omega_m)^{r_m}$, where $\widehat{\Omega}_+$ is the subgroup of $\widehat{\Omega}$ generated by the set $\Omega_+ := \{\omega \in \Omega \mid V(\omega) \neq 0^{\mathcal{A}}\}$. This allows us to analyze numerical relationships holding between different $V(\omega)$. Thereby, it will be possible to elaborate the conditionals whose structures V follows, that means, to determine sets of conditionals $\mathcal{R} \subseteq (\mathcal{L} \mid \mathcal{L})$ with respect to which V is *indifferent* :

Definition 6.1 (indifference wrt $\mathcal{R}$). *Suppose $V : \mathcal{L} \to \mathcal{A}$ is a conditional valuation function and $\mathcal{R} \subseteq (\mathcal{L} \mid \mathcal{L})$ is a set of conditionals such that $V(A) \neq 0^{\mathcal{A}}$ for all $(B|A) \in \mathcal{R}$.*

V is indifferent with respect to $\mathcal{R}$ iffthe following two conditions hold:

(i) If $V(\omega) = 0^{\mathcal{A}}$ then there is $(B|A) \in \mathcal{R}$ such that $V(\omega') = 0^{\mathcal{A}}$ for all ω' with $\sigma_{(B|A)}(\omega') = \sigma_{(B|A)}(\omega)$.

(ii) $V(\widehat{\omega}_1) = V(\widehat{\omega}_2)$ whenever $\sigma_{\mathcal{R}}(\widehat{\omega}_1) = \sigma_{\mathcal{R}}(\widehat{\omega}_2)$ for $\widehat{\omega}_1 \equiv_T \widehat{\omega}_2 \in \widehat{\Omega}_+$.

If V is indifferent with respect to $\mathcal{R} \subseteq (\mathcal{L} \mid \mathcal{L})$, then it does not distinguish between different elements $\widehat{\omega}_1, \widehat{\omega}_2$ which are equivalent modulo $\widehat{\Omega}_0$ and have the same conditional structure with respect to $\mathcal{R}$. Conversely, for each $\widehat{\omega} \in \widehat{\Omega}_0$, any deviation $V(\widehat{\omega}) \neq 1^{\mathcal{A}}$ can be explained by the conditionals in $\mathcal{R}$ acting on $\widehat{\omega}$ in a non-balanced way. Condition (i) in Definition 6.1 is necessary to deal with worlds $\omega \notin \Omega_+$. It says that $0^{\mathcal{A}}$-values in an indifferent valuation function V are established only in according with the partitionings induced by the conditionals in $\mathcal{R}$.

The following proposition rephrases conditional indifference by establishing a relationship between the kernels of $\sigma_{\mathcal{R}}$ and V:

Proposition 6.2. Let $\mathcal{R} \subseteq (\mathcal{L} \mid \mathcal{L})$ be a set of conditionals, and let $V : \mathcal{L} \to \mathcal{A}$ be a conditional valuation function with $V(A) \neq 0^{\mathcal{A}}$ for all $(B|A) \in \mathcal{R}$.

V is indiffrent with respect to $\mathcal{R}$ iffcondition (i) of Defiition 6.1 holds, and $\ker_0 \sigma_{\mathcal{R}} \cap \widehat{\Omega}_+ \subseteq \ker_0 V$.

We will close this section by characterizing probability functions, ordinal conditional functions and possibility distributions with indifference properties:

Theorem 6.1. Let $\mathcal{R} = \{(B_1|A_1), \ldots, (B_n|A_n)\} \subset (\mathcal{L} \mid \mathcal{L})$ be a (finite) set of conditionals.

1. A probability function P is indiffrent with respect to $\mathcal{R}$ iff $P(A_i) \neq 0$ for all $i, 1 \leqslant i \leqslant n$, and there are non-negative real numbers $\alpha_0, \alpha_1^+, \alpha_1^-, \ldots, \alpha_n^+$, $\alpha_n^- \in \mathbb{R}^+, \alpha_0 > 0$ such that, for all $\omega \in \Omega$,

$$P(\omega) = \alpha_0 \prod_{\substack{1 \leqslant i \leqslant n \\ \omega \models A_i B_i}} \alpha_i^+ \prod_{\substack{1 \leqslant i \leqslant n \\ \omega \models A_i \overline{B_i}}} \alpha_i^- \tag{5}$$

2. An ordinal conditional function κ is indiffrent with respect to $\mathcal{R}$ iff $\kappa(A_i) \neq \infty$ for all $i, 1 \leqslant i \leqslant n$, and there are rational numbers $\kappa_0, \kappa_i^+, \kappa_i^- \in \mathbb{Q}, 1 \leqslant i \leqslant n$, such that, for all $\omega \in \Omega$,

$$\kappa(\omega) = \kappa_0 + \sum_{\substack{1 \leqslant i \leqslant n \\ \omega \models A_i B_i}} \kappa_i^+ + \sum_{\substack{1 \leqslant i \leqslant n \\ \omega \models A_i \overline{B_i}}} \kappa_i^- \tag{6}$$

3. A possibility distribution π is indiffrent with respect to $\mathcal{R}$ iffthere are non-negative real numbers $\alpha_0, \alpha_1^+, \alpha_1^-, \ldots, \alpha_n^+, \alpha_n^- \in \mathbb{R}^+, \alpha_0 > 0$, such that for all $\omega \in \Omega$,

$$\pi(\omega) = \alpha_0 \prod_{\substack{1 \leqslant i \leqslant n \\ \omega \models A_i B_i}} \alpha_i^+ \prod_{\substack{1 \leqslant i \leqslant n \\ \omega \models A_i \overline{B_i}}} \alpha_i^- \tag{7}$$

Note that conditional indifference is a structural notion, without making any reference to degrees of certainty which may be assigned to the conditionals in $\mathcal{R}$. Theorem 6.1, however, also provides simple schemata how to obtain indifferent probabilistic, OCF and possibilistic representations of quantified conditionals: One has to simply set up functions of the corresponding type according to (5), (6) or (7), respectively, and to determine the constants $\alpha_0, \alpha_1^+, \alpha_1^-, \ldots, \alpha_n^+, \alpha_n^-$ or $\kappa_0, \kappa_i^+, \kappa_i^-$, respectively, appropriately so as to ensure that all necessary numerical relationships are established. Conditional valuation functions which represent a set $\mathcal{R}^{(*)}$ of (quantified) conditionals and are indifferent to it, are called *c-representations of* $\mathcal{R}^{(*)}$ (for further details and examples, cf. [21,25,29]; see also Section 7).

Theorem 6.1 also shows, that most important and well-behaved inductive representation methods realize conditional indifference: Namely, the principle of maximum entropy in probabilistics [34], system-Z^* in the OCF-framework [17], and the LCD-functions of Benferhat, Saffiotti and Smets [4] all give rise to conditionally indifferent functions (cf. [21,25,28]). The system-Z^* approach and that of LCD-functions can easily be derived by postulating conditional indifference and further plausibility assumptions (for a more detailed discussion, cf. [28]). Indeed, the crucial meaning of all these formalisms for adequate inductive knowledge representation is mainly due to this indifference property. It should be emphasized, that, to study interactions of conditionals, conditionals here are not reduced to material implications, as for system-Z^*, or for LCD-functions. Instead, the full dynamic, non-classical power of conditionals is preserved, and highly complex conditional interactions can be dealt with.

Therefore, the theory of conditional structures and conditional indifference presented so far proves to be of fundamental importance both for theoretical and practical issues in inductive knowledge representation. In the next section, we will show that it also provides an appropriate framework for revising quantified beliefs.

7   A Principle of Conditional Preservation in a (Semi-)quantitative Framework

When we revise an epistemic state Ψ – which is supposed to be represented by a conditional valuation function V – by a set of (quantified) conditionals $\mathcal{R}$ to obtain a posterior epistemic state $\Psi * \mathcal{R} \equiv V^* = V * \mathcal{R}$, conditional structures and/or interactions must be observed with respect to the prior state Ψ as well as to the new conditionals in $\mathcal{R}$. The theory of conditional structures can only be applied with respect to $\mathcal{R}$, since we usually do not know anything about the history of Ψ, or V, respectively. Conditional relationships within Ψ, however, are realized via the operation $\odot$ of V, so we base our definition of a principle of conditional preservation on an indifference property of the *relative change function* $V^* \odot V^{-1}$, in the following written as V^*/V. Taking into regard prior knowledge V and the worlds ω with $V(\omega) = 0^{\mathcal{A}}$ appropriately, this gives rise to the following definitions:

Definition 7.1 (V-consistency, indifference wrt $\mathcal{R}$ and V). *Let $V : \mathcal{L} \to \mathcal{A}$ be a conditional valuation function, and let $\mathcal{R}$ be a finite set of (quantified) conditionals. Let $V^* = V * \mathcal{R}$ denote the result of revising V by $\mathcal{R}$; in particular, suppose that $V^*(A) \neq 0^\mathcal{A}$ for all $(B|A) \in \mathcal{R}$.*

1. *V^* is called V-consistent iff $V(\omega) = 0^\mathcal{A}$ implies $V^*(\omega) = 0^\mathcal{A}$; V^* is called strictly V-consistent iff $V(\omega) = 0^\mathcal{A} \Leftrightarrow V^*(\omega) = 0^\mathcal{A}$;*

2. *If V^* is V-consistent, then the relative change function $(V^*/V) : \Omega \to \mathcal{A}$ is defined by*

$$(V^*/V)(\omega) = \begin{cases} V^*(\omega) \odot V(\omega)^{-1} & \text{if } V(\omega) \neq 0^\mathcal{A} \\ 0^\mathcal{A} & \text{if } V(\omega) = 0^\mathcal{A} \end{cases}$$

3. *V^* is indifferent with respect to $\mathcal{R}$ and V iff V^* is V-consistent and the following two conditions hold:*
   (i) If $V^*(\omega) = 0^\mathcal{A}$ then $V(\omega) = 0^\mathcal{A}$, or there is $(B|A) \in \mathcal{R}$ such that $V^*(\omega') = 0^\mathcal{A}$ for all ω' with $\sigma_{(B|A)}(\omega') = \sigma_{(B|A)}(\omega)$.
   (ii) $(V^*/V)(\widehat{\omega}_1) = (V^*/V)(\widehat{\omega}_2)$ whenever $\sigma_\mathcal{R}(\widehat{\omega}_1) = \sigma_\mathcal{R}(\widehat{\omega}_2)$ and $\widehat{\omega}_1 \widehat{\Omega}_0 = \widehat{\omega}_2 \widehat{\Omega}_0$ for $\widehat{\omega}_1, \widehat{\omega}_2 \in \widehat{\Omega}_+^*$, where $\widehat{\Omega}_+^* = \langle \omega \in \Omega \mid V^*(\omega) \neq 0^\mathcal{A} \rangle$.

Although the relative change function (V^*/V) is not a conditional valuation function, it may nevertheless be extended to a homomorphism $(V^*/V) : \widehat{\Omega}_+^* \to (\mathcal{A}, \odot)$. Therefore, Definition 7.1 is an appropriate modification of Definition 6.1 for revisions.

We are now ready to formalize appropriately a principle of conditional preservation for belief revision in a (semi-)quantitative framework:

Definition 7.2 (principle of conditional preservation wrt $\mathcal{R}$ and V). *A revision $V^* = V * \mathcal{R}$ of a conditional valuation function by a set $\mathcal{R}$ of (quantified) conditionals is said to satisfy the principle of conditional preservation with respect to $\mathcal{R}$ and V iff V^* is indiffrent with respect to $\mathcal{R}$ and V.*

Thus in a numerical framework, the principle of conditional preservation is realized as an indifference property.

From Theorem 6.1, we immediately obtain a concise characterization of revisions preserving conditional beliefs, which may also serve in practice as a schema to set up appropriate revision formalisms:

Theorem 7.1. *Let $\mathcal{R} = \{(B_1|A_1)([x_1]), \ldots, (B_n|A_n)([x_n])\} \subset (\mathcal{L} \mid \mathcal{L})$ be a (finite) set of (quantified) conditionals. Let P be a probability distribution, κ an ordinal conditional function, and π a possibility distribution, all serving as prior knowledge.*

1. *A probability distribution $P^* = P * \mathcal{R}$ satisfies the principle of conditional preservation with respect to $\mathcal{R}$ and P if and only if there are real numbers $\alpha_0, \alpha_1^+, \alpha_1^-, \ldots, \alpha_n^+, \alpha_n^-$ with $\alpha_0 > 0$ and $\alpha_1^+, \alpha_1^-, \ldots, \alpha_n^+, \alpha_n^-$ satisfying $\alpha_i^+, \alpha_i^- \geqslant 0$, $\alpha_i^+ = 0$ iff $x_i = 0$, $\alpha_i^- = 0$ iff $x_i = 1$, $1 \leqslant i \leqslant n$, such that, for all $\omega \in \Omega$,*

$$P^*(\omega) = \alpha_0 P(\omega) \prod_{\substack{1 \leqslant i \leqslant n \\ \omega \models A_i B_i}} \alpha_i^+ \prod_{\substack{1 \leqslant i \leqslant n \\ \omega \models A_i \overline{B_i}}} \alpha_i^- \tag{8}$$

2. A revision $\kappa^* = \kappa * \mathcal{R}$ satisfies the principle of conditional preservation with respect to $\mathcal{R}$ and κ iff $\kappa^*(A_i) \neq \infty$ for all $i, 1 \leqslant i \leqslant n$, and there are numbers $\kappa_0, \kappa_i^+, \kappa_i^- \in \mathbb{Q}, 1 \leqslant i \leqslant n$, such that, for all $\omega \in \Omega$,

$$\kappa^*(\omega) = \kappa(\omega) + \kappa_0 + \sum_{\substack{1 \leqslant i \leqslant n \\ \omega \models A_i B_i}} \kappa_i^+ + \sum_{\substack{1 \leqslant i \leqslant n \\ \omega \models A_i \overline{B_i}}} \kappa_i^- \qquad (9)$$

3. A revision $\pi^* = \pi * \mathcal{R}$ satisfies the principle of conditional preservation with respect to $\mathcal{R}$ and π iff there are positive real numbers $\alpha_0, \alpha_1^+, \alpha_1^-, \ldots, \alpha_n^+, \alpha_n^- \in \mathbb{R}^+$ such that for all $\omega \in \Omega$,

$$\pi^*(\omega) = \alpha_0 \pi(\omega) \prod_{\substack{1 \leqslant i \leqslant n \\ \omega \models A_i B_i}} \alpha_i^+ \prod_{\substack{1 \leqslant i \leqslant n \\ \omega \models A_i \overline{B_i}}} \alpha_i^- \qquad (10)$$

Note that the principle of conditional preservation is based only on observing conditional structures, without using any acceptance conditions or taking quantifications of conditionals into account. It is exactly this separation of numerical from structural aspects that results in a wide applicability of this principle within a quantitative framework. Revisions of epistemic states Ψ by sets $\mathcal{R}$ of (quantified) conditionals that also fulfill the so-called *success postulate* $\Psi * \mathcal{R} \models \mathcal{R}$ are termed *c-revisions*:

Definition 7.3 (c-revision). *A revision $V^* = V * \mathcal{R}$ of a conditional valuation function by a set $\mathcal{R}$ of (quantified) conditionals is called a* c-revision *iff V^* satisfies the principle of conditional preservation with respect to V and $\mathcal{R}$, and $V^* \models \mathcal{R}$.*

C-revisions can easily be obtained by using the schemata provided by Theorem 7.1 and choosing the constants $\alpha_0, \alpha_1^+, \alpha_1^-, \ldots, \alpha_n^+, \alpha_n^-$, and $\kappa_0, \kappa_i^+, \kappa_i^-$, respectively, appropriately so as to establish the necessary numerical relationships. For instance, for ordinal conditional functions, a c-revision $\kappa^* = \kappa * \mathcal{R}$ of an OCF κ by $\mathcal{R} = \{(B_1|A_1), \ldots, (B_n|A_n)\}$ has the form (9), and the postulate $\kappa^* \models \mathcal{R}$ yields the following conditions for κ_i^+, κ_i^- in a straightforward way:

$$\kappa_i^- - \kappa_i^+ > \min_{\omega \models A_i B_i} \left(\kappa(\omega) + \sum_{\substack{j \neq i \\ \omega \models A_j B_j}} \kappa_j^+ + \sum_{\substack{j \neq i \\ \omega \models A_j \overline{B_j}}} \kappa_j^- \right) \qquad (11)$$

$$- \min_{\omega \models A_i \overline{B_i}} \left(\kappa(\omega) + \sum_{\substack{j \neq i \\ \omega \models A_j B_j}} \kappa_j^+ + \sum_{\substack{j \neq i \\ \omega \models A_j \overline{B_j}}} \kappa_j^- \right)$$

Moreover, quantifications of conditionals can be taken easily into account by modifying (11) slightly, so as to comply with the representation postulate $\kappa^* \models (B|A) [m_i]$:

$$\kappa_i^- - \kappa_i^+ > m_i + \min_{\omega \models A_i B_i} \left(\kappa(\omega) + \sum_{\substack{j \Box i \\ \omega \models A_j B_j}} \kappa_j^+ + \sum_{\substack{j \Box i \\ \omega \models A_j \overline{B}_j}} \kappa_j^- \right) \tag{12}$$

$$- \min_{\omega \models A_i \overline{B}_i} \left(\kappa(\omega) + \sum_{\substack{j \Box i \\ \omega \models A_j B_j}} \kappa_j^+ + \sum_{\substack{j \Box i \\ \omega \models A_j \overline{B}_j}} \kappa_j^- \right)$$

We will illustrate this by an example.

Example 7.1. Let the ordinal conditional function κ, as shown in Table 1, represent epistemic knowledge about the atoms f - *flying*, b - *birds*, p - *penguins*, w - *winged animals*, and k - *kiwis*. Among others, κ represents the conditionals $(f|b)$

ω	$\kappa(\omega)$	$\kappa^*(\omega)$	ω	$\kappa(\omega)$	$\kappa^*(\omega)$	ω	$\kappa(\omega)$	$\kappa^*(\omega)$	ω	$\kappa(\omega)$	$\kappa^*(\omega)$
$pbfwk$	2	3	$\overline{p}bfwk$	0	1	$pbf\overline{w}k$	2	2	$\overline{p}bf\overline{w}k$	0	0
$pbf\overline{w}k$	3	3	$\overline{p}bf\overline{w}k$	1	1	$pbf\overline{w}k$	3	3	$\overline{p}bf\overline{w}k$	1	1
$pb\overline{f}wk$	1	2	$\overline{p}b\overline{f}wk$	1	2	$pb\overline{f}wk$	1	1	$\overline{p}b\overline{f}wk$	1	1
$pb\overline{f}\overline{w}k$	2	2	$\overline{p}b\overline{f}\overline{w}k$	2	2	$pb\overline{f}\overline{w}k$	2	2	$\overline{p}b\overline{f}\overline{w}k$	2	2
$p\overline{b}fwk$	5	6	$\overline{p}\overline{b}fwk$	1	2	$p\overline{b}fwk$	4	4	$\overline{p}\overline{b}fwk$	0	0
$p\overline{b}f\overline{w}k$	5	5	$\overline{p}\overline{b}f\overline{w}k$	1	1	$p\overline{b}f\overline{w}k$	4	4	$\overline{p}\overline{b}f\overline{w}k$	0	0
$p\overline{b}\,\overline{f}wk$	3	4	$\overline{p}\overline{b}\,\overline{f}wk$	1	2	$p\overline{b}\,\overline{f}wk$	2	2	$\overline{p}\overline{b}\,\overline{f}wk$	0	0
$p\overline{b}\,\overline{f}\overline{w}k$	3	3	$\overline{p}\overline{b}\,\overline{f}\overline{w}k$	1	1	$p\overline{b}\,\overline{f}\overline{w}k$	2	2	$\overline{p}\overline{b}\,\overline{f}\overline{w}k$	0	0

Fig. 1. OCF κ, and revised $\kappa^* = \kappa * \{(\overline{w}|k)\}$ for Example 7.1

$(birds\ fly)$, $(b|p)$ (*penguins are birds*), $(\overline{f}|p)$ (*penguins do not fly*), $(w|b)$ (*birds have wings*), and $(b|k)$ (*kiwis are birds*). This is checked easily by comparing the rankings $\kappa(\omega)$ of verifying and falsifying worlds ω, respectively, for each of the conditionals. (Actually, κ is a c-representation of these conditionals.)

Moreover, we have $\kappa \models (w|k)$ – from their superclass *birds*, kiwis inherit the property of having wings. Suppose now that we come to know that this is false – kiwis do *not* possess wings, – and we want to revise our knowledge κ by this new information. The revised epistemic state $\kappa^* = \kappa * \{(\overline{w}|k)\}$ should be a c-revision of κ by $\{(\overline{w}|k)\}$. Then due to (9), κ^* has the form

$$\kappa^*(\omega) = \begin{cases} \kappa_0 + \kappa(\omega) + \kappa^+ & \text{if } \omega \models k\overline{w} \\ \kappa_0 + \kappa(\omega) + \kappa^- & \text{if } \omega \models kw \\ \kappa_0 + \kappa(\omega) & \text{if } \omega \models \overline{k} \end{cases}$$

and (11) yields $\kappa^- - \kappa^+ > \min_{\omega \models k\overline{w}} \kappa(\omega) - \min_{\omega \models kw} \kappa(\omega) = 1 - 0 = 1$, i.e. $\kappa^- > \kappa^+ + 1$. Any such pair of κ^+, κ^- will give rise to a c-revision, but, in order to keep numerical changes minimal, we choose $\kappa^+ := 0, \kappa^- := 1$. No further normalization is necessary, so $\kappa_0 := 0$. The revised κ^* is shown in Table 1, too[1]. κ^* still represents the conditionals $(f|b), (b|p), (\overline{f}|p)$ and $(w|b)$, but it no longer satisfies $(b|k)$, since $\kappa^*(bk) = \kappa^*(\overline{b}k) = 1$ – the property of not having wings casts (reasonably) doubt on kiwis being birds. Note that no external knowledge, such as "*typically*, birds have wings", and no quantifications of the inferential strength of conditionals is needed to bring forth this reasonable behavior. So, this example illustrates strikingly, how adequately conditional interrelationships are dealt with by c-revisions.

In a probabilistic framework, Theorem 7.1 proves that revisions following the *principle of minimum cross-entropy* (so-called *MINENT-principle* or, briefly, *ME-principle*) [37,35,34,21] are also c-revisions. This principle is a method to revise a prior distribution P by a set $\mathcal{R}^* = \{(B_1|A_1)\,[x_1], \ldots, (B_n|A_n)\,[x_n]\}$ of probabilistic conditionals, so that the "dissimilarity" between P and the resulting distribution $P^* \models \mathcal{R}^*$ is minimal. A measure for this dissimilarity is given by the information-theoretical concept of *cross-entropy* $R(Q,P) = \sum\limits_{\omega\in\Omega} Q(\omega)\log\frac{Q(\omega)}{P(\omega)}$. If $\mathcal{R}^*$ is compatible with the prior P, in the sense that there is a P-consistent distribution Q representing $\mathcal{R}^*$, this optimization problem has a unique solution $P^* = P *_{ME} \mathcal{R}^*$ (cf. [7]), which can be written in the form

$$P^*(\omega) = \alpha_0 P(\omega) \prod_{\substack{1\leqslant i\leqslant n \\ \omega\models A_i B_i}} \alpha_i^{1-x_i} \prod_{\substack{1\leqslant i\leqslant n \\ \omega\models A_i \overline{B_i}}} \alpha_i^{-x_i} \tag{13}$$

with the α_i's being exponentials of the Lagrange multipliers, appropriately chosen so as to satisfy all conditionals in $\mathcal{R}^*$ (cf. [27]). Comparing (13) to (8), it is obvious that $P *_{ME} \mathcal{R}^*$ satisfies the principle of conditional preservation, and hence is a c-revision.

By Definition 7.2, we obtain a technically clear and precise formalization of the intuitive idea of conditional preservation in a very general framework, making it applicable to probabilistic, possibilistic and OCF-revisions. Note that, as abstract and technical as it appears, this principle is not a formal artifact but has been effectively guiding probabilistic revisions via the principle of minimum cross-entropy for many decades. Indeed, the first steps towards formalizing this principle have been taken when extracting the most basic and crucial properties of minimum cross-entropy methods in [21]. Therefore, the axiomatization provided by Definition 7.2 allows us to carry over a most successful information-theoretical idea from probabilistics to other frameworks when designing adequate revision methods. No explicit reference to ME-probability distributions is needed, as was done for system-Z^* (cf. [17]). Moreover, generalizations of system-Z^* and LCD-functions for belief revision are straightforward and can be theoretically justified within the corresponding framework.

---

[1] κ^* can also be regarded as the result of an *update process*, following evolution.

8   Linking Qualitative and Quantitative Approaches

In Sections 5 and 7, the idea of preserving conditional beliefs under revision have been formalized in two (apparently) different ways: In Section 5, we made use of the two relations $\sqsubseteq$ and $\perp\!\!\!\perp$, describing quite simple ways of conditional interactions. In Section 7, we based our formalization upon observing conditional structures. In any case, the principal idea was to focus on conditional (not logical) interactions, considering the effects conditionals may exert when being established. We will now show, that both approaches essentially coincide in the case that a conditional valuation function (as a quantitative representation of epistemic beliefs, like e.g. ordinal conditional functions or possibility distributions) is revised by only one conditional. More exactly, we will prove that a revision following the quantitative principle of conditional preservation (see Definition 7.2 in Section 7) satisfy the postulates (CR5)-(CR7) in Section 5, describing a qualitative principle of conditional preservation.

We begin by characterizing revisions $V^* = V * \mathcal{R} = V * (B|A)$ of a conditional valuation function V which satisfy the (quantitative) principle of conditional preservation with respect to $\mathcal{R} = \{(B|A)\}$ and V. As a basic requirement for such revisions, we will only presuppose that $V^*(A) \neq 0^{\mathcal{A}}$, instead of the (stronger) success postulate $V^* \models (B|A)$. This makes the results to be presented independent of acceptance conditions and helps concentrating on conditional structures; in particular, it will be possible to make use of these results even when conditionals are assigned numerical degrees of acceptance.

Proposition 8.1. *Let $V : \mathcal{L} \to \mathcal{A}$ be a conditional valuation function, and let $\mathcal{R} = \{(B|A)\}, (B|A) \in (\mathcal{L} \mid \mathcal{L})$, consist of only one conditional. Let $V^* = V * \mathcal{R} = V * (B|A)$ denote a revision of V by $(B|A)$ such that $V^*(A) \neq 0^{\mathcal{A}}$. V^* satisfies the principle of conditional preservation with respect to V and $\mathcal{R}$ iffthere are constants $\alpha_0, \alpha^+, \alpha^- \in \mathcal{A}$ such that*

$$V^*(\omega) = \begin{cases} \alpha^+ \odot V(\omega) & if \quad \omega \models AB \\ \alpha^- \odot V(\omega) & if \quad \omega \models A\overline{B} \\ \alpha_0 \odot V(\omega) & if \quad \omega \models \overline{A} \end{cases} \tag{14}$$

If V^* is strictly V-consistent, then all constants $\alpha_0, \alpha^+, \alpha^- \in \mathcal{A}$ may be chosen $\neq 0^{\mathcal{A}}$.

As an obvious link between the qualitative and the quantitative frameworks, we now strengthen the central postulate (CR5) to comply with the numerical information provided by conditional valuation functions V:

(CR5^{quant}) If $(D|C) \perp\!\!\!\perp (B|A)$ and $V(CD), (V * (B|A))(CD) \neq 0^{\mathcal{A}}$, then

$$V(C\overline{D}) \odot V(CD)^{-1} = (V * (B|A))(C\overline{D}) \odot (V * (B|A))(CD)^{-1}.$$

(CR5^{quant}) ensures that essentially, the values assigned to conditionals which are perpendicular to the revising conditional are not changed under revision:

Lemma 8.1. *Suppose the revision $V*(B|A)$ is strictly V-consistent and satisfies $(CR5^{quant})$. Then for any conditional $(D|C) \perp\!\!\!\perp (B|A)$ with $V(C) \neq 0^{\mathcal{A}}$, it holds that $V(D|C) = (V * (B|A))(D|C)$.*

The next proposition shows that indeed, $(CR5^{quant})$ is stronger than its qualitative counterpart (CR5):

Proposition 8.2. *Let $V^* = V * \mathcal{R} = V * \{(B|A)\}$ denote a strictly V-consistent revision of V by $(B|A)$ such that $V^*(A) \neq 0^{\mathcal{A}}$. If V^* fulfills $(CR5^{quant})$, then it also satisfies (CR5).*

The following theorem states that essentially, any revision of a conditional valuation function which satisfies the quantitative principle of conditional preservation (as specified by Definition 7.2), is also in accordance with the qualitative principle of conditional preservation (as described by (CR5)-(CR7)):

Theorem 8.1. *Let $V : \mathcal{L} \to \mathcal{A}$ be a conditional valuation function, and let $\mathcal{R} = \{(B|A)\}, (B|A) \in (\mathcal{L} \mid \mathcal{L})$, consist of only one conditional. Let $V^* = V * \mathcal{R}$ denote a strictly V-consistent revision of V by $\mathcal{R}$ fulfilling the postulates (CR1) (success) and (CR2) (stability).*

If V^* satisfies the principle of conditional preservation, then the revision also satisfies postulate $(CR5^{quant})$ and the postulates (CR6) and (CR7); in particular, it satisfies all of the postulates (CR5)-(CR7).

Therefore, Theorem 8.1 identifies the principle of conditional preservation, as formalized in Definition 7.2, as a fundamental device to guide reasonable changes in the conditional structure of knowledge.

9   Conclusion

In this paper, we presented axiomatizations of a principle of conditional preservation for belief revision operations in qualitative as well as in (semi-)quantitative settings. In both cases, we dealt with revisions of epistemic states by sets of conditional beliefs, thus studying belief revision in a most general framework. As the inductive representation of a set of conditionals (or default rules, respectively) can be considered as a special instance of a revision problem, this paper also provides an approach for adequate knowledge induction.

The crucial point in preserving conditional beliefs is to observe conditional interactions, which can be described by two relations, *subconditionality* and *perpendicularity*, in the qualitative framework, and are based on the algebraic notion of conditional structures in the quantitative framework. Since subconditionality and perpendicularity can also be defined via conditional structures, the theory of conditional structures developed in this paper proves to be a most basic and powerful tool for handling conditionals in knowledge representation and belief revision. We applied this theory to *conditional valuation functions* as basic representations of (semi-) quantitative epistemic states, covering probability distributions, ranking functions (ordinal conditional functions), and possibility distributions. Therefore, the results presented in this paper are of relevance for a wide range of revision problems in very different environments. Moreover, apart from theoretical aspects, our approach also yields practical schemata for setting up revision and representation operations in probabilistic, possibilistic and ordinal frameworks.

As the main result of this paper, we showed that the quantitative principle of conditional preservation implies the qualitative principle in semi-quantitative settings. This not only closes the gap between qualitative and quantitative approaches to belief revision, but also may give new impetus to classical belief revision theory.

References

1. C.E. Alchourrón, P. Gärdenfors, and P. Makinson. On the logic of theory change: Partial meet contraction and revision functions. *Journal of Symbolic Logic*, 50(2):510–530, 1985.
2. S. Benferhat, D. Dubois, and H. Prade. Representing default rules in possibilistic logic. In *Proceedings 3th International Conference on Principles of Knowledge Representation and Reasoning KR'92*, pages 673–684, 1992.
3. S. Benferhat, D. Dubois, and H. Prade. Nonmonotonic reasoning, conditional objects and possibility theory. *Artificial Intelligence*, 92:259–276, 1997.
4. S. Benferhat, A. Saffiotti, and P. Smets. Belief functions and default reasoning. *Artificial Intelligence*, 122:1–69, 2000.
5. C. Boutilier and M. Goldszmidt. Revision by conditional beliefs. In *Proceedings 11th National Conference on Artificial Intelligence (AAAI'93)*, pages 649–654, Washington, DC., 1993.
6. P.G. Calabrese. Deduction and inference using conditional logic and probability. In I.R. Goodman, M.M. Gupta, H.T. Nguyen, and G.S. Rogers, editors, *Conditional Logic in Expert Systems*, pages 71–100. Elsevier, North Holland, 1991.
7. I. Csiszár. I-divergence geometry of probability distributions and minimization problems. *Ann. Prob.*, 3:146–158, 1975.
8. A. Darwiche and J. Pearl. On the logic of iterated belief revision. *Artificial Intelligence*, 89:1–29, 1997.
9. B. DeFinetti. *Theory of Probability*, volume 1,2. John Wiley and Sons, New York, 1974.
10. J.P. Delgrande and T. Schaub. A consistency-based model for belief change: Preliminary report. In *Proceedings AAAI-2000*, pages 392–398, Austin, TX, 2000.
11. D. Dubois, J. Lang, and H. Prade. Possibilistic logic. In D.M. Gabbay, C.H. Hogger, and J.A. Robinson, editors, *Handbook of Logic in Artificial Intelligence and Logic Programming*, volume 3. Oxford University Press, 1994.
12. D. Dubois and H. Prade. A survey of belief revision and updating rules in various uncertainty models. *Intern. Journal of Intelligent Systems*, 9:61–100, 1994.
13. B. Fine and G. Rosenberger. *Algebraic Generalizations of Discrete Groups*. Dekker, New York, Basel, 1999.
14. M. Freund. Preferential orders and plausibility measures. *J. Logic Computat.*, 8:147–158, 1998.
15. N. Friedman and J.Y. Halpern. Plausibility measures and default reasoning. In *Proceedings 13th National Conference on Artificial Intelligence, AAAI-96*, volume 2, 1996.

16. P. Gärdenfors. *Knowledge in Flux: Modeling the Dynamics of Epistemic States.* MIT Press, Cambridge, Mass., 1988.
17. M. Goldszmidt, P. Morris, and J. Pearl. A maximum entropy approach to non-monotonic reasoning. *IEEE Transactions on Pattern Analysis and Machine Intelligence*, 15(3):220–232, 1993.
18. M. Goldszmidt and J. Pearl. Qualitative probabilities for default reasoning, belief revision, and causal modeling. *Artificial Intelligence*, 84:57–112, 1996.
19. H. Katsuno and A. Mendelzon. Propositional knowledge base revision and minimal change. *Artificial Intelligence*, 52:263–294, 1991.
20. H. Katsuno and A.O. Mendelzon. On the difference between updating a knowledge base and revising it. In *Proceedings Second International Conference on Principles of Knowledge Representation and Reasoning, KR'91*, pages 387–394, San Mateo, Ca., 1991. Morgan Kaufmann.
21. G. Kern-Isberner. Characterizing the principle of minimum cross-entropy within a conditional-logical framework. *Artificial Intelligence*, 98:169–208, 1998.
22. G. Kern-Isberner. Postulates for conditional belief revision. In *Proceedings Sixteenth International Joint Conference on Artificial Intelligence, IJCAI-99*, pages 186–191. Morgan Kaufmann, 1999.
23. G. Kern-Isberner. *A unifying framework for symbolic and numerical approaches to nonmonotonic reasoning and belief revision.* Department of Computer Science, FernUniversität Hagen, 1999. Habilitation thesis.
24. G. Kern-Isberner. Solving the inverse representation problem. In *Proceedings 14th European Conference on Artificial Intelligence, ECAI'2000*, pages 581–585, Berlin, 2000. IOS Press.
25. G. Kern-Isberner. Conditional preservation and conditional indifference. *Journal of Applied Non-Classical Logics*, 11(1-2):85–106, 2001.
26. G. Kern-Isberner. Conditionals in knowledge representation and belief revision. In *Proceedings Fifth Dutch-German Workshop on Nonmonotonic Reasoning Techniques and their applications, DGNMR'01*, Potsdam, Germany, 2001.
27. G. Kern-Isberner. *Conditionals in nonmonotonic reasoning and belief revision.* Springer, Lecture Notes in Artificial Intelligence LNAI 2087, 2001.
28. G. Kern-Isberner. Handling conditionals adequately in uncertain reasoning. In *Proceedings European Conference on Symbolic and Quantitative Approaches to Reasoning with Uncertainty, ECSQARU'01*, pages 604–615. Springer LNAI 2143, 2001.
29. G. Kern-Isberner. Representing and learning conditional information in possibility theory. In *Proceedings 7th Fuzzy Days, Dortmund, Germany*, pages 194–217. Springer LNCS 2206, 2001.
30. R. Kruse, E. Schwecke, and J. Heinsohn. *Uncertainty and Vagueness in Knowledge Based Systems.* Springer, Berlin Heidelberg New York, 1991.
31. I. Levi. Iteration of conditionals and the Ramsey test. *Synthese*, 76:49–81, 1988.
32. R.C. Lyndon and P.E. Schupp. *Combinatorial group theory.* Springer, Berlin Heidelberg New York, 1977.
33. D. Makinson and P. Gärdenfors. Relations between the logic of theory change and nonmonotonic logic. In *Proceedings Workshop The Logic of Theory Change, Konstanz, Germany, 1989*, pages 185–205, Berlin Heidelberg New York, 1991. Springer.
34. J.B. Paris. *The uncertain reasoner's companion – A mathematical perspective.* Cambridge University Press, 1994.
35. J.B. Paris and A. Vencovská. A method for updating that justifies minimum cross entropy. *International Journal of Approximate Reasoning*, 7:1–18, 1992.

36. F.P. Ramsey. General propositions and causality. In R.B. Braithwaite, editor, *Foundations of Mathematics and other logical essays*, pages 237–257. Routledge and Kegan Paul, New York, 1950.

37. J.E. Shore and R.W. Johnson. Axiomatic derivation of the principle of maximum entropy and the principle of minimum cross-entropy. *IEEE Transactions on Information Theory*, IT-26:26–37, 1980.

38. W. Spohn. Ordinal conditional functions: a dynamic theory of epistemic states. In W.L. Harper and B. Skyrms, editors, *Causation in Decision, Belief Change, and Statistics, II*, pages 105–134. Kluwer Academic Publishers, 1988.

Query Rewriting with Symmetric Constraints

Christoph Koch

Database and Artificial Intelligence Group
Technische Universität Wien, A-1040 Vienna, Austria
koch@dbai.tuwien.ac.at

Abstract. We address the problem of answering queries using expressive *symmetric* inter-schema constraints which allow to establish mappings between several heterogeneous information systems. This problem is of high relevance to data integration, as symmetric constraints are essential for dealing with true concept mismatch and are generalizations of the kinds of mappings supported by both local-as-view and global-as-view approaches that were previously studied in the literature. Moreover, the flexibility gained by using such constraints for data integration is essential for virtual enterprise and e-commerce applications. We first discuss resolution-based methods for computing maximally contained rewritings and characterize computability aspects. Then we propose an alternative but semantically equivalent perspective based on a generalization of results relating to the database-theoretic problem of answering queries using views. This leads to a fast query rewriting algorithm, which has been implemented and experimentally evaluated.

1 Introduction

This paper addresses the *query rewriting problem* in semantic data integration in a very general form, as a proper generalization of the well-known local-as-view (e.g., [17,11,2]) and global-as-view approaches (e.g., [10,1,5]). To start somewhere, we focus on the relational case. Given a conjunctive query Q, we attempt to find a *maximally contained rewriting* in terms of a set of distinguished *source predicates* **S** only – under a given set of constraints, the positive relational queries as the output query language (i.e., a rewriting is a set of conjunctive queries), and the classical logical semantics. Under the classical semantics,

1. for each conjunctive query Q' in the maximally contained rewriting of Q, the constraints taken as a logical theory imply $Q \supseteq Q'$ and Q' uses predicates of **S** only, and
2. for each conjunctive query Q'' over predicates in **S** only for which the constraints imply that $Q \supseteq Q''$, there is a conjunctive query Q' in the rewriting such that the constraints imply $Q' \supseteq Q''$.

We support inter-schema constraints in the form of what we call *Conjunctive Inclusion Dependencies* (cind's), containment relationships between conjunctive queries. We refer to cind's as *symmetric* because they are syntactically symmetric with respect to the inclusion resp. implication symbol, while for instance materialized view definitions used for local-as-view query rewriting are not.

T. Eiter and K.-D. Schewe (Eds.): FoIKS 2002, LNCS 2284, pp. 130–147, 2002.

Example 1.1. Consider a conjunctive query

$$Q(x_1) \leftarrow \text{parent}(x_1, x_2), \text{ parent}(x_2, x_3), \text{ parent}(x_3, x_4).$$

asking for great-grandparents in terms of a schema which contains a predicate "parent". Now let "parent" be a "logical" relation to which database relations first need to be mapped before any queries over it can be answered. Let "parent" be conceived to represent parent-child relationships between living persons only. We want to rewrite Q into a query over source predicates in **S** = {grandparent, alive}, where "grandparent" contains grandparent relationships between persons of which the grandparents may possibly have deceased and the source relation "alive" holds persons still alive. We may assert the cind

$$\{\langle x, z \rangle \mid \exists y : \text{parent}(x, y) \wedge \text{parent}(y, z)\} \supseteq \{\langle x, z \rangle \mid \text{grandparent}(x, z) \wedge \text{alive}(x)\}$$

between the schema of "parent" and **S**, i.e., a mapping formulated as a containment relationship between conjunctive queries. Then,

$$Q'(x_1) \leftarrow \text{grandparent}(x_1, x_3), \text{ alive}(x_1), \text{ grandparent}(x_3, z), \text{ alive}(x_3).$$

is the maximally contained rewriting of Q, i.e. the largest query logically contained in Q with respect to the constraint given (and thus cannot return any wrong answers) that can be computed by only considering query and constraint, but not the data in the relations of **S**, and which only uses relations from **S**. □

Note that the problem we attack in this paper is different from work on query answering using integrity constraints [8,9,12] or the problem of optimizing queries in mediated systems. Our constraints are meant to encode mappings between the schemata of several information systems as in [4,3]; as such, they compare to materialized view *definitions* in the local-as-view approach rather than to classical *integrity constraints*.

cind's may represent mappings between complex networks of information systems in which each information system may have its own schema and make use of integrated data. We are thus not restricted to a single layer of constraints (which map sources against a so-called "global" schema) as in the local-as-view approach. Starting from a set of actual source relations which contain data, views or "logical relations" can be defined and used to extend any of the schemata. To facilitate practical usability, a logical relation may map to sources through several indirections. Such an architecture is essential for large and open environments such as experienced in the modern e-economy [4,14].

The relevance of query rewriting with symmetric constraints stems from the observation that both local-as-view and global-as-view approaches to data integration are unable to deal with concept mismatch requiring mappings between pairs of complex query expressions. This problem is particularly common in complex technical domains [14].

Example 1.2. Assume that we have a number of sources holding information about computer models as-built (in fact, we only consider computer mainboards in this short example), their constituent parts, and technical specifications. We want to integrate these sources against a reference design view $\mathbf{R}$ with predicates "mb" (for mainboards), "cpu", "cache", "conn" (for connections or part-of relationships between component parts), and possibly others. Let a source schema $\mathbf{S}$ represent mainboards using a CPU model called "p1" which has an on-chip cache. We cannot directly map cache components in this example, but we can map characteristics represented by both schemata (say, MHz rates r and cache sizes s) to mainboards and CPUs and mediate useful queries over $\mathbf{R}$. We encode the desired mapping using the cind

$$\{\langle x,y,r,s\rangle \mid \exists z : \mathbf{R}.\mathrm{mb}(x), \mathbf{R}.\mathrm{conn}(x,y), \mathbf{R}.\mathrm{conn}(x,z), \mathbf{R}.\mathrm{cpu}(y,r), \mathbf{R}.\mathrm{cache}(z,s)\} \supseteq$$
$$\{\langle x,y,r,s\rangle \mid \mathbf{S}.\mathrm{mb}(x), \mathbf{S}.\mathrm{conn}(x,y), \mathbf{S}.\mathrm{p1}(y,r,s)\} \qquad \square$$

Local-as-view and global-as-view approaches assume that mediated schemata can be designed beforehand using intuitions concerning the likely sources to be added to an integration system later. Both large data integration settings and changing requirements render such an assumption unsustainable (see [14]). Our approach allows to "patch" local-as-view or global-as-view integration systems when sources need to be integrated whose particularities have not been foreseen when designing the schemata against which data are to be integrated.

The only previous work dealing with symmetric constraints is the description logics approach to data integration (e.g., [3,4]), which, however, requires high-complexity reasoning over the data (thus, there is a scalability issue) and to import all data to be integrated into the description logics reasoner. This is usually not an option in open e-economy or WWW data integration environments. Solving the integration problem on the level of queries and mappings *only* is essential for being able to deal with large amounts of data and restricted (e.g., screen-scraping) query interfaces.

Contributions and Structure.   After some preliminaries (Section 2), we discuss a simple resolution-based method for generating rewritings and provide characterizations of the main theoretical properties of our problem in Section 3. Unfortunately, positive (and thus non-recursive) maximally contained rewritings may be infinite and the major decision problems (such as the non-emptiness or boundedness of the result) are undecidable. However, given that the predicate dependency graph (with respect to the inclusion direction) of a set of constraints is acyclic, we can guarantee to find the maximally contained rewritings, which are finite. The acyclic case is a proper generalization of both local-as-view and global-as-view approaches.

In Section 4, we propose an alternative algorithm for computing maximally contained rewritings which is based on a generalization of the MiniCon Algorithm [18] for the problem of answering queries using views, and demonstrate its soundness and completeness. When using this algorithm, all intermediate rewritings are guaranteed to be function-free and thus conjunctive queries. Because of that, one can make use of classical database techniques for optimizing the rewriting process. Section 5 presents refinements of the algorithm of Section 4, which we have implemented in a practical system.

We evaluate our implementation, which is publicly available, experimentally in Section 6. It turns out that it scales to thousands of constraints and realistic applications. Section 7 concludes with a discussion of our new algorithm.

2   Preliminaries

We define a *conjunctive inclusion dependency* (cind) as a constraint of the form $Q_1 \subseteq Q_2$ where Q_1 and Q_2 are conjunctive queries of the form

$$\{\langle x_1, \ldots, x_n \rangle \mid \exists x_{n+1} \ldots x_m : (p_1(\bar{X}_1) \wedge \ldots \wedge p_k(\bar{X}_k))\}$$

with a set of *distinct*[1] unbound variables $x_1, \ldots, x_n$, without arithmetic comparisons, but possibly with constants. We may write $\{Q_1 \equiv Q_2\}$ as a short form of $\{Q_1 \subseteq Q_2, \ Q_1 \supseteq Q_2\}$. The *normal form* $NF(\Sigma)$ of a set Σ of cind's – i.e., Σ taken as a logical formula transformed into (implication) normal form – is a set of Horn clauses of a simple pattern. Every cind σ of the form $Q_1 \subseteq Q_2$ with

$$Q_1 = \{\langle x_1, \ldots, x_n \rangle \mid \exists x_{n+1} \ldots x_m : v_1(\bar{X}_1) \wedge \ldots \wedge v_k(\bar{X}_k)\}$$
$$Q_2 = \{\langle y_1, \ldots, y_n \rangle \mid \exists y_{n+1} \ldots y_{m'} : p_1(\bar{Y}_1) \wedge \ldots \wedge p_{k'}(\bar{Y}_{k'})\}$$

translates to k' Horn clauses $\quad p_i(\bar{Z}_i) \leftarrow v_1(\bar{X}_1) \wedge \ldots \wedge v_k(\bar{X}_k))$. where each $z_{i,j}$ of $\bar{Z}_i$ is determined as follows: If $z_{i,j}$ is a variable y_h with $1 \leq h \leq n$, replace it with x_h. If $z_{i,j}$ is a variable y_h with $n < h \leq m'$, replace it with Skolem function $f_{\sigma, y_h}(x_1, \ldots, x_n)$ (the subscript assures that the Skolem functions are unique for a given constraint and variable).

Example 2.1. Let σ be the cind

$$\{\langle y_1, y_2 \rangle \mid \exists y_3 : p_1(y_1, y_3) \wedge p_2(y_3, y_2)\} \supseteq \{\langle x_1, x_2 \rangle \mid \exists x_3 : v_1(x_1, x_2) \wedge v_2(x_1, x_3)\}$$

Then, $NF(\{\sigma\})$ is

$$p_1(x_1, f_{\sigma, y_3}(x_1, x_2)) \leftarrow v_1(x_1, x_2) \wedge v_2(x_1, x_3).$$
$$p_2(f_{\sigma, y_3}(x_1, x_2), x_2) \leftarrow v_1(x_1, x_2) \wedge v_2(x_1, x_3).$$ □

Whenever a cind translates into a function-free clause in normal form, we write it in datalog notation. This is the case for cind's $\{\langle \bar{X} \rangle \mid p(\bar{X})\} \supseteq Q$, i.e., where the subsumer queries are $\exists$-free single-literal queries.

The dependency graph of a set C of Horn clauses is the directed graph constructed by taking the predicates of C as nodes and adding, for each clause in C, an edge from each of the body predicates to the head predicate. The diameter of a directed acyclic graph is the longest directed path occurring in it. The dependency graph of a set of cind's Σ is the dependency graph of the logic program $NF(\Sigma)$. A set of cind's is *cyclic* if its dependency graph is cyclic. An acyclic set Σ of cind's is called *layered* if the predicates appearing in Σ can be partitioned into n disjoint sets $P_1, \ldots, P_n$ such that there is an index i for each cind $\sigma : Q_1 \subseteq Q_2 \in \Sigma$ such that $Preds(Body(Q_1)) \subseteq P_i$ and $Preds(Body(Q_2)) \subseteq P_{i+1}$ and $Sources = P_1$.

---

[1] Note that if we would not require unbound variables in constituent queries to be distinct, the transformation into normal form would result in Horn clauses with equality atoms as heads.

3   Query Containment and Rewriting

Let us begin with a straightforward remark on the containment problem for conjunctive queries under a set of cind's Σ, which, since they are themselves containment relationships between conjunctive queries, is the implication problem for this type of constraint. If we want to check a containment $\{\langle \bar{X} \rangle \mid \exists \bar{Y} : \phi(\bar{X}, \bar{Y})\} \supseteq \{\langle \bar{X} \rangle \mid \exists \bar{Z} : \psi(\bar{X}, \bar{Z})\}$ of two conjunctive queries under Σ by refutation (without loss of generality, we assume $\bar{Y}$ and $\bar{Z}$ to be disjoint and the unbound variables in the two queries above to be the same, $\bar{X}$), we have to show $\Sigma, \neg(\forall \bar{X} : (\exists \bar{Y} : \phi(\bar{X}, \bar{Y})) \leftarrow (\exists \bar{Z} : \psi(\bar{X}, \bar{Z}))) \vDash \bot$ i.e. the inconsistency of the constraints and the negation of the containment taken together. In normal form, ψ becomes a set of ground facts where all variables have been replaced *one-to-one* by new constants and ϕ becomes a clause with an empty head, where all distinguished variables x_i have been replaced by constants also used in ψ.

Example 3.1. For proving

$$\Sigma \vDash \{\langle x_1, x_2 \rangle \mid \exists x_3 : (p_1(x_1, x_3) \wedge p_2(x_3, x_2))\} \supseteq \{\langle y_1, y_2 \rangle \mid \exists y_3 : (r_1(y_1, y_3) \wedge r_2(y_3, y_2))\}$$

for a set of cind's Σ, we have to create the logic program

$$\mathcal{P} := NF(\Sigma) \cup \{ \leftarrow p_1(\alpha_1, x_3) \wedge p_2(x_3, \alpha_2).\ \ r_1(\alpha_1, \alpha_3) \leftarrow .\ \ r_2(\alpha_3, \alpha_2) \leftarrow . \}$$

where $\alpha_1, \alpha_2, \alpha_3$ are constants not appearing elsewhere. By the correctness of resolution for logic programs, the containment above holds iff there is a refutation of the goal $\leftarrow p_1(\alpha_1, x_3) \wedge p_2(x_3, \alpha_2).$ with the remaining clauses in $\mathcal{P}$.   □

Definition 3.1. A set of conjunctive queries $\mathcal{Q}$ is a maximally contained positive rewriting of a conjunctive query Q with respect to a set of cind's Σ and a set of source predicates **S** iff

1. for each $Q' \in \mathcal{Q}$, $\Sigma \vDash Q \supseteq Q'$ and $Preds(Q') \subseteq \mathbf{S}$ and
2. for each conjunctive query Q'' with $\Sigma \vDash Q \supseteq Q''$ and $Preds(Q'') \subseteq \mathbf{S}$, there is a $Q' \in \mathcal{Q}$ such that $\Sigma \vDash Q \supseteq Q' \supseteq Q''$.   □

In the finite case, a minimal[2] such set $\mathcal{Q}$ is of course unique up to reordering and variable renaming.

For simplicity, we assume that no source predicates appear in any heads of Horn clauses in $NF(\Sigma)$ throughout this paper. This does not cause any loss of generality, since we can always replace a source predicate that violates this assumption by a new virtual predicate in all cind's and then add a cind that maps the source predicate to that new virtual predicate.

Informally, we can obtain such a maximally contained rewriting by a method based on SLD resolution in the following way. Given a conjunctive query Q, a set of cind's Σ, and a set of source predicates **S**, we first create a logic program

---

[2] A set of conjunctive queries is minimal if and only if the constituent queries are individually minimal and pairwise non-redundant.

$NF(\Sigma)$ and add a unit clause $s(\bar{X}) \leftarrow$. (with a tuple $\bar{X}$ of *distinct* variables) for each predicate $s \in \mathbf{S}$. Then we try to refute the body of Q. (Differently from what we do for containment, we do not freeze any variables.) If we have found a refutation with a most general unifier θ, we collect the unit clauses used and create a Horn clause with $\theta(Head(Q))$ as head and the application of θ to the copies of unit clauses involved in the proof as body. If this clause is function-free, we output it. After that *we go on* as if we had not found a "proof" to compute more rewritings. Given an appropriate selection rule or a breath-first strategy for computing derivations, it is easy to see that this method will compute a maximally contained rewriting of Q in terms of multi-sets of conjunctive queries in the sense that for each conjunctive query Q'' contained in Q, a subsumer Q' will eventually be produced s.t. $\Sigma \models Q \supseteq Q' \supseteq Q''$. See Example 4.2 for query rewriting by an altered refutation proof.

Computability and Complexity.

Theorem 3.1. Let Σ be a set of cind's, $\mathbf{S}$ a set of predicates, and Q and Q' be conjunctive queries. Then the following problems are undecidable:

1. $\Sigma \models Q \subseteq Q'$, the containment problem.
2. $\exists Q' : \Sigma \models Q \supseteq Q'$ s.t. $Preds(Q') \subseteq \mathbf{S}$, i.e. it is undecidable whether the maximally contained rewriting of a conjunctive query Q w.r.t. Σ and $\mathbf{S}$ is nonempty (that is, it contains at least one conjunctive query).   □

Moreover, the boundedness problem for maximally contained positive rewritings is undecidable, as any datalog program can be written as a set of cind's.

We next give an intuition for the undecidability results of Theorem 3.1. Post's Correspondence Problem (PCP, see e.g. [20]), a simple and well-known undecidable problem, is defined as follows. Given nonempty words $x_1, \ldots, x_n$ and $y_1, \ldots, y_n$ over the alphabet $\{0, 1\}$, the problem is to decide whether there are indexes $i_1, \ldots, i_k$ (with $k > 0$) s.t. $x_{i_1} x_{i_2} \ldots x_{i_k} = y_{i_1} y_{i_2} \ldots y_{i_k}$. Pairs of words $\langle x_i, y_i \rangle$ are also called *dominos*. In the following example, we show, by an example, an encoding of PCP in terms of our query rewriting problem.

Example 3.2. Let s be a source, $q \leftarrow inc(0, 0)$. a boolean query, and

$$\text{inc}(x, y) \leftarrow \text{one}(x, x_1), \text{ zero}(x_1, x_2), \text{ one}(x_2, x_3), \text{ one}(y, y_1), \text{ inc}(x_3, y_1). \tag{1}$$

$$\begin{aligned}\text{inc}(x, y) \leftarrow &\text{ one}(x, x_1), \text{ zero}(y, y_1), \text{ one}(y_1, y_2), \\ &\text{ one}(y_2, y_3), \text{ one}(y_3, y_4), \text{ zero}(y_4, y_5), \text{ inc}(x_1, y_5).\end{aligned} \tag{2}$$

$$\text{inc}(x, y) \leftarrow \text{dec}(x, y). \tag{3}$$

$$\{\langle x, y \rangle \mid \text{dec}(x, y)\} \subseteq \{\langle x, y \rangle \mid \exists x_1, y_1 : \text{zero}(x, x_1) \wedge \text{zero}(y, y_1) \wedge \text{dec}(x_1, y_1)\} \tag{4}$$

$$\{\langle x, y \rangle \mid \text{dec}(x, y)\} \subseteq \{\langle x, y \rangle \mid \exists x_1, y_1 : \text{one}(x, x_1) \wedge \text{one}(y, y_1) \wedge \text{dec}(x_1, y_1)\} \tag{5}$$

$$\text{dec}(0, 0) \leftarrow s. \tag{6}$$

six cind's of which the leading two stand for the instance

$$\mathcal{I} = \{\langle x_1 = 101, \ y_1 = 1 \rangle, \langle x_2 = 1, \ y_2 = 01110 \rangle\}$$

and the remaining four constitute the core PCP encoding. The constraints (1) and (2) "guess" two words represented as chains of "one" and "zero" atoms by the nondeterminism by which resolution (or MCD rewriting using Algorithm 4.1, for that matter) chooses a clause to resolve an "inc" atom, (3) finalizes the guess phase, constraints (4) and (5) "check" whether the two words are equal (which indicates the existence of a solution to the PCP problem) by proceeding from the right to the left, and constraint (6) "terminates" if the search was successful.

For showing the PCP instance $\mathcal{I}$ satisfiable, one can compute a contained rewriting by applying the constraints in the following order (we only describe the proof but no dead-end branches): (guess phase) (1), (2), (1), (3), (check phase) (5), (4), (5), (5), (5), (4), (5), (termination) (6)[3]. We find a solution $x_1 x_2 x_1 = y_1 y_2 y_1 = 1011101$ to $\mathcal{I}$. Generally, a PCP instance is satisfiable iff the maximally contained rewriting is $\{q \leftarrow s.\}$. (Furthermore, a PCP instance is satisfiable iff $\Sigma \vDash \{\langle\rangle \mid inc(0,0)\} \supseteq \{\langle\rangle \mid s\}$.)   □

For the important case that Σ is acyclic, the above problems are decidable (and those of Theorem 3.1 are *NEXPTIME*-complete).

Theorem 3.2. Let Σ be an acyclic set of cind's and Q and Q' be conjunctive queries. Then the containment problem $\Sigma \vDash Q \subseteq Q'$ and the query rewriting problem for conjunctive queries (under acyclic sets of cind's) are NEXPTIME-complete.   □

Membership in NEXPTIME follows from the more general result on nonrecursive logic programming [7,21] and hardness can be shown by a modification of the reduction from the TILING problem of [7]. For lack of space, we have refer to [14] for a proof.

4   Generalizing Local-as-View Rewriting

The results of this section generalize from work on algorithms for the problem of answering queries using views [16], for instance the Bucket Algorithm [17], the Inverse Rules Algorithm [8], OCCAM [15], the Unification-join Algorithm [19], and particularly the MiniCon Algorithm [18]. For space reasons, we introduce necessary notions as needed and refer to [18] for a discussion and comparison of such algorithms.

We adapt the notion of MiniCon descriptions [18] to our framework based on query rewriting with cind's decomposed into Horn clauses.

Definition 4.1. (Inverse MiniCon Description). Let Q be a conjunctive query with $n = |Body(Q)|$ and Σ be a set of cind's. An (inverse) MiniCon description for Q is a pair of a tuple $\langle c_1, \ldots, c_n \rangle \in (NF(\Sigma) \cup \{\epsilon\})^n$ with at least one $c_i \neq \epsilon$ and a substitution θ that satisfies the following two conditions.

---

[3] One can easily verify this proof using the intuition of fully replacing parts of (intermediate) goals by subsumed queries of cind's whose subsumer queries fully match those parts. Due to the special structure of the cind's, at any point, all MCDs are "isomorphic" to some subsumer query of a cind.

1. For the most general unifier $\theta \neq fail$ arrived at by unifying the heads of all the $c_i \neq \epsilon$ with $Body_i(Q)$, the unfolding of Q and $\langle c_1, \ldots, c_n \rangle$ under θ is function-free and
2. there is no tuple $\langle c'_1, \ldots, c'_n \rangle \in \{c_1, \epsilon\} \times \ldots \times \{c_n, \epsilon\}$ with fewer entries different from ϵ than in $\langle c_1, \ldots, c_n \rangle$, such that the unfolding of Q with $\langle c'_1, \ldots, c'_n \rangle$ is function free.   □

Example 4.1. Consider again the query Q and the constraint (which we now call σ) of Example 1.1. $NF(\{\sigma\})$ is

$$c_1 : \text{parent}(x, f_{\sigma,y}(x, z)) \leftarrow \text{grandparent}(x, z) \wedge \text{alive}(x).$$
$$c_2 : \text{parent}(f_{\sigma,y}(x, z), z) \leftarrow \text{grandparent}(x, z) \wedge \text{alive}(x).$$

We have two MCDs, $\langle\langle c_1, c_2, \epsilon \rangle, \theta\rangle$ with the unifier

$$\theta = \{[x_1/x^{(1)}],\ [x_2/f_{\sigma,y}(x^{(1)}, z^{(1)})],\ [x_2/f_{\sigma,y}(x^{(2)}, z^{(2)})],\ [x_3/z^{(2)}]\}$$

and $\langle\langle \epsilon, \epsilon, c_1 \rangle, \theta'\rangle$ with $\theta' = \{[x_3/x^{(3)}], [x_4/f_{\sigma,y}(x^{(3)}, z^{(3)})]\}$. Note that $\langle c_1, c_2, c_1 \rangle$ violates condition 2 of Definition 4.1, while all other MCD candidates violate condition 1.   □

Note that the inverse MiniCon descriptions of Definition 4.1 exactly coincide with the MCDs of [18] in the local-as-view case. Algorithm 4.1 shown below can easily be reformulated so as to use a slight generalization of the notation of [18] to cover clause bodies consisting of several atoms. That way, one can even escape the need to transform cind's into Horn clauses and can reason completely without the introduction of function terms. However, to support the presentation of our results (particularly the equivalence proof of the following section), we do not follow this path in this paper.

Algorithm 4.1 (Query rewriting with MCDs).
Input. A conjunctive query Q, a set of cind's Σ, and a set **S** of source predicates
Output. A maximally contained rewriting of Q w.r.t. Σ and **S**

$Qs := [Q]$;
while Qs is not empty **do** {
    $[Q, Qs] := Qs$;
    if $Preds(Q) \subseteq$ **S then output** Q;
    else {
        $M :=$ compute the set of all inverse MCDs for Q and Σ;
        for each $\langle\langle c_1, \ldots, c_n \rangle, \theta\rangle \in M$ **do** {
            $Q' := \text{unfold}(Q, \theta, \langle c_1, \ldots, c_n \rangle)$;
            $Qs := [Qs, Q']$;
} } }   □

In Algorithm 4.1, maximally contained rewritings of a conjunctive query Q are computed by iteratively unfolding queries with *single* MiniCon descriptions[4]

---

[4] In this respect, Algorithm 4.1 differs from the MiniCon algorithm for the problem of answering queries using views, where MCDs are packed so as to rewrite all body atom at once.

until a rewriting contains only source predicates in its body. In order to handle cyclic sets of cind's (and attain completeness), we manage intermediate rewritings using a queue and, consequently, follow a breath-first strategy.

The function "unfold" accepts a conjunctive query Q with $|Body(Q)| = n$, a unifier θ and a tuple of n Horn clauses or ϵ s.t. if $c_i \neq \epsilon$, θ unifies $Body_i(Q)$ with $Head(c_i)$. It produces a new clause from Q (which in fact is again guaranteed to be function-free and thus a conjunctive query) by replacing $Head(Q)$ by $\theta(Head(Q))$ and each of the non-source body atoms $Body_i(Q)$, with $c_i \neq \epsilon$, by $\theta(Body(c_i))$. (i.e. after applying substitutions from the unifier). If $c_i = \epsilon$, $Body_i(Q)$ is replaced by $\theta(Body_i(Q))$. Of course, for each MCD $\langle\langle\ldots, c_i, \ldots, c_j, \ldots\rangle, \theta\rangle$ we have $\theta(Body(c_i)) = \theta(Body(c_j))$, and thus only one rule body needs to be added for each MCD during unfolding.

Theorem 4.2. Let Q be a conjunctive query, Σ be a set of cind's, and **S** be a set of "source" predicates. Then, for each conjunctive query Q' with $Preds(Q') \subseteq \mathbf{S}$ we have $\Sigma \vDash Q \supseteq Q'$ iff Algorithm 4.1 eventually computes a conjunctive query Q'' with $Preds(Q'') \subseteq \mathbf{S}$ and $\Sigma \vDash Q \supseteq Q'' \supseteq Q'$. $\Box$

In other words, Algorithm 4.1 enumerates the maximally contained positive rewriting of Q under Σ in terms of **S**. Note that given our requirement that predicates of **S** do not appear in heads of $NF(\Sigma)$, we of course have $\Sigma \vDash Q'' \supseteq Q'$ iff $Q'' \supseteq Q'$ (that is, classical conjunctive query containment [6]).

It is easy to see that the rewriting process of Algorithm 4.1 simply is equivalent to resolution where only some of the subgoals of a goal may be rewritten in a single step and each intermediate rewriting has to be function-free. Every proof generated by Algorithm 4.1 is thus a correct resolution proof. Thus,

Lemma 4.1. (Soundness of Algorithm 4.1) Let Q be a conjunctive query, Σ a set of cind's, and **S** a set of source predicates. Then, for each conjunctive query Q' generated by Algorithm 4.1 for Q, Σ, and **S**, we have $\Sigma \vDash Q \supseteq Q'$ and $Preds(Q') \subseteq \mathbf{S}$. $\Box$

Completeness is a consequence of the following result.

Lemma 4.2. Let $\mathcal{P}$ be a resolution proof establishing a logically contained rewriting of a conjunctive query Q under a set of cind's Σ. Then, there is always a proof $\mathcal{P}'$ establishing the same contained rewriting such that each intermediate rewriting is function-free. $\Box$

Proof.   Let us assume that each new subgoal a derived using resolution receives an identifying index $idx(a)$. Then, given the proof $\mathcal{P}$, there is a unique *next premise to be applied* $c_{idx(a)}$ out of the Horn clauses in $NF(\Sigma)$ for each subgoal a. This is the Horn clause from our constraints base that will be unfolded with a to resolve it in $\mathcal{P}$.

Note that the proof $\mathcal{P}$ is fully described by some unique indexing $idx(a)$ of all subgoals a appearing in the proof (while we do not need to know or remember the atoms themselves), the clauses $c_{idx(a)}$, and a specification of which indexes the subgoals in the bodies of these clauses are attributed with when they are unfolded with subgoals.

In our original proof $\mathcal{P}$, each subgoal a of a goal is rewritten with $c_{idx(a)}$ in each step, transforming g_0, the body of Q and at the same time the initial goal, via $g_1, \ldots, g_{n-1}$ to g_n, the body of the resulting rewriting. We maintain the head of Q separately across resolution steps and require that variables in the head are not unified with function terms, but apply other unifications effected on the variables in the goals in parallel with the rewriting process. Already $\mathcal{P}$ must assure *at any step* that no variable from the head of Q is unified with a function term, as otherwise no conjunctive query can result.

We know that resolution remains correct no matter in which order the next due resolution steps $c_{idx(a)}$ are applied to the subgoals, and that we even may unfold, given e.g. a goal with two atoms, the first goal and then a subgoal from the unfolding of that first goal (and may do that any finite number of times) before we unfold our second original subgoal.

Coming back to deriving a function-free proof starting from $\mathcal{P}$, all we now have to show is that at any intermediate step of a resolution proof with cind's, a nonempty set of subgoals $X = \{a_{i_1}, \ldots, a_{i_k}\} \subseteq g_i$ of the function-free intermediate goal g_i exists such that, when only these subgoals are unfolded with their next due premises to be applied $c_{idx(a_{i_1})}, \ldots, c_{idx(a_{i_k})}$, the overall new goal g_{i+1} produced will be function-free[5]. The emphasis here lies on finding a *nonempty* such set X, as the empty set automatically satisfies this condition. If we can guarantee that such a nonempty set always exists until the function-free proof has been completed, our lemma is shown.

Let there be a dependency graph $G_{g_i} = \langle V, E \rangle$ for each (intermediate) goal g_i with the subgoals as vertices and a directed edge $\langle a, b \rangle \in E$ iff a contains a variable v that is unified with a function term $f(\bar{X})$ in $Head(c_{idx(a)})$ and v appears in b and is unified with a variable (rather than a function term with the same function symbol) in $Head(c_{idx(b)})$. (Intuitively, if there is an edge $\langle a, b \rangle \in E$, then b must be resolved *before* a if a proof shall be obtained in which all intermediate goals are function-free.) As mentioned, query heads are guaranteed to remain function-free by the correctness of $\mathcal{P}$. For instance, the dependency graph of the goal $\leftarrow a(x)^{(0)}, b(x,y)^{(1)}, c(y,z)^{(2)}, d(z,w)^{(3)}$.   with

$$c_0 : a(x) \leftarrow a'(x). \qquad c_1 : b(f(x), x) \leftarrow b'(x).$$
$$c_2 : c(x, x) \leftarrow c'(x). \qquad c_3 : d(g(x), x) \leftarrow d'(x).$$

would be $G = \langle \{0, 1, 2, 3\}, \{\langle 1, 0 \rangle, \langle 3, 2 \rangle\} \rangle$, i.e. the first subgoal must be resolved before the second and the third subgoal must be resolved before the fourth.

We can now show that such a dependency graph G *is always acyclic*. In fact, if it were not, $\mathcal{P}$ could not be a valid proof, because unification would fail when trying to unify a variable in such a cycle with a function term that *contains that variable*. This is easy to see because each function term given our construction used for obtaining Horn clauses from cind's contains *all* variables appearing in that same (head) atom. Consider for instance

---

[5] The correctness of the proof $\mathcal{P}$ alone assures that the query head will be function-free as well.

$$q(x) \leftarrow a(x,y), \; a(y,z), \; b(w,z), \; b(z,y).$$

$$\{\langle x,y\rangle \mid \exists z : a(x,z) \wedge a(z,y)\} \supseteq \{\langle x,y\rangle \mid s(x,y)\}$$
$$\{\langle x,y\rangle \mid \exists z : b(x,z) \wedge b(z,y)\} \supseteq \{\langle x,y\rangle \mid s(x,y)\}$$

where s is a source. There is no rewriting under our two semantics, because the dependency graph of our above construction is cyclic already for our initial goal, the body of q.

However, since G is acyclic given a proof $\mathcal{P}$, we can unfold a nonempty set of atoms (those unreachable from other subgoals in graph G) with our intermediate goals until the proof has been completed.   □

As an immediate consequence of Lemma 4.2 (which assures that for each resolution proof $\mathcal{P}$ showing $\Sigma \vDash Q \supseteq Q'$ we can produce an equivalent function-free proof $\mathcal{P}'$ that will be covered by Algorithm 4.1), we have

Lemma 4.3. (Completeness of Algorithm 4.1) If $\Sigma \vDash Q \supseteq Q'$ and $Preds(Q') \subseteq \mathbf{S}$, then Algorithm 4.1 computes a conjunctive query Q'' s.t. $\Sigma \vDash Q \supseteq Q'' \supseteq Q'$.
    □

Lemma 4.1 and Lemma 4.3 taken together imply Theorem 4.2. Let us visualize the implications of Lemma 4.2 with an example.

Example 4.2. Given a boolean conjunctive query $q \leftarrow b(x,x,0)$. and the following set of Horn clauses which, as is easy to see, are the normal form of a set of cind's, which we do not show in order to reduce redundancy.

$b(x',y',0) \leftarrow a(x,y,2), \; e_\epsilon(x,x'), \; e_1(y,y').$	c_0
$b(x',y',2) \leftarrow a(x,y,0), \; e_1(x,x'), \; e_0(y,y').$	c_4, c_{10}, c_{11}
$b(x',y',0) \leftarrow a(x,y,1), \; e_0(x,x'), \; e_\epsilon(y,y').$	c_{12}, c_{18}, c_{19}
$b(x',y',1) \leftarrow a(x,y,0), \; e_1(x,x'), \; e_1(y,y').$	c_{20}, c_{25}
$e_\epsilon(x,x) \leftarrow v(x).$	c_2, c_{17}
$e_1(x,f_1(x)) \leftarrow v(x).$	c_3, c_8, c_{23}, c_{24}
$e_0(x,f_0(x)) \leftarrow v(x).$	c_2, c_{17}
$v(x) \leftarrow b(x,y,s).$	c_5, c_{13}, c_{21}
$v(y) \leftarrow b(x,y,s).$	c_6, c_{14}
$a(x,y,s) \leftarrow b(x,y,s).$	c_1, c_7, c_{15}

where x,y,x',y',s are variables. Let $\mathcal{P}$ be the resolution proof

(0) $\leftarrow b(x,x,0)^{(0)}$.
(1) $\leftarrow a(x,y,2)^{(1)}, \; e_\epsilon(x,z)^{(2)}, \; e_1(y,z)^{(3)}$.
(2) $\leftarrow b(f_1(y),y,2)^{(4)}, \; v(f_1(y))^{(5)}, \; v(y)^{(6)}$.
(3) $\leftarrow a(x_1,y_1,0)^{(7)}, \; e_1(x_1,f_1(y))^{(8)}, \; e_0(y_1,y)^{(9)}, \; b(f_1(y),v_1,2)^{(10)},$
      $b(v_2,y,2)^{(11)}$. $\dagger_{10}, \dagger_{11}$
(4) $\leftarrow b(f_0(y_1),y_1,0)^{(12)}, \; v(f_0(y_1))^{(13)}, \; v(y_1)^{(14)}$.
(5) $\leftarrow a(x_2,y_2,1)^{(15)}, \; e_0(x_2,f_0(y_1))^{(16)}, \; e_\epsilon(y_2,y_1)^{(17)}, b(f_0(y_1),v_1,0)^{(18)},$
      $b(v_2,y_1,0)^{(19)}$. $\dagger_{18}, \dagger_{19}$
(6) $\leftarrow b(y_1,y_1,1)^{(20)}, \; v(y_1)^{(21)}$.
(7) $\leftarrow a(x,x,0)^{(22)}, \; e_1(x,f_1(x))^{(23)}, \; e_1(x,f_1(x))^{(24)}, \; b(y_1,v_1,1)^{(25)}$. $\dagger_{25}$
(8) $\leftarrow a(x,x,0)^{(22)}, \; v(x)^{(26)}$.

which rewrites our query into $q \leftarrow a(x, x, 0), v(x)$. and in which we have superscribed each subgoal with its assigned index. In each resolution step, a goal $\leftarrow A^{(i_1)}, \ldots, A^{(i_n)}$. is unfolded with the clauses $c_{i_1}, \ldots, c_{i_n}$, as annotated above. To keep things short, we have eliminated subgoals (marked with a dagger † and their index) that are redundant with a different branch of the proof. As claimed in our theorem, $\mathcal{P}$ can be transformed into the following proof in which each intermediate step is function-free.

(0) $\leftarrow b(x, x, 0)^{(0)}$.
(1) $\leftarrow a(x, y, 2)^{(1)}$, $e_\epsilon(x, z)^{(2)}$, $[e_1(y, z)^{(3)}]$.
(2) $\leftarrow b(x, y, 2)^{(4)}$, $v(x)^{(5)}$, $[e_1(y, x)^{(3)}]$.
(3) $\leftarrow a(x_1, y_1, 0)^{(7)}$, $e_1(x_1, x)^{(8)}$, $e_0(y_1, y)^{(9)}$, $b(x, v_1, 2)^{(10)}$, $[e_1(y, x)^{(3)}]$. †$_{10}$
(4) $\leftarrow a(x_1, y_1, 0)^{(7)}$, $e_1(x_1, x)^{(8)}$, $[e_0(y_1, y)^{(9)}]$, $\cancel{e_1(y, x)^{(3)}}$.
(5) $\leftarrow b(y, y_1, 0)^{(12)}$, $v(y)^{(14)}$, $[e_0(y_1, y)^{(9)}]$.
(6) $\leftarrow a(x_2, y_2, 1)^{(15)}$, $e_0(x_2, y)^{(16)}$, $e_\epsilon(y_2, y_1)^{(17)}$, $b(y, v_1, 0)^{(18)}$, $\cancel{e_0(y_1, y)^{(9)}}$. †$_{18}$
(7) $\leftarrow b(y_1, y_1, 1)^{(20)}$, $v(y_1)^{(21)}$.
(8) $\leftarrow a(x_3, y_3, 0)^{(22)}$, $e_1(x_3, y_1)^{(23)}$, $e_1(y_3, y_1)^{(24)}$, $b(y_1, v_1, 1)^{(25)}$. †$_{25}$
(9) $\leftarrow a(x_3, x_3, 0)^{(22)}$, $v(x_3)^{(26)}$.

The subgoals that we have marked with brackets [ ] had been blocked at a certain step to keep the proof function-free.   □

Note that Example 4.2 constitutes another encoding of PCP that shows the undecidability of query rewriting with cind's. The PCP instance

$$\mathcal{I} = \{\langle x_1 = 10, y_1 = 1 \rangle, \langle x_2 = 1, y_2 = 01 \rangle\}$$

is encoded in the first four Horn clauses, which can be viewed as realizing a nondeterministic automaton that accepts two words $x_{i_1} \ldots x_{i_k}$ and $y_{i_1} \ldots y_{i_k}$ if they can be constructed using the dominos of $\mathcal{I}$. In the start state s_0, a domino $\langle x_i, y_i \rangle$ out of $\mathcal{I}$ is chosen. The symbols in x_i and y_i are then accepted one by one. If one of the two words x_i, y_i is longer than the other one, the shorter one is appended ϵ symbols. We return to the state s_0 no sooner than all symbols of a domino have been accepted. For the instance of Example 4.2, we thus have an automaton with three states.

The encoding again allows to show the undecidability of our query rewriting problem (A PCP instance is satisfiable iff the maximally contained rewriting of $q \leftarrow b(x, x, 0)$. under Σ is nonempty.) as well as the undecidability of query containment under a set of cind's. (A PCP instance is satisfiable if and only if $\Sigma \models \{\langle\rangle \mid \exists x : v(x) \wedge a(x, x, 0)\} \subseteq \{\langle\rangle \mid \exists x : b(x, x, 0)\}$.)

Of course this correspondence between function-free and general resolution proofs does not hold for Horn clauses in general.

Example 4.3. The boolean query $q \leftarrow a_1(u, v), b_1(u, v)$. and the Horn clauses

$$a_1(f(x), y) \leftarrow a_2(x, y). \qquad a_2(x, g(y)) \leftarrow a_3(x, y).$$
$$b_1(x, g(y)) \leftarrow b_2(x, y). \qquad b_2(f(x), y) \leftarrow b_3(x, y).$$

taken together entail $q \leftarrow a_3(x, y), b_3(x, y)$.   even though one cannot arrive at a function-free intermediate rewriting by either unfolding the left subgoal (resulting in $q \leftarrow a_2(x, y)$, $b_1(f(x), y)$.) or the right subgoal (which would result in $q \leftarrow a_1(x, g(y))$, $b_2(x, y)$.) of our query first, neither by unfolding both at once (resulting in $q \leftarrow a_2(x, g(y))$, $b_2(f(x), y)$.). $\square$

5   Implementation

Our implementation is based on Algorithm 4.1, but makes use of several optimizations. Directly after parsing, Horn clauses whose head predicates are unreachable from the predicates of the query are filtered out. The same is done with clauses not in the set X computed by

$X := \emptyset;$
do $X := X \cup$
$\qquad \{c \in C \mid Preds(Body(c)) \subseteq (Sources \cup \{Pred(Head(c')) \mid c' \in X\})\};$
while X changed;

We have implemented the simple optimizations known from the Bucket Algorithm [17] and the Inverse Rules Algorithm [11] for answering queries using views which are used to reduce the branching factor in the search process. Beyond that, MiniCon descriptions are computed with an intelligent backtracking method that always chooses to cover subgoals first for which this can be done deterministically (i.e., the number of Horn clauses that are candidates for unfolding with a particular subgoal can be reduced to one), thereby reducing the amount of branching.

In the implementation of the deterministic component of our algorithm for generating MiniCon descriptions, we first check whether the corresponding pairs of terms of two atoms to match unify independently before doing full unification. This allows to detect most violations with very low overhead. Given an appropriate implementation, it is possible to check this property in logarithmic or even constant time.

Our unification algorithm allows to pre-specify variables that may in no case be unified with a function term (e.g., for head variables of queries or atoms already over source predicates). This allows to detect the impossibility to create a function-free rewriting as early as possible.

Every time an MCD m is unfolded with a query to produce an *intermediate* rewriting Q, we compute a query Q' (a partial rewriting) as follows.

$Body(Q') := \{Body_i(Q) \mid m_i \neq \epsilon\}$
$Head(Q') := \langle x_1, \ldots, x_n \rangle$ s.t. each $x_i \in Vars(Head(Q)) \cap Vars(Body(Q'))$

Q' is thus created from the new subgoals of the query that have been introduced using the MCD. If Q' contains non-source predicates, the following check is performed. We check if our rewriting algorithm produces a nonempty rewriting on Q'. This is carried out in depth-first fashion. If the set of cind's is cyclic, we use a maximum lookahead distance to assure that the search terminates. If Q' is not further rewritable, Q does not need to be further processed but can be dropped. Subsequently, (intermediate) rewritings produced by unfolding queries with MiniCon descriptions are simplified using tableau minimization.

An important performance issue in Algorithm 4.1 is the fact that MCDs are only applied one at a time, which leads to redundant rewritings as e.g. the same MCDs may be applicable in different orders (as is true for the classical problem of answering queries using views, a special case) and thus a search space that may be larger than necessary. We use dependency graph-based optimizations to check if a denser packing of MCDs is possible. For the experiments with layered sets of cind's reported on in Section 6 (Figures 2 and 3), MCDs are packed exactly as densely as in the MiniCon algorithm of [18].

Distribution. The implementation of our query rewriter consists of about 9000 lines of C++ code. Binaries for several platforms as well as examples and a Web demonstrator that allows to run limited-size problems online are available on the Web at [13].

6   Experiments

A number of experiments have been carried out to evaluate the scalability of our implementation. These were executed on a 600 MHz dual Pentium III machine running Linux. A benchmark generator was implemented that randomly generated example chain queries and sets of chain cind's[6]. Chain queries are conjunctive queries of the form

$$q(x_1, x_{n+1}) \leftarrow p_1(x_1, x_2), \ p_2(x_2, x_3), \ \ldots, \ p_{n-1}(x_{n-1}, x_n), \ p_n(x_n, x_{n+1}).$$

Thus, chain queries are constructed by connecting binary predicates via variables to form chains, as shown above. In our experiments, the distinguished (head) variables were the first and the last. The chain cind's had between 3 and 6 subgoals in both the subsuming and the subsumed queries.

In all experiments, the queries had 10 subgoals, and we averaged timings over 50 runs. Sets of cind's were always acyclic. This was ascertained by the use of predicate indexes such that the predicates in a subsumer query of a cind only used indexes greater than or equal to a random number determined for each cind, and subsumed queries only used indexes smaller than that number. Times for parsing the input were excluded from the diagrams, and redundant rewritings were not eliminated[7]. Diagrams relate reasoning times on the (logarithmic-scale) vertical

---

[6] Experiments with various kinds of random queries and constraints were carried out, too. In this paper, we only report on chain queries, but the experiments with random queries were similarly favorable.

[7] Note that our implementation optionally can make finite rewritings non-redundant and minimal. However, for our experiments, these options were not active.

axis to the problem size expressed by the number of cind's on the horizontal axis.

We report on three experiments.

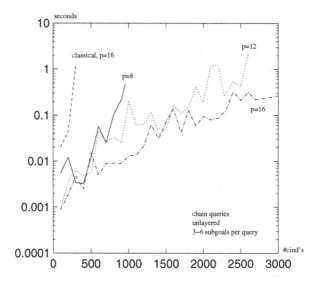

Fig. 1. Experiments with chain queries and nonlayered chain cind's.

Figure 1 shows timings for non-layered sets of constraints. By the steep line on the left we report on an alternative query rewriting algorithm that we have implemented and which follows a traditional resolution strategy. This algorithm (evaluated using instances with 16 predicates) is compared to and clearly outperformed by our new algorithm (with three different numbers of predicates; 8, 12, and 16). Clearly, the more predicates are available, the sparser the constraints get. Thus, more predicates render the query rewriting process simpler.

In Figure 2, we report on the execution times of our new algorithm with cind's generated with an implicit layering[8] of predicates (with 2 layers). This experiment is in principle very similar to local-as-view rewriting with $p/2$ global predicates and $p/2$ source predicates (where the subsumer queries of cind's correspond to logical views in the problem of answering queries using views), followed by view unfolding to account for the subsumed sides of cind's. We again report timings for three different total numbers of predicates, 8, 12, and 16.

In Figure 3, the new algorithm computes maximally contained rewritings for 20 and 40 predicates, which are grouped into stacks of five layers of 4 and 8 predicates each, respectively. Of the five sets of predicates, one constitutes the sources and one the "integration schema" over which queries are asked, and four equally sized sets of cind's bridge between these layers.

---

[8] See Section 2 for our definition of layered sets of cind's.

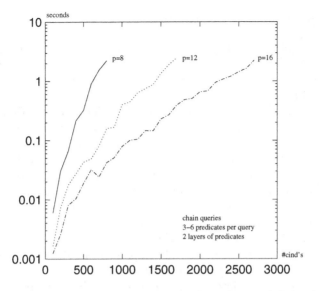

Fig. 2. Experiments with chain queries and two layers of chain cind's.

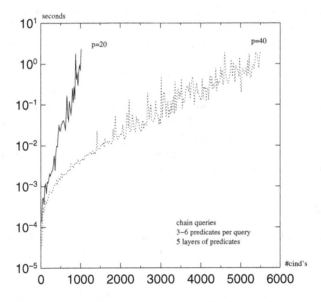

Fig. 3. Experiments with chain queries and five layers of chain cind's.

As can be seen by comparing the second and third diagrams with the first, the hardness of the layered problems is more homogeneous. Particularly in Figure 1 and Figure 2, one can also observe subexponential performance. Note that in the experiment of Figure 3, timings were taken in steps of 20 cind's, while in the other experiments, this step length was 100.

7 Discussion and Conclusions

This paper has addressed the query rewriting problem in data integration from a fresh perspective. We compute maximally contained rewritings with expressive symmetric constraints, which we call Conjunctive Inclusion Dependencies. We have proposed a new query rewriting algorithm based on techniques developed for the problem of answering queries using views (i.e., the MiniCon algorithm), which allows to apply time-tested (e.g., tableau minimization) techniques and algorithms from the database field to the query rewriting problem.

The main advantage of the new algorithm is that intermediate results are (function-free) queries and can be immediately made subject to query optimization techniques. As a consequence, further query rewriting may start from simpler queries, leading to an increase in performance and fewer redundant results that have to be found and later be eliminated. Thus, it is often possible to detect dead ends early. As a trade-off (as can be seen in Algorithm 4.1), an additional degree of nondeterminism is introduced compared to resolution-based algorithms that may temporarily introduce function terms.

In the context of data integration, there are usually a number of regularities in the way constraints are implemented and queries are posed. We expect to have a number of schemata, each one containing a number of predicates. Between the predicates of one schema, no constraints for data integration uses are defined. Moreover, we expect inter-schema constraints to be of the form $Q_1 \subseteq Q_2$ where most (or all) predicates in Q_1 belong to one and the same schema, while the predicates of Q_2 belong to another one. Queries issued against the system are usually formulated in terms of a single schema, and such a layering often propagates along intermediate rewritings. Given these assumptions, we suspect our approach – when optimization techniques from the database area are applied to intermediate results – to have a performance advantage over classical resolution-based algorithms, which do not exploit such techniques.

Our experiments show that our approach scales to very large and complex data integration settings with many schemata.

References

1. S. Adali, K. S. Candan, Y. Papakonstantinou, and V. S. Subrahmanian. "Query Caching and Optimization in Distributed Mediator Systems". In *Proceedings of the 1996 ACM SIGMOD International Conference on Management of Data (SIGMOD'96)*, pages 137–146, Montreal, Canada, June 1996.
2. Y. Arens and C. A. Knoblock. "Planning and Reformulating Queries for Semantically-Modeled Multidatabase Systems". In *Proceedings of the First International Conference on Information and Knowledge Management (CIKM'92)*, Baltimore, MD USA, 1992.
3. D. Calvanese, G. De Giacomo, and M. Lenzerini. "On the Decidability of Query Containment under Constraints". In *Proc. PODS'98*, pages 149–158, 1998.
4. D. Calvanese, G. De Giacomo, M. Lenzerini, D. Nardi, and R. Rosati. "Information Integration: Conceptual Modeling and Reasoning Support". In *Proc. CoopIS'98*, pages 280–291, 1998.

5. M. Carey, L. Haas, P. Schwarz, M. Arya, W. Cody, R. Fagin, M. Flickner, A. Luniewski, W. Niblack, D. Petkovic, J. Thomas, J. Williams, and E. Wimmers. "Towards Heterogeneous Multimedia Information Systems: The Garlic Approach". In *Proceedings of the Fifth International Workshop on Research Issues in Data Engineering: Distributed Object Management (RIDE-DOM'95)*, 1995.

6. A. K. Chandra and P. M. Merlin. "Optimal Implementation of Conjunctive Queries in Relational Data Bases". In *Conference Record of the Ninth Annual ACM Symposium on Theory of Computing (STOC'77)*, pages 77–90, Boulder, USA, 1977.

7. E. Dantsin and A. Voronkov. "Complexity of Query Answering in Logic Databases with Complex Values". In *LFCS'97, LNCS 1234*, pages 56–66, 1997.

8. O. M. Duschka and M. R. Genesereth. "Answering Recursive Queries using Views". In *Proc. PODS'97*, Tucson, AZ USA, 1997.

9. O. M. Duschka, M. R. Genesereth, and A. Y. Levy. "Recursive Query Plans for Data Integration". *Journal of Logic Programming*, **43**(1):49–73, 2000.

10. H. Garcia-Molina, Y. Papakonstantinou, D. Quass, A. Rajaraman, Y. Sagiv, J. D. Ullman, V. Vassalos, and J. Widom. "The TSIMMIS Approach to Mediation: Data Models and Languages". *Journal of Intelligent Information Systems*, **8**(2), 1997.

11. M. R. Genesereth, A. M. Keller, and O. M. Duschka. "Infomaster: An Information Integration System". In *Proceedings of the 1997 ACM SIGMOD International Conference on Management of Data (SIGMOD'97)*, pages 539–542, 1997.

12. J. Gryz. "Query Rewriting Using Views in the Presence of Functional and Inclusion Dependencies". *Information Systems*, **24**(7):597–612, 1999.

13. C. Koch. "Cindrew Home Page". http://cern.ch/chkoch/cindrew/.

14. C. Koch. *"Data Integration against Multiple Evolving Autonomous Schemata"*. PhD thesis, TU Wien, Vienna, Austria, 2001.

15. C. T. Kwok and D. S. Weld. "Planning to Gather Information". In *Proc. AAAI'96*, Portland, OR USA, Aug. 1996.

16. A. Y. Levy, A. O. Mendelzon, Y. Sagiv, and D. Srivastava. "Answering Queries Using Views". In *Proc. PODS'95*, San Jose, CA USA, 1995.

17. A. Y. Levy, A. Rajaraman, and J. J. Ordille. "Querying Heterogeneous Information Sources Using Source Descriptions". In *Proceedings of the 1996 International Conference on Very Large Data Bases (VLDB'96)*, pages 251–262, 1996.

18. R. Pottinger and A. Y. Levy. "A Scalable Algorithm for Answering Queries Using Views". In *Proceedings of the 26th International Conference on Very Large Data Bases (VLDB'2000)*, 2000.

19. X. Qian. "Query Folding". In *Proceedings of the 12th IEEE International Conference on Data Engineering (ICDE'96)*, pages 48–55, New Orleans, LA USA, 1996.

20. M. F. Sipser. *Introduction to the Theory of Computation*. PWS Publishing, 1997.

21. S. Vorobyov and A. Voronkov. "Complexity of Nonrecursive Logic Programs with Complex Values". In *Proc. PODS'98*, 1998.

A Privacy-Enhanced Microaggregation Method[*]

Yingjiu Li, Sencun Zhu, Lingyu Wang, and Sushil Jajodia

Center for Secure Information Systems, George Mason University,
Fairfax VA 22030-4444, USA
{yli2,szhu1,lwang3,jajodia}@gmu.edu

Abstract. Microaggregation is a statistical disclosure control technique for protecting microdata (i.e., individual records), which are important products of statistical offices. The basic idea of microaggregation is to cluster individual records in microdata into a number of mutually exclusive groups prior to publication, and then publish the average over each group instead of individual records. Previous methods require fixed or variable group size in clustering in order to reduce information loss. However, the security aspect of microaggregation has not been extensively studied. We argue that the group size requirement is not enough for protecting the privacy of microdata. We propose a new microaggregation method, which we call *secure-k-Ward*, to enhance the individual's privacy. Our method, which is optimization based, minimizes information loss and overall mean deviation while at the same time guarantees that the security requirement for protecting the microdata is satisfied.

1 Introduction

Microdata are relatively new products of statistical offices. Different from their traditional products of tabular data, which consist of *aggregate* information, microdata sets are groups of records containing information about *individual* respondents, such as persons, households, and companies [16]. Information about each individual respondent is recorded in microdata with two types of variables: identification variables (e.g., name) and sensitive variables (e.g., salary). Both identification and sensitive variables are confidential and thus need to be protected due to the "right of the individual to privacy." On the other hand, the "right of society to information" requires that adequate statistical information be supplied in the released data, which may lead to disclosure of individual data. Therefore, it is important to publish microdata so that individual information is sufficiently protected, while at the same time providing society with as much information as possible.

Microaggregation is a family of disclosure control methods for protecting numerical variables in microdata sets that have been recently studied [6,9,10,1]. The basic idea of microaggregation is to cluster individual records in microdata in a number of mutually exclusive groups prior to publication, and then publish

---

[*] This work was partially supported by the National Science Foundation under the grant CCR-0113515.

T. Eiter and K.-D. Schewe (Eds.): FoIKS 2002, LNCS 2284, pp. 148–159, 2002.
© Springer-Verlag Berlin Heidelberg 2002

the average over each group instead of individual records. A similar idea has also been discussed in statistical database literature where a database is partitioned into atomic populations (i.e., mutually exclusive groups) that constitute the raw materials available to the database users [3,2,13,17].

Previous microaggregation methods require that the size of each partition group be a fixed constant k, called *fixed-size microaggregation* [5,4]. Recent developments [6,9] have concentrated on reducing information loss by allowing the size of each partition group to vary (with lower bound k) to preserve natural data aggregates, called *data-oriented microaggregation* [6,9]. Following the setting used in Domingo-Ferrer and Mateo-Sanz [6], *information loss* can be defined as follows. Consider a microdata set with p continuous variables $X_1, \ldots, X_p$ and n individual records where each record can be considered as an instance of $X^T = (X_1, \ldots, X_p)$. Assume that these individual records are partitioned into g groups and the i-th group consists of n_i individuals x_{ij} ($j = 1, \ldots, n_i$) where $n_i \geq k$ and $\sum_{i=1}^{g} n_i = n$. Denote $\bar{x}_i$ the average vector over the i-th group and $\bar{x}$ the average of all individuals. The information loss is defined to be

$$L = \frac{SSE}{SST} \tag{1}$$

where SSE is the within-groups sum of squares:

$$SSE = \sum_{i=1}^{g} \sum_{j=1}^{n_i} (x_{ij} - \bar{x}_i)^T (x_{ij} - \bar{x}_i), \tag{2}$$

and SST is the total sum of squares:

$$SST = \sum_{i=1}^{g} \sum_{j=1}^{n_i} (x_{ij} - \bar{x})^T (x_{ij} - \bar{x}). \tag{3}$$

In the following discussion, we focus on *univariate microaggregation* [6], which refers to either of the two following cases: (1) the microdata set consists of a single variable (i.e., $p = 1$), or (2) the microdata set consists of several variables, but these variables are considered independently in turn. It is also possible to extend our method for multivariate microaggregation, which allows simultaneous microaggregation of several variables so that a single partition for the whole data set is obtained. We leave this as a possible future work area.

While using variable group size in microaggregation reduces the information loss in some cases[1], it could compromise the "privacy" of microdata sets. The microaggregation tries to preserve natural data aggregates; that is, the individuals with similar values are clustered together. Therefore, substituting the averages for the individuals in some groups has little effect on protecting the "privacy" of these individuals. For an extreme example, if the individual records in each group are the same, then a naive application of microaggregation dangerously publishes the original data set.

---

[1] According to the experiments in [6], the information loss decreases up to 0.2% after using variable group size in microaggregation for a single variable.

The security aspect (or "privacy") of microdata has not been studied extensively for microaggregation. Previous studies on microaggregation include (i) assessing the information loss caused by microaggregation [1], (ii) reducing the information loss by using variable group size [6], and (iii) applying microaggregation directly on multidimensional (unprojected) microdata [10]. In these studies, the security aspect of microdata is reflected on the requirement of minimum value of group size (i.e., k). Indeed, an attacker might not be able to discriminate among the individuals within a single group; therefore, with a larger group size, the "privacy" of microdata roughly increases. However, the group size is not a unique factor for the "privacy" aspect; the actual values of individuals within each group also count. In some cases (e.g., most individuals have similar values), the latter factor is more important.

In the following sections, we first review previous microaggregation methods and discuss the security issue of microaggregation. Then, we propose a secure microaggregation method based on optimization techniques. We employ two phases: intra-group optimization and inter-group optimization to minimize information loss and overall mean deviation and to guarantee that the security requirement for the microdata is satisfied. In the intra-group optimization phase, we model the problem of minimizing information loss within each group using nonlinear constrained programming. In the inter-group optimization phase, we prove that minimizing the overall mean deviation is an NP-hard problem and propose our heuristic algorithm. The paper concludes with a brief summary.

2   Previous Microaggregation Methods

Previous microaggregation methods can be classified into two categories: fixed-size microaggregation [5,4] and data-oriented microaggregation [6,9]. Both require individual records to be sorted according to some criterion before being partitioned. For the fixed-size microaggregation, the partition is done by combining successive k records into groups. If the total number of individual records n is not a multiple of k, the last group will contain more than k records. For the data-oriented microaggregation, the partition is done by allowing groups to be of size $\geq k$, depending on the structure of data, to attain the least information loss. The partition with group size $\geq k$ is called k-partition.

Intuitively, the finer the partition, the lower the information loss. For a given data set, a *finer than* relationship can be defined among different partitions: A partition p is said to be finer than another partition p' iff every group in p is contained by a group in p'. It has been proved in [6] that an optimal k-partition p (i.e., the one that achieves the least information loss) exists and that no k-partition $p' \neq p$ exists such that p' is finer than p. It has also been proved that the group size must be less than $2k$ (otherwise, we can split it to further reduce information loss) in the optimal k-partition. Unfortunately, no exact polynomial algorithms have been reported for the optimal k-partition to date.

Domingo-Ferrer and Mateo-Sanz [6] developed a heuristic algorithm, which they call k-Ward, for candidate optimal k-partitions based on Ward hierarchical clustering [15]. Given n individual records, algorithm k-Ward and Ward's method can be described respectively as follows:

Algorithm k-Ward

1 Initial phase: Form a group with the first k records of the microdata set and another group with the last k records. Other records constitute single-vector groups.

2 Merge phase: Use Ward's method (see below) until every group contains k or more records. When using Ward's method, never merge two groups that both have sizes $\geq k$.

3 Recursive phase: For each group in the final partition that contains $2k$ or more records, apply this algorithm (i.e., k-Ward) recursively.

It has been proven in [6] that the k-Ward algorithm ends after a finite number of recursion steps and that the computational complexity is quadratic (i.e., $O(n^2)$). The Ward's method used by k-Ward is an agglomerative hierarchical clustering method that produces a series n partitions. The first partition consists of n single-record groups; the last partition consists of a single group containing all n records. The algorithm for this method can be described as follows:

Ward's Method

1 Consider each single vector as a group. Then we have n groups $g_1, \ldots, g_n$.

2 Find the nearest pair of distinct groups, g_i and g_j, merge them to be one group, and decrement the number of groups by one.

3 If the number of groups is one, then stop; else, return to step 2.

3 The Security Issue of Microaggregation

The ultimate objective of the optimal microaggregation mentioned above is to minimize the information loss through grouping of the most similar records. However, as a consequence, the "privacy" of the microdata could be compromised. For example, assume that all the individual records within each group are almost the same (therefore, the information loss is very small) and there is little protection of the original data because the individual records are substituted in each group by the group average, which is almost the same as the individual records. In such a case, a database attacker is able to obtain either exact values or good approximate estimations for some original values of individual records. Intuitively, the lower the information loss, the less the microdata is protected, though the relationship between them is not explicit because both are data-oriented.

The security aspect in previous microaggregation is reflected in the requirement of the minimum group size k. With larger group size k, the security of microdata is roughly higher because an attacker needs to discriminate among more individuals within a group. However, no matter how large the group size, it is still possible that all the individuals in some groups are similar, depending on the data, leading to serious security problems.

Gaussian distribution with mean 5000			Uniform distribution with mean 5000		
standard deviation	$k = 4$	$k = 8$	half of scale parameter	$k = 4$	$k = 8$
1000	98.99%	94.87%	1000	100%	100%
2000	95.23%	88.21%	2000	100%	100%
5000	75.88%	62.05%	5000	91.35%	77.27%
10,000	58.79%	40%	10,000	67.18%	57.27%

Fig. 1. Percentage of "unsafe" groups in microaggregation for synthetic data sets

To show the motivation for studying the security issue of microaggregation, we perform a series of experiments using synthetic data sets. In the first set of experiments, we generate data sets with 2000 individual values using Gaussian distribution with mean 5000 and standard deviation 1000, 2000, 5000, and 10,000 respectively. We use the k-Ward algorithm to partition the data sets in which k equals 4 and 8, respectively. We consider a particular group of partitions "unsafe" if *all* the individual values in this group are at a distance from the group average of less than 1% of the group average. We show the percentage of groups that are "unsafe" in figure 1. In the same figure, we also show the result for synthetic data sets generated by uniform distribution with mean 5000 and the half-of-scale parameters 1000, 2000, 5000, and 10,000, respectively.

The above experiments show that microaggregation generates a significant percentage of "unsafe" groups that may be considered unacceptable for highly sensitive information. In our experiments, the less the standard deviation or scale parameter, and the less the minimum group size k, the more likely the microaggregation is "unsafe", because the individual values in each partition group are more similar to each other. For the same reason, the more individual values we generate in an experiment, the higher the percentage of groups are "unsafe." We also ran some experiments on data sets with more than 2000 individuals and found that the "unsafe" percentage was higher than those listed in figure 1.

In the following discussion, we consider an additional security measure in microaggregation. For numerical (continuous) variables, it is reasonable to protect the original data from approximate estimation in which an attacker need not know the exact value but a good estimation. We define *tolerance level* to measure such estimation:

Definition 3.1. *(Tolerance level ϵ) For any group in microaggregation, if an individual vector in the group is at a distance less than a scalar ϵ from its substituted value, then it is considered to be "dangerous"; otherwise, it is "safe".*

In general, different tolerance level ϵ_i can be used for different group i (e.g., a certain percentage of $\hat{x}_i$). To be simple, we assume that the tolerance level is a constant unless otherwise declared. Then we define *security ratio* as our new security measure.

Definition 3.2. *(Security ratio γ) For any group in microaggregation, the security ratio γ indicates the percentage of individual records in this group that are*

at a distance greater than ε from their substituted value, where ε is the tolerance level.

The security ratio is used to evaluate the effectiveness of substitution in microaggregation in terms of security, that is, the percentage of individual records in each group that is considered "safe." In our secure microaggregation method, we require that the security ratio γ be greater than a predetermined threshold γ_0 while at the same time we optimize the information loss and the overall mean deviation. We will discuss our method in detail in the next section.

4 A Secure Microaggregation Method

We study a secure microaggregation method based on k-Ward. The basic idea is as follows. Given a data set of n individual records and a threshold γ_0 for the security ratio, we assume that k-partition has been done by k-Ward which partitions the data set into g groups. After the k-partition is done, we can easily compute the security ratio γ for each group in the partition. For each group i, if $\gamma \geq \gamma_0$, then the substitution for this group using the group average $\bar{x}_i$ is considered to be "safe." Otherwise, we change the group average $\bar{x}_i$ to another value $\hat{x}_i$ and use the latter in substitution. In this case, we also use $\hat{x}_i$ (instead of $\bar{x}_i$) in computation of SSE (see formula (2); note that formulae (1) and (3) remain unchanged). We choose the value $\hat{x}_i$ to minimize the information loss (or SSE) for this group while at the same time satisfy the security constraint $\gamma \geq \gamma_0$. We also require that the average of all individuals changes as small as possible. The algorithm, which we call *secure-k-Ward*, is described as follows:

Algorithm secure-k-Ward

1 Initial phase: Apply k-Ward to the input data set. Assume that the data set is partitioned into g groups with the i-th group consisting of n_i individuals x_{ij} $(j = 1, \ldots, n_i)$, where $n_i \geq k$ and $\sum_{i=1}^{g} n_i = n$. Denote the average over the i-th group $\bar{x}_i$ $(i = 1, \ldots, g)$.

2 Checking phase: For each group i, compute the security ratio γ based on the data and the tolerance level ϵ. If $\gamma \geq \gamma_0$, then use the average $\bar{x}_i$ to substitute the individual values in this group and continue this checking phase for the next group; else, deliver the current group i to the intra-group optimization phase.

3 Intra-group optimization phase: Compute two optimal values $\overleftarrow{x_i}$ and $\overrightarrow{x_i}$ for the current group i and use them respectively instead of $\bar{x}_i$ in substitution of individuals in group i such that the information loss of substitution in this group is minimized with the constraints $\{\gamma \geq \gamma_0 \wedge \overleftarrow{x_i} \leq \bar{x}_i\}$ and $\{\gamma \geq \gamma_0 \wedge \overrightarrow{x_i} \geq \bar{x}_i\}$, respectively. Then go back to the checking phase for the next group.

4 Inter-group optimization phase: For each group j that has been optimized by phase 3, determine either $\overleftarrow{x_j}$ or $\overrightarrow{x_j}$ to be $\hat{x}_j$ and use $\hat{x}_j$ in substitution of values in this group such that the average over all substituted values of all groups is as close as possible to the original average $\bar{x}$.

One of the advantages of secure-k-Ward is that it is "compatible" with k-Ward; that is, if the k-partition finished by k-Ward has no security problem in terms of the security ratio, then secure-k-Ward works exactly the same way as k-Ward. In this case, secure-k-Ward terminates once the checking phase is finished.

However, if the security requirement is not satisfied for some groups, secure-k-Ward invokes the intra-group optimization phase and the inter-group optimization phase to search for an optimal substitution. The optimal substitution satisfies the security requirement while at the same time minimizes the information loss and the overall mean deviation. The purpose of intra-group optimization is to seek a trade-off between the security ratio and the information loss, while the inter-group optimization balances the security ratio and information loss with the overall mean deviation. We discuss those two phases in detail in the following subsections.

Note that secure-k-Ward is a heuristic method (i.e., suboptimal method) that minimizes the information loss and the overall mean deviation while at the same time satisfies the requirement of the security ratio. We mention that polynomial exact algorithms do not exist for obtaining the optimal solution. We will show in section 4.2 that even optimizing a particular phase in secure-k-Ward is NP-hard.

4.1   Intra-group Optimization

Given a particular group i of n_i individual data, the security ratio γ is a function of the group average $\bar{x}_i$ and the tolerance level ϵ, thus denoted as $\gamma(\bar{x}_i, \epsilon)$. More specifically,

$$\gamma(\bar{x}_i, \epsilon) = \frac{|S_i - S_i \cap I(\bar{x}_i, \epsilon)|}{|S_i|}, \tag{4}$$

where $S_i = \{x_{ij} : j = 1, \ldots, n_i\}$ and $I(\bar{x}_i, \epsilon) = \{x : |x - \bar{x}_i| < \epsilon\}$. If $\gamma(\bar{x}_i, \epsilon)$ is less than the threshold γ_0, then the substitution of $\bar{x}_i$ in group i is considered "unsafe". Then the intra-group optimization phase is invoked to compute two candidates $\overleftarrow{x_i}$ and $\overrightarrow{x_i}$ to replace $\bar{x}_i$ in substitution, where $\overleftarrow{x_i} \le \bar{x}_i$ and $\overrightarrow{x_i} \ge \bar{x}_i$. The candidates $\overleftarrow{x_i}$ and $\overrightarrow{x_i}$ are chosen—by minimizing the information loss in substitution—to be the solutions to the following nonlinear constrained programming problems $\overleftarrow{\mathcal{P}_i}$ and $\overrightarrow{\mathcal{P}_i}$, respectively:

$\overleftarrow{\mathcal{P}_i}$:   minimize $L(\overleftarrow{x_i})$ $\overrightarrow{\mathcal{P}_i}$:   minimize $L(\overrightarrow{x_i})$

　　　subject to $\gamma(\overleftarrow{x_i}, \epsilon) \ge \gamma_0$ subject to $\gamma(\overrightarrow{x_i}, \epsilon) \ge \gamma_0$

　　　　　　　　　$\overleftarrow{x_i} \le \bar{x}_i$ 　　　　　　　$\overrightarrow{x_i} \ge \bar{x}_i$

---

where $L(\overleftarrow{x_i}) = \frac{\sum_{j=1}^{n_i}(x_{ij} - \overleftarrow{x_i})^2}{\sum_{j=1}^{n_i}(x_{ij} - \bar{x}_i)^2}$ and $L(\overrightarrow{x_i}) = \frac{\sum_{j=1}^{n_i}(x_{ij} - \overrightarrow{x_i})^2}{\sum_{j=1}^{n_i}(x_{ij} - \bar{x}_i)^2}$. To assure that the solutions of these problems satisfy the security requirement, we require that all constraints in the above formulation must be "hard" constraints; that is, we must use feasible algorithms to solve these optimization problems. Note that the optimal solutions always exist. From section 2, we know that at least k and at most $2k - 1$ individuals are in each group. We can always set $\overleftarrow{x_j}$ (or $\overrightarrow{x_j}$) at a distance far away from the minimum (or maximum) value of the individuals in group i such that the security ratio γ is greater than γ_0. Therefore, the feasible sets of the above optimization problems are not empty and the optimal solutions exist.

Nonlinear constrained programming has been studied over fifty years in the literature of mathematical programming. Though it is a difficult field (even quadratic programming[2] is NP-hard), researchers have developed many practically efficient methods, such as penalty, barrier, augmented Lagrangian, sequential quadratic programming, and direct methods [12]. Some robust methods, such as SWIFT [14], have been used in mature software packages (e.g., MATLAB) that are publicly available and can be easily used to solve the above problems.

4.2   Inter-group Optimization

Without loss of generality, we assume that the two candidates $\overleftarrow{x_i}$ and $\overrightarrow{x_i}$ have been obtained for group $i = 1, \ldots, g'$, where $g' \leq g$. The inter-group optimization phase is to determine either $\overleftarrow{x_i}$ or $\overrightarrow{x_i}$ to be $\hat{x}_i$ such that the overall sum deviation (or overall mean deviation) is minimized. This problem can be formulated as follows:

$$
\mathcal{P}: \quad \text{minimize} \quad s = \left| \sum_{i=1}^{g'} u_i \cdot \overleftarrow{\Delta_i} + v_i \cdot \overrightarrow{\Delta_i} \right|
$$
$$
\text{subject to} \quad u_i, v_i \in \{0, 1\},
$$
$$
u_i + v_i = 1,
$$
$$
i = 1, \ldots, g'.
$$

where $\overleftarrow{\Delta_i} = (\overleftarrow{x_i} - \bar{x}_i) \cdot n_i$ is the sum deviation caused by using $\overleftarrow{x_i}$ instead of $\bar{x}_i$ in substitution; similarly, $\overrightarrow{\Delta_i} = (\overrightarrow{x_i} - \bar{x}_i) \cdot n_i$ is the sum deviation caused by using $\overrightarrow{x_i}$. We have $\overleftarrow{\Delta_i} \leq 0$ and $\overrightarrow{\Delta_i} \geq 0$. Denote $\hat{x}_i$ to be either $\overleftarrow{x_i}$ or $\overrightarrow{x_i}$: If $u_i = 1$ $(v_i = 0)$ is in the solution to the above problem $\mathcal{P}$, then $\hat{x}_i = \overleftarrow{x_i}$; otherwise, $\hat{x}_i = \overrightarrow{x_i}$. It is easy to know that the objective function s is the overall sum deviation caused by using $\hat{x}_i$ instead of $\bar{x}_i$ in substitution.

We have mentioned before that there is no polynomial exact algorithm that minimizes the information loss and overall mean deviation while at the same time satisfies the requirement of the security ratio. The following proposition shows that even optimizing a particular phase in secure-k-Ward is NP-hard.

Proposition 4.1. *Problem $\mathcal{P}$ is NP-hard.*

Proof. We restrict problem $\mathcal{P}$ to another problem $\mathcal{P}'$ by allowing only instances in which $\overleftarrow{\Delta_i} = -\overrightarrow{\Delta_i}$ and $\overrightarrow{\Delta_i}$ $(i = 1, \ldots, g')$ are positive integers. We only need to prove that the problem $\mathcal{P}'$ is NP-hard.

We claim the NP-hardness of another problem $\mathcal{P}''$: given a set $A = \{\overrightarrow{\Delta_1}, \ldots, \overrightarrow{\Delta_{g'}}\}$ of positive integers, determine if there is a subset $A' \subseteq A$ such that

---

[2] Quadratic programming refers to linearly constrained optimization with a quadratic objective function.

$\sum_{\overrightarrow{\triangle}_i \in A^{\square}} \overrightarrow{\triangle}_i = \sum_{\overrightarrow{\triangle}_i \in A - A^{\square}} \overrightarrow{\triangle}_i$. Problem $\mathcal{P}''$ is a well-known NP-hard problem called PARTITION.

Now we prove the NP-hardness of problem $\mathcal{P}'$ by contradiction. Suppose that a polynomial algorithm exists for problem $\mathcal{P}'$. Then, we can obtain a subset $A'' \subseteq A$ such that $s = \left| \sum_{\overrightarrow{\triangle}_i \in A^{\blacksquare}} \overrightarrow{\triangle}_i - \sum_{\overrightarrow{\triangle}_i \in A - A^{\blacksquare}} \overrightarrow{\triangle}_i \right|$ is the minimum for all possible subsets of A. Clearly, iff $s = 0$, the answer to problem $\mathcal{P}''$ is positive and A equals A''; otherwise, the answer to problem $\mathcal{P}''$ is negative. Therefore, problem $\mathcal{P}''$ can be solved in polynomial time. This is a contradiction. $\quad\square$

In order to solve problem $\mathcal{P}$ practically, we develop a heuristic method. Let $s^+ = \sum_i v_i \cdot \overrightarrow{\triangle}_i$ and $s^- = \sum_i u_i \cdot \overleftarrow{\triangle}_i$. The heuristic method is described as follows:

Heuristic Method for Problem $\mathcal{P}$
1 $s^+ \leftarrow 0$, $s^- \leftarrow 0$.
2 **for** $i \leftarrow 1$ **to** g' **do**
3 $\qquad$ **if** $s^+ \geq -s^-$ **then** $u_i \leftarrow 1$, $v_i \leftarrow 0$, $s^- \leftarrow s^- + \overleftarrow{\triangle}_i$
4 $\qquad$ **else** $u_i \leftarrow 0$, $v_i \leftarrow 1$, $s^+ \leftarrow s^+ + \overrightarrow{\triangle}_i$

Once the heuristic algorithm terminates, we have $s^+ = \sum_{i=1}^{g^{\square}} v_i \cdot \overrightarrow{\triangle}_i$ and $s^- = \sum_{i=1}^{g^{\square}} u_i \cdot \overleftarrow{\triangle}_i$ and the objective function $s = |s^+ + s^-|$. Clearly, the heuristic algorithm is linear. In regard to the overall sum deviation, we have the following result:

Proposition 4.2. *If problem $\mathcal{P}$ is solved by the heuristic method, then the overall sum deviation s satisfies*

$$s \leq max(-\overleftarrow{\triangle}_1, \ldots, -\overleftarrow{\triangle}_{g^{\square}}, \overrightarrow{\triangle}_1, \ldots, \overrightarrow{\triangle}_{g^{\square}}). \tag{5}$$

Proof. Denote $s(g') = \sum_{i=1}^{g^{\square}} (u_i \cdot \overleftarrow{\triangle}_i + v_i \cdot \overrightarrow{\triangle}_i)$, then $s = |s(g')|$ and $s(g') = s^+ + s^-$. We prove by mathematical induction that, for all $g' \geq 1$, formula (5) is true.

Basis step. Formula (5) is obviously true.
Induction step. If formula (5) is true for any k groups, which means

$$|s(k)| \leq max(-\overleftarrow{\triangle}_1, \ldots, -\overleftarrow{\triangle}_k, \overrightarrow{\triangle}_1, \ldots, \overrightarrow{\triangle}_k), \tag{6}$$

then

$$s(k+1) = s(k) + u_{k+1} \cdot \overleftarrow{\triangle_{k+1}} + v_{k+1} \cdot \overrightarrow{\triangle_{k+1}}. \tag{7}$$

According to our heuristic method, if $s(k) \geq 0$, then $u_k = 1$ and $v_k = 0$; else, $u_k = 0$ and $v_k = 1$. Therefore,

$$s(k+1) \leq max(max(-\overleftarrow{\triangle}_1, \ldots, -\overleftarrow{\triangle}_k, \overrightarrow{\triangle}_1, \ldots, \overrightarrow{\triangle}_k), max(-\overleftarrow{\triangle_{k+1}}, \overrightarrow{\triangle_{k+1}}))$$
$$\leq max(-\overleftarrow{\triangle}_1, \ldots, -\overleftarrow{\triangle_{k+1}}, \overrightarrow{\triangle}_1, \ldots, \overrightarrow{\triangle_{k+1}}). \tag{8}$$

$\quad\square$

It is guaranteed by proposition 4.2 that the overall sum deviation is bounded by the sum deviation within a particular group. Recall that the total number of individuals (i.e., the size of microdata) is n ($n = \sum_{i=1}^{g} n_i$), so we have the following corollary regarding to the overall mean deviation:

Corollary 4.1. *If problem $\mathcal{P}$ is solved by the heuristic method, then the overall mean deviation m satisfies*

$$m \leq \frac{max(-\overleftarrow{\Delta_1}, \ldots, -\overleftarrow{\Delta_{g^{\square}}}, \overrightarrow{\Delta_1}, \ldots, \overrightarrow{\Delta_{g^{\square}}})}{n}. \tag{9}$$

The above corollary indicates that the overall mean deviation is bounded by the sum deviation within a particular group divided by the total number of individuals in microdata. Consider that each group consists of k to $2k$ individuals and that k is usually small (e.g., $k = 3$); therefore, for large size microdata, the overall mean deviation indicated by formula (9) is negligible.

4.3   Discussion

The above study is done in the context of microaggregation, which is usually performed off-line and for the purpose of data publication. The same method can also be applied to a statistical database, where a database is partitioned into atomic populations (i.e., mutually exclusive groups) and each query set is restricted to some undivided groups (user queries are under control). In this case we can apply our heuristic algorithm to any legitimate query and the query response satisfies proposition 4.2 and corollary 4.1.

We notice that the previously studied k-Ward is a special case of our secure-k-Ward, where the threshold of the security ratio is $\gamma_0 = 0$. This explains our approach in three different aspects: (1) our approach works not only if the individuals in a group are similar, but also if the individuals are quite different (in the latter case our approach resorts to k-Ward); (2) we do not form new groups (there may exist some efficient grouping methods that are not based on k-Ward but satisfy our security requirements; however, to our knowledge, such methods have not been proposed); and (3) our approach could be "over secure" in that the public does not know that the microdata in a group are similar. However, as indicated in our experiments in section 3, a significant percentage of groups may be considered "unsafe" if the public simply assumes that the microdata in each group are similar.

In practice, the microaggregation method should be assessed with the security ratio, together with some other measures, such as the correlation matrix and the first principal component [6].

Besides microaggregation, we may also consider other methods for protecting numerical microdata. These methods include but are not limited to the following:

- *Additive-noise approach* [7]. Random noise is added to the protected variables and then, when necessary, a reidentification/swapping methodology is employed to assure confidentiality.
- *Data distortion by probability distribution* [8]. The underlying probability distribution function of the original data set is identified, and then a data set is generated from the estimated distribution function to replace the original data set.

- *Data swapping* [11]. The data records are ranked in ascending order and then each ranked value is swapped with another ranked value that is randomly chosen within a restricted range.

These methods are complementary to the microaggregation method. In practice, which method to be used should be decided by the charateristics of a particular application.

5   Summary

In this paper, we discussed the security issue of microaggregation and proposed a privacy-enhanced microaggregation method that is compatible with the previous k-Ward method. The proposed method, which we call secure-k-Ward, employs two phases, intra-group optimization and inter-group optimization, to minimize the information loss and the overall mean deviation and also to guarantee that the security requirement for the microdata is satisfied.

Acknowledgments

We thank the anonymous referees for their valuable comments.

References

1. Baeyens, Y., Defays, D.: Estimation of variance loss following microaggregation by the individual ranking method. Proc. of Statistical Data Protection (1998)
2. Chin, F.Y., Özsoyoglu, G.: Security in partitioned dynamic statistical databases. Proc. of the IEEE COMPSAC (1979) 594-601
3. Chin, F.Y., Özsoyoglu, G.: Statistical database design. ACM Trans. on Database Systems **6(1)** (1981) 113-139
4. Defays, D., Anwar, N.: Micro-aggregation: a generic method. Proc. of the 2nd Int'l Symp. on Statistical Confidentiality (1995) 69-78
5. Defays, D., Nanopoulos, P.: Panels of enterprises and confidentiality: the small aggregates method. Proc. of Symp. on Design and Analysis of Longitudinal Surveys (1993) 195-204
6. Domingo-Ferrer, J., Mateo-Sanz, J. M.: Practical data-oriented microaggregation for statistical disclosure control. IEEE Trans. Knowledge and Data Engineering (to appear)
7. Kim, J., Winkler, W.: Masking Microdata Files. American Statistical Association, Proceedings of the Section on Survey Research Methods (1995) 114-119
8. Liew, C.K., Choi, U.J., Liew, C.J.: A data distortion by probability distribution. ACM Trans. on Database Systems **10(3)** (1985) 395-441
9. Mateo-Sanz, J. M., Domingo-Ferrer, J.: A comparative study of microaggregation methods. Qüestiió **22** (1998)
10. Mateo-Sanz, J. M., Domingo-Ferrer, J.: A method for data-oriented multivariate microaggregation. Proc. of Statistical Data Protection (1998) 89-99

11. Moore Jr., R.A.: Controlled data-swapping techniques for masking public use microdata sets. Research Report, Statistical Research Division, U.S. Bureau of the Census (1996)
12. Nocedal, J., Wright, S.J.: Numerical Optimization. Springer (1999)
13. Schlörer, J.: Information loss in partitioned statistical databases. Comput. J. **26(3)** (1983) 218-223
14. Sheela, B.V., Ramamoorthy, P.: SWIFT – a contrained optimization technique. Computer Methods in Applied Mechanics and Engineering **6** 309-318
15. Ward, J.H.: Hierarchial grouping to optimize an objective function. J. American Stat. Asso. **58** (1963) 236-244
16. Willenborg, L., Waal, T. de: Statistical disclosure control in practice. Springer Verlag. (1996)
17. Yu, C.T., Chin, F.Y.: A study on the protection of statistical databases. Proc. of ACM SIGMOD Int'l Conf. on Management of Data (1977) 169-181

Towards a Tailored Theory
of Consistency Enforcement in Databases

Sebastian Link

Massey University, Department of Information Systems,
Private Bag 11222, Palmerston North, New Zealand
S.Link@massey.ac.nz

Abstract. The idea to enforce consistency in databases tries to overcome widely known weaknesses for consistency checking and verification
techniques. In general terms, a database transition S is systematically
modified to a new transition $S_\mathcal{I}$ (greatest consistent specialization, GCS)
that is provably consistent with respect to a given static constraint $\mathcal{I}$,
preserves the effects of S and is maximal with these properties.
Effect preservation has been formalized by the operational specialization
order $\sqsubseteq$ on (semantic equivalence classes of) database transitions. Its simplicity makes it possible to establish a well-founded theory for reasonably
large classes of database programs and static constraints. However, the
specialization order may be criticized in some aspects, in particular in
its coarseness.
We characterize specialization of a database transition S by the preservation of all transition constraints that S satisfies (δ-constraints). This
enables us to weaken the original order $\sqsubseteq$ leading to the central definition
of maximal consistent effect preservers (MCEs). We proof a normal form
result for MCEs that relates them to GCSs and implies existence and
uniqueness. This close relationship suggests the conjecture that there is
a theory for MCEs similar to the GCS theory. We support this statement
by showing that an MCE with respect to a set of static constraints can
be enforced sequentially, and independently from the given order.

1 Introduction

Integrity constraints play an important role in database design. If the set of
legal database states is restricted, then we speak of static integrity constraints.
Dynamic integrity constraints refer to the restriction of legal state sequences. The
article considers static integrity constraints only. A database program S is called
to be *consistent* with respect to a given static constraint $\mathcal{I}$, if all terminating
executions of S starting in a state satisfying $\mathcal{I}$ lead to a state which validates $\mathcal{I}$,
too.

Various approaches have been studied to guarantee consistency, e.g., *consistency checking* at run-time or *consistency verification* at compile-time. However,
changes to the database program are not permitted in neither of them. The program is either accepted or not. Another shortcoming is the missing feedback to
the designers on how to change the program in order to achieve consistency.

T. Eiter and K.-D. Schewe (Eds.): FoIKS 2002, LNCS 2284, pp. 160–177, 2002.

Consistency Enforcement is intended to provide an alternative. If we are given a database program S and a static constraint $\mathcal{I}$, we are looking for a new database transition $S_{\mathcal{I}}$ that is consistent with respect to $\mathcal{I}$. However, there are many programs with this property, for instance the effectless operation *skip* or the never terminating program *loop*. A reasonable choice for $S_{\mathcal{I}}$ would be close to the original database program S in some sense. In [17,18,20] *operational specialization* has been introduced, a partial order $\sqsubseteq$ on semantic equivalence classes of database transitions. Whenever $T \sqsubseteq S$ holds, state changes due to S are preserved as state changes due to T. On one hand, we consider state variables affected by the given database transiton S and require—with respect to these state variables— a specialization $T \sqsubseteq S$ to allow only executions that already appear with S. On the other hand, state variables not affected by S may be handled arbitrarily. Operational specialization can be formalized quite easily exploiting *predicate transformer semantics* in the style of Dijkstra and Nelson [15]. The work in [18] introduces $S_{\mathcal{I}}$ as the greatest consistent specialization of S with respect to $\mathcal{I}$. That is, $S_{\mathcal{I}}$ is as $\mathcal{I}$-consistent specialization maximal with these properties.

Moreover, [18] establishes first fundamental results on GCSs such as existence and uniqueness (up to semantic equivalence). A *commutativity* result states that the GCS $S_{\mathcal{I}_1 \wedge \cdots \wedge \mathcal{I}_n}$ can be built sequentially taking any order of the invariants $\mathcal{I}_i$. It therefore suffices to concentrate on one invariant.

A second result concerns *compositionality*. Using guarded commands as in [15] complex database programs can be built from basic ones, e.g., assignments or constants such as *skip*. In general, replacing simply the very basic specifications within S by their respective GCSs will not result in the GCS $S_{\mathcal{I}}$. However, under some mild technical restrictions we obtain at least an upper bound (with respect to $\sqsubseteq$) of the GCS, and the GCS itself results from adding a precondition.

The studies in [8,9,10] are based on arithmetic logic and aim to relate the theory to classical recursion theory. More specifically, *computability* of $(S, \mathcal{I}) \mapsto S_{\mathcal{I}}$ and *decidability* of the precondition have been investigated to bring the theory to practice. Apart from the very general case it could be shown that the class of database programs and invariants for which it is justified to talk of a computational approach is reasonably large. Therefore, the GCS formulation is a theoretically well-founded approach to consistency enforcement with a wide range of applicability. In Section 2 we briefly review the achievements of the GCS theory but dispense with effectivity issues. Instead we refer to either of [8,9,10] to discuss this topic.

Despite its theoretical strength the GCS approach is still debatable from a pragmatic point of view. The changes to state variables not affected by the original program specification allow too much freedom, whereas the formulation may be too restrictive for the other state variables. In particular, when state variables take set values, then the insertion of a value into a set should not disable the insertion of another value into the same set.

The idea persued in this article is to weaken the notion of effect preservation and instead of looking at the specialization order to consider the set of transition invariants that are satisfied by the original database program. These are called

δ-*constraints.* As operational specialization is equivalent to the preservation of all δ-constraints of S involving only the state variables affected by S, the simple idea is to preserve a different set of δ-constraints. This leads to the definition of a *maximal consistent effect preserver* (MCE). Informally, an MCE arises as the GCS of a slightly extended program specification. There is no more need to explicitly consider the set of affected state variables.

In Section 3, we introduce the notion of maximal consistent effect preservers, show that they cover reasonable examples and that they are closely related to GCSs.

We then argue that a naive reformulation of the commutativity result will fail within the MCE framework. Nevertheless, we prove an adequate version that allows to enforce MCEs sequentially and also independently from the order of the given set of invariants.

Section 4 outlines some of the related research that has been undertaken in this field. Finally, we remark that the MCE approach has already been studied according to its practicality, i.e., computability and decidability issues are investigated on the basis of arithmetic logic (see [11]).

2 The Theory of Greatest Consistent Specializations

In order to develop a theory of consistency enforcement we adapt the state-based approach to formal database specifications. This means that we support explicitly the concepts of state and state transition. Database programs will be taken in the form of extended guarded commands as defined by Nelson [15]. Semantics will be expressed by predicate transformers that are defined over infinitary logic [13] as in [18].

2.1 Database Programs

The theory [18] of consistency enforcement has been developed with respect to the many-sorted, infinitary, first-order logic $\mathcal{L}^{\omega}_{\infty\omega}$. Therefore, we assume a fixed interpretation structure (D, ω), where $D = \bigcup_{T type} T$ is the semantic domain and ω assigns type-compatible functions $\omega(f) : T_1 \times \ldots \times T_n \to T$ and $\omega(p) : T_1 \times \ldots \times T_n \to \{true, false\}$ to n-ary function symbols f and n-ary predicate symbols p, respectively [13]. We extend ω in the usual way to the terms and formulae of $\mathcal{L}^{\omega}_{\infty\omega}$. This logic restricts the set of formulae on those with finitely-many free variables and finitely-many quantors. In addition, we assume the *domain closure property*, i.e., for each $d \in D$ there is some closed term t in $\mathcal{L}^{\omega}_{\infty\omega}$ with $\omega(t) = d$. This property can be easily achieved by extending the set of constants.

Definition 2.1. A *state space* is a finite set X of variables of $\mathcal{L}^{\omega}_{\infty\omega}$ such that for each $x \in X$ there is an associated type $\sharp x$. A *state* on X is a type-compatible variable assignment $x \mapsto \sigma(x) \in \sharp x$ for each $x \in X$. Let Σ denote the set of all states on X such that $\infty \notin \Sigma$. A *state transition set* is a subset $\Delta(S) \subseteq \Sigma \times (\Sigma \cup \{\infty\})$.   □

The special symbol ∞ is used to model non-termination.

Static constraints are formulae that can be evaluated in states. This enables us to distinguish between legal states, i.e., those satisfying the constraints, and non-legal states.

Definition 2.2. A *static invariant* on a state space X (short: an X-constraint or X-formula) is a formula $\mathcal{I}$ of $\mathcal{L}^{\omega}_{\infty\omega}$ with free variables in X ($fr(\mathcal{I}) \subseteq X$). □

Given an X-formula $\mathcal{I}$, a state σ on X suffices to interpret $\mathcal{I}$. We write $\models_{\sigma} \mathcal{I}$ if and only if the interpretation of $\mathcal{I}$ by σ is *true*. Next we define database transitions on a given state space.

Definition 2.3. Let X be a state space. The language of *guarded commands* contains *skip, fail, loop*, simultaneous assignment $x_{i_1} := t_{i_1} \parallel \ldots \parallel x_{i_k} := t_{i_k} \in \mathcal{S}(X)$ for state variables $x_{i_j} \in X$ and terms t_{i_j} (of corresponding type $\natural x_{i_j}$), sequential composition $S_1; S_2$, choice $S_1 \square S_2$, restricted choice $S_1 \boxtimes S_2$, guard $\mathcal{P} \to S$ with an X-formula $\mathcal{P}$, unbounded choice $@y(:: \natural y) \bullet S$ with a variable y, and least fixed points $\mu S.f(S)$, with a program variable S and a guarded command expression $f(S)$, in which S may occur at the place of a basic command, i.e., *skip, fail, loop* or an assignment. □

Please note that the inclusion of the *restricted choice*-operator $\boxtimes$ is necessary to retain *orthogonality*. For a deeper justification see [15].

In order to define the semantics of guarded commands on the basis of $\mathcal{L}^{\omega}_{\infty\omega}$, we associate with S two *predicate transformers* $wlp(S)$ and $wp(S)$—i.e., functions from (equivalence classes) of formulae to (equivalence classes) of formulae—with the standard informal meaning:

- $wlp(S)(\varphi)$ characterizes those initial states σ such that each terminating execution of S starting in σ results in a state τ satisfying φ, i.e., $\models_{\sigma} wlp(S)(\varphi)$ holds iff for all $\tau \in \Sigma$ with $(\sigma, \tau) \in \Delta(S)$ we have $\models_{\tau} \varphi$.
- $wp(S)(\varphi)$ characterizes those initial states σ such that each execution of S starting in σ terminates and results in a state τ satisfying φ, i.e., $\models_{\sigma} wp(S)(\varphi)$ holds iff for all $(\sigma, \tau) \in \Delta(S)$ we have $\models_{\tau} \varphi$.

The notation $wlp(S)(\varphi)$ and $wp(S)(\varphi)$ corresponds to the usual *weakest (liberal) precondition* of S with respect to the postcondition φ. In order to save space we shall often use the notation $w(l)p(S)(\varphi)$ to refer to both predicate transformers at a time. If this occurs in an equivalence, then omitting everything in parentheses gives the wp-part, whereas omitting just the parentheses results in the wlp-part. Moreover, we define *dual* predicate transformers $w(l)p(S)^*$ by $wlp(S)^*(\varphi) \Leftrightarrow \neg wlp(S)(\neg\varphi)$ and $wp(S)^*(\varphi) \Leftrightarrow \neg wp(S)(\neg\varphi)$.

Now consider the following definition of predicate transformers for our language of guarded commands (for a justification see [15,18])

$$w(l)p(skip)(\varphi) \Leftrightarrow \varphi$$
$$w(l)p(fail)(\varphi) \Leftrightarrow true$$
$$w(l)p(loop)(\varphi) \Leftrightarrow false(\lor true)$$

$$w(l)p(x_{i_1} := t_{i_1} \| \ldots \| x_{i_k} := t_{i_k})(\varphi) \Leftrightarrow \{x_{i_1}/t_{i_1}, \ldots, x_{i_k}/t_{i_k}\}.\varphi$$

$$w(l)p(S_1; S_2)(\varphi) \Leftrightarrow w(l)p(S_1)(w(l)p(S_2)(\varphi))$$

$$w(l)p(S_1 \square S_2)(\varphi) \Leftrightarrow w(l)p(S_1)(\varphi) \wedge w(l)p(S_2)(\varphi)$$

$$w(l)p(S_1 \boxtimes S_2)(\varphi) \Leftrightarrow w(l)p(S_1)(\varphi) \wedge (wp(S_1)^*(true) \vee w(l)p(S_2)(\varphi))$$

$$w(l)p(@x_j \bullet S)(\varphi) \Leftrightarrow \forall x_j.w(l)p(S)(\varphi)$$

$$w(l)p(\mathcal{P} \rightarrow S)(\varphi) \Leftrightarrow \mathcal{P} \Rightarrow w(l)p(S)(\varphi)$$

$$wlp(\mu S.f(S))(\varphi) \Leftrightarrow \bigwedge_{\alpha \in \mathcal{O}rd} wlp(f^\alpha(loop))(\varphi)$$

$$wp(\mu S.f(S))(\varphi) \Leftrightarrow \bigvee_{\alpha \in \mathcal{O}rd} wp(f^\alpha(loop))(\varphi) \quad .$$

In this definition we used $\mathcal{O}rd$ to denote the ordinal numbers. Two database programs S and T are *semantically equivalent* iff $w(l)p(S) = w(l)p(T)$.

Note that database transitions may only affect parts of the state space. For consistency enforcement it will be necessary to "extend" such operations. Therefore, we need to know for each transition S the subspace $Y \subseteq X$ such that S does not change the values in $X - Y$. In this case we call S a Y-*operation*. Formally, if X is a state space and S a database transition on X, then S is called a Y-operation for $Y \subseteq X$ iff $w(l)p(S)(\varphi) \Leftrightarrow \varphi$ holds for each $(X - Y)$-formulae φ and Y is minimal with this property.

2.2   Consistency and GCSs

We would like to derive a proof obligation that characterizes consistency of a database transition S with respect to a static constraint $\mathcal{I}$ (see [10,18]). Consistency means that whenever $\models_\sigma \mathcal{I}$ for a state σ and $(\sigma, \tau) \in \Delta(S)$ for $\tau \neq \infty$, then $\models_\tau \mathcal{I}$. In other words, $\models_\sigma \mathcal{I}$ implies $\models_\sigma wlp(S)(\mathcal{I})$.

Definition 2.4. Let S be a database transition and $\mathcal{I}$ a static constraint, both on X. Then S is *consistent* with respect to $\mathcal{I}$ (short: $\mathcal{I}$-consistent) iff $\mathcal{I} \Rightarrow wlp(S)(\mathcal{I})$ holds.   □

Operational specialization aims at reducing existing executions and at the same time extending the state space and allowing arbitrary additional changes on new state variables [18]. The following definition captures the idea of effect preservation using predicate transformers. It is fundamental for the entire theory of GCS consistency enforcement.

Definition 2.5. Let S and T be database transitions on X and Y, respectively, with $X \subseteq Y$. Then S is *specialized* by T ($T \sqsubseteq S$) iff $w(l)p(S)(\varphi) \Rightarrow w(l)p(T)(\varphi)$ holds for all X-formulae φ.   □

We remark that for the wp-part it is enough to require that $wp(S)(true) \Rightarrow wp(T)(true)$ holds. Operational specialization defines a partial order $\sqsubseteq$ on semantic equivalence classes of database transitions with a minimum *fail*.

The proof obligation for consistency and the definition of operational specialization are sufficient to define the central notion of the approach.

Definition 2.6. Let S be a Y-command and $\mathcal{I}$ a constraint on X with $Y \subseteq X$. The *greatest consistent specialization* (GCS) of S with respect to $\mathcal{I}$ is an X-command $S_{\mathcal{I}}$ with $S_{\mathcal{I}} \sqsubseteq S$ such that $S_{\mathcal{I}}$ is consistent with respect to $\mathcal{I}$ and each $\mathcal{I}$-consistent specialization $T \sqsubseteq S$ satisfies $T \sqsubseteq S_{\mathcal{I}}$. □

The first important result concerns the *commutativity*, i.e., GCSs with respect to conjunctions can be built successively using any order of the constraints.

Proposition 2.1. *For two constraints $\mathcal{I}$ and $\mathcal{J}$ we always obtain that $\mathcal{I} \wedge \mathcal{J} \rightarrow S_{\mathcal{I} \wedge \mathcal{J}}$ and $\mathcal{I} \wedge \mathcal{J} \rightarrow (S_{\mathcal{I}})_{\mathcal{J}}$ are semantically equivalent.* □

It would be nice, if building the GCS for a complex database transition S simply required the basic operations in S to be replaced by their GCSs. Let $S'_{\mathcal{I}}$ denote the result of such a naive syntactic replacement. However, in general $S'_{\mathcal{I}}$ is not the GCS $S_{\mathcal{I}}$. It may not even be a specialization of S, or it may be a consistent specialization but not the greatest one.

There exists a technical condition which implies at least $S_{\mathcal{I}} \sqsubseteq S'_{\mathcal{I}}$ holds. The corresponding result was called the *upper bound theorem* in [18]. On the way to formulate this purely technical notion we define several concepts that we will need later on again.

We need the notion of a *deterministic branch* S^+ of a command S, which requires $S^+ \sqsubseteq S$, $wp(S)^*(true) \Leftrightarrow wp(S^+)^*(true)$ and $wlp(S^+)^*(\varphi) \Rightarrow wp(S^+)(\varphi)$ to hold for all φ. Herein, the last condition expresses that S^+ is indeed deterministic, i.e., whenever $(\sigma, \tau) \in \Delta(S^+)$ for a $\tau \in \Sigma$ then $(\sigma, \infty) \notin \Delta(S^+)$ and whenever $(\sigma, \tau_1), (\sigma, \tau_2) \in \Delta(S^+)$ then $\tau_1 = \tau_2$. Together, a deterministic branch S^+ of S is a deterministic specialization of S which comprises executions if and only if S does.

Transition constraints are a device for reducing the allowed set of transition pairs. A pair $(\sigma, \tau) \in \Sigma \times \Sigma$ is sufficient to interpret this kind of constraints.

Definition 2.7. A *transition constraint* on a state space X is a formula $\mathcal{J}$ with free variables in $X \cup X'$ using a disjoint copy X' of X, i.e., $fr(\mathcal{J}) \subseteq X \cup X'$. □

We define δ-constraints as transition constrains that are satisfied by a specification. In order to save space we use $\{x/x'\}$ to refer to a simultaneous substitution with respect to the set of state variables of state spaces X and X', respectively.

Definition 2.8. Let S be a database program on X. A δ-*constraint* for S is a transition constraint $\mathcal{J}$ on X such that $\{x'/x\}.wlp(S')(\mathcal{J})$ holds, where S' results from S by renaming all x_i to x'_i. □

Example 2.1. Look at the insertion S of a new tuple t into a relation r, i.e., $S = r := r \cup \{t\}$. Then the following formulae are δ-constraints for S:

- $t \in r'$
- $\forall u. \, u \in r \Rightarrow u \in r'$
- $\forall u. u \in q \Leftrightarrow u \in q'$ for all relation schemata $q \neq r$ and
- $\forall u. \, u \neq t \wedge u \in r' \Rightarrow u \in r$. □

We write φ_σ to denote the characterizing formula of a state σ.

Definition 2.9. Let $S = S_1; S_2$ be a Y-command such that S_i is a Y_i-command for $Y_i \subseteq Y$ ($i = 1, 2$). Let $\mathcal{I}$ be some X-constraint with $Y \subseteq X$. Let $X - Y_1 = \{y_1, \ldots, y_m\}$, $Y_1 = \{x_1, \ldots, x_l\}$ and assume that $\{x_1', \ldots, x_l'\}$ is a disjoint copy of Y_1 disjoint also from X. Then S is in $\mathcal{I}$-*reduced form* iff for each deterministic branch S_1^+ of S_1 the following two conditions – with $\boldsymbol{x} = (x_1, \ldots, x_l)$, $\boldsymbol{x}' = (x_1', \ldots, x_l')$ – hold:

- For all states σ with $\models_\sigma \neg\mathcal{I}$ we have, if $\varphi_\sigma \Rightarrow \{\boldsymbol{x}/\boldsymbol{x}'\}.(\forall y_1 \ldots y_m.\mathcal{I})$ is a δ-constraint for S_1^+, then it is also a δ-constraint for S_1^+ ; S_2.
- For all states σ with $\models_\sigma \mathcal{I}$ we have, if $\varphi_\sigma \Rightarrow \{\boldsymbol{x}/\boldsymbol{x}'\}.(\forall y_1 \ldots y_m.\neg\mathcal{I})$ is a δ-constraint for S_1^+, then it is also a δ-constraint for S_1^+ ; S_2. $\quad\square$

Informally, $\mathcal{I}$-reducedness is a property of sequences $S_1; S_2$ which rules out occurences of interim states that wrongly cause an enforcement within any branch of S_1 but which is not relevant for the entire specification.

Example 2.2. Consider the database program $S = x := x - a; x := x + a$ with $x :: \mathbb{N}$ and some constant $a \geq 1$ and $\mathcal{I} = x \geq 1$. Then the GCS of S with respect to $\mathcal{I}$ is certainly *skip*. However, $(x := x - a)_\mathcal{I} = (x = 0 \lor x > a) \to x := x - a$. A simple replacement of basic commands by their respective GCSs leads in this case to $(x = 0 \lor x > a) \to x := x - a; x := x + a$ which is just a proper specialization of *skip*. The reason is that S is not in $\mathcal{I}$-reduced form. $\quad\square$

It is straightforward to extend the definition of $\mathcal{I}$-reducedness to arbitrary commands other than sequences. Although the upper bound theorem already has a flavour of compositionality it does not yet give the GCS. The idea of the main theorem on GCSs is to add a precondition $\mathcal{P}(S, \mathcal{I}, \cdot)$ to $S_\mathcal{I}'$ which cuts out those executions from $S_\mathcal{I}'$ that are not allowed to occur in a specialization of S. This leads to the following theorem [18].

Theorem 2.1. *Let $\mathcal{I}$ be an invariant on X and let S be some $\mathcal{I}$-reduced Y-command with $Y \subseteq X$. Let $S_\mathcal{I}'$ result from S as follows:*

- *Each restricted choice $S_1 \boxtimes S_2$ occurring within S will be replaced by*

$$S_1 \square wlp(S_1)(false) \to S_2 .$$

- *Then each basic command will be replaced by its GCS with respect to $\mathcal{I}$.*

Let Z be a disjoint copy of the state space Y. With the formulae

$$\mathcal{P}(S, \mathcal{I}, \boldsymbol{x}') = \{\boldsymbol{z}/\boldsymbol{y}\}.wlp(S_\mathcal{I}''; \boldsymbol{z} = \boldsymbol{x}' \to skip)(wlp(S)^*(\boldsymbol{z} = \boldsymbol{y})) \quad,$$

where $S_\mathcal{I}''$ results from $S_\mathcal{I}'$ by renaming the Y to Z, the GCS $S_\mathcal{I}$ is semantically equivalent to $@\boldsymbol{x}' \bullet \mathcal{P}(S, \mathcal{I}, \boldsymbol{x}') \to (S_\mathcal{I}'; \boldsymbol{y} = \boldsymbol{x}' \to skip)$. $\quad\square$

Note that if we consider deterministic branches as a pragmatic approach suggested in [18], then the unbounded choice in Theorem 2.1 disappears. We omit further details.

The characterization of GCSs according to Theorem 2.1 makes it possible to reduce consistency enforcement to a simple syntactical replacement (the forming of $S_\mathcal{I}'$) and to an investigation of a guard, namely $\mathcal{P}(S, \mathcal{I}, \boldsymbol{x}')$.

2.3   GCS Branches

Due to the definition of the specialization preorder, GCSs in general are highly non-deterministic, even if the original database transition was not. From a pragmatic point of view, however, it will be enough to have a deterministic result. Therefore, it is a natural idea to consider *deterministic GCS branches* or at least *quasi-deterministic GCS branches*. Here quasi-determinism means determinism up to the selection of values [18].

Let us now look at an example how to construct GCS branches on the basis of Theorem 2.1.

Example 2.3. Consider the state space $X = \{x_1, x_2\}$. Although types have been left implicit so far, let us assume that values for both state variables are sets of pairs. We consider the following three X-constraints:

$$
\begin{aligned}
\mathcal{I}_1 &\equiv \pi_1(x_1) \subseteq \pi_1(x_2) \\
\mathcal{I}_2 &\equiv \forall x, y. x \in x_2 \wedge y \in x_2 \wedge \pi_2(x) = \pi_2(y) \Rightarrow \pi_1(x) = \pi_1(y) \qquad \text{and} \\
\mathcal{I}_3 &\equiv \pi_2(x_1) \cap \pi_2(x_2) = \emptyset
\end{aligned}
$$

with the projection functions π_i onto the i'th components. Then we consider a database transition S on $\{x_1\}$ defined by the simple assignment $x_1 := x_1 \cup \{(a, b)\}$ with some constants a and b.

Step 1. First consider the constraint $\mathcal{I}_1$. Since S is just an assignment, it is $\mathcal{I}_1$-reduced. We then replace S by a quasi-deterministic branch of its GCS with respect to $\mathcal{I}_1$ and obtain

$$
x_1 := x_1 \cup \{(a, b)\} \; ; \; (a \notin \pi_1(x_2) \to @c \bullet x_2 := x_2 \cup \{(a, c)\} \boxtimes skip) \quad ,
$$

which is an X-operation. Let this be our new S_1.

Step 2. Now consider the constraint $\mathcal{I}_2$. It can be shown that S_1 is $\mathcal{I}_2$-reduced. We have to remove the restricted choice and then replace the assignment to x_2 by the deterministic GCS branch $c \notin \pi_2(x_2) \to x_2 := x_2 \cup \{(a, c)\}$ with respect to $\mathcal{I}_2$. For the resulting operation $S'_{\mathcal{I}}$ we compute $\mathcal{P}(S_1, \mathcal{I}_2) \Leftrightarrow true$. After some rearrangements we obtain the following GCS branch of S with respect to $\mathcal{I}_1 \wedge \mathcal{I}_2$:

$$
x_1 := x_1 \cup \{(a, b)\} \; ; \; ((a \notin \pi_1(x_2) \to @c \bullet c \notin \pi_2(x_2) \to x_2 := x_2 \cup \{(a, c)\})
$$
$$
\square \; a \in \pi_1(x_2) \to skip)
$$

Let this be our new program S_2.

Step 3. Now regard the constraint $\mathcal{I}_3$. Again we can show $\mathcal{I}_3$-reducedness, but dispense with the formal proof. We replace the assigment to x_1 in S_2 by the deterministic GCS branch $x_1 := x_1 \cup \{(a, b)\} \; ; \; x_2 := x_2 - \{x \in x_2 \mid \pi_2(x) = b\}$.

Analogously, we replace the assignment to x_2 in S_2 by the deterministic GCS branch $x_2 := x_2 \cup \{(a, c)\} \; ; \; x_1 := x_1 - \{x \in x_1 \mid \pi_2(x) = c\}$. Then we compute

$$
\mathcal{P}(S_2, \mathcal{I}_3) \; \Leftrightarrow \; b \notin \pi_2(x_2) \wedge (a \notin \pi_1(x_2) \Rightarrow \forall c. (c \notin \pi_2(x_2) \Rightarrow c \notin \pi_2(x_1) \cup \{b\})) .
$$

After some rearrangements the final result is

$$b \notin \pi_2(x_2) \ \rightarrow \ x_1 := x_1 \cup \{(a,b)\} \ ; \ ((a \notin \pi_1(x_2) \rightarrow @c\bullet$$
$$c \notin \pi_2(x_2) \wedge c \notin \pi_2(x_1) \rightarrow x_2 := x_2 \cup \{(a,c)\}) \square \ a \in \pi_1(x_2) \rightarrow skip \ ) \ ,$$

which is a branch of the GCS of S with respect to $\mathcal{I}_1 \wedge \mathcal{I}_2 \wedge \mathcal{I}_3$. □

2.4   Major Problems with the Specialization Order

Let us look at consistency enforcement from a more practical point of view and ask whether GCSs really coincide with our intution. In general, GCSs are non-deterministic, which reflects various strategies for consistency enforcement. The approach in [18] selects a branch of the GCS which is related to an interactive support for the values to be selected.

E.g., take an inclusion constraint $x \in p \Rightarrow x \in q$ and an insertion into p, then GCS branches offer the freedom to chose any new value for q provided it is a superset of $p \cup \{x\}$. Intuitively, we prefer this value to be $q \cup \{x\}$, i.e., to keep change propagation as simple as possible. For GCS branches, however, there is no such "preference" or otherwise said:

For a database operation on $Y \subseteq X$ the GCS approach is too liberal on $X - Y$.

On the other hand, multi-valued dependencies, which concern only set-valued state variables lead to preconditions, although we might expect additional changes instead. Otherwise said:

For a database operation on $Y \subseteq X$ the GCS approach is too restrictive on Y.

This demonstrates that the specialization order might still be too coarse for enforcement purposes.

3   Maximal Consistent Effect Preservers

In the introduction we already explained that GCSs are not the only possible choice for formalizing consistency enforcement. If a database transition S affects state variables in Y and the constraint is defined on X with $Y \subseteq X$, then specialization may be too restrictive on Y and too liberal on $X - Y$. We develop the notion of maximal consistent effect preservers (MCEs) that intends to overcome both these weaknesses of the GCS approach.

3.1   A Motivating Example

The key concept is the one of a δ-constraint introduced in Section 2. This is a transition constraint $\mathcal{J}$ satisfied by the given database transition S. Thus, the δ-constraints of S express some kind of effect of S. Consequently, "preservation of effects" could be formalized by the preservation of δ-constraints. Let us first look at an example.

Example 3.1. Let us look back again at the enforcement strategies in Example 2.3 underlying the construction of a GCS branch. With respect to the inclusion constraint $\mathcal{I}_1$ the GCS branch was chosen in such a way that an insertion into x_1 was followed by an insertion into x_2, if necessary. Alternatively, we may like to replace $x_1 := x_1 \cup \{(a,b)\}$ by $a \notin \pi_1(x_2) \to x_1 := x_1 \cup \{(a,b)\} \boxtimes skip$. This would mean to restrict insertions by adding a precondition and to do nothing, if this condition is violated. Such a strategy is not possible with the GCS-approach.

Analogously, for the assignment $x_2 := x_2 \cup \{(a,c)\}$ and the constraint $\mathcal{I}_2$ from Example 2.3 on the state space $\{x_2\}$ we may like to replace it by $x_2 := \{(x,y) \in x_2 \mid y \neq c\} \cup \{(a,c)\}$. Taking these ideas together we would first replace S by S_1, which is $a \notin \pi_1(x_2) \to x_1 := x_1 \cup \{(a,b)\} \boxtimes skip$ in order to enforce consistency with respect to $\mathcal{I}_1$. Then there is nothing to do to enforce $\mathcal{I}_2$. Finally, we replace $b \notin \pi_2(x_2) \to x_1 := x_1 \cup \{(a,b)\} \boxtimes skip$ for the assignment $x_1 := x_1 \cup \{(a,b)\}$ to enforce the constraint $\mathcal{I}_3$. Thus, the final result would be $a \notin \pi_1(x_2) \wedge b \notin \pi_2(x_2) \to x_1 := x_1 \cup \{(a,b)\} \boxtimes skip$, which appears to be a reasonable alternative to the result obtained in Example 2.3. □

3.2 Replacing the Specialization Order

We are starting now to formalize the preservation of effects. The goal in this section is to obtain a characterization of the specialization order $\sqsubseteq$.

The first idea is to construe a transition constraint $\mathcal{J}$ as a database transition itself. This way we can make use of predicate transformers again.

Definition 3.1. Each transition constraint $\mathcal{J}$ gives rise to a database transition $S(\mathcal{J})$ that can be written as

$$S(\mathcal{J}) = (@x'_1, \ldots, x'_n \bullet \mathcal{J} \to x_1 := x'_1 \parallel \ldots \parallel x_n := x'_n) \,\square\, loop$$

using guarded commands. □

Note that $S(\mathcal{J})$ comprises state pairs (σ, ∞), i.e., non-terminating executions are included. The specialization order can be used to express that a database transition S is consistent with respect to a transition constraint.

Definition 3.2. A database transition S is *consistent* with respect to a transition constraint $\mathcal{J}$ if and only if $S \sqsubseteq S(\mathcal{J})$ holds. □

We can interpret this definition as saying that S is an extended database transition which preserves the effect of $\mathcal{J}$.

In order to establish the correspondence between δ-constraints and transition-consistent programs (Lemma 3.1) we need the following result from the GCS-theory. It gives a normal form for the specialization order. For a proof see [18, App. B].

Proposition 3.1. *Let S and T be database transitions on $X = \{x_1, \ldots, x_n\}$ and Y, respectively, with $X \subseteq Y$ and a disjoint copy $Z = \{z_1, \ldots, z_n\}$ of X. Then $wlp(S)(\varphi) \Rightarrow wlp(T)(\varphi)$ holds for all state formulae φ on X if and only if $\{z/x\}.wlp(T')(wlp(S)^*(x = z))$ is valid, where T' results from T by renaming all x_i to z_i.* □

Lemma 3.1. *A database transition S is consistent with respect to a transition constraint $\mathcal{J}$ on X if and only if $\mathcal{J}$ is a δ-constraint for S.*

Proof. The specialization condition $S \sqsubseteq S(\mathcal{J})$ means nothing else than

$$wlp(S(\mathcal{J}))(\varphi) \Rightarrow wlp(S)(\varphi) \tag{1}$$

for all X-formulae φ and $wp(S(\mathcal{J}))(true) \Rightarrow wp(S)(true)$. As $wp(S(\mathcal{J}))(\varphi) \Leftrightarrow false$ for arbitrary X-formulae φ, the second condition is always satisfied. Applying Proposition 3.1 to equation (1) leads to $\{z/x\}.wlp(S')(wlp(S(\mathcal{J}))^*(x = z))$. We further simplify $wlp(S(\mathcal{J}))^*(x = z)$ according to Definition 3.1 and obtain $\mathcal{J}(x, z)$. Together, we yield the equivalence

$$S \sqsubseteq S(\mathcal{J}) \quad \text{iff} \quad \{z/x\}.wlp(S')(\mathcal{J}(x, z))$$

which proves the lemma.   □

Finally, we are ready to characterize the specialization order by preservation of δ-constraints.

Proposition 3.2. *Let S and T be database transitions on Y and X, respectively, where $Y \subseteq X$. Then we have $T \sqsubseteq S$ if and only if each $\delta-$constraint $\mathcal{J}$ for S with $fr(\mathcal{J}) \subseteq Y \cup Y'$ is also a $\delta-$constraint for T and $wp(S)(true) \Rightarrow wp(T)(true)$ holds.*

Proof. We consider the only-if direction first. The condition $wp(S)(true) \Rightarrow wp(T)(true)$ is already part of the specialization condition $T \sqsubseteq S$ we assume to hold. Let $\mathcal{J}$ be an arbitrary δ-constraint for S with $fr(\mathcal{J}) \subseteq Y \cup Y'$. Following Lemma 3.1, we have $S \sqsubseteq S(\mathcal{J})$. As $T \sqsubseteq S$ holds by assumption, we use the transitivity of $\sqsubseteq$ to conclude that $T \sqsubseteq S(\mathcal{J})$ holds as well. Again, Lemma 3.1 implies that $\mathcal{J}$ must be a δ-constraint for T, too.

For the reverse direction we just have to show that $wlp(S)(\varphi) \Rightarrow wlp(T)(\varphi)$ holds for each φ with $fr(\varphi) \subseteq Y$. We assume that $\{y'/y\}.wlp(S')(\mathcal{J}) \Rightarrow \{x'/x\}.wlp(T')(\mathcal{J})$ is valid for all $\mathcal{J}$ with $fr(\mathcal{J}) \subseteq Y \cup Y'$. Now, let us consider all φ' with $fr(\varphi') \subseteq Y'$. Then, we are able to conclude $\{y'/y\}.wlp(S')(\varphi') \Rightarrow \{x'/x\}.wlp(T')(\varphi')$. The substitutions can be omitted since they are only renamings with $fr(\varphi') \subseteq Y'$. Finally, we rename y''s to y's yielding $wlp(S)(\varphi) \Rightarrow wlp(T)(\varphi)$ for all φ with $fr(\varphi) \subseteq Y$ as demanded.   □

Proposition 3.2 tells us that a specialization of a given program S preserves the effects given by all δ-constraints of S and terminates if S does. We have argued and demonstrated that the specialization order is too coarse. The characterization above allows to weaken this order in a natural way.

3.3   Definition of MCEs

The basic idea of the tailored operational approach is now to consider not all δ-constraints but only some of them. Thus, we do not build the GCS of S with respect to $\mathcal{I}$ but the GCS of some $S(\mathcal{J})$. An arbitrary conjunction $\mathcal{J} = \bigwedge \mathcal{J}'$ of δ-constraints $\mathcal{J}'$ for S is again a δ-constraint for S. If some δ-constraints of S are omitted in $\mathcal{J}$, then $S(\mathcal{J})$ will allow executions that do not occur in any specialization of S. This way we can circumvent the problems that were mentioned in Section 2.4. However, taking any such δ-constraint is much too weak. $S(\mathcal{J})$ should only add executions that are consistent with $\mathcal{I}$. This justifies to define δ-constraints that are compatible with a given static constraint $\mathcal{I}$ on X. Therefore, we are only interested in terminating executions of $S(\mathcal{J})$, i.e., programs of the form $S'(\mathcal{J}) = @\boldsymbol{x}' \bullet \mathcal{J} \rightarrow \boldsymbol{x} := \boldsymbol{x}'$. Compatibility with $\mathcal{I}$ then means that building the GCS $S'(\mathcal{J})_{\mathcal{I}}$ does not increase partiality. Thus, if $S'(\mathcal{J})_{\mathcal{I}}$ was not total, then $S'(\mathcal{J})$ is not total.

Definition 3.3. A transition constraint $\mathcal{J}$ is *compatible* with respect to a static constraint $\mathcal{I}$ (short: $\mathcal{I}$-compatible) if and only if $wp(\mathcal{I} \rightarrow S'(\mathcal{J})_{\mathcal{I}})(false) \Rightarrow wp(S'(\mathcal{J}))(false)$ holds. □

Example 3.2. It is easy to see that each of the δ-constraints in Example 2.1 is compatible with $\mathcal{I}$ chosen to be a multivalued dependency. Furthermore, the conjunction of three of these constraints is also compatible with $\mathcal{I}$ but the conjunction of all four δ-constraints is not. □

Definition 3.3 allows to show the following technical lemma. Basically, it applies the commutativity result for GCS (Proposition 2.1).

Lemma 3.2. *Let $\mathcal{J}$ be a transition constraint that is $\mathcal{I}_1 \wedge \mathcal{I}_2$-compatible. Then $\mathcal{J}$ is both $\mathcal{I}_1$- and $\mathcal{I}_2$-compatible.*

Proof.

$$\mathcal{J} \text{ is } \mathcal{I}_1 \wedge \mathcal{I}_2\text{-compatible} \qquad\qquad\qquad\qquad\qquad\qquad\qquad\qquad \text{iff}$$
$$wp(S'(\mathcal{J}))^*(true) \Rightarrow wp(\mathcal{I}_1 \wedge \mathcal{I}_2 \rightarrow S'(\mathcal{J})_{\mathcal{I}_1 \wedge \mathcal{I}_2})^*(true) \qquad\qquad \text{iff}$$
$$wp(S'(\mathcal{J}))^*(true) \Rightarrow wp(\mathcal{I}_1 \wedge \mathcal{I}_2 \rightarrow (S'(\mathcal{J})_{\mathcal{I}_1})_{\mathcal{I}_2})^*(true) \wedge$$
$$wp(\mathcal{I}_1 \wedge \mathcal{I}_2 \rightarrow (S'(\mathcal{J})_{\mathcal{I}_2})_{\mathcal{I}_1})^*(true) \qquad\qquad \Rightarrow$$
$$wp(S'(\mathcal{J}))^*(true) \Rightarrow wp(\mathcal{I}_1 \wedge \mathcal{I}_2 \rightarrow S'(\mathcal{J})_{\mathcal{I}_1})^*(true) \wedge$$
$$wp(\mathcal{I}_1 \wedge \mathcal{I}_2 \rightarrow S'(\mathcal{J})_{\mathcal{I}_2})^*(true) \qquad\qquad\qquad \text{iff}$$
$$wp(S'(\mathcal{J}))^*(true) \Rightarrow \mathcal{I}_1 \wedge \mathcal{I}_2 \wedge wp(S'(\mathcal{J})_{\mathcal{I}_1})^*(true) \wedge wp(S'(\mathcal{J})_{\mathcal{I}_2})^*(true) \quad \text{iff}$$
$$wp(S'(\mathcal{J}))^*(true) \Rightarrow wp(\mathcal{I}_1 \rightarrow S'(\mathcal{J})_{\mathcal{I}_1})^*(true) \wedge wp(\mathcal{I}_2 \rightarrow S'(\mathcal{J})_{\mathcal{I}_2})^*(true) \quad \text{iff}$$
$$wp(S'(\mathcal{J}))^*(true) \Rightarrow wp(\mathcal{I}_1 \rightarrow S'(\mathcal{J})_{\mathcal{I}_1})^*(true) \quad \text{and}$$
$$wp(S'(\mathcal{J}))^*(true) \Rightarrow wp(\mathcal{I}_2 \rightarrow S'(\mathcal{J})_{\mathcal{I}_2})^*(true) \qquad\qquad\qquad \text{iff}$$
$$\mathcal{J} \text{ is compatible with respect to } \mathcal{I}_1 \text{ and with respect to } \mathcal{I}_2 \qquad\qquad\qquad \square$$

The last example suggests to consider the implication order on δ-constraints. We say that $\mathcal{J}_1$ is *stronger* than $\mathcal{J}_2$ if and only if $\mathcal{J}_1 \Rightarrow \mathcal{J}_2$ holds. Unfortunately, there is no smallest δ-constraints for S but we may consider minimal elements in this order.

Definition 3.4. A δ-constraint $\mathcal{J}$ for S is *low* with respect to a static constraint $\mathcal{I}$ (short: $\mathcal{I}$-low) iff it is $\mathcal{I}$-compatible and there is no strictly stronger $\mathcal{I}$-compatible δ-constraint for S. □

Now we are prepared to define maximal consistent effect preservers for a database transition S. For these we choose a low δ-constraint $\mathcal{J}$ which formalizes effects of S to be preserved. Then we take a consistent database operation $S^{\mathcal{I},\mathcal{J}}$ that preserves this effect but remains undefined, wherever S is undefined. Finally, we require $S^{\mathcal{I},\mathcal{J}}$ to be a greatest operation with these properties with respect to the specialization order.

Definition 3.5. Let S be a database transition and $\mathcal{I}$ a static constraint on X. Let $\mathcal{J}$ be a δ−constraint of S that is $\mathcal{I}$-compatible. A database transition $S^{\mathcal{I},\mathcal{J}}$ on X is called a *consistent effect preserver (CE)* of S with respect to $\mathcal{I}$ and $\mathcal{J}$ if and only if

1. $\mathcal{J}$ is a δ−constraint for $S^{\mathcal{I},\mathcal{J}}$,
2. $wp(S)(false) \Rightarrow wp(S^{\mathcal{I},\mathcal{J}})(false)$ holds,
3. $S^{\mathcal{I},\mathcal{J}}$ is consistent with respect to $\mathcal{I}$ and
4. any other database transition T with these properties specializes $S^{\mathcal{I},\mathcal{J}}$.

If $\mathcal{J}$ is even a low δ-constraint for S with respect to $\mathcal{I}$, then $S^{\mathcal{I},\mathcal{J}}$ *is called maximal consistent effect preserver (MCE).* □

Note that in this definition the state space on which S is defined is no longer of importance. It "vanishes" inside the chosen $\mathcal{J}$. Then it is easy to see that informal enforcement strategies are captured by MCEs for basic database operations.

3.4   A Normal Form for MCEs

The last property of (maximal) consistent effect preservers (Definition 3.5) employs the specialization order $\sqsubseteq$ again. This seems to be surprising for the first moment but it turns out to be a natural definition as shown in the following theorem which gives a normal form for maximal consistent effect preserver.

Theorem 3.1. *Let S be a database transition and $\mathcal{I}$ a static constraint on X. Let $\mathcal{J}$ be a low δ−constraint of S with respect to $\mathcal{I}$. Then $wp(S)^*(true) \to S(\mathcal{J})_\mathcal{I}$ is the MCE $S^{\mathcal{I},\mathcal{J}}$ with respect to $\mathcal{I}$ and $\mathcal{J}$.*

Proof. We take $wp(S)^*(true) \to S(\mathcal{J})_\mathcal{I}$ as a definition for $S^{\mathcal{I},\mathcal{J}}$ and verify each single condition of Definition 3.5.
First, we show that $\mathcal{J}$ is a δ−constraint for $S^{\mathcal{I},\mathcal{J}}$. This follows immediately from $S(\mathcal{J})_\mathcal{I} \sqsubseteq S(\mathcal{J})$ (definition GCS) and $S^{\mathcal{I},\mathcal{J}} \sqsubseteq S(\mathcal{J})_\mathcal{I}$. The second condition results from the following computation:

$$\begin{aligned}
wp(S)(false) \quad &\Leftrightarrow \quad \neg wp(S)^*(true) \\
&\Rightarrow \quad \neg wp(S)^*(true) \vee wp(S(\mathcal{J})_\mathcal{I})(false) \\
&\Leftrightarrow \quad wp(S^{\mathcal{I},\mathcal{J}})(false) \quad .
\end{aligned}$$

The $\mathcal{I}$-consistency of $S^{\mathcal{I},\mathcal{J}}$ follows immediately from the $\mathcal{I}$-consistency of $S(\mathcal{J})_\mathcal{I}$, namely $\mathcal{I} \Rightarrow wlp(S(\mathcal{J})_\mathcal{I})(\mathcal{I})$ implies $\mathcal{I} \Rightarrow (wp(S)^*(true) \Rightarrow wlp(S(\mathcal{J})_\mathcal{I})(\mathcal{I}))$, which is equivalent to $\mathcal{I} \Rightarrow wlp(S^{\mathcal{I},\mathcal{J}})(\mathcal{I})$. Finally, let T be a database transition such that

- $\mathcal{J}$ is a δ-constraint for T,
- $wp(S)(false) \Rightarrow wp(T)(false)$ and
- T consistent with respect to $\mathcal{I}$ is.

According to Lemma 3.1 we receive $T \sqsubseteq S(\mathcal{J})$ since $\mathcal{J}$ is a δ-constraint for T. Together with the $\mathcal{I}$-consistency of T, it follows by definition of greatest consistent specializations that even $T \sqsubseteq S(\mathcal{J})_{\mathcal{I}}$ holds. We then also apply $wp(T)^*(true) \Rightarrow wp(S)^*(true)$ to obtain

$$T = wp(T)^*(true) \to T \sqsubseteq wp(S)^*(true) \to S(\mathcal{J})_{\mathcal{I}} .$$

This establishes the validity of $T \sqsubseteq S^{\mathcal{I},\mathcal{J}}$ and completes the proof. $\square$

Remark 3.1. $S(\mathcal{J})$ allows non-termination in all start states. If we require only terminating database transitions with properties one to three to specialize $S^{\mathcal{I},\mathcal{J}}$ (Definition 3.5), then its normal form becomes $wp(S)^*(false) \to S'(\mathcal{J})_{\mathcal{I}}$. $\square$

The proof suggests even a normal form for consistent effect preservers as we do not need to make use of the lowness of $\mathcal{J}$.

Corollary 3.1. *Let S be a database transition and $\mathcal{I}$ a static constraint on X. Let $\mathcal{J}$ be a δ-constraint of S that is $\mathcal{I}$-compatible. Then $wp(S)^*(true) \to S(\mathcal{J})_{\mathcal{I}}$ is the CE $S^{\mathcal{I},\mathcal{J}}$ with respect to $\mathcal{I}$ and $\mathcal{J}$.* $\square$

From Theorem 3.1 we may draw first conclusions:

- For a chosen (low) δ-constraint with respect to $\mathcal{I}$ the (M)CE $S^{\mathcal{I},\mathcal{J}}$ always exists and is uniquely determined (up to semantic equivalence) by $S, \mathcal{I}$ and $\mathcal{J}$.
- (M)CEs are closely related to GCSs. The (M)CE is the GCS of a slightly extended database transition apart from the precondition $wp(S)^*(true)$, i.e., possible changes have been incorporated into $S(\mathcal{J})$.

The theorem suggests that there is also a strict theory for (M)CEs leading to commutativity and compositionality results. This theory, however, has not yet been developed but we can check that the construction in Example 3.1 led indeed to an MCE.

3.5 A Commutativity Result

A strong theory should feature a result similar to the commutativity for GCS consistency enforcement (Proposition 2.1). For a given complex static constraint $\mathcal{I}_1 \wedge \cdots \wedge \mathcal{I}_n$ we would like to break down the process of enforcement to its single conjuncts $\mathcal{I}_i$. The result just mentioned goes even a little bit further and allows to build the greatest consistent specialization independently from the given order.

If we reformulate Proposition 2.1 within the MCE framework, we conjecture the semantic equivalence of $\mathcal{I}_1 \wedge \mathcal{I}_2 \to (S^{\mathcal{I}_1,\mathcal{J}_1})^{\mathcal{I}_2,\mathcal{J}_2}$ and $\mathcal{I}_1 \wedge \mathcal{I}_2 \to S^{\mathcal{I}_1 \wedge \mathcal{I}_2,\mathcal{J}_{12}}$. Herein, $\mathcal{J}_1$ is a low δ-constraint for S with respect to $\mathcal{I}_1$, $\mathcal{J}_2$ is a low δ-constraint for $S^{\mathcal{I}_1,\mathcal{J}_1}$ with respect to $\mathcal{I}_2$ and $\mathcal{J}_{12}$ is a low δ-constraint for S with respect to $\mathcal{I}_1 \wedge \mathcal{I}_2$.

Within $(S^{\mathcal{I}_1,\mathcal{J}_1})^{\mathcal{I}_2,\mathcal{J}_2}$ we have $S^{\mathcal{I}_1,\mathcal{J}_1} = wp(S)^*(true) \to S(\mathcal{J}_1)_{\mathcal{I}_1}$ which is certainly $\mathcal{I}_1$-consistent. However, then we take the δ-constraint $\mathcal{J}_2$ for $S^{\mathcal{I}_1,\mathcal{J}_1}$, i.e. $S^{\mathcal{I}_1,\mathcal{J}_1} \sqsubseteq S(\mathcal{J}_2)$, and enforce $\mathcal{I}_2$-consistency on $S(\mathcal{J}_2)$. In general, we will loose consistency with respect to $\mathcal{I}_1$ within this step. Therefore, the result $(S^{\mathcal{I}_1,\mathcal{J}_1})^{\mathcal{I}_2,\mathcal{J}_2}$ is not necessarily $\mathcal{I}_1$-consistent. Thus, the commutativity statement for the MCE-theory fails.

Proposition 3.3. *In general, $\mathcal{I}_1 \wedge \mathcal{I}_2 \to (S^{\mathcal{I}_1,\mathcal{J}_1})^{\mathcal{I}_2,\mathcal{J}_2}$ and $\mathcal{I}_1 \wedge \mathcal{I}_2 \to S^{\mathcal{I}_1 \wedge \mathcal{I}_2,\mathcal{J}_{12}}$ are not semantically equivalent.* $\qquad\square$

In order to keep the theoretical strength we look at a different way to build the MCE $S^{\mathcal{I}_1 \wedge \mathcal{I}_2,\mathcal{J}_{12}}$ gradually. We are able to proof the following.

Theorem 3.2. *Let S be a database transition on Y, $\mathcal{I}_1,\mathcal{I}_2$ be static constraints on X with $Y \subseteq X$. Let $\mathcal{J}$ be a low δ-constraint for S with respect to $\mathcal{I}_1 \wedge \mathcal{I}_2$. Then $\mathcal{I}_1 \wedge \mathcal{I}_2 \to (S^{\mathcal{I}_1,\mathcal{J}})_{\mathcal{I}_2}$ and $\mathcal{I}_1 \wedge \mathcal{I}_2 \to S^{\mathcal{I}_1 \wedge \mathcal{I}_2,\mathcal{J}}$ are semantically equivalent.*

Proof. First, Lemma 3.2 tells us that $\mathcal{J}$ is a δ-constraint for S with respect to $\mathcal{I}_1$ and with respect to $\mathcal{I}_2$. The consistent effect preserver $\mathcal{I}_1 \wedge \mathcal{I}_2 \to S^{\mathcal{I}_1,\mathcal{J}}$ is equivalent to $\mathcal{I}_1 \wedge \mathcal{I}_2 \wedge wp(S)^*(true) \to S(\mathcal{J})_{\mathcal{I}_1}$. Enforcing $\mathcal{I}_2$-consistency on $S^{\mathcal{I}_1,\mathcal{J}}$ results in $\mathcal{I}_1 \wedge \mathcal{I}_2 \wedge wp(S)^*(true) \to (S(\mathcal{J})_{\mathcal{I}_1})_{\mathcal{I}_2}$. Finally, we apply Proposition 2.1 and obtain $\mathcal{I}_1 \wedge \mathcal{I}_2 \wedge wp(S)^*(true) \to S(\mathcal{J})_{\mathcal{I}_1 \wedge \mathcal{I}_2}$ which is exactly $\mathcal{I}_1 \wedge \mathcal{I}_2 \to S^{\mathcal{I}_1 \wedge \mathcal{I}_2,\mathcal{J}}$. $\qquad\square$

Remark 3.2. The last theorem suggests a strategy combining GCS and MCE theory to enforce $S^{\mathcal{I}_1 \wedge \mathcal{I}_2,\mathcal{J}}$. First, lowness of $\mathcal{J}$ is given up and the consistent effect preserver $S^{\mathcal{I}_1,\mathcal{J}}$ is enforced. Notice that $\mathcal{J}$ is even a δ-constraint for $S^{\mathcal{I}_1,\mathcal{J}}$. Building the GCS of this intermediate result with respect to $\mathcal{I}_2$ results in $S^{\mathcal{I}_1 \wedge \mathcal{I}_2,\mathcal{J}}$. The theorem shows even independence from the given order of the static constraints. That is, it does not matter whether $S^{\mathcal{I}_1,\mathcal{J}}$ is built first and the GCS with respect to $\mathcal{I}_2$ is enforced or whether $S^{\mathcal{I}_2,\mathcal{J}}$ is built first and the GCS with respect to $\mathcal{I}_1$ is enforced. Hence, the theorem shows also the equivalence of $\mathcal{I}_1 \wedge \mathcal{I}_2 \to (S^{\mathcal{I}_1,\mathcal{J}})_{\mathcal{I}_2}$ and $\mathcal{I}_1 \wedge \mathcal{I}_2 \to (S^{\mathcal{I}_2,\mathcal{J}})_{\mathcal{I}_1}$. We have therefore obtained an adequate replacement for the GCS commutativity result. $\qquad\square$

Remark 3.3. The precondition $\mathcal{I}$ in the Definition 3.3 of $\mathcal{I}$-compatible transition constraints has been added to prove Lemma 3.2. If we omit this precondition we can still prove that an $\mathcal{I}_1 \wedge \mathcal{I}_2$-compatible transition constraint is $\mathcal{I}_1$-compatible or $\mathcal{I}_2$-compatible. In this case, however, we loose the independence of Theorem 3.2 from the given order of static constraints.

Again, we do not make any use of $\mathcal{J}$'s lowness and achieve therefore also a result for consistent effect preservers only.

Corollary 3.2. *Let S be a database transition on Y, $\mathcal{I}_1,\mathcal{I}_2$ be static constraints on X with $Y \subseteq X$. Let $\mathcal{J}$ be a δ-constraint for S with respect to $\mathcal{I}_1 \wedge \mathcal{I}_2$. Then $\mathcal{I}_1 \wedge \mathcal{I}_2 \to (S^{\mathcal{I}_1,\mathcal{J}})_{\mathcal{I}_2}$ and $\mathcal{I}_1 \wedge \mathcal{I}_2 \to S^{\mathcal{I}_1 \wedge \mathcal{I}_2,\mathcal{J}}$ are semantically equivalent.* $\qquad\square$

The proof of Theorem 3.2 concludes the investigation for the time being. We have seen that the notion of maximal consistent effect preservers is very promising.

4   Related Work

The idea to systematically modifying a program such that the result is consistent has some tradition in the field of deductive databases [3,4,5,6,12,14,21,22] and also appears as one of the goals of active databases [2,7,16,19]. The first group of articles investigates additional insertions, deletions and sometimes also updates that guarantee consistency; the latter group of articles emphasizes the use of triggers.

Instead of explaining the work in the context of deductive databases we refer to [14] that contains a comparison with the rest of the articles mentioned. The major difference with these articles is in the run-time approach that allows to reduce investigations to update requests. As a special case δ-constraints that are formulated in [14] should indeed lead to MCEs. A closer study of this relationship, however, is future work.

The use of rule trigger systems (RTSs) has been suggested from the very beginning as an approach to consistency enforcement [2,7]. However, there has never been a satisfactory theory behind this. The work in [19] investigates the limitations of the approach.

- For each set of constraints we can always find a sequence of insertions and deletions that is *non-repairable*. Even worse, checking repairability is equivalent to the implication problem for the admitted class of constraints, i.e., in many cases it is undecidable.
- Even if we only consider repairable program executions, the RTS may contain so-called critical cycles, i.e., the triggers may undo some (or all) of the effects of the program, but nevertheless change the final state.

For the theoretical results we refer to [16,19].

The Active Consistent Specialization (ACS) approach (see [1]) tries to combine the theoretical strength of GCSs with the simplicity of RTSs. Central to the approach is the use of repair actions, i.e., operations transforming an inconsistent state into a consistent state. As in the RTS approach such repair actions are appended to the given operation. The ACS approach suggests an alternative precondition-less method for effect preservation that is based on syntactic characterization of effects.

Although some special cases can be handled that cannot be captured using GCSs, this approach looses the generality of the GCS theory and is too restrictive. In particular, the sufficient condition for effect preservation by additional repair actions is too weak. Therefore, this approach can be considered at most as a pragmatic attempt to Consistency Enforcement.

5   Conclusion

In this paper we have investigated a new approach to consistency enforcement in databases.

First, we summarized the GCS theory of consistency enforcement. The elegance of this theory is based on the simplicity of the specialization order. However, it must be admitted that it shows some weaknesses.

The idea of this article is to overcome these weaknesses by weakening the specialization order $\sqsubseteq$. This could be accomplished by the concept of δ-constraints. A specialization of S can be characterized by the preservation of all δ-constraints of S. Then, it was only natural to consider only δ-constraints that lead to a consistent state with respect to the given static constraint. This results in the definition of (maximal) consistent effect preservers (MCEs) $S^{\mathcal{I},\mathcal{J}}$ for database programs S, static invariants $\mathcal{I}$ and (low) δ-constraints $\mathcal{J}$ for S that are compatible with $\mathcal{I}$. These MCEs are closely related to GCSs which demonstrates that effect preservers are the right kind of notion that can lead to an improvement of the current theory.

Also, the commutativity result from the GCS theory finds its generalization in the MCE framework. Building the (M)CE can be done not only gradually but also independently from a given set of static constraints. Therefore, it is sufficient to consider the enforcement process with respect to a single static constraint.

A compositionality result similar to the one for GCSs is highly desirable. An arithmetic version of the results achieved (see [11]) rounds off the investigations with a practicality study and allows computability and decidability questions to be asked (see [8,9,10]).

References

1. M. Balaban, S. Jurk: A DT/RT/CT framework for Integrity Enforcement based on Dependency Graphs. *In Proceedings DEXA.* 2001.
2. S. Ceri, P. Fraternali, S. Paraboschi, L. Tanca: Automatic Generation of Production Rules for Integrity Maintenance. *ACM TODS* 19(3), 1994, 367-422.
3. I. A. Chen, R. Hull, D. McLeod. An Execution Model for Limited Ambiguity Rules and its Applications to Derived Data Update. *ACM ToDS* 20, 1995, 365-413.
4. L. Console, M. L. Sapino, D. Theseider. The Role of Abduction in Database View Updating. *Journal of Intelligent Information Systems* 4, 1995, 261-280.
5. H. Decker. One Abductive Logic Programming Procedure for two Kinds of Update. *Proc. DYNAMICS'97*, 1997.
6. M. Dekhtyar, A. Dikovsky, S. Dudakov, N. Spyratos. Maximal Expansions of Database Updates. In K.-D. Schewe, B. Thalheim (Eds.). *Foundations of Information and Knowledge Systems*, 72-87. Springer LNCS 1762, 2000.
7. M. Gertz. Specifying Reactive Integrity Control for Active Databases. *Proc. RIDE '94*, 1994, 62-70.
8. S. Link. *Eine Theorie der Konsistenzerzwingung auf der Basis arithmetischer Logik*. M.Sc. Thesis (in German). TU Clausthal 2000.
9. S. Link, K.-D. Schewe. An Arithmetic Theory of Consistency Enforcement. to appear in *Acta Cybernetica*.
10. S. Link, K.-D. Schewe. Computability and Decidability Issues in the Theory of Consistency Enforcement. *Electronic Notes in Theoretical Computer Science*. vol. 42 . 2001
11. S. Link, K.-D. Schewe. Towards an Arithmetic Theory of Consistency Enforcement based on Preservation of δ-constraints. to appear in *Electronic Notes in Theoretical Computer Science*. vol. 61 . 2002.
12. J. Lobo, G. Trajcevski. Minimal and Consistent Evolution in Knowledge Bases. *Journal of Applied Non-Classical Logics* 7, 1997, 117-146.

13. M. Makkai. Admissible Sets and Infinitary Logic. In J. Barwise (Ed). *Handbook of Mathematical Logic*. North Holland, Studies in Logic and Foundations of Mathematics. vol. 90: 233-281. 1977.

14. E. Mayol, E. Teniente. Dealing with Modification Requests During View Updating and Integrity Constraint Maintenance. In K.-D. Schewe, B. Thalheim (Eds.). *Foundations of Information and Knowledge Systems*, 192-212. Springer LNCS 1762, 2000.

15. G. Nelson. A Generalization of Dijkstra's Calculus. *ACM TOPLAS*. vol. 11 (4): 517-561. 1989.

16. K.-D. Schewe. Consistency Enforcement in Entity-Relationship and Object-Oriented Models. *Data and Knowledge Engineering* 28, 1998, 121-140.

17. K.-D. Schewe. Fundamentals of Consistency Enforcement. In H. Jaakkola, H. Kangassalo, E. Kawaguchi (eds.). *Information Modelling and Knowledge Bases* X: 275-291. IOS Press 1999.

18. K.-D. Schewe, B. Thalheim. Towards a Theory of Consistency Enforcement. *Acta Informatica*. vol. 36: 97-141. 1999.

19. K.-D. Schewe, B. Thalheim. Limitations of Rule Triggering Systems for Integrity Maintenance in the Context of Transition Specifications. *Acta Cybernetica*. vol. 13: 277-304. 1998.

20. K.-D. Schewe, B. Thalheim, J. Schmidt, I. Wetzel. Integrity Enforcement in Object Oriented Databases. In U. Lipeck, B. Thalheim (eds.). *Modelling Database Dynamics*: 174-195. Workshops in Computing. Springer 1993.

21. E. Teniente, A. Olivé. Updating Knowledge Bases while Maintaining their Consistency. *The VLDB Journal* 4, 1995, 193-241.

22. B. Wüthrich. On Updates and Inconsistency Repairing in Knowledge Bases. *Proc. ICDE'93*, 1993, 608-615.

Improving Supervised Learning
by Feature Decomposition

Oded Maimon and Lior Rokach

Tel-Aviv University
Department of Industrial Engineering
Ramat Aviv, Tel Aviv 69978, Israel
{maimon,liorr}@eng.tau.ac.il

Abstract. This paper presents the Feature Decomposition Approach for improving supervised learning tasks. While in Feature Selection the aim is to identify a representative set of features from which to construct a classification model, in Feature Decomposition, the goal is to decompose the original set of features into several subsets. A classification model is built for each subset, and then all generated models are combined. This paper presents theoretical and practical aspects of the Feature Decomposition Approach. A greedy procedure, called DOT (Decomposed Oblivious Trees), is developed to decompose the input features set into subsets and to build a classification model for each subset separately. The results achieved in the empirical comparison testing with well-known learning algorithms (like C4.5) indicate the superiority of the feature decomposition approach in learning tasks that contains high number of features and moderate numbers of tuples.

1 Introduction and Motivation

Supervised Learning is one of the most important tasks in knowledge discovery in databases (KDD). In supervised problems the induction algorithm is given a set of training instances and the corresponding class labels and outputs a classification model. The classification model takes an unlabeled instance and predicts its class. The classification techniques can be implemented on variety of domains like marketing, finance and manufacturing.

Fayyad et al. (see [13]) claim that the explicit challenges for the KDD research community is to develop methods that facilitate the use of data mining algorithms for real-world databases. One of the characteristics of a real world databases is high volume. The difficulties in implementing classification algorithms as-is on high volume databases derives from the increase in the number of records in the database and from the increase in the number of features or attributes in each record (high dimensionality). High numbers of records primarily create difficulties in storage and computing complexity. Approaches for dealing with high number of records include sampling methods; massively parallel processing and efficient storage methods. However high dimensionality increases the size of the search space in an exponential manner, and thus increases the chance that the algorithm will find spurious models that are not valid in general.

T. Eiter and K.-D. Schewe (Eds.): FoIKS 2002, LNCS 2284, pp. 178–196, 2002.

It is well known that the required number of labeled samples for supervised classification increases as a function of dimensionality (see [18]). Fukunaga ([16]) showed that the required number of training samples is linearly related to the dimensionality for a linear classifier and to the square of the dimensionality for a quadratic classifier. In terms of nonparametric classifiers, the situation is even more severe. It has been estimated that, as the number of dimensions increases, the sample size needs to increase exponentially in order to have an effective estimate of multivariate densities (see [17]).

Bellman [5] was the first to define this phenomenon as the "curse of dimensionality", while working on complicated signal processing. Techniques that are efficient in low dimensions fail to provide meaningful results when the number of dimensions goes beyond a 'modest' size. Furthermore smaller data mining models, involving less attributes (probably less than 10), are much more understandable by humans. Smaller models are also more appropriate for user-driven data mining, based on visualization techniques.

Most of the methods for dealing with high dimensionality focus on Feature Selection techniques, i.e. selecting some subset of attributes upon which the induction algorithm will run, while ignoring the rest. The selection of the subset can be done manually by using prior knowledge to identify irrelevant variables or by using proper algorithms.

In the last decade, Feature Selection has enjoyed increased interest by the data mining community. Consequently many Feature Selection algorithms have been proposed, some of which have reported remarkable accuracy improvement. The literature on this subject is too wide to survey here, however, we recommend Langley [23], Liu and Motoda [25] and Maimon and Last [26] on this topic. Despite its popularity, using feature selection methodology for overcoming the high dimensionality obstacles has several shortcomings:

- The assumption that a large set of input attributes can be reduced to a small subset of relevant attributes is not always true; in some cases the target attribute is actually affected by most of the input attributes, and removing attributes will cause a significant loss of important information.
- The outcome (i.e. the subset) of many algorithms for *Feature Selection* (for instance almost any of the algorithms that are based upon the wrapper model methodology) is strongly dependent on the training set size. That is, if the training set is small the size of the reduced subset will be small as well due to the elimination of relevant attributes.
- In some cases, even after eliminating a set of irrelevant attributes, the researcher is left with relatively large numbers of relevant attributes.
- The backward elimination strategy, used by some methods, is extremely inefficient for working with large-scale databases, where the number of original attributes is more than 100.

A number of linear dimension reducers have been developed over the years. The linear methods of dimensionality reduction include projection pursuit (see [14]), factor analysis (see [19]), and principal components analysis (see [12]). These methods are not aimed directly at eliminating irrelevant and redundant attributes, but are rather concerned with transforming the observed variables into a small number of "projections" or "dimensions." The underlying assumptions are that the variables are numeric and the dimensions can be expressed as linear combinations of the observed variables (and vice versa). Each discovered dimension is assumed to represent an unobserved factor and thus provide a new way of understanding the data (similar to the curve equation in the regression models).

The linear dimension reducers have been enhanced constructive induction systems that use a set of existing attributes and a set of predefined constructive operators to derive new attributes (see [31]). These methods are effective for high dimensionality applications only if the original domain size of the input attribute can be in fact decreased dramatically.

One way to deal with the aforementioned disadvantages is to use a very large training set (which should increase in an exponential manner as the number of input attributes increase). However, the researcher rarely enjoys this privilege, and even if it does happen, the researcher will probably encounter the aforementioned difficulties derived from high number of records.

The rest of the paper is organized into three parts. In the first part we introduce the *Feature Decomposition Approach* literally and theoretically. In the second part we develop a heuristic algorithm for implementing the decomposition approach. In the third part we examine the algorithm on several artificial data and real applications.

2   Feature Decomposition Approach

The purpose of decomposition methodology is to break down a complex problem into several manageable problems. In artificial intelligence, according to Michie [30], finding a good decomposition is a major tactic both for ensuring the transparent end-product and for avoiding the combinatorial explosion.

Decomposition methodology can be considered as effective strategy for changing the representation of a learning problem. In fact Kusiak [22] consider decomposition as the "most useful form of transformation of data set".

It is generally believed that problem decomposition's benefits from: conceptual simplification of the problem, making the problem more feasible by reducing its dimensionality, achieving clearer results (more understandable), reducing run time by solving smaller problems and by using parallel or distributed computation and allowing different solution techniques for individual sub problems.

The decomposition approach is frequently used for operations research and engineering design, however, as Buntine [7] states, it has not attracted as much attention in KDD and machine learning community. Most of the work in machine learning decomposition can be found either in practical attempts in specific real life applications (see [7]) or in treatments of closely related problems mainly in the context of distributed and parallel learning (see [42]) or multiple classifiers (see [1]).

Figure 1 illustrates our approach for arranging the different types of decomposition in supervised learning.

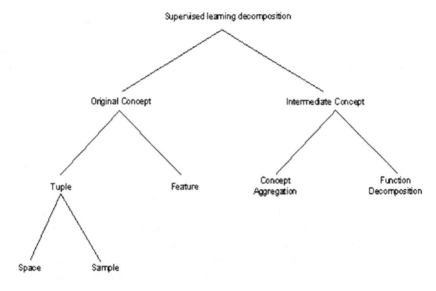

Fig. 1. Decomposition methods in supervised learning

In Intermediate Concept decomposition instead of learning a single complex classification model, several sub problems with different and simpler concepts are defined. The intermediate concepts can be based on aggregation of the original concept's values (concept aggregation) or not necessarily (function decomposition).

Buntine [7] used the concept aggregation to classify free text documents into predefined topics. Buntine [7] suggests breaking the topics up into groups (co-topics), and, instead of predicting the document's topic directly, first classifying the document to one of the co-topics and then using another model to predict the actual topic in that co-topic. Dietterich and Bakiri [9] have developed a general concept aggregation algorithm called Error-correcting output coding (ECOC) which decomposes multi-class problems into multiple two class problems. A classifier is build for each possible binary partition of the classes. Experiments show that ECOC improves the accuracy of neural networks and decision trees on several multi-class problems from the UCI repository.

Function decomposition was originally developed in 50's for improving the design of switching circuits. Recently this approach has been adopted by the machine learning community. Shapiro [38] and Michie [30] used a manual decomposition of the problem and an expert-assisted selection of examples to construct rules for the concepts in the hierarchy. In comparison with standard decision tree induction techniques, structured induction exhibits about the same classification accuracy with the increased transparency and lower complexity of the developed models. Zupan et al. [43] presented a general-purpose function decomposition approach for machine learning. According to this approach, attributes are transformed into new concepts in an iterative manner and create a hierarchy of concepts.

Original Concept decomposition, means dividing the original problem into several sub problems by partitioning the training set into smaller training sets. Each sub problem aims to solve the original problem, i.e. finding a classification model using only portion of the original training set. Then the classification models are combined in some fashion, either at learning or classification time.

There are two obvious ways to partition the data - tuples oriented or feature oriented which will be considered here.

Tuple decomposition by itself can be divided into two different types: sample and space. In sample decomposition (also known as partitioning) the goal is to partition the training set into several sample sets, such that each sub-learning task considers the entire space. In space decomposition on the other hand the original instance space is divided into several subspaces, each considered independently. In the last case no sophisticated combination is required.

For instance Chan and Stolfo [8] have used sample decomposition for reducing running time (as most of the inducers have running time that are quadratic in the sample size) as well as improving accuracy.

Bay [4] has presented a feature decomposition algorithm called MFS which combines multiple Nearest Neighbor classifiers each using only a subset random of features. It has shown that MFS can improve the standard Nearest Neighbor classifiers.

Blum and Mitchell [6] used a sort of feature decomposition for classification of Web pages. They suggested a Co-Training paradigm for learning with labeled and unlabeled data, especially when there is a large sample of data, which only small part of it is labeled. According to Blum and Mitchell paradigm of Co-Training the input space is divided to two different views (i.e. two independent and redundant sets of features). For each view they build a separated classifier that is then used to classify some unlabeled data. The new-labeled data of each classifier is then used to retrain the other classifier.

An important issue in decomposition is how its structure was obtained: It might be obtained manually based on expert's knowledge on a specific domain (like in [6], [38] or [30]) arbitrarily (as in [8]), due to some restrictions (like in the case of distributed learning) or induced without human interaction by a suitable algorithm (like in [43]).

Another important issue that differentiate between various decomposition implementations is whether the decomposition is mutually exclusive or partially overlapping, i.e. whether we utilize a certain data (a value of a certain attribute in a certain tuple) more than once. For instance in the case of sample decomposition, mutually exclusive means that a certain tuple cannot belong to more than one subset. (as in [8]). Bay [4] on the other hand, has used a non-exclusive feature decomposition. According to Bay exclusive feature decomposition may help avoid some of the error correlation problems.

In this paper we present new mutually exclusive feature decomposition where the attributes set is decomposed by an algorithm and not manually by the researcher. This method facilitates the creation of a classification model for high dimensionality databases. The idea we propose can be summarized as follows:

- The original input attribute set is decomposed to mutually exclusive subsets.
- An inducer algorithm is run upon the training data for each subset independently.
- The generated models are combined in order to make classification for new instances.

Variety of methods (like boosting or bagging), which also provide an improvement in classification performance by combining several simple classifiers produced by the same method, can be found in the literature. However, the resulting predictions are usually inscrutable to end-users ([34]), mainly due to the complexity of the generated models as well as the obstacles in transforming theses models into a single model. Moreover these methods do not attempt to use all relevant features, consequently in some cases especially when there are a lot of relevant attribute the researcher will not get the complete picture, of what attributes actually have an effect on the target attribute.

Other methods that deals directly with high dimensional data like support vector machines also suffer from inscrutability. The method proposed here improves classification performance, without jeopardizing the model's comprehensibility. Furthermore the *Feature Decomposition Approach* assists the researcher in discovering and understanding the relations between the different attributes, so it might lead to more comprehensible description of the learned concepts.

3   Notation

Throughout this paper we will use the following notation:

- $A = \{a_1, ..., a_i, ..., a_n\}$ - a set of n input attributes, where a_i is an attribute No. i.
- y - Represents the class variable or the target attribute.
- $G_k = \{a_{k,j(i)} \,|\, j = 1, ..., l_k\}$ - indicates a subset k that contains l_k input attributes where i is the original attribute index in the set A.
- $R_k = \{i/a_{k,j(i)} \in G_k, j = 1, ..., l_k\}$ denotes the correspondence indexes of subset k in the complete attribute set A.
- $Z = \{G_1, ...G_k..., G_\omega\}$ - A decomposition of the attribute set A into ω mutually exclusive subsets $G_k = \{a_{k,j(i)} \,|\, j = 1, ..., l_k\}$ $k = 1, ..., \omega\}$.
- $V_i = \{v_{i,j} \,|\, j = 1, ..., q_i\} \,\forall i = 1, ..., n$ - The domain of the attribute a_i with finite cardinality denoted q_i. We assume that each domain is a set of nominal values. For numeric attributes having continuous domains, each value represents an interval between two continuous values. In similar way V_y represents the domain of the target attribute.
- The *instance space* is defined as Cartesian product of all the input attributes domains: $X = V_1 \times V_2 \times ... \times V_n$. The *labeled instance space set* U is defined as Cartesian product of all input attribute domains and target attribute domain, i.e.:$U = X \times V_y$.

- $S = (< x_1, y_1 >, ..., < x_m, y_m >)$ - indicate the training set, containing m tuples (sometime called "instances," "records," "rows" or "observations") where $x_q \in X$ and $y_q \in V_y$. We assume that the tuples are generated according to some fixed and unknown joint probability distribution D over U. Note that this is a generalization of the deterministic case when a supervisor classifies a tuple using a function $y = f(x)$.
- $x_{q,i}$ - value of attribute i in an observation q. $\forall q, i$: $x_{q,i} \in V_i$. For discretized attributes, this means that any continuous value can be related to one of the intervals. Null (missing) values are not allowed (unless they are encoded as a special value.
- We use the notation I to represent a probabilistic induction algorithm (by probabilistic learning algorithm we refer to an algorithm that generates classifiers that also provide estimates to the conditional probability of the target attribute given the input attributes), and by $I(S, G_k)$ to represent a probabilistic classifier which was induced by activating the learning method I on a training set S using the input attributes in the subset G_k. Using $I(S, G_k)$ one can estimate the probability $\hat{P}_{I(S,G_k)}(y = v_{y,j} | a_i = x_{q,i} \ i \in R_k)$ of an observation x_q. Note we add a hat to the conditional probability estimation in order to distinguish it form the actual conditional probability.

4   The Problem Formulation

The problem of decomposing the input attribute set is that of finding the best decomposition, such that if a specific induction algorithm is run on each attribute subset data, then the combination of the generated classifiers will have the highest possible accuracy.

In this paper we focus on Naive Bayesian combination, which is an extension of the *Naive Bayesian* classifier. The *Naive Bayesian* classifier ([10]) uses Bayes rule to compute the probability of each possible value of the target attribute given the instance, assuming the input attributes are conditionally independent given the target attribute. The predicted value of the target attribute is the one, which maximizes the calculated probability, i.e.:

$$v_{MAP}(x_q) = \underset{v_{y,j} \in V_y}{\arg\max} \ \hat{P}_I(y = v_{y,j}) \cdot \prod_{i=1}^{n} \hat{P}_I(a_i = x_{q,i} | y = v_{y,j})$$

Despite its naive assumption, a variety of empirical research shows surprisingly that the Naive Bayesian classifier can perform quite well compared to other methods even in domains where clear attribute dependencies exist. Furthermore, Naive Bayesian classifiers are also very simple and easy to understand (see [20]).

In the Feature Decomposition approach with Naive Bayesian combination we use a similar idea, namely the prediction of a new instance x_q is based on the product of the conditional probability of the target attribute, given the values of the input attributes in each subset. Mathematically it can be formulated as follows:

$$v_{MAP}(x_q) = \underset{v_{y,j} \in V_y}{\arg\max} \frac{\prod_{k=1}^{\omega} \hat{P}_{I(S,G_k)}(y{=}v_{y,j}|a_i{=}x_{q,i} \; i{\in}R_k)}{\hat{P}_{I(S,G_k)}(y{=}v_{y,j})^{\omega\blacksquare 1}}$$

In fact extending the Naive Bayesian classifier by joining attributes is not new. Kononenko [21] have suggested the Semi-Naive Bayesian Classifier that use a conditional independence test to join attributes. Domingos and Pazzani [10] used estimated accuracy (as determined by leave-one-out cross validation on the training set). In both cases, the suggested algorithm finds the single best pair of attributes to join by considering all possible joins. Friedman et al [15] have suggested *Tree Augmented Naive Bayesian classifier* (TAN) which extends Naive Bayes taking into account dependencies among input attributes. Selective Bayesian Classifier ([24]) preprocesses data using a form of feature selection to delete redundant attributes.

However these methods have not noticeably improved accuracy. The reasons for the moderate results are two-fold. First both algorithms used a limited criterion for joining attributes. Second and more importantly, attributes are joined by creating a new attribute, whose values are the Cartesian product of its ingredients' values, specifically the number of attributes that can be joined together is restricted to a small number.

Duda and Hart ([11]) showed that Bayesian classifier has highest possible accuracy (i.e. Bayesian classifier predicts the most probable class of a given instance based on the complete distribution). However in practical learning scenarios, where the training set is very small compared to the whole space, the complete distribution can hardly be estimated directly.

According to the decomposition concept the complete distribution is estimated by combining several partial distributions. Bear in mind that it is easier to build a simpler model from limited number of training instances because it has less parameters. This makes classification problems with many input attributes more feasible.

This problem can be related to the bias-variance tradeoff (see for example [15]). The bias of a learning algorithm for a given learning problem is the persistent or systematic error that the learning algorithm is expected to make. A concept closely related to bias is variance. The variance captures random variation in the algorithm from one training set to another. This variation can result from variation in the training sample, from random noise in the training data, or from random behavior in the learning algorithm itself. The smaller each subset is, the less probabilities we have to estimate and potentially less variance in the estimation of each one of them. On the other hand, when there are more subsets, we expect that the approximation of the full distribution using the partial distributions is less accurate (i.e. higher bias error). Formally the problem can be phrased as follows:

Given a learning method I, and a training set S with input attribute set $A = \{a_1, a_2, ..., a_n\}$ *and target attribute y from a distribution D over the labeled instance space, the goal is to find an optimal decomposition* Z_{opt} *of the input attribute set A into* ω *mutually exclusive subsets* $G_k = \{a_{k,j(i)} | j = 1, ..., l_k\}$ $k =$

$1, ..., \omega$ not necessarily exhaustive such that the generalization error of the Naive Bayesian combination of the induced classifiers $I(S, G_k), k = 1, ..., \omega$ will be minimized over the distribution D.

It should be noted that the optimal is not necessarily unique. Furthermore it is not obligatory that all input attributes will actually belong to one of the subsets. Because of that the problem can be treated as an extension of the feature selection problem, i.e. finding the optimal decomposition of the form $Z_{opt} = \{G_1\}$, as the non-relevant features are in fact $NR=A$-G_1.

Moreover, when using a Naive Bayes for combining the models as described above, the Naive Bayes Classifier can be treated as specific decomposition: $Z = \{G_1, G_2, ..., G_n\}$, where $G_i = \{A_i\}$.

5   The Single Oblivious Decision Tree for Feature Selection

Oblivious Decision Trees are decision trees, in which all nodes at the same level test the same attribute. Despite its restriction, oblivious decision trees found to be effective as a feature selection procedure. Almuallim and Dietterich [2]) as well as Schlimmer [37] have proposed forward feature selection procedure by constructing oblivious decision trees.

Recently Maimon and Last [26] have suggested a new algorithm for constructing oblivious decision trees, called *IFN* that is based on information theory. Figure 2 represents a typical oblivious decision tree with three input attributes: glucose level, age and blood pressure of a certain patient and the Boolean target attribute representing whether that patient suffer from diabetes. Each layer is uniquely associated with an input attribute by representing the interaction of that attribute and the input attributes of the previous layers. The first layer (layer No. 0) includes only the root node and is not associated with any input attribute. The oblivious decision tree can also be used to predict values of target attributes in a disjunctive manner, similar to the decision-tree. The principal difference between the oblivious decision tree and a regular decision tree structure (see [33]) is the *constant ordering* of input attributes at every terminal node of the oblivious decision tree, the property which is necessary for minimizing the overall subset of input attributes (resulting in dimensionality reduction). The arcs that connect the terminal nodes and the nodes of the target layer are labeled with the number of records that fit this path. For instance there are twelve patients in the training set whose their glucose level is less than 107 but who still suffer from diabetes.

6   The DOT Algorithm

As the oblivious decision tree approach and more specifically the IFN algorithm were found to be effective in discovering the relevant attributes and their relations to the target attribute, we further extended it aiming to approach the

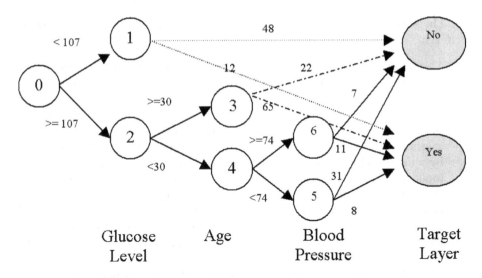

Fig. 2. Illustration of Oblivious Decision Tree

optimal feature decomposition (Z_{opt}). For our purpose each subset is represented by a different oblivious decision tree, while each attribute in this subset is located in a different layer. Attributes in the same tree should be dependent, while independent attributes should be in different trees as the independent assumption suggests. However it does not mean that attributes in different trees are necessarily independent. In some cases assigning dependent attributes into different groups contributes to the overall classification accuracy.

DOT (Decomposed Oblivious decision Trees) is an algorithm that instantiates this idea. The DOT learning algorithm begins with a single tree with a single node (the root node), representing an empty subset of input attributes. In each iteration the algorithm decides which attribute should be added to the current tree as a new layer, and to what nodes on the previous layer it will be connected (the splitted nodes). The nodes of a new layer are defined as all Cartesian product combinations of the splitted nodes with the values of the new input attribute, which have at least one observation associated with it.

Obviously DOT can construct up to n trees (in the extreme case where each tree may represent one input attribute) and up to n attributes in each tree (in the case where we have one tree that include all input attributes).

Each valid instance (instance that belongs to the instance space), is associated in each tree with exactly one path between the root node and the target layer. We make the following two assumptions:

- There are no missing values. Either they are replaced with valid values or the observation should be ignored.
- All attributes have discretely valued domains. Continuous attributes should be made discreet before using them in the algorithm.

The selection of the a new input attribute is made according the following criteria:

- The selected attribute should maximize the total significant decrease in the conditional entropy, as a result of adding it as a new layer. In order to calculate the total significant decrease in the conditional entropy, we estimate for each node in the last layer, the decrease in the conditional entropy as a result of splitting that node according the candidate attribute values. Furthermore the decrease in the conditional entropy is tested for significance by a likelihood-ratio test ([3]). The null hypothesis (H_0) is that a candidate input attribute and a target attribute are conditionally independent, given the node (implying that their conditional mutual information is zero). If H_0 holds, the test statistic is distributed as χ^2 with degrees of freedom equal to the number of independent proportions estimated from the observations associated with this node. Finally all significant decreases of specific nodes are summed up to achieve the total significant decrease.
- The attribute is conditionally dependent on the splitted nodes (nodes with significant decrease in the conditional entropy) given the target attribute. For testing the conditional independency we use a χ^2 test as described in [41]. The null hypothesis (H_0) is that a candidate input attribute and all splitted nodes are conditionally independent, given the target attribute.
- Adding the attribute to the current tree should decrease the generalization error bound of the combined trees so far. The bound is discussed in the following section. In this case there are two purposes for using it; First of all as adding a new attribute to the current tree increases this tree's complexity. Under the Occam's-razor assumption that simplicity is a virtue in conflict with training accuracy, we verify whether the decrease in the entropy worth the addition in complexity. Moreover the addition of the attribute to the current tree, contributes to the performance of the combined trees structure as a whole.

If no input attribute was selected an attempt is made to construct a new tree (a new subset) with the input attributes that were not used by previous trees. This procedure continues until there is no more unused attributes or until the last tree is left empty.

7   Generalization Error Bound for Multiple Oblivious Decision Trees

Over-fitting and under-fitting are well known problems in learning. A conventional approach to overcome these problems is to use a generalization error bound in terms of the training error and concept size.

As stated before, a oblivious decision tree can be considered as restricted decision tree, for that reason we might use one of the generalization error bound that were developed for decision trees in the literature (see [28]). However there are several reasons to develop a specific bound. First, we can utilize the fact that oblivious structure is more restricted, in order to develop a tighter bound. Second we are required to extend the bound for several oblivious trees combined using Naive Bayesian combination.

Due to the fact that we use probabilistic classification tree (represented by real value weights on the terminal nodes), the hypothesis space is infinite. A typical bound for infinite hypothesis space which makes use of VC (Vapnik and Chervonenkis) dimension, and holds with probability at least $1 - \delta$, has the following form ([39]):

$$|\varepsilon(h) - \hat{\varepsilon}(h)| \leq \sqrt{\frac{d \cdot (\ln \frac{2m}{d} + 1) - \ln \frac{\delta}{4}}{m}} \quad \begin{array}{l} \forall h \in H \\ \forall \delta > 0 \end{array}$$

Where d is the VC-Dimension of hypothesis class H, $\hat{\varepsilon}(h)$ is the error of h on training set of cardinality m.

The VC dimension for a set of indicator functions is defined as the maximum number of data points that can be shattered by the set of admissible functions. By definition, a set of m points is shattered by a concept class if there are concepts (functions) in the class that split the points into two classes in all of the 2^m possible ways. The VC dimension might be difficult to compute accurately. Here we introduce an upper bound and a lower bound of the VC dimension. The functions that we consider as a hypothesis class are computed by classes of multiple mutually exclusive oblivious decision trees. We characterize such a class by two vectors and one scalar: $L = (l_1, ..., l_\omega)$, $T = (t_1, ..., t_\omega)$ and n. Where l_k is the numbers of layers (not including the root and target layers) in the tree k, t_k is the number of terminal nodes in the tree k and n is the number of input attributes.

For the sake of simplicity the bound described in this section is developed assuming that the input attributes and the target attribute are both binary. However the bound can be extended for other cases in a straightforward manner. Note that each oblivious decision tree with non-binary input attributes can be converted to a corresponding binary oblivious decision tree by using appropriate artificial attributes.

Before presenting the main theorem we first consider two lemmas:

Lemma 7.1. *The VC dimension of oblivious decision tree on n binary input attributes with l layers and t terminal nodes is not greater than:* $t + \log_2(\frac{n!}{(n-l)!} \cdot \frac{(2t-4)!}{(t-2)! \cdot (t-2)!})$

Proof. Any oblivious decision tree can be converted to a suitable classification tree with leafs labeled $\{0,1\}$ according to the highest weight of each of the terminal node in the original tree. Because the probabilistic oblivious tree and its corresponded classification tree shattered the same subsets, their VC dimensions are identical.

The hypothesis space size of a classification oblivious tree with l layers, t terminal nodes and n input attributes to choose from is not greater than:

$$\frac{n!}{(n-l)!} \cdot 2^t \cdot \frac{(2t-4)!}{(t-2)! \cdot (t-2)!}$$

The first multiplier indicates the number of combinations for selecting with order l attributes from n. The second multiplier corresponds to the different classification options of the terminal nodes. The third multiplier represents the number of different binary tree structures that contains t leaves. The last multiplier is calculated using Wallace tree structure (see [40]). Note that in the case of binary tree there are exactly one more leaves than inner nodes. Furthermore the tree string always begins with an inner nodes (when $l \geq 1$) and end with at least two leaf nodes.

Based on the familiar relation $VC(H) \leq \log_2(|H|)$ for finite H, we proved the Lemma.

Lemma 7.2. *Consider ω mutually exclusive oblivious decision trees that are combined with Naive Bayesian and that has a fixed structure containing $T = (t_1, ..., t_\omega)$ terminal nodes. The number of dichotomies it induces on a set of cardinality m is at most:*

$$2\left(\frac{em}{1 + \sum\limits_{i=1}^{\omega} t_i}\right)^{1+\sum\limits_{i=1}^{\omega} t_i}.$$

Proof. For proving the lemma, we use a similar lemma introduced by Schmitt [36] for the number of dichotomies that a higher order threshold neuron with k monomials induces on a set of cardinality m.

A definition of a higher-order threshold neuron has the form:

$$w_1 M_1 + w_2 M_2 + ... + w_k M_k - t$$

Where $M_1, M_2, ..., M_k$ are monomials.

ω binary and oblivious decision trees which are combined with Naive Bayesian, can be converted to a higher order threshold neuron, where the set of terminal nodes constitutes the neuron's monomials and the log-odds in favor of $y = 1$ in each terminal node is the corresponded neuron's weight. Furthermore to be able to use the sign activation function we use a threshold that equals to the sum of all other monomials.

Theorem 7.1. *The VC-Dimension of ω mutually exclusive oblivious decision trees on n binary input attributes that are combined using Naive Bayesian combination and that have $\boldsymbol{L} = (l_1, ..., l_\omega)$ layers and $\boldsymbol{T} = (t_1, ..., t_\omega)$ terminal nodes is not greater than:*

$$\begin{cases} F + \log U & \omega = 1 \\ 2(F+1)\log(2e) + 2\log U & \omega > 1 \end{cases}$$

and at least:

$$F - \omega + 1$$

where:

$$U = \frac{n!}{(n - \sum\limits_{i=1}^{\omega} l_i)!} \cdot \prod_{i=1}^{\omega} \frac{(2t_i - 4)!}{(t_i - 2)! \cdot (t_i - 2)!} \; ; \; F = \sum_{i=1}^{\omega} t_i$$

Proof. We first discuss the upper bound. If $\omega = 1$ we can use Lemma 1 directly. For the case $\omega > 1$ we first bound the number of dichotomies induced by ω mutually exclusive oblivious decision trees on an arbitrary set of cardinality m. Because the biggest shattered set follows this bound as well, we derive the statement of theorem.

There are at most:

$$\frac{n!}{(n - \sum\limits_{i=1}^{\omega} l_i)!} \cdot \prod_{i=1}^{\omega} \frac{(2t_i - 4)!}{(t_i - 2)! \cdot (t_i - 2)!}$$

different structures for ω mutually exclusive oblivious trees on n binary input attributes with $\boldsymbol{L} = (l_1, ..., l_\omega)$ layers and $\boldsymbol{T} = (t_1, ..., t_\omega)$ terminal nodes.

According to Lemma 2 a fixed structure and variable weights can induce at most:

$$2 \left(\frac{em}{1 + \sum\limits_{i=1}^{\omega} t_i} \right)^{1 + \sum\limits_{i=1}^{\omega} t_i}$$

dichotomies on a given set of cardinality m. Enumerating over all structures, we derive that there are at most:

$$\frac{n!}{(n - \sum\limits_{i=1}^{\omega} l_i)!} \cdot \prod_{i=1}^{\omega} \frac{(2t_i - 4)!}{(t_i - 2)! \cdot (t_i - 2)!} \cdot 2 \left(\frac{em}{\sum\limits_{i=1}^{\omega} t_i} \right)^{\sum\limits_{i=1}^{\omega} t_i}$$

dichotomies on a given set of cardinality m that are induce by the class considered. If the above class shatters the given set, we must have:

$$2^m \le \frac{n!}{(n - \sum\limits_{i=1}^{\omega} l_i)!} \cdot \prod_{i=1}^{\omega} \frac{(2t_i - 4)!}{(t_i - 2)! \cdot (t_i - 2)!} \cdot 2 \left(\frac{em}{1 + \sum\limits_{i=1}^{\omega} t_i} \right)^{1 + \sum\limits_{i=1}^{\omega} t_i}$$

However the last inequality will not be true If we choose $m \ge 2F \log(2e) + 2 \log U$ where F and U defined above. The lower bound is true due to the fact that any set of ω trees with fixed structure has the above VC dimension. The result can be achieved by setting in each tree (beside one) a neutralized terminal node (i.e. a terminal node with posteriori probabilities that are equal to the apriority probabilities). This concludes our proof.

Our preliminary experiments have shown that estimating the generalization error by using the lower bound of the VC Dimension provides a better performance.

8   Making a Classification

The oblivious decision trees constructed by DOT algorithm can be used for classification of unlabeled instances, by performing the the following steps:

- In each tree locate the relevant node (final or unsplitted) that satisfies the unseen instance.
- Extract from the located node, the frequency vector (how many instances relate to each possible value of the target attribute.)
- Transform the frequency vector to probability vector. Using the frequency as is will typically over-estimate the probability so we use the Laplace correction to avoid this phenomenon (See [10]). According to Laplace's law of succession, the probability of the event $a_i = v_{i,j}$ which has been observed m_i times of m instances is $(m_i + 1)/(m + d_i)$ where d_i denotes the domain size of attribute a_i.
- Combine the probability vectors using Naive Bayesian combination.
- Select the target value maximizing the Naive Bayesian combination.

9   Evaluation of DOT on Variety Classification Problems

In order to validate the DOT algorithm and to illustrate the usefulness of the decomposition approach in classification problems, we apply our method to various domains and compare the results to other methods. In this paper we decided to compare the DOT algorithm to the following algorithms: IFN, Naive Bayes and C4.5. We have special interest in both IFN and Naive Bayes as they represent specific points in the search space of the DOT algorithm. We also compare the DOT to C4.5, a state-of-the-art heuristic machine learning algorithm, because its similarity to IFN (in the model structure) and due to its popularity in many other comparative studies.

The *DOT* approach has been applied to 15 representative public domain data sets from the UCI Machine learning and KDD Repository ([29]). Although we recognize the limitations of using this repository for comparing algorithms (see [35]), we use it here because it is considered as an objective method for comparing algorithms since the published results can be validated.

The databases passed a simple preprocessing stage. In this stage missing values are replaced by a distinctive value, and numeric attributes are made discrete by dividing their original range to ten equal-size intervals (or one per observed value, whichever was least). We could improve the results by using more sophisticated discretization. However, since the main purpose of this trial is to verify whether the *DOT* is capable of approximating optimal Feature Decomposition, we decided that any non-relevant differences between the algorithms should be

Table 1. Summary of experimental results

Database	Naive Bayes	C4.5	IFN	D-IFN
Aust	84.93±2.7	85.36±5.1	84.49±5.1	84.49±2.9
Bcan	97.29±1.6	+92.43±3.5	+94.39±3.5	97.29±1.6
LED17	+63.18±8.7	+59.09±6.9	+55.55±6.3	73.64±5.5
LETTER	+73.29±1	+74.96±0.8	+69.56±0.7	79.07±0.9
Monks1	+73.39±6.7	+75.81±8.2	+75.00±10.7	92.74±11
Monks2	+56.21±6.1	+52.07±8.6	63.87 ±6.4	62.13±6.4
Monks3	93.44±3.7	93.44±3.7	92.38±3.3	92.62±3.3
MUSH	+95.48±0.9	100±0	100±0	100±0
Nurse	+65.39±24	‾97.65±0.4	92.47±0.5	92.67±0.6
OPTIC	91.73±1.3	+62.42±2	+48.90±2.5	91.73±1.4
Sonar	75.48±7.3	69.71±5.4	76.48±6.8	77.12±8.7
SPI	+94.2±0.9	+91.2±1.9	+87.00±2.6	95.8±0.9
TTT	+69.27±3.2	‾85.31±2.7	73.19±3.9	73.33±4
Wine	96.63±3.9	+85.96±6.9	+91.45±5	96.63±3.9
Zoo	89.11±7	93.07±5.8	90.89±9.7	92.71±7.3

neutralized. Furthermore after DOT create a decomposition, one may use any other state-of-the-art data mining algorithms for constructing the appropriate models.

Table 1 shows the average accuracy and sample standard deviation obtained by using 10-fold-cross-validation. One tailed paired t-test with confidence level of 95% was used in order to verify whether the differences in accuracy are statistically significant. The results of our experimental study are very encouraging. In fact there was no significant case where Naive Bayes or IFN were more accurate than DOT, on the other hand DOT was more accurate than Naive Bayes and IFN in 8 databases, and 7 databases respectively. Furthermore DOT was significantly more accurate than C4.5 in 9 databases, and less accurate in only 2 databases.

The contribution of feature decomposition in real life applications can be found in [27].

10   The Link between Error Reduction and the Problem Complexity

In order to understand when the suggested approach introduces considerable performance enhancement, we checked the correlation between error reduction and the problem complexity.

There are two obvious alternatives for measuring the error reduction achieved by using Feature Decomposition approach: measuring the error difference between IFN and DOT or measuring the error ratio (i.e. the error of DOT divided by the error of single IFN). Following [1] we use error ration because it manifests the fact that it becomes gradually more difficult to achieve error reduction as the error of single IFN converge to zero.

In order to estimate the problem complexity we used the following ratio $\log(|H|)/m$. Where m is the training set size and $|H|$ is the hypothesis space size of all possible functions of the investigated problem. Note that the problem complexity increases as the problem dimensionality grows.

The estimated linear correlation coefficient (r) is 0.9. This result is quite encouraging as it evidently indicates when should we potentially use Feature Decomposition.

11   Summary and Future Work

In this paper we presented a new concept of Feature Decomposition for classification problems and proposed the DOT algorithm for discovering the appropriate decomposition. The algorithm has been implemented on variety of datasets, and has generated models with higher classification accuracy than other comparable methods.

Finally, the issues to be further studied include: considering other search methods for the problem defined, examining how the Feature Decomposition concept can be implemented using other classification methods like Neural Networks, examining other techniques to combine the generated classifiers, and exploring different decomposition paradigms other than Feature Decomposition.

Along with performing more empirical, we hope to better understand when it will be appropriate to use attributes decomposition.

References

1. Ali K. M., Pazzani M. J., Error Reduction through Learning Multiple Descriptions, Machine Learning, 24(3): 173-202, 1996.
2. Almuallim H. and Dietterich T.G., Learning boolean concepts in the presence of many irrelevant features. Artificial Intelligence, 69(1-2):279–306, 1994.
3. Attneave, F., Applications of Information Theory to Psychology. Holt, Rinehart and Winston, 1959.
4. Bay, S. Nearest neighbor classification from multiple feature subsets. Intelligent Data Analysis, 3(3): 191-209, 1999.
5. Bellman, R., Adaptive Control Processes: A Guided Tour, Princeton University Press, 1961.
6. Blum, A. and Mitchell, T., "Combining Labeled and Unlabeled Data with Cotraining", COLT: Proceedings of the Workshop on Computational Learning Theory, Morgan Kaufmann Publishers, 1998.
7. Buntine, W., "Graphical Models for Discovering Knowledge", in U. Fayyad, G. Piatetsky-Shapiro, P. Smyth, and R. Uthurusamy, editors, Advances in Knowledge Discovery and Data Mining, pp 59-82. AAAI/MIT Press, 1996.
8. Chan, P.K. and Stolfo, S.J., A Comparative Evaluation of Voting and Meta-learning on Partitioned Data, Proc. 12th Intl. Conf. on Machine Learning ICML-95, 1995.
9. Dietterich, T. G., and Bakiri, G., Solving multiclass learning problems via errorcorrecting output codes. Journal of Artificial Intelligence Research, 2:263-286, 1995.

10. Domingos, P., and Pazzani, M., "On the Optimality of the Simple Bayesian Classifier under Zero-One Loss," Machine Learning, 29: 103-130, 1997.
11. Duda, R., and Hart, P., Pattern Classification and Scene Analysis, New-York, NY: Wiley, 1973.
12. Dunteman, G.H., Principal Components Analysis, Sage Publications, 1989.
13. Fayyad, U., Piatesky-Shapiro, G., and Smyth P., "From Data Minig to Knowledge Discovery: An Overview," in U. Fayyad, G. Piatetsky-Shapiro, P. Smyth, and R. Uthurusamy, editors, Advances in Knowledge Discovery and Data Mining, pp 1-30, MIT Press, 1996.
14. Friedman, J.H., and Tukey, J.W., "A Projection Pursuit Algorithm for Exploratory Data Analysis," IEEE Transactions on Computers, 23 (9): 881-889, 1974.
15. Friedman, J.H., "On bias, variance, 0/1 - loss and the curse of dimensionality," Data Mining and Knowledge Discovery, 1 (1): 55-77, 1997.
16. Fukunaga, K., Introduction to Statistical Pattern Recognition. San Diego, CA: Academic, 1990.
17. Hwang J., Lay S., and Lippman A., "Nonparametric multivariate density estimation: A comparative study," IEEE Trans. Signal Processing, vol. 42, pp. 2795–2810, Oct. 1994.
18. Jimenez, L. O., and Landgrebe D. A., "Supervised Classification in High- Dimensional Space: Geometrical, Statistical, and Asymptotical Properties of Multivariate Data." IEEE Transaction on Systems Man, and Cybernetics — Part C: Applications and Reviews, 28:39-54, 1998.
19. Kim J.O., and C.W. Mueller, Factor Analysis: Statistical Methods and Practical Issues. Sage Publications, 1978.
20. Kononenko, I., "Comparison of inductive and naive Bayesian learning approaches to automatic knowledge acquisition". In Current Trends In reply to: Knowledge Acquisition, IOS Press, 1990.
21. Kononenko, I., "Semi-naive Bayesian classifier," in Proceedings of the Sixth European Working Session on Learning, Springer-Verlag, pp. 206-219, 1991.
22. Kusiak, A., Decomposition in Data Mining: An Industrial Case Study, IEEE Transactions on Electronics Packaging Manufacturing, Vol. 23, No. 4, 2000, pp. 345-353
23. Langley, P., "Selection of relevant features in machine learning," in Proceedings of the AAAI Fall Symposium on Relevance. AAAI Press, 1994.
24. Langley, P. and Sage, S., Oblivious decision trees and abstract cases. Working Notes of the AAAI-94 Workshop on Case-Based Reasoning, Seattle, WA: AAAI Press, 113-117.
25. Liu and H. Motoda, Feature Selection for Knowledge Discovery and Data Mining, Kluwer Academic Publishers, 1998.
26. Maimon, O., and M. Last, Knowledge Discovery and Data Mining: The Info-Fuzzy network (IFN) methodology, Kluwer Academic Publishers, 2000.
27. Maimon, O. and Rokach, L., "Data Mining by Attribute Decomposition with semiconductors manufacturing case study" in D. Bracha, Editor, Data Mining for Design and Manufacturing: Methods and Applications, Kluwer Academic Publishers, 2001.
28. Mansour, Y., and McAllester, D., Generalization Bounds for Decision Trees, COLT 2000: 220-224.
29. Merz, C.J, and Murphy. P.M., UCI Repository of machine learning databases. Irvine, CA: University of California, Department of Information and Computer Science, 1998.
30. Michie, D., "Problem decomposition and the learning of skills," in Proceedings of the European Conference on Machine Learning, Springer-Verlag, PP. 17-31, 1995.

31. Pfahringer, B., "Controlling constructive induction in CiPF," in Proceedings of the European Conference on Machine Learning, Springer-Verlag, pp. 242-256. 1994.

32. Pickard, L., B. Kitchenham, and S. Linkman., "An investigation of analysis techniques for software datasets", in Proc. 6th IEEE Intl. Software Metrics Symposium. Boca Raton, FL: IEEE Computer Society, 1999.

33. Quinlan, J.R., C4.5: Programs for Machine Learning, Morgan Kaufmann, 1993.

34. Ridgeway, G., Madigan, D., Richardson, T. and O'Kane, J. (1998), "Interpretable Boosted Naive Bayes Classification", Proceedings of the Fourth International Conference on Knowledge Discovery and Data Mining, pp 101-104.

35. Salzberg. S. L. (1997), "On Comparing Classifiers: Pitfalls to Avoid and a Recommended Approach". Data Mining and Knowledge Discovery, 1, 312-327, Kluwer Academic Publishers, Boston.

36. Schmitt, M. On the complexity of computing and learning with multiplicative neural networks, to appear in Neural Computation, 2001.

37. Schlimmer, J. C. Efficiently inducing determinations: A complete and systematic search algorithm that uses optimal pruning. In Proceedings of the 1993 International Conference on Machine Learning, pages 284–290, San Mateo, CA, 1993. Morgan Kaufmann.

38. Shapiro, A. D., Structured induction in expert systems, Turing Institute Press in association with Addison-Wesley Publishing Company, 1987.

39. Vapnik, V.N., 1995. The Nature of Statistical Learning The-ory. Springer-Verlag, New York.

40. Wallace, C. S., 1996. MML Inference of Predictive Trees, Graphs and Nets. In Computational Learning and Probabilitic Reasoning, A., Gammerman (ed), Wiley, pp43-66.

41. Walpole, R. E., and Myers, R. H., Probability and Statistics for Engineers and Scientists, pp. 268-272, 1986.

42. Zaki, M. J., and Ho, C. T., Eds., Large- Scale Parallel Data Mining. New York: Springer- Verlag, 2000.

43. Zupan, B., Bohanec, M., Demsar, J., and Bratko, I., "Feature transformation by function decomposition," IEEE intelligent systems & their applications, 13: 38-43, 1998.

Extremal Theorems for Databases

Krisztián Tichler

Alfréd Rényi Institute of Mathematics
1053 Budapest, Hungary
`krisz@renyi.hu`

Abstract. We say, that a database relation represents a Sperner system $\mathcal{K}$ on the set of attributes, if the system of minimal keys is exactly $\mathcal{K}$. It is known, that such a representation always exsists. In this paper we show, that the maximum of the minimal number of tuples, that are needed to represent a Sperner system of only two element sets is $3^{(n/3+o(n))}$. We consider this problem for other classes of Sperner systems (e.g for the class of trees, i.e. each minimal key has cardinality two, and the keys form a tree), too.

Keywords: Relational database model, keys, antikeys, maximal independent sets, labelled directed tree, cliques, extremal problems

1   Introduction

Consider a database relation R of arity n in the relational database model. The set of *attributes* (i.e. column-names) is denoted by Ω. Usually attributes correspond to a certain type of data (e.g. name, date of birth, place of birth, etc.), while n-*tuples* correspond to the data of a given individual.

A *key dependency* is an expression of the form $K \rightarrow \Omega$, where $K \subseteq \Omega$ is called a *key*. A relation instance I over Ω *satisfies* $K \rightarrow \Omega$, denoted $I \vDash K \rightarrow \Omega$, if for each pair u and v of tuples in I, $\pi_K(u) = \pi_K(v)$ imply $\pi_{\Omega \setminus K}(u) = \pi_{\Omega \setminus K}(v)$. Here $\pi_X(u)$ is an $|X|$-tuple, namely the *projection* of u to the attributes of X.

A key is called a *minimal key,* if it does not include other keys. Keys play an important role in the theory of databases. If we know the connection between the attributes of a key and the other attributes (and this connection is stored efficiently), it is clearly sufficient to store the attributes of the key. Since the set of keys and minimal keys determines each other, it is natural to investigate the system of minimal keys, which in most cases contains much fewer elements.

The system of minimal keys is clearly a non-empty *Sperner system* (i.e. no member can include another member). For a Sperner system $\mathcal{K}$ let us use the notation

$$I(\mathcal{K}) = \{I | I \vDash K \rightarrow \Omega \text{ if and only if } \exists K', K' \subseteq K, K' \in \mathcal{K}\}.$$

We call an element of $I(\mathcal{K})$ a *representation* of $\mathcal{K}$. The following basic theorem of W.W. Armstrong and J. Demetrovics states, that for every non-empty Sperner system, there is always a representation of it, i.e. there exists a relation, in which the system of minimal keys is exactly the given family of sets.

T. Eiter and K.-D. Schewe (Eds.): FoIKS 2002, LNCS 2284, pp. 197–211, 2002.
© Springer-Verlag Berlin Heidelberg 2002

Theorem 1.1 *[1,4,5]*
  If $\mathcal{K}$ is non-empty, then $I(\mathcal{K}) \neq \emptyset$.

In view of Theorem 1.1 it is natural to ask what is the minimal size of a relation, that represents a given system of keys. Formally let $s(\mathcal{K}) = \min\{|I| \mid I \in I(\mathcal{K})\}$ denote this minimum.

Suppose, that little a priori information is known about the structure of a given database instance. If some theorem ensures the validity of certain inequalities among some parameters of databases and we have information on the actual values of a part of these parameters then some statement may be deduced for the other parameters of a given instance. In our case, we have a theorem between the number of attributes, system of minimal keys and the size of the relation. So if the size of the instance is less than the minimal representation of the given family of sets, then the system of minimal keys can not be this one.

The goal of this paper is to deduce results on the maximum of $s(\mathcal{K})$ if $\mathcal{K}$ is choosen from a given class of Sperner systems. The most interesting result is determining the magnitude of this maximum for the class, that consists of all graphs,

$$\max\{s(\mathcal{K}) \mid |K| = 2, \forall K \in \mathcal{K}\} = 3^{n/3+o(n)}. \tag{1.1}$$

We shall present further results on other graph classes and a lower estimation for the class, that consists of all k-graphs. Typically the proof of these theorems consists of two parts. First, apply a theorem from combinatorics on the maximum number of maximal independent sets of graphs, where the graph is chosen from a given class of graphs. Second, try to apply Theorem 5.1 for the extremal graphs. It will turn out, that this theorem or the idea of the proof can be applied in surprisingly many cases. The heart of the proof of Theorem 5.1 is a combinatorial lemma on labelled directed trees.

These questions can also be asked in the following way. How worse the worst representable Sperner systems (of a certain class) are? The answer is rather dissapointing in the investigated cases. The results show families of sets with exponential minimal representation in the number of attributes. For rather simple key systems containing only 2-element keys we are unable to find relations of reasonable size.

The paper is organized as follows. In Section 2 we present earlier results on minimal representation and some useful lemmas as well. In Section 3 we discuss a combinatorial lemma on labelled directed trees. In Section 4 we show some theorems on independent sets of graphs. These two sections can be considered as the combinatorial background of the paper. Readers, who are interested only in the database theoretical results may skip these sections at first read. In Section 5 we prove Theorem 5.1, our main tool in determining the magnitude of several minimum representation. In Section 6 we just put together the results of the previous two sections. Finally, in Section 7 we present some open problems.

For further combinatorial problems in database theory, see the survey [13]. We shall use frequently the following abbreviation. If n is an integer we write briefly $[n]$ for the set $\{1, \ldots, n\}$.

2   Previous Results

In this section we present some useful lemmas on minimal representation and list some earlier result.

$A \subseteq \Omega$ is an *antikey* if it is not a key. An antikey is called a *maximal antikey*, if other antikeys do not include it. If $\mathcal{K}$ is the system of minimal keys, denote the system of maximal antikeys by $\mathcal{K}^{-1}$. There is a strong connection between $s(\mathcal{K})$ and $|\mathcal{K}^{-1}|$, namely the magnitude of $s(\mathcal{K})$ is between $|\mathcal{K}^{-1}|$ and its square root.

Theorem 2.1 *[6]*

If $\mathcal{K} \neq \emptyset$ is a Sperner system, then the following two inequalities hold,

$$|\mathcal{K}^{-1}| \leq \binom{s(\mathcal{K})}{2} \quad and \quad s(\mathcal{K}) \leq 1 + |\mathcal{K}^{-1}|. \tag{2.1}$$

We shall use in Section 5 the following two basic observations on minimal representations.

Proposition 2.2 *Suppose, that $I \in I(\mathcal{K}), |I| = s(\mathcal{K})$ is a minimum representation of the Sperner system $\mathcal{K}$, then the following properties hold,*

(i) *for every $A \in \mathcal{K}^{-1}$ there exist two tuples, u and v in I, such that $\pi_A(u) = \pi_A(v)$,*
(ii) *there are no two diffrent tuples u and v in I, such that $\pi_K(u) = \pi_K(v)$ holds for some $K \in \mathcal{K}$.*

Proof. Suppose, that (i) is not true. Then $\pi_A(u) = \pi_A(v)$ never holds, so A is a key, which contradicts the choice of A. Suppose, that a pair of tuples, u and v violates (ii). So $\pi_K(u) = \pi_K(v)$ holds. Since K is a key, it means $u = v$. Delete u from I, so we get a representation of $\mathcal{K}$ with fewer tuples, which is a contradiction.   □

Note, that this statement can be reversed in a certain sense, see [6]. The problem of determining $s(\mathcal{K})$ was widely studied, if $|\Omega| = n$ and $\mathcal{K} = \mathcal{K}_k^n$ consists of all subsets of Ω of k elements. In many cases the exact value was determined. Further results can be found in [2].

Theorem 2.3 *[7]*

$$s(\mathcal{K}_1^n) = 2, \quad s(\mathcal{K}_2^n) = \lceil (1 + \sqrt{1 + 8n})/2 \rceil, \quad s(\mathcal{K}_{n-1}^n) = n, \quad s(\mathcal{K}_n^n) = n + 1.$$

Theorem 2.4 *[3,10]*

$$n \geq 7, n \neq 8 \Rightarrow s(\mathcal{K}_3^n) = n.$$

Theorem 2.5 *[6]*

$$2 \leq k < n \Rightarrow \exists c_1 = c_1(k), c_2 = c_2(k)$$

$$c_1 n^{(k-1)/2} < s(\mathcal{K}_k^n) < c_2 n^{(k-1)/2}.$$

Theorem 2.6 *[8]*

$$n > n_0(k), k \geq 1 \implies \exists c_3 = c_3(k), c_4 = c_4(k)$$

$$c_3 n^{(2k+1)/3} < s(\mathcal{K}^n_{n-k}) < c_4 n^k, \qquad \frac{1}{12} n^2 < s(\mathcal{K}^n_{n-2}) < \frac{1}{2} n^2.$$

Except for $s(\mathcal{K}^n_n)$ and Theorem 2.6 the values are around (or equal to) the lower bound of (2.1). We will show several Sperner systems with minimal representation near to the upper bound.

Note, that these results present such minimal representations, that are not exponential at all. For example Theorem 2.3 show a minimal representation of 2-element keys of magnitude $\sqrt{n}$.

3   Labelled Directed Trees

The heart of this work is a combinatorial lemma. Here we present a generalized version, despite we shall need only a special case of it (for $k = 1$). The proof is a slight modification of the special case $k = 1$, $l = 2$, see [17].

A tree F is called a *directed tree*, if there is a direction on the edges, so that a vertex v_0 *(root)* has only out-neighbours, and an arbitrary vertex $v \neq v_0$ has a uniquely determined in-neighbour $n(v)$. $N(v)$ denotes the out-neighbourhood of v. The set of the leaves of a tree F is denoted by $l(F)$. Let U be a (finite) set. A tree $F = F(U)$ is called *labelled*, if a subset $A(v)$ of U is associated with each vertex v of F.

For two fixed integers $k \geq 1$, $l \geq 2$ and $U = \{1, 2, ..., m\}$ ($m \geq k+1$) consider the family of labelled directed trees $\mathcal{F} = \mathcal{F}^{(m)}_{k,l}$, for which the vertices of each tree $F \in \mathcal{F}$ are labelled as follows. The label of the root v_0 of F is $A(v_0) = U$. For an arbitrary vertex v of F there is a disjoint partition $N(v) = \bigcup_{i=1}^{l} N_i(v)$ of its out-neighbourhood and the following hold:

$$A(v) \subseteq A(n(v)) \quad (v \neq r), \tag{3.1}$$

$$|A(v)| \geq k + 1, \tag{3.2}$$

$$w_1, w_2 \in N_i(v) \Rightarrow A(w_1) \cap A(w_2) = \emptyset \quad (1 \leq i \leq l), \tag{3.3}$$

$$w_1 \in N_i(v), w_2 \in N_j(v) \Rightarrow |A(w_1) \cap A(w_2)| \leq k \quad (1 \leq i < j \leq l). \tag{3.4}$$

As an example, consider the following labelled directed tree F of $\mathcal{F}^{(9)}_{1,2}$.

Example 3.1 $A(v_0) = \{1, 2, 3, 4, 5, 6, 7, 8, 9\}$, $N(v_0) = \{v_1, v_2, v_3\}$, $A(v_1) = \{1, 2, 3, 4, 5\}$, $A(v_2) = \{6, 7\}$, $A(v_3) = \{3, 6, 8\}$, $N(v_1) = \{v_4, v_5, v_6, v_7\}$, $A(v_4) = \{1, 2, 3\}$, $A(v_5) = \{4, 5\}$, $A(v_6) = \{1, 5\}$, $A(v_7) = \{3, 4\}$, $N(v_4) = \{v_8, v_9\}$, $A(v_8) = \{1, 3\}$, $A(v_9) = \{2, 3\}$, $l(F) = \{v_2, v_3, v_5, v_6, v_7, v_8, v_9\}$. *Easy to check, that F satisfies the properties (3.1)-(3.4).*

Introduce the notation $T_{k,l}(m) = \max\{|l(F)| \mid F \in \mathcal{F}^{(m)}_{k,l}\}$. We shall need the following observations

Proposition 3.2 *For arbitrary integers* $m_1, m_2, \ldots, m_r \geq k+1$ *the following hold:*

$$T_{k,l}(m_1) + T_{k,l}(m_2) + \ldots + T_{k,l}(m_r) \leq T_{k,l}(m_1 + m_2 + \ldots + m_r), \qquad (3.5)$$

$$\text{if } m_1 < m_2 \text{ then } T_{k,l}(m_1) < T_{k,l}(m_2), \qquad (3.6)$$

$$T_{k,l}(m) \leq \binom{m}{k+1}. \qquad (3.7)$$

Proof. In order to prove (3.5) it is sufficient to see that $T_{k,l}(m_1) + T_{k,l}(m_2) \leq T_{k,l}(m_1 + m_2)$. Let two labelled directed trees, F_1 and F_2 be given with the disjoint labels U_1 and U_2 at their roots respectively, $|U_i| = m_i$, $|l(F_i)| = T_{k,l}(m_i)$ (i=1, 2). Suppose, that these trees have properties (3.1)-(3.4). Now consider the following labelled directed tree F. Its root has degree 2, and connected with the roots of F_1 and F_2, which are subtrees of F. The label of the root of F is $U_1 \cup U_2$, the other labels are unchanged. It is clear, that F has properties (3.1)-(3.4) and $|l(F)| = T_{k,l}(m_1) + T_{k,l}(m_2)$.

In order to prove (3.6) take a directed tree F satisfying properties (3.1)-(3.4) and suppose, that the label of the root is U, $|U| = m_1$, $|l(F)| = T_{k,l}(m_1)$. Then consider the following labelled directed tree F'. Let the set U_1 satisfy $|U_1| = m_2 - m_1 + 1 (\geq 2)$, $|U_1 \cap U| = 1$. The root of the tree F' has label $U \cup U_1$ and degree 2, and connected with the root of F and a new point of label U_1. It is obvious, that F' has properties (3.1)-(3.4) and $|l(F')| = T_{k,l}(m_1) + 1$.

In order to prove (3.7) we only need to observe, that by (3.2) and (3.4) the leaves are different. So by (3.4) a $(k+1)$-element subset of U determines the leaf. $\qquad \square$

Lemma 3.3 $\forall 0 < \varepsilon < \frac{1}{2} \exists C = C(\varepsilon, k, l)$, *so that for every integer* $m \geq k+1$,

$$T_{k,l}(m) \leq Cm^{1+\varepsilon}. \qquad (3.8)$$

Proof. Let $0 < \varepsilon < \frac{1}{2}$ be fixed. We shall define constants $c = c(\varepsilon, k, l), M = M(c, k, l)$ and $C = C(M)$ later. Note, that expressions (3.9), (3.11), (3.17), (3.19), (3.21) and (3.24) define these constants.

We use induction on m. By (3.7) if we choose

$$C > M^{k+1} \qquad (3.9)$$

(3.8) will be true for $m \leq M$.

Let $m > M$ be an arbitrary integer. Suppose, that (3.8) is true, for every integer less than m. Consider a tree $F \in \mathcal{F}_{k,l}^{(m)}$, for which $|l(F)|$ is maximal. If v_0 denotes the root, then let $N(v_0) = \{v_1, v_2, \ldots, v_t\}$ where $N_1(v_0) = \{v_1, v_2, \ldots, v_{t_1}\}, \ldots, N_l(v_0) = \{v_{t_{l-1}+1}, v_{t_{l-1}+2}, \ldots, v_{t_l}\}$ ($t_1 \leq t_2 \leq \ldots \leq t_{l-1} \leq t_l = t$) is the decomposition in the definition of F. Choose $m_i = |A(v_i)|$ and let F_i be a subtree of F, defined by v_i as a root ($1 \leq i \leq t$). Observe, that $|l(F)|$ can be maximal only if $T_{k,l}(m_i) = |l(F_i)|$ for every $1 \leq i \leq t$. So it is sufficient to prove the inequality

$$\sum_{i=1}^{t} T_{k,l}(m_i) \leq Cm^{1+\varepsilon}. \qquad (3.10)$$

Now let us decompose the set of indices $1 \leq i \leq t$ into 4 parts:

$$P = \{i|\ m_i \leq k(l{-}1)c^2\},$$
$$Q = \{i|\ k(l{-}1)c^2 < m_i \leq \tfrac{m}{c}\},$$
$$R = \{i|\ \tfrac{m}{c} < m_i \leq m(1 - \tfrac{1}{c})^{1/\varepsilon}\},$$
$$S = \{i|\ m(1 - \tfrac{1}{c})^{1/\varepsilon} < m_i\}.$$

If we choose

$$M > (l{-}1)kc^3, \quad \text{and} \quad \frac{1}{c} < (1 - \frac{1}{c})^{1/\varepsilon} \tag{3.11}$$

these sets will be disjoint.

Case 1: $S \neq \emptyset$. Let $j \in S$. By the symmetry of the definition of F we may assume, that $1 \leq j \leq t_1$. (3.3) obviously implies

$$\sum_{\substack{i=1 \\ i \neq j}}^{t_1} m_i \leq m{-}m_j$$

and (3.2)-(3.4) imply

$$\sum_{i=t_1+1}^{t} m_i \leq m{-}m_j + k(t{-}t_1) \leq (1{+}k(l{-}1))(m{-}m_j).$$

These inequalities and (3.5) lead to

$$\sum_{i=1}^{t} T_{k,l}(m_i) = T_{k,l}(m_j) + \sum_{\substack{i=1 \\ i \neq j}}^{t} T_{k,l}(m_i) \leq T_{k,l}(m_j) + T_{k,l}(m{-}m_j){+}$$
$$+ T_{k,l}((kl{-}k{+}1)(m{-}m_j)). \tag{3.12}$$

Using the induction hypothesis we obtain

$$T_{k,l}(m_j) \leq Cm_j^{1+\varepsilon} \leq C(m^{1+\varepsilon} - (m{-}m_j)m^\varepsilon), \tag{3.13}$$
$$T_{k,l}(m{-}m_j) \leq C(m{-}m_j)^{1+\varepsilon}, \tag{3.14}$$
$$T_{k,l}((kl{-}k{+}1)(m{-}m_j)) \leq C((kl{-}k{+}1)(m{-}m_j))^{1+\varepsilon}. \tag{3.15}$$

We have

$$((kl{-}k+1)(m{-}m_j))^{1+\varepsilon} = (kl{-}k{+}1)^{1+\varepsilon} \cdot (m{-}m_j)^{1+\varepsilon} \leq (\gamma{-}1) \cdot (m{-}m_j)^{1+\varepsilon}. \tag{3.16}$$

where

$$\gamma = \gamma_{k,l} = (kl{-}k{+}1)^{1.5} + 1. \tag{3.17}$$

By (3.16) we have

$$(m-m_j)^{1+\varepsilon} + \big((kl-k+1)(m-m_j)\big)^{1+\varepsilon} \leq \gamma \cdot (m-m_j)^{1+\varepsilon} =$$
$$= (m-m_j)m^\varepsilon \Big(\gamma \cdot \big(\tfrac{m-m_j}{m}\big)^\varepsilon\Big). \quad (3.18)$$

Observe, that if we choose c so large that

$$\big(1 - \big(\tfrac{1}{\gamma}\big)^{1/\varepsilon}\big)^\varepsilon < 1 - \frac{1}{c} \quad (3.19)$$

holds, the choice of S will imply, that the expression in the big parantheses of (3.18) can be upperestimated by 1. Now comparing (3.12)-(3.15) and (3.18) we get inequality (3.10).

Case 2: $S = R = \emptyset$. Then the summation from 1 to t acts on $P \cup Q$. By the induction hypothesis we have

$$\sum_{i=1}^{t} T_{k,l}(m_i) \leq C \sum_{i \in P \cup Q} m_i^{1+\varepsilon} = C \sum_{i \in P \cup Q} m_i \big(\tfrac{m_i}{m}\big)^\varepsilon m^\varepsilon. \quad (3.20)$$

If we choose c so large that

$$l < c^\varepsilon \quad (3.21)$$

holds, the definition of Q will imply $m_i/m^\varepsilon \leq 1/l$ for $1 \leq i \leq t$. On the other hand (3.3) implies

$$\sum_{i=1}^{t} m_i = \sum_{j=1}^{l} \sum_{i=t_{j_0 1}+1}^{t_j} m_i \leq lm \quad (\text{where } t_0 = 0).$$

These two inequalities and (3.20) prove (3.10).

Case 3: $S = \emptyset, R \neq \emptyset$. Then

$$\sum_{i=1}^{t} T_{k,l}(m_i) = \sum_{i \in P} T_{k,l}(m_i) + \sum_{i \in Q} T_{k,l}(m_i) + \sum_{i \in R} T_{k,l}(m_i)$$

holds. By the induction hypothesis and the definition of R we have

$$\sum_{i \in R} T_{k,l}(m_i) \leq C \sum_{i \in R} m_i^{1+\varepsilon} = C \sum_{i \in R} m_i \big(\tfrac{m_i}{m}\big)^\varepsilon m^\varepsilon \leq \frac{C}{l} \sum_{i \in R} lm_i(1 - \tfrac{1}{c})m^\varepsilon =$$
$$= \frac{C}{l}\Big(\sum_{i \in R}(m_i + (l-1)(m_i - \tfrac{m_i}{c}))\Big)m^\varepsilon - \frac{C}{l}\Big(\sum_{i \in R} \tfrac{m_i}{c}\Big)m^\varepsilon. \quad (3.22)$$

By the definition of R and the condition $R \neq \emptyset$

$$\frac{1}{l}\Big(\sum_{i \in R} \tfrac{m_i}{c}\Big)m^\varepsilon \geq \frac{1}{lc^2}m^{1+\varepsilon} \quad (3.23)$$

can be obtained. If we choose

$$M^{k+1+\varepsilon} > \frac{l^2 c^2}{k+1} T_{k,l}(k(l-1)c^2) \tag{3.24}$$

then (3.6) and $|P| \le lm/(k+1)$ ensures

$$\sum_{i\in P} T_{k,l}(m_i) \le \frac{lm}{k+1} T_{k,l}(k(l-1)c^2) < \frac{M^{k+1}}{lc^2} m \cdot M^\varepsilon < \frac{C}{lc^2} m^{1+\varepsilon}. \tag{3.25}$$

So, by (3.23)-(3.25) the last term of (3.22) can be lowerestimated in absolute value by $\sum_{i\in P} T_{k,l}(m_i)$. The summation on Q can be made as in *Case 2*:

$$\sum_{i\in Q} T_{k,l}(m_i) \le C \sum_{i\in Q} m_i \left(\frac{m_i}{m}\right)^\varepsilon m^\varepsilon \le \frac{C}{l} \sum_{i\in Q} m_i m^\varepsilon. \tag{3.26}$$

We need to prove the inequality

$$\sum_{i\in Q} m_i + \sum_{i\in R} (m_i + (l-1)(m_i - \tfrac{m_i}{c})) \le lm. \tag{3.27}$$

Let us denote shortly the sets of indices satisfying $t_{r-1}+1 \le i \le t_r$ by T_r, $1 \le r \le l$. Consider an $i \in R$. It may be assumed without loss of generality, that $i \in T_1$. By (3.3), the set $A(v_i)$ can have a non-empty intersection only with $A(v_j)$s satisfying $j \notin T_1$. The sets $A(v_j)$, $j \in T_r$ for some fixed $2 \le r \le l$ are disjoint. Here $m_j > k(l-1)c^2$ holds for $j \in Q \cup R$, hence the number of sets $A(v_j)$, $j \in T_r \cap (Q \cup R)$, having a non-empty (at most k) intersection with $A(v_i)$ is at most $m/(k(l-1)c^2)$ in T_r. The choice $i \in R$ implies $|A(v_i)| > m/c$. So by (3.4) at most one cth of the elements of $A(v_i)$ can be an element of some $A(v_j)$, $j \in T_r \cap (Q \cup R)$. In other words for each $2 \le r \le l$ at least $m_i - m_i/c$ elements of U are not covered by some $A(v_j)$, $T_r \cap (Q \cup R)$, $2 \le r \le l$. These "holes" are of course disjoint for different elements of R. Hence we have

$$\sum_{i\in T_r\cap(Q\cup R)} m_i + \sum_{i\in R\setminus T_r} \left(m_i - \tfrac{m_i}{c}\right) \le m \qquad (1 \le r \le l).$$

The sum of these l inequalities gives (3.27).

By (3.22)-(3.27) inequality (3.10) is valid in this case, too.   □

4   Graphs with a Lot of Maximal Independent Sets

In this section we present some results on how many maximal independent sets a graph can have if it is chosen from a given class of graphs. If $G = (V, \mathcal{E})$ is a graph (or $\mathcal{H} = (V, \mathcal{E})$ is a hypergraph), $I \subseteq V$ is called an *independent set*, if $\forall E \in \mathcal{E}$, $E \not\subseteq I$. An independent set is called maximal if other independent sets do not include it. Note, that $\mathcal{K}^{-1}$ is just the set of maximal independent sets of the (hyper)graph $\mathcal{K}$.

The number of maximal independent sets will be denoted by $i(G)$ (or by $i(\mathcal{H})$). For a class of Sperner systems (graphs, hypergraphs) $\mathbf{H}$, let us intoduce the notation $i(n, \mathbf{H}) = \max\{i(\mathcal{H}) \mid |V(\mathcal{H})| = n, \mathcal{H} \in \mathbf{H}\}$.

For $\mathbf{G} = \{\,\text{graphs}\,\}$ the question of determining $i(n, \mathbf{G})$ is equivalent to maximize the number of cliques (i.e. maximal complete subgraphs) a graph can have. (Take the complements of the graphs.) The same argument can be applied for other graphclasses closed under complement.

This question was asked for $\mathbf{G}$ by P.Erdős and L.Moser. P.Erdős answered the question with an inductive argument. J.W.Moon and L.Moser used a different argument characterizing the extremal graphs. Also R.E. Miller and D.E. Muller answered the question independently. The vertex disjoint union of graphs G_1 and G_2 is denoted by $G_1 + G_2$, the vertex disjoint union of t copies of a graph G is denoted by tG. The complete graph on n vertices is denoted by K_n. Let

$$G_n = \begin{cases} tK_3 & \text{for } n = 3t, \\ (t{-}1)K_3 + 2K_2 \text{ or } (t{-}1)K_3 + K_4 & \text{for } n = 3t + 1, \\ tK_3 + K_2 & \text{for } n = 3t + 2, \end{cases}$$

so for $n = 3t + 1$ G_n denotes two graphs.

Theorem 4.1 *[15]*

$$i(n, \mathbf{G}) = \begin{cases} 3^t & \text{for } n = 3t, \\ 4 \cdot 3^{t-1} & \text{for } n = 3t + 1, \\ 2 \cdot 3^t & \text{for } n = 3t + 2, \end{cases}$$

and $i(G) = i(n, \mathbf{G}), G \in \mathbf{G}, |V(G)| = n$ *holds if and only if* $G \cong G_n$

Let us consider two more examples in detail. Let $\mathbf{T} = \{\,\text{trees}\,\}$ and for an integer n let us denote by P_n the path of n vertices. T_n^k is the following tree of n vertices. A special vertex v_0 is connected with an edge to one of the two endpoints of a P_k and with one edge to the $(n{-}k{-}1)/2$ copies of P_2. Of course, T_n^k exists only if $(n{-}k{-}1)/2$ is an integer. Let

$$T_n = \begin{cases} T_n^2 & \text{for odd } n, \\ T_n^1 \text{ or } T_n^3 & \text{for even } n, \end{cases}$$

so for even n T_n denotes two graphs.

Theorem 4.2 *[18,16]*

$$i(n, \mathbf{T}) = \begin{cases} 2^{(n-1)/2} & \text{if } n \text{ is odd}, \\ 2^{(n-2)/2} + 1 & \text{if } n \text{ is even}. \end{cases}$$

and $i(T) = i(n, \mathbf{T}), T \in \mathbf{T}, |V(T)| = n$ *holds if and only if* $T \cong T_n$

This number was proved by H.S. Wilf [18], the extremal graphs was determined by B.E. Sagan [16] and also by J.R. Griggs and C.M. Grinstead independently.

Let $\mathbf{C} = \{$ connected graphs $\}$. If n is fixed, let C_n be the following graph on n vertices. For $n = 3t$ let $G = tK_3$ and $x \in V(G)$. We obtain C_n from G by joining x with one edge to each of the other $(t-1)$ components. For $n = 3t + 1$ let $G = K_1 + tK_3$ and denote the isolated point by x. We obtain C_n by joining x with 3 edges to the first copy of K_3 and with one edge to the other $(t-1)$ copies of it. For $n = 3t + 2$ consider $G = K_4 + (t-1)K_3 + K_1$. We obtain C_n by joining the isolated point with an edge to each component and with 3 edges to one K_3.

Theorem 4.3 *[9,11]*

$$i(n, \mathbf{C}) = \begin{cases} 2 \cdot 3^{t-1} + 2^{t-1} & \text{for } n = 3t, \\ 3^t + 2^{t-1} & \text{for } n = 3t + 1, \\ 4 \cdot 3^{t-1} + 3 \cdot 2^{t-2} & \text{for } n = 3t + 2, \end{cases}$$

and $i(C) = i(n, \mathbf{C}), C \in \mathbf{C}, |V(C)| = n$ holds if and only if $C \cong C_n$

The question for $\mathbf{C}$ was asked by H.S. Wilf, and the above theorem was proved independently by Z. Füredi (for $n > 50$ only, but with a simpler proof) and J.R. Griggs - C.M. Grinstead - D.R. Guichard.

There are further results. E.g. in [12,14] there are theorems on the maximum number of maximal independent sets of bipartite, connected bipartite, forest and triangle-free graphs. The magnitude of the results are $2^{n/2}$. The extremal graphs were also determined and Consequence 5.2 can be applied to them to derive the analogous results.

5   Badly Representable Sperner Systems

In this section the main idea of the paper will be presented. We prove, that certain Sperner systems can not be well represented, i.e. their minimal representation is closer to the upper bound of (2.1).

Theorem 5.1 *Let $\mathcal{K}_n$ be a sequence of Sperner systems over the underlying set Ω_n and $\preceq$ is an ordering of the attributes. Suppose furthermore, that for every n, a subset $\mathcal{K}_n^*$ of $\mathcal{K}_n^{-1}$ of cardinality*

$$|\mathcal{K}_n^*| \geq |\mathcal{K}_n^{-1}|^{1-o(1)} \tag{5.1}$$

is given. For every $A \in \mathcal{K}_n^*$ let us fix a partition $A = A_1 \cup \ldots \cup A_{t=t(A)}$, that satisfies the condition

$$t_1 \in A_i, t_2 \in A_j, i < j \; \Rightarrow \; t_1 \prec t_2.$$

Let us introduce the notation

$$\mathcal{K}_n^*\{A_1, \ldots, A_r\} = \{B \subseteq \Omega \mid \exists A \in \mathcal{K}_n^*, A = A_1 \cup \ldots \cup A_t, r < t, A_{r+1} = B\},$$

and fix a constant l. If for every $\mathcal{K}_n^*\{A_1, \ldots, A_r\}$

$$|\mathcal{K}_n^*\{A_1, \ldots, A_r\}| \leq l, \tag{5.2}$$

and

$$\forall B_1, B_2 \in \mathcal{K}_n^*\{A_1, \ldots, A_r\} \; \exists K \in \mathcal{K}_n, \; such \; that \; K \subseteq B_1 \cup B_2, \qquad (5.3)$$

hold, then we have

$$s(\mathcal{K}_n) = |\mathcal{K}_n^{-1}|^{1-o(1)}. \qquad (5.4)$$

Before the proof, we present here a short explanation of theorem. Informally it says, that if we can select a big part of the antikeys, can order the attributes in an appropriate order and can partition the selected antikeys in a "good" way then the Sperner system is badly representable. "Good" way means two things. First, all initial segments (the meaning of initial is according to the order of attributes and the partition) can be continued only in at most l ways (for some global constant l). Second, the union of each two continuations forms a key.

Proof. Suppose that the conditions of the theorem hold, and $I_n \in I(\mathcal{K}_n), |I| = s(\mathcal{K}_n)$ is a minimal representation of $\mathcal{K}_n$. Let $U_n = [s(\mathcal{K}_n)]$ denote the set of indices of the tuples and let $u_i^{(n)} = \langle u_{i1}^{(n)}, \ldots, u_{in}^{(n)} \rangle$ be the ith tuple of I_n, $1 \leq i \leq s(\mathcal{K}_n)$. The jth attribute is simply denoted by j.

The projections of the tuples to a given set of attributes J determine a partition of U or more generally of its arbitrary subset W. Let us collect the elements of cardinality at least 2 of this partition in $\mathcal{P}_W^J$. Formally let $W \subseteq U$ and $J \subseteq \Omega_n$. Let us introduce the notation (subscripts n are omitted)

$$\mathcal{P}_W^J = \{A \subseteq W \mid |A| \geq 2; i_1, i_2 \in A \Rightarrow \forall j \in J \; u_{i_1j} = u_{i_2j};$$
$$i_1 \in A, i_2 \in W \backslash A \Rightarrow \exists j \in J \; u_{i_1j} \neq u_{i_2j}\},$$

We shall define recursively a labelled directed tree F. Let the label of the root v_0 of F be $A(v_0) = U$. If $\bigcup \{\mathcal{P}_U^B \mid B \in \mathcal{K}_n^*\{\}\} = \{U_1, U_2, \ldots U_s\}$ for some integer s, then let $N(v_0) = \{v_1, v_2, \ldots v_s\}$ and its labels $A(v_i) = U_i$, $1 \leq i \leq s$. Suppose, that we have already defined a vertex v of the tree, and its label $A(v)$. Furthermore assume, that $A(v)$ was chosen as an element of $\mathcal{P}_W^{A_r}$ for some integer r, $W \subseteq U$, $A_r \in \mathcal{K}_n^*\{A_1, \ldots, A_{r-1}\}$. If $\bigcup \{\mathcal{P}_{A(v)}^B \mid B \in \mathcal{K}_n^*\{A_1, \ldots, A_r\}\} = \{V_1, V_2, \ldots, V_s\}$ for some integer s, then let $N(v) = \{v_1, v_2, \ldots, v_s\}$ and $A(v_k) = V_k$ $(1 \leq k \leq s)$. The leaves of the tree F will be those vertices, for which $s = 0$. It is easy to see, that $F \in \mathcal{F}_{1,l}^{(s(\mathcal{K}_n))}$: (3.1)-(3.3) holds by the definition of F, (3.4) holds by (5.2), (5.3) and (ii) of Proposition 2.2.

For $A \in \mathcal{K}_n^*$ consider a set U_A with the property $|U_A| \geq 2, U_A \subseteq U_n, \forall u, v \in U_A \; \pi_A(u) = \pi_A(v)$. Such a set exists by (i) of Proposition 2.2. By the definition of the tree F it is a equal to some $A(v)$, $v \in l(F)$.

On the other hand, $|U_A \cap U_{A^\bullet}| \leq 1$ for different elements A and A' of $\mathcal{K}_n^*$. Otherwise there would be two tuples u and v, such that $\pi_{A \cup A^\bullet}(u) = \pi_{A \cup A^\bullet}(v)$, contradicting (ii) of Proposition 2.2 since $A \cup A'$ is a key. So by (3.1) and (3.2) the labels are different for different elements of $\mathcal{K}_n^*$. We obtained the following inequality

$$|l(F)| \geq |\mathcal{K}_n^*|. \qquad (5.5)$$

By Lemma 3.3 we have for a fixed $0 < \varepsilon \leq \frac{1}{2}$

$$|l(F)| \leq T_{1,l}(s(\mathcal{K}_n)) \leq C(\varepsilon)s(\mathcal{K}_n)^{1+\varepsilon}. \tag{5.6}$$

So from (5.1), (5.5), (5.6) and (2.1) we obtained, if n is large enough, the inequality

$$|\mathcal{K}_n^{-1}| \leq s(\mathcal{K}_n)^{1+4\varepsilon},$$

which is equivalent to (5.4).   □

A special case of the theorem is the following.

Consequence 5.2 *Suppose, that all the maximal antikeys of $\mathcal{K}_n^*$ are partitioned into one element sets. Then instead of the condition on the partition we can consider sets $\varphi(Z)$, where*

$$\varphi(Z) = \Big\{ \min\{t|\ t > \max Z, t \in A\| A \in \mathcal{K}_n^*, A \cap [\max Z] = Z \Big\}.$$

Here simply j denotes the jth attribute. (5.2) and (5.3) can be modified as follows. Suppose, that there exists a constant l, such that for every $Z \subseteq \Omega$

$$|\varphi(Z)| \leq l \tag{5.7}$$

and

$$t_1, t_2 \in \varphi(Z) \Rightarrow \{t_1, t_2\} \in \mathcal{K}_n \tag{5.8}$$

holds. Then (5.4) holds.   □

6   Maxima of Minimal Representations

In [17] it was shown, that a relation of size $2^{\lambda+o(1)}$, where $\lambda = 0.4056\ldots$, is needed to represent a cycle (i.e. a Sperner system of 2-element sets that form a cycle).

Since this number is quite large, naturally arises the question, whether there is any graph (i.e. a Sperner system of 2-element sets), that need a larger minimal representation.

More generally, let $\mathbf{K}$ be a class of Sperner systems (e.q. the class of all Sperner systems of 2-element sets). We suppose, that for every $\mathcal{K} \in \mathbf{K}$ its underlying set $\Omega(\mathcal{K})$ is given, too. For every integer n let us introduce the notation $s(n, \mathbf{K}) = \max\{s(\mathcal{K}) \,|\, |\Omega(\mathcal{K})| = n, \mathcal{K} \in \mathbf{K}\}$.

Using the notations of Section 4, we have the following theorem (note, that it is a reformulation of (1.1))

Theorem 6.1

$$\frac{\log_2 s(n, \mathbf{G})}{n} \longrightarrow \frac{\log_2 3}{3}.$$

Proof. Let $\mathcal{K} = \mathcal{E}(G_n)$. By (2.1) and Theorem 4.1 it is sufficient to prove, that (5.4) holds. We check, whether the conditions of Consequence 5.2 are satisfied.

Let $n = 3t$, the proof is similar in the other cases. First we need to give an order of the attributes. Let the $(3j-2)$th, $(3j-1)$th and $(3j)$th attribute correspond to the vertices of the jth copy of K_3 $(1 \leq j \leq t)$. The maximal antikeys are those sets that contain exactly one element from each copy of K_3. Z can be an initial segment of a maximal antikey (in other cases $\varphi(Z) = \emptyset$) only if it contain exactly one attribute from the first $j-1$ copies of K_3, and contain no elements from the others. Then $\varphi(Z)$ contain exactly the attributes of the jth copy of K_3. So (5.7) (with $l = 3$) and (5.8) are satisfied and Consequence 5.2 can be applied. $\qquad\square$

The proofs of the following theorems are similar to the proof of Theorem 6.1. One can easily check that the extremal graphs T_n and C_n of Theorem 4.2 and Theorem 4.3 respectively satisfy the conditions of Consequence 5.2.

Theorem 6.2
$$\frac{\log_2 s(n, \mathbf{T})}{n} \longrightarrow \frac{1}{2}$$
$\qquad\square$

Theorem 6.3
$$\frac{\log_2 s(n, \mathbf{C})}{n} \longrightarrow \frac{\log_2 3}{3}$$
$\qquad\square$

Finally, consider the following class of Sperner systems, which does not consist of graphs. Let us introduce the notation $\mathbf{G}^r = \{\, r\text{-uniform hypergraphs}\,\}$. We give a lower estimation on the magnitude of $s(n, \mathbf{G}^r)$ and show a direct application of Theorem 5.1.

Let K_n^r denote the complete r-uniform hypergraph on n vertices $(n \geq r)$. For some constants $\sum_{i=1}^{t(n)} n_i = n, r \leq n_i \leq s$ let $G_n^{(r)} = K_{n_1}^r + \ldots + K_{n_t}^r$.

Proposition 6.4 $G_n^{(r)}$ *satisfies the conditions of Theorem 5.1.*

Proof. The maximal antikeys are those sets, that contain exactly $r - 1$ elements from each copy of K_n^r. So each maximal antikey consists of $t(r-1)$ elements. Let the order of the attributes be such an order, that list the vertices of the complete r-graphs one after the other. Let the partitons of the maximal antikeys consist of the intersections the complete r-graphs. So each partition consists of t parts, each part has size $r-1$. If $A_1 \cup \ldots \cup A_j$ is an initial segment of a maximal antikey, then there are $\binom{n_{j+1}}{r-1} \leq \binom{s}{r-1}$ possible continuation of it and the union of any two continuations forms a key. So the conditions of Theorem 5.1 is satisfied (with $l = \binom{s}{r-1}$) $\qquad\square$

Consequence 6.5
$$\limsup \frac{\log_2 s(n, \mathbf{G}^r)}{n} \geq \max_{s \in \mathbb{N}} \frac{1}{s} \log_2 \binom{s}{r-1}. \qquad (6.1)$$

We have already seen, that this value is $0.528\ldots$ for $r = 2$. For $r = 3, r = 4$ and $r = 5$ (6.1) gives $0.664\ldots$, $0.733\ldots$ and $0.775\ldots$ respectively.

7 Open Problems

To get sharper results, it would be of interest to improve on the main lemma.

Conjecture 7.1

$$T_{1,2}(m) = \Theta(m \log m) \tag{7.1}$$

The lower bound can be achieved if every vertex of label size h have 2 set of around $\sqrt{h}$ new neighbours each. The size of their labels are around $\sqrt{h}$, and each label intersects (nearly) all labels from the other set of neighbours.

Problem 7.2 *Determine $s(n, \mathbf{K})$ for other classes of Sperner systems $\mathbf{K}$. Also determining $s(\mathcal{K})$ for other Sperner systems $\mathcal{K}$ would be of great interest.*

In order to advance in these problems we may need to know more on maximal independent sets of hypergraphs.

Problem 7.3 *Determine the maximal number of maximal independent sets for other classes of (hyper)graphs.*

Acknowledgements

I would like to thank for the help of my supervisor, Professor G.O.H Katona, and every other people who helped me writing this paper including the referees, who had several useful comments on how to reorganize the paper.

References

1. W.W. Armstrong, Dependency structures of database relationship, Information Processing 74 (North Holland, Amsterdam, 1974) 580-583.
2. F.E. Bennett, LiSheng Wu, Minimum matrix representation of Sperner-systems, Discrete Appl. Math. 81 (1998), no. 1-3., 9-17.
3. F.E. Bennett, LiSheng Wu, On minimum matrix representation of closure operations, Discrete Appl. Math. 26 (1990) 25-40.
4. J. Demetrovics, Candidate keys and antichains, SIAM J. Algebraic Methods 1 (1980) 92.
5. J. Demetrovics, On the equivalence of candidate keys with Sperner systems, Acta Cybernet. 4 (1979) 247-252.
6. J. Demetrovics, Z. Füredi, G.O.H. Katona, Minimum matrix representation of closure operations, Discrete Appl. Math. 11 (1985) 115-128.
7. J. Demetrovics, G.O.H. Katona, Extremal combinatorial problems in relational database, in Fundamentals of Computation Theory 81, Proc. of the 1981 International FCT-Conference, Szeged, Hungary, 1981, Lecture Notes in Computer Science 117 (Springer, Berlin 1981) 110-119.
8. Z. Füredi, Perfect error-correcting databases, Discrete Appl. Math. 28 (1990) 171-176.
9. Z. Füredi, The Number of Maximal Independent Sets in Connected Graphs, Journal of Graph Theory 11 (1987) 463-470.

10. B.Ganter, H-D.O.F. Gronau, Two conjectures of Demetrovics, Füredi and Katona, concerning partitions, Combinatorics of ordered sets (Oberwolfach, 1988), Discrete Math. 88 (1991), no. 2-3., 149-155.
11. J.R. Griggs, C.M. Grinstead, D.R. Guichard, The maximum number of maximal independent sets in a connected graph, Discrete Math. 68 (1988), no. 2-3., 211-220.
12. M. Hujter, Zs. Tuza, The number of maximal independent sets in triangle-free graphs, SIAM J. Discrete Math. 6 (1993), no. 2, 284–288.
13. G.O.H. Katona, Combinatorial and algebraic results for database relations, in J. Biskup, R. Hull, ed., Database Theory - ICDT '92, Berlin, 1992, Lecture Notes in Comput. Science, 646 (Springer Verlag, Berlin, 1992) 1-20.
14. Jiuqiang Liu, Maximal independent sets in bipartite graphs. J. Graph Theory 17 (1993), no. 4, 495–507.
15. J.W. Moon, L. Moser, On cliques in graphs, Israel J. Math. 3 (1965) 23-28.
16. B.E. Sagan, A note on independent sets in trees, SIAM J. Discrete Math. 1 (1988) 105-108.
17. K. Tichler, Minimum matrix representation of some key systems, in K.-D. Schewe, B. Thalheim ed., Proc. of FoIKS 2000 Conference, Burg, Germany, 2000, Lecture Notes in Computer Science 1762 (Springer-Verlag, Berlin, 2000) 275-287.
18. H.S. Wilf, The number of maximal independent sets in a tree, SIAM J. Alg. Disc. Meth. 7 (1986) 125-130.

Relational Databases and Homogeneity
in Logics with Counting[*]

José María Turull Torres

Universidad Tecnológica Nacional, F.R.B.A.
Universidad Nacional de San Luis
Perón 2315, piso 4, depto. P
1040 Capital Federal, Argentina
jmturull@hotmail.com, turull@mail.unlu.edu.ar

Abstract. We define a new hierarchy in the class of computable queries to relational databases, in terms of the preservation of equality of theories in fragments of first order logic with bounded number of variables with the addition of counting quantifiers (C^k). We prove that the hierarchy is strict, and it turns out that it is orthogonal with the TIME-SPACE hierarchy defined with respect to Turing machine complexity. We introduce a model of computation of queries to characterize the different layers of our hierarchy which is based on the reflective relational machine of S. Abiteboul, C. Papadimitriou, and V. Vianu and where databases are represented by their C^k theories. Then we define and study several properties of databases related to homogeneity in C^k getting various results on the increase of computation power of the introduced machine.

1 Introduction

Given a relational database schema, it is natural to think in the whole class of queries which might be computed over databases of that schema, if we do not restrict ourselves to a given implementation of certain query language on some computer, in the same way as the notion of computable function over the natural numbers was raised in computability theory. In [7], A. Chandra and D. Harel devised a formalization for that notion. They defined a *computable query* as a function over the class of databases of some given schema which is not only recursive but preserves isomorphisms as well. Isomorphism preservation is what formalizes the intuitive property of representation independence.

In [27] a strict hierarchy was defined, in the class of computable queries ($\mathcal{CQ}$) of A. Chandra and D. Harel, in terms of the preservation of equivalence in bounded variable fragments of first order logic (FO), which we denote as FO^k. The logic FO^k is the fragment of FO which consists of the formulas with up to k different variables. We denote the whole hierarchy as $\mathcal{QCQ}^\omega$. For every natural k, the layer denoted as $\mathcal{QCQ}^k$ was proved to be a semantic characterization of

---

[*] This work has been partially supported by Grants of Universidad CAECE and Universidad de Luján, Argentina.

T. Eiter and K.-D. Schewe (Eds.): FoIKS 2002, LNCS 2284, pp. 212–229, 2002.

the computation power of the reflective relational machine of [2] with variable complexity k (RRM^k). The RRM^k is a model of computation of queries to relational databases which has been proved to be incomplete, i.e., it does not compute all computable queries. Then, we defined and studied in [27] several properties of relational databases, related to the notion of homogeneity in model theory ([8]), as properties which increase the computation power of the RRM^k when working on databases having those properties.

That research was enrolled in a very fruitful research program in the field of finite model theory considered as a theoretical framework to study relational databases. In that program different properties of the databases have been studied, which allow incomplete computation models to increase their expressive power when computing queries on databases with those properties. Order ([3],[10]), different variants of rigidity ([9], [25], [26]), and different notions related to homogeneity ([27]) are properties which turned out to be quite relevant to that regard.

In the present paper, and following the same research program, we define a new hierarchy in the class of computable queries, which we denote as QCQ^{C^ω}. We define this hierarchy in terms of the preservation of equivalence in bounded variable logics with *counting quantifiers* (C^k). For every natural k, we denote as QCQ^{C^k} the layer of the hierarchy QCQ^{C^ω} which consists of those queries that preserve equivalence in C^k. The logic C^k is obtained by adding quantifiers "there exists at least m different elements in the database such that..." to the logic FO^k for every natural m. The logic C^k has been deeply studied during the last decade ([6], [12], [15], [24]).

Defining the classes QCQ^{C^k} appears to be rather natural, since in the definition of *computable query* of [7] the property of preservation of isomorphisms is essential, and, as it is well known, isomorphism in finite databases coincides with equivalence in first order logic. Moreover, it is also well known that for every natural k, the logic C^k is strictly weaker than FO as to expressive power. So, when we define subclasses of computable queries by the preservation of equivalence in C^k, with different values of the parameter k, we are actually defining *diffrent levels with respect to the amount of information on the database which every query really needs* to be evaluated on that database.

The hierarchy QCQ^{C^ω} turns out to have a quite similar structure and behavior as the hierarchy QCQ^ω in [27]. The results of Sections 3 and 4 are analogous to the results in [27] regarding QCQ^ω, and their proofs follow a similar strategy. However, there is a very important difference in the "size" of layers in both hierarchies, which is derived naturally by the well known relation between the two logics FO^k and C^k regarding their expressiveness. For every $k \geq 2$ the subclass QCQ^{C^k} is "big", whereas each subclass QCQ^k is "small", in a sense which we will make precise in Section 5 using results on asymptotic probabilities. Roughly, we can say that for every $k \geq 2$ and for every computable query q there is a query q' in the layer QCQ^{C^k} which is equivalent to q over *almost all* databases. And this is not true for any layer in QCQ^ω, and not even for the whole hierarchy.

We prove that the hierarchy $\mathcal{QCQ}^{C^\omega}$ is strict, and that it is strictly included in the class $\mathcal{CQ}$ of computable queries. Furthermore, it turns out to be *orthogonal* with the TIME-SPACE hierarchy defined with respect to Turing machine complexity, as it was also the case with the hierarchy $\mathcal{QCQ}^\omega$. Hence, we can define finer classifications in the class $\mathcal{CQ}$ by intersecting $\mathcal{QCQ}^{C^\omega}$ with the Turing machine complexity hierarchy (see [28] for a preliminary discussion of this approach). As an illustrating example, we include a classification of some problems in finite group theory at the end of Section 5. This may be derived from results in [19] and [20] together with our characterization of the layers of $\mathcal{QCQ}^\omega$ in terms of fragments of the infinitary logic $\mathcal{L}^\omega_{\infty\omega}$.

Having defined the different classes $\mathcal{QCQ}^{C^k}$ in a semantic way we look next for a syntactic characterization of these classes in terms of a computation model. For that sake we define a machine which we call *reflective counting machine* with bounded variable complexity k (RCM^k), as a variant of the reflective relational machine of [2]. In our model, dynamic queries are formulas in the logic C^k, instead of FO^k. In [23] a similar model has been defined to characterize the expressibility of fixed point logics with counting terms, but it was based in the relational machine of [3], instead. Then we prove that for every natural k, the class $\mathcal{QCQ}^{C^k}$ characterizes exactly the expressive power of the machine RCM^k.

As the model RCM^k turns out to be incomplete, we define several properties related to homogeneity (which are quite analogous to the properties studied in [27] regarding the model RRM^k), and we study them as a means to increase the computation power of the model RCM^k. Such properties are C^k-*homogeneity*, *strong* C^k-*homogeneity* and *pairwise* C^k-*homogeneity*. A database is C^k-*homogeneous* if the properties of every k-tuple in the database, up to automorphism, can be expressed by C^k formulas (i.e., whenever two tuples satisfy the same properties expressed by FO formulas with k variables and with counting quantifiers, then there is an automorphism in the database mapping each tuple onto each other). We prove that, for every natural number k, RCM^k machines augment drastically their computability power when working on such classes of databases. A database is *strongly* C^k-*homogeneous* if it is C^r-homogeneous for every $r \geq k$. Here we show that, roughly speaking, for every $r > k \geq 1$, the class of queries computable by RCM^r machines working on such classes of databases strictly includes the class of queries computable by the same machines on classes of databases which are C^k-homogeneous but which are not strongly C^k-homogeneous. As to the third notion, we say that a class of databases is *pairwise* C^k-*homogeneous* if for every pair of databases in the class, and for every pair of k-tuples taken respectively from the domain of the two databases, if both k-tuples satisfy the same properties expressible by C^k formulas, then the two databases are isomorphic and there is an isomorphism mapping one tuple onto the other. We show that for every k, machines in RCM^k working on such classes achieve completeness provided the classes are recursive.

Considering that equivalence in C^k is decidable in polynomial time ([24]), a very important line of research, which is quite relevant to complexity theory, is the identification of classes of graphs where C^k equivalence coincides with isomorphism. These classes are the classes which we define as *pairwise C^k-homogeneous*, and include the class of trees ([17]) and the class of planar graphs ([14]). In the study of C^k-homogeneity we intend to generalize this approach by defining a formal framework, and by considering not only those "optimal" classes, but also other properties which, still not being so powerful as to equate C^k equivalence with isomorphism, do increase the computation power of the model RCM^k to an important extent.

In Section 5, we investigate the relationship between our classes $\mathcal{QCQ}^{C^k}$ and recursive fragments of the infinitary logic $C^\omega_{\infty\omega}$. We prove that for every natural k, the restriction of $\mathcal{QCQ}^{C^k}$ to Boolean queries characterizes the expressive power of $C^k_{\infty\omega}$ restricted to sentences with a recursive class of models. As a corollary, we get a characterization of the expressive power of the model RRM^k restricted to Boolean queries, for every natural k, in terms of the infinitary logic $\mathcal{L}^k_{\infty\omega}$. The characterization for the whole class of *relational machines* (RM) (and, hence, also of $RRM^{O(1)}$, given the equivalence of the two classes which was proved in [3]) in terms of the infinitary logic $\mathcal{L}^\omega_{\infty\omega}$ was proved in [4], but the expressive power of each subclass of machines RRM^k in terms of the corresponding fragment of the infinitary logic was unknown up to the author's knowledge.

Some of the results presented here have been included in [28].

Due to space limitations, some proofs have been omitted. They are included in the full version of the present paper.

2   Preliminaries

We define a *relational database schema*, or simply *schema*, as a set of relation symbols with associated arities. We do not allow constraints in the schema, and we do not allow constant symbols neither. If $\sigma = \langle R_1, \ldots, R_s \rangle$ is a schema with arities $r_1, \ldots, r_s$, respectively a *database instance* or simply *database* over the schema σ, is a structure $I = \langle D^I, R_1^I, \ldots, R_s^I \rangle$ where D^I is a finite set which contains exactly all elements of the database, and for $1 \le i \le s$, R_i^I is a relation of arity r_i, i.e., $R_i^I \subseteq (D^I)^{r_i}$. We will often use $dom(I)$ instead of D^I. We define the *size* of the database I as the size of D^I, i.e., $|D^I|$. We will use $\simeq$ to denote isomorphism. A *k-tuple* over a database I, with $k \ge 1$, is a tuple of length k formed with elements from $dom(I)$. We will denote a k-tuple of I as $\bar{a}_k$. We use $\mathcal{B}_\sigma$ to denote the class of all databases of schema σ.

Computable Queries and Relational Machines: In this paper, we will consider *total* queries only. Let σ be a schema, let $r \ge 1$, and let R be a relation symbol of arity r. A *computable query of arity r and schema σ* ([7]), is a total recursive function $q^r : \mathcal{B}_\sigma \to \mathcal{B}_{\langle R \rangle}$ which preserves isomorphisms such that for every database I of schema σ, $dom(q(I)) \subseteq dom(I)$. A Boolean query is a 0-ary query. We denote the class of computable queries of schema σ as $\mathcal{CQ}_\sigma$, and $\mathcal{CQ} = \bigcup_\sigma \mathcal{CQ}_\sigma$. Relational machines ($RM$) have been introduced in [3]. A RM is a one-tape Turing machine (TM) with the addition of a *relational store* (rs) formed by a possibly infinite set of relations whose arity is *bounded* by some integer. The *only* way to access the relations in the rs is through FO (first order logic) formulas in the finite control of the machine. The input database as well as the output relation are in rs. Each of these FO formulas is evaluated in rs according to the transition function of the machine. The resulting relation can be assigned to some relation symbol of the appropiate arity in the rs. Reflective relational machines (RRM) have been introduced in [2] as an extension of RMs. In an RRM, FO queries are generated *during the computation* of the machine, and they are called *dynamic queries*. Each of these queries is written in a *query tape* and it is evaluated by the machine in one step. A further important difference to RM is that in RRM relations in the rs can be of *arbitrary arity*. The *variable complexity* of an RRM is the maximum number of variables which may be used in the dynamic queries generated by the machine throughout any computation. We will denote as RRM^k, with $k \geq 1$, the sub-class of RRM with variable complexity k. Furthermore, we define $RRM^{O(1)} = \bigcup_{k \geq 1} RRM^k$.

Finite Model Theory and Databases: We will use the notion of a *logic* in a general sense. A formal definition would only complicate the presentation and is unnecessary for our work. As usual in finite model theory, we will regard a logic as a language, that is, as a set of formulas (see [10], [1]). We will only consider signatures, or vocabularies, which are purely *relational*. We will always assume that the signature includes a symbol for equality. We consider *finite* structures only. Consequently, if $\mathcal{L}$ is a logic, the notions of *satisfaction*, denoted as $\models_{\mathcal{L}}$, and *equivalence* between structures or databases, denoted as $\equiv_{\mathcal{L}}$, will be related to only finite structures. If $\mathcal{L}$ is a logic and σ is a signature, we will denote as $\mathcal{L}_\sigma$ the class of formulas from $\mathcal{L}$ with signature σ. If I is a structure of signature σ, or σ-*structure*, we define the $\mathcal{L}$ *theory of* I as $Th_{\mathcal{L}}(I) = \{\varphi \in \mathcal{L}_\sigma : I \models_{\mathcal{L}} \varphi\}$. A *database schema* will be regarded as a *relational signature*, and a *database instance* of some schema σ as a finite and relational σ-*structure*. If φ is a sentence in $\mathcal{L}_\sigma$, we define $MOD(\varphi) = \{I \in \mathcal{B}_\sigma : I \models \varphi\}$. By $\varphi(x_1, \ldots, x_r)$ we denote a formula of some logic whose free variables are *exactly* $\{x_1, \ldots, x_r\}$. Let $free(\varphi)$ be the set of free variables of the formula φ. If $\varphi(x_1, \ldots, x_k) \in \mathcal{L}_\sigma$, $I \in \mathcal{B}_\sigma$, $\bar{a}_k = (a_1, \ldots, a_k)$ is a k-tuple over I, let $I \models \varphi(x_1, \ldots, x_k)[a_1, \ldots, a_k]$ denote that φ is TRUE, when interpreted by I, under a valuation v where for $1 \leq i \leq k$ $v(x_i) = a_i$. Then we consider the set of all such valuations as follows: $\varphi^I = \{(a_1, \ldots, a_k) : a_1, \ldots, a_k \in dom(I) \wedge I \models \varphi(x_1, \ldots, x_k)[a_1, \ldots, a_k]\}$. That is, φ^I is the relation defined by φ in the structure I, and its arity is given by the number of free variables in φ. Sometimes, we will use the same notation when the set of free variables of the formula is *strictly* included in $\{x_1, \ldots, x_k\}$. We will also deal with *extensions* of structures. If R is a relation of arity k in the domain of a structure I, we denote as $\langle I, R \rangle$ the τ-structure resulting by adding the relation R to I, where τ is obtained from σ by adding a relation symbol of arity k. Similarly, if $\bar{a}_k$ is a k-tuple over I, we denote as $\langle I, \bar{a}_k \rangle$ the τ-structure resulting by adding the k-tuple $\bar{a}_k$ to I, where τ is obtained from σ by adding k constant symbols $c_1, \ldots, c_k$, and where for $1 \leq i \leq k$, the constant symbol c_i of τ is interpreted in I by the i-th component of $\bar{a}_k$. This is the only case where we allow constant symbols in a signature. We denote as FO^k with some integer $k \geq 1$ the fragment of FO where only formulas whose variables are in $\{x_1, \ldots, x_k\}$ are allowed. In this setting, FO^k itself is a logic. This logic is obviously *less expressive* than FO. We denote as C^k the logic which is obtained by adding to FO^k *counting quantifiers*, i.e., all existential quantifiers of the form $\exists^{\geq m} x$ with $m \geq 1$. Informally, $\exists^{\geq m} x(\varphi)$ means that there are at least m diffrent elements in the database which satisfy φ.

Types: Given a database I and a k-tuple $\bar{a}_k$ over I, we would like to consider *all* properties of $\bar{a}_k$ in the database I including the properties of every component of the tuple and the properties of all different sub-tuples of $\bar{a}_k$. Therefore, we use the notion of *type*. Let $\mathcal{L}$ be a logic. Let I be a database of some schema σ and let $\bar{a}_k = (a_1, \ldots, a_k)$ be a k-tuple over I. The $\mathcal{L}$ type of $\bar{a}_k$ in I, denoted $tp_I^{\mathcal{L}}(\bar{a}_k)$, is the set of formulas in $\mathcal{L}_\sigma$ with free variables *among* $\{x_1, \ldots, x_k\}$ such that every formula in the set is TRUE when interpreted by I for any valuation which assigns the i-th component of $\bar{a}_k$ to the variable x_i, for every $1 \leq i \leq k$. In symbols $tp_I^{\mathcal{L}}(\bar{a}_k) = \{\varphi \in \mathcal{L}_\sigma : free(\varphi) \subseteq \{x_1, \ldots, x_k\} \wedge I \models \varphi[a_1, \ldots, a_k]\}$.

Note that we may also regard an $\mathcal{L}$ type as a *set of queries*, and even as a *query*. We can think of a type *without having a particular database in mind*. That is, we add properties (formulas with the appropiate free variables) as long as the resulting set remains consistent. Let us denote as $Tp^{\mathcal{L}}(\sigma, k)$ for some $k \geq 1$ the class of all $\mathcal{L}$ types for k-tuples over databases of schema σ. In symbols, $Tp^{\mathcal{L}}(\sigma, k) = \{tp_I^{\mathcal{L}}(\bar{a}_k) : I \in \mathcal{B}_\sigma \wedge \bar{a}_k \in (dom(I))^k\}$. Hence, $Tp^{\mathcal{L}}(\sigma, k)$ is a class of properties, or a set of sets of formulas. Let $\alpha \in Tp^{\mathcal{L}}(\sigma, k)$ (i.e., α is the $\mathcal{L}$ type of some k-tuple over some database in $\mathcal{B}_\sigma$). We say that a database I *realizes* the type α if there is a k-tuple $\bar{a}_k$ over I whose $\mathcal{L}$ type is α. That is, if $tp_I^{\mathcal{L}}(\bar{a}_k) = \alpha$. We denote as $Tp^{\mathcal{L}}(I, k)$ the class of all $\mathcal{L}$ types for k-tuples which are realized in I. That is, it is the class of properties of all the k-tuples over the database I which can be expressed in $\mathcal{L}$. In symbols, $Tp^{\mathcal{L}}(I, k) = \{tp_I^{\mathcal{L}}(\bar{a}_k) : \bar{a}_k \in (dom(I))^k\}$. The following is a well known result.

Proposition 2.1. *For every schema σ and for every pair of (finite) databases I, J of schema σ the following holds: $I \equiv_{FO} J \Longleftrightarrow I \simeq J$.*

Although types are infinite sets of formulas, a *single* C^k formula is equivalent to the C^k type of a tuple over a given database. The equivalence holds for all databases of the same schema. This result has been proved by M. Otto.

Proposition 2.2. *([23]): For every schema σ, for every database I of schema σ, for every $k \geq 1$, for every $1 \leq l \leq k$, and for every l-tuple $\bar{a}_l$ over I, there is a C^k formula $\chi \in tp_I^{C^k}(\bar{a}_l)$ such that for any database J of schema σ and for every l-tuple $\bar{b}_l$ over J $J \models \chi[\bar{b}_l] \Longleftrightarrow tp_I^{C^k}(\bar{a}_l) = tp_J^{C^k}(\bar{b}_l)$*

Moreover, such a formula χ can be built inductively for a given database. If a C^k formula χ satisfies the condition of Proposition 2.2, we call χ an *isolating formula* for $tp_I^{C^k}(\bar{a}_l)$. Let $\bar{a}_k = (a_1, \ldots, a_k)$ be a k-tuple over I. We say that the type $tp_I^{\mathcal{L}}(\bar{a}_k)$ is an *automorphism type* in the database I if for every k-tuple $\bar{b}_k = (b_1, \ldots, b_k)$ over I, if $tp_I^{\mathcal{L}}(\bar{a}_k) = tp_I^{\mathcal{L}}(\bar{b}_k)$, then there exists an automorphism f in the database I which maps $\bar{a}_k$ onto $\bar{b}_k$, i.e., for $1 \leq i \leq k$, $f(a_i) = b_i$. Regarding the tuple $\bar{a}_k$ in the database I, the logic $\mathcal{L}$ is therefore sufficiently expressive with respect to the properties which might make $\bar{a}_k$ distinguishable from other k-tuples in the database I. We say that the type $tp_I^{\mathcal{L}}(\bar{a}_k)$ is an *isomorphism type* if for every database $J \in \mathcal{B}_\sigma$, and for every k-tuple $\bar{b}_k = (b_1, \ldots, b_k)$ over J, if $tp_I^{\mathcal{L}}(\bar{a}_k) = tp_J^{\mathcal{L}}(\bar{b}_k)$, then there exists an isomorphism $f : dom(I) \to dom(J)$ which maps $\bar{a}_k$ in I onto $\bar{b}_k$ in J, i.e., for $1 \leq i \leq k$, $f(a_i) = b_i$.

Asymptotic Probabilities: See [10], among other sources. Let φ be a sentence in $\mathcal{L}_\sigma$. We define $MOD_n(\varphi) = \{I \in \mathcal{B}_\sigma : dom(I) = \{1, \ldots, n\} \wedge I \models \varphi\}$. Let's denote as $\mathcal{B}_{\sigma,n}$ the sub-class of databases of schema σ with domain $\{1, \ldots, n\}$. We define the following limit, which we call *asymptotic probability of φ*: $\mu_\varphi = lim_{n \to \infty}(|MOD_n(\varphi)|/|\mathcal{B}_{\sigma,n}|)$. We say that a logic $\mathcal{L}$ has a 0-1 *Law* if for every sentence $\varphi \in \mathcal{L}$ μ_φ is defined, and is either 0 or 1. The same notion can also be defined on classes of databases, or Boolean queries. This means that the asymptotic probability of every property which can be expressed in the formalism (or of the given class) always exists, and is either 0 or 1. Among other logics, FO has this Law.

3   Definition of the Hierarchy

One of the main reasons for the weakness of FO^k regarding expressibility of queries, is its inability to count beyond the bound given by k. For instance, note that we need $k + 2$ different variables to express that a node in a graph has out-degree at least k. Hence, it seems quite natural to add to FO^k the capability to count beyond that bound, while still restricting the number of different variables which may be used in a formula. In this way we get the logic C^k (see Section 2), which turned out to be much more expressive than FO^k (see [10] and [18]). In logics with counting, 2 variables are enough to express *any* output degree of a node in a graph. Then, we define in this section a hierarchy which is similar to the one defined in [27], but for which we consider the logics C^k instead of FO^k. In this way we get a new hierarchy whose layers are much bigger than the corresponding layers in the hierarchy of [27]. In Section 5 we compare the two hierarchies.

Definition 3.1. *Let σ be a database schema and let $k \geq 1$ and $k \geq r \geq 0$. Then we define*

$$\mathcal{QCQ}_\sigma^{C^k} = \{f^r \in \mathcal{CQ}_\sigma \mid \forall I, J \in \mathcal{B}_\sigma :$$

$$Tp^{C^k}(I, k) = Tp^{C^k}(J, k) \Longrightarrow Tp^{C^k}(\langle I, f(I) \rangle, k) = Tp^{C^k}(\langle J, f(J) \rangle, k)\}$$

where $\langle I, f(I) \rangle$ and $\langle J, f(J) \rangle$ are databases of schema $\sigma \cup \{R\}$, with R being a relation symbol of arity r. We define further $\mathcal{QCQ}^{C^k} = \bigcup_\sigma \mathcal{QCQ}_\sigma^{C^k}$ and $\mathcal{QCQ}^{C^\omega} = \bigcup_{k \geq 1} \mathcal{QCQ}^{C^k}$.

That is, a query is in the sub-class $\mathcal{QCQ}^{C^k}$ if it *preserves realization of C^k types for k-tuples*. It is well known that equality in the set of C^k types for k-tuples realized in two given databases is equivalent to $\equiv_{C^k}$, i.e., equality of C^k

theories (see [24], [10]). Moreover, the size of the tuples which we consider for the types is irrelevant to that regard. Thus, queries in $\mathcal{QCQ}^{C^k}$ may also be regarded as those which *preserve equality of* C^k *theories*. Note that the different classes $\mathcal{QCQ}^{C^k}$ form a hierarchy, i.e., for every $k \geq 1$, $\mathcal{QCQ}^{C^k} \subseteq \mathcal{QCQ}^{C^{k+1}}$. This follows from the notion of C^k type and from the definition of the classes $\mathcal{QCQ}^{C^k}$. It can be also got as a straightforward corollary to Theorem 3.1.

Hence, queries in $\mathcal{CQ}$ may be considered as ranging from those, which need to consider every property of the database up to isomorphism (i.e., every *FO* property), to those for which it is enough to consider the C^k properties of the database, for some fixed k. Different sub-classes $\mathcal{QCQ}^{C^k}$ in the hierarchy $\mathcal{QCQ}^{C^\omega}$ correspond to different degrees of "precision" with which its queries *need* to consider the database for them to be evaluated.

Next, we give an important result from [6] which we will use in most of our proofs. Then, we show that the hierarchy defined by the sub-classes $\mathcal{QCQ}^{C^k}_\sigma$, for $k \geq 1$, is *strict*.

Proposition 3.1. *([6]) For every $k \geq 1$, there are two non isomorphic graphs G_k, H_k, such that $G_k \equiv_{C^k} H_k$.*

Proposition 3.2. *For every $k \geq 1$, there is some $h > k$ such that $\mathcal{QCQ}^{C^h}_\sigma \supset \mathcal{QCQ}^{C^k}_\sigma$.*

Proof. The inclusion is trivial and can also be easily obtained as a corollary to Theorem 3.1. For the strict inclusion we will use the graphs G_k, H_k of Proposition 3.1. Note that by Proposition 2.1, for every pair of the graphs G_k, H_k there exists an integer $h > k$ such that the C^h types are *FO* types for both graphs. Let us write h as $h(k)$. Then, by Proposition 3.1, for every $k \geq 1$ in one of the graphs, say G_k, there are nodes whose $C^{h(k)}$ types are not realized in the other graph H_k. Then we define for every $k \geq 1$, the query f_k in the schema of the graphs, say σ, as the nodes of the input graph whose $C^{h(k)}$ types are not realized in H_k. We will show first that $f_k \in \mathcal{QCQ}^{C^{h(k)}}_\sigma$. Let I, J be an arbitrary pair of graphs with $I \equiv_{C^{h(k)}} J$. If they are $C^{h(k)}$ equivalent to H_k, then the result of f_k will be the empty set for both graphs. If they are not $C^{h(k)}$ equivalent to H_k, then clearly the nodes in the result of f_k will have the same $C^{h(k)}$ types in both graphs. So, f_k preserves realization of $C^{h(k)}$ types and hence $f_k \in \mathcal{QCQ}^{C^{h(k)}}_\sigma$. Now, we will show that $f_k \notin \mathcal{QCQ}^{C^k}_\sigma$. To see that, note that $f_k(H_k) = \emptyset$ by definition of f_k, but by Proposition 3.1 and by our assumption $f_k(G_k) \neq \emptyset$ and $H_k \equiv_{C^k} G_k$. Thus, f_k does not preserve realization of C^k types and hence $f_k \notin \mathcal{QCQ}^{C^k}_\sigma$.

Proposition 3.3. $\mathcal{QCQ}^{C^\omega} \subset \mathcal{CQ}$.

Proof. Straightforward, using the graphs G_k, H_k of Proposition 3.1.

3.1 A Reflective Machine for Logics with Counting

We will now define a model of computation to characterize the sub-classes $\mathcal{QCQ}^{C^k}_\sigma$.

In [23], M. Otto defined a new model of computation of queries inspired in the RM of [3], to characterize the expressive power of fixed point logic with the addition of *counting terms* (see [18]). Here, we define a machine which is similar to the model of Otto, but which is inspired in the RRM of [2], instead. In this paper, we will not compare the expressive power between the model of Otto and ours. However, it is straightforward to prove that the machine of Otto can be simulated in our model. The other direction should be further studied, though the simulation seems to be possible as well.

Definition 3.2. *For every $k \geq 1$, we define the* reflective counting machine of variable complexity k *which we denote by RCM^k, as a reflective relational machine RRM^k where dynamic queries are C^k formulas, instead of FO^k formulas. In all other aspects, our model works in exactly the same way as RRM^k. We define $RCM^{O(1)} = \bigcup_{k \geq 1} RCM^k$.*

We need first a technical result whose proof is straightforward. Then, we can prove the characterization of the expressive power of the model RCM^k.

Lemma 3.1. *Let $k \geq 1$, let σ be a schema, let I be a database of schema σ and let $\mathcal{M}$ be an RCM^k which computes a query of schema σ. Then, the result of the computation of $\mathcal{M}$ on input I is equivalent to the evaluation of a formula $\varphi_{\mathcal{M},I}$ in C^k on the database I. Moreover, $\varphi_{\mathcal{M},I}$ depends only on $\mathcal{M}$ and I.*

Theorem 3.1. *For every $k \geq 1$, the class of total queries which are computable by RCM^k machines is exactly the class $\mathcal{QCQ}^{C^k}$.*

Proof. **a)** ($\subseteq$): Straightforward. **b)** ($\supseteq$): Let $f \in \mathcal{QCQ}^{C^k}$ be an r-ary query of schema σ for some $k \geq r$. We build an RCM^k machine $\mathcal{M}_f$, which will compute f. We use a countably infinite number of k-ary relation symbols in its relational store. With the input database I in its relational store, $\mathcal{M}_f$ will build an encoding of a database I' in its TM tape such that $Tp^{C^k}(I, k) = Tp^{C^k}(I', k)$. For this purpose, $\mathcal{M}_f$ will work as follows: **b1):** $\mathcal{M}_f$ finds out the size of I, say n. Note that this can be done through an iteration by varying m in the query $\exists^{\geq m} x(x = x) \wedge \neg \exists^{\geq m+1} x(x = x)$ which is in C^1. Then $\mathcal{M}_f$ builds an encoding of every possible database I' of schema σ and of size n in its TM tape with domain $\{1, \ldots, n\}$. **b2):** For every k-tuple s_i over I', $\mathcal{M}_f$ builds in its TM tape the isolating formula χ_{s_i} (as in Proposition 2.2) for the C^k type of s_i in the database I', and in this way we get isolating formulas for the types in $Tp^{C^k}(I', k)$. **b3):** $\mathcal{M}_f$ evaluates as dynamic queries the formulas χ_{s_i}, for every i, which are in C^k and assigns the results to the working k-ary relation symbols S_i in the relational store, respectively (note that these queries are evaluated on the input database I). **b4):** If every relation S_i is non-empty, and if the union of all of them is the set of k-tuples over I, then it means that $Tp^{C^k}(I, k) = Tp^{C^k}(I', k)$ and I' is the database we were looking for; otherwise, we try another database I'. **b5):** Now $\mathcal{M}_f$ computes $f(I')$ in its TM tape and then expands the r-ary relation $f(I')$ to a k-ary relation $f^k(I')$ with cartesian product with $dom(I')$. **b6):** $\mathcal{M}_f$ builds $f^k(I)$ in the relational store as the union of the relations S_i which correspond to the C^k types χ_{s_i} of the k-tuples s_i which form $f^k(I')$, and finally it reduces the k-ary relation $f^k(I)$ to an r-ary relation $f(I)$.

Corollary 3.1. $RCM^{O(1)} = \mathcal{QCQ}^{C^\omega}$.

Corollary 3.2. *The computation model $RCM^{O(1)}$ is incomplete.*

Remark 3.1. The hierarchy defined by the classes $\mathcal{QCQ}^{C^k}$ is not only *strict*, but it is *orthogonal* with respect to the hierarchy of complexity classes defined in terms of TIME and SPACE in Turing machines (like $LOGSPACE \subseteq PTIME \subseteq NP \subseteq PSPACE \subseteq EXPTIME$). This is also the case with the classes $\mathcal{QCQ}^k$ of [27]. Note that *any* recursive predicate, evaluated on the number of equivalence classes in the (equivalence) relation defined by equality of C^k types in the set of k-tuples of a database, is in $\mathcal{QCQ}^{C^k}$. Therefore, there is no complexity class defined in terms of TIME or SPACE in Turing machines which includes $\mathcal{QCQ}^{C^k}$. And this is the case for every $k \geq 1$. In Section 5 we make some considerations to this regard.

4   Homogeneity in Logics with Counting

First, we will give some definitions. Let k, l be positive integers such that $k \geq l \geq 1$. Let us denote by $\equiv_k$ the (equivalence) relation induced on the set of l-tuples over a given database I by equality of C^k types of l-tuples. That is, for every pair of l-tuples $\bar{a}_l$ and $\bar{b}_l$ over I, $\bar{a}_l \equiv_k \bar{b}_l$ iff $tp_I^{C^k}(\bar{a}_l) = tp_I^{C^k}(\bar{b}_l)$.

As it is well known (see [24]), allowing more variables in isolating formulas for C^k types of tuples results in a preciser view of the properties which identify a given sub-set of tuples among the whole set of tuples which may be built over the database. By Proposition 2.1, we know that the limit is FO which includes the logic C^k for every natural k. Types in FO are isomorphism types (and, hence, also automorphism types) for tuples of every length in every database. So, we want to consider the number of variables which are needed for a given database and for a given integer k to express the properties of k-tuples in that database up to automorphism with a counting logic. For this matter we define different variants of the notion of homogeneity from model theory (see [10] and [8]) in the context of logics with counting. For every $k \geq 1$ and for any two k-tuples $\bar{a}_k$ and $\bar{b}_k$ over a given database I, we will denote as $\equiv_\sim$ the (equivalence) relation defined by the existence of an automorphism in the database I mapping one k-tuple onto the other. That is, $\bar{a}_k \equiv_\sim \bar{b}_k$ iff there exists an automorphism f on I such that, for every $1 \leq i \leq k$, $f(a_i) = b_i$.

Let $k \geq 1$. A database I is C^k-*homogeneous* if for every pair of k-tuples $\bar{a}_k$ and $\bar{b}_k$ over I, if $\bar{a}_k \equiv_k \bar{b}_k$, then $\bar{a}_k \equiv_\sim \bar{b}_k$. Let σ be a schema. A class $\mathcal{C}$ of databases of schema σ is C^k-*homogeneous* if every database $I \in \mathcal{C}$ is C^k-homogeneous.

We define next a presumably stronger notion regarding homogeneity: *strong C^k-homogeneity*. To the author's knowledge it is not known whether there exist examples of classes of databases which are C^k-homogeneous for some k, but which are not strongly C^k-homogeneous. This was also the case with the analogous notions in [27]. However, the consideration of strong C^k-homogeneity makes sense not only because of the intuitive appeal of the notion, but also because this is the property which we use in Proposition 4.3 to prove that the class QCQ^C (see Definition 4.2) is a lower bound with respect to the increment in computation power of the machine RCM^k when working on strongly C^k-homogeneous databases. Up to know, we could not prove that this result holds for C^k-homogeneous databases as well. Let $k \geq 1$. A database I is *strongly C^k-homogeneous* if it is C^r-homogeneous for every $r \geq k$. Let σ be a schema. A class C of databases of schema σ is *strongly C^k-homogeneous* if every database $I \in C$ is strongly C^k-homogeneous.

Note that, by Proposition 2.1, every database is strongly C^k-homogeneous for some $k \geq 1$. However, it is clear that this is not the case with *classes* of databases.

In [23] it was noted that the discerning power of the machine defined there, and that is similar to our machine RCM^k (see discussion before Definition 3.2), is restricted to C^k types for k-tuples. So, the following result seems quite natural, and is somehow implicit in Otto's work. If f is a query of schema σ, and C is a class of databases of schema σ, we will denote as $f|_C$ the restriction of f to the class C.

Theorem 4.1. *For every schema σ and for every $k \geq 1$, there is a set of queries F of schema σ such that if C and C' are any two classes of databases of schema σ such that C is C^k-homogeneous and C' is not C^k-homogeneous, then for every $f \in F$, $f|_C$ is computable by an RCM^k machine but it is not the case that for every $f \in F$, $f|_{C'}$ is computable by an RCM^k machine.*

Proof. For every given k, we will exhibit a set of queries F for which we will prove that there is at least one which is not computable by any RCM^k machine on classes of databases which are not C^k-homogeneous. For every database I, let us define the k-ary query q_i for $i \geq 1$, as the set of k-tuples over I which form the i-th equivalence class in the relation $\equiv_{\sim}$ for k-tuples over I, considering some order in the set of equivalence classes of $\equiv_{\sim}$. These queries are clearly computable by RCM^k machines on classes of databases which are C^k-homogeneous. Now, for arbitrary classes of databases, let us fix a natural number $k \geq 1$ and let C' be a class of databases which is *not* C^k-homogeneous. Let $I \in C'$ such that I is not C^k-homogeneous neither. Then, there are two k-tuples $\bar{a}_k$ and $\bar{b}_k$ in $(dom(I))^k$ such that $\bar{a}_k \equiv_k \bar{b}_k$ but $\bar{a}_k \not\equiv_{\sim} \bar{b}_k$. Let q_i be the query such that $\bar{a}_k$ is in $q_i(I)$ but $\bar{b}_k$ is not in $q_i(I)$. It is not hard to prove that there is no k-ary query f computable by an RCM^k machine such that f on input I includes in its result the tuple $\bar{a}_k$, but it does not include the tuple $\bar{b}_k$. Consequently, q_i is not computable by any RCM^k machine on arbitrary classes of databases.

Remark 4.1. Note that the sub-class of queries which can be computed by RCM^k machines on C^k-homogeneous classes of databases but which *cannot* be computed by such machines on arbitrary classes of databases, is quite big. An RCM^k machine can count the number of equivalence classes in $\equiv_{\sim}$ for k-tuples on a

C^k-homogeneous database as an intermediate result in its TM tape. This can be done by following the same process as we did in the proof of Theorem 3.1 and then by counting the isolating formulas for the C^k types in $Tp^{C^k}(I, k)$. And clearly, for any schema σ, this number cannot be computed by any RCM^k machine on the whole class $\mathcal{B}_\sigma$. Then we can use this parameter, which we will call C^k *type index for k-tuples* following [3], as the argument for *any* partial recursive predicate in an RCM^k machine. Thus, the *whole* class of partial recursive predicates, evaluated on the C^k type index for k-tuples of the input database, is included in the sub-class of queries which can be computed with RCM^k machines, due to C^k-homogeneity.

However, we still do not know whether the machine RCM^k can achieve *completeness* when computing queries on databases which are C^k-homogeneous. This problem has important consequences in query computability and complexity, and is also related to the expressibility of fixed point logics (see [23]). In particular, it is related to the problem of knowing whether whenever two databases are C^k-homogeneous, and are also C^k equivalent then they are isomorphic.

Next, we will show that the property of *strong* C^k-homogeneity will allow $RCM^{O(1)}$ machines to extend their power with respect to computability of queries. Let us denote by $\{F_r\}_{r \geq k}$ a countably infinite class of sets of queries F_r, for every $r \geq k$. The proof is similar to the proof of the corresponding result in [27] regarding the class $\mathcal{QCQ}$ and strong k-homogeneity.

Proposition 4.1. *For every schema σ and for every $k \geq 1$, there is a class of sets of queries $\mathcal{F} = \{F_r\}_{r \geq k}$ of schema σ such that, if $\mathcal{C}$ and $\mathcal{C}'$ are any two classes of databases of schema σ such that $\mathcal{C}$ is strongly C^k-homogeneous and $\mathcal{C}'$ is not strongly C^k-homogeneous, then for every $F_r \in \mathcal{F}$ and for every $f \in F_r$, $f|_{\mathcal{C}}$ is computable by an RCM^r machine, but it is not the case that for every $F_r \in \mathcal{F}$ and for every $f \in F_r$, $f|_{\mathcal{C}'}$ is computable by an RCM^r machine.*

With the next notion of homogeneity we intend to formalize the property of the classes of databases where C^k equivalence coincides with isomorphism. Among other classes, this is the case with the class of trees ([17]), the class of planar graphs ([14]) and the class of databases of bounded tree-width ([11]). With this stronger notion we can achieve *completeness* with RCM^k machines.

Definition 4.1. *Let σ be a schema and let $\mathcal{C}$ be a class of databases of schema σ. Let $k \geq 1$. We say that $\mathcal{C}$ is* pairwise C^k-homogeneous, *if for every pair of databases I, J in $\mathcal{C}$, and for every pair of k-tuples $\bar{a}_k \in (dom(I))^k$ and $\bar{b}_k \in (dom(J))^k$, if $\bar{a}_k \equiv_k \bar{b}_k$, then there exists an isomorphism $f : dom(I) \longrightarrow dom(J)$ such that $f(a_i) = b_i$ for every $1 \leq i \leq k$.*

Proposition 4.2. *For every schema σ, for every $k \geq 1$ and for every query f of schema σ in $\mathcal{CQ}$, if $\mathcal{C}$ is a recursive and pairwise C^k-homogeneous class of databases of schema σ, then there is an RCM^k machine which computes $f|_{\mathcal{C}}$.*

Proof. We use the same strategy to build an RCM^k machine $\mathcal{M}_f$ which computes a given query $f \in \mathcal{CQ}$, as we did in the proof of Theorem 3.1. In this case we must also check that the database I' which we build in the TM tape is in the class $\mathcal{C}$.

4.1   A Lower Bound for Strong Homogeneity

The queries which preserve realization of FO types for tuples (i.e., the computable queries), but which do not preserve realization of C^k types for k-tuples for any k, do not belong to *any* QCQ^{C^k} class. Thus, we define next a new class of queries, following the same strategy as in [27] regarding FO^k. The intuitive idea behind this new class is that queries which belong to it preserve, for any two databases of the corresponding schema, the realization of types in C^k where k is the number of variables which is *enough* for *both* databases to define tuples up to automorphism.

Definition 4.2. *For any schema σ, let us denote as $arity(\sigma)$ the maximum arity of a relation symbol in the schema. We define the class QCQ^C as the class of queries $f \in CQ$ of some schema σ and of any arity, for which there exists an integer $n \geq max\{arity(f), arity(\sigma)\}$ such that for every pair of databases I, J in $\mathcal{B}_\sigma$, if $Tp^{C^h}(I, h) = Tp^{C^h}(J, h)$, then $Tp^{C^h}(\langle I, f(I)\rangle, h) = Tp^{C^h}(\langle J, f(J)\rangle, h)\}$ where $\langle I, f(I)\rangle$ and $\langle J, f(J)\rangle$ are databases of schema $\sigma \cup \{R\}$ with R being a relation symbol with the arity of the query f, and $h = max\{n, min\{k : I \text{ and } J \text{ are strongly } C^k\text{-homogeneous}\}\}$.*

Clearly, $QCQ^C \supseteq QCQ^{C^\omega}$. But, unlike the analogous class QCQ in [27], we do not know neither whether the inclusion is strict, nor whether CQ strictly includes QCQ^C. Both questions seem to be non trivial since they are related to the problem which we mentioned after Remark 4.1, by Proposition 4.3 below.

Note that the queries based on the C^k type index for k-tuples which we mentioned in Remark 4.1 are in QCQ^C. Therefore, the increment in the computability power of $RCM^{O(1)}$ machines when working on classes of databases which are C^k homogeneous is actually quite big. So, the next result is rather intuitive. The proof is analogous to the proof of the corresponding result in [27] regarding the class QCQ and k-homogeneity.

Proposition 4.3. *Let f be a query of schema σ in QCQ^C, with parameter n according to Definition 4.2. Let C be a class of databases of schema σ which is strongly C^k-homogeneous for some $k \geq 1$. Then, the restriction of f to C is computable by an RCM^h machine where $h = max\{n, k\}$.*

Thus, the class QCQ^C is quite meaningful since Proposition 4.3 shows that it is a *lower* bound for the increment in the power of computation which machines in RCM^k gain when working on classes of databases which are strongly C^k-homogeneous.

5   Further Considerations

5.1   Infinitary Logics with Counting

The *infinitary logic* $\mathcal{L}^k_{\infty\omega}$, for every $k \geq 1$, has the usual first order rules for the formation of formulas. In addition, it is closed under infinitary conjunctions and disjunctions. Formulas in $\mathcal{L}^k_{\infty\omega}$ contain at most k different variables. We write $\mathcal{L}^\omega_{\infty\omega} = \bigcup_k \mathcal{L}^k_{\infty\omega}$. Similarly, we define *infinitary logics with counting*, denoted as $C^k_{\infty\omega}$ and $C^\omega_{\infty\omega}$, respectively. These logics are defined in the same way as $\mathcal{L}^k_{\infty\omega}$ and $\mathcal{L}^\omega_{\infty\omega}$ with the addition of all *counting quantifiers*. That is, $C^k_{\infty\omega}$ has the same formation rules as $\mathcal{L}^k_{\infty\omega}$ plus the following one: if ψ is a formula in $C^k_{\infty\omega}$, x is a variable and $m \geq 1$, then $\exists^{\geq m} x(\psi)$ is also a formula in $C^k_{\infty\omega}$, provided the number of different variables in $\exists^{\geq m} x(\psi)$ is $\leq k$. Then $C^\omega_{\infty\omega} = \bigcup_{k \geq 1} C^k_{\infty\omega}$.

Let $C^k_{\infty\omega}|_{rec}$ denote the fragment of the infinitary logic $C^k_{\infty\omega}$ that contains exactly all sentences with a recursive class of models. We also define $\mathcal{L}^k_{\infty\omega}|_{rec}$ in the same way. Now we give a characterization of the expressive power of the computation model RCM^k (and, hence, also of each subclass $\mathcal{QCQ}^{C^k}$) in terms of the fragment $C^k_{\infty\omega}|_{rec}$, regarding only *Boolean queries*.

Theorem 5.1. *For every $k \geq 1$, the expressive power of the RCM^k machine, restricted to Boolean queries, is exactly $C^k_{\infty\omega}|_{rec}$.*

Proof. $\subseteq$): Let $\mathcal{M}$ be an RCM^k of schema σ for some natural k. It is known that every database I is characterized up to $\equiv_{C^k_\omega}$ by a C^k formula (see Lemma 1.33 and Corollary 2.4 in [24]). Let α_I be such a formula. On the other hand, by Lemma 3.1, the computation of $\mathcal{M}$ on a database I is equivalent to a C^k formula $\varphi_{\mathcal{M},I}$. Then we build the $C^k_{\infty\omega}$ formula $\Psi_{\mathcal{M}} \equiv \bigvee_{I \in \mathcal{B}_\sigma}(\alpha_I \wedge \varphi_{\mathcal{M},I})$. Clearly, the models of the formula $\Psi_{\mathcal{M}}$ are the databases accepted by $\mathcal{M}$. To see that the formula is in the fragment $C^k_{\infty\omega}|_{rec}$, note that we can build a Turing machine M which simulates $\mathcal{M}$ and which accepts a database iff it is accepted by $\mathcal{M}$. $\supseteq$): Let Ψ be a $C^k_{\infty\omega}$ formula of schema σ such that its class of models is recursive, i.e., it is decidable by some Turing machine M. We build an RCM^k machine $\mathcal{M}$ which works as follows. On input I it builds on the TM tape an encoding of every possible database I' of schema σ building the corresponding isolating formulas for the C^k types realized in I', as in the proof of Theorem 3.1, until $I \equiv_{C^k} I'$. Since in finite databases C^k equivalence coincides with $C^k_{\infty\omega}$ equivalence (see [24] and also [28]), we have $I \models \Psi$ iff $I' \models \Psi$. Hence, $\mathcal{M}$ simulates the TM M in its tape on input I' and $\mathcal{M}$ accepts I iff M accepts I'.

We can use the same strategy to characterize the expressive power of the model RRM^k (and, hence also of each subclass $\mathcal{QCQ}^k$ of [27]) in terms of the corresponding fragment $\mathcal{L}^k_{\infty\omega}|_{rec}$. For the proof, we use Corollary 2.3 of [24] and a result from [3] which is analogous to our Lemma 3.1 for RRM^k machines.

Theorem 5.2. *For every $k \geq 1$, the expressive power of the RRM^k machine, restricted to Boolean queries, is exactly $\mathcal{L}^k_{\infty\omega}|_{rec}$.*

5.2   The Relevance of Counting in the Hierarchy

Note, that the hierarchy defined by the sub-classes $\mathcal{QCQ}^{C^k}$ by using k as a parameter, has some similar properties with respect to the hierarchy defined by $\mathcal{QCQ}^k$ classes of [27]. However, the expressive power of every logic C^k is much bigger than the expressive power of the corresponding logic FO^k ([24]). It turns out that the sub-classes QCQ^k are *"very small"*, while the sub-classes QCQ^{C^k} are *"very big"*, in a certain precise sense which we define next. This fact can be clearly noted by using the notion of asymptotic probability (see Section 2). Recall from [27] that each sub-class QCQ^k, as well as the whole hierarchy QCQ^ω, have a 0–1 Law. This implies a strong limitation with respect to expressive power. It is well known that a query as simple as the *parity*[1] query has not a 0–1 Law, and this means that this query does not even belong to the whole hierarchy QCQ^ω. On the other hand, the parity query belongs to the first layer of the hierarchy QCQ^{C^ω}. Recall the second part of the proof of Theorem 3.1. There, we defined a machine RCM^k which in first place computed the size of the input database. This was done using a dynamic query in C^1, so that the parity query can be computed by an RCM^1 machine. Hence, it belongs to the sub-class QCQ^{C^1}. Then the next result follows immediately.

Proposition 5.1. *For any $k \geq 1$, QCQ^{C^k} does not have a 0–1 Law. Hence, the whole hierarchy QCQ^{C^ω} does not have a 0–1 Law either.*

The next two results (see [13]) will help us in trying to understand the extent of the difference in the size of the corresponding sub-classes, as well as of the hierarchies.

Proposition 5.2. *([5] and [17]) There is a class C of graphs with $\mu_C = 1$ such that for all graphs $I, J \in C$ we have $I \simeq J \iff I \equiv_{C^2} J$. Moreover, for all $I \in C$ and $a, b \in dom(I)$, there is an automorphism mapping a to b iff $tp_I^{C^2}(a) = tp_I^{C^2}(b)$.*

Note that the class C of Proposition 5.2 is C^k-homogeneous. Further note that this result is quite relevant not only in our context, but also in complexity theory, since the isomorphism problem is well known to be in NP, whereas M. Grohe has proved that for every $k \geq 1$, C^k equivalence is $PTIME$ complete under quantifier free reductions ([12]). Examples of classes of well known graphs, though not having asymptotic probability 1, where C^k equivalence coincides with isomorphism are the class of planar graphs ([14]) and the class of trees ([17]). On the other hand, the class of linear graphs is an example of a class where FO^2 equivalence coincides with isomorphism (see [10]).

Proposition 5.3. *([21]) Let $k \geq 1$. If C is a class of graphs such that for all graphs $I, J \in C$ we have $I \simeq J \iff I \equiv_{FO^k} J$, then $\mu_C = 0$.*

Next and following [16] though using a slightly different perspective, we define the notion of equality of queries *almost everywhere*. Let σ be a schema, and let q, q' be two computable queries of schema σ. Let $\mu_{(q=q^a)}$ be as follows:

$$\mu_{(q=q^a)} = \lim_{n \to \infty} \frac{|\{I \in \mathcal{B}_\sigma : dom(I) = \{1, \ldots, n\} \wedge q(I) = q'(I)\}|}{|\{I \in \mathcal{B}_\sigma : dom(I) = \{1, \ldots, n\}\}|}$$

---

[1] $q(I) = true$ iff $|dom(I)|$ is even.

By Proposition 5.2 for *every* computable query q there is a query q' in $\mathcal{QCQ}^{C^2}$ (and, hence in each layer $\mathcal{QCQ}^{C^k}$, for $k \geq 2$) such that $\mu_{(q=q')} = 1$, i.e., such that q' coincides with q over *almost all* databases. On the other hand, by Proposition 5.3, this cannot be true for any layer in $\mathcal{QCQ}^{\omega}$, and not even for the whole hierarchy.

On the other hand, regarding expressive power, the following result shows that the number of variables remains more powerful than both together, infinity of formulas and existence of counting quantifiers. Moreover, as it is well known (see [13]), if we consider only *ordered* databases, then $\mathcal{L}^{\omega}_{\infty\omega} = C^{\omega}_{\infty\omega}$, and hence, $\mathcal{QCQ}^{\omega} = \mathcal{QCQ}^{C^{\omega}}$.

Proposition 5.4. *([24]) For every $k \geq 1$, there is a Boolean query which is expressible in FO^{k+1}, but which is not expressible in $C^k_{\infty\omega}$, thus $\mathcal{QCQ}^{k+1} \not\subseteq \mathcal{QCQ}^{C^k}$.*

Finally, we give some examples of known classifications of queries in the infinitary logics $C^{\omega}_{\infty\omega}$ and $\mathcal{L}^{\omega}_{\infty\omega}$ and, hence, by Theorems 5.1 and 5.2, in the hierarchies $\mathcal{QCQ}^{C^{\omega}}$ and $\mathcal{QCQ}^{\omega}$, respectively.

Example 5.1. **1)**: *The size of a database is even* $\in \mathcal{QCQ}^{C^1}$ and $\notin \mathcal{QCQ}^{\omega}$ (see observation before Proposition 5.1). **2)**: *A graph is regular* $\in \mathcal{QCQ}^{C^2}$ and $\notin \mathcal{QCQ}^{\omega}$ ([24]). **3)**: *A graph is Eulerian* $\in \mathcal{QCQ}^{C^2}$ and $\notin \mathcal{QCQ}^{\omega}$ ([24]). **4)**: *A graph is the disjoint union of an even number of cliques* $\in \mathcal{QCQ}^{C^2}$ and $\notin \mathcal{QCQ}^{\omega}$ ([22]). **5)**: *A graph is connected* $\in \mathcal{QCQ}^3$, $\notin \mathcal{QCQ}^2$, and $\notin \mathcal{QCQ}^{C^2}$, either ([13]). **6)**: *A graph has an even number of connected components* $\in \mathcal{QCQ}^{C^{\omega}}$ and $\notin \mathcal{QCQ}^{\omega}$ ([22]). **7)**: *A projective plane is Desargian* $\notin \mathcal{QCQ}^{C^3}$ ([13], see there also the definition of projective planes).

5.3   Relation with Complexity Theory

As we pointed out in Remark 3.1 (see also [27]), the hierarchies $\mathcal{QCQ}^{\omega}$ and $\mathcal{QCQ}^{C^{\omega}}$ are *orthogonal* with respect to the hierarchy of complexity classes defined in terms of TIME and SPACE in Turing machine complexity. Then, we can use these hierarchies to refine the TIME and SPACE complexity classes by intersecting these classes with the different hierarchies $\mathcal{QCQ}^{\omega}$ and $\mathcal{QCQ}^{C^{\omega}}$. In this way, we obtain complexity classes which are much finer. This results in a deeper and more subtle understanding on the nature of queries. Next, we give some examples to illustrate this point.

Combining results from [19] and [20] with known results in descriptive complexity and with Theorem 5.2, we have the following classification regarding some Boolean queries in the class of finite groups.

Proposition 5.5. a): *The next Boolean queries, defined in the class of finite groups, belong to the sub-class $(\mathcal{QCQ}^4 \cap NLOGSPACE)$: 1): Given a group G, it is completely reducible and centreless; 2): Given a group G and a pair of* *elements a, b, the subgroup generated by a is a subgroup of the subgroup generated by b; 3): Given a group G and a pair of elements a, b, the two elements generate the same subgroup.* **b):** *The next Boolean query, defined in the class of finite groups, belongs to the sub-class QCQ^4: given a group G and an element a, the subgroup generated by a is minimal normal.* **c):** *In the class of finite groups, the Boolean queries defined by the properties simplicity, nilpotency and solvability, belong to some layers in the hierarchy QCQ^ω.* **d):** *The isomorphism problem of finite abelian groups does not belong to the hierarchy QCQ^ω.*

As to the hierarchy QCQ^{C^ω}, combining known results in descriptive complexity (see [24]) with results from computational complexity and with Theorem 5.1, we have the following classification regarding two Boolean queries in the class of finite graphs.

Proposition 5.6. *The next Boolean queries, defined in the class of finite graphs, belong to the sub-class $(QCQ^{C^2} \cap PTIME)$: a) A graph is Eulerian; b) A graph is regular.*

Acknowledgements

I am deeply grateful to Lauri Hella, Kerko Luosto and Ari Koponen for the interesting and stimulating discussions we had on this subject. The comments of the anonymous referees were very helpful in improving both the contents and the presentation of this article.

References

1. Abiteboul, S., Hull, R. and Vianu, V.: Foundations of Databases. Addison-Wesley (1994)
2. Abiteboul, S., Papadimitriou, C. and Vianu, V.: Reflective Relational Machines. Information and Computation **143** (1998) 110–136
3. Abiteboul, S. and Vianu, V.: Computing with first-order logic. Journal of Computer and System Sciences **50(2)** (1995) 309–335
4. Abiteboul, S., Vardi, M. and Vianu, V.: Computing with Infinitary Logic. Theoretical Computer Science **149(1)** (1995) 101–128
5. Babai, L., Erdös, P. and Selkow, S.: Random Graph Isomorphism. SIAM Journal on Computing **9** (1980) 628–635
6. Cai, J. Y., Fürer, M. and Immerman, N.: An Optimal Lower Bound on the Number of Variables for Graph Identification. Combinatorica **12(4)** (1992) 389–410
7. Chandra, A. K. and Harel, D.: Computable Queries for Relational Data Bases. Journal of Computer and System Sciences **21(2)** (1980) 156–178
8. Chang, C. and Keisler, H.: Model Theory, 3rd ed. Elsevier North Holland (1992)
9. Dawar, A., Lindell, S. and Weinstein, S.: Infinitary Logic and Inductive Definability over Finite Structures. Information and Computation **119(2)** (1995) 160–175
10. Ebbinghaus, H. and Flum, J.: Finite Model Theory, 2nd ed. Springer (1999)
11. Grohe, M. and Mariño, J.: Definability and Descriptive Complexity on Databases of Bounded Tree-Width. Proc. of International Conference on Database Theory (1999). Springer, LNCS 1540 (1998) 70–82

12. Grohe, M.: Equivalence in Finite Variable Logics is Complete for Polynomial Time. Proc. of 37th IEEE Symposium on Foundations of Computer Science (1996) 264–273

13. Grohe, M.: Finite Variable Logics in Descriptive Complexity Theory. Preliminary version (1998)

14. Grohe, M.: Fixed Point Logics on Planar Graphs. Proc. of 13th IEEE Symposium on Logic in Computer Science (1998) 6–15

15. Hella, L.: Logical Hierarchies in PTIME. Information and Computation **129(1)** (1996) 1–19

16. Hella, L., Kolaitis, P. and Luosto, K.: Almost Everywhere Equivalence of Logics in Finite Model Theory. The Bulletin of Symbolic Logic **2, 4** (1996) 422–443

17. Immerman, N. and Lander, E.: Describing Graphs: A First Order Approach to Graph Canonization. Complexity Theory Retrospective, A. Selman, ed. Springer (1990) 59–81

18. Immerman, N.: Descriptive Complexity. Springer (1999)

19. Koponen, A. and Luosto, K.: Definability of Group Theoretic notions. Research Report **227** of the Department of Mathematics of the University of Helsinki (1999)

20. Koponen, A. and Luosto, K.: personal comunication (2000)

21. Kolaitis, P. and Vardi, M.: Infinitary Logic and 0–1 Laws. Information and Computation **98** (1992) 258–294

22. Kolaitis, P. and Väänänen, J.: Generalized Quantifiers and Pebble Games on Finite Structures. Annals of Pure and Applied Logic **74** (1995) 23–75

23. Otto, M.: The Expressive Power of Fixed Point Logic with Counting. Journal of Symbolic Logic **61, 1** (1996) 147–176

24. Otto, M.: Bounded Variable Logics and Counting. Springer (1997)

25. Turull Torres, J. M.: Partial Distinguishability and Query Computability on Finite Structures. Communicated in the XI Brazilean Symposium on Logic, Salvador, Brazil (1996). Abstract published in the Bulletin of the IGPL, London, **3** (1996)

26. Turull Torres, J. M.: Query Completeness, Distinguishability and Relational Machines. Models, Algebras and Proofs: Selected Papers from the X Latin American Symposium on Mathematical Logic, Bogotá 1995. Marcel-Dekker (1998) 135–163

27. Turull Torres, J. M.: A Study of Homogeneity in Relational Databases. To appear in Annals of Mathematics and Artificial Intelligence (2001)

28. Turull Torres, J. M.: Semantic Classifications of Queries to Relational Databases. L. Bertossi, G. Katona, K.-D. Schewe, B. Thalheim (Eds.): Semantics in Databases. Springer LNCS, submitted

Uniqueness of Update Strategies
for Database Views

Stephen J. Hegner

Umeå University
Department of Computing Science
SE-901 87 Umeå, Sweden
hegner@cs.umu.se
http://www.cs.umu.se/~hegner

Abstract. The problem of supporting updates to views of a database schema has been the focus of a substantial amount of research over the years. Since the mapping from base schema to view schema is seldom injective, there is usually a choice of possibilities for the reflection of view updates to base-schema updates. This work presents a solution to this problem which augments the constant-complement strategy of Bancilhon and Spyratos with order-theoretic properties to guarantee unique reflection of view updates. Specifically, most database formalisms endow the database states with a natural order structure, under which update by insertion is an increasing operation, and update by deletion is decreasing. Upon augmenting the original constant-complement strategy with compatible order-based notions, the reflection to the base schema of any update to the view schema which is an insertion, a deletion, or a modification which is realizable as a sequence of insertions and deletions is shown to be unique and independent of the choice of complement.

1. Introduction

Database management systems are typically large and complex, and it is seldom the case that an individual user is granted full access to the entire system. Rather, user access is via windows to the entire system, called *views*. Consequently, a great deal of research has been devoted to the various issues surrounding such views. Among these issues, perhaps none is thornier than the update problem. In general, the mapping from states in the main (or *base*) schema to states in the view schema is not injective; rather, a single view state can be the image of many different base states. At the very least, this leads to the question of which of the many alternatives should be selected as the appropriate reflection of an update to the view. However, more comprehensively, it leads to serious questions about providing a view in which the family of supported updates is systematic, appropriate, and effectively manageable. This, in turn, suggests that not all possible updates to a view should be allowed.

1.1 Open vs. Closed Update Strategies. Not surprisingly, a wide selection of approaches to the view update problem has evolved. In [Heg90], the extremes

T. Eiter and K.-D. Schewe (Eds.): FoIKS 2002, LNCS 2284, pp. 230–249, 2002.

have been termed open and closed update strategies. Roughly speaking, an *open* strategy is very liberal; as many updates as possible are allowed, with the user expected to be aware of the consequences of such a strategy. A *closed* strategy, on the other hand, is very conservative and systematic. The view appears as a schema unto itself, and the family of updates which is allowed looks exactly as would a family of updates to a base schema.

As the focus of this paper is support for updates under closed strategies, it is fair to ask why one should consider such strategies at all, given that open strategies invariably allow a wider range of updates to the view. The short answer is that open strategies inevitably give rise to certain anomalies which render them less than suitable in certain situations. A few examples will illustrate this point. Let $\mathbf{C}_0$ denote the schema with the single relation symbol $P[\mathsf{Name}, \mathsf{Dept}, \mathsf{Proj}]$, and the initial instance $M_0 = \{(\mathrm{Smith}, 1, \mathrm{A}), (\mathrm{Jones}, 2, \mathrm{A}), (\mathrm{Jones}, 2, \mathrm{B})\}$. The informal semantics of a tuple such as $(\mathrm{Smith}, 1, \mathrm{A})$ is that employee Smith works in department 1 and on project A. It is furthermore assumed that the functional dependency $\mathsf{Name} \rightarrow \mathsf{Dept}$ holds; i.e., that an individual works in only one department. On the other hand, an individual may work on several projects.

First, let $\Pi_{\mathsf{NP}} = (P[\mathsf{Name}, \mathsf{Proj}], \pi_{(\mathsf{Name}, \mathsf{Proj})})$ denote the view which retains just the Name and Proj attributes; the image of M_0 under this view is $\{(\mathrm{Smith}, \mathrm{A}), (\mathrm{Jones}, \mathrm{A}), (\mathrm{Jones}, \mathrm{B})\}$. Consider deletion of the tuple $(\mathrm{Smith}, \mathrm{A})$. Under an open strategy, it might be argued that such an operation should be allowed, as the only reasonable reflection is to delete $(\mathrm{Smith}, 1, \mathrm{A})$ from M_0. While this reflection is unique and unambiguous, there are nonetheless at least two points of caution. First of all, this update involves a *hidden trigger*, in that information about the department in which Smith works is also deleted. The user must have access to information beyond the view Π_{NP} itself in order to be aware of this. Furthermore, this update is *irreversible*, in the sense that it is not possible to undo its effect by re-inserting $(\mathrm{Smith}, \mathrm{A})$ into the view, since the information regarding the department of Smith has been lost. For these reasons, this update would not be allowed in a closed view. On the other hand, these difficulties do not arise in the deletion of $(\mathrm{Jones}, \mathrm{A})$; in this case the view update may be realized via deletion of $(\mathrm{Jones}, 2, \mathrm{A})$ in M_0. Since information about the department of Jones is retained in the tuple $(\mathrm{Jones}, 2, \mathrm{B})$, and since $\mathsf{Name} \rightarrow \mathsf{Dept}$ holds, re-insertion of $(\mathrm{Jones}, \mathrm{A})$ is unambiguous and restores the initial state M_0. Thus, deletion of $(\mathrm{Jones}, \mathrm{A})$ would be allowed, even in a closed strategy, from the view state resulting from M_0.

Next, consider the schema $\mathbf{C}_1$, a slight modification of $\mathbf{C}_0$ in which nulls are allowed for the attribute Proj. A state such as $M_1 = \{(\mathrm{Smith}, 1, \mathrm{A}), (\mathrm{Jones}, 2, \mathrm{A}), (\mathrm{Jones}, 2, \mathrm{B})(\mathrm{Wilson}, 1, \mathrm{NULL})\}$ is now allowed. The interpretation is that Wilson does not work on any projects. Let $\Pi_{\mathsf{N\tilde{P}}} = (P[\mathsf{Name}, \mathsf{Proj}], \pi_{(\mathsf{Name}, \widetilde{\mathsf{Proj}})})$ denote the view which projects only those tuples on $(\mathsf{Name}, \mathsf{Proj})$ which do not contain any null values. Thus, the image of M_1 under this view is $\{(\mathrm{Smith}, \mathrm{A}), (\mathrm{Jones}, \mathrm{A}), (\mathrm{Jones}, \mathrm{B})\}$; the tuple $(\mathrm{Wilson}, \mathrm{NULL})$ is not included. In comparison to the previous example, many of the complications surrounding deletion of the tuple $(\mathrm{Smith}, \mathrm{A})$ disappear. Indeed, this deletion may be realized in M_1 by modifying the tuple (Smith, 1, A) to (Smith, 1, NULL). This update is reversible, and involves no hidden triggers. However, there remains a difficulty; namely, the admissibility of an insertion into the state of the view depends upon information not visible within that view. More specifically, it is clear that the tuple (Wilson, C) may be inserted into the view state by replacing (Wilson, 1, NULL) with (Wilson, 1, C) in M_1. On the other hand, the tuple (Young, C) may not be so inserted, since no department information is available for Young. This situation involves a *hidden dynamic constraint*, in the sense that whether or not the insertion is permitted depends upon information not contained in the view itself. For this reason, under a closed interpretation, insertion of (Wilson, C) would be disallowed, although it might be allowed under some open strategies.

Finally, consider the view $\Pi_{\mathsf{N}\widehat{\mathsf{P}}} = (P[\mathsf{Name}, \mathsf{Proj}], \pi_{(\mathsf{Name}, \widehat{\mathsf{Proj}})})$ of $\mathbf{C}_1$ which does allow for the projection of null values; the image of M_1 under this view is $\{(\mathsf{Smith}, \mathsf{A}), (\mathsf{Jones}, \mathsf{A}), (\mathsf{Jones}, \mathsf{B})(\mathsf{Wilson}, \mathsf{NULL}\}$. Now, even under a closed interpretation, insertion of (Wilson, C) is allowed; the tuple (Wilson, NULL) is simply replaced with this new value. Insertion of (Young, C) is still not allowed; however, this information necessary to make this distinction is now embodied in the view.

It is not the purpose of this paper to argue that closed update strategies are better than open ones, or that one should be used to the exclusion of the other. Indeed, no such argument seems possible, as they each have their place. Open strategies are useful as tools for experienced users who have wide access to the database, but wish, for convenience, to represent certain operations within a view. Such users can and will understand the more global implications of view updates, and so issues such as hidden triggers, irreversibility, and hidden dynamic constraints pose no real difficulties. On the other hand, there is also a clear need for views which are totally encapsulated. Many users, for reasons of security, lack of expertise, or simply effective management of complex schemata, need to work with views which, for operational purposes, are self contained. In particular, in such situations, the admissibility and effects of updates must be understandable within, and restricted entirely to, the view itself. In this context, anomalies such as hidden triggers, hidden dynamic constraints, and irreversibility must be avoided. It is to such closed update strategies which this paper is directed.

1.2 The Constant-Complement Strategy. The preceding discussion provides only an anecdotal characterization of the notion of a closed view; it remains to formalize this concept. Fortunately, to a large degree, this has already been done. The seminal work on closed strategies is the *constant-complement* approach, developed some twenty years ago by Bancilhon and Spyratos [BS81]. The idea is quite simple. To support updates to the view Γ_1 of the main schema $\mathbf{D}$, a view Γ_2 which is complementary to Γ_1 is identified; i.e., $\{\Gamma_1, \Gamma_2\}$ forms a lossless decomposition of $\mathbf{D}$. Then, the only updates to Γ_1 which are allowed are those which hold the state of Γ_2 fixed. Intuitively, the changes are isolated in Γ_1; the "rest" of the schema, which is Γ_2, cannot change. This freezing of the state of the complement under view update eliminates the possibility of hidden triggers and hidden dynamic constraints. Remarkably, it also eliminates the possibility of anomalies such as irreversibility.

An example will help illustrate. Let the base schema $\mathbf{E}_1$ have the single relation $R[ABC]$, governed by the functional dependency $B \to C$. Let the view to be updated be $\Pi_{AB} = (R[AB], \pi_{AB})$, the projection of the main relation onto the attributes AB. (In the context of the example of 1.1, just take $A = \mathsf{Proj}$, $B = \mathsf{Name}$, and $C = \mathsf{Dept}$.) A natural complement to Π_{AB} is the view $\Pi_{BC} = (R[BC], \pi_{BC})$. It is easy to see that updates to Π_{AB} which keep Π_{BC} constant are precisely those which hold the projection $\Pi_B = (R[B], \pi_B)$ of the relation $R[AB]$ constant. The common view Π_B is called the *meet* of Π_{AB} and Π_{BC}, and the latter two views are called Π_B-complements. In [Heg90, 2.10], it is established that every constant-strategy in the sense of [BS81] is in fact based upon a meet complement, and the updates which are allowed are precisely those which hold that meet constant.

This situation is illustrated diagrammatically in Fig. 1 to the right. The area with up-to-right crosshatch is to be held constant; this includes in particular the meet $\Pi_B = \Pi_{AB} \wedge \Pi_{BC}$. The rest of Π_{AB}, with down-to-right crosshatching, may be updated without restriction.

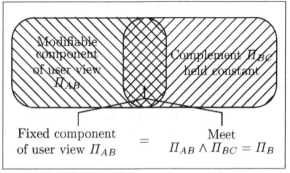

Fig. 1: Visualization of the constant complement strategy

1.3 Overview and Scope of This Work. Part of the appeal of the constant-complement strategy is its generality; it is formulated in a framework in which database schemata are sets and database mappings are functions. Thus, it is applicable, in principle, to almost any data model. With this generality comes a certain lack of uniqueness. In general, there are many complements to choose from, and distinct complements yield distinct update strategies. As illustrated in [BS81, Sec. 6], this ability to choose can sometimes be useful. If Γ_2 and Γ_3 are both meet complements of the view Γ_1 to be updated, and the meet of $\{\Gamma_1, \Gamma_2\}$ is different than that of $\{\Gamma_1, \Gamma_3\}$, then selecting Γ_2 as the constant complement for an update strategy will result in a different set of allowable updates than will choosing Γ_3 as the complement. On the other hand, if the pairs $\{\Gamma_1, \Gamma_2\}$ and $\{\Gamma_1, \Gamma_3\}$ have the same meet, then the allowable updates to Γ_1 will be the same for each complement; the difference will lie solely in how they are reflected into the base schema $\mathbf{D}$. This is almost never a desirable situation; a continuation of the above relational example will illustrate the problems which can ensue. Let $\mathsf{Dom}(C)$ denote the set of allowable domain values for attribute C, let $\alpha : \mathsf{Dom}(C) \to \mathsf{Dom}(C)$ be any permutation of $\mathsf{Dom}(C)$, and define the view $\Pi'_{BC} = (R'[BC], \pi'_{BC})$ as follows. States of Π'_{BC} are binary tuples on the domains of B and C, just as are states of the projection $R[BC]$. However, the tuples which are in the instance of $R'[BC]$ have their C-position values translated by α. Specifically, let M be a state of E_1. For any $b \in \mathsf{Dom}(B)$, let $\#_A(b)$ denote the number of distinct values of for attribute A associated with b in the relation $\pi_{AB}(M)$. Define $\pi'_{BC}(M) = \{(b,c) \mid (b,c) \in \pi_{BC}(M)$ and $\#_A(b)$ is odd$\} \cup \{(b, \alpha(c)) \mid (b,c) \in \pi_{BC}(M)$ and $\#_A(b)$ is even$\}$. It is easy to see that Π'_{BC} is a Π_B-complement of Π_{AB}, and the updates permitted to Π_{AB} under constant complement Π'_{BC} are exactly the same as those permitted under constant complement Π_{BC}. However, the translation is quite different. As a specific example, suppose that $\mathsf{Dom}(C) = \{c_0, c_1, c_2\}$, and let $\alpha(c_i) = c_{(i+1) \bmod 3}$. Let $M = \{(a_0, b_0, c_0), (a_1, b_1, c_1), (a_2, b_1, c_1)\}$. Then $\pi'_{BC}(M) = \{(b_0, c_0), (b_1, \alpha(c_1))\} = \{(b_0, c_0), (b_1, c_2)\}$. Now suppose that the tuple (a_1, b_0) is to be added to the state of Π_{AB}. Under constant complement Π_{BC}, the translation is simply to insert (a_1, b_0, c_0) to M. However, under constant complement Π'_{BC}, the translation is to insert the tuple $(a_1, b_0, \alpha^{-1}(c_0)) = (a_1, b_0, c_2)$, and to change the tuple (a_0, b_0, c_0) to $(a_0, b_0, \alpha^{-1}(c_0)) = (a_1, b_0, c_2)$, so that the state of E_1 after the update is $\{(a_0, b_0, c_2), (a_1, b_0, c_2), (a_1, b_1, c_1), (a_2, b_1, c_1)\}$.

It is difficult to imagine a circumstance under which update to Π_{AB} with constant complement Π'_{BC} would be desirable. It is clear that Π_{BC} is *the* complement to be kept constant. Yet, the constant-complement approach itself gives no preference to Π_{BC} over Π'_{BC}. The goal of the work reported here is to augment that approach so that only updates with respect to the "natural" complement (Π_{BC} in the example) are permitted, while preserving, to the greatest extent possible, the generality and data-model independence of the original work of Bancilhon and Spyratos. Principally, such a theory is useful not because one might be led to select Π'_{BC} over Π_{BC} as a complement to Π_{AB} (clearly, based upon aesthetics alone, one would not), but rather because it is useful to have a theory which provides a sound foundation as to why Π_{BC} is preferable. Furthermore, it eliminates the possibility that some other view Γ_1 of some schema **S** might have two apparently equally aesthetically reasonable complementary views Γ_2 and Γ'_2 from which to choose.

The solution utilizes natural order structure. Most data models admit an order on the states under which insertions increase the position of the state in the order, while deletions decrease it. Furthermore, basic data morphisms are typically monotonic under this ordering. For example, in the relational model, the natural ordering is defined by relation-by-relation inclusion, while the basic morphism operations of projection, selection, and join are monotonic with respect to this ordering. The context of this work is that of ordered schemata and monotonic morphisms. The central result is that, within this restricted context, the translation of insertions and deletions is unique, and independent of the particular choice of complement. This is a very versatile result, in that it does not depend upon establishing the uniqueness of a complement; indeed, it holds even across complements with different meets.

Relative to the relational example above, with relation-by-relation inclusion defining the ordering, it is easy to see that the view mappings π_{AB} and π_{BC} are monotonic, while π'_{BC} is not. Thus, Π'_{BC} is not a suitable complement to Π_{AB} for constant-complement update within the framework presented here. Furthermore, since every update to Π_{AB} which holds Π_B constant may be realized as a sequence of insertions and deletions (the family of updates is *order realizable* in the terminology of 4.1), translation of these updates via constant complement Π_{BC} is the only strategy allowed under order-based constant complement.

The results presented here are limited in that they apply only to updates which are insertions, deletions, or realizable as sequences of such. They do not apply, in general, to modifications. For example, let $\mathbf{E}_2$ be the relational schema which is identical to $\mathbf{E}_1$, save that the additional functional dependency $B \to A$ holds. With constant complement Π_{BC}, the only updates which are allowed to Π_{AB} are those which replace the A component of a tuple (a, b) with a new value. It is not possible to realize such an update as an insertion followed by a deletion, since the insertion would result in a violation of the functional dependency $B \to A$, which embeds in $R[AB]$. Thus, with the natural relation-by-relation inclusion, the theory developed here has nothing to say about updates to this view. It is an order-based theory, and updates which sidestep the order are not covered. Fortunately, there is still a way to establish uniqueness of the update strategy. In many cases, including this one, it is possible to find another order which will render these updates to be order-based, while retaining the monotonicity of the underlying view mappings. A full solution is presented in 4.5.

1.4 Applicability and Relationship to Previous Work. Over the years, there has been a substantial amount of research on the topic of view updates, a majority of which has focused upon the relational model; some quite recent [BL98]. The problem has also been studied, to a limited extent, in the context of the ER model [Tha00, Sec. 8.3] and the object-oriented model [Bel00]. However, except for the seminal work of Bancilhon and Spyratos [BS81] and that of the author [Heg90], most of this research has the flavor of open strategies.

The work reported here depends only upon the data model possessing a natural order structure, and so is potentially applicable to any of the contexts identified above. Although the examples used in this paper are all relational, the theory is not tied to that model in any way. Nonetheless, it does presume a situation in which the state of the database is represented by a single structure, rather than as a set of constraints, so applicability to deductive models is not clear. In any case, research on updates to deductive databases has taken a direction quite its own; see [MT99] for a recent survey.

The choice of order as a tool to establish uniqueness results is motivated by earlier work [Heg94], in which such tools were used to show that decompositions into independent components are unique when databases are suitably ordered. However, the techniques employed in this paper are vastly different than those of [Heg94], since independence is not a property which most user views have. This paper is in some way part of a long overdue sequel to [Heg90], which laid out principles for the support of closed views, but never unified the results to fruition.

1.5 The Results and the Relational Model. Although the results are not specific to the relational model, it remains not only the most widely used data model, but the one with, by far, the most extensive theoretical foundation. Therefore, it is important to show applicability to that model. To this end, several examples set within the classical relational context which illustrate the use of the results developed here are presented. Unfortunately, it is not practical to summarize even the full notation and terminology from that model; rather, it must be assumed that the reader is familiar with the standard terminology, notation, and results within that context. The monograph [AHV95] provides a relatively recent survey and the necessary background. Only a few key points which are necessary to show how this model fits into the order-based framework are presented here. Furthermore, due to space limitations, proofs of results which are specific to the relational context are only sketched, with many details omitted.

2.   Database Concepts in the Order-Based Context

In this section, the fundamental ideas of database schemata, morphisms, views, and complements are formulated within the context of order. That is, database schemata are presumed to have an underlying order to their states, and database mappings are assumed to preserve this order. A few of the ideas are related to those presented in [Heg94]; however, the details are quite different, since that work dealt with a much more specialized context.

2.1 Posets. Familiarity with the fundamental ideas of posets, such as presented in [DP90], is presumed; only a few notational and terminological points are reviewed here. A *partially ordered set* (*poset*) is pair $\mathbf{P} = (P, \leq)$ in which P is a set and $\leq$ is a reflexive, transitive, and antisymmetric relation on P. Given posets $\mathbf{P} = (P, \leq)$ and $\mathbf{Q} = (Q, \leq)$, a *morphism* $f : \mathbf{P} \to \mathbf{Q}$ is a *monotone* function $f : P \to Q$; i.e., $p_1, p_2 \in P$ with $p_1 \leq p_2$ implies that $f(p_1) \leq f(p_2)$. The morphism f is *open* if, for any $q_1, q_2 \in Q$ with $q_1 \leq q_2$, there are $p_1 \in f^{-1}(q_1)$, $p_2 \in f^{-1}(q_2)$ with $p_1 \leq p_2$. In other words, f is open if Q carries the least order which renders f a morphism. Following the standard terminology of category theory [Mac98], the morphism f is an *isomorphism* iff it has both left and right inverses. It is easily verified that this is equivalent to being an open bijection.

2.2 Schemata and Morphisms. Mathematically, a database schema with order is just a partially ordered set, and a morphism of such schemata is a poset morphism. However, to emphasize the database aspects, a special notation is employed in this work. Specifically, a *database schema with order* is a poset $\mathbf{D} = (\mathsf{LDB}(\mathbf{D}), \leq_{\mathbf{D}})$ in which $\mathsf{LDB}(\mathbf{D})$ is a set, called the set of *legal databases* of $\mathbf{D}$.

In the case that the order $\leq_{\mathbf{D}}$ is the identity order in which $M \leq_{\mathbf{D}} N$ iff $M = N$, $\mathbf{D}$ is called a *flat* or *unordered* schema. In this case, the order relation $\leq_{\mathbf{D}}$ plays no rôle whatever, and the schemata and morphisms are just sets and functions, respectively.

To simplify terminology, throughout the rest of this paper, the term *schema* shall mean *schema with order*, unless specifically stated to the contrary.

Given database schemata $\mathbf{D}_1 = (\mathsf{LDB}(\mathbf{D}_1), \leq_{\mathbf{D}_1})$ and $\mathbf{D}_2 = (\mathsf{LDB}(\mathbf{D}_2), \leq_{\mathbf{D}_2})$, a *morphism* $h : \mathbf{D}_1 \to \mathbf{D}_2$ is a function $h : \mathsf{LDB}(\mathbf{D}_1) \to \mathsf{LDB}(\mathbf{D}_2)$ which is a poset morphism with respect to the orders $\leq_{\mathbf{D}_1}$ and $\leq_{\mathbf{D}_2}$. It is called an *open surjection* precisely in the case that it has that property as a poset morphism.

2.3 Views and Congruences. An *order view* of the schema $\mathbf{D}$ is a pair $\Gamma = (\mathbf{V}, \gamma)$ in which $\mathbf{V}$ is a schema and $\gamma : \mathbf{D} \to \mathbf{V}$ is an open surjection. Given order views $\Gamma_1 = (\mathbf{V}_1, \gamma_1)$ and $\Gamma_2 = (\mathbf{V}_2, \gamma_2)$ of $\mathbf{D}$, a *morphism* $h : \Gamma_1 \to \Gamma_2$ is a schema morphism $h : \mathbf{V}_1 \to \mathbf{V}_2$ with the property that $h \circ \gamma_1 = \gamma_2$, that is, such that the diagram to the right commutes. Since the morphisms γ_1 and γ_2 are open surjections, so too is h. The order views Γ_1 and Γ_2 are *isomorphic* just in case they satisfy the standard categorical notion of isomorphism [Mac98]; that is, there are morphisms $h_1 : \Gamma_1 \to \Gamma_2$ and $h_2 : \Gamma_2 \to \Gamma_1$ such that $h_1 \circ h_2$ and $h_2 \circ h_1$ are both identities. The *congruence* of order view $\Gamma = (\mathbf{V}, \gamma)$ is the equivalence relation $\mathsf{Congr}(\Gamma)$ on $\mathsf{LDB}(\mathbf{V})$ defined by $(M, N) \in \mathsf{Congr}(\Gamma)$ iff $\gamma(M) = \gamma(N)$. Given $M \in \mathsf{LDB}(\mathbf{D})$, the notation $[M]_\Gamma$ is shorthand for the more cumbersome $[M]_{\mathsf{Congr}(\Gamma)}$. Both denote the equivalence class of M under the equivalence relation $\mathsf{Congr}(\Gamma)$.

Throughout the remainder of this work, unless specifically stated to the contrary, the term *view* will mean *order view*, as defined above.

Before proceeding further, it is important to establish that the general notions introduced here are applicable to the classical relational setting. The result 2.5 below shows that the common *Select-Project-Join* mappings of the relational theory define order based views in the sense of 2.2 above. First, some clarification of terminology and notation is in order.

2.4 Order-Based Schemata and Morphisms in the Classical Relational Context. The *named perspective* [AHV95, Sec. 3.2] is used; this means that the columns if relations are identified by attribute names from a universe $\mathbf{U}$. For a given attribute A, $\mathsf{Dom}(A)$ denotes the set of all allowable values for that attribute. A *relational schema* $\mathbf{D}$ consists of a finite set of relational symbols $\mathsf{Rel}(\mathbf{D})$, each with an arity $\mathsf{Arity}(R) \subseteq \mathbf{U}$. An *unconstrained database* M over a relational schema $\mathbf{D}$ consists of a set of relations $\{M^R \mid R \in \mathsf{Rel}(\mathbf{D})\}$ of the appropriate arities. The set of all unconstrained databases on $\mathbf{D}$ is denoted $\mathsf{DB}(\mathbf{D})$. The *natural ordering* $\subseteq_{\mathbf{D}}$ on the databases of $\mathbf{D}$ is defined via relation-by-relation inclusion; i.e., $M_1 \subseteq_{\mathbf{D}} M_2$ iff $R^{M_1} \subseteq R^{M_2}$ for all relation symbols R of $\mathbf{D}$.

Relational schemata are commonly constrained by Horn sentences. If only universal quantifiers are allowed, such constraints are termed *full dependencies*; if existential quantifiers are allowed on positive atoms, they are termed *embedded dependencies* [AHV95, Chap. 10]. Functional dependencies (*fd*'s) and join dependencies (*jd*'s) are full dependencies. If there is a set Φ of full (resp. embedded) dependencies such that $\mathsf{LDB}(\mathbf{D}) = \{M \in \mathsf{DB}(\mathbf{D}) \mid M \models \mathsf{Dep}(\mathbf{D})\}$, then

D is said to be *constrained by full* (resp. *embedded*) *dependencies*; in both cases the notation $\mathsf{Dep}(\mathbf{D})$ is used to denote Φ.

It is critical to know that the most common types of morphisms within the relational framework define views in the order-based context. The database mappings which will be considered in this work are those which are built up from compositions of the primitives *selection, projection, join,* and *renaming*. Such compositions are termed *SPJR-morphisms.* [AHV95, Sec. 4.4]. It is clear that *SPJR*-mappings are monotonic with respect to the natural orderings, and so define morphisms in the order-based sense. It is equally important to note that database mappings which involve negation, such as difference and division, are not monotonic.

2.5 Proposition – *SPJR*-Morphisms Define Views. *Let* **D** *and* **V** *be relational schemata, and suppose furthermore that* **D** *is constrained by full dependencies. Let* $\gamma : \mathbf{D} \to \mathbf{V}$ *be a surjective SPJR-morphism. Then* **V** *is also constrained by full dependencies, and* γ *is an open poset morphism with respect to the natural orderings* $\subseteq_{\mathbf{D}}$ *and* $\subseteq_{\mathbf{V}}$, *so that* $\Gamma = (\mathbf{V}, \gamma)$ *is a view of* **D** *in the order-based sense.*

PROOF OUTLINE: First of all, that the class of full dependencies is closed under projection and join is established in [Hul84, Thm. 5.4]. Selection may be added easily using the submodel characterization of universal Horn sentences [Mon76, Thm. 25.13]. Thus, **V** is also constrained by full dependencies.

To establish that γ is open, break the problem into three cases, one each for projection, selection, and join, each with possible renaming. Let $N_1, N_2 \in \mathsf{LDB}(\mathbf{V})$ with $N_1 \subseteq_{\mathbf{V}} N_2$. Now, reflect N_1 and N_2 back into **D** as minimal structures P_1 and P_2, respectively, possibly with variables, and apply the chase inference procedure [AHV95, Sec. 10.2] to generate legal databases of **D**. When variables occur (this will happen with projection), they must be the same in tuples which are in both N_1 and N_2, and their eventual bindings to domain values must be the same in each case. Let $\hat{P}_1, \hat{P}_2 \in \mathsf{LDB}(\mathbf{D})$ be the models generated from the chase on P_1 and P_2, respectively. Then $\hat{P}_1 \subseteq_{\mathbf{D}} \hat{P}_2$, with $\gamma(\hat{P}_1) = N_1$ and $\gamma(\hat{P}_2) = N_2$. □

2.6 Relational Projections. The key relational examples used in this work are projections. Although this framework has already been used in the introduction, it is important to crystallize the notation for the formal part of the paper. Let **D** be a relational schema which is constrained by full dependencies, let $R \in \mathsf{Rel}(\mathbf{D})$, let $\mathbf{A} = \mathsf{Arity}(R)$, and let $\mathbf{B} \subseteq \mathbf{A}$. The **B**-*projection* of R is the view $\Pi_{\mathbf{B}} = (R[\mathbf{B}], \pi_{\mathbf{B}})$ with $R[\mathbf{B}]$ the schema with a single relational symbol R on attribute set **B**, and $\pi_{\mathbf{B}} : \mathbf{D} \to R[\mathbf{B}]$ the morphism which sends $M \in \mathsf{LDB}(\mathbf{D})$ to the projection onto attributes in **B** of the relation R in **D**. $\mathsf{Dep}(R[\mathbf{B}])$ is taken to be the set of full dependencies which render $\pi_{\mathbf{A}}$ an open surjection. In view of 2.5 above, $\mathsf{Dep}(R[\mathbf{B}])$ is guaranteed to exist, and $\Pi_{\mathbf{B}}$ is guaranteed to be a view in the order-based sense.

The focus now returns to the more general context. The following proposition characterizes views and their isomorphism classes in terms of their congruences. The proof is completely straightforward, and so omitted.

2.7 Proposition. *Let* $\mathbf{D}$ *be a schema, and let* $\Gamma_1 = (\mathbf{V}_1, \gamma_1)$ *and* $\Gamma_2 = (\mathbf{V}_2, \gamma_2)$ *be views of* $\mathbf{D}$.

   (a) *Every view morphism* $\Gamma_1 \to \Gamma_2$ *is an open surjection of posets.*
   (b) *There is at most one morphism* $\Gamma_1 \to \Gamma_2$.
   (c) *There is a morphism* $\Gamma_1 \to \Gamma_2$ *iff* $\mathsf{Congr}(\Gamma_1) \subseteq \mathsf{Congr}(\Gamma_2)$.
   (d) *The views* Γ_1 *and* Γ_2 *are isomorphic iff* $\mathsf{Congr}(\Gamma_1) = \mathsf{Congr}(\Gamma_2)$. $\square$

2.8 View Equivalence and Order. The (equivalence) class of all views which are isomorphic to Γ is denoted $[\Gamma]$. In view of 2.7(d) above, $[\Gamma_1] = [\Gamma_2]$ iff $\mathsf{Congr}(\Gamma_1) = \mathsf{Congr}(\Gamma_2)$. The notation $[\Gamma_2] \leq [\Gamma_1]$ denotes that there is a morphism $\Gamma_1 \to \Gamma_2$, or, equivalently, that $\mathsf{Congr}(\Gamma_1) \subseteq \mathsf{Congr}(\Gamma_2)$. As a shorthand, $\Gamma_2 \leq \Gamma_1$ shall also be written to denote this fact, with the understanding that $\leq$ is not a partial order on the views themselves, but only on the underlying equivalence classes.

If $\Gamma_1 = (\mathbf{V}_1, \gamma_1)$ and $\Gamma_2 = (\mathbf{V}_2, \gamma_2)$ are views of the schema $\mathbf{D}$ with $\Gamma_2 \leq \Gamma_1$, then the unique morphism $\Gamma_1 \to \Gamma_2$ is denoted $\lambda\langle \Gamma_1, \Gamma_2 \rangle$. In this case, $\mathbf{V}_2$ may be regarded as a view of $\mathbf{V}_1$ under the view mapping $\lambda\langle \Gamma_1, \Gamma_2 \rangle$. Specifically, the *relativization* of Γ_2 to Γ_1 is the view $\Lambda(\Gamma_1, \Gamma_2) = (\mathbf{V}_2, \lambda\langle \Gamma_1, \Gamma_2 \rangle)$ of $\mathbf{V}_1$.

2.9 Order-Compatible Congruences. In the context of a flat schema $\mathbf{D}$ with no order relation, every equivalence relation R on $\mathsf{LDB}(\mathbf{D})$ gives rise to a view whose states are the equivalence classes of R, with the view mapping the natural projection of an element to its equivalence class. In the context of order-based schemata, an additional constraint mandating that the equivalence respect the order on the database states must be imposed.

Specifically, let $\mathbf{D}$ be an order-based schema, and let R be an equivalence relation on $\mathsf{LDB}(\mathbf{D})$. Call R *order compatible* for $\mathbf{D}$ if for every pair $(M_1, M_2) \in R$ with $M_1 \leq_{\mathbf{D}} M_2$ and every $M_3 \in \mathsf{LDB}(\mathbf{D})$ with $M_1 \leq_{\mathbf{D}} M_3 \leq_{\mathbf{D}} M_2$, $(M_1, M_3) \in R$ as well. Now, define $\Theta_R = (\mathsf{LDB}(\mathbf{D})/R, \theta_R)$ to be the view of $\mathbf{D}$ with $\mathsf{LDB}(\mathbf{D})/R$ the schema whose underlying set is $\mathsf{LDB}(\mathbf{D})/R$, the set of equivalence classes of R, with $\theta_R : \mathbf{D} \to \mathsf{LDB}(\mathbf{D})/R$ the morphism which sends each $M \in \mathsf{LDB}(\mathbf{D})$ to its equivalence class $[M]_R$ under R. The order $\leq_{\Theta_R}$ is given by $[M]_R \leq_{\Theta_R} [N]_R$ iff $(\exists M_1 \in [M]_R)(\exists N_1 \in [N]_R)(M_1 \leq_{\mathbf{D}} N_1)$. The order compatibility of R ensures that $\leq_{\Theta_R}$ is a partial order, and the construction itself ensures that θ_R is an open surjection. Thus, Θ_R is indeed an order-based view of $\mathbf{D}$.

Note, conversely, that for any view $\Gamma = (\mathbf{V}, \gamma)$, $\mathsf{Congr}(\Gamma)$ is an order-based congruence, since otherwise the order $\leq_{\mathbf{V}}$ would not be well defined.

2.10 Products and Complements of Views. Let $\Gamma_1 = (\mathbf{V}_1, \gamma_1)$ and $\Gamma_2 = (\mathbf{V}_2, \gamma_2)$ be views of the schema $\mathbf{D}$. The product view $\Gamma_1 \times \Gamma_2 = (\mathbf{V}_1 {}_{\gamma_1}\!\otimes_{\gamma_2} \mathbf{V}_2, \gamma_1 \otimes \gamma_2)$ has $\mathsf{LDB}(\mathbf{V}_1 {}_{\gamma_1}\!\otimes_{\gamma_2} \mathbf{V}_2) = \{(\gamma_1(M), \gamma_2(M)) \mid M \in \mathsf{LDB}(\mathbf{D})\}$. The morphism $\gamma_1 \otimes \gamma_2 : \mathbf{D} \to \mathbf{V}_1 {}_{\gamma_1}\!\otimes_{\gamma_2} \mathbf{V}_2$ is given on elements by $M \mapsto (\gamma_1(M), \gamma_2(M))$. The order on $\mathbf{V}_1 {}_{\gamma_1}\!\otimes_{\gamma_2} \mathbf{V}_2$ is that which renders $\gamma_1 \otimes \gamma_2$ an open poset morphism.

The pair $\{\Gamma_1, \Gamma_2\}$ of views is said to form a *subdirect complementary pair* just in case $\gamma_1 \otimes \gamma_2 : \mathbf{D} \to \mathbf{V}_1 \,_{\gamma_1}\!\otimes_{\gamma_2} \mathbf{V}_2$ is a poset isomorphism.

It is entirely possible for $\gamma_1 \otimes \gamma_2$ to be a bijection and a poset morphism without being a poset isomorphism, since the order on $\mathbf{V}_1 \,_{\gamma_1}\!\otimes_{\gamma_2} \mathbf{V}_2$ induced by the product order on $\mathbf{V}_1 \times \mathbf{V}_2$ is, in general, strictly stronger than that induced by the morphism $\gamma_1 \otimes \gamma_2$. Thus, two order-based views may be complementary in a "flat" environment in which order is ignored, without being complements in the order-based sense.

In the examples of 1.2 and 1.3, the common view Π_B was referred to as the *meet* of Π_{AB} and Π_{BC}. This notion of the common component of two views is extremely important in a number of contexts involving views and database decomposition, including the generalization of acyclic decompositions [Heg93] and decomposition into independent components [Heg94]. Not surprisingly, it is also central to the constant complement strategy. For it to be well defined, the congruences of the two views must commute; the definition follows.

2.11 Fully Commuting Views and Meet Complements. The pair $\{\Gamma_1, \Gamma_2\}$ of views of $\mathbf{D}$ is called a *fully commuting pair* if $\mathsf{Congr}(\Gamma_1) \circ \mathsf{Congr}(\Gamma_2) = \mathsf{Congr}(\Gamma_2) \circ \mathsf{Congr}(\Gamma_1)$, with "$\circ$" denoting ordinary relational composition. A subdirect complementary pair $\{\Gamma_1, \Gamma_2\}$ which is fully commuting is called a *meet-complementary pair*, and Γ_1 and Γ_2 are called *meet complements* of one another.

2.12 Generalized Dependencies. Let $\{\Gamma_1, \Gamma_2\}$ be a subdirect complementary pair.

(a) The $\{\Gamma_1, \Gamma_2\}$-*reconstruction dependency* on $\mathbf{V}_1 \,_{\gamma_1}\!\otimes_{\gamma_2} \mathbf{V}_2$, denoted $\otimes[\Gamma_1, \Gamma_2]$, is satisfied iff for any $M_1, N_1 \in \mathsf{LDB}(\mathbf{V}_1)$ and $M_2, N_2 \in \mathsf{LDB}(\mathbf{V}_2)$, if any three of the elements of the set $\{(M_1, M_2), (M_1, N_2), (N_1, M_2), (N_1, N_2)\}$ is in $\mathbf{V}_1 \,_{\gamma_1}\!\otimes_{\gamma_2} \mathbf{V}_2$, then so too is the fourth.

(b) Let $\Gamma_3 = (\mathbf{V}_3, \gamma_3)$ be a view of $\mathbf{D}$, with $[\Gamma_3] \le [\Gamma_1]$ and $[\Gamma_3] \le [\Gamma_2]$. The Γ_3-*independence dependency* on $\mathbf{V}_1 \,_{\gamma_1}\!\otimes_{\gamma_2} \mathbf{V}_2$, denoted $\otimes_{\Gamma_3}$, is satisfied iff for any $M_1 \in \mathsf{LDB}(\mathbf{V}_1)$ and $M_2 \in \mathsf{LDB}(\mathbf{V}_2)$, $((M_1, M_2) \in \mathsf{LDB}(\mathbf{V}_1 \,_{\gamma_1}\!\otimes_{\gamma_2} \mathbf{V}_2)) \Leftrightarrow (\lambda\langle\Gamma_1, \Gamma_3\rangle(M_1) = \lambda\langle\Gamma_2, \Gamma_3\rangle(M_2))$

The following characterization first appeared in [Heg90, 1.13]. Unfortunately, due to space constraints, no proof was presented. Because of its importance, the proof is sketched here. Note that this result is essentially independent of additional constraints imposed by the order-based context.

2.13 Theorem – Characterization of Meet-Complementary Pairs. *Let* $\{\Gamma_1, \Gamma_2\}$ *be a subdirect complementary pair. Then the following conditions are equivalent.*

(a) $\{\Gamma_1, \Gamma_2\}$ *is a meet-complementary pair.*

(b) $\mathsf{Congr}(\Gamma_1) \circ \mathsf{Congr}(\Gamma_2)$ *is an equivalence relation.*

(c) $\mathbf{V}_1 \,_{\gamma_1}\!\otimes_{\gamma_2} \mathbf{V}_2$ *satisfies* $\otimes[\Gamma_1, \Gamma_2]$.

(d) $\mathbf{V}_{1\,\gamma_1}\otimes_{\gamma_2}\mathbf{V}_2$ *satisfies* $\otimes_{\Gamma_3}$, *with* Γ_3 *the view (unique up to equivalence) whose congruence is the smallest equivalence relation on* $\mathsf{LDB}(\mathbf{D})$ *containing both* $\mathsf{Congr}(\Gamma_1)$ *and* $\mathsf{Congr}(\Gamma_2)$.

PROOF: The implications (a) $\Leftrightarrow$ (b) and (a) $\Rightarrow$ (c) are straightforward and left to the reader, while (a) $\Leftrightarrow$ (d) is a special case of the Chinese-remainder characterization for schema decomposability [Heg93, 2.1.5]. To show the implication, (c) $\Rightarrow$ (a) let $(M,N) \in \mathsf{Congr}(\Gamma_1) \circ \mathsf{Congr}(\Gamma_2)$. Then, there is a $P \in \mathsf{LDB}(\mathbf{D})$ with $(M,P) \in \mathsf{Congr}(\Gamma_1)$ and $(P,N) \in \mathsf{Congr}(\Gamma_2)$. Let (M_1, M_2), (N_1, N_2), and (P_1, P_2) denote the images, under $\gamma_1 \otimes \gamma_2$, of M, N, and P, respectively. Since $(M,P) \in \mathsf{Congr}(\Gamma_1)$, $M_1 = P_1$. Similarly, since $(P,N) \in \mathsf{Congr}(\Gamma_2)$, $N_2 = P_2$. Thus, $(P_1, P_2) = (M_1, N_2)$. In particular, $(M_1, N_2) \in \mathsf{LDB}(\mathbf{V}_{1\,\gamma_1}\otimes_{\gamma_2}\mathbf{V}_2)$. So, applying $\otimes[\Gamma_1, \Gamma_2]$ to the set $\{(M_1, M_2), (M_1, N_2), (N_1, N_2)\}$, it follows that $(N_1, M_2) \in \mathsf{LDB}(\mathbf{V}_{1\,\gamma_1}\otimes_{\gamma_2}\mathbf{V}_2)$. Thus, $((\gamma_1 \otimes \gamma_2)^{\bullet^{-1}}(M_1, M_2),\ (\gamma_1 \otimes \gamma_2)^{\bullet^{-1}}(N_1, M_2))$ $\in \mathsf{Congr}(\Gamma_2)$ and $((\gamma_1 \otimes \gamma_2)^{\bullet^{-1}}(N_1, M_2), (\gamma_1 \otimes \gamma_2)^{\bullet^{-1}}(N_1, N_2)) \in \mathsf{Congr}(\Gamma_1)$, so that $(M,N) \in \mathsf{Congr}(\Gamma_2)\circ\mathsf{Congr}(\Gamma_1)$, whence $\mathsf{Congr}(\Gamma_1)\circ\mathsf{Congr}(\Gamma_2)\subseteq\mathsf{Congr}(\Gamma_2)\circ\mathsf{Congr}(\Gamma_1)$. The opposite inclusion is proved in an analogous fashion, so that $\mathsf{Congr}(\Gamma_1) \circ \mathsf{Congr}(\Gamma_2) = \mathsf{Congr}(\Gamma_2) \circ \mathsf{Congr}(\Gamma_1)$. $\square$

2.14 Meets and Γ-Complements. Let $\Gamma_1 = (\mathbf{V}_1, \gamma_1)$ and $\Gamma_2 = (\mathbf{V}_2, \gamma_2)$ be views of $\mathbf{D}$ which form a subdirect complementary pair. In the case that the equivalent conditions of 2.13 above are satisfied, the view Γ_3 guaranteed by (d) is called the *meet* of $\{\Gamma_1, \Gamma_2\}$, and is denoted $\Gamma_1\wedge\Gamma_2 = (\mathbf{V}_{1\,\gamma_1}\wedge_{\gamma_2}\mathbf{V}_2, \gamma_1\wedge\gamma_2)$. The set $\{\Gamma_1, \Gamma_2\}$ is then said to form a *meet-complementary pair*, or Γ_3-*complementary pair*, and Γ_1 and Γ_2 are called Γ_3-*complements* of one another.

The meet view Γ_3 is defined only up to isomorphism of views, but this is no limitation for the work presented here. Also, since $\mathbf{V}_{1\,\gamma_1}\wedge_{\gamma_2}\mathbf{V}_2$ factors through both Γ_1 and Γ_2, it is immediate that the order on $\mathsf{LDB}(\mathbf{V}_{1\,\gamma_1}\wedge_{\gamma_2}\mathbf{V}_2)$ induced by either $\leq_{\mathbf{V}_1}$ or $\leq_{\mathbf{V}_2}$ is the same as that induced by $\leq_{\mathbf{D}}$, so there is no question that this order is well defined.

2.15 Products and Meets in the Relational Context. Let $\mathbf{D}$ be a relational schema, and let $\Gamma_1 = (\mathbf{V}_1, \gamma_1)$ and $\Gamma_2 = (\mathbf{V}_2, \gamma_2)$ be views of $\mathbf{D}$ defined by SPJR-morphisms. The relation names of $\mathbf{V}_{1\,\gamma_1}\otimes_{\gamma_2}\mathbf{V}_2$ will be the disjoint union of those in $\mathbf{V}_1$ and $\mathbf{V}_2$. Furthermore, if the pair $\{\Gamma_1, \Gamma_2\}$ forms a subdirect decomposition, then, in general, there will be interrelational constraints. For example, let $\mathbf{E}_1$ be the schema introduced in 1.2, with the single relation symbol $R[ABC]$, governed by the fd $B \rightarrow C$. Let $\Gamma_1 = \Pi_{AB}$ and $\Gamma_2 = \Pi_{BC}$. On $\mathbf{V}_{1\,\gamma_1}\otimes_{\gamma_2}\mathbf{V}_2$, which contains relation symbols $R_1[AB]$ and $R_2[BC]$ (the subscripts on the R's are used here to avoid name collision), the fd $B \rightarrow C$ holds on $R_2[BC]$, and the jd $R_1[AB] \bowtie R_2[BC]$ binds the two relations together. In this case, it is easy to see that $\{\Gamma_1, \Gamma_2\}$ are Π_B-complements, as condition (d) of 2.13 applies. On the other hand, if the fd $A \rightarrow C \in \mathsf{Dep}(\mathbf{D})$ as well, as in the schema $\mathbf{E}_2$ of 1.3, then while $\{\Gamma_1\Gamma_2\}$ remains a subdirect complementary pair, it is no longer a meet-complementary pair, as condition (d) of 2.13 fails [Heg90, 1.11].

The generalization of this idea makes use of the idea of dependency preservation. A decomposition $\{\Gamma_1 = (\mathbf{V}_1, \gamma_1), \Gamma_2 = (\mathbf{V}_2, \gamma_2)\}$ of a relational schema $\mathbf{D}$ is *dependency preserving* if $\mathsf{Dep}(\mathbf{D})$ is recoverable from the reconstruction dependency (usually a join dependency), together with $\mathsf{Dep}(\mathbf{V}_1) \cup \mathsf{Dep}(\mathbf{V}_2)$. If $\mathsf{Dep}(\mathbf{D})$ consists of fd's, this means that a cover of $\mathsf{Dep}(\mathbf{D})$ embeds in the relations of the view schemata. For details, see [AHV95, Sec. 11.2]. The formalization is then the following.

2.16 Proposition – Meets of Projections in the Relational Context. *Let* $\mathbf{D}$ *be a relational schema consisting of a single relation* $R[\mathbf{U}]$, *and let* $\mathbf{A}, \mathbf{B} \subseteq \mathbf{U}$. *Assume further that* $\mathsf{Dep}(\mathbf{D})$ *is generated by full dependencies, and that* $\bowtie [\mathbf{A}, \mathbf{B}] \in \mathsf{Dep}(\mathbf{D})$. *Then the pair* $\{ \Pi_{\mathbf{A}}, \Pi_{\mathbf{B}} \}$ *forms a meet-complementary pair iff the decomposition is dependency preserving. In this case,* $\Pi_{\mathbf{A}} \wedge \Pi_{\mathbf{B}} = \Pi_{\mathbf{A} \cap \mathbf{B}}$.

PROOF OUTLINE: It is straightforward to verify that condition (d) of 2.13 is satisfied for these projections. $\square$

3. Updates in the Order-Based Context

Using the context established in the previous section, the ideas of constant-complement update within an order-based framework are now established. These results extend those of Bancilhon and Spyratos [BS81] to the order-based case. Because this extension is far from trivial, and because the formalism employed here is different than that of [BS81], all results are proven directly. The results presented here strengthen those of [BS81], not only in extension to the order-based case, but also in that meet complementation is used to provide a complete bijective correspondence between update strategies and complements.

3.1 Update Strategies. Let $\mathbf{D}$ be a database schema. A *closed update family* for $\mathbf{D}$ is an order-compatible equivalence relation U on $\mathsf{LDB}(\mathbf{D})$. Think of a pair $(M_1, M_2) \in U$ as describing an update of the database from state M_1 to state M_2. The equivalence-relation requirement implies that the identity update is always allowable, that all updates are reversible, and that updates may be composed.

Now let $\Gamma = (\mathbf{V}, \gamma)$ be a view of $\mathbf{D}$, and let T be a closed update family for $\mathbf{V}$. An *update strategy* for T with respect to U is a partial function $\rho : \mathsf{LDB}(\mathbf{D}) \times \mathsf{LDB}(\mathbf{V}) \to \mathsf{LDB}(\mathbf{D})$ which has the eight properties listed below. The first five, (upt:1)-(upt:5), constitute an alternative formulation of those in the original work [BS81], while the last three, (upt:6)-(upt:8), are specific to the order-based context. The notation $\rho(M, N){\downarrow}$ means that ρ is defined on the argument (M, N). If a formula involving ρ appears in a formula, then it is implicitly assumed that it is defined.

(upt:1) $\rho(M, N){\downarrow}$ iff $(\gamma(M), N) \in T$.

(upt:2) If $\rho(M, N){\downarrow}$, then $(M, \rho(M, N)) \in U$ and $\gamma(\rho(M, N)) = N$.

(upt:3) For every $M \in \mathsf{LDB}(\mathbf{D})$, $\rho(M, \gamma(M)) = M$. [Identity updates are reflected as identities.]

(upt:4) If $\rho(M, N){\downarrow}$, then $\rho(\rho(M, N), \gamma(M)) = M$. [Every view update is globally reversible.]

(upt:5) If $\rho(M, N_1)\!\downarrow$ and $\rho(\rho(M, N_1), N_2)\!\downarrow$, then $\rho(M, N_2) = \rho(\rho(M, N_1), N_2)$. [View update reflection is transitive.]

(upt:6) If $\rho(M, N)\!\downarrow$ and $\gamma(M) \leq_{\mathbf{V}} N$, then $M \leq_{\mathbf{D}} \rho(M, N)$. [View update reflects order.]

(upt:7) If $\rho(M_1, N_1)\!\downarrow$ with $M_1 \leq_{\mathbf{D}} \rho(M_1, N_1)$, then for all $M_2 \in \mathsf{LDB}(\mathbf{D})$ with $M_1 \leq_{\mathbf{D}} M_2 \leq_{\mathbf{D}} \rho(M_1, N_1)$, there is an $N_2 \in \mathsf{LDB}(\mathbf{V})$ with $\rho(M_1, N_2) = M_2$. [This condition is called *chain reflection.*]

(upt:8) If $M_1, M_2 \in \mathsf{LDB}(\mathbf{D})$ with $\gamma(M_1) \leq_{\mathbf{V}} \gamma(M_2)$ and $(\exists N_1, N_2 \in \mathsf{LDB}(\mathbf{V}))(\rho(M_1, N_1) \leq_{\mathbf{D}} \rho(M_2, N_2))$, then $M_1 \leq_{\mathbf{D}} M_2$. [This condition is called *order inheritance.*]

The *induced update family* on $\mathbf{D}$ is the smallest subset of U which will support the updates in T. It is denoted $\equiv_\rho$ and is given by $\{(M_1, M_2) \in \mathsf{LDB}(\mathbf{D}) \mid (\exists N \in \mathsf{LDB}(\mathbf{V}))(\rho(M_1, N) = M_2)\}$.

While conditions (upt:7) and (upt:8) are somewhat technical, it will be seen in the following that they are exactly what is required to ensure that the update strategy defines an order-based complement, and conversely.

3.2 Notational Convention. For 3.3 through 3.6 below, $\mathbf{D}$ will be a database schema, $\Gamma = (\mathbf{V}, \gamma)$ will be a view of $\mathbf{D}$, U and T will be closed update families for $\mathbf{D}$ and $\mathbf{V}$, respectively, and ρ will be an update strategy for T with respect to U.

3.3 Proposition. $\equiv_\rho$ *is a an order-compatible equivalence relation for* $\mathbf{D}$.

PROOF: The reflexivity, symmetry, and transitivity of $\equiv_\rho$ follow from conditions (upt:3), (upt:4), and (upt:5), respectively. Order compatibility follows from (upt:7). $\square$

3.4 The Complementary View for an Update Strategy. The ρ-*complement* of Γ, denoted $\tilde{\Gamma}^\rho = (\tilde{\mathbf{V}}^\rho, \tilde{\gamma}^\rho)$, is defined to have $\mathsf{LDB}(\tilde{\mathbf{V}}^\rho) = \mathsf{LDB}(\mathbf{D})/\!\equiv_\rho$, with the morphism $\tilde{\gamma}^\rho : \mathbf{D} \to \tilde{\mathbf{V}}^\rho$ given by $M \mapsto [M]_{\equiv_\rho}$. The order $\leq_{\tilde{\mathbf{V}}^\rho}$ is just that which makes $\tilde{\gamma}^\rho$ an open surjection. More specifically, $[M_1]_{\equiv_\rho} \leq_{\tilde{\mathbf{V}}^\rho} [M_2]_{\equiv_\rho}$ iff there are $M_3 \in [M_1]_{\equiv_\rho}$, $M_4 \in [M_2]_{\equiv_\rho}$, with the property that $M_3 \leq_{\mathbf{D}} M_4$.

The *reflection of* T *along* γ is defined to be the relation $\mathsf{Refl}_\gamma(T) = \{(M_1, M_2) \in \mathsf{LDB}(\mathbf{D}) \times \mathsf{LDB}(\mathbf{D}) \mid (\gamma(M_1), \gamma(M_2)) \in T\}$.

3.5 Proposition. $\{\Gamma, \tilde{\Gamma}^\rho\}$ *forms a meet-complementary pair, with meet* $\Theta_{\mathsf{Refl}_\gamma(T)} = (\mathsf{LDB}(\mathbf{D})/\mathsf{Refl}_\gamma(T), \theta_{\mathsf{Refl}_\gamma(T)})$.

PROOF: First, it will be shown that $\gamma \otimes \tilde{\gamma}^\rho : \mathbf{D} \to \mathbf{V}_{,\otimes_{\tilde{\gamma}^\rho}} \tilde{\mathbf{V}}^\rho$ is a bijection. It suffices to establish that it is an injection, i.e., that $\mathsf{Congr}(\Gamma) \cap \mathsf{Congr}(\tilde{\Gamma}^\rho) = \{(M, M) \mid M \in \mathsf{LDB}(\mathbf{D})\}$. Let $(M_1, M_2) \in \mathsf{LDB}(\mathbf{D}) \times \mathsf{LDB}(\mathbf{D})$. If $(M_1, M_2) \in \mathsf{Congr}(\tilde{\Gamma}^\rho)$, then $(\exists N \in \mathsf{LDB}(\mathbf{V}))(\rho(M_1, N) = M_2)$; in particular, $N = \gamma(M_2)$. Since $(M_1, M_2) \in \mathsf{Congr}(\Gamma)$ iff $\gamma(M_1) = \gamma(M_2)$, condition (upt:3) ensures that $(M_1, M_2) \in \mathsf{Congr}(\Gamma)$ iff $M_1 = M_2$.

Next, it will be shown that $\gamma \otimes \tilde{\gamma}^\rho$ is open. Let $M_1, M_2 \in \mathsf{LDB}(\mathbf{D})$ be such that $([M_1]_\Gamma, [M_1]_{\tilde{\Gamma}^\rho}) \leq_{\Gamma \otimes \tilde{\Gamma}^\rho} ([M_2]_\Gamma, [M_2]_{\tilde{\Gamma}^\rho})$; i.e., $\gamma(M_1) \leq_{\mathbf{V}} \gamma(M_2)$ and $\tilde{\gamma}^\rho(M_1) \leq_{\tilde{\mathbf{V}}^\rho}$

$\tilde{\gamma}^\rho(M_2)$. The latter inequality implies that there are $M_3 \in [M_1]_{\tilde{\Gamma}^\rho}$ and $M_4 \in [M_2]_{\tilde{\Gamma}^\rho}$ with the property that $M_3 \leq_D M_4$. By the definition of $\mathsf{Congr}(\tilde{\Gamma}^\rho)$, there are $N_1, N_2 \in \mathsf{LDB}(\mathbf{V})$ with the property that $M_3 = \rho(M_1, N_1)$ and $M_4 = \rho(M_2, N_2)$, whence condition (upt:8) mandates that $M_1 \leq_D M_2$, as required.

Finally, it will be established that $\mathsf{Congr}(\Gamma) \circ \mathsf{Congr}(\tilde{\Gamma}^\rho) = \mathsf{Congr}(\tilde{\Gamma}^\rho) \circ \mathsf{Congr}(\Gamma) = \mathsf{Refl}_\gamma(T)$. It is immediate that $\mathsf{Congr}(\Gamma) \subseteq \mathsf{Refl}_\gamma(T)$ and $\mathsf{Congr}(\tilde{\Gamma}^\rho) \subseteq \mathsf{Refl}_\gamma(T)$. To establish the converse, let $(M_1, M_2) \in \mathsf{Refl}_\gamma(T)$. Then there is a $N_1 \in \mathsf{LDB}(\mathbf{D})$ with $\gamma(M_1) = \gamma(N_1)$ and $\rho(M_2, \gamma(M_1)) = N_1$. In other words, $(M_1, N_1) \in \mathsf{Congr}(\Gamma)$ and $(N_1, M_2) \in \mathsf{Congr}(\tilde{\Gamma}^\rho)$. Thus, $\mathsf{Refl}_\gamma(T) \subseteq \mathsf{Congr}(\gamma) \circ \mathsf{Congr}(\tilde{\Gamma}^\rho)$, and so $\mathsf{Congr}(\Gamma) \circ \mathsf{Congr}(\tilde{\Gamma}^\rho) \subseteq \mathsf{Refl}_\gamma(T) \circ \mathsf{Refl}_\gamma(T) = \mathsf{Refl}_\gamma(T)$ i.e., $\mathsf{Refl}_\gamma(T) = \mathsf{Congr}(\Gamma) \circ \mathsf{Congr}(\tilde{\Gamma}^\rho)$. Since $\mathsf{Refl}_\gamma(T)$ is an equivalence relation, condition (b) of 2.13 is satisfied, and so $\{\Gamma, \tilde{\Gamma}^\rho\}$ is a meet-complementary pair with meet $\Theta_{\mathsf{Refl}_\gamma(T)}$. $\square$

The following theorem is the order-based analog of the characterization first reported by Bancilhon and Spyratos in their seminal paper [BS81, Thm. 7.3].

3.6 Theorem – Constant Complement Representation of Update. *For every* $(N_1, N_2) \in T$ *and* $M \in \mathsf{LDB}(\mathbf{D})$ *with* $\gamma(M) = N_1$, $\rho(M, N_2) = (\gamma \otimes \tilde{\gamma}^\rho)^{\mathbf{a}-1}(N_2, [M]_{\tilde{\Gamma}^\rho})$.

PROOF: Follows from 3.5 and the definition of $\tilde{\Gamma}^\rho$. $\square$

Bancilhon and Spyratos also present a result which associates an update strategy for a closed update family T of $\Gamma_1 = (\mathbf{V}_1, \gamma_1)$ to each complement view Γ_2 which admits a translation of T (Γ_2-*translatable* in their terminology) [BS81, Thm. 7.1]. However, their characterization does not provide conditions under which Γ_2 admits such a translation. The result 3.8 below makes this characterization precise in terms of the existence and character of the meet $\Gamma_1 \wedge \Gamma_2$.

3.7 The Update Strategy Associated with a Meet Complement. Let $\{\Gamma_1 = (\mathbf{V}_1, \gamma_1), \Gamma_2 = (\mathbf{V}_2, \gamma_2)\}$ be a meet-complementary pair of the schema $\mathbf{D}$.

(a) Define $\mathsf{UpdStr}\langle\Gamma_1, \Gamma_2\rangle : \mathsf{LDB}(\mathbf{D}) \times \mathsf{LDB}(\mathbf{V}_1) \to \mathsf{LDB}(\mathbf{D})$ by $(M, N) \mapsto (\gamma_1 \otimes \gamma_2)^{\mathbf{a}-1}(N, \gamma_2(M))$. $\mathsf{UpdStr}\langle\Gamma_1, \Gamma_2\rangle$ is called the *update strategy* for Γ_1 with respect to Γ_2.

(b) Define $\mathsf{UpdFam}\langle\Gamma_1, \Gamma_2\rangle = \{(N_1, N_2) \in \mathsf{LDB}(\mathbf{V}_1) \times \mathsf{LDB}(\mathbf{V}_1) \mid \lambda\langle\Gamma_1, \Gamma_1 \wedge \Gamma_2\rangle(N_1) = \lambda\langle\Gamma_1, \Gamma_1 \wedge \Gamma_2\rangle(N_2)\}$. $\mathsf{UpdFam}\langle\Gamma_1, \Gamma_2\rangle$ is called the *update family* induced by Γ_2 on Γ_1.

3.8 Theorem. *Let* $\{\Gamma_1 = (\mathbf{V}_1, \gamma_1), \Gamma_2 = (\mathbf{V}_2, \gamma_2)\}$ *be a meet-complementary pair of the schema* $\mathbf{D}$. *Then* $\mathsf{UpdFam}\langle\Gamma_1, \Gamma_2\rangle$ *is a closed update family for* Γ_1, *and* $\mathsf{UpdStr}\langle\Gamma_1, \Gamma_2\rangle$ *is an update strategy for* $\mathsf{UpdFam}\langle\Gamma_1, \Gamma_2\rangle$ *with respect to* $\mathsf{LDB}(\mathbf{D}) \times \mathsf{LDB}(\mathbf{D})$.

PROOF: First of all, $\mathsf{UpdFam}\langle\Gamma_1, \Gamma_2\rangle$ must be an order-compatible equivalence relation, since it is the congruence of a view. Next, it is completely straightforward to verify that $\mathsf{UpdStr}\langle\Gamma_1, \Gamma_2\rangle$ satisfies conditions (up1:1)-(upt:6) of 3.1. To show (upt:7), let $M_1, M_2 \in \mathsf{LDB}(\mathbf{D})$, $N_1 \in \mathsf{LDB}(\mathbf{V}_1)$, be such that $\mathsf{UpdStr}\langle \Gamma_1, \Gamma_2 \rangle \!\downarrow$ with $M_1 \leq_{\mathbf{D}} M_2 \leq_{\mathbf{D}} \mathsf{UpdStr}\langle \Gamma_1, \Gamma_2 \rangle (M_1, N_1)$. Then $(\gamma_1 \otimes \gamma_2)(M_1)$ is of the form $(\gamma(M_1), P)$ for some $P \in \mathsf{LDB}(\mathbf{V}_2)$, and $(\gamma_1 \otimes \gamma_2)(\mathsf{UpdStr}\langle \Gamma_1, \Gamma_2 \rangle (M_1, N_1)) = (N, P)$. Thus, $(\gamma_1 \otimes \gamma_2)(M_2) = (\gamma(M_2), P)$, whence $(\gamma(M_1), \gamma(M_2)) \in T$.

Finally, to show that (upt:8) holds, let $M_1, M_2 \in \mathsf{LDB}(\mathbf{D})$ with $\gamma_1(M_1) \leq_{\mathbf{V}} \gamma_2(M_2)$. Then $(\gamma_1 \otimes \gamma_2)^{\square 1}(M_1)$ is of the form $(\gamma_1(M_1), P_1)$ and $(\gamma_1 \otimes \gamma_2)^{\square 1}(M_2)$ is of the form $(\gamma_1(M_2), P_2)$ for some $P_1, P_2 \in \mathsf{LDB}(\mathbf{V}_1)$. Now if $(\exists N_1, N_2 \in \mathsf{LDB}(\mathbf{V}_1))(\mathsf{UpdStr}\langle \Gamma_1, \Gamma_2 \rangle (M_1, N_1) \leq_{\mathbf{D}} \mathsf{UpdStr}\langle \Gamma_1, \Gamma_2 \rangle (M_2, N_2))$, then $(\gamma_1 \otimes \gamma_2)^{\square 1}(\mathsf{UpdStr}\langle \Gamma_1, \Gamma_2 \rangle (M_1, N_1)) = (Q_1, P_1)$ and $(\gamma_1 \otimes \gamma_2)^{\square 1}(\mathsf{UpdStr}\langle \Gamma_1, \Gamma_2 \rangle (M_2, N_2)) = (Q_2, P_2)$, with $Q_1, Q_2 \in \mathsf{LDB}(\mathbf{V}_1)$ and $(Q_1, P_1) \leq_{\mathbf{V}_1 \gamma_1 \otimes \gamma_2 \mathbf{V}_2} (Q_2, P_2)$. In particular, $P_1 \leq_{\mathbf{V}_2} P_2$, whence $(\gamma_1(M_1), P_1) \leq_{\mathbf{V}_1 \gamma_1 \otimes \gamma_2 \mathbf{V}_2} (\gamma_1(M_2), P_2)$, and so $M_1 \leq_{\mathbf{D}} M_2$. $\square$

Note carefully the definition of $\mathsf{UpdFam}\langle \Gamma_1, \Gamma_2 \rangle$ in the above. The allowable updates to Γ_1 under constant complement Γ_2 are precisely those which hold the meet $\Gamma_1 \wedge \Gamma_2$ constant. Thus, only $\Gamma_1 \wedge \Gamma_2$, and no further properties of Γ_2, influence which updates are allowed. However, it may very well influence how those updates are reflected, as illustrated by the Π_B-complement views Π_{BC} and Π'_{BC} to Π_{AB} in the example schema $\mathbf{E}_1$ in 1.2 and 1.3. This uniqueness issue will be addressed in the next section.

To close, the following corollary, which identifies explicitly the natural association between meet complements and update strategies, is presented. It follows from the combination of 3.6 and 3.8.

3.9 Corollary. *Let $\mathbf{D}$ be a database schema, and let Γ be a view of $\mathbf{D}$. There is natural bijective correspondence between update strategies for the view Γ and (equivalence classes of) meet complements that view. Specifically:*

(a) *For any update strategy ρ, $\mathsf{UpdStr}\langle \Gamma, \tilde{\Gamma}^{\rho} \rangle = \rho$.*

(b) *For any meet complement Γ_1 of Γ, $\tilde{\Gamma}^{\mathsf{UpdStr}\Gamma, \Gamma_1 \square} = \Gamma_1$. $\square$*

4. Uniqueness Results for Update Strategies

The necessary background having been established, the main results on the uniqueness of view update strategies and meet complements in the order-based context are presented. First, it is necessary to make precise the relationship between the order properties and types of updates.

4.1 Types of Updates. Let $\mathbf{D}$ be a database schema, and let U be a closed update family for $\mathbf{D}$.

(a) A pair $(M_1.M_2) \in U$ is called:

(i) a *formal insertion* with respect to U if $M_1 \leq_{\mathbf{D}} M_2$;

(ii) a *formal deletion* with respect to U if $M_2 \leq_{\mathbf{D}} M_1$;

(iii) an *order-based update* with respect to U if there exists a nonempty sequence $(N_1, N_2), (N_2, N_3), \ldots (N_{k-2}, N_{k-1}), (N_{k-1}, N_k)$ of elements of U with the properties that $N_1 = M_1$, $N_k = M_2$, and each pair (N_i, N_{i+1}), $1 \leq i \leq k-1$, is either a formal insertion or else a formal deletion with respect to U.

(b) The update family U is called *order realizable* if every pair in U is an order-based update.

The main theorem of this paper states that within the constant-complement order-based framework, the reflection of an order-based update of a view to the base schema is unique, period. It does not depend upon the choice of complement, and it does not matter whether other updates are or are not order based. In short, the reflection of order-based updates is unique in a strong and global sense.

4.2 Theorem – Uniqueness of Reflection of Order-Based View Updates. *Let* $\mathbf{D}$ *be a database schema, let* $\Gamma = (\mathbf{V}, \gamma)$ *be a view of* $\mathbf{D}$, *and let* U *and* T *be a closed update families for* $\mathbf{D}$ *and* $\mathbf{V}$, *respectively. Let* ρ_1 *and* ρ_2 *be update strategies for* T *with respect to* U. *Then, for any* $M \in \mathsf{LDB}(\mathbf{D})$ *and* $N \in \mathsf{LDB}(\mathbf{V})$ *with* $(\gamma(M), N) \in T$ *an order-based update, it must be the case that* $\rho_1(M, N) = \rho_2(M, N)$. *In particular, if* T *is order realizable, then* $\rho_1 = \rho_2$.

PROOF: The diagram to the right provides a general view of how updates are processed under the two different strategies. From top to bottom, the first leg of each path corresponds to translation from $\mathbf{D}$ to the corresponding subdirect complement representation, the second leg (μ_1 and μ_2) corresponds to the actual update, and the final leg corresponds to translation back to $\mathbf{D}$. The horizontal

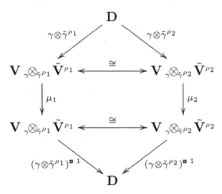

arrows marked with "$\cong$" indicate the natural isomorphism between the two decompositions of the schema $\mathbf{D}$. Suppose that the state of the schema $\mathbf{D}$ is M, and that it is desired to update the state of the view Γ from $\gamma(M)$ to N, with $(\gamma(M), N) \in T$. Relative to the diagram above and to the right, the two diagrams on the next page show how this update proceeds on elements. The diagram to the left below corresponds to ρ_1 or constant complement $\tilde{\Gamma}^{\rho_1}$, and the diagram to the right below to ρ_2 or constant complement $\tilde{\Gamma}^{\rho_2}$. Thus, in the diagram to the left, μ_1 corresponds to update under constant complement $\tilde{\Gamma}^{\rho_1}$, while μ_2 gives the corresponding update in the schema $\mathbf{V}_{\gamma \otimes_{\tilde{\gamma}\rho_2} \tilde{\mathbf{V}}^{\rho_2}}$. In the diagram to the right, the situation is reversed; μ_2 gives the update under constant complement $\tilde{\Gamma}^{\rho_2}$, while μ_1 gives the corresponding update in the schema $\mathbf{V}_{\gamma \otimes_{\tilde{\gamma}\rho_1} \tilde{\mathbf{V}}^{\rho_1}}$

The goal is to show that, in these diagrams, $P_1 = \tilde{\gamma}^{\rho_1}(M)$, and $P_2 = \tilde{\gamma}^{\rho_2}(M)$, which in turn forces $\rho_1(M, N) = \rho_2(M, N)$. First of all, assume that the update $(\gamma(M), N) \in T$ is a formal insertion. Since $(\gamma(M), \tilde{\gamma}^{\rho_1}(M)) \leq_{\mathbf{V}_{\gamma \otimes_{\tilde{\gamma}\rho_1} \tilde{\mathbf{V}}^{\rho_1}}} (N, \tilde{\gamma}^{\rho_1}(M))$, the order isomorphisms guarantee that $(\gamma(M), \tilde{\gamma}^{\rho_2}(M)) \leq_{\mathbf{V}_{\gamma \otimes_{\tilde{\gamma}\rho_1} \tilde{\mathbf{V}}^{\rho_1}}} (N, P_2)$ as well. Thus $\rho_2(M, N) = (\gamma \otimes \tilde{\gamma}^{\rho_2})^{\square 1}((N, \tilde{\gamma}^{\rho_2}(M))) \leq_{\mathbf{V}_{\gamma \otimes_{\tilde{\gamma}\rho_2} \tilde{\mathbf{V}}^{\rho_2}}} (\gamma \otimes \tilde{\gamma}^{\rho_2})^{\square 1}((N, P_2)) = (\gamma \otimes \tilde{\gamma}^{\rho_1})^{\square 1}((N, \tilde{\gamma}^{\rho_1}(M))) = \rho_1(M, N)$; i.e., $\rho_2(M, N) \leq_{\mathbf{D}} \rho_1(M, N)$. An analogous argument establishes that $\rho_1(M, N) \leq_{\mathbf{D}} \rho_2(M, N)$, so that $\rho_2(M, N) = \rho_1(M, N)$. The proof is now finished easily. A formal deletion is handled analogously, and a general order-based update is managed by gluing together the insertions and deletions of which it is composed. □

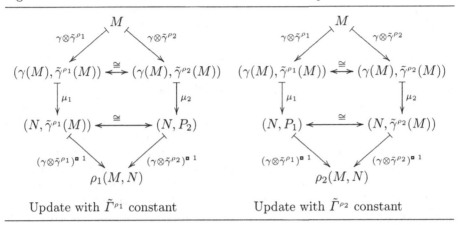

Update with $\tilde{\Gamma}^{\rho_1}$ constant   Update with $\tilde{\Gamma}^{\rho_2}$ constant

Although it is primarily uniqueness of view update strategies which is the focus of this work, it is nonetheless worthwhile to note that in the case that the update family in the view is order realizable, the view complement defined by that update family is unique.

4.3 Corollary – Uniqueness of Meet Complements. *Let* **D** *be a database schema, let* $\Gamma = (\mathbf{V}, \gamma)$ *be a view of* **D**, *and* T *be an order-realizable closed update family for* **V**. *Then there is at most one view of* **D** *which is a* Θ_T-*complement of* Γ.

PROOF: Follows immediately from 3.9 and the above theorem. □

4.4 Example. Recall the schema $\mathbf{E}_1$ from 1.2, with relation schema $R[ABC]$, constrained by the fd $B \to C$. The view to be updated is Π_{AB}. From 2.16, it follows that Π_{BC} is a Π_B-complement of Π_{AB}, and the corresponding update family on Π_{AB} is precisely that which holds Π_B constant. This update family is order realizable, since there are no constraints on Π_{AB}. Any change can be realized by first inserting the new tuples, and then deleting the ones which are no longer wanted. Thus, in view of 4.2, the only update strategy in the sense of 3.1 which supports these updates is that which holds Π_{BC} constant. Furthermore, 4.3 above guarantees that Π_{BC} is the only order-based Π_B-complement of Π_{AB}. In particular, in view of 2.5, Π_{BC} is the only SPJR-view of $\mathbf{E}_1$ which is a Π_B-complement of Π_{AB}. In short, the theory has very strong things to say about $\mathbf{E}_1$.

4.5 Example – Using Tuple Ordering to Force Order Realizability. Now, revisit the example schema $\mathbf{E}_2$ from 1.3. It is identical to $\mathbf{E}_1$, save that it is constrained by the additional fd $B \to A$. Π_{BC} is still a Π_B-complement of Π_{AB}, since the dependency $B \to A$ embeds in Π_{AB}. Thus, the update family in which Π_B is held constant is again that induced on Π_{AB} by the complement

Π_{BC}. However, this time the states in Π_{AB} are constrained by the fd $B \to A$. This has the consequence that none of the allowable updates on Π_{AB} is order based; thus, under the natural order, the theory developed above has nothing to say either about updates to or about Π_B-complements of Π_{AB}.

Fortunately, in this situation, there is a way to establish results similar to those for $\mathbf{E}_1$. The trick is to add additional order to the relational states. Let $\preceq_A$, $\preceq_B$ and $\preceq_C$ be partial orders on $\mathsf{Dom}(A)$, $\mathsf{Dom}(B)$ and $\mathsf{Dom}(C)$, respectively. Define the ordering $\preceq_{ABC}$ on tuples over ABC by $(a_0, b_0, c_0) \preceq_{ABC} (a_1, b_1, c_1)$ iff $a_0 \preceq_A a_1$, $b_0 \preceq_B b_1$, and $c_0 \preceq_C c_1$. Finally, extend the ordering $\preceq_{ABC}$ to relations on ABC by $M_1 \preceq_{ABC} M_2$ iff $(\forall t_0 \in M_1)(\exists t_1 \in M_2)(t_0 \preceq_{ABC} t_1)$. It is easy to see that this induces a partial order on the relations of $R[ABC]$ which is stronger than $\leq_{\mathbf{E}_2}$ in general, and the same as $\leq_{\mathbf{E}_2}$ if each of the three orders $\preceq_A$, $\preceq_B$, and $\preceq_C$ is flat (i.e., no ordering at all). Define a similar ordering, using the same base orders $\preceq_A$, $\preceq_B$, and $\preceq_C$, on the states of $R[AB]$ and $R[BC]$.

Now, for the specific problem at hand, let $\preceq_A$ be any *total* order on $\mathsf{Dom}(A)$, and let $\preceq_B$ and $\preceq_C$ be the flat orders on $\mathsf{Dom}(B)$ and $\mathsf{Dom}(C)$, respectively. Using the orders $\preceq_{ABC}$ on $R[ABC]$, $\preceq_{AB}$ on $R[AB]$, and $\preceq_{BC}$ on $R[BC]$, every allowable update to Π_{AB} under constant complement Π_{BC} becomes order realizable. Furthermore, Π_{BC} is completely unchanged. Thus, the above results apply; update with constant complement Π_{BC} is the unique order-based update strategy on Π_{AB} with constant complement Π_B, and Π_{BC} is the unique order-based Π_B-complement of Π_{AB}.

5.   Conclusions and Further Directions

It has been shown that the use of order as a central property of database schemata and morphisms leads to strong uniqueness results for view updates under the constant-complement strategy. In many cases, the natural order defined by inclusion is adequate for uniqueness; however, it has also been shown (4.5) that an "artificial" order may be used to achieve uniqueness in certain other situations.

In terms of future theoretical directions for this work, the most immediate one is to examine the circumstances under which update strategies may be combined to yield a single, larger strategy. Ultimately, it would be interesting and useful to identify circumstances under which a given view Γ_1 has a least meet complement Γ_2, in the sense that for any other meet complement Γ_3, $\Gamma_1 \wedge \Gamma_2 \leq \Gamma_1 \wedge \Gamma_3$. This would imply that Γ_1 has a largest update family which can be supported via the constant-complement strategy. Other theoretical directions to consider include a more systematic treatment of the kind of artificial orders used in 4.5, as well as study of the complexity of these forms of updates under specific data models.

In terms of more practical follow-up work, certainly a closer examination of how this work might be applied to data models other than the relational is high on the list. However, it seems that there is a more fundamental issue which must be addressed first. Most of the research on the view update problem has focused upon open strategies, with the goal to support the largest possible family of updates, even at the expense of violating the isolation principles which are implicit in the constant-complement strategy. Indeed, very little work has been done which builds upon the constant complement strategy, and even in the few cases in which it has, the axioms have been weakened so that critical properties, such as reversibility, have been sacrificed [GPZ88]. In the opinion of the author, this situation exists because in traditional database design, the main schema is established first, and only afterwards are views fitted to it. Therefore, *view-centered schema design*, a research direction in which schema design is focused upon the support of views, including view updates based upon the constant-complement strategy, is proposed. The conjecture is that, with the judicious use of null values, most view updates can be accommodated within the constant-complement strategy. The most natural framework in which to pursue these ideas would be within *HERM*, the *H*igher-order *E*ntity-*R*elationship *M*odel [Tha00]. Since HERM is a meta model, conclusions about most modern data models could be extracted from a study based upon it.

References

[AHV95] Abiteboul, S., Hull, R., and Vianu, V., *Foundations of Databases*, Addison-Wesley, 1995.

[BS81] Bancilhon, F. and Spyratos, N., "Update semantics of relational views," *ACM Transactions on Database Systems*, **6**(1981), pp. 557–575.

[Bel00] Bellahsène, Z., "Updates and object-generating views in ODBS," *Data & Knowledge Engr.*, **34**(2000), pp. 125–163.

[BL98] Bentayeb, F. and Laurent, D., "View updates translations in relational databases," in: *Proc. DEXA '98, Vienna, Sept. 24-28, 1998*, pp. 322–331, 1998.

[DP90] Davey, B. A. and Priestly, H. A., *Introduction to Lattices and Order*, Cambridge University Press, 1990.

[GPZ88] Gottlob, G., Paolini, P., and Zicari, R., "Properties and update semantics of consistent views," *ACM Trans. Database Systems*, **13**(1988), pp. 486–524.

[Heg90] Hegner, S. J., "Foundations of canonical update support for closed database views," in: *Proc. ICDT'90, Paris, Dec. 1990*, Springer-Verlag, 1990.

[Heg93] Hegner, S. J., "Characterization of desirable properties of general database decompositions," *Ann. Math. Art. Intell.*, **7**(1993), pp. 129–195.

[Heg94] Hegner, S. J., "Unique complements and decompositions of database schemata," *J. Comput. System Sci.*, **48**(1994), pp. 9–57.

[Hul84] Hull, R., "Finitely specifiable implicational dependency families," *Journal of the Association for Computing Machinery*, **31**(1984), pp. 210–226.

[Mac98] Mac Lane, S., *Categories for the Working Mathematician*, Springer-Verlag, second edition, 1998.

[MT99] Mayol, E. and Teniente, E., "A survey of current methods for integrity constraint maintenance and view updating," in: *Proc. ER '99 Workshops, Paris, Nov. 15-18, 1999*, Springer-Verlag, 1999.

[Mon76] Monk, J. D., *Mathematical Logic*, Springer-Verlag, 1976.

[Tha00] Thalheim, B., *Entity-Relationship Modeling*, Springer-Verlag, 2000.

Knowledge Representation in Extended Pawlak's Information Systems: Algebraic Aspects

Jānis Cīrulis

University of Latvia,
Raiņa b., 19
Riga LV-1586, Latvia
jc@fmf.lu.lv

Abstract. The notion of an information system in Pawlak's sense is extended by introducing a certain ordering on the attribute set, which allows to treat some attributes as parts of others. With every extended information system **S** associated is the set $K(\mathbf{S})$ of those pieces of information that, in a sense, admit a direct access in **S**. The algebraic structure of the "information space" $K(\mathbf{S})$ is investigated, and it is shown, in what extent the structure of **S** can be restored from the structure of its information space. In particular, an intrinsic binary relation on $K(\mathbf{S})$, interpreted as entailment, is isolated, and an axiomatic description of a knowledge revision operation based on it is proposed.

1 Introduction

An information system in Pawlak's sense is a quadruple (Ob, At, Val, f), where

- Ob is a non-empty set of *objects*,
- At is a set of their *attributes*,
- Val is a family $(Val_a, a \in At)$ of sets: each Val_a is considered as the set of possible *values of* a,
- f is a function $Ob \times At \to \bigcup(P_0(Val_a): a \in At)$ such that $f(o,a) \in P_0(Val_a)$, where $P_0(X)$ stands for the set of nonempty subsets of X; it is called the *information function*.

The system is said to be *deterministic* if each $f(o,a)$ is a singleton.

This notion of information system goes back to 70'ies [17,26]. It is somewhat surprisingly that such a simple concept (a deterministic information system is nothing else as a one-relational database) has turned out to be very fruitful and has given rise to rough set theory and other approaches to approximation of information, to applications to concept analysis, to logical foundations of knowledge representation, to attribute dependency; this list by no means is complete. See, e.g., [2,6,11,18,20,21,22,24,25,26,27,30,36,37].

Usually attributes in an information system are thought of as formally independent: the information function may be quite arbitrary. The actual dependencies between attributes are supposed to be caused by the behaviour of the

T. Eiter and K.-D. Schewe (Eds.): FoIKS 2002, LNCS 2284, pp. 250–267, 2002.

information function on the object set as a whole. Namely, an attribute b is considered as dependent on a subset $A \subset At$ if the value of b for every object turns out to be uniquely determined by values of attributes in A for this object [11,22,27]:

$$A \to b \text{ iff for all } o_1, o_2 \in Ob, \ f(o_1, b) = f(o_2, b) \text{ whenever}$$
$$f(o_1, a) = f(o_2, a) \text{for every } a \in A.$$

We note that this particular way of defining functional dependencies becomes somewhat problematic if the information systems under consideration are non-deterministic.

However, there could be also dependencies *a priori*, for example, those determined by some ontological presuppositions, or those caused by the "construction" of the system or its objects. In relational database theory such presuppositions are sometimes even included as constraints in the scheme of a database, and this could, and should, be done also in the case of information systems. Dependencies of this latter kind occur, in particular, if some attributes are considered as parts of others, and it is just these inclusion dependencies that we deal with in this paper. Let us consider two examples.

Example 1.1. Let $\mathbf{S} := (Ob, At, Val, f)$ be a Pawlak's information system. Subsets of At can be treated as complex attributes. Suppose that we are interested in a certain collection of complex attributes; let us denote it by At^+. There is a natural part_of relation on At^+, viz., the set inclusion.

Given a complex attribute A, we put Val_A^+ to be the cartesian product $\prod(Val_a \colon a \in A)$, i.e. the set of functions φ on A such that $\varphi(a) \in Val_a$ for all $a \in A$. Let f^+ be a function on $Ob \times At^+$ defined as follows:

$$f^+(o, A) := \{\varphi \in Val_A^+ \colon \varphi(a) \in f(o, a) \text{ for all } a \in A\}.$$

Then the quadruple $\mathbf{S}^+ := (Ob, At^+, Val^+, f^+)$ is again an information system. If $At^+ = At$ (we identify here every attribute a with its unit set $\{a\}$), the system $\mathbf{S}^+$ coincides with $\mathbf{S}$. However, in theoretical investigations also subsets of At are traditionally taken into account; then it is natural to take $P_0(At)$ or even the set $P(At)$ of all subsets of At for At^+. There may well be intermediate choices. In any case, the information function f^+ now reflects possible interdependencies between complex attributes in A^+.   □

Remark 1.1. We might consider the system $\mathbf{S}^+$ as a relational database if its components are interpreted as follows. Think of the complex attributes and the set At^+ as of relation schemes and a database scheme, respectively. Then subsets of Val_A^+ are relations (instances of A). For each $o \in Ob$, the collection $(f^+(o, A) \colon A \in At^+)$ of relations is an instance of At^+. Thus, under this interpretation objects are peculiar database states indexing the instances of the database scheme. The real distinction from the database theory lies in the understanding of a relation: in the present context it should be perceived in an unusual manner as a vague specified record rather than a presentation of a class of entities or of a relationship between such classes.

If the underlying system **S** is deterministic, another, more traditional interpretation is possible. In this case we may consider the set $\{f^+(o, At): o \in Ob\}$ as a universal relation in $\mathbf{S}^+$, each row of which is a description of some object (perceived now as an entity). Then the relation $\{f^+(o, A): o \in Ob\}$ is merely an A-projection of the universal relation.

In this paper, we shall develop further neither of these relation-theoretical points of view. □

Most concrete information systems with ordered attribute set arise as in the example above. The following example of a system of another kind was more extensively discussed in [35].

Example 1.2. We can relate an information system with every finite or infinite automaton $(X, Y, S, \delta, \lambda)$, where X is the input set, Y is the output set, S is the set of states, $\delta: S \times X \to S$ is the next-state function, and $\lambda: S \times X \to Y$ is the next-output function. In the standard fashion, the automaton induces a function $\Lambda: S \times X^* \to Y^*$. Let I be a prefix-closed set of input sequences, and let O stands for the family $(O_i, i \in I)$, where each O_i consists of all output sequences of the same length as i. Then (S, I, O, Λ) is a deterministic information system. The role of attributes is played by the chosen input sequences; this set of attributes is naturally tree-ordered by the prefix_of relation. Any non-deterministic automaton (see [34]) gives rise to an information system in a similar way. □

The primary goal of the paper is to contribute to better understanding of the structure of information represented by values of attributes. Our aim is three-fold:

- at first, to generalise the concept of an information system taking account of part_of dependencies between attributes. This is done in Sect. 3, where the attribute set is endowed with an order relation of certain kind; this leads also to fixing up connections between the value sets Val_a. Sect. 2 contains the needed preliminaries.
- at second, to study the structure of the set of those pieces of information, or knowledge, that can be regarded as directly accessible in an information system "by name". Our motivation for selection of such pieces is given at the end of Sect. 3, and the algebraic (order-theoretic) structure of the "information space" is clarified in Sect. 4.
- at third, to demonstrate that the mentioned information space deserves to be called the knowledge space of the system. We briefly show in Sect. 5 that a certain entailment-like relation can be extracted out of the structure of the information space and that an axiomatic description (resembling the so called AGM-postulates) of a knowledge revision operation in the latter can then be carried out in this algebraic setting.

The information retrieval systems in the sense of Salton [32] are not based on attributes. An extensive study of these systems was undertaken by Raś in [31]. In particular, he demonstrated that attributes can, in fact, be introduced in Salton's systems (not uniquely). Analysis of the constructions show that certain ordering is then implicitly induced on the attribute set. It seems, however, that the idea of ordered attribute sets has been completely abandoned in the theory of Pawlak's information systems. On the other hand, the notion of an extended information system in the sense of Sect. 4 is a specific particular case of the concept recently discussed by the present author in [5], where arbitrary functional dependencies between attributes were admitted.

Algebraic approach to various problems in the theory of Pawlak's information system (and related fields of database theory) by no means is a novelty – see [3,6,7,11,13,16,19,22], but we are not aware of other investigations of algebraic aspects of knowledge representation and knowledge revision in such systems. In other context, an domain theoretic approach to knowledge representation was proposed in [4]. It seems that the abstract geometrical approach to databases and knowledge bases proposed by B.Plotkin [28,29] can also be put in the framework of extended Pawlak's information systems, where attributes generate some term algebra.

2   Type Systems and Their Models

We first recall some definitions from [23]. Their motivation, based on analysis of flat descriptions in the relational model, is discussed in Sect. 2 of [23].

A partially ordered set is said to possess the *pairwise bounded join* property (the pbj property, for short), if every pair x, y of its elements bounded from above has the join (i.e. least upper bound) $x \vee y$. We shall call a set ordered this way a *pbj-poset*.

Example 2.1 (see Example 1 in [4]). Assume that some set M is equipped with an irreflexive and symmetric relation $\sharp$ ($m \sharp n$ may be read as 'm rejects n'). A subset X of M is said to be *coherent* if $m \sharp n$ for no $m, n \in X$.

Any collection of coherent sets that is closed under existing finite joins is a pbj-poset under set inclusion.   □

By the way, any pbj-poset P is an event structure [38] of a special kind. Indeed, the relation $\#$ defined on it as follows:

$$x \# y \text{ iff } x \vee y \text{ does not exist}$$

is irreflexive and symmetric; moreover, $x \# y \leq z$ implies that $x \# z$. So, it is a conflict relation on P. We shall say that elements p and q of P are *compatible* if, in opposite, the join $p \vee q$ does exist, and shall write $p \downarrow q$ in this case. A subset of P is said to be *conflict-free* if every two of its elements are compatible.

Following [23], we define a *(database) type system* to be any pbj-poset. A *(description) domain* is a pbj-poset that has the bottom element. In fact, it is also required in Def. 3.1 and Def. 3.2 of [23] that both type systems and domains must be effective in a natural sense, but we shall not concern ourselves with effectiveness matters here. However, to avoid technical difficulties concerning infinite joins, we shall regard thorough the paper that every type system T is *locally finite* in the following sense: every subset $\downarrow t := \{s \in T: s \leq t\}$ is finite.

A model of a type system T was defined in [23] to be (in effect) a T-indexed family of domains interconnected by Galore insertions. We shall deal here with models of simpler structure.

Definition 2.1. A *model of a type system* T is a system $V := (V_s, p_s^t)_{s \leq t \in T}$, where

- $(V_t: t \in T)$ is a family of nonempty sets,
- each p_s^t is a surjective mapping $V_t \to V_s$ such that

$$p_s^s = \mathrm{id}_{V\,s}, \quad p_r^s p_s^t = p_r^t, \tag{1}$$

and, whenever $s \vee t$ exists,

$$p_s^{s \vee t}(x) = p_s^{s \vee t}(y), \ p_t^{s \vee t}(x) = p_t^{s \vee t}(y) \ \Rightarrow \ x = y. \tag{2}$$

□

Thus, a model of T can be viewed as a T-shaped many-sorted algebra with unary operations of mixed types. The condition (2) attains that the set $V_{s \vee t}$ is injectively embedded into $V_s \times V_t$ and, hence, can be identified with a subset of the latter; then $p_s^{s \vee t}$ and $p_t^{s \vee t}$ become the usual cartesian projections.

Example 2.2. A model of totally unordered set L is just a L-indexed family of sets $V := (V_l: l \in L)$.

□

Example 2.3. Let L and V be as in the preceding example. Elements of L a called labels and those of each V_l are values. Suppose that T is a collection of subsets of L that is a type system under set inclusion. Given a type X, put Rec_X to be the set of flat records of this type, i.e. the set of functions φ on X satisfying the condition $\varphi(l) \in V_l$ for all $l \in X$ (this is the same construction we used for Val_A^+ in Example 1.1). If $X \subset Y$ and $\psi \in Rec_Y$, let $p_X^Y(\psi)$ be the restriction $\psi[X]$ of the record ψ to X. The system $Rec := (Rec_X, p_X^Y)_{X \subset Y \in T}$ is a model of T. If $\emptyset \in T$, then there is only one "empty" record in $Rec_\emptyset$.

□

Example 2.4 (see Remark 1.1). Let V be a model of T. We generalize some constructions appearing in the classical relational database theory. Consider types from T as relation schemes, subsets of V_t as instances of t (i.e. relations with scheme t), and the type system T itself as a database scheme. Given a scheme t, put Rel_t to be the set of all relations having this scheme. If $s \leq t$ and $r \in Rel_t$, let $\pi_s^t(r)$ be the projection of r onto s, i.e. $\pi_s^t(r) := \{\psi[s]: \psi \in r\}$. The system $Rel := (Rel_X, \pi_X^Y)_{X \subset Y \in T}$ is one more model of T obtained by reinterpreting types in T as set (relational) types.

□

A class of more sophisticated type systems (involving variant and set constructors and recursive types) for complex objects in relational databases is described in [23, Sect 4]. See also [3,14,16].

Example 2.5 (continuation of Example 1.2). Any rooted tree is a type system. Take for instance the subset I of X^*. If $i \leq j$ means that the word i is a prefix of j, then $(I, \leq)$ is a rooted tree and, hence, a type system. Furthermore, if $i \leq j \in I$ and $w \in O_j$, let $p_i^j(w)$ be the prefix of w belonging to O_i. Then $O := (O_i, p_i^j)_{i \leq j \in I}$ is a model of I.   □

What we still need for further discussion is a rather technical lemma, which shows that any pbj-poset equipped with a binary relation of certain kind gives rise to a type system with a model attached to it.

Definition 2.2. A preorder $\sqsubset$ on a pbj-poset P is said to be an *overriding relation* ($p \sqsubset q$ is read as 'p is overridden by q') if it satisfies the conditions

$$x \leq y \Rightarrow x \sqsubset y, \quad x \sqsubset y, x \downarrow y \Rightarrow x \leq y, \tag{3}$$

$$x \sqsubset z, y \sqsubset z, x \downarrow y \Rightarrow x \vee y \sqsubset z, \tag{4}$$

$$x \sqsubset z \Rightarrow x \parallel y \leq z \text{ for some } y, \tag{5}$$

where $\parallel$ is the equivalence relation induced by the preorder $\sqsubset$. Two elements of P are *alternative* if they lie in the same $\parallel$-class.   □

For example, $\leq$ itself is a trivial overriding relation. A natural overriding lives on a pbj-poset consisting of partial functions.

Example 2.6. Let L and V be as in Example 2.2. Clearly, the set $\mathcal{F}(L, V)$ of all partial functions f on L with $f(l) \in V(l)$ is a pbj-poset with respect to set inclusion, if a function is considered set-theoretically as a set of ordered pairs. (By the way, then $\mathcal{F}(L, V)$ is just the set of all coherent subsets of the labelled sum $U := \bigcup(\{l\} \times V_l : l \in L)$ under the rejection relation $\sharp$ defined as follows:

$$(k, u) \sharp (l, v) :\equiv k = l \text{ and } u \neq v$$

– see Example 2.1.) Now suppose that P is a subset of $\mathcal{F}(L, V)$ closed under existing unions; then both P and $T := \{\operatorname{dom} f : f \in P\}$ are pbj-posets. If P is closed also under restrictions, i.e. $f[X] \in P$ for every $f \in P$ and all $X \in T$ such that $X \subset \operatorname{dom} f$, then the relation $\sqsubset$ defined by

$$f \sqsubset g \text{ iff } \operatorname{dom} f \subset \operatorname{dom} g$$

is overriding on P.   □

In particular, the set of all records $\bigcup(Rec_X : X \in T)$ of Example 2.3 can be taken for such a P. Here, two records are alternative if they are of the same type. Theorem 4.1 generalises this example.

It is easily shown, using (3) and (4), that the element y in (5) is uniquely determined; let us denote it by $x \flat z$. Furthermore, $x \parallel y$ and $x \downarrow y$ imply that $x = y$.

Now assume that $(P, \sqsubset)$ is an pbj-poset with overriding, and suppose that τ is any mapping from P onto some set T with $\parallel$ the kernel equivalence. Let P_t stand for the $\parallel$-class $\tau^{-1}(t)$. The preorder $\sqsubset$ induces an order relation $\leq$ on T:

$$s \leq t \text{ iff } x \sqsubset y \text{ for some } x \in P_s \text{ and } y \in P_t. \tag{6}$$

Therefore, $p \sqsubset q$ ifs $\tau(p) \leq \tau(q)$. Clearly, the poset T is determined uniquely up to isomorphism (in fact, it is isomorphic to the quotient $P/\parallel$). We may call it a *scheme for P*.

Finally, if $s \leq t \in T$, let p_s^t be the mapping $P_t \to P_s$ defined by $p_s^t(y) = x \flat y$, where x is any element from P_s. The definition is correct, as an easy calculation shows that $x_1 \flat y = x_2 \flat y$ if x_1 and x_2 are alternative.

Lemma 2.1. *Suppose that P is locally finite. Then T is type system, and the system $M(P, \sqsubset) := (P_t, p_s^t)_{s \leq t \in T}$ is a model of T.*

Proof. By axiom checking. Note that the supposition is essential for T to be locally finite.   □

Example 2.7 (continuation of Example 2.6). In the situation of the preceding example, τ is the mapping dom, the order $\leq$ on T introduced by (6) coincides with $\subset$, and $M(P, \sqsubset)$ (with W chosen as noted just after the Example 2.6) coincides with the model *Rec* from Example 2.3.   □

Remark 2.1. We are, actually, interested in the alternation relation $\parallel$ rather than in $\sqsubset$. However, its axiomatic definition is less transparent. The overriding relation can be defined in terms of alternation:

$$x \sqsubset y \text{ iff } x \parallel x' \text{ and } y \parallel y' \text{ for some } x', y' \text{ with } x' \leq y'.$$

□

3   Information Systems Reconsidered

An information system may be thought of as consisting of two components: its "frame", comprised of the attribute set and respective value sets, and its "content", presented by the object set and information function. We first extend the concept of a frame.

Definition 3.1. A *frame* is a pair (T, V) consisting of a type system and its model. A *(total) description* in (T, V) is a function δ on T that assigns a non-empty subset of V_t to every $t \in T$ so that

 - if $s \leq t$, then $\delta(s) = \{p_s^t(v) : v \in \delta(t))\}$,
 - if $s \vee t$ exists, then $\delta(s \vee t) = \{w \in V_{s \vee t} : p_s^{s \vee t}(w) \in \delta(s) \text{ and } p_t^{s \vee t}(w) \in \delta(t)\}$.

A description δ is said to be *proper* if there is no other description δ' with $\delta'(t) \subset \delta(t)$ for all $t \in T$, and *flat* if every $\delta(t)$ is a singleton.   □

Let $F := (T, V)$ be a frame. Clearly, the function λ defined by $\lambda(t) = V_t$ is a description.

Note that a proper description need not be flat. The following example shows that there are simple frames that do not permit flat descriptions at all.

Example 3.1. Let $T = \{s1, s2, t1, t2\}$, and let, for $i = 1, 2$, $V_{si} = \{u_{i1}, u_{i2}\}$, $V_{ti} = \{v_{i1}, v_{i2}\}$. Assume that $s1, s2 \leq t1, t2$, and set

$$ p_{si}^{t1}(v_{1j}) = u_{ij}, \quad p_{s1}^{t2}(v_{2j}) = u_{1j}, \quad p_{s2}^{t2}(v_{21}) = u_{22}, \quad p_{s2}^{t2}(v_{22}) = u_{21}. $$

This frame has only the trivial description λ: if, for instance, $v_{11} \in \delta(t1)$, then $u_{11} \in \delta(s1)$ and $u_{21} \in \delta(s2)$. But then the only possible choice for $\delta(t2)$ is $\{v_{21}, v_{22}\}$. $\quad\square$

We present two more examples of descriptions in frames considered earlier.

Example 3.2 (continuation of Example 2.3; see also Example 2.4). The pair (T, Rec) is a frame. An instance of T (the type system being considered as a database scheme) is a family $\mathbf{r} := (r_X, X \in T)$, where r_X is an instance of X. We may consider such a family as a function from T to the set of all relations. This function is a description in the frame (T, Rec) (or, equivalently, a flat description in (T, Rel)) if and only if r_X is the projection $\pi_X(r_Y)$ whenever $X \subset Y$, and $r_{X \cup Y}$ is the natural join $r_X \bowtie r_Y$ whenever $X \cup Y \in T$. $\quad\square$

Example 3.3 (continuation of Example 2.5). In the terminology of [34, Def. 4.3], descriptions in the frame (I, O) are just sequential ND-operators on $[X, Y]$. $\quad\square$

We are now prepared to introduce the notion of an information system with an ordered set of attributes.

Definition 3.2. An *information system* is a quadruple $\mathbf{S} := (Ob, At, Val, f)$, where

- Ob is a nonempty set,
- At is a type system,
- Val is a model of At,
- f is a function $Ob \times At \to \bigcup(P_0(Val_a) : a \in At)$ such that for each $o \in Ob$ the mapping δ_o of At defined by $\delta_o(a) = f(o, a)$ is a description.

The frame (At, Val) is said to be the *frame of* $\mathbf{S}$ and denoted by $F(\mathbf{S})$, and the attribute system At, the *scheme* of $F(\mathbf{S})$ and of $\mathbf{S}$. $\quad\square$

Of course, types in At will now be called attributes. Recall that At, being a type system, has to be locally finite. If a and b are two attributes and $a \leq b$ in At, let us consider the attribute a as a part of b, and the function p_a^b as a tool for computing values of a from those of b. Under another reasonable interpretation of components of $\mathbf{S}$, elements of Ob, At and Val could be called states, requests and answers, respectively.

For a trivially ordered attribute set, this notion of an information system formally reduces to the original one described in the introduction. Let us call such systems *unordered*. On the other hand, the system $\mathbf{S}^+$ from Example 1.1 (with At^+ appropriately chosen) serves as an example of an information system in the sense of above definition. We call $\mathbf{S}^+$ a *power-set system* if $At+ = \mathcal{P}(At)$. The system (S, I, O, Λ) of Example 1.2 is another illustration to Definition 3.2. Let as consider one more example.

Example 3.4 (continuation of Example 3.2). Let $(\mathbf{r}_s\colon s \in S)$ be a family of descriptions in (T, Rec), where S is any set. If f is the function on $S \times T$ that assigns the relation r_X from $\mathbf{r}_s$ to every pair (s, X), then the system (S, T, Rec, f) is an information system. Note that the information system $\mathbf{S}^+$ from Example 1.1 was constructed, as a matter of fact, this way.   □

Let $\mathbf{S} := (Ob, At, Val, f)$ be a fixed information system. It seems natural to conceive of that the only pieces of information, or knowledge, available in $\mathbf{S}$ are those saying that certain attributes have certain values. This idea leads us to the notion of a knowledge set considered below. Here, we note that a piece of information about an object in consideration can be directly available "by name" only if it concerns a single attribute, i.e. is presented by a *descriptor* (a, u) (where $u \in Val_a$). Of course, we may be interested also in more extensive pieces of information; however, there may be no real possibility to get to know values of several attributes simultaneously. For instance, imagine a system in which John stores information about his three televisors (Ob is a three-element set of televisors). He has chosen for At the set of (names of) buttons of a televisor. He then can simultaneously fix the "values" of, say, the volume button (the loudness level), the picture format button (e.g. *wide*) and the programme button 5 (the TV station), but cannot test at a time, which TV stations are stored under distinct programme numbers. One might object that the "concurrent" attributes of a televisor can be tested one after the other, for their values do not change during this procedure. But this argument certainly does not work in Example 1.2: generally, there is no way to observe the output sequences emitted by an automaton, even in a fixed initial state, in response to two input sequences none of which is an initial segment of the other (unless the automaton has the restart button which allows to return it to the initial state after each observation). Likewise, if properties of objects in $\mathbf{S}$ are influenced by any quantum phenomena, it may happen that some of their attributes are not commensurable.

Be it as it may, we regard a set A of attributes as simultaneously observable if and only if there is an attribute b such that all attributes in A are parts of b: the values of attributes in A are then figured out from those of b by means of functions p_a^b. This assumption involves an implicit presupposition that the attribute set of a system (for instance, the set At^+ of complex attributes in Example 1.1) has been chosen to be rich enough to draw a principal conclusion that the phrase 'simultaneous values of attributes $a, b, c, \ldots$' makes sense in it if and only if the attributes under consideration have a common upper bound in.

Due to the pbj property (and the local finiteness condition for type systems), the set A has the least upper bound, which could be regarded as the complex attribute "consisting" of the elements of A. This is one of reasons why we wanted type systems to have this property. In effect, we see that our starting position (only descriptors are directly available pieces of information) is not a real loss of generality – rather, it is a change of language: one complex attribute or descriptor instead of a set of attributes, resp., descriptors.

Now we define the *information space of* S to be the set

$$K(S) := \{(a, u): a \in At, u \in Val_a)\}$$

of all descriptors in (At, Val). It is, actually, completely determined by the frame of S, so we may denote it also by $K(At, Val)$. Moreover, we even can speak of an information space $K(F)$ of a frame F regardless of any information system based on it.

Example 3.5. The information space of the frame (T, Rec) (see Example 3.2) is essentially the set $\bigcup(Rec_X: X \in T)$ of all records, for each piece of information here is of the form $(\mathrm{dom}\,\varphi, \varphi)$. □

4   Structure of Information Spaces

We first shall study the structure of a information space of a fixed frame $F :=$ (At, Val), and then shall find out what is added to this structure when the frame is complemented by objects and information function.

A descriptor (a, u) is said to be a *restriction of* (b, v) (in symbols, $(a, u) \leq$ (b, v)) if $a \leq b$ and $u = p_a^b(v)$. Clearly, the relation $\leq$ is a partial order on $K(F)$.

Theorem 4.1. *The poset $K(F)$ has the pbj property and, for all (a, u), (b, v) and (c, w)*

$$(a, u) \vee (b, v) = (a \vee b, p_{a \vee b}^c(w))$$

whenever $(a, u) \leq (c, w)$ and $(b, v) \leq (c, w)$. Moreover, $K(F)$ is locally finite, and the relation $\angle$ on $K(F)$ defined by

$$(a, u) \angle (b, v) \quad \textit{iff} \quad a \leq b$$

is overriding.

Proof. The proof is by direct axiom-checking. We only note that the first assertion heavily depends on (2) (see Sect 2). □

In particular, if At is unordered (as in Example 2.2), then so is the space $K(F)$, and $\angle$ becomes an equivalence relation in this event. On the other hand, $K(F)$ is a domain if and only if At has the least element 0 and Val_0 is a singletons (as in Example 2.3). If it is the case, then the description $(0, \imath)$, where $\imath$ is the single element of Val_0, is the bottom element in $K(F)$. We shall see in the subsequent section that the alternation relation allows us to introduce certain relation on a knowledge space that could be interpreted as entailment.

The next theorem states that there is, up to isomorphisms, a one-to-one correspondence between the class of frames and that of locally finite pbj-posets with an overriding relation. See Lemma 2.1 above and the discussion preceding it for the definition of $M(P, \sqsubset)$.

Theorem 4.2. *Suppose that (At, Val) is a frame and that $(P, \sqsubset)$ is a pbj-poset with overriding. Then $(P, \sqsubset)$ is isomorphic to $(K(At, Val), \angle)$ if and only if At is a scheme for P and Val is isomorphic to $M(P, \sqsubset)$.*

Proof. To prove the 'if' part, we should to demonstrate that $(P, \sqsubset)$ is isomorphic to $(K(T, M), \angle)$, where T is a locally finite scheme for P and $M = M(P, \sqsubset)$. But $K := K(T, M)$ is just the union of components $\{t\} \times P_t$ with $t \in T$. In K,

$$(s, p) \leq (t, q) \text{ iff } s \leq t \text{ and } p = p_s^t(q) = p \flat q,$$
$$\text{iff } p \sqsubset q \text{ (by (6)) and } p \leq q,$$
$$\text{iff } p \leq q \text{ (by (3))}.$$

So, the mapping $(s, p) \mapsto p$ is an isomorphism between the posets K and P. Furthermore, $(s, p) \angle (t, q)$ in K ifs $s \leq t$ ifs $p \sqsubset q$.

To prove the 'only if' part, we first note that At is a scheme for $K := K(At, Val)$ relatively to the mapping $\tau : (a, u) \mapsto a$. Furthermore, $K_a = \{a\} \times Val_a$ and $(a, u) \flat (b, v) = (a, p_a^b(v))$. Thus, $M(K, \angle)$ is isomorphic to Val, as needed. $\square$

In the light of this theorem, it is reasonable to introduce the term '*abstract information space*' for locally finite pbj-posets with overriding relation. The information spaces of frames could then be called *concrete*. Thus, the concept of an abstract information space is the order-theoretic equivalent of that of a frame. We now shall look for such equivalent of the notion of a description.

Imagine some agent whose knowledge is presented by pieces of information in K. We assume that

- if the agent knows a piece of information, then he also knows every part of the piece,
- if the agent knows two pieces of information which can be pooled together, then he also knows the combined piece.

Therefore, the pieces of information known by the agent form a subset of K that is both downward closed and closed under existing joins. Such subsets of a pbj-poset are known as its ideals.

There is one more reasonable (though not compulsory) assumption as to the agent's knowledge in a concrete information space:

- if the attribute a is a part of b, and if the agent is aware of b, then all what he knows about a is included in his knowledge about b.

In more details: if $a \leq b$ and the agent knows a piece (b, v), then he knows a piece (a, u) only if it knows some piece (b, v') such that $u = p_a^b(v')$.

We sum up the above discussion in following definition of a knowledge set in an abstract information space K.

Definition 4.1. A *knowledge set* in K is any ideal of K. We call the knowledge set I

- *flat* if $x \parallel y$ for no distinct $x, y \in I$,
- *full* if every $x \in I$ can be extended in the following sense: if $x \sqsubset z$ for some $z \in I$, then there is $y \in I$ such that $x \leq y$ and $y \parallel z$, and
- *extensive* if, for every $x \in K$, there is $y \in I$ with $y \parallel x$.   □

Proposition 4.1. *A description in F, if considered set-theoretically as a set of ordered pairs (descriptors), is a full and extensive knowledge set in $K(F)$, and the converse also holds. A description is flat if and only if so is the corresponding knowledge set.*

We conclude that each object $o \in Ob$ in an information system induces an extensive knowledge set $I_o := \{(a, u): u \in f(o, a)\}$ in the information space of its frame. Therefore, the information system gives rise to a family of such knowledge sets on its information space. Let us present this family in a distinctive form.

We refine Definition 4 from [4] and say that a pair $(W, \Vdash)$ consisting of a nonempty set W and a binary relation in $W \times P$ is a *possible world space* for a pbj-poset P if every subset $\{x: w \Vdash x\}$ is a knowledge set in P. If elements of P are interpreted as pieces of information, then we may consider the connection $w \Vdash d$ as asserting that the piece d is valid in a sense in the possible world w.

Let us call a possible world space *extensive* if the knowledge sets induced by its possible worlds are all extensive.

Proposition 4.2. *Suppose that (Ob, At, Val, f) is an information system If the relation $\Vdash$ is defined on $Ob \times K(At, Val)$ by the condition*

$$o \Vdash (a, u) :\equiv u \in f(o, a) \ ,$$

then $(Ob, \Vdash)$ is an extensive possible world space for $K(At, Val)$.

Therefore, every information system can adequately be presented as a triple $(W, P, \Vdash)$, where P is a information space and $(W, \Vdash)$ is an extensive possible world space for it. In addition, every such a triple presents some information system. The correspondence between information systems and triples is easily seen to be one-to-one up to isomorphisms; this conclusion justifies the next definition.

Definition 4.2. An *information system in triple form* is a system $(W, P, \Vdash)$, where P is an abstract information space and $(W, \Vdash)$ is an extensive possible world space for P. (If needed, we then call the information systems in the sense of our previous definition *attribute information systems*.)   □

We could remove the extensiveness requirement of the possible world space in this definition. The weakened triples correspond to attribute systems with partially defined descriptions (some attributes of some objects have not values at all). The triple corresponding to a partial unordered attribute system may be interpreted as a formal context [8], where the role of *Merkmalen* are played by descriptions rather than the initial attributes. If we replace the relation $|{\vdash}$ in a triple by the function $U\colon P \to \mathcal{P}(W)$, where

$$U(p) := \{w \in W\colon w \,|{\vdash}\, p\},$$

we come to an ordered information retrieval system (W, P, U) like those studied in [31]. There considered are the cases when P is an arbitrary poset, a lattice, and a Boolean algebra, not equipped with an overriding relation or any of its equivalents.

5   Logic in Information Spaces

We shall continue the study of knowledge sets in an abstract information space P. In this section, we develop some ideas from Sects 5 and 6 of [4] concerning entailment relations. However, we must first clarify the meaning of the knowledge presented by a set of alternative pieces of knowledge.

Up to now, we did not use any ontological presumptions in this respect (apart from Introduction, where, according to tradition, a Pawlak's system was treated as indeterministic, or incomplete, if some of the sets $f(o, a)$ were not a singletons). However, actually there are several possible ways of interpreting a non-flat descriptions in a frame.

If the set $\delta(t)$ for some $t \in T$ contains at least two elements, it may be interpreted either as an or-set or as an and-set, and then it presents either a vaguely defined or an overdefined element from V_t, respectively. For example, consider a bibliographical information system, where objects are books and a is the attribute 'the number of pages in'; then the information $f(o, a) = \{121, 122, 123, 124\}$ is read either as '121 or 122 or 123 or 124' or '121 and 122 and 123 and 124', respectively. Thus, the information is either incomplete (in the first case) or inconsistent (in the second case). The same happens if b means 'the author of' (as far as one-author books are retrieved) and $f(o, b) = \{Brown, Smith\}$. But if b means 'the author(s) of', the same information may be interpreted as a collective set: 'both Brown and Smith are authors of o'. Formally, b has been now treated as a set type without extending the value set V_a with such objects as $\{Brown, Smith\}$. (By the way, this explains the virtual collision of views noticed at the end of first paragraph of Remark 1.1 in Introduction.) Likewise, b could be understood as a variant type ('an author'). However, it is not a good idea to reinterpret a type t this way without including sets, resp, variants in V_t as regular values.

Under the or-set interpretation, adding a new piece q to a knowledge set I is perceived as increasing information, if I does not contains alternatives of q or its parts, and as increasing uncertainty in the opposite case. Under the and-set interpretation, adding a new piece is always adding new information, probably, inconsistent with that already contained in I. In the following, this latter interpretation will be more useful for our purposes.

Definition 5.1. A relation $\prec$ between subsets of P and elements of P is said to be an *entailment* if it satisfies the following conditions, where $I \prec q$ should be read as 'I entails q':

- for every $I \subset P$, the set $\{x \in P: I \prec q\}$ is a knowledge set,
- if $q \in I$, then $I \prec q$,
- if $I \prec q$ and $I \subset J$, then $J \prec q$,
- if $I \prec q$ and $J \prec p$ for all $p \in I$, then $J \prec q$.

Entailment $\prec$ is *finitary* if, whenever $I \prec q$, there is a finite subset $J \subset I$ that entails q.   □

In [4] such a relation was considered only between pieces of information. We shall say that I entails J if I entails every element of J.

Example 5.1. Let $(W, \Vdash)$ be a possible world space for a pbj-poset P. The the relation $\models$ defined by

$$I \models q \ :\equiv \ (\forall w \in W)(w \Vdash I \Rightarrow w \Vdash q)$$

is entailment ($w \Vdash I$ means that $w \Vdash p$ for all $p \in I$).   □

This entailment, when applied to an abstract information system $(W, P, \Vdash)$, could be termed *semantical*, for it is determined by the "content" of the system. We now shall describe another particular example of entailment which is completely determined by the structure of our information space P only.

Definition 5.2. A *knowledge state* in an abstract information space P is defined to be a minimal (relatively to $\subset$) full and extensive knowledge set. We say that a subset I of K *internally entails* q, and write $I \vdash q$ in this case, if q belongs to every knowledge state including I. A knowledge set is said to be *closed* if it is closed under $\vdash$. The *closure* $[I]$ of a subset I is the least closed knowledge set including I.   □

Therefore, knowledge states of an attribute information system correspond to its proper descriptions, and conversely. The relation $\vdash$ is an entailment relation indeed, for its definition can be rendered as in Example 5.1, taking knowledge states in the role of possible worlds. Every knowledge state itself is closed; however a closed knowledge set need not be extensive, neither even full. Another example of a closed knowledge set is whole P. The closure $[I]$ is nothing else than the intersection of all closed knowledge sets including I. Equivalently, $[I]$ can be described as the intersection of all knowledge states including I, if we take P for the intersection of an empty family of states.

A pair of incompatible elements (see the beginning of Sect. 2) of K can intuitively be considered as a contradiction. Then it is reasonable to consider some subset I of K as consistent with respect to the introduced entailment relation if its closure does not contains such contradictions, i.e. is conflict-free. However, an inconsistent set may be paraconsistent in the sense that its closure does not coincide with whole K. This is the case ifs it is included in some knowledge state. Note that we have not excluded inconsistent knowledge states: we already know, that there are frames with no consistent states (see Example 3.1).

We consider I as consistent with another subset J if adding I to J does not yield new contradictions. More formally: $I \in C(J)$ if and only if

$$I \cup J \vdash x, y, \ x \# y \ \Rightarrow \ J \vdash x, y.$$

Using this concept, we now can model the so called AGM postulates for knowledge revision [1,9] in information spaces. Where I is a knowledge set, let as denote by $I + q$ the closure of $I \cup \{q\}$ (the *expansion* of I by q), and by $I \dotplus q$ the knowledge set representing the revision of I by q. Actually, we apply here the revision operation $\dotplus$ only to closed knowledge sets. The following axioms of revision mimic the postulates (K+1)–(K+8) in [9].

$\dotplus$1: For every closed knowledge set I and $q \in I$, $I \dotplus q$ is a closed knowledge set.

$\dotplus$2: The piece q is accepted in $I \dotplus q$: $q \subset I \dotplus q$.

$\dotplus$3: Revision is stronger operation than expansion: $I \dotplus q \subset I + q$,

$\dotplus$4: If I is consistent with q, then whole I is accepted in $I \dotplus q$: if $I \in C(q)$, then $I \subset I \dotplus q$.

$\dotplus$5: The result of revision is consistent with q: $I \dotplus q \in C(q)$,

$\dotplus$6: Revision by equivalent pieces of information have same effect: if $p \prec q$ and $p \prec q$, then $I \dotplus p = I \dotplus q$.

The two final axioms concern composite revisions. If $p \downarrow q$, then

$\dotplus$7: $I \dotplus (p \vee q) \subset (I \dotplus p) + q$.

$\dotplus$8: If $(I \dotplus p) \in C(q)$, then $(I \dotplus p) + q \subset I \dotplus (p \vee q)$.

Of course, similar constructions can be based also on the semantic entailment of Example 5.1, although the significance of them seems to be more discussible. It may be of interest to find out in what extent the ideas behind the construction of the maxichoise revision operator of [4] can be transferred to the information spaces.

6   Conclusion

We have proposed a more general concept of information system that allows to take into account 'part of' like dependencies between attributes, and have associated a certain set of pieces of information, called the information space, with every such an information system. Examples show that extended information systems naturally can be extracted out of several well-known structures, including databases and automata. Moreover, we suggest that every Pawlak's information system can, and should, be treated as a powerset system (if there are not attributes rejecting each other) rather than an unordred one. The used algebraic methodology seems to be appropriate for qualitative reasoning about the knowledge presentable in attribute systems

Of course, the traditional directions of investigation in the theory of Pawlak's information systems (see Introduction) can be developed also for the extended information systems. We would like to call attention to some possible directions of investigations specific to the present approach.

The definition of $\models$ in Exercise 5.1 suggests that we could try to eliminate possible world spaces in favor of entailment relations. An *entailment space*, i.e. a pair $(K, \prec)$ consisting of an abstract information space and an arbitrary entailment relation on it could be considered as even more general presentation of an information system. However, not every entailment relation on K is induced by some possible world space. Nevertheless, entailment spaces may be of interest as abstract models of knowledge; for example, they might provide a basis of semantics for logical approaches to knowledge representation and revision. We also remind that the kernel of an information system in the sense of Scott is an abstract consequence relation between finite subsets of some set of tokens; see [33,7]. Various other kinds on abstract consequence relations have also been studied in the context of information systems [36,37].

We introduced a natural notion of a scheme for a pbj-poset with overriding in the paragraph just before Lemma 1. See [3, Sect. 4] and [16, Sect. 3] for another approach to the mathematics of schemes for domains. These approaches are related to each other, but not very close; the interconnections between them require further investigation.

Finally, we pose two concrete problems:

Problem 6.1. Call two information systems equivalent if they have same information space and same entailment $\models$ of Example 5.1. Characterise information systems that are equivalent to a system with flat descriptions.   □

Problem 6.2. Characterise the information systems embeddable (in any reasonable sense) in a powerset system.

References

1. Alchaurrón C.E., Gárdenfors P., Makinson D.: On the logic of theory change: Partial meet contraction and revision functions. J. Symb. Logic **50** (1985), 512–530.
2. Archangelsky, D.A., Taitslin, M.A.: A logic for information systems. Stud. Log. **58** (1997), 3–16.
3. Buneman P., Jung A., Ohori A.: Using powerdomains to generalize relational databases. Theor. Comput. Sci. **91** (1991), 23–55.
4. Cīrulis, J.: An algebraic approach to knowledge representation. MFCS'99, LNCS **1672** (1999), 299–309.
5. Cīrulis, J.: Are there essentially incomplete knowledge representation systems? FCT'01, LNCS **2138** (2001), 94–105.
6. Comer, S.D.: An algebraic approach to the approximation of information. Fund. Inform. **14** (1991), 492–502.

7. Davey, B.A., Priestley, H.A.: Introduction to Lattices and Order. Cambridge UP, 1994.
8. Ganter, B, Wille, R.: Formale Begriffsanalyse. Mathematishe Grundlagen. Springer, 1996.
9. Gärdenfors P.: Belief revision: an introduction. In: Gärdenfors P. (ed.), Belief revision. Cambr. Univ. Press, 1992, 1–28.
10. Grätzer G.: Lattice Theory. Academie-Verlag, Berlin, 1978.
11. Düntsch, I., Gediga, G.: Algebraic aspects of attribute dependencies in information systems. Fund. Inform. **29** (1997), 119–133.
12. Jaederman, M.: Information storage and retrieval systems IV. Systems with incomplete information. CC PAS Report **214**, Warszaw, 1975.
13. Jung, A., Libkin, L., Puhlmann, H.: Decomposition of domains. MFPS'91, LNCS **598**, 1992, 235–250.
14. Jung, A., Puhlmann, H.: Types, Logic, and Semantics for Nested Databases. Electr. Notes in Theoret. Comp. Sci. **1** (1995), URL: http://www.elsevier.nl /locate/entcs/volume1.html.
15. Kryszkiewicz, M.: Rules in incomplete information systems. Inf. Sci. **113** (1999), 271–292.
16. Libkin, L.: A relational algebra for complex objects based on partial information. MFDBS'91, LNCS **495** (1991), 29–43.
17. Marek, W., Pawlak, Z.: Information storage and retrieval systems: Mathematical foundations. Theor. Comp. Sci. **1** (1976), 331–354.
18. Marek, W., Truszszyński, M.: Contributions to the theory of rough sets. Fund. Inform. **39** (1999), 389–409.
19. Novotný, J., Novotný, M.: Notes on the algebraic approach to dependencies in information systems. Fund. Inform. **16** (1992), 263–273.
20. Novotný, M., Pawlak, Z.: On a representation of rough sets by means of information systems. Fund. Inform. **6** (1983), 289–296.
21. Novotný, M., Pawlak, Z.: Concept forming and black boxes. Bull. Polish Acad. Sci. Math. **35** (1987), 133–141.
22. Novotný, M., Pawlak, Z.: Algebraic theory of independence in information systems. Fund. Inform. **14** (1991), 454–476.
23. Ohori, A.: Semantics of types for database objects. Theor. Comput. Sci. **76** (1990), 53–91.
24. Orlowska, E.: Logic approach to information systems. Fund. Inform. **8** (1985), 359–378.
25. Orłovska, E., Pawlak, Z.: Representation of nondeterministic information. Theoret. Comput. Sci. **29** (1984), 27–39.
26. Pawlak, Z.: Information systems – theoretical foundations. Inform. Systems **6** (1981), 205–218.
27. Pawlak, Z., Rauszer, C.: Dependency of attributes in information systems. Bull. Polish. Acad. Sci. Math. **33** (1985), 561–569.
28. Plotkin, T., Plotkin, B.: Geometrical aspect of databases and knowledge bases. Algebra Univers. **46** (2001), 131–161.
29. Plotkin, B., Plotkin, T.: Universal algebra and computer science. FCT'01, LNCS **2138** (2001), 35–44.
30. Polkowski, L., Skowron, A.: Rough mereology in information systems with applications to qualitative reasoning. Fund. Inform. **43** (2000), 291–320.
31. Raś, Z.: Information retrieval systems, an algebraic approach, I, II. Fund Inform. **4** (1981), 551–603, 777–818.

32. Salton, G.: Automathic Information Organization and Retrieval. McGill, N.Y., 1968.
33. Scott, D.S.: Domains for denotational semantics. Automata, Languages and Programs, LNCS **173**, 1982, 577–613.
34. Starke, P.H.: Abstrakte Automaten. WEB Deutscher Verl. Wissensch., Berlin, 1969.
35. Tsirulis, Ya.P.: Variations on the theme of quantum logic (in Russian). In: Algebra i Diskretnaya Matematika, Latv. State Univ., Riga, 1984, 146–158.
36. Vakarelov, D.: Consequence relations and information systems. In: R. Slowinski (ed.), Intelligent Decision Support. Handbook of Applications and Advances of Rough Sets Theory, Kluwer, 1992.
37. Vakarelov, D.: A duality between Pawlak's knowledge representation systems and BI-Consequence Systems. Stud. Log. **55** (1995), 205–228.
38. Winskel, G.: An introduction to event structures. LNCS **354** 1989, 364–397.

Minimal Sample Databases
for Global Cardinality Constraints

Konrad Engel and Sven Hartmann

FB Mathematik, Universität Rostock, 18051 Rostock, Germany

Abstract. Cardinality constraints are a popular way of imposing restrictions to the structure of a database. In this paper, we consider global
cardinality constraints which specify lower and upper bounds on the total
number of relationships an entity of a fixed type may be involved in. It
is natural to ask for the smallest database with non-empty domains that
satisfies a given set of these constraints. For global cardinality constraints
this problem is proved to be $\mathcal{NP}$-complete. However, the problem can
be tackled via branch & bound. In many cases, the relaxed optimization problem can be solved with the help of min-cost flow methods in a
suitable network depending on the given database schema.

1   Introduction

The motivation of this study is the entity-relationship model (ERM) introduced
by Chen [1], which is one of the most popular approaches in high-level database
design. It provides a convenient description of objects to be stored in a database.

Let us briefly summarize basic concepts of the ERM. For a complete definition
we refer to [1,11]. Let $\mathcal{E}$ be a non-empty, finite set. In the context of the entity-
relationship approach, the elements of $\mathcal{E}$ are the *entity types*. At moment t,
every entity type $\underline{e}$ is associated with its *domain* $\mathrm{dom}^t(\underline{e})$. The members of the
set $\mathrm{dom}^t(\underline{e})$ are *entities* of type $\underline{e}$. Intuitively, entities can be seen as individuals,
which occur in the target of the database system to be designed. By classifying
them and specifying their significant properties, we obtain the entity types in $\mathcal{E}$,
which are used to model the individuals in their domains.

Whenever entity types $\underline{e}_1, \ldots, \underline{e}_n$ are related to each other, this can be ex-
pressed by a *relationship type* $\underline{r}$ with *components* $\underline{e}_1, \ldots, \underline{e}_n$. By $|\underline{r}| = n$ we
denote the arity of $\underline{r}$. Relationship types model connections between entities. A
relationship of type $\underline{r}$ is defined as the image of $\underline{r}$ under a function assigning
items from $\mathrm{dom}^t(\underline{e}_i)$ to the components $\underline{e}_i$. At moment t, every relationship type
$\underline{r}$ is associated with its *population* of $\underline{r}$. The members of the multiset $\mathrm{pop}^t(\underline{r})$ are
relationships of type $\underline{r}$.

Let $\mathcal{R}$ be a set of relationship types defined on $\mathcal{E}$. Further, put $\mathcal{E}^t = \cup_{\underline{e} \in \mathcal{E}}$
$\mathrm{dom}^t(\underline{e})$ and $\mathcal{R}^t = \cup_{\underline{r} \in \mathcal{R}} \mathrm{pop}^t(\underline{r})$. The pair $\mathfrak{G} = (\mathcal{E}, \mathcal{R})$ is called a *database
schema*, and is used to model the target of the database system. Every pair
$\mathfrak{G}^t = (\mathcal{E}^t, \mathcal{R}^t)$ is a *database* or *instance* of the schema $\mathfrak{G}$. From the graph-
theoretic point of view, both $\mathfrak{G}$ and $\mathfrak{G}^t$ can be considered as hypergraphs, where
the schema $\mathfrak{G}$ is the homomorphic image of each of its databases $\mathfrak{G}^t$.

T. Eiter and K.-D. Schewe (Eds.): FoIKS 2002, LNCS 2284, pp. 268–287, 2002.

Often, database schemas come along with restrictions that limit the possible combinations of entities participating in relationships. These restrictions are expressed by integrity constraints. A database correctly reflects the underlying domain of interest only if it respects these constraints. Thus, we are usually given a database schema $\mathfrak{G}$ together with an application-dependent constraint set Σ declared on it. A database $\mathfrak{G}^t$ is only meaningful if it satisfies all constraints in Σ. We call such a database *legal* for $(\mathfrak{G}, \Sigma)$.

Cardinality constraints are among the most popular integrity constraints used in conceptual design. They impose restrictions on the number of relationships an entity of a given type may be involved in. Cardinality constraints have already been discussed for a longer period, cf. [6]. A general approach towards cardinality constraints was developed in [11]. Combinatorial aspects were considered e.g. in [3,4,10].

In this paper, we study a particular class of cardinality constraints, namely global cardinality constraints. A *global cardinality constraint* $\text{gcard}(\underline{e}) = (a, b)$ specifies that in each admissible database $\mathfrak{G}^t$ of a schema $\mathfrak{G}$ every entity of type $\underline{e}$ participates in at least a and at most b relationships. Note, that (a, b) denotes an *interval* of non-negative integers. That is, a may be chosen from $\mathbb{N}_{\geq 0}$ and b from $\mathbb{N}_{\geq 0} \cup \{\infty\}$ such that $a \leq b$ holds. A database $\mathfrak{G}^t$ *satisfies* this constraint if the degree $\deg_{\mathfrak{G}^t}(e)$ lies in the interval (a, b) for every entity e of type $\underline{e}$ in $\mathfrak{G}^t$.

Originally, cardinality constraints were introduced to restrict the number of relationships of a fixed (single) type, that an entity may be involved in, see [1,9,11]. Global cardinality constraints, on the other hand, are used to bound the total number of relationships an entity participates in. First results on global cardinality constraints were given in [2,11]. Trivially, the empty database is always legal for global cardinality constraints. In practice, however, we are interested in legal databases where each of the domains $\text{dom}^t(\underline{e})$ is non-empty. Such a database is said to be a *sample database* for $(\mathfrak{G}, \Sigma)$.

This paper is organized as follows. Section 2 contains a couple of examples for the use of global cardinality constraints in database design. In Sections 3 and 4, we formulate the problem of finding sample databases in the context of graph theory. Unfortunately, the problem of finding small sample databases turns out to be $\mathcal{NP}$-complete as shown in Section 6. In Section 7, we provide a branch & bound algorithm to generate minimal sample databases for a large variety of schemas. Within this approach, each relaxed subproblem can be solved using min-cost-flow methods.

2 Some Examples

In this section we present some applications of global cardinality constraints to illustrate their use in conceptual design. Our first example deals with partnerships and common research activities. Assume a number of universities and private research institutes is going to organize a catalogue of multilateral activities such as workshops and projects. In addition, the universities offer tutorials in the fields of common interest. Using the entity-relationship approach, we obtain the database schema shown in Fig.1 with the vertices UNIVERSITY, INSTITUTE, WORKSHOP, PROJECT and TUTORIAL. As usual, the entity types, i.e. vertices, are drawn as rectangles, while the relationship types, i.e. edges, are represented by diamonds.

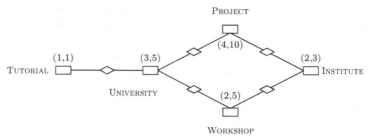

Fig. 1. A database schema for the research network.

Due to financial and time limitations several restrictions have to be considered. Each university shall be involved in at least 3 and at most 5 activities (workshops, projects, tutorials), each research institute in at least 2 and at most 3 activities (workshops or projects). On the other hand, each workshop shall be organized by at least 2 and at most 5 partners (universities or institutes), each tutorial by exactly one university. In each project, at least 4 and at most 10 partners shall be involved in. Note that all these restrictions are global cardinality constraints.

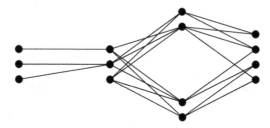

Fig. 2. A sample database of the database schema in Fig.1.

As a second example consider a part of a company-wide database that keeps track of the company's stuff. Some of the employees have special job titles such as manager, secretary, engineer or scientist. This is modelled with the help of is-a relationship types as shown in Fig.3.

The entity types MANAGER, SECRETARY, ENGINEER, SCIENTIST may be regarded as subtypes of the entity type EMPLOYEE. The global cardinality constraint gcard(EMPLOYEE) = (0, 1) says that every employee belongs to at most one of these subtypes. Thus, global cardinality constraints can be used to express exclusion constraints. Alternatively, if every employee in the company belongs to exactly one of the four subtypes, we should use the constraint

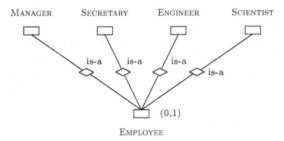

Fig. 3. A database schema with is-a relationships.

gcard(EMPLOYEE) = (1, 1). In this case, a global cardinality constraint may be used to express a closure constraint (cf. [11]), too.

   Finally, consider a part of a schema for a conference database shown in Fig.4, which is used to gather information on scheduled talks. Of course, a submitted paper is only scheduled for presentation if it has been accepted before. Within a session, their shall be between one and three talks. Moreover, the programme committee asks participants to serve as a responder for the talks. Every responder is responsible for exactly one talk.

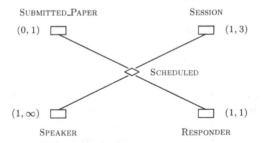

Fig. 4. A database schema to capture information on scheduled talks.

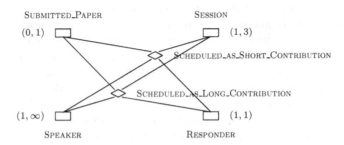

Fig. 5. The database schema in Fig.4 after vertical decomposition.

   Talks may be scheduled as short contributions or as long ones. Due to database requirements, it might be useful to split the population of the relationship type SCHEDULED according to this criterion. In the database schema, we simply replace the old relationship type, i.e. edge, SCHEDULED by two new ones. This transformation is known as vertical decomposition. Fortunately, it is not necessary to modify the global cardinality constraints. Thus, the vertical decomposition is constraint-preserving with respect to global cardinality constraints. Note that this observation does not hold for ordinary cardinality constraints.

3   Sample Databases

The acquisition of the constraint set Σ is a key activity during conceptual modelling. Checking that the specified constraints describe the target of the database system correctly can be quite difficult. Therefore, sample databases are used as test data to support the evaluation of design decisions. Moreover, applications can be tested partly by using sample databases, and sample databases are also an excellent tool during discussions between designers and potential users of the database system.

A constraint set Σ is said to be *consistent* if it admits at least one sample database. Obviously, consistency is a basic requirement for the correctness of chosen constraints. To avoid trivial cases, we now discuss some situations that hinder a constraint set to be consistent. Suppose we have two constraints $\text{gcard}(\underline{e}) = (a_1, b_1)$ and $\text{gcard}(\underline{e}) = (a_2, b_2)$ declared for the same entity type $\underline{e}$. Obviously, we may conclude the new constraint $\text{gcard}(\underline{e}) = (a_1, b_1) \cap (a_2, b_2)$, where $(a_1, b_1) \cap (a_2, b_2)$ denotes the intersection of the two intervals. If the intersection is empty, the given constraints *compete* each other. In this case, every legal database has an empty domain $\text{dom}^t(\underline{e})$, since no entity of type $\underline{e}$ is able to satisfy two competing constraints.

Consider an entity type $\underline{e}$ which does not participate in any relationship type, i.e. an isolated vertex in the database schema. We immediately derive $\text{gcard}(\underline{e}) = (0,0)$. Conversely, suppose we have a constraint $\text{gcard}(\underline{e}) = (0,0)$, that is, entities of type $\underline{e}$ must not participate in any relationship. Consequently, all relationship types containing the entity type $\underline{e}$ are superfluous: Their population will always be empty, and thus they may be removed from the schema. As a result of this transformation, the entity type $\underline{e}$ will become an isolated vertex in the schema.

When declaring global cardinality constraints for a database schema $\mathfrak{G}$, it is reasonable to take the observations above into consideration. We call a set Σ of global cardinality constraints *conflict-free* if Σ does not contain constraints $\text{gcard}(\underline{e}) = (a_1, b_1)$ and $\text{gcard}(\underline{e}) = (a_2, b_2)$ which compete each other, and Σ contains a constraint $\text{gcard}(\underline{e}) = (0,0)$ if and only if the entity type $\underline{e}$ is an isolated vertex in the schema $\mathfrak{G}$. As we shall see later on, conflict-free sets of global cardinality constraints are always consistent, that is, admit sample databases.

For practical purposes, however, it is often not enough to prove the mere existence of sample databases. The partners in our research network in Fig.1, for example, will not be interested in databases with some hundreds of thousands of workshops or tutorials. Due to obvious limitations the number of entities should be bounded from above. Thus, the following question naturally arises: Given a set Σ of global cardinality constraints, what is the smallest sample database.

Knowing such a minimal example provides us a lower bound on the size of the databases to be handled, and thus, enables us to decide whether the semantic information used to describe the modelled real world is well-chosen or not.

4   A Graph-Theoretic Approach to Find Sample Databases

In this section, we are going to develop a graph-theoretic approach to construct sample databases. Let $\mathfrak{G} = (\mathcal{E}, \mathcal{R})$ be a database schema, and Σ be a conflict-free set of global cardinality constraints declared on $\mathfrak{G}$. As mentioned above two (non-competing) constraints $\mathrm{gcard}(\underline{e}) = (a_1, b_1)$ and $\mathrm{gcard}(\underline{e}) = (a_2, b_2)$ may be replaced by a single constraint $\mathrm{gcard}(\underline{e}) = (\max\{a_1, a_2\}, \min\{b_1, b_2\})$. On the other hand, if no constraint is given for some entity type, we have the trivial constraint $\mathrm{gcard}(\underline{e}) = (0, \infty)$ which is always valid.

In practice, we may assume that Σ contains exactly one global cardinality constraint per entity type. This enables us to define two functions $a : \mathcal{E} \to \mathbb{N}_{\geq 0}$ and $b : \mathcal{E} \to \mathbb{N}_{\geq 0} \cup \{\infty\}$, whose values $a(\underline{e})$ and $b(\underline{e})$ are specified by the global cardinality constraint $\mathrm{gcard}(\underline{e}) = (a, b)$ in Σ. We call a and b the *constraint functions* determined by Σ. As mentioned, we require $a(\underline{e}) \leq b(\underline{e})$ for all entity types $\underline{e}$, and $a(\underline{e}) = b(\underline{e}) = 0$ holds just when $\underline{e}$ is isolated.

The problem of constructing a sample database for $(\mathfrak{G}, \Sigma)$ consists in finding a hypergraph $\mathfrak{G}^t = (\mathcal{E}^t, \mathcal{R}^t)$ such that there exists a *surjective* mapping $\phi : \mathcal{E}^t \to \mathcal{E}$ and a mapping $\psi : \mathcal{R}^t \to \mathcal{R}$ with:

(C1) $\psi(r) = \{\phi(e) : e \in r\}$ and $|\psi(r)| = |r|$ hold for all edges $r \in \mathcal{R}^t$,
(C2) the degree $\deg_{\mathfrak{G}^t}(e)$ of e is bounded by $a(\phi(e)) \leq \deg_{\mathfrak{G}^t}(e) \leq b(\phi(e))$ for all vertices $e \in \mathcal{E}^t$.

We call every hypergraph $\mathfrak{G}^t$ satisfying these two conditions an *instance of* $(\mathfrak{G}, a, b)$. By (C1), the schema $\mathfrak{G}$ is the homomorphic image of $\mathfrak{G}^t$ under some homomorphism (ϕ, ψ). Clearly, every instance of $(\mathfrak{G}, a, b)$ corresponds to a sample database for $(\mathfrak{G}, \Sigma)$, and vice versa.

Given an instance $\mathfrak{G}^t$ with associated mappings ϕ and ψ, we put

$$\phi^{-1}(\underline{e}) := \{e \in \mathcal{E}^t : \phi(e) = \underline{e}\} \quad \text{and} \quad x(\underline{e}) := |\phi^{-1}(\underline{e})|,$$
$$\psi^{-1}(\underline{r}) := \{r \in \mathcal{R}^t : \psi(r) = \underline{r}\} \quad \text{and} \quad y(\underline{r}) := |\psi^{-1}(\underline{r})|,$$

for all $\underline{e} \in \mathcal{E}$ and all $\underline{r} \in \mathcal{R}$. From (C2) we derive

$$\sum_{e \in \phi^{-1}(\underline{e})} a(\underline{e}) \leq \sum_{e \in \phi^{-1}(\underline{e})} \deg_{\mathfrak{G}^t}(e) \leq \sum_{e \in \phi^{-1}(\underline{e})} b(\underline{e}),$$

for all $\underline{e} \in \mathcal{E}$, that is,

$$a(\underline{e})x(\underline{e}) \leq \sum_{\underline{r} \in \mathcal{R} : \underline{e} \in \underline{r}} y(\underline{r}) \leq b(\underline{e})x(\underline{e}) \text{ for all } \underline{e} \in \mathcal{E}. \tag{1}$$

Moreover, since ϕ is surjective, we have

$$x(\underline{e}) \geq 1 \text{ for all } \underline{e} \in \mathcal{E}, \tag{2}$$

$$y(\underline{r}) \geq 0 \text{ for all } \underline{r} \in \mathcal{R}, \tag{3}$$

and the functions x and y are both integral. It is worth mentioning that the conditions (1) to (3) are sufficient to ensure the existence of a sample database.

Proposition 1 *Let $(\mathfrak{G}, a, b)$ be given as above, and let $x : \mathcal{E} \to \mathbb{N}_{\geq 0}$ and $y : \mathcal{R} \to \mathbb{N}_{\geq 0}$ be two functions satisfying (1) to (3). Then there exists an instance $\mathfrak{G}^t = (\mathcal{E}^t, \mathcal{R}^t)$ of $(\mathfrak{G}, a, b)$ with some associated homomorphism (ϕ, ψ) such that*

$$x(\underline{e}) = |\phi^{-1}(\underline{e})| \text{ for all } \underline{e} \in \mathcal{E}, \tag{4}$$

$$y(\underline{r}) = |\psi^{-1}(\underline{r})| \text{ for all } \underline{r} \in \mathcal{R}. \tag{5}$$

Proof. For each $\underline{e} \in \mathcal{E}$, choose $\mathrm{dom}^t(\underline{e}) := \{e_1, \ldots, e_{x(\underline{e})}\}$, and let $\mathcal{E}^t := \bigcup_{\underline{e} \in \mathcal{E}} \mathrm{dom}^t(\underline{e})$. Next, we construct the edge set $\mathcal{R}^t$ of the claimed instance $\mathfrak{G}^t$ by the following algorithm in which edges are added step by step.

```
{Initialization}
R^t ← ∅;
for e ∈ E do counter(e) ← 0; od;
{Construction}
for r ∈ R do
     pop^t(r) ← ∅;
     for j ← 1 to y(r) do
        r ← ∅;
        for e ∈ r do
             counter(e) + +;
             if counter(e) > x(e) then counter(e) ← 1; fi;
             r ← r ∪ {e_counter(e)};
        od;
        pop^t(r) ← pop^t(r) ∪ {r};
     od;
     R^t ← R^t ∪ pop^t(r);
od.
```

Clearly, we choose the desired mappings $\phi : \mathcal{E}^t \to \mathcal{E}$ and $\psi : \mathcal{R}^t \to \mathcal{R}$ such that $\phi(e) = \underline{e}$ holds whenever $e \in \mathrm{dom}^t(\underline{e})$, and $\psi(r) = \underline{r}$ holds whenever $r \in \mathrm{pop}^t(\underline{r})$. By construction, $\mathfrak{G}$ is a homomorphic image of $\mathfrak{G}^t = (\mathcal{E}^t, \mathcal{R}^t)$, and (4) and (5) are fulfilled. It remains to verify the second condition (C2). Since the edges are added "cyclically" with respect to the corresponding vertex sets, in each step of the algorithm the degrees of the vertices within a domain $\mathrm{dom}^t(\underline{e})$ differ by at most one. This holds in particular after the final step. Hence, for all $\underline{e} \in \mathcal{E}$ and all $e \in \mathrm{dom}^t(\underline{e})$, we have

$$\left\lfloor \frac{1}{x(\underline{e})} \sum_{\underline{r} \in \mathcal{R}: \underline{e} \in \underline{r}} y(\underline{r}) \right\rfloor \leq \deg_{\mathfrak{G}^t}(e) \leq \left\lceil \frac{1}{x(\underline{e})} \sum_{\underline{r} \in \mathcal{R}: \underline{e} \in \underline{r}} y(\underline{r}) \right\rceil. \tag{6}$$

Thus (1) implies $a(\underline{e}) \leq \deg_{\mathfrak{G}^t}(e) \leq b(\underline{e})$ for all $e \in \mathrm{dom}^t(\underline{e})$. $\qquad\square$

Proposition 1 suggests a two-step approach to construct sample databases. In a first step, we look for suitable functions x and y which determine the sizes of the domains and populations, respectively, in the sample database. Afterwards, in a second step, we arrange the entities to form relationships. By this approach, we immediately derive the following result.

Theorem 2 *Let $\mathfrak{G} = (\mathcal{E}, \mathcal{R})$ be a hypergraph, and $a : \mathcal{E} \to \mathbb{N}_{\geq 0}$, $b : \mathcal{E} \to \mathbb{N}_{\geq 0} \cup \{\infty\}$ be functions satisfying $a(\underline{e}) \leq b(\underline{e})$ for all $\underline{e} \in \mathcal{E}$, and $a(\underline{e}) = b(\underline{e}) = 0$ just when $\underline{e}$ is an isolated vertex. Then there exists an instance $\mathfrak{G}^t$ of $(\mathfrak{G}, a, b)$.*

Proof. By Proposition 1 we only have to verify that there is an integral solution x, y of (1) to (3). For every non-isolated vertex $\underline{e}$, we choose some non-zero integer $\lambda(\underline{e})$ such that $a(\underline{e}) \leq \lambda(\underline{e}) \leq b(\underline{e})$ holds. Afterwards, let

$$\Lambda := \prod_{\underline{e} \in \mathcal{E}:\ \underline{e}\ \text{is not isolated}} \lambda(\underline{e}).$$

Further, we put for all vertices $\underline{e} \in \mathcal{E}$ and all edges $\underline{r} \in \mathcal{R}$

$$x(\underline{e}) := \begin{cases} 1 & \text{if } \underline{e} \text{ is isolated,} \\ \frac{\deg_{\mathfrak{G}}(\underline{e})}{\lambda(\underline{e})} \Lambda & \text{otherwise,} \end{cases}$$

$$y(\underline{r}) := \Lambda.$$

Then

$$a(\underline{e})x(\underline{e}) = \frac{a(\underline{e})\deg_{\mathfrak{G}}(\underline{e})}{\lambda(\underline{e})}\Lambda \leq \deg_{\mathfrak{G}}(\underline{e}) \cdot \Lambda \leq \frac{b(\underline{e})\deg_{\mathfrak{G}}(\underline{e})}{\lambda(\underline{e})}\Lambda = b(\underline{e})x(\underline{e}).$$

Hence (1) holds for all non-isolated vertices. For isolated vertices, however, (1) trivially holds due to the assumption of the theorem. Clearly, the conditions (2) and (3) are satisfied, too, and the functions x, y are integral as desired.   □

5   Consistency and Implication

Recall, that a constraint set Σ is consistent if there exists a sample database $\mathfrak{G}^t$ for $(\mathfrak{G}, \Sigma)$. Due to the correspondence between sample databases and instances of $(\mathfrak{G}, a, b)$, where a and b are the constraint functions determined by Σ, we obtain the following consequence of Theorem 2.

Corollary 3 *Each conflict-free set of global cardinality constraints is consistent.*

In general, the constraints satisfied by a database $\mathfrak{G}^t$ are not independent. A single constraint σ *follows* from a given constraint set Σ if σ holds in every database which is legal for Σ. We also say that Σ *semantically implies* σ, and denote this by $\Sigma \models \sigma$. The following three rules describe trivial implications for global cardinality constraints:

(I1) $\Sigma \models \mathrm{gcard}(\underline{e}) = (0, \infty)$.
(I2) (*Monotonicity.*) If Σ contains $\mathrm{gcard}(\underline{e}) = (a, b)$, and $(a, b) \subset (a', b')$, then $\Sigma \models \mathrm{gcard}(\underline{e}) = (a', b')$.
(I3) (*Closedness under intersection.*) If Σ contains $\mathrm{gcard}(\underline{e}) = (a, b)$ and $\mathrm{gcard}(\underline{e}) = (a', b')$, then $\Sigma \models \mathrm{gcard}(\underline{e}) = (a, b) \cap (a', b')$.

It is well-known that the solution of the implication problem for ordinary cardinality constraints also requires non-trivial rules, see [3]. For global cardinality constraints, however, the rules (I1) to (I3) are not only correct, but form a complete system of implication rules. A set Σ of global cardinality constraints is *closed under implication* if it contains every global cardinality constraint σ which is implied by Σ. The characterization of closed sets within a constraint class is of special interest in database theory.

Theorem 4 *Let Σ be a conflict-free set of global cardinality constraints. Then Σ is closed under implication if and only if it contains every constraint derivable from Σ due to (I1), (I2) or (I3).*

Proof. The correctness of (I1) to (I3) is obvious. Thus it remains to show that the rules are sufficient to characterize closed sets of global cardinality constraints. Consider an entity type $\underline{e}$. Due to (I1) to (I3), the family of intervals (a', b'), such that $\mathrm{gcard}(\underline{e}) = (a', b')$ belongs to Σ, forms an upper ideal in the family of all intervals of non-negative integers (ordered by inclusion), and has a unique minimum, say some interval (a, b). We used this observation already to introduce the constraint functions a and b determined by Σ.

We have to verify that Σ does not imply any constraint $\mathrm{gcard}(\underline{e}) = (a'', b'')$ with $(a, b) \not\subseteq (a'', b'')$. Consider an integer $\delta \in (a, b)$. We are looking for a sample database $\mathfrak{G}^t$ containing an entity e of type $\underline{e}$ participating in exactly δ relationships. That is, we want to have $\deg_{\mathfrak{G}^t}(e) = \delta$. If $\delta = 0$, we take the sample database constructed in Theorem 2 and add a new isolated vertex e to the domain of $\underline{e}$. Since $a = \delta = 0$, the enlarged hypergraph is still a sample database of $(\mathfrak{G}, \Sigma)$. If $\delta \neq 0$, we choose $\lambda(\underline{e}) := \delta$ in the proof of Theorem 2. An easy calculation and (6) prove $\deg_{\mathfrak{G}^t}(e) = \delta$ for every entity e of type $\underline{e}$. $\qquad\square$

6   The Complexity of Constructing Minimal Sample Databases

Sample databases are a useful tool for checking the correctness of a chosen database schema and the constraints declared on it. The examples help to detect missing or extraneous requirements. For practical reasons we are interested in small sample databases. This is of special importance if we intend to use sample databases for the dialogue between designers and potential users of the database system. Thus the question arises whether there exist sample databases of reasonable size. As a measure for the size of a sample database $\mathfrak{G}^t = (\mathcal{E}^t, \mathcal{R}^t)$, we shall use the total number $|\mathcal{E}^t|$ of entities.

Suppose we are given a database schema $\mathfrak{G}$ together with a conflict-free set Σ of global cardinality constraints. As in Section 4, let a and b denote the constraint functions determined by Σ. An *optimal instance* $\mathfrak{G}^t = (\mathcal{E}^t, \mathcal{R}^t)$ of $(\mathfrak{G}, a, b)$ satisfies the additional condition $|\mathcal{E}^t| \to \min$. By Proposition 1 the problem of constructing an optimal instance of $(\mathfrak{G}, a, b)$ reduces to the solution of the discrete linear programming problem (1) to (3) with the objective function

$$\sum_{\underline{e} \in \mathcal{E}} x(\underline{e}) \to \min. \tag{7}$$

We call it the *Global Cardinality Constraints Problem (GCCP)*. Unfortunately, this problem cannot be solved in polynomial time, unless $\mathcal{P} = \mathcal{NP}$. To verify this claim, we have to show that the corresponding decision problem is $\mathcal{NP}$-complete:

GCCP-decision: Given $(\mathfrak{G}, a, b)$ and a positive integer L, do there exist integral functions x, y such that (1) to (3) hold as well as

$$\sum_{\underline{e} \in \mathcal{E}} x(\underline{e}) \le L. \tag{8}$$

Theorem 5 *The Global Cardinality Constraints Decision Problem (GCCP-decision) is $\mathcal{NP}$-complete.*

Proof. Clearly, the problem belongs to $\mathcal{NP}$, since for guessed x and y, the inequalities (1) to (3) and (8) can be tested in polynomial time. To prove the $\mathcal{NP}$-completeness we proceed by reduction from Subset Sum to Restricted Subset Sum to GCCP-decision. Let us recall the Subset Sum Problem which is well-known to be $\mathcal{NP}$-complete (cf. [7, p.137]):

Subset Sum: Given positive integers $s_1, \ldots, s_n, T$, does there exist a 0-1 vector $\boldsymbol{x}$ such that $\sum_{j=1}^{n} s_j x_j = T$?

Obviously, we may suppose that $s_j \le T$ for all j without disturbing the $\mathcal{NP}$-completeness. As an intermediate problem we investigate the following one:

Restricted Subset Sum: Given positive integers $c_1, \ldots, c_n, K$ such that $\max\{c_1, \ldots, c_n\} \le 2\min\{c_1, \ldots, c_n\}$, does there exist a vector $\boldsymbol{z} \in \mathbb{N}_{\ge 1}^n$ such that $\sum_{j=1}^{n} c_j z_j = K$?

First of all, note that in the proof of the $\mathcal{NP}$-completeness of Restricted Subset Sum we may replace the condition $\boldsymbol{z} \in \mathbb{N}_{\ge 1}^n$ by the condition $\boldsymbol{z} \in \mathbb{N}_{\ge 0}^n$ since, for $\boldsymbol{z} \in \mathbb{N}_{\ge 1}^n$, we have $\sum_{j=1}^{n} c_j z_j = K$ if and only if $\sum_{j=1}^{n} c_j(z_j - 1) = K - \sum_{j=1}^{n} c_j$ holds. Now we show that Subset Sum polynomially reduces to Restricted Subset Sum. Given an instance $(s_1, \ldots, s_n, T)$ of Subset Sum (with $s_j \le T$ for all j) we define an instance $(c_1, \ldots, c_{2n}, K)$ of Restricted Subset Sum by

$$M' := 2n(n+1)T,$$

$$M := 2^m \text{ where } m \text{ is the smallest integer with } 2^m > M',$$

$$K := nM^{n+1} + \sum_{j=1}^{n} M^j + T = nM^{n+1} + \frac{M^{n+1} - M}{M - 1} + T,$$

$$c_j := \begin{cases} M^{n+1} + M^j + s_j & \text{if } 1 \le j \le n, \\ M^{n+1} + M^{j-n} & \text{if } n < j \le 2n. \end{cases}$$

This construction is motivated by a related construction presented e.g. in [8, ch.15.7]. It should be mentioned, that all the numbers above can be computed in polynomial time. In order to see this easier, we replaced M' by M, since M^{n+1} can then be calculated in a trivial way if the computations are carried out in binary code. Note that

$$\frac{\max\{c_1, \ldots, c_{2n}\}}{\min\{c_1, \ldots, c_{2n}\}} < \frac{M^{n+1} + M^n + T}{M^{n+1}} = 1 + \frac{1}{M} + \frac{T}{M^{n+1}} \le 2.$$

Now, if $(s_1, \ldots, s_n, T)$ is feasible with corresponding vector $\boldsymbol{x}$, then we may define

$$z_j := \begin{cases} x_j & \text{if } 1 \le j \le n, \\ 1 - x_{j-n} & \text{if } n < j \le 2n. \end{cases}$$

It is easy to see that the constructed tuple $(c_1, \ldots, c_{2n}, K)$ is feasible with corresponding vector $\boldsymbol{z}$. Conversely, let the constructed tuple $(c_1, \ldots, c_{2n}, K)$ from Restricted Subset Sum be feasible with corresponding vector $\boldsymbol{z}$. Then we have

$$\left(\sum_{j=1}^{2n} z_j\right) M^{n+1} + \sum_{j=1}^{n} (z_j + z_{n+j}) M^j + \sum_{j=1}^{n} s_j z_j = n M^{n+1} + \sum_{j=1}^{n} M^j + T. \quad (9)$$

Since $\sum_{j=1}^{2n} c_j z_j = K$, we derive for all j

$$z_j \le \frac{K}{c_j} < \frac{1}{M^{n+1}} \left(n M^{n+1} + \sum_{j=1}^{n} M^j + T\right) < n + 1 < \frac{M}{2nT}.$$

Hence,

$$\sum_{j=1}^{2n} z_j < 2n \frac{M}{2nT} < M,$$

$$z_j + z_{n+j} < 2 \frac{M}{2nT} < M \text{ for all } j,$$

and, as $s_j \le T$ for all j,

$$\sum_{j=1}^{n} s_j z_j < \frac{nTM}{2nT} < M,$$

that is, all coefficients of the LHS of (9) are smaller than M. Comparison of coefficients yields

$$\sum_{j=1}^{2n} z_j = n,$$

$$z_j + z_{n+j} = 1 \text{ for all } j,$$

$$\sum_{j=1}^{n} s_j z_j = T.$$

Thus $z_j \in \{0,1\}$ for all j. The vector z shows that the instance $(s_1, \ldots, s_n, T)$ is feasible.

It remains to prove that Restricted Subset Sum polynomially reduces to GCCP-decision. Given an instance $(c_1, \ldots, c_n, K)$ of Restricted Subset Sum we define an instance $(\mathfrak{G}, a, b, L)$ of GCCP-decision as follows: Let

$$\mathcal{E} := \{\underline{e}_1, \ldots, \underline{e}_n, \underline{e}_{n+1}\},$$
$$\mathcal{R} := \{\{\underline{e}_1, \underline{e}_{n+1}\}, \ldots, \{\underline{e}_n, \underline{e}_{n+1}\}\},$$
$$a(\underline{e}_j) := b(\underline{e}_j) := c_j, \ j = 1, \ldots, n,$$
$$a(\underline{e}_{n+1}) := b(\underline{e}_{n+1}) := K,$$
$$L := \left\lceil \frac{K}{\min\{c_1, \ldots, c_n\}} \right\rceil + 1.$$

Here the hypergraph $\mathfrak{G} = (\mathcal{E}, \mathcal{R})$ is a star with central vertex $\underline{e}_{n+1}$. Clearly, this instance can be constructed in polynomial time. Let $(c_1, \ldots, c_n, K)$ be feasible with corresponding vector $z \in \mathbb{N}_{\geq 1}^n$. Then we define

$$x(\underline{e}_j) := z_j, \ j = 1, \ldots, n,$$
$$x(\underline{e}_{n+1}) := 1,$$
$$y(\{\underline{e}_j, \underline{e}_{n+1}\}) := c_j z_j, \ j = 1, \ldots, n.$$

It is easy to see that (1) to (3) are satisfied and, with $\mu := \min\{c_1, \ldots, c_n\}$,

$$\sum_{j=1}^{n+1} x(\underline{e}_j) = \sum_{j=1}^{n} z_j + 1 \leq \sum_{j=1}^{n} \frac{c_j z_j}{\mu} + 1 = \frac{K}{\mu} + 1 \leq L,$$

i.e., $(\mathfrak{G}, a, b, L)$ is feasible. Conversely, let the constructed $(\mathfrak{G}, a, b, L)$ be feasible with corresponding functions $x : \mathcal{E} \to \mathbb{N}_{\geq 0}$ and $y : \mathcal{R} \to \mathbb{N}_{\geq 0}$. Assume that $x(\underline{e}_{n+1}) > 1$ holds. Since

$$\sum_{j=1}^{n} c_j x(\underline{e}_j) = \sum_{j=1}^{n} y(\{\underline{e}_j, \underline{e}_{n+1}\}) = K x(\underline{e}_{n+1}),$$

we have, with the abbreviation $\nu := \max\{c_1, \ldots, c_n\}$,

$$\sum_{j=1}^{n} x(\underline{e}_j) \geq \sum_{j=1}^{n} \frac{c_j x(\underline{e}_j)}{\nu} = \frac{K x(\underline{e}_{n+1})}{\nu} \geq \frac{2K}{\nu} \geq \frac{K}{\mu}.$$

It follows that

$$\sum_{j=1}^{n+1} x(\underline{e}_j) \geq \left\lceil \frac{K}{\mu} \right\rceil + 2 = L + 1,$$

which gives a contradiction. Consequently, we have $x(\underline{e}_{n+1}) = 1$, and therefore

$$\sum_{j=1}^{n} c_j y(\{\underline{e}_j, \underline{e}_{n+1}\}) = K.$$

The vector $\boldsymbol{z}$ with $z_j := y(\{\underline{e}_j, \underline{e}_{n+1}\})$ shows that $(c_1, \ldots, c_n, K)$ is feasible.   □

By the preceding result, it is $\mathcal{NP}$-complete to decide whether there exists a sample database with less than L entities. Note, that due to the instance of GCCP-decision constructed in the proof of Theorem 5, it is even $\mathcal{NP}$-complete to decide the existence of an Armstrong database for $(\mathfrak{G}, \Sigma)$ with less than L entities.

7   Exact Solution via Branch & Bound

Within this section, we restrict ourselves to database schemas containing only binary relationship types, i.e., to database schemas $\mathfrak{G}$ which are graphs. Of course, the GCCP can be solved via any solver for integer linear programming problems (ILP). But in many cases, we can drastically improve the efficiency of constructing minimal sample databases. This is due to the nice structure of the system of inequalities (1) to (3).

If an entity type $\underline{e}$ is an isolated vertex in the database schema, then its domain $\operatorname{dom}^t(\underline{e})$ will be of size 1 in every minimal sample database. Thus, the best we can do for isolated vertices, is to choose $x(\underline{e}) = 1$. Clearly, this has no influence on the choice of the x-values for the other entity types. For the sake of simplicity, we shall assume that the database schema $\mathfrak{G}$ does not contain isolated vertices. This gives us $b(\underline{e}) > 0$ for all entity types $\underline{e} \in \mathcal{E}$.

As pointed out in Section 4, the first step to construct a sample database consists in finding *integral* functions x, y satisfying the conditions (1) to (3). Under some weak assumptions, however, it suffices to force the function x to be integral.

Theorem 6 *Let $(\mathfrak{G}, a, b)$ be given such that every cycle of odd length in the graph $\mathfrak{G}$ contains at least one vertex $\underline{e}$ with $a(\underline{e}) < b(\underline{e})$. Let x, y be a solution of (1) to (3) and let x be integral. Then there exists an integral function y' such that x, y' is a solution of (1) to (3), too.*

Proof. First let $\mathfrak{G}$ be bipartite. For fixed x, the system (1), (3) has the form

$$\begin{pmatrix} A \\ -A \end{pmatrix} \boldsymbol{y} \leq \boldsymbol{c}, \tag{10}$$

$$\boldsymbol{y} \geq \boldsymbol{0}, \tag{11}$$

where $\boldsymbol{c}$ is an integral vector and A is the incidence matrix of $\mathfrak{G}$. By the supposition, the polytope described by (10), (11) is non-empty. For $\boldsymbol{y}'$ (the vector with components $y'(\underline{r})$, $\underline{r} \in \mathcal{R}$) we may take any extremal point of this polytope since A is well-known to be totally unimodular and hence the polytope is integral.

If $\mathfrak{G}$ is not bipartite we conclude as follows. The idea is to construct a bipartite graph $\mathfrak{G}_B = (\mathcal{E}_1 \cup \mathcal{E}_2, \mathcal{R}_B)$ whose color classes $\mathcal{E}_1, \mathcal{E}_2$ are copies of $\mathcal{E}$ and where $\{\underline{v}_1, \underline{w}_2\}$ and $\{\underline{w}_1, \underline{v}_2\}$ are edges in $\mathcal{R}_B$ whenever $\{\underline{v}, \underline{w}\}$ is an edge in $\mathcal{R}$. Here $\underline{v}_1, \underline{w}_1 \in \mathcal{E}_1$ and $\underline{v}_2, \underline{w}_2 \in \mathcal{E}_2$ are the corresponding copies of original vertices $\underline{v}$ and $\underline{w}$.

Next we put $y_B(\{\underline{v}_1, \underline{w}_2\}) := y_B(\{\underline{w}_1, \underline{v}_2\}) := y(\{\underline{v}, \underline{w}\})$ for every edge $\{\underline{v}, \underline{w}\} \in \mathcal{R}$. For every $\underline{e} \in \mathcal{E}$, we trivially derive

$$a(\underline{e})x(\underline{e}) \leq \sum_{\underline{r}_B \in \mathcal{R}_B : \underline{e}_1 \in \underline{r}_B} y_B(\underline{r}_B) \leq b(\underline{e})x(\underline{e}),$$

$$a(\underline{e})x(\underline{e}) \leq \sum_{\underline{r}_B \in \mathcal{R}_B : \underline{e}_2 \in \underline{r}_B} y_B(\underline{r}_B) \leq b(\underline{e})x(\underline{e}),$$

for the copies $\underline{e}_1$ and $\underline{e}_2$ of $\underline{e}$, as well as $y_B(\underline{r}_B) \geq 0$ for all $\underline{r}_B \in \mathcal{R}_B$.

Due to our investigation for bipartite graphs above, there exists some integral function y'_B satisfying these inequalities, too. Consequently, the inequalities (1) and (3) are satisfied by the intermediate function y'' which is given by

$$y''(\{\underline{v}, \underline{w}\}) := \frac{1}{2}(y'_B(\{\underline{v}_1, \underline{w}_2\}) + y'_B(\{\underline{w}_1, \underline{v}_2\})) \text{ for all } \{\underline{v}, \underline{w}\} \in \mathcal{R}.$$

Finally, a slight modification makes the function y'' integral. Let $\mathfrak{G}_{mod} = (\mathcal{E}, \mathcal{R}_{mod})$ be the subgraph of $\mathfrak{G}$ whose edge set is

$$\mathcal{R}_{mod} := \{\underline{r} \in \mathcal{R} : y''(\underline{r}) \text{ is not integral (but then half-integral)}\}.$$

In a standard way, we partition the edge set of $\mathfrak{G}_{mod}$ into vertex-disjoint closed walks and into some paths (such that every vertex occurs at most once as an end vertex of a path). Now we make y'' integral, that is, modify y'' by adding and substracting $\frac{1}{2}$ on the edges in $\mathcal{R}_{mod}$. Along the paths and along the closed walks of even length we do this in any alternating way. This procedure does not violate (1) or (3), since the lower and upper bounds in (1) are integral.

Afterwards we handle the closed walks $(\underline{e}_1, \ldots, \underline{e}_k, \underline{e}_1)$ of odd length. For them the situation is slightly more involved. Due to our assumption, we may suppose that $\underline{e}_1$ is a vertex with $a(\underline{e}_1) < b(\underline{e}_1)$. Again we proceed in an alternating way, but we have to decide for the first edge $\{\underline{e}_1, \underline{e}_2\}$ on the closed walk whether to start with adding or substracting $\frac{1}{2}$. The difficulty is that the integral sum $\sum_{\underline{e}_1 \in \underline{r}} y''(\underline{r})$ increases or decreases by one, since this time the y''-values for both edges incident with $\underline{e}_1$ are revised in the same way. In fact, we add $\frac{1}{2}$ on the edge $\{\underline{e}_1, \underline{e}_2\}$ if and only if $\sum_{\underline{e}_1 \in \underline{r}} y''(\underline{r}) < x(\underline{e}_1)b(\underline{e}_1)$. Due to the integrality of the constraint functions a and b, conditions (1) and (3) will not be violated: If $\sum_{\underline{e}_1 \in \underline{r}} y''(\underline{r}) = x(\underline{e}_1)b(\underline{e}_1)$ holds, our assumption $a(\underline{e}_1) < b(\underline{e}_1)$ implies $\sum_{\underline{e}_1 \in \underline{r}} y''(\underline{r}) > x(\underline{e}_1)a(\underline{e}_1)$. In this case, we substract $\frac{1}{2}$ on both edges incident with $\underline{e}_1$.

As a result of this procedure we obtain a revised function y' which is integral and still satisfies (1) and (3).   □

The proof above shows that Theorem 6 remains true for many situations, where the database schema $\mathfrak{G}$ does not meet the assumption of Theorem 6. It suffices to ensure a decomposition of $\mathfrak{G}_{mod}$ into closed walks and paths such that every closed walk of odd length contains some vertex $\underline{e}_1$ with $a(\underline{e}_1) < b(\underline{e}_1)$. Though it is rather easy to find further classes of graphs admitting such a decomposition, we shall not proceed this discussion here due to the lack of space.

Within this paper, we rather concentrate on the algorithmic aspects of constructing y' (respectively y'_B and hence y''). Following the standard branch & bound approach for ILP (cf. [7, p.356]), we solve the LP-relaxation of each occurring subproblem and branch always at some variable $x(\underline{e})$ where $\xi := x(\underline{e})$ is not integral. This raises two new subproblems with the additional inequalities

$$x(\underline{e}) \leq \lfloor \xi \rfloor \text{ or } x(\underline{e}) \geq \lfloor \xi \rfloor + 1, \tag{12}$$

respectively. Thus the LP-relaxation of each occurring subproblem has the following form:

We are given constraint functions $a : \mathcal{E} \rightarrow \mathbb{N}_{\geq 0}$, $b : \mathcal{E} \rightarrow \mathbb{N}_{\geq 1}$, and two auxiliary functions $\alpha, \beta : \mathcal{E} \rightarrow \mathbb{N}_{\geq 1}$ with $\alpha(\underline{e}) \leq \beta(\underline{e})$ for all $\underline{e} \in \mathcal{E}$. The problem is to find functions $x : \mathcal{E} \rightarrow \mathbb{R}$ and $y : \mathcal{R} \rightarrow \mathbb{R}$ satisfying (1), (3), (7), and additional inequalities

$$\alpha(\underline{e}) \leq x(\underline{e}) \leq \beta(\underline{e}) \text{ for all } \underline{e} \in \mathcal{E}. \tag{13}$$

We call this problem the *Relaxed Global Cardinality Constraints Problem (RGCCP)*. A major observation is the fact that RGCCP can be solved efficiently via a min-cost-flow algorithm. Moreover, it should be emphasized that RGCCP provides a new, interesting example where at each node of the branch & bound tree there is a *nicely solvable subproblem* and where the variables are *not only binary*.

First we discuss our approach for a bipartite database schema $\mathfrak{G} = (\mathcal{E}, \mathcal{R})$. Let $\mathcal{E}_1$ and $\mathcal{E}_2$ be its color classes. By orienting every edge $\underline{r} = \{\underline{e}_1, \underline{e}_2\}$ in $\mathfrak{G}$ from $\underline{e}_1 \in \mathcal{E}_1$ to $\underline{e}_2 \in \mathcal{E}_2$ we obtain a digraph $(\mathcal{E}, \mathcal{A})$ with arcs $\underline{a}_r = (\underline{e}_1, \underline{e}_2) \in \mathcal{A}$.

Starting with this digraph, we construct a network $\mathfrak{N} = (\mathcal{E}_N, \mathcal{A}_N; \underline{q}, \underline{s}; \ell, u, c)$. Here $\underline{q}$ and $\underline{s}$ are two new vertices, known as the *source* and the *sink* of the network. Thus we have $\mathcal{E}_N = \mathcal{E} \cup \{\underline{q}, \underline{s}\}$. Afterwards we add two new (parallel) arcs $\underline{a}'_e$ and $\underline{a}''_e$ for every vertex $\underline{e} \in \mathcal{E}$. In fact, we choose

$$\underline{a}'_e := \underline{a}''_e := \begin{cases} (\underline{q}, \underline{e}) & \text{if } \underline{e} \in \mathcal{E}_1, \\ (\underline{e}, \underline{s}) & \text{if } \underline{e} \in \mathcal{E}_2. \end{cases}$$

The set of all the edges $\underline{a}'_e$ is denoted by $\mathcal{A}'$, and the set of all arc $\underline{a}''_e$ by $\mathcal{A}''$. With that, the arcs of the network form the multi-set $\mathcal{A}_N = \mathcal{A} \cup \mathcal{A}' \cup \mathcal{A}''$.

Furthermore, we define a *lower* and an *upper capacity function* ℓ and u, respectively, on $\mathcal{A}_N$ by

$$\ell(\underline{a}) := \begin{cases} a(\underline{e})\alpha(\underline{e}) & \text{if } \underline{a} = \underline{a}'_e \in \mathcal{A}', \\ 0 & \text{if } \underline{a} \in \mathcal{A}'' \text{ or } \underline{a} \in \mathcal{A}, \end{cases}$$

$$u(\underline{a}) := \begin{cases} b(\underline{e})\alpha(\underline{e}) & \text{if } \underline{a} = \underline{a}'_{\underline{e}} \in \mathcal{A}', \\ b(\underline{e})(\beta(\underline{e}) - \alpha(\underline{e})) & \text{if } \underline{a} = \underline{a}''_{\underline{e}} \in \mathcal{A}'', \\ \infty & \text{if } \underline{a} \in \mathcal{A}. \end{cases}$$

Finally, c is the *cost function* defined on $\mathcal{A}_N$ by

$$c(\underline{a}) := \begin{cases} 0 & \text{if } \underline{a} \in \mathcal{A}', \\ \frac{1}{b(\underline{e})} & \text{if } \underline{a} = \underline{a}''_{\underline{e}} \in \mathcal{A}'', \\ 0 & \text{if } \underline{a} \in \mathcal{A}. \end{cases}$$

For an arc $\underline{a} = (\underline{v}, \underline{w})$ let $\underline{a}^- := \underline{v}$ and $\underline{a}^+ := \underline{w}$ be its initial and its terminal vertex. A *flow* on the network $\mathfrak{N}$ is a function $f : \mathcal{A}_N \to \mathbb{R}$ such that

$$\sum_{\underline{a}^+ = \underline{e}} f(\underline{a}) = \sum_{\underline{a}^\square = \underline{e}} f(\underline{a}) \text{ for all } \underline{e} \in \mathcal{E}, \text{ and } \sum_{\underline{a}^\square = \underline{q}} f(\underline{a}) = \sum_{\underline{a}^+ = \underline{s}} f(\underline{a}).$$

We call the flow *admissible* if

$$\ell(\underline{a}) \le f(\underline{a}) \le u(\underline{a}) \text{ for all } \underline{a} \in \mathcal{A}_N$$

holds, too. The *cost of the flow* f is defined by

$$c(f) := \sum_{\underline{a} \in \mathcal{A}_N} c(\underline{a}) f(\underline{a}),$$

which equals $\sum_{\underline{a} \in \mathcal{A}^\square} c(\underline{a}) f(\underline{a})$ for our network $\mathfrak{N}$. We obtain a solution of the Relaxed Global Cardinality Constraints Problem via the following theorem and by applying any min-cost-flow algorithm.

Theorem 7 *Let $\mathfrak{G}$ be bipartite, and let f^* be an admissible flow of minimum cost on the corresponding network $\mathfrak{N}$. Then an optimal solution of RGCCP is given by*

$$x^*(\underline{e}) := \alpha(\underline{e}) + \frac{1}{b(\underline{e})} f^*(\underline{a}''_{\underline{e}}) \text{ for all } \underline{e} \in \mathcal{E},$$

$$y^*(\underline{r}) := f^*(\underline{a}_{\underline{r}}) \text{ for all } \underline{r} \in \mathcal{R},$$

where $\underline{a}_{\underline{r}} \in \mathcal{A}$ is the arc obtained from the edge $\underline{r}$.

If there is no admissible flow on the network $\mathfrak{N}$, then there is no admissible solution of RGCCP.

Proof. It is an easy exercise to verify that x^*, y^* is an admissible solution of RGCCP. As an example, we prove only the first inequality in (1) for some vertex $\underline{e} \in \mathcal{E}_1$. We have

$$\sum_{\underline{r} \in \mathcal{R}: \underline{e} \in \underline{r}} y^*(\underline{r}) = \sum_{\underline{a}_{\underline{r}}^\square = \underline{e}} f^*(\underline{a}_{\underline{r}}) = \sum_{\underline{a}^\square = \underline{e}} f^*(\underline{a}) = \sum_{\underline{a}^+ = \underline{e}} f^*(\underline{a}) = f^*(\underline{a}'_{\underline{e}}) + f^*(\underline{a}''_{\underline{e}})$$

$$\geq a(\underline{e})\alpha(\underline{e}) + b(\underline{e})(x^*(\underline{e}) - \alpha(\underline{e}))$$
$$\geq a(\underline{e})\alpha(\underline{e}) + a(\underline{e})(x^*(\underline{e}) - \alpha(\underline{e})) = a(\underline{e})x^*(\underline{e}).$$

Note that the value of the objective function of RGCCP, see (7), equals

$$\sum_{\underline{e} \in \mathcal{E}} x^*(\underline{e}) = \sum_{\underline{e} \in \mathcal{E}} \alpha(\underline{e}) + \sum_{\underline{e} \in \mathcal{E}} \frac{1}{b(\underline{e})} f^*(\underline{a}''_{\underline{e}}) = \sum_{\underline{e} \in \mathcal{E}} \alpha(\underline{e}) + c(f^*). \qquad (14)$$

To show that x^*, y^* is an optimal solution of RGCCP we shall construct for an arbitrary admissible solution x, y of RGCCP an admissible flow f such that its cost satisfies

$$c(f) \leq \sum_{\underline{e} \in \mathcal{E}} (x(\underline{e}) - \alpha(\underline{e})). \qquad (15)$$

Since f^* is a flow of minimum cost we conclude by (14) and (15)

$$\sum_{\underline{e} \in \mathcal{E}} x^*(\underline{e}) - \sum_{\underline{e} \in \mathcal{E}} \alpha(\underline{e}) = c(f^*) \leq c(f) \leq \sum_{\underline{e} \in \mathcal{E}} x(\underline{e}) - \sum_{\underline{e} \in \mathcal{E}} \alpha(\underline{e}),$$

that is,

$$\sum_{\underline{e} \in \mathcal{E}} x^*(\underline{e}) \leq \sum_{\underline{e} \in \mathcal{E}} x(\underline{e}).$$

Moreover, this construction then verifies that there is no admissible solution of RGCCP if there is no admissible flow on the network $\mathfrak{N}$.

It remains to present the claimed construction of the admissible flow f: Consider the auxiliary function

$$h(\underline{e}) := \sum_{\underline{r} \in \mathcal{R}: \underline{e} \in \underline{r}} y(\underline{r}) - a(\underline{e})(x(\underline{e}) - \alpha(\underline{e})) - b(\underline{e})\alpha(\underline{e}).$$

We put

$$f(\underline{a}) := \begin{cases} b(\underline{e})\alpha(\underline{e}) + \min\{0, h(\underline{e})\} & \text{if } \underline{a} = \underline{a}_{\underline{e}} \in \mathcal{A}', \\ a(\underline{e})(x(\underline{e}) - \alpha(\underline{e})) + \max\{0, h(\underline{e})\} & \text{if } \underline{a} = \underline{a}_{\underline{e}} \in \mathcal{A}'', \\ y(\underline{r}) & \text{if } \underline{a} = \underline{a}_{\underline{r}} \in \mathcal{A}. \end{cases}$$

For every vertex $\underline{e} \in \mathcal{E}_1$ we then have

$$\sum_{\underline{a}^+ = \underline{e}} f(\underline{a}) - \sum_{\underline{a}^\circ = \underline{e}} f(\underline{a}) =$$

$$= b(\underline{e})\alpha(\underline{e}) + \min\{0, h(\underline{e})\} + a(\underline{e})(x(\underline{e}) - \alpha(\underline{e})) + \max\{0, h(\underline{e})\} - \sum_{\underline{r} \in \mathcal{R}: \underline{e} \in \underline{r}} y(\underline{r})$$

$$= b(\underline{e})\alpha(\underline{e}) + a(\underline{e})(x(\underline{e}) - \alpha(\underline{e})) + h(\underline{e}) - \sum_{\underline{r} \in \mathcal{R}: \underline{e} \in \underline{r}} y(\underline{r})$$

$$= 0,$$

and analogously this holds for vertices $\underline{e} \in \mathcal{E}_2$. Hence f is indeed a flow on the network. The inequality $\ell(\underline{a}) \leq f(\underline{a}) \leq u(\underline{a})$ is trivially satisfied for the arcs $\underline{a} \in \mathcal{A}$. For arcs $\underline{a}'_{\underline{e}} \in \mathcal{A}'$ we have

$$
\begin{aligned}
\ell(\underline{a}'_{\underline{e}}) &= a(\underline{e})\alpha(\underline{e}) = \min\{b(\underline{e})\alpha(\underline{e}), a(\underline{e})\alpha(\underline{e})\} \\
&= \min\{b(\underline{e})\alpha(\underline{e}), a(\underline{e})(x(\underline{e}) - x(\underline{e}) + \alpha(\underline{e}))\} \\
&\leq \min\{b(\underline{e})\alpha(\underline{e}), \sum_{\underline{r} \in \mathcal{R}: \underline{e} \in \underline{r}} y(\underline{r}) - a(\underline{e})(x(\underline{e}) - \alpha(\underline{e}))\} = f(\underline{a}'_{\underline{e}}) \\
&\leq b(\underline{e})\alpha(\underline{e}) = u(\underline{a}'_{\underline{e}}),
\end{aligned}
$$

and for arcs $\underline{a}''_{\underline{e}} \in \mathcal{A}''$ we have

$$
\begin{aligned}
\ell(\underline{a}''_{\underline{e}}) &= 0 \leq a(\underline{e})(x(\underline{e}) - \alpha(\underline{e})) \\
&\leq \max\{a(\underline{e})(x(\underline{e}) - \alpha(\underline{e})), \sum_{\underline{r} \in \mathcal{R}: \underline{e} \in \underline{r}} y(\underline{r}) - b(\underline{e})\alpha(\underline{e})\} = f(\underline{a}''_{\underline{e}}) \\
&\leq \max\{b(\underline{e})(\beta(\underline{e}) - \alpha(\underline{e})), b(\underline{e})(x(\underline{e}) - \alpha(\underline{e}))\} \\
&= b(\underline{e})(\beta(\underline{e}) - \alpha(\underline{e})) = u(\underline{a}''_{\underline{e}}).
\end{aligned}
$$

Hence f is an admissible flow. Finally, the cost of f is given by

$$
\begin{aligned}
c(f) &= \sum_{\underline{a}''_{\underline{e}} \in \mathcal{A}''} c(\underline{a}''_{\underline{e}}) f(\underline{a}''_{\underline{e}}) = \sum_{\underline{e} \in \mathcal{E}} \frac{1}{b(\underline{e})}(a(\underline{e})(x(\underline{e}) - \alpha(\underline{e})) + \max\{0, h(\underline{e})\}) \\
&\leq \sum_{\underline{e} \in \mathcal{E}} \frac{1}{b(\underline{e})} \max\{b(\underline{e})(x(\underline{e}) - \alpha(\underline{e})), \sum_{\underline{r} \in \mathcal{R}: \underline{e} \in \underline{r}} y(\underline{r}) - b(\underline{e})\alpha(\underline{e})\} \\
&\leq \sum_{\underline{e} \in \mathcal{E}} \max\{(x(\underline{e}) - \alpha(\underline{e})), (x(\underline{e}) - \alpha(\underline{e}))\} = \sum_{\underline{e} \in \mathcal{E}} (x(\underline{e}) - \alpha(\underline{e})),
\end{aligned}
$$

i.e., (15) holds, and the proof is complete. $\square$

Since all capacities are integral, standard min-cost-flow algorithms yield integral optimal flows. Therefore, the function y^* constructed in Theorem 7 is always integral. Only the function x^* need not be integral, and this just motivates the branching into subproblems as described in (12). Since the investigation obviously may be restricted to a polytope (that is, a bounded polyhedron), the finiteness of the branch & bound algorithm is ensured, and our approach terminates with some integral function x^*.

Now we study the case where the database schema $\mathfrak{S}$ is not necessarily bipartite, but meets the assumption of Theorem 6. As in the proof of Theorem 6 we associate with $\mathfrak{S}$ the bipartite graph $\mathfrak{S}_B = (\mathcal{E}_1 \cup \mathcal{E}_2, \mathcal{R}_B)$ whose color classes $\mathcal{E}_1, \mathcal{E}_2$ are copies of $\mathcal{E}$ and where the edges $\{\underline{v}_1, \underline{w}_2\}$ and $\{\underline{w}_1, \underline{v}_2\}$ are in $\mathcal{R}_B$ whenever the edge $\{\underline{v}, \underline{w}\}$ is in $\mathcal{R}$. Moreover, we extend the constraint function a to a new function a_B defined on the set $\mathcal{E}_1 \cup \mathcal{E}_2$ by setting

$$
a_B(\underline{e}_1) := a_B(\underline{e}_2) := a_B(\underline{e})
$$

where $\underline{e}_1, \underline{e}_2$ are the two copies of $\underline{e}$. Similarly, the functions b, α and β are extended to functions b_B, α_B and β_B. The following proposition is obvious.

Proposition 8 *(i) If x_B, y_B is an admissible solution of RGCCP on $\mathfrak{G}_B$, then the functions x, y defined by*

$$x(\underline{e}) := \tfrac{1}{2}(x_B(\underline{e}_1) + x_B(\underline{e}_2)) \text{ for all } \underline{e} \in \mathcal{E},$$
$$y(\{\underline{v}, \underline{w}\}) := \tfrac{1}{2}(y_B(\{\underline{v}_1, \underline{w}_2\}) + y_B(\{\underline{w}_1, \underline{v}_2\})) \text{ for all } \{\underline{v}, \underline{w}\} \in \mathcal{R},$$

form an admissible solution of RGCCP on $\mathfrak{G}$.

(ii) If x, y is an admissible solution of RGCCP on $\mathfrak{G}$, then the functions x_B, y_B defined by

$$x_B(\underline{e}_1) := x_B(\underline{e}_2) := x(\underline{e}) \text{ for all } \underline{e} \in \mathcal{E},$$
$$y_B(\{\underline{v}_1, \underline{w}_2\}) := y_B(\{\underline{w}_1, \underline{v}_2\}) := y(\{\underline{v}, \underline{w}\}) \text{ for all } \{\underline{v}, \underline{w}\} \in \mathcal{R},$$

form an admissible solution of RGCCP on $\mathfrak{G}_B$.

Note that we have

$$2\sum_{\underline{e} \in \mathcal{E}} x(\underline{e}) = \sum_{\underline{e}_1 \in \mathcal{E}_1} x_B(\underline{e}_1) + \sum_{\underline{e}_2 \in \mathcal{E}_2} x_B(\underline{e}_2)$$

in this correspondence, and thus optimal solutions of RGCCP on $\mathfrak{G}$ and on $\mathfrak{G}_B$ can be bijectively mapped onto each other due to the formulas in Proposition 8.

Consequently, we may use the approach described for bipartite graphs (and verified by Theorem 7) to solve RGCCP on $\mathfrak{G}$, too. The branch & bound algorithm leads to an optimal solution under the additional condition of integrality of $x(\underline{e})$, $\underline{e} \in \mathcal{E}$. By the integrality of all flows the variables $y(\underline{r})$ will be integral or half-integral in this solution. Using the method proposed in the proof of Theorem 6, we derive an optimal solution of GCCP, which has integral values $y(\underline{r})$, too. As pointed out, this method works well when every cycle of odd length contains some vertex $\underline{e}$ with $a(\underline{e}) < b(\underline{e})$, but also in many other situations.

8 Conclusion and Further Research

In the present paper, we studied global cardinality constraints which have been introduced as a variation of ordinary cardinality constraints. While ordinary cardinality constraints impose restrictions on the participation in relationships of a single type, global cardinality constraints do the same with respect to relationships of all types. Clearly, in practice it will more likely happen that we need to model restrictions that are somewhere 'between' these two extremes. Thus we propose to continue the investigation by studying constraints $\text{gcard}(\mathcal{R}', \underline{e}) = (a, b)$ where $\mathcal{R}'$ denotes some subset of all relationship types involving the entity type $\underline{e}$. Note that this question, in particular, raises the question of interactions between different versions of cardinality constraints.

Of course, cardinality constraints themselves will usually not be sufficient to describe all the requirements a database has to satisfy in order to represent the underlying domain of interest correctly. Therefore, it would be desirable to study global cardinality constraints in the presence of constraints from other classes, such as functional or inclusion dependencies.

The problem of finding small sample databases (and, in particular, small Armstrong databases) turned out to be computationally hard for global cardinality constraints. This is a bad news, since sample databases are a popular tool in conceptual design and frequently used to support the communication between designers and users. It should be emphasized that a similar result is not available so far for ordinary cardinality constraints.

The major objective of the paper was to develop an efficient approach to construct minimal sample databases for a large class of database schemas. We presented a branch & bound algorithm whose subproblems are tackled via methods from combinatorial optimization. We proved that the LP-relaxation of each occurring subproblem can be solved by finding a minimum-cost flow in a suitable network. Algorithms for minimum-cost-flow problems have been widely studied in literature and are well-tested. For up-to-date surveys, see [5,7]. These monographs also discuss efficient implementations of the algorithms.

References

1. P.P. Chen. The entity-relationship model: towards a unified view of data. *ACM Trans. Database Systems*, 1:9–36, 1976.
2. S. Hartmann. Global cardinality constraints. In M. Klettke, and B. Thalheim, editors, Proc. *Workshops on Challenges of Design and Challenges of Application, 17th Int. Conference on Conceptual Modeling*, pages 196–206, 1996.
3. S. Hartmann. On the implication problem for cardinality constraints and functional dependencies. *Ann. Math. Artificial Intelligence*, 33:253–307, 2000.
4. M. Lenzerini and P. Nobili. On the satisfiability of dependency constraints in entity-relationship schemata. *Inform. Systems*, 15:453–461, 1990.
5. B. Korte and J. Vygen: *Combinatorial optimization: theory and algorithms*, Springer, Berlin, 2000.
6. S. W. Liddle, D. W. Embley, and S. N. Woodfield. Cardinality constraints in semantic data models. *Data Knowledge Eng.*, 11:235–270, 1993.
7. G.L. Nemhauser and L.A. Wolsey: *Integer and combinatorial optimization*, Wiley, New York, 1988.
8. C.H. Papadimitriou and K. Steiglitz: *Combinatorial optimization: algorithms and complexity*, Prentice-Hall, Englewood Cliffs, N.J., 1982.
9. A. Rochfeld and H. Tardieu: Merise: An information system design and development methodology, *Information Management*, 6: 143–159, 1983.
10. B. Thalheim. Fundamentals of cardinality constraints. *LNCS*, 645:7–23, 1992.
11. B. Thalheim. *Entity-relationship modeling*. Springer, Berlin, 2000.

Author Index

Lecture Notes in Computer Science

For information about Vols. 1–2189
please contact your bookseller or Springer-Verlag